Religion in America

Expansion of the United States with Dates When New States Became Part of the Union

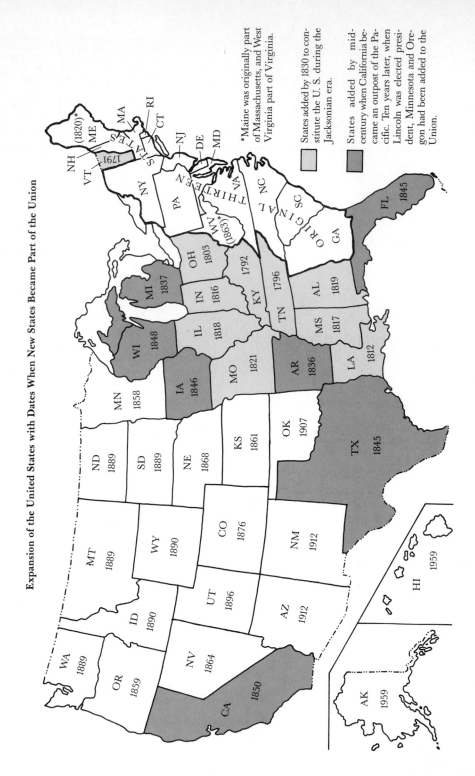

*Maine was originally part of Massachusetts, and West Virginia part of Virginia.

States added by 1830 to constitute the U. S. during the Jacksonian era.

States added by mid-century when California became an outpost of the Pacific. Ten years later, when Lincoln was elected president, Minnesota and Oregon had been added to the Union.

WINTHROP S. HUDSON
JOHN CORRIGAN

Religion in America

An Historical Account of the Development of American Religious Life

FIFTH EDITION

MACMILLAN PUBLISHING COMPANY
NEW YORK

Maxwell Macmillan Canada
TORONTO

Maxwell Macmillan International
NEW YORK   OXFORD   SINGAPORE   SYDNEY

Editor: Margaret Barbieri
Production Supervisor: George Carr
Production Manager: Linda Greenberg
Text and Cover Designer: Eileen Burke

This book was set in Baskerville by Digitype, Inc.
and was printed and bound by Book Press.
The cover was printed by New England Book Components.

Macmillan Publishing Company
866 Third Avenue, New York, New York 10022

Macmillan Publishing Company is part of
the Maxwell Communication Group of Companies.

Maxwell Macmillan Canada, Inc.
1200 Eglinton Avenue East
Suite 200
Don Mills, Ontario M3C 3N1

LIBRARY OF CONGRESS CATALOGING-IN-PUBLICATION DATA

Hudson, Winthrop Still, 1911–
    Religion in America : an historical account of the development of
American religious life / Winthrop S. Hudson, John Corrigan. — 5th
ed.
        p. cm.
    Includes bibliographical references and index.
    ISBN 0-02-357830-0 (paper)
    1. United States — Religion. I. Corrigan, John, 1952–
    II. Title.
BL2525.H83 1992   91-3853
    291'.0973 — dc20   CIP

Printing: 1 2 3 4 5 6 7   Year: 2 3 4 5 6 7 8

To
CHARLES M. NIELSEN
friend and colleague

Preface

The historian Herbert Butterfield wrote that we study the past not only because we wish to understand the present, but because good history is a good story, capable of satisfying what he referred to as a "basic human demand for narrative." My experiences in the classroom have prompted me to restate Butterfield's theory with a variant emphasis: We demand narrative because it teaches so effectively. A good story is a good teacher of history.

In preparing *Religion in America* for publication in a fifth edition I have endeavored above all to sustain the narrative that has made the book so serviceable in the classroom. In some cases I have grafted new material onto the vine in order to add texture and breadth to the story, at other times to focus and reinforce the historical account. In all cases I have been guided by my regard for the classroom value of a concise historical survey that allows the assignment of supplementary reading. Accordingly, where previous themes have been revised or new ones added, regard for brevity and integration has regulated the writing.

This story of religion in America unfolds one step at a time, as the cast of persons, settings, ideas, and events develop characteristic patterns of interrelatedness in four chronological periods. Some of those patterns endure, carrying the story from one period to the next, while others disappear completely, and still others lose visibility only to reemerge in high profile later. The narrative is not a mere chronicling of the deeds of various actors as they operated against a fixed background of social institutions and structures. History is never so simple. This is a story of adaptation and acculturation, but it is a complex story that also tells about material change over time, about shifting backgrounds and new revelations, about religion conserving tradition and departing from it. It is about the emergence of a thoroughgoing religious pluralism as well as the survival of shared meanings.

Three overlapping contexts frame the story. First, religion is pictured in its relations with other aspects of American life. Religious traditions and communities exercise a profound influence on the formation of culture in America. Religion in turn is constantly being shaped by forces external to it. *Religion in America* addresses religious life as a whole as it arises in the context of this reciprocal relationship.

Second, the transatlantic dimension forms a key part of the story. While religion in America exhibits distinct features, it bears the mark of its predominantly European background. After the initial migrations to America, the European influence was sustained in various ways, and most conspicuously through successive waves of immigration. It is true as well that in the course of being translated to an American context, religion that originated in Europe (or Asia or Africa) was modified. In some cases the change was minimal, and in other cases the process of adaptation resulted in a dramatic recasting of religious life.

Third, the story of religion in America emerges out of the interaction of many religious groups. At times, that interaction was manifest in cooperative projects of missionizing, education, and reform. On other occasions conflict in the form of nativism, heresy accusations, and regional differences (particularly between north and south) broke the surface of denominational life. In early America, patterns of interaction were relatively simple because the religious spectrum was narrow. As religious and ethnic diversity increased during the nineteenth century, relations between religious groups invariably became more complex. In the late twentieth century complexity born of a broad pluralism appears as an exclamation point to the story thus far.

To these observations on the approach of *Religion in America* and its classroom advantages, I add a note about my effort to prepare this edition for publication. My enthusiasm for the book and my desire to see that it remains available in updated form stem also from my regard for its long view of history. The pluralism that has emerged as the prominent feature of religion in America in recent decades is understandable only against the background of over four hundred years of religious history. Recognizing that history is essential for gauging the nature and extent of religious innovation, for comprehending the constants, and especially for appreciating adaptation as a process involving both change and resistance to change. In that process, new arrivals became Americanized and, until the 1960s, the nation periodically reaffirmed its faith in a collective religious mission. *Religion in America* is more than an assemblage of snapshots of religious denominations, social groups, political events, and cultural developments. It is a moving picture of the constantly evolving interrelationship of those parts in the whole.

Winthrop Hudson made my work in revising this book a pleasure. This edition stands as an improvement because I began with an excellent, proven text and received expert guidance from its author as I revised it.

My work on this book has required that I constantly attempt to see the material as would a person just beginning the study of religion in America.

I am grateful to those colleagues who, from their positions in the classroom trenches, communicated to me suggestions on how to avoid unnecessarily complicating the story. I am especially grateful to my graduate students Mike Ashcraft, Cathie Cookson, Eric Mazur, Rodger Payne, Marianne Perciaccante, and Briane Turley. I also am happily obliged to Helen McInnis for all that she did to keep the project on track.

J. C.
Cambridge, Massachusetts

Contents

Introduction: Profile of an Evolving Nation

"Where shall I begin?" asked the White Rabbit of the King in *Alice's Adventures in Wonderland*. "Begin at the beginning, and go on till you come to the end: then stop." This is sensible advice for anyone who wishes to understand the United States in all its variety. If the story is to be understood, one must be clear when and where and with whom it all began. One must also have some notion of the changes that were introduced along the way. The United States, as it nears the end of the twentieth century, is a vast land with a multiplicity of peoples drawn from every quarter of the globe and exhibiting a fascinating tapestry of many differing religious faiths. But it was not so at the beginning.

The Geography of the Nation

The United States was a land of small geographical beginnings. It began as a slender fringe of 13 states along the Atlantic coast that declared their independence from Britain in 1776. Even this is deceptive, for the colonists inhabited mostly a fringe of a fringe. Settlement in Georgia was limited to the coastal lowlands and up one bank of the Savannah River not far beyond Augusta; Massachusetts' district of Maine was mostly wilderness; western Virginia above the Shenandoah was unsettled; and central, western, and northern New York had not been opened to settlement.

By 1840 13 more states—mostly carved out of the territory east of the Mississippi River ceded by Britain in 1783—had been added to the new nation. Thereafter the United States became a patchwork quilt with many of the patches yet missing. In 1845 Texas and Florida became part of the Union, but Oklahoma did not until 1907. When California became a state in 1850, a foothold on the Pacific was gained, but it was a foothold far removed from the rest of the nation. The southern tier of states was not

1

completed until 1912, when Arizona and New Mexico were received as members of the Union. Two decades earlier, in 1889 and 1890, the empty spaces of the northern frontier had been filled when the Dakotas, Montana, Idaho, and Washington became member states of the nation. Utah remained a missing patch of the quilt until 1896. Not until 1959 did Alaska and Hawaii become constituent parts of the United States.

The Ethnography of the Nation

If the United States at the outset was small in geographical extent, it was also limited in the diversity of its population. It is true that at the beginning there were the Native Americans, the "Indians," who were treated (mostly mistreated) in a variety of ways and progressively displaced. Of the white population at the end of the colonial period, 85 percent came from the British Isles. By the latter part of the twentieth century, however, the United States was a land of minorities, with a population drawn from every continent and almost every country of the world. Thirty million of its citizens have distant antecedents in Africa. Much more recent are the 22.4 million people referred to by the Census Bureau as of Spanish origin, but more commonly known as Hispanics.

Few of the 22.4 million Hispanics came from Spain. More than half are of Mexican origin, and most Mexicans insist that Mexico is an Indian (i.e., American Indian) nation. Many (2 million) are Puerto Ricans and a surprising number (900,000) are Cubans. The rest are from other countries of Latin America, the numbers swelling in proportion to the hazards of life in their homelands — a reason many from all parts of the world became Americans, blacks being the notable exception.

The Spanish presence in the United States came relatively late. When Florida became one of the United States in 1845, only a few archeological survivals remained of early Spanish settlements on this then-desolate peninsula. Texas under Spanish and then Mexican rule also was virtually an unoccupied land (the Indians, as usual, were ignored) with only three small permanent settlements. First Spain and then Mexico sought to entice settlers to Texas from the United States and Germany with grants of land. In 1845 when the republic of Texas, after nine years of independence, was annexed and admitted as a state, the Mexican population that remained was far outnumbered by the newer arrivals. The 1850 census reported a Texas population of 212,595, with Protestants (mainly Baptists and Methodists) predominant among the religiously affiliated. The report added laconically that the annexation "only brought back into the Union those who had migrated thither a short time before." California thus was the first state to introduce an established Spanish presence into the life of the nation.

In this land of minorities, in addition to the Scots, Welsh, English, and Irish from the British Isles, major segments of the population were drawn from every area of Europe. One need only call the roll: Germany, Italy, Scandinavia, eastern Europe, and the Balkans—with Greece, Portugal, and the Netherlands each making its own important contribution. Descendants of the early French Huguenots constitute a remote French connection, and the twentieth-century influx of French Canadians supplied a more tangible presence.

Nearly seven and a half million Americans are from east and south Asia and the islands of the Pacific, and the number keeps increasing: Chinese, Filipinos, Japanese, (east) Indians, Koreans, Vietnamese, to name the largest groupings. A medley of peoples also have come from what technically should be regarded as part of Asia and Africa but is more commonly labeled the Near East or Middle East. And then, to return to the beginning, half-forgotten by many, are the two million survivors of the Native Indians of the forests and plains who were displaced and isolated and yet continued to exist, as did the blacks for so many years, on the periphery of the "white man's world."

From Religious Diversity to Religious Pluralism

There was religious diversity (and much irreligion) from the start. But it was a diversity mostly within the confines of a common faith diversely expressed. By the twentieth century, however, the diversity was so expanded that it was renamed "pluralism" as a term more appropriate to describe the situation when a nation had become a sampler of all the religions of the globe. These include all the major faiths in their multifarious expressions as well as lesser-known religions and innovative constructs of belief and devotion of independent and often indigenous origin.

Apart from the obvious concentrations of specific religious groups in early New England, Pennsylvania, and Virginia, differences within and between separate denominations were not so noticeable in the early years of the republic, a fact attested to by Tocqueville as late as the Jacksonian era. Traveling itinerants in the colonial period, such as Francis Makemie, Samuel Davies, Henry M. Muhlenberg, Shubal Stearns, Francis Asbury, and a host of others—including above all "the grand itinerant," George Whitefield—blurred the boundaries between the colonies and often between the churches. New England, to be sure, retained a distinctive character as it moved from a Puritan to a Yankee society, but it shared much of its religious ethos with other sections of the evolving nation through migration, missionary activity, and educational influence. It was not until the 1830s that a north side and a south side of religion began to develop and to divide the republic. In spite of this cleavage, Protestants north and Protestants south in the late 1850s were still able to join in sponsoring "union prayer meetings."

Real religious pluralism began to emerge in a small way with the inno-
vating groups produced by the indigenous religious ferment of the 1830s
and 1840s, and with the beginning of what was to be a mounting tide of
immigration from abroad following the revolutions of 1830 and 1848 as
well as the potato famine in Ireland. Decade by decade the immigration
increased, until it reached its peak in the years preceding the outbreak of
war in 1914. The full spectrum of religious belief, however, did not
become apparent until a major influx of peoples from Asia begun after
World War II contributed both directly and indirectly to a mushrooming
pluralism. Asian faiths became more prominent and helped foster in part
additional home-grown religious groups or communes during the troubled years of the late 1960s and early 1970s.

Departures from the General Pattern: Regionalism in Religion

Following the Civil War, regional differences in religious faith and practice were accentuated. The Old South remained a bastion of an evangelical Protestantism untouched by the changing patterns and relationships
introduced by growing urbanization and large-scale immigration in other
parts of the country. Immigration also created enclaves of Roman Catholics and Lutherans which in the course of time expanded to become what
Martin Marty called "empires," centers of predominant regional strength.
The concentration of Lutherans in Wisconsin, Minnesota, and the Dakotas is an obvious example of such regional strength. There are also
urban areas of Jewish concentration which in similar fashion have given a
distinctive tone or ethos to these localities. By the middle of the twentieth
century, the most tightly knit regional religious bastion was the intramountain Mormon empire that had spilled over the border of Utah into
neighboring states. Two additional areas of regional religion have been
commonly overlooked, namely southern Appalachia and the Pacific coast.

Catherine Albanese has called attention to southern Appalachia as an
area of regional religion. Unlike the mountains of New England and New
York, which were largely denuded of population—and unlike northern
Appalachia in Pennsylvania as well as in much of West Virginia and
Kentucky, which was robbed of its innocence by coal mines, coke ovens,
and steel mills—southern Appalachia had mountaineers who remained
where they were, isolated from the rest of the world in their narrow
valleys behind rugged ridges for a century and more. Even the architecture of their cabins remained unchanged, betraying the pilgrimages of
their ancestors from Scotland and Ireland. In the same way, their folk
religion preserved a faith and practice that reflected eighteenth-century
religious life, with some embellishments of their own that had developed
over the years. This is the reason, one assumes, that in the twentieth

century the whole region, when discovered by holiness and pentecostal preachers, yielded a ready harvest once the seed was sown and that thereafter its own home-grown brands of pentecostalism flourished.

The Pacific coast, most notably California, provides a quite different example of geographically and culturally conditioned regional religion. Culturally it is, to use a colloquial expression, "laid-back" and future-oriented. Southern California as early as the 1920s and 1930s gained the reputation in religion of being the twentieth-century equivalent of the "burned-over district" of central and western New York in the 1830s and 1840s. A profusion of novelties flourished, and interest in the new and exotic spread up the coast in the decades that followed.

Why this should be so is difficult to determine. Only a series of "perhaps," with a focus on California, can suggest a partial answer. Perhaps the distance across the plains was too great and the difficulty in breaching the mountains too arduous to give ready access for the old-line churches to become as deeply rooted as elsewhere. Perhaps the get-rich-quick spirit of those who participated in the Gold Rush and the quick wealth amassed by the railroad and banking elite of Sacramento and San Francisco contributed to a cosmopolitan mood and an entrepreneurial lack of interest in rootage. The early settlers were not stay-at-homes. They were people on the move and, unlike the settlers who came later to the plains east of the mountains, were uninterested in replicating the farms and villages whence they had come. Perhaps the fact that southern California became old-folks territory in the 1920s — people who were far removed and cut off from the former securities of family and church back in Iowa and elsewhere — had something to do with receptivity to religious novelty. Perhaps the influx of refugees from the "dust bowl" in the 1930s helped augment a pervasive restless and rootless spirit. Perhaps early trading contact with the Orient and Eastern religions made a difference. Perhaps the movement of troops through the ports and of their wives into the munitions plants during World War II gave an added complexity to West Coast society. The presence of Hispanics (Chicanos) and Asians after the war as major segments of the population added another element to an already cosmopolitan region. Perhaps it was the attractive power of Hollywood with its own tinsel vision of life that helped set the tone, at least in California, for more than half a century.

Pluralism and Regionalism as Less than the Whole Story

Although differences between religious groups and between regions should not be ignored, equally important is the evolving religious life of the American people as a whole in interaction with other dimensions of their experience — the unity exhibited in American religious life as well as its particularities. In spite of regionalism and in spite of the seemingly rampant pluralism that developed under conditions of religious freedom, at a deeper level of American experience there remained an underlying unity. Churches of various traditions in many ways were Americanized and reduced to a common pattern. The life that centered in a Jewish temple, for example, differed little from the activities characteristic of Christian churches.

Quite apart from the churches, there was a national faith—a belief in providence and the mission of America—which was shared by Catholics and Jews as well as Protestants. It was a faith even former slaves did not reject; they rather sought to have practice match profession so that they too could become inheritors of the national faith's promises. Though sorely tested, often perverted, and increasingly diluted, this national faith retained sufficient health, prior to the spreading disenchantment of the late 1960s, for Martin Luther King, Jr., to be able to touch the conscience of much of the nation by reminding Americans of it.

There have been and are, as has been noted, regional differences in the United States, just as there have been regional differences in England, France, Germany, and other nations. The differences in each of these countries have resulted in armed conflict, but in the long run the differences were gradually subordinated and, with a few striking exceptions, became less important than the continuities that made them nations. Evidence of continuity in the United States, less so in southern Appalachia and the Southwest, can most easily be seen in surviving architecture. Indeed, the moving population tended to recreate not only the architecture, but the layout and design of the villages from whence the participants in the migration came. Place names provide equally eloquent testimony to continuity. Evidence of continuity stretches from the Atlantic to the Pacific. It was no accident that Berkeley, even in California, was chosen as the name for the site of the University of California.[1] On the other hand, influences moved back east from the west, and moved north as well as south. The striking feature of individual continuities in the molding of the nation, however, is the way in which they became mingled in the course of transit. They became enriched by local modifications and by new patterns of life and understanding introduced by successive waves of immigration. Tensions were ample enough, but the new infusions as well as the old continuities all became part of the fabric of the new nation. Religion in America shared in this process, becoming a tapestry woven of many different strands.

---

[1] George Berkeley, philosopher and educational theorist, was an adopted son of Yale and admired and esteemed by Samuel Johnson who sought to put his theories into practice in the founding of King's College (Columbia University) in New York.

PART I

The Formative Years

1607–1789

1589	The Protestant reformed religion established by law as the official religion in England
1607	Jamestown founded
1611	King James Bible published
1612	Tobacco planted in Virginia
1613–14	English colonists in Virginia block French colonization of Nova Scotia, Maryland, and Maine
1614	Indian Princess Pocahontas marries John Rolfe
1619	First African slaves in North America arrive in Virginia
1619	First representative colonial assembly in America held at Jamestown, Virginia
1620	Miles Standish and Pilgrims found Plymouth Colony
1622	William Bradford begins 30 years as governor of Plymouth
1623	First English settlement in New Hampshire
1624	Virginia Company dissolved and Virginia becomes crown colony
1626	Dutch traders found New Amsterdam
1628	Dutch Reformed minister Jonas Michaelius organizes church in New Amsterdam
1630	English Archbishop Laud enforces religious conformity
1630	John Winthrop helps found Massachusetts Bay Colony
1633	First Baptist Church formed at Southwark, London
1634	Maryland founded by Lord Baltimore
1635	Windsor, Connecticut, founded by religious refugees from Massachusetts
1635	Connecticut founded by Thomas Hooker
1636	Harvard College founded
1636	Welsh Puritan Roger Williams banished from Massachusetts; establishes Rhode Island and proclaims religious freedom
1637	Anne Hutchinson flees to Rhode Island
1638	Swedes settle on Delaware River
1639	First printing press in North America at Cambridge, Massachusetts
1640–60	Civil wars in England
1641	French settle in Michigan
1642	Montreal, Canada, founded
1643	Confederation of New England formed by Connecticut, New Haven, Plymouth, and Massachusetts Bay Colony
1644	Roger Williams writes "Queries of Highest Consideration" on separation of church and state
1647	Peter Stuyvesant becomes director of New Amsterdam
1648	*Cambridge Platform* adopts Westminster Confession
1648	George Fox founds the Society of Friends (Quakers)
1649	Maryland Assembly passes Act of Toleration professing belief in the Holy Trinity
1650	Beginning of extermination of North American Indians
1654	Jews fleeing from Brazil arrive in New Amsterdam
1655	Cromwell prohibits Anglican services in England
1656	Quakers Mary Fisher and Ann Austin arrive in Boston
1660	Stuarts restored to English throne
1664	English take control of New Netherlands
1668	Government of Maine passes to Massachusetts
1672	Quaker missionary George Fox tours eastern seaboard
1674	New Jersey founded
1676	"Declaration of the People of Virginia" by Nathaniel Bacon gains support for rebellion against authorities
1676	Settlement of boundary between eastern and western New Jersey
1679	New Hampshire separated as special province from Massachusetts
1680	French Colonial Empire from Quebec to mouth of Mississippi River
1681	Pennsylvania founded by William Penn
1682	Louisiana Territory for France

1682	Delaware founded
1683	Mennonites begin arriving in Pennsylvania
1684	Massachusetts Bay charter revoked
1688	Glorious Revolution; William and Mary ascend throne
1689	Act of Toleration accepts religious diversity
1691	Witchcraft accusations and executions at Salem, Massachusetts
1699	Brattle Street Church formed in Boston
1701	Yale founded
1701	Society for the Propagation of the Gospel organized to promote Anglicanism
1702	Anglican Church established in Maryland
1703	German Lutheran Church organized at New Hanover, Pennsylvania
1703	John Wesley, founder of Methodism, born (d. 1791)
1704	Anglican Church established in South Carolina
1706	Francis Makemie helps form Presbytery of Philadelphia
1707	Philadelphia Baptist Association formed
1707	England and Scotland unite to form Great Britain
1708	*Saybrook Platform* centralizes control of churches
1712	Last execution for witchcraft in England
1715	Anglican Church established in North Carolina
1719	Dutch Reformed minister Theodore Frelinghuysen arrives in New Jersey
1720s	First stirrings of Great Awakening in middle colonies
1721	Regular postal service between London and New England
1723	Dunker Church formed at Germantown, Pennsylvania
1726	Gilbert Tennent arrives in New Brunswick Presbyterian Church
1727	William Tennent establishes "log college"
1729	Presbyterian Synod of Philadelphia adopts Westminster Confession
1730	John and Charles Wesley found Methodism at Oxford
1732	Benjamin Franklin issues "Poor Richard's Almanac"
1733	Jewish congregation at Savannah, Georgia, founded
1734	Revival breaks out in Jonathan Edwards' church in Northampton
1734–37	Revival in Connecticut River valley
1735	Moravians settle in Georgia; move to Pennsylvania in 1740
1737	John Wesley's "Psalms and Hymns" published in Charleston
1739	George Whitefield arrives in Philadelphia
1740–41	Whitefield visits New England; Gilbert Tennent preaches in New England; peak of Great Awakening
1741	Charles Chauncy objects to excesses of revival
1741	James Davenport denounces unconverted ministers
1741–43	Moravian Count von Zinzendorf organizes German churches in Pennsylvania
1742	Henry Muhlenberg arrives in Pennsylvania; helps form Lutheran Ministerium in 1748
1746	Jonathan Edwards writes "A Treatise Concerning Religious Affections"
1748	Presbyterian Samuel Davies sent to Virginia
1749	Jewish congregation at Charleston, South Carolina
1749	Settlement of West undertaken by Ohio Company
1750	Jonathan Edwards ejected from Northampton church
1754	Baptist preachers Shubal Stearns and Daniel Marshall begin preaching in Virginia
1758	Anglican Church established in Georgia
1756–63	French and Indian War; treaty of Paris accepts French in Canada
1763	Deveraux Jarratt installed as rector at Bath, Virginia, and leads local revival
1775–83	War of American Independence
1786	Thomas Jefferson's "Bill for Establishing Religious Freedom" in Virginia
1791	Jesuits found Georgetown Academy

CHAPTER 1

The American Context

Our roots as a nation go back to the remarkable burst of colonizing activity that transformed the Atlantic Ocean into the *Mare Nostrum* of western Europe. There is little that we, as Americans, can claim as exclusively our own. Our language is not our own, nor are our tables of weights and measures. Our most familiar proverbs and nursery rhymes have been inherited from others. Our concept of trial by jury came to us from abroad. Indeed, our whole legal system, with its guarantees of liberty and provisions for constitutional government, is the product of a longer history than ours. Even after our declaration of political independence, we remained part of this larger society—reading the works of European poets, studying the writings of European philosophers, listening to the music of European composers, utilizing the discoveries of European scientists, reaping the benefits of European capital invested in our railroads and mines, recruiting European "hands" for our mills and factories. In almost every respect we have been part of Europe. This is as true in religion as it is in literature, law, philosophy, art, or science.

The religious heritage that links us to Europe is immediately apparent to any visitor to the British Isles. When Americans walk down the street of an English city, they will be reminded of home as they pass Anglican (Protestant Episcopal), Presbyterian, Baptist, Methodist, and Roman Catholic churches. They may be handed a Plymouth Brethren tract, encounter a Salvation Army lassie, or find a Quaker meetinghouse or Jewish synagogue half hidden in a side street. Traveling north of the Tweed, they will discover that many of the Presbyterian divisions at home had their origin in Scotland.

But it is not from the British Isles only that our churches have come, for there are German, Swedish, Danish, Norwegian, and Finnish Lutheran churches; German, Dutch, and Hungarian Reformed churches; Mennonite, Moravian, and Dunker communities. And more recent immigration from central and eastern Europe has swelled the Roman Catholic and Jewish populations in the United States and has introduced the numerous national churches of Eastern Orthodoxy into the American scene.

With only a few exceptions, the varied religious groups of America have their rootage abroad. The continuing European religious influence is no more than barely suggested by the names of Kant, Schleiermacher, and Ritschl; Pascal, Kierkegaard, and Von Hügel; Newman, Maurice, and Temple; Barth, Buber, and Bultmann. In religion, as in other areas of our common life, we have been and we have continued to be part of a larger European society.

The recognition that the United States, in all the fundamental features of its life save geographical location, is a part of Europe must not obscure the parallel fact that we are Americans as well as Europeans. European society has never been a monolithic whole. Within the common culture there have always been diverse local and national traditions; and this is as true in America as it is in England and France and Germany. America has drawn most heavily, as the mere fact of language so eloquently testifies, from the English-speaking segment of European society. But it is far from an exact transcript that has been reproduced on American soil. There have been modifications and adaptations of the European inheritance from the beginning.

In part the changes that have occurred in America have been a result of the differing circumstances of life in a new land; in part they have been the product of the mingling in varying proportion of several European traditions; in part they have been the consequence of the constitutional arrangements that were effected to bring 13 newly independent and somewhat recalcitrant colonies together under one government; and in part they have been the result of the evolving life that is characteristic of any intimately related segment of a larger community. Thus, although we have been and continue to be debtors to Europe, we also developed, within the larger context, a distinctive life of our own and have made contributions of our own to the European society of which we are a part.

Although the European heritage has given American religious life its basic shape and substance, the purpose here is to focus attention upon the distinctive ethos and character of religion in America.

England as the "Bridge" from the Old World to the New

As early as 1622 John Donne was asserting with remarkable prescience that England, which hitherto as an island had been "but as the suburbs" of Europe, was destined to occupy a much more central position in the future as the "bridge" between the Old World and the New.[1] His words were prophetic as far as the Atlantic coast of North America was concerned,

---

[1] Louis B. Wright, *Religion and Empire* (Chapel Hill, N.C., 1943), 111.

and the most obvious conditioning factor in American religious life has been its English beginnings. The 13 colonies were English colonies, the vast proportion of the population was of English stock, and the American Revolution was fought — so the colonists asserted — to defend and preserve their rights as Englishmen.

Protestant Predominance

The fact that the American colonies were English colonies meant, first of all, that the colonists in background if not always in active affiliation would be predominantly Protestant. Even the non-English minorities — Scots, Scotch Irish, Germans, Dutch, French, and Swedes — were almost wholly Protestant in background. Only in Maryland were there a significant number of Roman Catholics, and even in Maryland they were a minority. Judaism was limited to a handful of tiny congregations. Thus, to the extent that the mind of colonial America was shaped by a religious faith, it was shaped perforce by Protestantism.

This overwhelmingly Protestant religious orientation was equally true of the new nation as its borders pushed westward. The French trading posts on the Great Lakes were not rooted deeply enough to become centers of a continuing cultural or religious tradition, and a permanent non-Protestant area of settlement was confined to a relatively small enclave at the southern tip of the vast area embraced in the Louisiana Purchase of 1803. It was not until the nineteenth century was well advanced, when their numbers began to be augmented by large-scale immigration, that Roman Catholics became a numerically significant segment of American life; and it was not until the end of the nineteenth century that major Jewish and Eastern Orthodox communities came into existence.

As a consequence of Protestant predominance, even non-Protestant groups tended to take on a somewhat Protestant coloration in the American environment. The earnest "moralism" of American Roman Catholicism has often been attributed to the influence of a Protestant culture; and on occasion American Roman Catholics have had to defend themselves against charges of undue "Americanism," a term that usually implied the adoption of Protestant presuppositions. A more complete adjustment was represented by Reform Judaism, which initially adopted even the forms of Protestant Sunday worship. Nor has Eastern Orthodoxy remained unaffected. A spokesman for the Greek church, after staunchly defending at an ecumenical gathering the unchanging integrity of the Orthodox witness, commented privately that the Orthodox in America scarcely dare admit even to themselves the extent to which their life has been modified by an encounter with Protestantism.

After World War I, to be sure, the older Protestant predominance had been so greatly reduced by the shifting tide of immigration that influences that once moved only in one direction tended to become reciprocal. Not the least of the influences — for example, reshaping the Protestant understanding of the pastoral office and Protestant liturgical practice — has been the influence exerted by Roman Catholicism.

The Puritan Heritage

Although the United States by virtue of its English antecedents and character was predominantly Protestant throughout its early history, it was an English Protestantism with a difference. At home the great majority of the people were Anglicans, members of the Church of England; and the "Dissenting" interest composed of Presbyterians, Congregationalists, Baptists, and Quakers was relatively small. In the colonies this situation was reversed. By the end of the colonial period the Congregationalists and the Presbyterians were the two largest American denominations. The Baptists and the Anglicans were roughly equal in size, and the Quakers — widely dispersed throughout all the colonies — ranked fifth in number of adherents. It was this difference in the religious make-up of the population that Edmund Burke had in mind when he noted in his speech *On Conciliation with the American Colonies* (1775) that "the people [of the colonies] are Protestants, and of that kind which is the most adverse to all implicit subjection of mind and opinion."

What was the character of this early American Protestantism? Although diverse in outward ecclesiastical form, its diversity found expression mostly within the limits of the common faith of English Puritanism.[2] The tendency in popular mythology to stress the priority of Plymouth at the expense of Jamestown is not historically accurate, but in a deeper sense it is a true recognition that the American people have had their fundamental rootage in a Puritanism that they have found most easy to identify in terms of New England.

André Siegfried, a French observer of twentieth-century America, confirmed the estimate that is implicit in the prominence given to the story of the landing of the Pilgrims when he asserted: "If we wish to understand the real sources of American inspiration we must go back to the English Puritanism of the seventeenth century." James Bryce also emphasized this feature of American life in 1888 as he sought to describe the American commonwealth to his fellow countrymen at home. "There is a hearty Puritanism in the view of human nature which pervades the instrument of

[2] See David Hall, "Understanding the Puritans," in J. M. Mulder and J. F. Wilson, eds., *Religion in American History* (Englewood Cliffs, N.J., 1978), 1–16.

Mr. John Rodgers, minister of the gospel in London, was the first martyr in Queen Mary's reign, and was burnt at Smithfield, February the 14th, 1554. His wife, with nine small children, and one at her breast, followed him to the stake; with which sorrowful sight he was not in the least jaunted, but with wonderful patience died courageously for the Gospel of Jesus Christ.

1787," he wrote. "It is the work of men who believed in original sin, and were resolved to leave open for transgressors no door which they could possibly shut. Compare this spirit with the enthusiastic optimism of the Frenchmen of 1789. It is not merely a difference of race and temperaments; it is a difference of fundamental ideas."[3]

The same verdict had been expressed by Philip Schaff in 1844 when, shortly after his arrival from Germany, he sought to analyze the main features of American religious life. "Puritan Protestantism forms properly the main trunk of our North American church," he declared in his inaugural address as professor of church history in the Mercersburg Theological Seminary. "Viewed as a whole," the American church "owes her general characteristic features, her distinctive image, neither to the German or Continental Reformed, nor to the English Episcopal communion," but to the Puritans of New England. "To this New England influence must be added indeed the no-less important weight of Presbyterianism, as derived subsequently from Scotland and Ireland. But this may be regarded as in all essential respects the same life. The reigning theology of the country . . . is the theology of the Westminster Confession." A few years later he asserted that "the six northeastern states included under the

---

[3] André Siegfried, *America Comes of Age* (N.Y., 1927), 33. James Bryce, *The American Commonwealth* (N.Y., 1910), I, 306.

name of New England . . . are . . . in regard to culture and Christianity, the garden of America" and from this seedbed has come "the leading religious influence in the Union," exerting "a powerful influence upon the religious, social, and political life of the whole nation."[4]

Schaff's only error was to identify this Puritanism so exclusively with New England. Puritanism was far from monolithic. In England it was a many-faceted movement that embraced Presbyterians, Congregationalists, Baptists, large numbers of Episcopalians, and even the Quakers. It is a mistake, therefore, to limit Puritan influence in America to New England Congregationalism, for in other forms of English dissent it was strongly represented in all the colonies. As Schaff noted, the Presbyterians—including those from Scotland and Ireland—stood shoulder-to-shoulder with the Congregationalists at every important point. This was equally true of the Baptists who also had adopted a modified form of the 1647 Westminster Confession[5] as their statement of faith. Nor was colonial Anglicanism for the most part "the high-flying Anglicanism" of the Restoration divines; it was "the Calvinistic Low Church Anglicanism of the period before Laud."[6] Whether in Virginia or in New England, the same books of religious edification were read, the same doctrines were taught from the pulpits, and the same laws were passed to enforce religious duties. When the Quakers, who represented the left wing of the Puritan movement, are brought into the picture, it is evident that the Puritan influence in early America was dominant. So pervasive was its influence that, as Schaff reports, even many of the Lutheran churches were remade in the Puritan image.[7]

---

[4] Philip Schaff, *The Principle of Protestantism as Related to the Present State of the Church* (Chambersburg, Pa., 1845), 114; quoted by J. H. Nichols, *Romanticism in American Theology* (Chicago, 1961), 2. Philip Schaff, *America: A Sketch of Its Political, Social, and Religious Character*, ed. Perry Miller (Cambridge, Mass., 1961), 54, 89, 107; see also 116–17.

[5] The Westminster Confession, with modifications made by Congregationalists, is reproduced in Williston Walker, *The Creeds and Platforms of Congregationalism* (N.Y., 1893). The Baptist recension is in W. L. Lumpkin, *Baptist Confessions of Faith* (Philadelphia, 1959). John Witherspoon, president of Princeton, noted the basic unity of the denominations in this tradition when he described the religious situation in New Jersey at the close of the Revolution. "The Baptists," he said, "are Presbyterians in all other respects, only differing in the point of infant baptism, their political weight goes the same way as the Presbyterians." *Essays on Important Subjects* (Edinburgh, 1805), IV, 203.

[6] The comment is William Haller's in *The Constitution Reconsidered*, ed. Conyers Read (N.Y., 1938), 136. This "Calvinism" owed more perhaps to Zurich than Geneva, the term being used as shorthand for the whole Reformed tradition.

[7] Schaff, *America*, 93, 150–54.

One further word of caution needs to be spoken. What was labeled as Puritan by Schaff, Bryce, and Siegfried was not a static theological point of view.[8] As the Calvinism of the early Puritans was not precisely the same as the Calvinism of Geneva, so the Puritanism of nineteenth-century America was not that of seventeenth-century England, and it might more properly be described as Evangelicalism. There was constant modification and change and development. But there were also large elements of continuity; and even when theological foundations were altered or eroded, habitual ways of thinking and feeling persisted and continued to give form and structure to the common life.

Religious Diversity

The fact that the American colonies were English colonies also explains in large measure the multiplicity of religious bodies that was so prominent a feature of the English colonial scene in contrast to the religious uniformity that prevailed in the French and Spanish domains, for a deliberate policy of religious toleration was adopted by the English colonial authorities.

At the outset, to be sure, it was assumed that there would be and should be uniformity of religion in the new settlements; but in keeping with the whole system — or lack of system — of English colonial administration, the instructions at this point were not always observed. The Separatists who landed at Plymouth in 1620, for example, had set sail with the permission of the Virginia Company to establish a settlement within its territory, even though the second Virginia charter stated that no one, such as the Separatists, who refused to take the Oath of Supremacy should be allowed to embark for Virginia. In colonies other than Virginia, English administrative laxity was transformed into an explicit policy of toleration, and in no colony other than Virginia did the English authorities even attempt to impose a pattern of religious uniformity. When such attempts were made, as in Massachusetts Bay, it was by the colonists themselves, and it was in spite of rather than because of English policy.

One important factor determining the tolerant attitude of the English government was the economic advantage to be gained by a policy of toleration. The colonies were regarded as commercial ventures designed to contribute to the wealth and prosperity of the mother country. The great need if they were to be profitable was to attract settlers who would provide the labor to exploit the untapped resources of field and forest. Jails were emptied to provide colonists, the impoverished were sent out, adventurers were enlisted. But it soon became obvious that those who suffered from disabilities at home because of their religious profession

---

[8] Some recent scholarship has stressed the imprecision of the label "Puritan." See David D. Hall, *Worlds of Wonder, Days of Judgement* (N.Y., 1989), and Charles Lloyd Cohen, *God's Caress* (N.Y., 1986).

would be prime recruits if they could be induced to leave the homeland by the prospect of greater freedom abroad.

The Dutch had early discovered the economic folly of adopting rigorous measures to suppress religious dissent, and Peter Stuyvesant was rebuked for attempting to institute such a policy in New Amsterdam. The Dutch authorities informed him that his "vigorous proceedings" should be discontinued lest he "check and destroy" the population. The secret of the prosperity of old Amsterdam, he was reminded, was the moderation displayed by the magistrates in dealing with religious minorities, with the result that "people have flocked" from every land "to this asylum." He was informed that a similar policy should be pursued in New Amsterdam. "It is our opinion that some connivance would be useful; that the consciences of men, at least, ought ever to remain free and unshackled."[9]

English policy was of a piece with the Dutch. This is self-evident in the grants that were made to Lord Baltimore and William Penn, but the clearest statement of the motivation that lay behind the policy is to be found in a communication from the Lords of Trade in London to the Council of Virginia: "A free exercise of religion . . . is essential to enriching and improving a trading nation; it should be ever held sacred in His Majesty's colonies. We must, therefore, recommend it to your care that nothing be done which can in the least affect that great point."[10] Non-English settlers were welcomed and some were even recruited with the promise of freedom to establish their own religious institutions. Most of these non-English groups arrived relatively late in the colonial period[11] and constituted, proportionately, a small segment of the total population, but they did serve to give added variety to the religious spectrum.

Economic advantage alone, however, does not explain the relative equanimity with which dissent was viewed by both the Dutch and the English. A major contributing factor was the fact that the "maxims of moderation" were already being practiced at home. The English were more halting in their progress in this direction, but throughout the colonial period England was moving steadily toward an ever-broadening toleration of religious dissent. At times the toleration at home was within narrow limits. At other times, as during the two decades following the meeting of the Long Parliament in 1640, it was very broad. For brief periods under Charles I and Charles II there were efforts to impose a rigid conformity, but these efforts were never wholly successful and were not long pursued. With the adoption of the Act of Toleration in 1689, the acceptance of religious diversity within the limits of trinitarian Protestantism became the settled

---

[9] The text of the letter is printed in W. W. Street, *Religion in Colonial America* (N.Y., 1942), 151–52.

[10] *Historical Collections Relating to the American Colonial Church*, ed. William S. Perry (Hartford, Conn., 1871–1878), I, 379–81.

[11] The great influx of the Germans and Scotch Irish, the major non-English elements in the population, occurred during the last third of the colonial period.

domestic policy of the English government. Thus its religious policy in the colonies was in many ways merely a reflection of a policy that was being developed at home, and in the end England did little more than export her own religious diversity.

A New Beginning in a New Land

Although the English inheritance was the most important single influence determining the form and substance of religious life in the colonies, both the necessities and the opportunities of life in the New World introduced changes of emphasis and modifications of practice. Faced with the task of beginning anew, the leaders of the churches found themselves far more dependent upon the laity than had hitherto been true, and they were forced to concede to the laity far greater powers than the laity had previously enjoyed. Furthermore, the long sea journey had removed many of the inhibitions and restraints to which most of the churches had been subject, leaving them free to experiment in reshaping their life to conform more closely to long-cherished convictions than had been possible at home. Finally, given the view of history that prevailed, the mere fact that a new beginning could be made cultivated an eager expectancy that this was "the Lord's doing" and was but a foretaste of the near-approaching time when all things would be made new.

The Importance of the Laity

The Protestant Reformation with its emphasis upon the priesthood of believers and its appeal to the plain testimony of Scripture tended to elevate the laity in the life of the church. This tendency was arrested, however, by the establishment of national churches, sanctioned and maintained by the state. The clergy, being appointed by and responsible to the state, took charge and left to the people a passive role. Thus, within the limits of state control, the church tended to become a clerically dominated institution. In England, to be sure, the post-Reformation struggle for dominance between contending parties within the church necessitated appeals for lay support and gave added influence to the laity,[12] but this influence was always limited by ordered structures of church life. In the colonies, on the other hand, the restraint of an established church order was reduced to a minimum.

One of the facts of life in the New World was that a new beginning had to be made, and for most of the churches this new beginning had to be made by individual clergymen recruiting their own congregations out of a population that was largely unchurched. The ready-made congregations

[12] See James F. Maclear, "The Making of the Lay Tradition," *Journal of Religion*, 33 (1953), 113–36.

rugged individualism *rugged congregationalism*

of early New England and the parishes created by legislative fiat in Virginia were not typical. Elsewhere there were neither closely knit bodies of believers already in existence nor parishes established by law. Nor was there any ecclesiastical body close at hand to supervise and regulate the life of the churches. Furthermore, because of the diversity that prevailed, the clergy often had to compete for the allegiance of the people. Far removed from the status-giving context of an ordered church life and dependent upon what support they could enlist among the laity for both the formation and the maintenance of the congregations they served, the only real authority the clergy possessed was the authority they could command by their powers of persuasion and the force of their example. Given these circumstances, it is not surprising that the laity began to exercise a decisive voice in church affairs, with "everything," as Pennsylvanian Henry M. Muhlenberg explained, dependent "on the vote of the majority."[13]

Even in New England, where churches had been constituted at the outset with ministers as a "speaking aristocracy" and congregations reduced to a "silent democracy," this state of affairs did not long persist. Men who had gained independent status as property holders by clearing their own land with flintlocks close at hand were not the type to be unduly submissive, and their self-assertiveness soon stripped the New England clergy of much of their independence. The same process was at work in Virginia, where lay vestries gained effective control by neglecting to present the clergy to the governor for permanent induction into office, thus retaining, as the Archbishop of Canterbury complained, the right to hire and fire them like "domestic servants."[14]

A further consequence of lay predominance in church affairs was the strong support that was given to what was later described as "local autonomy." With single congregations beginning of necessity as independent self-governing units, resistance developed when attempts were made to subordinate them to larger units of ecclesiastical control. This was especially true in places where church structures tended to be relatively weak, as in the middle colonies. The laity were fearful of losing the prerogatives they possessed in the local church. Thus in Virginia and other southern colonies, where the Anglican laity had gained decisive powers in local "vestries," there was vigorous opposition to the attempt to establish an episcopate in America. A similar apprehension among the Congregational laity in Massachusetts thwarted the proposal to complete the Congregational structure there with a yearly consultative synod, and the Presbyterians in 1758 were forced to come to terms with this sentiment by conced-

[13] *The Journals of Henry Melchior Muhlenberg* (Philadelphia, 1942), I, 67. For a perceptive discussion of this point, see Sidney E. Mead in *The Ministry in Historical Perspectives*, ed. H. Richard Niebuhr and D. D. Williams (N.Y., 1956), 212–18.

[14] Elizabeth Davidson, *The Establishment of the English Church in Continental American Colonies* (Durham, N.C., 1936), 19.

ing extensive powers to local presbyteries at the expense of synodical authority.

Thus, whatever the denomination and whatever the polity that was ostensibly professed, all colonial churches tended to be characterized by a strong emphasis upon local autonomy and lay control. This emphasis persisted and was only partially curtailed in the nineteenth and twentieth centuries through strenuous efforts of Presbyterian, Methodist, and Roman Catholic clergy alike to have all church property transferred to and vested in presbytery, conference, or bishop. The objective was to limit local lay power by gaining control of the church property.

The Breakdown of the Parish System

A further consequence of the conditions that prevailed in the New World was the shattering of the parish system of ecclesiastical organization and the transformation of all the churches into what are usually described as "gathered" churches.

For almost a thousand years in western Europe, it had generally been assumed that every member of society was automatically a member of the church. Richard Hooker (1554?–1600), speaking of the situation in England, had voiced this common assumption in these words: "There is not any member of the Church of England but the same man is also a member of the commonwealth; nor any member of the commonwealth which is not also [a member] of the Church of England."[15] For purposes of worship, instruction, and discipline, people were divided geographically into parishes. This was the basic unit of church life, established and maintained by the state. It was in marked contrast to a self-supporting congregation whose membership was defined by voluntary affiliation.

Only in Virginia and in New England did a parish system, designed to embrace a total community, function with any success, and in Virginia the success was limited. The pattern of settlement in Virginia was the major problem. With population thinly distributed on large plantations bordering navigable rivers, a single parish could be 30 miles in length. In such a situation, it was difficult for the parish incumbent even to keep in touch with his parishioners, to say nothing of maintaining regular services of worship and a systematic program of instruction for them. In New England the pattern of settlement on small landholdings gathered about a village center was more conducive to an effective parish system, and it was maintained largely unimpaired until the inroads of dissent destroyed the religious homogeneity of the population.

Elsewhere in the colonies, the religious diversity that was present from the beginning compromised any attempt to establish a system that presupposed that the whole community would belong to a single church. A thin

---

[15] *Hooker's Ecclesiastical Polity: Book VIII*, ed. R. A. Houk (N.Y., 1931), 156.

façade of parish structure was maintained by legislative action in Maryland, the Carolinas, Georgia, and the environs of New York City, but none of these parish churches could claim more than a minority of the population. South of Virginia most parishes existed only on paper, never having been supplied with clergymen. The only thing that made possible even the pretense of maintaining a parish system was governmental authority, and the moment it was withdrawn the whole flimsy structure toppled. By this time the Anglicans had become a minority even in Virginia, and the adoption of Thomas Jefferson's "Bill for Establishing Religious Freedom" (1786) was equally effective in exposing as fiction the notion that the Anglican parishes there were anything more than "gathered" churches composed of voluntary adherents.

The New England story was somewhat more complex, for in New England the attempt was made to preserve "gathered" churches within a parish structure. This posed no great problem during the early years when the total population was largely a "sifted" people. But when the children of believers were unable to exhibit the minimum qualifications for church membership, the problem became acute. In an effort to preserve the parish concept, a form of "birthright" membership was adopted, and by this means the collapse of the parish system in New England was deferred until the increase of dissent made its defense a hopeless cause. A full century before disestablishment stripped away the lingering traces of the parish structure in New England, Jonathan Edwards (1703–58) recognized that its days were numbered and called upon his fellow Congregationalists to return to their initial emphasis upon the church as a covenanted community of convinced believers. Although certain privileges were retained until the first decades of the nineteenth century, the defenders of the attenuated "establishment" that survived during these final years found it necessary to adopt all the techniques of the "gathered" churches in order to carry on a rear-guard defense of its few remaining prerogatives.

The "techniques of the 'gathered' churches" is a key phrase, for it calls attention to the necessity that was laid upon the churches to win support and gain recruits by voluntary means. No longer could they depend upon people automatically being members of the church and subject to its discipline. The churches had to utilize all their powers of persuasion if they were to maintain and perpetuate themselves. The techniques they devised to this end were many and varied: the fostering of revivals, the organization of mission societies, the establishment of Sunday schools, the development of programs of visitation, the publication of tracts, and later the utilization of advertisements in periodicals. But above all, preaching was the means by which churches survived as voluntary organizations. Effective preaching was the very cornerstone of Protestantism, and it played an important role as well in the development of Roman Catholicism and Judaism in America. This vigorous evangelistic and instructional

activity, imposed upon the churches by their status as "gathered" groups
of convinced believers, was to become one of the most distinctive features
of American church life. And in the end, in order to maintain themselves
on this basis, some of the churches—most notably the Roman Catholic
Church—felt compelled to embark on the even more ambitious venture
of establishing weekday schools for the complete education of their
children.

The Possibility of Thoroughgoing Reform

The prominence of religious radicals and left-wing groups in America has
frequently been noted, and it is not surprising that they should have come
to the New World in disproportionate numbers. Members of the established churches in Europe could only view the situation in America with
some dismay, for the necessity to make a new beginning forced them to
improvise and served to shatter many of their previously cherished patterns of ecclesiastical life. In New Amsterdam, for example, Jonas Michaelius was acutely conscious of the coercions imposed by the conditions of
life in a new land, and he felt compelled to explain the irregularities that
attended the formation of his church. "One cannot," he wrote to the
authorities at home, "observe strictly all the usual formalities in making a
beginning under such circumstances."[16] The nonestablished churches of
Europe, however, were in a reverse situation. They welcomed the opportunity to make a new beginning free from the restraints to which they
were subjected at home. This was the great attraction that enticed the
Mennonites and the Moravians to risk the hazards of beginning life anew
in the American wilderness. It was this prospect also that exerted so strong
an appeal to that hardy band of Pilgrims who settled at Plymouth in 1620
and encouraged the founders of Massachusetts Bay Colony in 1629 to
undertake their "great migration."

The necessity to make a new beginning was seen by these minority
groups as more than mere negative release. It was an opportunity to
undertake a positive work of construction. William Penn never could have
launched his "holy experiment" in England where the existing patterns
and institutions of a settled community would have dictated compromises
from the start. He needed a place to begin anew where there would be
"room," as he put it, for "such an experiment." It was this opportunity
that was given him in America.

The significance of the opportunity to make a new beginning can be
seen most clearly through the eyes of those who sailed with the Winthrop
fleet to Massachusetts Bay. Michaelius had to "make do" in New Amsterdam, but the early New Englanders had had to "make do" at home. In
England they had been compelled to adjust to the irregularities imposed

---

[16] His letter is printed in *A Documentary History of Religion in America*, ed. E. S. Gaustad
(Grand Rapids, Mich., 1982–83), I, 82–83.

upon them by the requirements of the established church, and the shift to the New World was viewed by them as a release from this bondage. "It is one thing," explained John Cotton, "for . . . members of the church loyally to submit unto any form of [church] government when it is above their calling to reform it"; it is quite another matter for them to "choose a form of government and governors discrepant from the rule." The Great Migration had been organized with the specific purpose of providing them with this freedom to "choose." John Winthrop standing on the deck of the *Arbella* made explicit the duty that was laid upon them. It was to "bring into familiar and constant practice" that which they previously had been able to "maintain as truth in profession only." The purpose was clear. "We go," said Francis Higginson, "to practice the positive part of church reformation."[17]

America was for them, as it was to become for others, a land of opportunity, a land where a "wide door" of "liberty" had been set open before them. No longer were they to be compelled to resort to devious expedients, as they had been at home, in order to avoid "corruptions." This necessity had been lifted. But more important was the freedom they possessed to undertake a radical reconstruction of church life to conform to what they regarded as the plain prescriptions of God's "most holy Word." The goal was a full and complete restoration of the primitive church in all its pristine glory. This was their opportunity, and they were determined to take advantage of it. Looking back in 1677 to the early days of settlement, Increase Mather declared: "There never was a generation that did so perfectly shake off the dust of Babylon . . . as the first generation of Christians that came to this land for the Gospel's sake."[18]

The early New Englanders were seeking freedom for themselves alone, but others found in America an equal freedom to "shake off the dust of Babylon." There was and there continued to be space enough for everyone.[19] It was this sense of being freed from the necessity to give heed to compromising restraints in making a new beginning that was to give a perfectionist cast to much of American religious life and to foster the uninhibited experimentation by smaller fringe groups that was to be the dismay of European churchmen.)

The Sense of Expectancy

A new beginning is always a heady experience that breeds an eager expectancy among those who participate in it. Hopes are kindled and, as imagination takes over, the future becomes pregnant with possibility. This

[17] See Perry Miller, *Orthodoxy in Massachusetts* (Cambridge, Mass., 1933), 137, 146. Winthrop's address, "A Model of Christian Charity," is printed in *The Puritans*, ed. Perry Miller and T. H. Johnson (N.Y., 1963), I, 195–99.

[18] Quoted by W. W. Sweet, *Religion in Colonial America* (N.Y., 1950), 2.

[19] For a discussion of the significance of geographical space, see S. E. Mead, *The Lively Experiment* (N.Y., 1963), 2–15.

was doubly true of the new beginning that was made in America, for European peoples had always lived with the hope — sometimes faint but never absent — that the Lord's promise in Isaiah and Revelation to "make all things new" would some day be fulfilled. And the very term "New World," which was used to describe the setting in which they were making their new beginning, was calculated to remind them of the Lord's promise.

Since every Englishman had been taught from childhood to view the course of history as predetermined by God's overruling providence, no one could regard the colonizing activity in America as an ordinary venture. As early as 1613, William Strachey was insisting that God had kept America hidden for a purpose and that those who had established the small settlement in Virginia were but pursuing a course of action that God had foreseen and willed and was now carrying to its foreordained completion.[20] This purpose of necessity was related to God's final act of redemption, for this was the end toward which all history was directed.

The specific understanding of the past that illumined God's activity in the present was that which had been made the common possession of all Englishmen by John Foxe's "Book of Martyrs" — a volume that in 1571 had been placed by official decree in every cathedral church for all to read and was later to have a place of honor beside the Bible in every Protestant home.[21] Through the eyes of Foxe the shifting course of past events was seen to be a movement within a set pattern that God had adopted as a means of instructing mankind in the ways of righteousness. Throughout the centuries there had been alternating periods of impiety and faithfulness, corruption and reform, decline and renewal. After a long period of decline in which darkness had been demonstrated to be the only result of the folly of unrighteousness, Foxe pointed out that by 1300 God had begun to summon his servants to a renewed witness to him and thus to serve as harbingers of the new dispensation that was to be inaugurated with the Protestant Reformation.

When a full century had passed after the posting of the "Ninety-five Theses" by Martin Luther, it had become clear to scattered groups in England that Foxe had been overoptimistic in his estimate of the immediate outcome of the Reformation. The godly forces in Europe had proved to be unequal to the task to which God had summoned them. Why this should be so, they could only speculate; it was evident that God intended to pursue a new tactic to effect the final thrust into the new age.

Early New Englanders shared this sense of disappointment. As they reflected upon the significance of their venture in the New World, they felt certain that it was to implement God's overall design that they had been sent on an "errand into the wilderness." When old England "began

---

[20] Perry Miller, *Errand into the Wilderness* (Cambridge, Mass., 1956), 111, 117.
[21] See William Haller's *The Elect Nation* (N.Y., 1963).

to decline in religion," declared Edward Johnson (1598–1672), Christ raised "an army out of our English nation, for freeing his people from their long servitude" and created "a new England to muster up the first of his forces in." This new England, he continued, "is the place where the Lord will create a new heaven and a new earth in, new churches and a new commonwealth together."[22]

God had "sifted a whole nation" in order to plant his "choice grain" in the American wilderness, but his purpose was more far-ranging than merely to enable them to escape the inhibitions they had suffered at home. They were not fleeing from persecution; they were executing a flank attack upon the forces of unrighteousness everywhere. Their role, John Winthrop had reminded them, was to be "a city set on a hill" to demonstrate before "the eyes of the world" what the result would be when a whole people was brought into open covenant with God. As part of God's program of instruction, they were to provide the nations with a working model of a godly society and by the contagion of their example were to be God's instruments in effecting the release from bondage of all mankind.[23]

The New Englanders, however, were not alone in the conviction that America had a decisive role to play in God's plan of redemption. William Penn was equally convinced that God intended his "holy experiment" to be "an example . . . to the nations" and a means of forwarding the remodeling of life everywhere. And Samuel Purchas' history of Virginia, written in 1625, began its account of that colony's varied experiences with Adam and Eve in order to "show how God had so managed the past that English colonization in the present was the fulfillment of his plan."[24] Even Roger Williams, "the New England firebrand" who dissented at several crucial points from his neighbors in the Bay Colony, lived in daily expectation of a new dispensation.

This understanding of the decisive role America was to have was appropriated and popularized in the eighteenth century by leaders of the Great Awakening. (For the Awakening, see Chapter 3.) Jonathan Edwards, reflecting upon the outbreak of the revival, was convinced that "this work of God's Spirit, so extraordinary and wonderful, is the dawning or at least a prelude of that glorious work of God so often foretold in Scripture, which in the progress and issue of it shall renew the world of mankind." He saw

[22] *Johnson's Wonder-working Providence, 1628–1651*, ed. J. F. Jameson (N.Y., 1910), 23, 25. A portion of Johnson's narrative is in *The Puritans*, ed. Perry Miller and T. H. Johnson (N.Y., 1963), I, 143–62.

[23] Perry Miller discusses this "errand" in *Errand into the Wilderness*, 11 ff. It should not be overlooked, however, that many Puritans discovered themselves unable to negotiate the demands of life in the New World and returned to England. Others, weary from their struggles with English authorities, merely sought in America refuge from their problems. See Andrew Delbanco, *The Puritan Ordeal* (Cambridge, Mass., 1989) and Theodore Dwight Bozeman, *To Live Ancient Lives: The Primitivist Dimension in Puritanism* (Chapel Hill, NC, 1988).

[24] Miller, *Errand into the Wilderness*, 115. See also Wright, *Religion and Empire*, 115–33.

the Awakening, after so many successive disappointments, as the vindication of the expectation that the final act of God's work of redemption would begin in America. And if "in any part of America," he continued, "I think if we consider the circumstances of the settlement of New England, it must needs appear the most likely of all American colonies to be the place whence this work shall principally take its rise."[25] Whatever other leaders of the revival may have thought of Edwards' speculation as to the point at which the new age would first manifest itself, they shared his belief that God's Spirit was making itself felt in an unusual way and that God had a special destiny in store for America.

This mood of eager expectancy was to continue to be characteristic of American religious life. Having escaped in so many ways the limitations of a bounded existence, men and women were easily persuaded of the reality of unlimited possibilities. The hope of all things being made new, in the course of time, was often subtly secularized and frequently restated in political terms (America as the agent for the establishment of democratic liberties around the globe; mandate to settle territories to the West). But the conviction remained that somehow this was God's country with a mission to perform. For the churches this sense of mission was the source of much of their restless energy as they sought to keep abreast of the western tide of migration and to make sure that the United States would fulfill its calling as a godly nation.

The Outsiders

One should keep in mind, as a continuing feature of the American context, two segments of the population that were unable to share the eager expectation of the dominant majority. The Native Americans quickly became strangers in the land with no heady vision of the future to sustain them. To evangelize the Indians and make them joint-heirs of the promise had been one of the motives of colonization, and there was intermittent missionary activity. For the most part, however, Indians were treated as an alien presence to be pushed back beyond the forward-moving edge of "civilization." In similar fashion captives brought from Africa as slaves were outsiders who had little reason to view the future as pregnant with the possibility of all things being made new.

Mostly only at times of sporadic revolt did the outsiders achieve momentary visibility as persons. It is true that some Indian missions were successful, with converts being accepted and assimilated to new modes of life, but this was not the typical outcome of the encounter between the colonists and the first Americans. A few blacks also gained visibility in churches of their own in the years surrounding the American Revolution.

[25] *The Works of Jonathan Edwards,* Vol. IV, *The Great Awakening,* ed. C. C. Goen (New Haven, 1972), 353, 358.

The dating is shadowy, but two black Baptist preachers, David George and George Liele, gathered a congregation in 1775 at Silver Bluff, South Carolina. Three years later there was a black congregation down river in Savannah. With the British evacuation, David George was carried to Nova Scotia where he gathered a church in 1784, and Liele escaped to Jamaica to carry on Baptist activity there. The first permanent African Baptist church in Savannah was established in 1788 by Andrew Bryan.[26] Meanwhile, in 1776, a black church was founded at Williamsburg, and in 1780 another black Baptist church was formed in Petersburg, Virginia. By the 1790s there were also black Methodist churches in Philadelphia and New York City. Despite these beginnings, a century and a half elapsed before either Native Americans or blacks achieved sufficient visibility to become participants in the shaping of a common destiny for all Americans.

[26] See Albert J. Raboteau, *Slave Religion* (N.Y., 1978).

CHAPTER 2

Transplanted Churches

Where to begin an account of the various religious groups in colonial America is a puzzling question. There was no single dominant group to provide a logical point of departure and to serve as a foil for the discussion of the others. The Congregationalists were the largest of the denominations, but they were a regional group. The Anglicans were the first to establish themselves on the American scene, but they were to be neither the largest nor the most influential of the colonial religious bodies. The Presbyterians and the Baptists were to be both numerous and widely dispersed by the end of the colonial period, but their growth was relatively late and presupposed in part the founding of Pennsylvania by the Quakers. The most satisfactory solution would seem to be to provide a brief review of the founding and the religious complexion of each of the colonies, and then to deal with each of the English-speaking denominations in roughly chronological order before giving attention to the highly significant but much less numerous groups of Continental origin.

Religious Characteristics of the Different Colonies

The 13 colonies came into being as a result of two great waves of English colonizing activity separated by the 20 distracting years (1640–60) of the English civil wars and the regime of Oliver Cromwell. Virginia, Maryland, and the several New England colonies were products of the early years. Following the restoration of the Stuarts to the English throne in 1660, the gap between Maryland and New England on the Atlantic coast was closed by the capture of New Netherlands from the Dutch in 1664 and by the founding of New Jersey in 1674 and of Pennsylvania and Delaware in 1681 and 1682. The southern frontier was extended by the settlement of

Charleston in 1670 in accordance with a proprietary patent to the territory which was later divided into the royal colonies of South and North
Carolina. Georgia, the last of the 13 colonies, was founded in 1733.

The Southern Colonies

Virginia, the earliest of the colonies, was unique in several other respects.
In Virginia alone of all the colonies did the Anglicans command a clear
majority of the religious population; in Virginia alone was Anglicanism the
established religion from the beginning; and in Virginia alone was provision made to enforce conformity to the Church of England. The instructions of James I in the first charter of Virginia were explicit. "The true
word and service of God" was to be "preached, planted, and used" in the
new colony "according to the doctrine, rights [rites?], and religion now
professed and established within our realm of England."[1] Chaplains were
appointed by the Company, and repeated legislation required everyone to
attend the services of the church. It is true that these laws were seldom
rigorously enforced, but the intention was that there should be no toleration of dissent.

The first major break in the pattern of religious uniformity in Virginia
came after 1660 when Quaker missionaries were successful in establishing
scattered communities of adherents, but it was not until the later decades
of the colonial period that the Anglican predominance was sharply reduced and then surpassed as new population flowed into the area that lay
beyond the tidewater region. The surge of non-Anglican strength was
partially the result of Anglican neglect to provide a ministry for the new
arrivals, but it was more largely due to other factors. Many of the new
settlers who spread out in the territory adjacent to the Shenandoah were
Scots from northern Ireland, some were Germans, others were from New
England. The potential Presbyterian strength represented by the Scotch
Irish was marshaled with great effectiveness by Samuel Davies, who had
been sent to Virginia by the Synod of New York in 1748 and who continued to spearhead the Presbyterian advance until 1759 when he became
president of the College of New Jersey (now Princeton). The moderate
growth of the Baptists was transformed into a phenomenal expansion by
the exciting preaching of a transplanted New Englander, Shubal Stearns,
who began his activity in Virginia in 1754. The success of these dissenting
groups was facilitated by the tension that existed between the older and
the newer areas of settlement. Anglicanism suffered because of its identification with the early planters of the tidewater region, whose descendants

---

[1] Peter G. Mode, *Source Book . . . for American Church History* (Menasha, Wis., 1920), 10.

had become a ruling aristocracy that controlled the Assembly, denied full representation to the upcountry districts, and refused to heed their grievances. Moreover, attempts to suppress dissent by this time could be countered by an appeal to rights guaranteed by the English Act of Toleration of 1689.

From the standpoint of religion, North Carolina, South Carolina, and Georgia had little in common with Virginia beyond a nominal establishment of Anglicanism as the official faith of the three colonies. Religious toleration was granted at the outset and the population had little homogeneity. The settlement of North Carolina was haphazard, and it resembled Pennsylvania in its religious diversity. The early inhabitants were runaway servants from Virginia. For many years Quakers were the largest religious group. Later the Scotch Irish sweeping up the Shenandoah valley gave Presbyterians major strength in the southern colonies, and Baptists were active and growing rapidly at the close of the colonial period. Strong German communities — mostly Lutherans and Moravians — were found in both North Carolina and Georgia. Only in South Carolina was there any significant Anglican strength south of Virginia. In 1704 "by dint of political trickery" an act was passed by the South Carolina Assembly providing for an Anglican establishment. Its provisions, however, were never fully carried out because of lack of clergymen, and at best it was a highly precarious establishment depending upon shifting majorities in an Assembly controlled at intervals by the dissenting groups. A similar establishment was secured in North Carolina in 1715 and in Georgia in 1758, but in neither colony did the establishment become operative in more than a handful of parishes.

Maryland, founded in 1634 by the second Lord Baltimore, had many affinities with the middle colonies, both geographic and otherwise. Its proprietor was Roman Catholic; and like the Quaker William Penn, he was as interested in providing a place where his co-religionists could settle as he was in making his colony a profitable financial investment. For both these reasons, like Penn, he pursued a forthright policy of religious toleration. For the first decade or two, Roman Catholics were the only persons in Maryland who received any benefit from this toleration, for there were no other dissenting groups. The non-Catholic Christians there were Anglicans, and one can scarcely speak of tolerating in English territory a church whose "supreme governor" was the English monarch. Indeed, the charter presupposed that churches would be "dedicated and consecrated according to the ecclesiastical laws of our kingdom of England."

The Roman Catholics who participated in the colonization of Maryland were a minority of even the first contingent that sailed for the new colony; and in order not to jeopardize the charter they were instructed by the proprietor that "no scandal nor offense" was "to be given any of the Protestants." On shipboard they were "to cause all acts of the Roman

Catholic religion to be done as privately as may be" and were "to be silent upon all occasion of discourse concerning matters of religion."[2]

The wise precautions by which the proprietor sought to secure the toleration of his co-religionists were not entirely successful, for Roman Catholics were disenfranchised for a brief period in the 1650s after their leaders had proclaimed allegiance to Charles II in opposition to the authority of English Parliament. And after the explusion of James II from the English throne because of his efforts to subvert the Protestant faith, Roman Catholics in Maryland were again subjected to various disabilities. Nevertheless, they remained one of the most important and influential segments of Maryland society.

By 1677 both Roman Catholics and Anglicans had been reduced to the status of minority groups if credence is given Lord Baltimore's report to the Privy Council concerning the shifts that had occurred in the religious affiliations of the Maryland populace. The greatest part of the inhabitants of that province (three of four at least) "do consist of Presbyterians, Independents, Anabaptists, and Quakers; those of the Church of England, as well as those of the Romish, being the fewest."[3] In spite of this numerical inferiority, the overthrow of James II in 1688 marked the beginning of a vigorous campaign to secure an Anglican establishment in Maryland, an objective achieved in 1702 when the Board of Trade and Plantations in London was finally satisfied that the rights of other minorities would be safeguarded. By this time Presbyterians, Baptists, and Quakers were becoming more numerous, and German Protestants were soon to spill over the border from Pennsylvania.

The New England Colonies

Plymouth, the first New England colony, was almost immediately overshadowed by and in 1691 absorbed into Massachusetts Bay Colony, and its religious history differed little from its larger neighbor. Both colonies were established by Congregationalists — Plymouth by Separatist Congregationalists; Massachusetts Bay by Nonseparatist Congregationalists — but in the New World this difference was not of great moment.

A degree of intrigue and perhaps deception lay behind the establishment of Massachusetts Bay. In 1629, when the repressive ecclesiastical measures of William Laud, bishop of London (later archbishop of Canterbury) and chief advisor to the king, were making life in England difficult for them, a group of Nonseparatist Congregationalists obtained from Charles I a royal charter for the Massachusetts Bay Company. For some

---

[2] "The Calvert Papers," no. 1, *Maryland Historical Society Proceedings,* (Baltimore, 1889), 132.

[3] L. J. Trinterud, *The Forming of an American Tradition* (Philadelphia, 1949), 26.

reason the usual clause that required the headquarters of such a company to be in England and thus subject to the immediate control of the crown was omitted from the charter. This could scarcely have been an oversight, for when the great Winthrop fleet sailed in the summer of 1630 it carried with it all the officers and stockholders of the company together with the charter itself. With charter and company in America, the colony was in effect an independent republic. The stockholders were called "freemen" and they became the electorate; the directors or "deputies" became legislators; and the governor of the company became the chief executive of the colony. When it became inconvenient for the whole body of freemen to attend the annual meeting or "general court" of the company, a representative system was devised whereby their "assistants" became a second house of the legislative assembly. When the English authorities finally discovered what had occurred, efforts were made to have the charter returned and the status of the colony regularized. Tactics of delay, however, were adopted; the turmoil of the two decades from 1640 to 1660 intervened, and it was not until 1684 that the charter was finally revoked and a royal governor appointed.

With freedom to pursue an independent course, the early settlers of Massachusetts Bay were in no mood to permit dissent from the "due form" of ecclesiastical government they had established. Having forsaken their homes to found a new Zion in the American wilderness, they saw no reason why their endeavor should be compromised by dissidence. Others, they contended, had full liberty to stay away; and they noted that there was ample room elsewhere in America for them to establish settlements of their own. As early as 1635 the first of a long succession of heresy trials imposing banishment as the most common penalty was held.[4]

The attempt to suppress dissent in Massachusetts Bay was never wholly successful for several reasons. The mere fact of space, even in Massachusetts, made policing difficult. And the policy of banishment created centers just across its borders from which the contagion of dissent filtered back to the older settlements. Furthermore, their fellow Congregationalists in England were embarrassed by their proceedings and exerted constant pressure upon them to adopt a more liberal policy. But the major reason was the fact that within the heart of New England Puritanism there was a steady and persistent acknowledgment that "the Lord hath more light yet to break forth out of his Holy Word" and that therefore they must ever be ready "to receive whatever truth shall be made known . . . from the written Word of God." These were the words of John Robinson (1576–1625), pastor of those who came to Plymouth in 1620 when they were exiles at Leyden, but they represent the basic assumption upon which the whole Congregationalist enterprise was founded. In the

---

[4] Among those banished were Roger Williams, Samuel Gorton, William Coddington, John Wheelwright, and Anne Hutchinson.

Protestantism forever spawns Protesters ! [handwritten annotation]

light of this fundamental principle, it is not surprising that Congregation-alism was forever spawning its own dissidents — men and even women who defended themselves by appealing to the truth that had been made known to them from "the written Word of God." Moreover, given the fact that the average New Englander heard over seven thousand sermons preached in the course of a lifetime, there was more than ample opportunity for men and women to hear and reflect upon Scripture.[5]

Although these factors reduced the effectiveness of the attempt by Massachusetts Bay to enforce conformity, the leaders persisted in their endeavor until 1684 when the loss of the charter made it impossible to proceed independently of English authority. Three years later the end of Congregational monopoly in the colony was dramatically signalized in Boston when the governor forced the Congregationalists to permit the Old South meetinghouse to be utilized for Anglican worship. By the end of the century, Massachusetts had been drawn by the terms of a new charter into a closer orbit around old England, and this included having to come to terms with religious diversity, as a consequence of the English Act of Toleration (1689).

New Hampshire, in its pattern of church life, was little more than an extension of Massachusetts Bay. This was also largely true of Connecticut, founded by Thomas Hooker in 1635 and later incorporating the smaller colony of New Haven. Connecticut in one respect was more conservative than Massachusetts. The *Saybrook Platform* of 1708 provided a more centralized control over the churches.

Rhode Island was a different story. The territory around Narragansett Bay had become the refuge for many of those expelled for reasons of religious dissent from Massachusetts Bay. Roger Williams, who was to be briefly a Baptist and then a Seeker, made his way there in 1636.[6] Anne Hutchinson, the "antinomian" prophetess whose trial shook the whole ruling hierarchy of the Bay colony, arrived with a number of her adherents in 1637. John Coggeshall and William Aspinwell came in 1638, and a little later were joined by John Clarke and William Coddington. Williams, fearful lest the leading of God's Spirit and one's faithfulness to Christ be impaired by the sinful corruption of men, was a firm advocate of complete religious freedom. On this basis he succeeded in bringing together the

---

[5] Cotton Mather, *Magnalia Christi Americana* (Hartford, 1855), I, 64. For a discussion of the frequency with which New Englanders heard sermons preached, see Harry S. Stout, *The New England Soul: Preaching and Religious Culture in Colonial New England* (New York, 1986), 4.

[6] For Williams, see Perry Miller, *Roger Williams: His Contribution to the American Tradition* (Indianapolis, 1953), and W. C. Gilpin, *The Millenarian Piety of Roger Williams* (Chicago, 1979). For a brief account, see Introduction to his *Experiments of Spiritual Life and Health*, ed. W. S. Hudson (Philadelphia, 1951). For a discussion of Roger Williams set in the context of religious liberty in America, see William Lee Miller, *The First Liberty: Religion and the American Republic* (N.Y., 1986).

disparate religious elements represented in the communities at Providence, Portsmouth, Newport, and Warwick to form the colony of Rhode Island and Providence Plantations, traveling to England in 1643 to secure the necessary patent from the English Parliament. Although Baptists initially were the largest group in Rhode Island, they were soon rivaled and then surpassed by the Quakers who utilized the freedom the colony afforded as a base from which to attempt the evangelization of other parts of New England.

The Middle Colonies

When the English took over control of New Netherlands in 1664, the new colony was the most religiously heterogeneous area in America. The Dutch Reformed church quite understandably was the largest single religious group, and throughout the seventeenth century it was to continue to have more adherents than all other groups combined. But, as Governor Dongan (a Roman Catholic) reported in 1687, there were also French Calvinists, German Lutherans, Congregationalists from New England, several varieties of Quakers, Mennonites, Baptists, some Roman Catholics, and a few Jews. "In short," he explained, "of all sorts of opinion there are some, and of the most part none at all."

The terms of capitulation to England provided that the Dutch should have freedom of conscience, worship, and church discipline. This was interpreted to mean that the Dutch Reformed church retained a measure of its established character, and the early English governors considered that the Dutch Reformed ministers were entitled to support from public funds. The Duke of York, to whom the colony had been granted by royal patent, also issued instructions that no one who professed the Christian faith was to be in any way disturbed for differing judgment in religious matters. Thus the policy of religious toleration that hitherto had prevailed was continued, with only the status of the Jews left in doubt.

After the Glorious Revolution of 1688, which brought William and Mary to the English throne, the governor of New York was instructed to secure an Anglican establishment in the colony. After repeated rebuffs, the Assembly was finally induced in 1693 to adopt a measure that stipulated only that a "sufficient Protestant minister" should be supported by an annual tax in each of six parishes to be set up in New York City and three adjoining counties. The governor interpreted the act (contrary to the intention of the Assembly) as a legal establishment of the Church of England. It was a small victory, for there were too few Anglicans in the colony to give it much substance. As the chaplain of the English garrison reported, there were only 90 Anglican families in the entire colony, in contrast to the 1,754 Dutch Reformed families and the 1,355 families of various types of English dissent.

The colony of New Jersey had a checkered development. Initially it was part of the grant to the Duke of York in 1664, but almost immediately he gave it to two friends. A few hundred Dutch and New England emigrês were already there, and to attract more settlers laws were promulgated that provided for freedom of conscience and an assembly. In 1674 West New Jersey was sold to two Quakers, who let William Penn become one of the proprietors. It was not until 1702, when New Jersey became a royal colony, that the two sections were reunited. Delaware was purchased by Penn from the Duke of York in 1682 and was administered jointly with Pennsylvania until given a separate assembly in 1704.

William Penn founded Pennsylvania in 1681. Son of an admiral, Penn was converted to Quakerism in 1667 at the age of 23. Penn was eager to secure a colony where, free from the pressure of bad example and worldly corruption, he could carry out a "holy experiment" in establishing a society fashioned in accordance with Quaker ideals. His share of West (New) Jersey did not satisfy his ambitions; a tactful reminder to the Duke of York of a debt to his father that had not been repaid led to his becoming the proprietor of the vast slice of territory that was given the name Pennsylvania.

The settlement of the new colony began without delay. A few Swedes, Finns, and Dutch were already there, and large-scale Quaker immigration set in at once. Other English-speaking inhabitants were enticed by the easy terms for the purchase of land described in Penn's promotional brochure, *Some Account of the Province of Pennsylvania* (1681). The prospect of religious freedom attracted several German minority religious groups (see pp. 52–57); the lure of economic advantage drew other Germans from the economically depressed Palatinate. Large numbers of Scotch-Irish Presbyterians also arrived driven from home by the economic consequences of the Woolens Act of 1699 and by religious disabilities imposed in 1704. Quakers, however, continued to set the tone of the colony and, due to unbalanced representation in the Assembly, Quakers long maintained political dominance.

The English-Speaking Denominations

The Church of England was drastically reformed at the time of the Protestant Reformation. Ties with Rome were severed, monasteries suppressed, prayers for the dead abolished, altars replaced by tables, the liturgy reshaped and rewritten, worship conducted in English, and the monarch acknowledged as "supreme governor" of the church. Although the English church was indebted to the major Reformed theologians— Bucer, Bullinger, and Calvin—for its theology, the impact of the variant form of Calvinism known as Arminianism[7] began to be felt soon after the first colonies were settled. During the reigns of Elizabeth (1558–1603) and James I (1603–25), a strong Puritan movement developed within the church which sought to remove a few remaining popish "ornaments," to promote godly preaching throughout the land, and to secure greater self-government for the church. A policy that gave Puritan consciences considerable latitude avoided, except for a few small separatist groups, any open break until after Charles I came to the throne. In the 1630s, however, Archbishop Laud's attempt to enforce rigid conformity by means of extra-legal royal prerogative courts helped fuel the flames that resulted in civil war between King and Parliament in the 1640s. When the Long Parliament met in 1640, almost everyone was opposed to the "prelacy" represented by Laud. Beyond that, there was no agreement. Some favored a reformed episcopacy, some favored a presbyterian system of church government after the Scottish model, some became independents (congregationalists) who stressed the rights of local congregations. Some of the latter advocated believers' baptism. In the confusion following the defeat and execution of the king, still other groups appeared, the Quakers being the most prominent. When the Stuart line was restored in 1660, a new attempt was made to enforce a rigid conformity, a policy that ended with the Glorious Revolution of 1688 when James II was expelled and the Act of Toleration of 1689 was adopted. Henceforth the Church of England was to be in fact and in law the church of only part of the English people. A further anomaly for an "established" or "state church" was the fact that the monarch when in Scotland ceased to be an Anglican and became a Presbyterian.

The Anglicans

In colonial America, Virginia was the great center of Anglican strength. And Anglicanism served well to promote stability and social solidarity in the tidewater, beginning with the arrival of the first minister in Jamestown, who brought spiritual milk to those who had survived the "starving time" of the settlement's first years. The first ministers were chaplains sent out by the Virginia Company, but between 1619 and 1622 a rudimentary parish system was set up with assessments levied and land set aside for parochial support. Lay vestries with responsibility for ordering parish life probably were introduced at this time. They were given statutory authority in 1643 when the Assembly ordered that vestrymen should be

---

[7] Jacob Arminius (1560–1609) was a Dutch Calvinist who opposed the hyper-Calvinism of the late sixteenth century. Later the term *Arminian* was used in England to designate a "Romish" tendency to stress the human role in redemption. A century later John Wesley used the term with a still different connotation. See the portion of his "What Is an Arminian?" printed in H. E. Fosdick, *Great Voices of the Reformation* (N.Y., 1952), 514–17.

chosen by the voters of each parish. Later the vestries became self-perpet-uating bodies, the preserves of the socially and economically privileged.

There was a perennial shortage of ministers throughout the colonial years. This was partly due to the fact that the establishment of a college to train a native ministry, though earnestly sought, was long delayed. Although Harvard College was founded as early as 1636, it was not until 1693 that Virginia was able to secure a similar institution for training its clergy. Even after William and Mary opened its doors, the problem was not wholly solved. Since a bishop alone could ordain, young Anglicans who wished to enter the ministry were compelled to undertake the long and hazardous journey to England to secure ordination.

Among expedients used to entice ministers to Virginia was the payment of a bounty of 20 pounds to anyone who would transport a "sufficient minister" to the colony. Later the bounty was paid directly to the minister. Clergymen secured by such means were of uneven quality. Several were of unusual ability, although many were not. But even the competent and faithful had a difficult time. Parishes were large, population was scattered, and a legal technicality frequently deprived them of security and author-ity. A 1629 act directed the governor to "induct" a minister "into any parish that shall make presentation of him." Vestries discovered that by neglecting to present their ministers for induction, the parish remained technically vacant and the minister could be made subservient by hiring him on a yearly basis. If the faithful and competent had a difficult time by being subjected to the whims of the vestry, clergy of less zeal and devotion found the absence of episcopal supervision a distinct advantage. Charges of indolence, drunkenness, and immorality were not uncommon. Although abuses were not as widespread as some suggested, there were few means by which they could be corrected. In this regard there was a significant difference from New England, and it stemmed partly from the fact that Virginia was settled primarily as a trading colony, not as a refuge for religious visionaries.

The Anglican clergy in the colonies were nominally under the supervi-sion of the bishop of London, but, apart from certain formalities, his jurisdiction was not given practical implementation until after the Revolu-tion of 1688 when Bishop Compton began to delegate his disciplinary authority to resident "Commissaries," the most notable of whom were James Blair in Virginia and Thomas Bray in Maryland. Although they did much to improve the condition of both church and clergy, they lacked the full episcopal powers that were indispensable to a fully developed church life. Bray was one of the first to make an earnest plea for an American episcopate, but despite continuing agitation this was to remain an unreal-ized hope throughout the whole colonial period. Much of the opposition to the appointment of a bishop came from the laity, who felt that he would jeopardize their prerogatives. William White, who became one of the first bishops of the newly formed Protestant Episcopal Church after the American Revolution, declared in 1782 that "there cannot be produced an instance of laymen in America, unless in the very infancy of the settlements, soliciting the introduction of a bishop." Even the clergy in the southern parishes were opposed to the establishment of an American episcopate, Samuel Auchmuty reported, since without a bishop they were "their own pastors."[8]

The missionaries sent out by the Society for the Propagation of the Gospel (S.P.G.) after 1701 presented a brighter picture than did the general run of the parish clergy. The primary objective of the Society was to provide for "the administration of God's Word and the sacraments" in those areas where there were no settled Anglican clergy. From the time of its inception until 1783 when it officially ceased operations in the newly independent colonies, 84 of its missionaries labored in New England, 58 in New York, 54 in South Carolina, 47 in Pennsylvania, 44 in New Jersey, 33 in North Carolina, 13 in Georgia, 5 in Maryland, and only 2 in Virginia. In all, 309 missionaries were recruited to serve in these colonies, and well over $1 million (£227,454) was raised in England for their support.[9]

The S.P.G. missionaries constituted a superior caste among the Anglican clergy. A measure of idealism and devotion was required of those whose only prospect of financial remuneration was the relatively small stipend provided by the Society. A life of ease and modest comfort might be envisioned by those who sought appointment to established parishes, but this was never the lot of the missionaries. Furthermore, the absence of episcopal authority and discipline was in a measure remedied by the Society. The Society, to be sure, could not unfrock an erring minister, but it could and did dismiss the indolent, the disobedient, and the immoral from its service. Everywhere, even in New England and Pennsylvania, the missionaries had the advantage of varying degrees of official support, an advantage they were not slow to exploit. The advantage, of course, became a liability with the coming of the American Revolution. The missionaries almost to a man identified themselves completely with the English cause, and in the end few of them remained to carry on the ministry of the Protestant Episcopal Church in the United States.

Since the S.P.G. missionaries were to disappear with the coming of independence, a development of greater long-range significance was the emergence of an indigenous Anglicanism in New England. The break came on the day after commencement in September 1722, when Timothy Cutler, president of Yale College, announced to the astonished trustees that he and one of the tutors and three neighboring ministers had been

---

[8] William White, *The Case of the Episcopal Churches in the United States Considered*, ed. R. G. Salomon (Philadelphia, 1954), 29. Carl Bridenbaugh, *Mitre and Sceptre* (N.Y., 1962), 249.

[9] C. S. Pascoe, *An Historical Account of the Society for the Propagation of the Gospel* (London, 1901), 86–87.

persuaded that their congregational ordinations were invalid. This change of view went back in part to a gift of books to the library, some of which detailed the Anglican claim to be the lineal descendant of the apostolic church. A more decisive factor perhaps was the influence exerted by an S.P.G. missionary stationed at Stratford, for Cutler and his friends did not reveal their new sentiments until they had been assured of support by the Society. Four of the converts went abroad to seek episcopal ordination. One of them died there of the smallpox, but the others returned to serve as missionaries of the Society — Cutler becoming the first rector of Christ Church in Boston, James Whetmore serving the mission station at Rye, and Samuel Johnson ultimately becoming the first president of King's College (Columbia University) in New York.

The apostasy of the president of Yale was a traumatic shock to New England Congregationalism, and as a result of his influence and example there were continuing conversions among the students at New Haven. These conversions gave the Church of England in the colonies a nucleus of native-born and native-trained ministers who were "convinced" rather than "birthright" Anglicans, and they brought to their pastoral endeavors all the zeal and ardor that is commonly found among converts.

The Congregationalists

The "congregationalism" of the early New Englanders was the product of the peculiar history of the English Reformation, which in several respects was an "arrested" reformation. Some of the early advocates of a more thoroughgoing reform, especially liturgical reform, broke from the parish churches and established independent churches of their own. These were the Separatists.[10] They restricted church membership to convinced believers and insisted that, since all members were equally priests, all should share in the determination of church affairs. Others who were dissatisfied with the slow pace of official reform found a considerable measure of freedom to carry out their desired reforms within the established parishes. As long as they engaged in no concerted organizational activity, both Elizabeth and James I were content for the most part to leave them to their own devices. When pressure was applied they found patrons to aid them, and they became adept at defending their rights in the common-law courts. They did not reject the Church of England as a false church, although they acknowledged that in many ways it was deformed and tainted with corruptions.

This point of view was made explicit in the words Francis Higginson is reported to have said on shipboard as the shores of England faded from view:

---

[10] Robert Browne (1550?–1633?), author of *Reformation without Tarrying for Any[one]* (1582), was the early leader.

> We will not say as the Separatists are wont to say at their leaving England, "Farewell Babylon, Farewell Rome" but we will say, "Farewell dear England, Farewell the Church of God in England and all the Christian friends there." We do not go to New England as Separatists from the Church of England, though we cannot be separate from the corruptions in it.[11]

Prior to Higginson's departure in 1629, these Nonseparatist Congregationalists had elaborated the theory that in the hidden essence of its constitution the Church of England was basically congregational in structure. They differed from the Presbyterians at two points. Since they had had unworthy and unwanted ministers thrust upon them in their parish churches, they were unwilling to concede the power of ordination even to a presbytery, reserving it to the local congregation alone. Furthermore, since they had been pressured on occasion by the threat of excommunication wielded by a bishop, they were insistent that this power also must be reserved to the local congregation so that an individual might be tried by those who knew him best and not by any higher judicatory.

The Separatists provided the nucleus of the settlement at Plymouth; those who came to Massachusetts Bay were Congregationalists of the Nonseparatist variety. The difference between the two groups was not great, and two factors served to obliterate it. First, shortly before their departure from their refuge in the Netherlands, the leader of this particular group of Separatists, John Robinson, had been persuaded of the validity of most of the Nonseparatist contentions. Second, in the New World the old issue that had divided them, whether or not the parish churches of England could in some way be viewed as true churches, was not of great significance, for they had to establish new churches of their own. Thus they became joint representatives of what was to be a single denomination. There were a few isolated individuals like Roger Williams, of course, who insisted that they should repudiate the Church of England in profession as well as in practice, but this counsel was rejected as politically inexpedient.

Unlike other religious groups, the Congregationalists in America were well supplied with ministers from the beginning, with no fewer than 130 graduates of Cambridge and Oxford having come out to serve the churches prior to 1647. "Such a concentration of educated men within a new settlement in proportion to the population," it has been stated, "has never occurred before or since," and one of the first concerns of the early settlers was to make provision for the future supply of educated ministers. *New England's First Fruits* (1643) emphasized this point in its account of the founding of Harvard in 1636.

> After God had carried us safe to New England and we had builded our houses, provided necessaries for our livelihood, reared convenient places for

---

[11] Cotton Mather, *Magnalia*, I, 362. For an elaboration of the Separatist–Nonseparatist distinction, see Perry Miller, *Orthodoxy in Massachusetts*, 53–101.

God's worship, and settled the civil government; one of the next things we longed for and looked after was to advance learning and perpetuate it to posterity, dreading to leave an illiterate ministry to the churches when our present ministers shall lie in the dust.[12]

So successful were they in this endeavor that of the 1,586 ministers who served the Congregational churches of New England during the colonial period, only 79 were not college graduates.

Elementary education was of equal concern, being "one chief project of that old deluder Satan to keep men from the knowledge of the Scriptures."[13] To counter this "project," a grammar school was established in every town. The consequence of this systematic effort, as Andrew Eliot informed Thomas Hollis in 1761, was that "scarce any are to be found among us, even in the obscurest parts, who are not able to read and write with tolerable propriety."

"The convenient places for God's worship" that were erected were called meetinghouses so that people would not be confused and make the mistake of thinking that the church was a building. These houses in which the church met were plain structures, often beautiful in their simplicity, with the people gathered about the table which stood at the center and with a high pulpit on one side for the reading and preaching of God's Word. The worship was equally plain, with the singing of psalms, a long prayer, the reading of Scripture, and a sermon being the principal features. The government of these churches was given its classic definition in the *Cambridge Platform* of 1648,[14] a document drafted and adopted in response to a "Remonstrance" that challenged the Congregational way of proceeding and threatened an appeal to the English Parliament if the restrictions upon church membership and voting were not liberalized. The synod that framed the *Platform* also adopted as a statement of the Congregationalist doctrinal position the Confession of Faith that had just been issued in England by the Westminster Assembly of Divines.

The *Cambridge Platform* had sidestepped one issue with regard to church membership that had begun to trouble the churches, and it proved to be an issue that could not long be ignored. According to Congregational theory, both the believing adult and his infant child belonged to the church, the latter being "federally holy" and entitled to receive baptism. On reaching the age of discretion, however, the child was required to give an account of his or her own repentance and faith in order to qualify for

---

[12] A portion of *New England's First Fruits* is printed in *The Puritans*, ed. Miller and Johnson, II, 70–77.

[13] S. E. Morison, *The Puritan Pronaos: Studies in the Intellectual Life of New England in the Seventeenth Century* (N.Y., 1936), 65.

[14] A portion is reprinted in H. S. Smith, R. T. Handy, and L. A. Loetscher, *American Christianity* (N.Y., 1960–63), I, 128–40. The full text is in Walker, *Creeds and Platforms of Congregationalism*.

full communicant standing, including the right to partake of the Lord's Supper and to vote at church meetings. It was understood that true faith, even among the weakest Christians, would be confirmed by some specific experience of God's redeeming grace, and that in the absence of such an experience a person was not to be admitted to full membership. This practice posed no problem until grandchildren began to be born whose parents were but "half-way" embraced within the convenant community and the question was raised as to whether their children were "federally" related to the church and qualified to receive baptism.

The controversy that ensued was heated—whatever the decision, one of two equally cherished "goods" would be sacrificed. If baptism were denied to children of unregenerate parents, the integrity of the churches as gathered communities of convinced believers would be preserved but an increasing proportion of the population would be removed from the discipline of the church, and the endeavor to fashion a holy commonwealth in the American wilderness would be endangered. If baptism were granted, the churches would be in danger of becoming "mixed multitudes" of the regenerate and unregenerate. Seventeen ministers from Massachusetts and Connecticut met in Boston in 1657 and announced that they were persuaded that the children of half-way convenanters should be baptized. Their action served only to inflame the opposition, which was led by Charles Chauncy, president of Harvard. Finally, the General Court of Massachusetts Bay intervened in 1662 and sought to end the controversy by summoning a synod of the churches to reach an authoritative decision. When the vote was taken after long debate, the earlier judgment of the 17 ministers was sustained.

The decision of the synod opened the door to further laxity. Within little more than a decade, the restriction that kept unregenerate church members from partaking of the Lord's Supper began to break down. Solomon Stoddard, pastor at Northampton, became the chief advocate of lowering the bar at this point. He insisted that the germ of grace is latent in all the children of the covenant and that it should be nourished by partaking of the Lord's Supper as soon as possible. To him it seemed contradictory that those who were in need of grace should be denied this means of grace because of their weakness in grace. His arguments were persuasive to many and his practice was widely adopted.

A further breach was effected in Boston toward the close of the century. The instigators were two Harvard tutors, William Brattle and William Leverett, who, while remaining Congregationalists, were attracted to certain aspects of Anglicanism. They insisted that all distinctions among church members should be discarded and that even those who could not testify to an experience of grace should be allowed to participate in the government of the church, including the right to vote in the selection of the minister. Without the consent of the other churches, they proceeded to organize a new church upon this basis. And so a process of "Anglicization" began in the New England churches.

The formation of the Brattle Street Church in 1699 stirred the conservatives to action. Their plan, embodied in the *Massachusetts Proposals* of 1705, was to bring the churches under a form of synodical control to hold further innovation in check. This proposal of the ministers received no support from the governor and council appointed under the new charter of 1691, for they had no intent of diminishing their power by setting up an instrument for independent action by the clergy. The *Proposals* received equally short shrift from many church members, whose fear that their rights and privileges might thereby be lost was articulated by John Wise of Ipswich in two tracts that later became part of the ideological arsenal of the American Revolution.[15]

Though defeated in Massachusetts, the conservative party was more successful in Connecticut, where Yale College had been founded in 1701 with the aid of the Mathers as a counter to the lax influences emanating from Harvard. The *Saybrook Platform* of 1708 embodied all the essential features of the *Massachusetts Proposals*. It provided that the churches of each county were to be formed into a Consociation which was to have disciplinary oversight over them and from whose decision there was to be no appeal. These churches were further bound together by a General Association made up of delegates from each of the local Associations. The approval of the colonial authorities was secured by including the proviso that no church should be compelled to join the "united churches" or hindered, if allowed by the general laws of Connecticut, from exercising discipline in its own way.

As a result of the stabilizing influence exerted by Yale and the achievement of a measure of disciplinary oversight of the churches, Connecticut became the citadel of Congregational orthodoxy. Over the course of time, many of the Connecticut Congregationalists came to feel a greater sense of kinship with the Presbyterians than they did with their fellow Congregationalists of Massachusetts, who had been unable to complete their system with any connectional body and thus pursued a more independent development.

The Presbyterians

The classic form of Presbyterianism, with its presbyteries, synods, and general assembly, took shape in Scotland, where the Reformation had been carried forward under the leadership of John Knox, after his return from John Calvin's Geneva. It did not differ greatly from the structures devised by the other Reformed churches on the Continent. Incipient presbyterian tendencies had long been present in English Puritanism, and they came to the fore when the Long Parliament met in 1640. One reason

---

[5] *The Churches Quarrel Espoused* (1713) and *A Vindication of the Government of New England Churches* (1717). An excerpt from the latter tract is in *The Puritans*, ed. Miller and Johnson, I, 257–69.

for the strength of the Presbyterian party that emerged at that time was the influence of the Scottish Commissioners. The meeting of Parliament had been precipitated by a Scottish invasion, which in turn had been occasioned by an attempt to impose "Laud's liturgy" upon the Scottish churches. The Scots supported Parliament in its controversy with the king, but they insisted, as a condition of their support, that the Church of England be brought into conformity with the Church of Scotland so that occasion for future strife might be avoided.

Presbyterian sentiment was constantly cropping out in early New England and gained strength from the course of events at home. Hingham and Newbury were two notable centers, and several Presbyterian churches were established by migrating New Englanders—first on Long Island and then in New Jersey, Pennsylvania, Maryland, and South Carolina. Several of these churches were brought together to form the Presbytery of Philadelphia in 1706. Ten years later three additional presbyteries were organized and the Synod of Philadelphia was established. Although there were scattered groups of Scotch Irish in the colonies as early as the 1680s, the great influx of population from northern Ireland which contributed so greatly to Presbyterian strength did not begin until 1720. Those who settled in the back country of New England tended to be absorbed into the Congregational churches, but the major flow of Scotch Irish was into the middle colonies and down the Shenandoah valley into the Piedmont region of the South, and these areas became the great centers of Presbyterian strength and influence.

Francis Makemie, a Scotch Irishman with strong ties to both England and New England, was the key figure in the early growth of American Presbyterianism. He was in effect a missionary-at-large, itinerating widely to gather churches and to supervise their work. He had been sent to the colonies in 1683 by the Presbytery of Laggan in Ireland, but after 1691 he served as an agent of the newly formed United Brethren (Congregationalists and Presbyterians) in London. Although he was the leading spirit in the formation of the Presbytery of Philadelphia in 1706, he did not think in terms of denominational aggrandizement and he insisted that it was the height of folly to magnify the small differences that existed among Protestants.

In 1707 Makemie became one of the heroes of the struggle for religious freedom. He had been arrested by the governor of New York for unlicensed preaching, and he responded that "to give bond not to preach" was one thing he did not dare do. He appealed to the Boston ministers for help; they enlisted the aid of the United Brethren in London, and the case became a *cause célèbre*.[16] Makemie was acquitted after a brilliant defense, but the governor forced him to pay the costs of his own prosecution—the

---

[16] An account of Makemie's apprehension and examination is printed in *The Presbyterian Enterprise: Sources of American Presbyterian History,* ed. M. W. Armstrong, L. A. Loetscher, and C. A. Anderson (Philadelphia, 1956), 13–18.

rather considerable sum of £83/7s/6d. This injustice so incensed the
colonial legislature that an act was passed prohibiting the assessment of
such costs in the future. Charges were also brought against the governor,
which led to his being recalled to London in disgrace.

Makemie died in 1708, and the subsequent history of the Presbyterians
in colonial America was to be inextricably entangled in the story of the
Great Awakening. This was true even of the Adopting Act of 1729[17] by
which the Synod of Philadelphia established the Westminster Confession
of Faith as the doctrinal standard of American Presbyterianism, since
freedom was given the presbyteries to distinguish between the essential
and nonessential doctrines contained therein.

The Baptists

The English Baptists were another offshoot of the Puritan movement.
Baptists were Congregationalists who had become convinced that if
churches were to be composed of believers only, then baptism should be
restricted to those who were able to give some account of their own faith.
Prior to 1640 the Baptists in England were few in number. It was during
the decade that followed that they became a significant and influential
group, with their most notable strength being gained among the officers
and men of Cromwell's army. Some of the Baptists—the General
Baptists—were Arminian in theology, deriving their name from their
adherence to the doctrine of a general atonement. What was destined to
be the major Baptist body, however, was firmly rooted in the Calvinistic
tradition that found its classic expression in the Westminster Confession of
Faith.[18]

Baptist beginnings in America closely paralleled those of the Presbyterians. It was not the intention of the founders of New England to foster
dissent, but dissent there was from the start, and the considerations that
had led some of the English Congregationalists to become Baptists were
equally persuasive to some New Englanders. Henry Dunster, for example,
rejected infant baptism in 1654 and was forced to resign as president of
Harvard. The key figure initially, however, was Roger Williams, who was
instrumental in forming a Baptist church at Providence in 1639, three
years after establishing a settlement there. Williams soon abdicated his
Baptist leadership, for he became convinced that all existing churches,
including the newly established Providence church, lacked a proper foundation, a defect that could be remedied only by a new apostolic dispensation in which new apostles, authoritatively commissioned and divinely
authenticated, would appear to reestablish the true church. A more im-

---

[17] Printed in *The Presbyterian Enterprise*, 30–32. See also Jonathan Dickinson's *Remarks* in
Smith, Handy, and Loetscher, *American Christianity*, I, 262–68.

[18] The several strands of Baptist life are discussed in *Baptist Concepts of the Church*, ed.
W. S. Hudson (Philadelphia, 1959), 11–29.

portant person in early Baptist history was John Clark, who had gathered a church at Newport, Rhode Island, in 1641. It was Clarke's *Ill News from New England* (1652) that gave notoriety to the case of Obadiah Holmes, who was publicly whipped by the Massachusetts authorities for conducting unauthorized worship in Lynn.

Although Rhode Island remained a center of Baptist activity and a Baptist church was organized in Boston as early as 1665, the major Baptist growth prior to the Great Awakening stemmed from the formation of the Philadelphia Baptist Association in 1707. This Association was founded almost simultaneously with the Presbytery of Philadelphia and was similar in character to the presbytery although it lacked the latter's "authoritative" judicial power. Initially the Association was composed of churches in New Jersey, Pennsylvania, and Delaware; later it also included churches in Connecticut, New York, Maryland, and Virginia; ultimately subsidiary Associations were formed in Massachusetts and Virginia, and a relationship was established with the Charleston Association in the Carolinas. The Association carried on vigorous missionary activity from Nova Scotia to Georgia, and it established the College of Rhode Island (Brown University) as a training center for its ministers. The Philadelphia Confession of Faith of these American Baptists was a slightly amended version of the Westminster Confession of Faith, following the changes introduced by the Savoy Declaration (1658) of the English Congregationalists with an additional modification at the point of baptism.[19]

Although the growth of the Baptists was substantial during the first half of the eighteenth century, the large-scale accessions which made them one of the major religious groups in America occurred just prior to and during the American Revolution.

The Quakers

The Society of Friends, as the Quakers are more properly termed, emerged in England around 1650 out of the turmoil and confusion of the religious controversies that had accompanied the English civil wars.[20] During these years many people had pursued what was in effect a spiritual pilgrimage from one group to another. In the end there were many who became completely disenchanted by the welter of competing claims and, like Roger Williams, became Seekers waiting for a new apostolic dispensation when the true Church would be restored. Others, whom Oliver Cromwell was to describe as "happy finders," believed that the new

[19] "The Platform of Government," which the English Congregationalists had appended to the Savoy Declaration, was incorporated in the body of the Confession by the Baptists.

[20] For the Puritan antecedents, see G. F. Nuttal, *The Holy Spirit in Puritan Faith and Experience* (Oxford, Eng., 1946). Two standard accounts of the Quakers are Howard Brinton, *Friends for 300 Years: The History and Beliefs of the Society of Friends* (N.Y., 1952), and F. B. Tolles, *Quakers and the Atlantic Culture* (N.Y., 1960).

dispensation, in the form of a new age of the Spirit, had already arrived. It was from among these "happy finders" that George Fox gathered the people known as Quakers. They were a plain people — plain in dress, plain in speech, and plain in behavior. They gathered in silence for worship until one of their number was led by the Spirit to speak. Many of them became itinerant "publishers of truth," moving from place to place to declare that Christ had already returned to reign, that he was rising up as the "Christ within" in innumerable sons and daughters, and that the terrible day of the Lord was at hand when the whole creation would be purged of dross and corruption.

Few groups exhibited the intense missionary zeal that characterized the early Quakers. In many ways they were a most attractive people of simple honesty and integrity, but in terms of their missionary activity they were frequently the most troublesome of people. It became customary for them to invade churches and to interrupt the sermon with denunciations of false worship and the folly of seeking God through empty forms and human inventions. A few felt called by the Spirit to even more bizarre behavior, such as going naked through the streets of a town as a "sign." By 1700, however, the early excesses had disappeared and Quakerism entered a period of "quietism." Henceforth they were to be the most restrained of people in their behavior and were to become increasingly esteemed for their humanitarian sympathies and concerns. John Woolman is the most famous representative of this latter tendency. The journal in which he tells of his itinerant ministry in bearing testimony against slavery is a moving testament of devotion.[21]

The first Quaker missionaries to reach the New World were two women, Mary Fisher and Ann Austin, who arrived in Boston in 1656 and were followed a few weeks later by eight additional publishers of truth. The following year Quaker missionaries made their appearance in New Amsterdam and Virginia. Everywhere, except in Rhode Island, they were harried with fines, imprisonment, and deportation. The most savage persecution occurred in Massachusetts, where a law was enacted subjecting Quaker missionaries who returned to the colony, after once having been banished, to the death penalty. Four suffered martyrdom before Charles II intervened in 1661 and put an end to the executions.

Rhode Island and Long Island, where the followers of Anne Hutchinson had been embryonic Quakers for 20 years, quickly became centers of Quaker strength. By the time George Fox arrived for a missionary tour in 1672, persecution had practically ceased and Quaker "meetings" were to be found in every colony from New Hampshire to South Carolina. Two years later, when West (New) Jersey came under the control of Quaker proprietors, the flow of Quaker settlers to the New World set in, and the number of Quaker immigrants swelled to a great tide after Pennsylvania

---

[21] *The Journal of John Woolman* (Chicago, 1950).

was established as a Quaker domain in 1681. As a result of the earlier missionary activity and the later migration, Quakers ranked fifth numerically among the various religious bodies at the close of the colonial period.

As the number of Quakers increased, zeal tended to diminish. The passage of time and growing prosperity took their toll. In 1764 an aged Quaker minister summarized the decline that had taken place over the past 60 years. He well remembered, he declared, that in the early days

> Friends were a plain lowly minded people and that there was much tenderness and contrition in their meetings; and that at the end of twenty years from that time, the Society increasing in wealth and in some degree conforming to the fashions of the world, true humility decreased and their meetings in general were not so lively and edifying; that at the end of forty years many of the Society were grown rich, that wearing of fine costly garments and with fashionable furniture, silver watches became customary with many and with their sons and daughters, and as these things prevailed in the Society and appeared in our meetings of ministers and elders so the powerful overshadowings of the Holy Spirit were less manifested amongst us . . . and that the weakness amongst us in not living up to our principles and supporting the testimony of truth in faithfulness was matter of much sorrow.[22]

With the passing of the first generation, there were many who were Quakers by birth rather than conviction. This tendency was both accelerated and sanctioned by the action of the London Yearly Meeting in 1737 which permitted "the wife and children to be deemed members of the Monthly Meeting of which the husband or father is a member, not only during his life but after his decease." Thus the Quakers with their "birthright membership" were pursuing the same path as New England Congregationalists with their progressive lowering of the bars to church membership after the adoption of the Half-way Covenant.

The Roman Catholics

Of all the churches that took definitive shape at the time of the Reformation, the Roman Catholic Church was by far the largest. As certain elements in the pre-Reformation church had been made normative for Lutherans by the Augsburg Confession and the Formula of Concord, so other elements were made normative for Roman Catholics by the decrees of the Council of Trent (1545–63). In spite of their predominance in many parts of Europe, the Roman Catholics were a small minority in England. Although their faith was proscribed by law, few Roman Catholics found the hard conditions of life in America an attractive prospect. In England they were mostly landed gentry and they had friends at Court to

---

[22] F. B. Tolles, *Meeting House* and *Counting House* (Chapel Hill, N.C., 1948), 123–24.

offer them protection. Consequently, enjoying at least modest comfort and relative security, these English Roman Catholics did not bulk large in the colonizing activity of their compatriots. Since there was to be no significant Roman Catholic immigration from the Continent until after the American Revolution, the Roman Catholic population in the colonies was largely limited to Maryland, where the proprietor had granted large manors to his Catholic friends. There were a few Roman Catholics in New York and a larger number in Pennsylvania, but elsewhere only isolated individuals were to be found.[23]

When the *Ark* sailed from England late in 1633 with the first contingent of settlers for Maryland, it stopped briefly at the Isle of Wight to pick up two Jesuit priests, Fathers Andrew White and John Altham, who were to distinguish themselves in the new colony by their earnest pastoral care and by their missionary activity among the Indians. Later they became involved in controversy with the proprietor because of their zeal in attempting to proselyte among non-Catholics and because of their purchase of land directly from the Indians. In different ways both of these proceedings appeared to threaten Lord Baltimore's authority, and when he carried the issue to Rome they were ordered to yield to his demands. The resolution of the controversy was hastened by the arrival of two secular priests in 1642 to replace the dissident Jesuits. In 1669 the proprietor complained that only two priests remained in the colony, and as a result two Franciscans were sent out in 1673; they were joined four years later by three additional Franciscans and three more Jesuits. Within a few years Catholic families were moving northward into Pennsylvania, and in 1706 the Jesuits opened a mission near the border of Pennsylvania and for a brief period conducted a school there. This school was apparently the only Catholic educational venture until the founding of Georgetown Academy in 1791.

Denominations of Continental Origin

With the exception of African slaves and native Americans who had little opportunity to develop independent religious institutions, there were only three nationality groups of measurable size at the end of the colonial period that were of non-British stock. These were the Germans with roughly 9 percent of the white population; the Dutch, 3 percent; and the French, 1.7 percent.[24] Of these, the Dutch and the French were the earliest arrivals, with most of the latter initially being French-speaking Walloons. Practically all these people, whether Dutch, French, or German, were of Protestant background.

[23] Ellis, *Catholics in Colonial America* (Baltimore, 1965).
[24] W. L. Sperry, *Religion in America* (N.Y., 1946), 266–70.

The Dutch and French Reformed

Reformed Protestantism had no single outstanding early leader. It originated in the reforming activity of such men as Huldreich Zwingli, Henry Bullinger, Martin Bucer, and William Farel. Later John Calvin emerged as the most influential of the Reformed theologians, and his *Institutes of the Christian Religion* became the most representative statement of the Reformed understanding of the Christian faith. Almost everywhere the Reformed churches had to struggle for existence, and in the face of unrelenting persecution they stressed the sovereignty of God and man's duty to glorify him by full and unyielding obedience.

The efforts to suppress the Reformed church in France led to a series of inconclusive Wars of Religion between 1562 and 1593. A resolution of the conflict was effected when Henry of Navarre, the Protestant (or Huguenot) leader, succeeded to the throne, declared himself a Catholic, and in 1598 issued the Edict of Nantes guaranteeing freedom of worship to the Protestants. During the same period, the Dutch were struggling to free themselves from the rule of Spain, a struggle that was intensified by the Spanish attempt to stamp out Dutch Protestantism. The armed revolt that broke out in 1566 culminated in a declaration of independence by the five northern provinces at Utrecht in 1581, and by 1609 the Dutch had made good their claim to independence.

With energies released by the winning of independence, the Dutch Republic became the great trading power of Europe with the largest and most efficient merchant marine in the world. Dutch traders were everywhere, reaching Java as early as 1595. In the next few decades they ejected the Portuguese from most of their trading posts in the Far East, conquered Brazil, and occupied several islands in the West Indies. Their attention had been called to the possibilities of the fur trade in North America by the pioneering voyages of Henry Hudson, and in the same year that they gained control of Brazil they established a trading post at the present site of Albany on the Hudson River. Two years later, in 1626, another trading post — New Amsterdam — was established on the tip of Manhattan Island.

Peter Minuit, the first director of New Netherlands, had been a ruling elder of the French Reformed church at Wesel, and he brought with him in 1626 two "comforters of the sick" to minister to the religious needs of the infant settlement. In 1628 the first minister, Jonas Michaelius, arrived and immediately organized a church. Michaelius reported that there were "fifty communicants, Walloons and Dutch," at the first administration of the Lord's Supper, it being observed with "great joy and comfort to many." Since few of the Walloons and others from French-speaking areas could not understand Dutch, Michaelius thought it unnecessary to have weekly services for them in their own tongue. Every four months, however, he did administer the Lord's Supper "in the French language and according to the French mode." On these occasions he read his sermon because, as he explained, he was not sufficiently fluent in French to speak extemporaneously. When Michaelius returned to Holland in 1632, he brought charges of incompetence and irregularity against the director, with the result that both men were replaced.

New Amsterdam was a typical sailors' town. Many of the inhabitants were rough and boisterous, and the lot of the early ministers was far from easy. Not until Peter Stuyvesant became the director of the colony in 1647 did they receive any real support from the governing authority. Stuyvesant, the son and son-in-law of Dutch Reformed ministers, was a zealous churchman and a strict disciplinarian. He restricted the sale of liquor, ordered strict observance of the Sabbath, and required all persons to attend the services of the church. Stuyvesant's zeal included an attempt to impose a rigid religious uniformity upon the colony, but his treatment of Lutherans, Quakers, and Jews earned him a stern rebuke and he was ordered to leave any dissenter "unmolested as long as he is modest, moderate, [and] his political conduct irreproachable."

By the time the colony was surrendered to the English in 1664, there were 11 Dutch Reformed churches in the colony which included settlements in what was to be New Jersey. Although the shift to English control involved problems of readjustment, the Dutch churches continued to grow with the natural increase in the Dutch population; and it is estimated that there were 120 Dutch Reformed congregations at the time of the Declaration of Independence.

For two decades prior to the revocation of the Edict of Nantes in 1685, increasing pressure by the government led many Huguenots to leave France and seek refuge in other European countries. Some made their way to America, with the largest number settling in New York and South Carolina. Several Dutch Reformed ministers made it a practice to preach in French, and the French Reformed in New York generally became members of the Dutch churches. In 1683, however, the French Reformed in New York secured a pastor of their own, and congregations also were formed at New Rochelle and New Paltz. By the end of the century there were five or six French Reformed churches in the vicinity of New York City. Another church had been formed in Boston, at least one in Virginia, and several in South Carolina. The tendency everywhere was for the Huguenots to disperse and to become denationalized, due partly perhaps to an eagerness to forget the language and customs of the land that had subjected them to such relentless persecution. In the South they tended to become Anglicans. In New York they were absorbed by the Dutch Reformed; the "French church" at New Paltz, for example, kept its records in Dutch after the first 50 years of its existence.

Mennonites, Dunkers, and Moravians

Pennsylvania was the great center of German immigration to the colonies, for William Penn's efforts to recruit settlers found an eager response among the inhabitants of the Palatinate (an area between the upper Rhine and France) which had repeatedly been ravaged and devastated by the armies of Louis XIV. This eager response was movingly expressed in a letter, dated February 6, 1681, from a father in Heilbron to his son, who had been among the first to arrive in the new colony.

> Dear Son:— Your letter from far away America . . . gave us great joy. . . . America, according to your writing, must be a beautiful land. . . .
>
> Dear Henry, since you have been away from us conditions in South Germany have become very much worse. The French have wrought much devastation . . ., and besides we now suffer from the plague of high taxes. Thousands would gladly leave the Fatherland if they had the means to do so.
>
> A merchant from Frankfort was with us last week and informed us how along the Rhine a number of families have banded together to accept the invitation of an Englishman named William Penn, who had recently visited that community, to settle in that beautiful land and there establish new homes.
>
> After I had received this information I went at once to our minister, whose parents live at Worms on the Rhine, and begged him earnestly to learn what truth there was in these reports and to find out, if possible, if there would be any opportunity for us to join them. . . . He then informed me that these reports were all true. . . .
>
> It is the good providence of God that has shown these burdened people so glorious a land. We . . . are only waiting for a good opportunity when the dear Lord will bring us to you. Your brother Peter is learning shoemaking and will soon be free. America is the only dream of Elizabeth. Catharine, only six years old, asks us daily, "Will we soon be going to our brother in America?"[25]

Although a half dozen different religious groups were to be represented in the German migration to Pennsylvania, the family at Heilbron were Mennonites, an Anabaptist group that took its name from Menno Simons (1492–1559).[26]

Of all the Reformation groups, none had been subjected to more bitter persecution than the Anabaptists. They were earnest people, deeply devout, who rejected infant baptism and sought to practice full obedience to the commands of Christ, refusing among other things to take oaths, hold public office, or bear arms. They had managed to survive in small scattered communities throughout the Rhineland from Rotterdam to the valleys of Switzerland. The earliest Mennonite group to arrive in Pennsyl-

[25] Smith, Handy, and Loetscher, *American Christianity,* I, 183.
[26] See C. Henry Smith, *The Mennonites of America,* 4th ed., rev. by Cornelius Krahn (Newton, Kans., 1957).

vania came from Krefeld in 1683. Most of this initial contingent had been won to Quaker views prior to their departure, and separate Mennonite worship was not established until 1690. The Swiss Mennonites who began arriving around 1710 settled in what is now Lancaster County and this became the principal Mennonite center. Each Mennonite congregation conducted its own affairs, frequently choosing its officers—a bishop, elders, and deacons—by lot. Consequently they were seldom troubled by lack of ministerial leadership and they never needed to await the arrival of a minister in order to organize their church life.

The Dunkers (Church of the Brethren) in many ways were not unlike the Mennonites. They also were a "plain" people who sought to live in strict obedience to New Testament precepts. Their founder was Alexander Mack, a man of some means who had come under Pietistic influences after reacting against the spiritual lethargy of the German Reformed church in which he had been reared. At Schwarzenau in Hesse-Kassel in 1708 he formed into a church the little group he had gathered for Bible study, and other congregations were soon formed in neighboring provinces. Unlike the Mennonites, many of whose practices they adopted, the Dunkers baptized by a threefold immersion rather than by pouring. It was this practice that gave them their popular name. Their worship centered in the Lord's Supper, which was preceded by a "love feast" and the washing of feet, and was concluded with the "holy kiss of charity" and the "right hand of fellowship." The Dunker migration to America was initiated in 1719 by the congregation at Krefeld, and four years later their first church in America was formed at Germantown.

A Saxon nobleman, Nicholas Ludwig, Count von Zinzendorf (1700–60) was the key figure in the story of the Moravians. He was a Lutheran who also had come under the influence of Pietism, a movement that, in reaction to the seeming lifelessness of Lutheran and Reformed orthodoxy, stressed the importance of religious experience and the devotional life.[27] Its most characteristic feature was the gathering of earnest Christians in small groups to study the Bible, sing hymns, and engage in prayer. The Pietists were neither hostile to the churches nor heterodox, but they found theological discussion distasteful and regarded it as a source of division and strife among Christians. Christianity was a life, they insisted, not a creed. Thus Pietists tended to sit loosely to their confessional traditions, to emphasize the common experience of Christ that bound all Christians together, and to possess a strong missionary fervor. It was this spirit that Zinzendorf imbibed, and it led him to welcome to his estates any refugees among whom he espied any signs of true piety.

[27] Pietism stemmed from the activities of Philip J. Spener (1635–1705) and August H. Francke (1663–1727). The former gathered small groups for Bible study in his home at Frankfort. The latter developed a similar ministry among students at the University of Leipzig. The founding of the University of Halle in 1691 by the Elector of Brandenburg provided them with a center for the dissemination of their views.

The Moravians, or the Unitas Fratrum, had their origin in the evangelical movement that sprang from the preaching of John Hus of Prague in the fifteenth century.[28] They had been buffeted by persecution for more than two centuries when Zinzendorf offered them asylum in 1722. Zinzendorf, together with other Lutheran Pietists whom he had gathered about him, soon became deeply involved in the activities of the Moravian community. He gradually emerged as their leader and was consecrated Bishop in 1737. Under his leadership the Moravians launched a far-flung missionary campaign that had several objectives — the conversion of the heathen, the renewal of spiritual life among nominal Christians, and the reuniting of all Christian groups in a single spiritual communion. An early project had been the establishment of a Moravian settlement in Georgia in 1735 where some missionary work was carried on among the Indians and blacks. Their refusal to bear arms, however, aroused the oppositon of the colonial authorities, and in 1740 the Moravians moved to Pennsylvania where they established the towns of Nazareth and Bethlehem. Later Salem, North Carolina, became a major Moravian center.

In the meantime Zinzendorf, having been charged with harboring religious fanatics and promoting views contrary to accepted Lutheran standards, had been banished in 1738 from his estates. He utilized his banishment as an opportunity to embark on a missionary tour that brought him to Pennsylvania in 1741. His immediate objective was to draw together the various German Protestant denominations in Pennsylvania to form what he called "the Church of God in the Spirit." His intention was to create spiritual ties among them by an acknowledgment of agreement in "essentials," but this intention was misunderstood and the project interpreted as a scheme to subordinate all the churches to Moravian control and direction. As a result the seven consultations that were held with representatives of the different denominations ended in failure. During the remaining months of his stay, Zinzendorf busied himself in establishing contact with the Indians and in organizing churches and schools at scattered points in Pennsylvania and New York. For a brief time he served as pastor of the Lutheran congregation in Philadelphia. Before his departure in 1743 he made arrangements for the orderly supervision of both the itinerant preachers and the rapidly expanding missionary activity among the Indians.

The German Lutherans and the German Reformed

The economic havoc wrought by Louis XIV's repeated spoliation of the Palatinate which had spurred the emigration of the small religious minori-

---

[28] See Edward Langton, *History of the Moravian Church* (London, 1956), and J. R. Weinlick, *Count Zinzendorf* (N.Y., 1956).

ties was equally effective in promotional efforts to recruit settlers for his new colony. There had been Germans of Reformed background in New Netherlands, and a Dutch Lutheran congregation had been formed there. There were also Swedish Lutherans who remained in America after the short-lived Swedish colony on the Delaware was taken over by the Dutch. The Lutherans and the German Reformed, however, derived their major strength from the flow of Palatine Germans into Pennsylvania.

Organized church life among the German Lutherans and German Reformed was not effected immediately for several reasons. For one thing, they migrated as individuals and not as religious communities. They generally had no financial resources of their own and they had no group to help provide the expense of travel. Many of them came as "redemptioners," given free passage by shipowners who recouped themselves financially by selling their passengers for a term of service as indentured servants. Others were assisted by the English government which recognized the need for settlers but had placed restrictions upon the emigration of English subjects lest the homeland should be impoverished. Most of these Germans had no strong religious interest, and neither the Reformed nor the Lutherans had a tradition of lay initiative in church affairs. Consequently their adherents tended to be dependent upon outside help for leadership in the formation of churches.

Although a Swedish Lutheran church had been formed in 1639 and the Dutch Lutheran church in New Amsterdam had secured a minister as early as 1658, the first German Lutheran church was not organized until 1703. This was at New Hanover, Pennsylvania, and it was established under the leadership of Daniel Falckner. In the same year his brother, Justus Falckner, became pastor of the Dutch Lutheran church in New York, where the growing German population became the primary concern of his pastoral labors. These were small beginnings and further work among the Germans was long delayed. There were a few other early ministers, but a decisive change did not occur until the arrival of Henry Melchior Muhlenberg in 1742.

Muhlenberg was sent to America by the Pietists at Halle in response to a plea for help that had been made much earlier by the Lutherans of Philadelphia. The failure to respond immediately had been occasioned by the unwillingness of the American congregations to commit themselves to a definite salary; but when news of Zinzendorf's activities reached Halle, the salary debate ceased and Muhlenberg set out without further delay. When he arrived he found the people badly divided. Some had been drawn away by Zinzendorf, and others had come under the influence of a minister of dubious character, Johann Valentin Kraft. Within six weeks Muhlenberg mastered the situation and was installed as pastor of the Philadelphia Lutherans. He soon took additional churches under his care, and ultimately seven churches looked to him for pastoral leadership. Whenever possible he responded to calls for help from more distant places and frequently was asked to arbitrate church quarrels. The regular reports that he sent to Halle stimulated further interest in his work and brought reinforcements in both men and money. Muhlenberg's most important achievement was the forming of the Ministerium of Pennsylvania in 1748. This was the first permanent Lutheran synod in America, and its influence became decisive in the developing life of the churches.

Whereas most of the Lutheran population in the colonies stemmed from the influx of Germans into Pennsylvania, being largely a dispersion from this center, the Salzburg Lutherans in Georgia were the product of an independent odyssey. They had been driven from their homes in Austria in 1731 by the Roman Catholic archbishop of Salzburg. Fourteen thousand of them in the dead of winter made the long trek to Prussia, where they had been promised refuge. Accounts of their sufferings aroused interest in England and provision was made to send some of them to Georgia, where they arrived in four contingents between 1734 and 1741. The first group was accompanied by two ministers who had been trained at Halle, and they had a vigorous church life from the beginning.

The plight of the German Reformed in America was much the same as that of the Lutherans. They also came without pastors and with meager resources. The first churches to be formed among them were an exception to the general rule of waiting until a minister appeared on the scene. John Philip Boehm had settled in Pennsylvania in 1720 as a farmer. He was the son of a Reformed minister at Frankfort-on-the-Main and he had taught school for a period of 12 years. After his arrival his neighbors persuaded him to conduct religious services for them. Five years later the three informal congregations he had gathered pressed him to assume the pastoral office. With some reluctance he agreed to do so, although he was not ordained. When a German Reformed minister, George Michael Weiss, arrived two years later, he was scandalized by Boehm's action, challenged his right to assume ministerial prerogatives, and attempted to take over his congregations. The people rallied to Boehm's support, appealed to the Dutch Reformed ministers in New York for advice, and were referred by them to the Classis of Amsterdam for a decision. In due time an answer was received that approved Boehm's emergency assumption of pastoral duties but advised him to seek ordination. He was ordained by the Dutch Reformed ministers of New York on November 23, 1729. Weiss was present at the ordination and afterward the two worked together in complete harmony.

People of German Reformed background were rapidly increasing in numbers, being augmented by an influx of settlers from Switzerland, and they were becoming widely dispersed in the back country of the colonies. Most were without either ministers or churches. The appeal to the Classis of Amsterdam had enlisted the interest of the synods of Holland in the plight of the German immigrants, and a committee of the synods was appointed to send aid. In 1746 Michael Schlatter, a Swiss who had been educated and ordained in the Netherlands, was sent to Pennsylvania as the representative of the Dutch synods with instructions to visit existing congregations, to form new ones where needed, and to bring them together as soon as possible in a presbytery (or "coetus") subject to the synods of Holland. He immediately made a tour of the churches and discovered that in Pennsylvania there were four ordained men to care for an estimated German Reformed population of 15,000. Within a year he had organized the "coetus," and in 1751 he returned to Europe to plead the cause of the German Reformed churches. When he returned he brought with him six young ministers, 700 Bibles, and the promise of an annual subsidy of 2,000 gulden from the states of Holland and West Friesland.

The Jews

With the exception of such transient groups as the Sandemanians, Rogerenes, and the Ephrata community, the Jews were the smallest of the religious minorities in colonial America.[29] Twenty-three Jews, fleeing from Brazil when the Portuguese regained control from the Dutch, arrived in New Amsterdam in 1654. Most of them failed to remain, but those who did were not permitted to maintain public worship until after the end of Dutch control. Their number gradually increased and by 1695 they were worshiping in a rented room. Thirty-five years later, in 1730, a synagogue was built and dedicated. There were isolated Jews in New England as early as 1649 and a community was gathered in Newport, Rhode Island, about 1658. This early congregation had disappeared by 1690 and was not revived until about 1750. The beautiful synagogue, which still survives in Newport, was erected in 1763. Apart from these two centers, the only other congregations in America prior to the American Revolution were at Savannah (1733), Philadelphia (1747), and Charleston (1749). Moreover, none of these congregations included a rabbi until the nineteenth century.

Popular Religious Beliefs

Not all of the religion that was transplanted to America was defined by denominational boundaries. Some religion took a "popular" form that supplemented and sometimes contradicted the religious life associated with the churches. This popular religion was in no ways organized, but instead was threaded through colonial American culture as an exceedingly broad set of beliefs and behaviors.

Colonists brought popular religion from Europe as part of their cultural baggage. In England and on the Continent during the centuries leading

---

[29] See Jacob R. Marcus, *Early American Jewry*, 2 vols. (Philadelphia, 1951–1953).

up to the settlement of North America, men and women viewed the world as a setting for manifestations of diverse supernatural forces. Life was marked by mysterious and unearthly events — some proved favorable to physical and spiritual health, and others crippled or destroyed life. Astrology, magic, prophecy, fortune telling, various forms of divination and supernatural healing, and witchcraft thrived in the religious atmosphere of Europe on the eve of the American colonization. Colonists also reported and closely followed stories of mermaids, rattlesnakes that hypnotized persons with their eyes, and sinister disappearing black dogs.[30]

In America the clergy condemned much popular religion, and especially witchcraft, as superstitious evil. This did not prevent the laity from believing in it, however. Americans and Europeans in the seventeenth century blamed witches for a host of scourges ranging from diseased livestock to hallucinations. In a few instances, entire communities were aroused to vigilance against witchcraft. Such was the case at Salem, Massachusetts, in the 1690s, when numerous suspected witches were imprisoned and some were executed.[31] Belief in witchcraft was as widespread in other North American colonies as it was in New England. Belief in occult healing also took root in American soil. Reverend Cotton Mather of Boston lamented in 1720 the widespread use of charms and magic words in attempts to cure disease. Among spoken charms, he singled out the word *Abracadabra* as a particularly "famous" example, while condemning as well attempts to cure toothaches by wearing around the neck a folded paper with strange sayings scrawled upon it. Particularly upsetting to Mather was his realization that even the faithful used charms to overcome illness: "But this impiety, how commonly it is practiced: Even among those who have been baptised for God. . . . "[32]

Not all popular religion earned the scorn of the clergy, however. Some aspects of popular religious belief did not directly challenge church doctrine and were not considered detrimental to the soul. Such was the case with wonder stories, or tales of remarkable and supernatural happenings. Protestants had long believed that it was through God's "providence" that the natural world in all of its operations was upheld. This included not only such regular events as the rising and setting of the sun, but the seemingly odd or freakish events that occurred in nature that amazed and bewildered mere mortals.[33]

[30] Herbert Leventhal, *In the Shadow of the Enlightenment: Occultism and Renaissance Science in Eighteenth-Century America* (N.Y., 1976); Jon Butler, *Awash in a Sea of Faith: Christianizing the American People* (Cambridge, Mass., 1990), 7–36; and David D. Hall, *Worlds of Wonder, Days of Judgment: Popular Religious Belief in Early New England* (N.Y., 1989), 71–116.

[31] See John Putnam Demos, *Entertaining Satan: Witchcraft and the Culture of Early New England* (N.Y., 1982).

[32] Cotton Mather, *The Angel of Bethesda*, ed. Gordon W. Jones (Barre, Mass., 1972), 293–301.

[33] Hall, *World of Wonder, Days of Judgment*, 75–80, 91–94.

The lore of wonders was generated in part from the New World'experiences of the colonists, but a substantial part of the lore was transmitted from England through newspapers, almanacs, and books. The clergy rarely opposed the lore because the telling and retelling of wonder stories served to keep persons' attention focused on the supernatural in general and oftentimes God in particular. When men and women repeated to each other stories of frightening earthquakes or destructive fires or extraordinary deliverances from lightning bolts or fateful carriage accidents, the clergy rested. In wonder stories, the God who ruled the universe saved from harm those who were steadfast in their faith, and punished those who strayed.

Popular religion, as represented by wonder lore, witchcraft beliefs, the use of magical charms, and numerous other ideas and behaviors, was one component of the religious life of Americans. It was more important at some times in the nation's history than at other times, and was more visible in certain social and geographic contexts than in others. It never replaced denominational religion, nor did it even challenge it in any significant way. In its various and ever-changing forms over the years, however, it consistently expressed the vitality and diversity of religious belief in ways that are not always apparent in more organized forms of religion in America. It also historically represented something of the fluidity and adaptability of religious faith in America, particularly when it was connected with patriotism in a kind of "civil religion."

This account of denominational beginnings in America can be misleading. Although there was a profusion of religious groups, most of the people belonged to no church at all. It was not until the Great Awakening, when America experienced its "national conversion,"[34] that this situation began to change.

---

[34] The term is supplied and explicated by H. Richard Niebuhr, *The Kingdom of God in America* (N.Y., 1959), 126.

CHAPTER 3

The Great Awakening

The Great Awakening, which was to exert a decisive and far-reaching influence upon the development of American religious life, was but one manifestation of a general spiritual quickening during the eighteenth century. There were scattered "awakenings" of new religious life in England, Scotland, and Wales, as well as in America. These several awakenings reinforced each other and initiated the great tide of evangelical religion that swept through the English-speaking world, reaching a crest of influence in the latter half of the nineteenth century before it began to ebb away. Churches of all denominations were caught up in the surge of religious fervor and were profoundly affected by its impact. A new type of preaching dominated the pulpits, the structure of public worship was altered, and the "revival" became the most widely accepted means of introducing people to the Christian life.

Although the immediate effect of the Awakening was to arouse opposition, split congregations, set minister against minister, and divide most of the denominations, the opposition in the end was almost everywhere overwhelmed and the ultimate consequence was to mold the various denominations to a common pattern, to subordinate differences, and to make possible wide-ranging cooperative endeavors.[1] Above all, this surging tide of evangelical religion supplied the dynamic that emboldened the Protestant churches of America to undertake the enormous task of Christianizing a continent, nerved those of the British Isles to assume a similar responsibility for an expanding population at home and overseas, and led both the British and the American churches to join forces in a vast mission to the entire non-Christian world.

[1] A common pattern of religious life in New England and elsewhere already existed in the form of popular religion, and this served to some degree to mitigate the effects of controversy over doctrine that took place during the Awakening and in the years immediately following. See David D. Hall, *Worlds of Wonder, Days of Judgment: Popular Religion in Early New England* (N.Y., 1989), and Jon Butler, *Awash in a Sea of Faith: Christianizing the American People* (Cambridge, Mass., 1990).

Why the spark provided by any one of the local quickenings should suddenly have ignited a general conflagration is something of a mystery. The early drive and enthusiasm of the Puritan movement sprang from a transforming experience of God's grace and a consequent dedication to warfare against sin, together with a strong tendency to introspection and self-critical reflection. This brand of Protestantism was transplanted to America in the seventeenth century, and guided the lives of the faithful there, such as New Englander Elizabeth White, who wrote in 1660: "When I have seen a spider, which of all things is most loathsome to me, I have been ready to wish myself such a one, esteeming of it to be in a far happier condition than I was."[2] But this religion had moved to the periphery of religious life. For some the consciousness of entering the Christian life through a "new birth" had been replaced by an insistence upon mere assent to orthodox beliefs as the foundation of the Christian life. Others stressed the reasonable character of the "grand essentials" of all religion and emphasized moral behavior as the distinguishing mark of the Christian. The theological problem faced by the successors of the Puritans was to draw the emotional component of religion inward from the periphery, and to blend it with doctrine and morality. In addressing this problem they were mostly unsuccessful, with "head" predominating over "heart." This is not to say that ministers and laypersons were satisfied with their efforts. When Jonathan Edwards spoke of "the time of extraordinary dullness in religion" that preceded the outbreak of the revival in Northampton, Massachusetts, he was but echoing the lament that had been voiced by many of the New England clergy for the better part of a century. And from time to time there had been local awakenings — even in Northampton under the preaching of Solomon Stoddard — when consciences would be touched, faith awakened, and people brought into the churches in unusual numbers. But no general revival had occurred.

Nor is the suggestion that the revivals were the product of the unsettled conditions of frontier life an adequate explanation of a phenomenon that was equally widespread in both Britain and America. Furthermore, the communities in America where the revivals first appeared were centers of an established agrarian economy rather than frontier settlements. Even after revivalism became an accepted feature of American religious life, revivals seldom occurred in an area until the frontier period was over;

---

[2] For the definition of Puritanism as a "revival," see Alan Simpson, *Puritanism in Old and New England*, (Chicago, 1962), 103–10. For an interpretation of revivalism as a "revitalization" of the Puritan "culture core," see William G. McLoughlin, *Revivals, Awakening and Reform: An Essay on Religion and Social Change in America, 1607–1977* (Chicago, 1978) Elizabeth White, *Experiences of God's Gracious Dealing* (Boston, 1741). White wrote the lines in the 1660's.

and they manifested themselves with equal power in many of the oldest communities.[3]

It is true that the revivals were initially welcomed and later eagerly promoted as an answer to the problem posed by the fact that a large part of the population, in both England and America, stood outside the churches altogether. In England the parish system, which through custom and tradition provided the possibility of long-term nurture and instruction in the Christian faith, had broken down.[4] And in America, with the possible exception of New England, the parish system had never been successfully established. Even in New England the loss of the charter in Massachusetts had made it clear that little confidence could be placed in external guarantees that were designed to ensure that at least the outward formalities of religion would continue to be observed. Thus the churches were confronted by a clear-cut summons to missionary endeavor. Given the circumstances that prevailed, the time was ripe for a type of preaching that would prick the conscience, convict people of sin, and lead them through the agony of repentance into a personally apprehended experience of the new life that was to be found in Christ. The mystery nonetheless remains, for such preaching had never completely disappeared. The novelty of the Awakening was the widespread response it suddenly elicited, a response so unexpected that it surprised even those who sought it.

Transatlantic Influences

The Transmission of Ritual Forms

A practice of great future significance was introduced at the beginning of the eighteenth century, when Scotch Irish Presbyterians began to migrate to America in large numbers. Some settled in New England, but the majority came to the middle colonies, and especially to northern New Jersey and to the area around Philadelphia. The new arrivals did not agree in all articles of religious doctrine. They did share, however, a belief in the importance of religious ritual, as it had emerged among Irish Presbyterians over the course of the previous half-century. And as they formed

---

[3] The appearance of revivals in postfrontier areas is documented in the illuminating study of Whitney R. Cross, *The Burned-over District: The Social and Intellectual History of Enthusiastic Religion in Western New York, 1800–1850* (Ithaca, N.Y., 1950), 75–76. See also Paul Johnson, *A Shopkeeper's Millennium: Society and Revivals in Rochester, New York, 1815–1837* (N.Y., 1978); Richard W. Pointer *Protestant Pluralism and the New York Experience: A Study of Eighteenth-Century Religious Diversity* (Bloomington, Ind., 1988).

[4] For the significance of unaltered parish boundaries in relationship to England's shifting population, see Winthrop S. Hudson, *The Great Tradition of the American Churches* (N.Y., 1963), 99–100.

communities and established churches along the Atlantic seaboard, they continued to organize their religious life around that ritual.

A key component of this Presbyterian ritual was the Lord's Supper, or "communion." In Scotland, it was an occasion that unfolded over the course of several days and attracted several thousand, and sometimes over 10,000 people. The ritual as it was performed differed in detail from one context to another, and the communion "season" could last anywhere from two days to ten days.

A typical performance of the ritual generally began with observance of a day of fasting together with one's own congregation. The following day persons from different congregations would travel to the outdoor site of the communion they were to have together to hear a group of ministers preach a series of sermons, lasting as long as 24 hours. This mostly extemporaneous preaching would be followed by a day of preparation for the Lord's Supper itself, a process that included personal prayer and soul searching, examination by ministers or church elders, and a renewal of commitment to piety and morality. On Sunday, following further preaching, prayer, and psalm singing, the participants were seated at tables arranged in front of the pulpit and were served the bread and the wine. On the last day, ministers preached thanksgiving sermons and reminded persons of the solemnity of their rededication to spiritual striving.[5]

Typically, in the course of the communion ritual some persons experienced religious conversions, and others rediscovered their faith. The ritual stage for these experiences — lengthy outdoor services attended by great crowds, extemporaneous preaching by numerous ministers, a mood of intense prayerful self-examination and reflection — also promoted an intense community piety.[6] In America, as the communion season was re-created, it helped to structure a context for the outburst of emotional religion known as the Great Awakening.

Theological Change and Public Piety in New England

By the beginning of the eighteenth century, new currents in English scientific and religious thought had crossed the Atlantic Ocean to the colonies. The scientific view of the world as a rational, ordered, interconnected whole was manifest in writings by Robert Boyle, William Derham, and John Ray, and in the works of English "latitudinarian" writers (so called because they promoted latitude, or tolerance, in religion) such as

---

[5] See Lee Leigh Eric Schmidt, *Holy Fairs: Scottish Communions and American Revivals in the Early Modern Period* (Princeton, 1989), 21–59, 70–73; Marilyn J. Westerkamp, *Triumph of the Laity: Scots-Irish Piety and the Great Awakening 1625–1760* (N.Y., 1988), 28–35, 136–44.

[6] Westerkamp, *Triumph of the Laity*, 31.

John Tillotson. Americans gradually became acquainted with these writings, and some of the clergy were profoundly influenced by them.

In New England, a group of ministers who had encountered the new thinking as students at Harvard College began to articulate a fresh theological viewpoint that emphasized the "whole person." These ministers, led by Benjamin Colman of the newly organized Brattle Street Church, proposed that reason and the emotions operated together in fostering spiritual development. Stressing the unity of creation, these ministers rejected the assumption—which had emerged within many of the churches in New England in the preceding decades—that emotion was essentially a private aspect of religion. Rather, they argued that public worship, and community life in general, ought to be animated by a heartfelt piety. For them, emotional piety and a rational morality grounded in Scripture were complementary components present in both private and public life.[7]

As part of their program to restore to religion a balance of head and heart, these Boston-area ministers promoted a style of worship aimed at arousing the emotions or "affections." Believing in a world wherein all things were interconnected in the whole, they proposed that the emotions of the soul could be enlivened through the stimulation of the senses. Accordingly, they argued for the institution of preaching techniques and forms of worship that suited that purpose. As Colman wrote, "Our spirits being imbodied are naturally come at by impressions from our senses, and more particularly by the eye and the ear."[8]

Colman and his colleagues promoted psalm singing, public recitation of prayer, expressive reading of scripture, and other methods they believed would serve to inflame the religious affections of their audiences. In addition, they advocated preaching that used colorful images and a direct, animated style of address. Most importantly, they stressed that the public gathering in the meetinghouse was the ideal setting for arousing the affections. As Colman's colleague Thomas Foxcroft wrote, "The union of many devout souls in a joint presence, mutually raises and enlivens their affections. As a collection of many dispersed *rays* into a narrow compass, gives them greater light and heat . . . even so the concurrence of a multitude in the solemnities of God's house tends to kindle and diffuse a common ardour in the worshipping assembly."[9]

The emphasis that Foxcroft and Colman and their Boston-area colleagues placed on emotional public worship helped prepare the New England soil for the itinerant ministers who scored such successes there. But even those members of the Boston clergy who endeavored to raise the

---

[7] John Corrigan, *The Prism of Piety: Catholick Congregational Clergy at the Beginning of the Enlightenment* (N.Y., 1991).

[8] Benjamin Colman, *The Government and Improvement of Mirth* (Boston, 1707), 152.

[9] Thomas Foxcroft, *The Character of Anna* (Boston, 1723), 35.

emotional temperature of their congregations could not have anticipated the suddenness or the magnitude of the revival of religion that was soon to take place.

The First Stirrings of Revival

The Great Awakening in America had its antecedents in local revivals that developed among the Dutch Reformed churches of northern New Jersey under the leadership of Theodore J. Frelinghuysen; among the Presbyterian churches of the same general area under the leadership of the Tennents, father and sons; and in Northampton and other communities of the Connecticut valley under the leadership of Jonathan Edwards. Although these local revivals were not consolidated into one great movement until George Whitefield arrived on the scene, they provided a foretaste of what was to come and did much to shape the subsequent outburst of religious fervor.

Theodore J. Frelinghuysen

The "beginner of the great work"[10] in America was a German born near the Dutch border, educated under Dutch auspices, ordained to the ministry of the Dutch Reformed church, and sent to America in 1719 to become a pastor in the Raritan valley of New Jersey. Although sometimes described as a German Pietist, his real affinities were with Dutch Calvinists who had been deeply influenced by the experiential piety of the English Puritans.[11]

When Frelinghuysen assumed his new responsibilities, he discovered, much to his dismay, that most of his parishioners were content with a perfunctory orthodoxy that had become for them more a symbol of their Dutch nationality than an expression of any deep-seated Christian conviction. He immediately embarked on a program of reform, seeking to rouse them from their lethargy by a strict enforcement of the provisions of the Reformed discipline with regard to admission to the Lord's Supper, by personal conferences in their homes, and above all by pointed evangelistic preaching that sought to induce the members of his congregations to take seriously the understanding of the Christian faith they ostensibly professed.[12] Many were scandalized by his bluntness, and his congregations were disrupted and thrown into turmoil. The cause of the disaffected was

---

[10] The phrase is Whitefield's; quoted by L. J. Trinterud, *The Forming of an American Tradition*, 34.

[11] For the absence of Pietist influence, see ibid., 54–57.

[12] His program of reform is illustrated in a sermon, a portion of which is printed in Smith, Handy, and Loetscher, *American Christianity*, I, 316–21.

championed by the Dutch ministers of New York, one of whom visited them in their homes to encourage their opposition. Frelinghuysen, however, refused to be daunted and conversions became so frequent in the heated atmosphere that opposition within his own congregations was silenced. By 1726 the revival was at its height and had spread to other Dutch communities; and within the next few years Frelinghuysen gained the support of the majority of the Dutch ministers.

The Tennents

William Tennent and his sons were key figures in the outbreak of the revival among the Presbyterians. A graduate of the University of Edinburgh and an unusually able teacher and scholar, the father followed Irish precedent in giving his sons their theological training in his own home while he was a pastor at Bedford, New York, from 1720 to 1727. Gilbert Tennent, his eldest son, received a Master's degree from Yale in 1725, perhaps in partial compensation for his father's disappointment in not being named to succeed Timothy Cutler as president of that institution. Two years later the father moved to Neshaminy, Pennsylvania, where he established an embryo college of his own. Deeply indebted to the Puritan devotional classics for his own understanding of the Christian faith, the elder Tennent succeeded in transmitting his earnest concern for a vital inward faith both to his sons and to the graduates of his "log college" at Neshaminy.

The chronology of the awakening among the Presbyterians is somewhat obscure, for Gilbert Tennent reports that his brother John had the first actual revival. This must have been sometime in 1727 or 1728. Later, when John Tennent was pastor at Freehold, New Jersey, another revival occurred that was carried forward after John's death by his brother William, Jr. The most important of the brothers, however, was Gilbert. He was the outstanding preacher and the natural leader of the men his father had trained.

In 1726 Gilbert Tennent was called to the Presbyterian church at New Brunswick, New Jersey, where the revival among the Dutch Reformed was at its height. He and Frelinghuysen immediately recognized each other as kindred spirts. Tennent's ministry, by his own account, was not conspicuously successful at first, but Frelinghuysen encouraged him and Frelinghuysen's success served both as a rebuke and as an inspiration. After a period of sickness, during which he was "exceedingly grieved" that he had "done so little for God" and had vowed to "promote his kingdom" with all his might if God would be pleased to spare him for this purpose, Tennent began to secure the response his father had taught him to seek.

The nub of the problem, as Tennent defined it, was what he called the "presumptuous security" of those who professed to be Christians. They had been baptized, catechized, and inducted into full membership in the church. They affirmed orthodox doctrines and were fully persuaded that one is saved by faith and not by works. But faith was interpreted as merely assent to orthodox ideas and was quite unrelated to most of the Christian graces. There was little of the inwardness and transforming power of the Christian faith to be found among them. To counter this complacency Tennent adopted the Puritan technique of preaching for "conviction" — an acknowledgment of one's own sinful estate. He insisted that no one ever became a Christian without first being subjected to the terrifying realization that one is not a Christian. One must first know oneself as a sinful creature, estranged from God and rightfully subject to condemnation, before one can apprehend and receive God's forgiveness and acceptance.

Tennent's preaching had the desired effect. By 1729 scattered Presbyterian congregations from New Brunswick to Staten Island began to throb with new life under his leadership. Other products of his father's tuition, notably Samuel Blair, were equally active. The participation of Presbyterian ministers of New England background, such as Jonathan Dickinson at Elizabeth and Aaron Burr at Newark, was also enlisted. By the end of the 1730s there had been eight or ten local revivals of some degree of intensity. In the meantime Gilbert Tennent was gaining a wider hearing through the 1735 publications of three of his sermons. Earlier in the same year two sermons by John Tennent with an account of the revival at Freehold had also been published.

Jonathan Edwards

The third manifestation of religious excitement occurred in the Connecticut valley with Jonathan Edwards playing the central role. Edwards, one of the most brilliant and original minds America has produced, scarcely conforms to the popular image of the revivalist. His interests seem to have been largely academic, and he spent long hours each day in his study. His sermons were tightly knit and closely reasoned expositions of theological doctrine which he read rather than speaking extemporaneously. But his preaching struck a nerve among his listeners, and from that sprang a revival of extraordinary power.

Edwards had been educated at Yale, graduating in 1720 at the age of 17. For some years he served there as a tutor, leaving in 1727 to assist his grandfather, Solomon Stoddard, who was pastor of the church at Northampton, Massachusetts, and succeeding him two years later when he died. Edwards was greatly distressed by the "licentiousness" that so generally prevailed among the youth of the town.

> Many of them [were] very much addicted to night walking, and frequenting the tavern, and lewd practices. . . . It was their manner very frequently to

get together in conventions of both sexes for mirth and jollity, which they called frolics, and they would often spend the greater part of the night in them.

Furthermore, many of them were "indecent in their carriage at meeting." Edwards began to meet with the young people in their homes. They in turn responded to his pastoral concern; reformation in behavior set in, and by 1733 Edwards was able to report that they had grown "observably more decent in their attendance on public worship."[13]

In the meantime he had become alarmed by the complacency engendered by the spread of "Arminian" principles. The notion of human ability, he believed, undercut a dependence upon divine grace, which was at the heart of the Christian faith. To counter this threat he preached a series of five sermons in 1734 on justification by faith alone. Those sermons, Edwards reported, were attended by "a very remarkable blessing of heaven to the souls of the people in this town." A young woman of questionable morals was converted, other young people were stirred by her example, the tempo of religious interest increased, and conversions multiplied.

> This work of God . . . made a glorious alteration in the town, so that in the spring and summer following (anno 1735) the town seemed to be full of the presence of God. It never was so full of love, nor so full of joy, and yet so full of distress, as it was then. There were remarkable tokens of God's presence in almost every house. It was a time of joy in families on the account of salvation being brought unto them; parents rejoicing over their children as new born, and husbands over their wives, and wives over their husbands.

There had been other revivals in the valley, most notably those that occurred under the ministry of Edwards' grandfather, Solomon Stoddard. None of them, however, proved to be contagious. With the quickening of 1734 it was otherwise. News was carried to other communities, visitors came to Northampton, Edwards was invited to preach in neighboring churches, and by 1736 the revival had spread throughout the Connecticut valley. But by 1737 the revival in Northampton had come to a halt, ceasing almost as abruptly as it had begun. Even this, Edwards interpreted as further evidence of God's mercy, for by withdrawing his Spirit to other places he was but demonstrating "how entirely and immediately the great work lately wrought was his" and "how little we can do and how little effect great things have without him."[14]

---

[13] *A Faithful Narrative of the Surprising Work of God in the Conversion of Many Hundred Souls in Northamption and Neighboring Towns* (London, 1737), reprinted in *The Works of Jonathan Edwards*, Vol. IV, *The Great Awakening*, ed. C. C. Goen (New Haven, 1972), 146–47.

[14] Quoted by Edwin S. Gaustad, *The Great Awakening in New England* (N.Y., 1957), 22.

Edwards' fame as a revivalist was the product in part of his *Faithful Narrative of the Surprising Work of God in the Conversion of Many Hundred Souls in Northampton,* published in London in 1737 and reprinted in Boston in 1738. John Wesley read it as he walked from London to Oxford, and George Whitefield read it during his first brief visit to Georgia in 1738; it had a decisive effect upon both men. More important than the stimulation the book provided was the way in which it shaped subsequent revival efforts by the precise and detailed account it gave of how the revival at Northampton actually developed. The duplication of this pattern, of course, became a major objective of those who followed him. Even the conversion process itself tended to become stereotyped. Less influential but of greater inherent significance was the series of writings — *The Distinguishing Marks of a Work of the Spirit of God* (1741), *Some Thoughts Concerning the Present Revival of Religion* (1742), and *A Treatise Concerning Religious Affections* (1746) — in which he analyzed with psychological insight and scientific detachment the twin phenomena of conversion and revival.

The Great Awakening

It was not until 1740 that the local manifestations of intense religious interest and concern were transformed into a Great Awakening that was to spread throughout every colony from Nova Scotia to Georgia and to touch every area — urban and rural, tidewater and back country — and every class — rich and poor, educated and uneducated — before its power was finally dissipated. There had been interconnections, to be sure, between the revival movements led by Frelinghuysen, the Tennents, and Edwards. Frelinghuysen and Gilbert Tennent actively supported one another. Edwards was at Yale when William Tennent was sufficiently well known there to think of himself as a possible choice for the presidency and when Gilbert Tennent received a degree. In his *Faithful Narrative* Edwards mentions an earlier revival "under the ministry of a very pious young gentleman, a Dutch minister, whose name as I remember was Frelinghuysen." But these were mostly tenuous connections and the revivals remained local in character until they were consolidated into a single movement by the itinerant activity of George Whitefield.

"The Grand Itinerant"

A recent graduate of Oxford University where he had been an intimate friend of the Wesleys and a member of the "Holy Club," Whitefield had spent a few months in Georgia in 1738. Upon his return to England he had adopted, much to the dismay of John Wesley, the expedient of preaching in the open air. Both men had come to look upon "all the

The Old Court House in Philadelphia. From this courthouse George
Whitefield preached to great throngs. Benjamin Franklin paced off the
distance at which Whitefield's voice could be heard and estimated that, on
the basis of two square feet per person, he could easily be heard by 25,000
people. *(Courtesy of the Library Company of Philadelphia.)*

world" as their "parish" to the extent that they were convinced that,
wherever they chanced to be, it was their "bounden duty to declare unto
all that are willing to hear the glad tidings of salvation"; hence, Whitefield's expedient had the distinct advantage of making it unnecessary to
secure an invitation from a local parish church in order to have an opportunity to preach. Moreover, Whitefield's preaching in the open air met
with such success that by the time he returned to America late in 1739 he
had persuaded Wesley to "become more vile" and to preach in his stead to
the great throngs he had assembled in the vicinity of Bristol.

Whitefield arrived in Philadelphia on November 2, 1739. He was a
"slim slender youth," 24 years of age, with a strong but mellow voice,
perfect enunciation, a keen sense of the dramatic, and an ability by subtle
inflection to clothe almost any word with emotion. Later it was said that by
merely pronouncing the word *Mesopotamia* he could bring tears to the eyes
of his listeners. Although his intention had been to proceed immediately
to Georgia to look after the affairs of his projected orphanage, Whitefield
was prevailed upon to preach first in the Anglican church and then in
other churches, and finally he spoke to great crowds each evening from
the steps of the courthouse. The response was astonishing. Even Benjamin

Franklin was impressed, both with the young man himself and with the good moral effect of his preaching. Franklin later reflected that "it seem'd as if all the world were growing religious." William Tennent visited him and persuaded him to make a rapid evangelistic tour of the area between Philadelphia and New York, which already had been stirred by revivals. Conscious of the new opportunity that had opened before him, Whitefield determined to preach his way to Georgia, traveling by land instead of going by ship. After a brief period in Savannah, he was back in the Philadelphia area from the middle of April to the middle of May to collect funds for the building of his orphanage, announcing his intention to visit New England in the autumn on a similar mission.

Whitefield arrived at Newport, Rhode Island, in September 1740, having sailed from Charleston three weeks before. His arrival had been well publicized, and the Boston newspapers carried advertisements of numerous books and tracts by and about Whitefield. During the next 73 days he traveled 800 miles and preached 130 sermons. He was met everywhere by great throngs. The ministers of Boston gave him an enthusiastic welcome (Charles Chauncy may have had some reservations); Harvard and Yale threw open their doors; the visit to Jonathan Edwards at Northampton was a triumphant pilgrimage; and by the time Whitefield had made his way through New York and New Jersey to Philadelphia, he was convinced that America was to be his "chief scene of action."[15] Although this was not to be true, he did make three other tours of the colonies and had embarked upon a fifth when he died at Newburyport, Massachusetts, on September 30, 1770.

If America was not the chief scene of his labors, Whitefield nonetheless did as much to shape the future of American religious life as anyone else. Previous to his coming, the "quickening" sermons had been preached in churches and at stated hours of public worship. And when sermons were delivered to congregations other than one's own it was at the invitation of the pastor. But Whitefield knew no such restrictions. He preached whenever and wherever he could find anyone to listen and in this, as well as in his extemporaneous preaching, he had many imitators. Through him also, with his incessant traveling and a catholicity of spirit that welcomed an opportunity to preach from any pulpit that was opened to him, the revival impulse permeated every denomination. America in turn did much to shape Whitefield. He was early indebted to Edwards, and Gilbert Tennent helped win him to a type of Calvinism that later cost him the friendship of the Wesleys.[16] Henceforth he was to be firmly convinced that the doctrine of election was the only sure guard against the notion that one is saved by one's own choice and decision.

---

[15] Joseph Tracy, *The Great Awakening* (Boston, 1842), 112. For Whitefield's life, see Stuart C. Henry, *George Whitefield: Wayfaring Witness* (N.Y., 1957).
[16] Trinterud, *Forming of an American Tradition*, 88.

The Mounting Opposition

Although the early revivals among the Dutch Reformed and Presbyterians had provoked discord and strife and although Whitefield had encountered vigorous opposition among his fellow Anglican ministers, the Edwardsean revival and the subsequent visit of Whitefield to New England had been viewed with remarkable equanimity and approval. In 1741, however, the storm broke.

Among the Presbyterians the occasion for the violent rupture was Gilbert Tennent's sermon on *The Danger of an Unconverted Ministry*, delivered at Nottingham, Pennsylvania, on March 8, 1740, and published at Philadelphia before the end of the year. It was an intemperate discourse. Even though he had been goaded into a denunciation of "pharisee-teachers" by the persistent efforts of unsympathetic preachers to sabotage his father's "log college," Gilbert Tennent's response only served further to inflame them. "Is a blind man," he asked,

> fit to be a guide in a very dangerous way? Is a dead man fit to bring others to life? . . . Is an ignorant rustic that has never been at sea in his life fit to be a pilot? . . . Isn't an unconverted minister like a man who would learn others to swim before he has learned it himself, and so is drowned in the act and dies like a fool?

The sermon ended with an open invitation for people to forsake the ministry of "natural" men and to seek out instead a congregation where they would receive profitable instruction.[17]

The result could have been predicted. The opposition was both consolidated and angered. At the meeting of the Synod of Philadelphia in 1741, the revivalist group was expelled, and they later formed the rival Synod of New York.[18] At the time of the expulsion the antirevivalist group was slightly stronger, with 27 ministers versus the 22 members of the Tennent party. Seventeen years later, in 1758, when the schism was finally healed with the formation of the Synod of New York and Philadelphia, the antirevivalist ministers in the old Synod of Philadelphia had dwindled in number to 23, whereas the ministers of the newer Synod of New York had more than tripled in number to 73. The initial defeat was turned into an ultimate triumph by the withering of the antirevivalist party and by the subsequent conciliatory spirit displayed by Gilbert Tennent.

When Whitefield left New England on his way to Philadelphia, he had met Gilbert Tennent and had insisted that Tennent must go to New

---

[17] A major portion of the sermon is reprinted in Smith, Handy, and Loetscher, *American Christianity*, I, 321–28.

[18] Technically the revivalists withdrew, but it was under duress. Furthermore, it is clear that the powers reserved to the presbyteries by the Adopting Act of 1729 had been usurped by the synod.

England in order to carry forward the work Whitefield had begun. Tennent's tour, from December 13, 1740, to March 3, 1741, was marked by the same large crowds that had greeted Whitefield, and at New Haven many of the students were converted. There was, however, an undercurrent of opposition among some of the clergy. Charles Chauncy (1705–87) in particular had had second thoughts that caused him to regard Tennent's preaching as unlearned, confused, ill-prepared, and ill-delivered. Rumors had begun to circulate concerning Tennent's Nottingham sermon which, if the rumors were true, was clearly calculated to undermine and foster disrespect for ministerial authority.

After Tennent's departure a sizable portion of the New England clergy exploded in indignation. Not only were the rumors concerning Tennent's sermon confirmed, but printed copies of Whitefield's journal of his New England tour were found to contain disparaging comments concerning the caliber of many New England ministers. Whitefield, to be sure, had paid tribute to the general level of religious life in New England which he regarded as exceeding that of any other part of the world, but many who preached did not "experimentally know Christ," and consequently their preaching was judged uninspired and uninspiring.

> The ministers' preaching almost universally by note is a certain mark they have in a great measure lost the old spirit of preaching. . . . It is a sad symptom of decay of vital religion when reading sermons becomes fashionable where extempore preaching did once almost universally prevail.

Whitefield echoed Tennent's denunciation of unconverted ministers. The reason that congregations have been dead, he wrote, is that "dead men preach to them," and "how can dead men beget living children?" God may, if he chooses, "convert people by the Devil," and he may also "by unconverted ministers," but "he seldom or never makes use of either of them for this purpose." Nor could one look to the New England colleges, Harvard and Yale, to supply ministers of different caliber, said Whitefield, for "their light is become darkness, darkness that may be felt and is complained of by the most godly ministers."[19]

Opposition was further aroused by the fanatical spirit and emotional extravagance of James Davenport, who projected himself on the scene at this junction. The revival preaching, to be sure, was highly emotional and on occasion people were known to cry out, to weep and sob, and even to faint and swoon. But the leaders of the revival were careful to restrain such public displays and to cast doubt upon them as evidence of conversion. Thomas Prince reported that he did not "remember any crying out or falling down or fainting, either under Mr. Whitefield's or Mr. Ten-

---

[19] Gaustad, *The Great Awakening in New England*, 30; C. C. Goen, *Revivalism and Separatism in New England, 1740–1800* (New Haven, 1962), 49.

nent's ministry all the while they were here [in Boston]."[20] It was otherwise with James Davenport, who did so much to bring the revival into disrepute by encouraging all manner of excess.

The grandson of the founder of New Haven and a graduate of Yale, Davenport had been called to a pastorate on Long Island in 1738. Stirred by the revival excitement, he crossed to Connecticut in the summer of 1741 to follow the itinerant path blazed by Whitefield and Tennent. His sermons were marked by invective, incoherent ejaculations, and indiscriminate denunciations of ministers. He sang as he made his way through the streets to the place of worship. He claimed to be able to distinguish infallibly the elect from the damned, publicly greeting the former as "brethren" and the latter as "neighbors." He was obviously unbalanced mentally, and the leaders of the revival immediately sought to dissociate themselves from him. But the damage was done, and the revival cause was brought into further disrepute when Davenport invaded Massachusetts the following summer. He had been arrested in Connecticut and transported under guard out of the colony. In Massachusetts he was jailed, again adjudged insane, and sent back to Long Island. In the end his sanity seems to have been restored, and through the friendly counsel of Eleazar Wheelock and Solomon Williams he came to see the error of his ways. In 1744 he published his *Confessions and Retractions*, expressing the hope that this would remove the prejudices that his extravagant behavior had evoked. It was a vain hope, for those who had been affronted by Whitefield's ill-considered observations were only too happy to utilize Davenport's excesses as a weapon to discredit the revivalists as a whole.

Charles Chauncy led the attack and blasted the revival from the pulpit of the First Church of Boston in a sermon entitled *Enthusiasm Described and Cautioned Against*. This was followed by 1743 by a more extended denunciation, *Seasonable Thoughts on the State of Religion in New England*. The Harvard faculty was also incensed. When Whitefield had first visited Boston he had been entertained and commended by the president of the college, and the overseers had set aside a day of thanksgiving for the beneficent effect of his labors. When he returned in 1744 the doors of the college were closed to him and the faculty issued a statement, later endorsed by the Yale faculty, blistering his message, his methods, and his character.

The situation was confused and the ministers badly divided. One group, under the leadership of Chauncy, feared that the enthusiasm of the revival might undermine the authority of the churches, and so for a time they emphasized the rational–moral aspects of religion as an antidote. Another group of ministers, loosely clustered around Edwards, favored the revival and participated wholeheartedly in it, but they also remained aware of its potential effects on the order of the Congregational churches. Only a handful were ready to insist upon emotional manifestations as evidence of

[20] Goen, *Revivalism and Separatism in New England*, 18.

conversion and to defend itinerancy and lay preaching. The others were uncommitted. These responses to the revival predicted the course of religion in New England well into the next century. At one end of the spectrum eventually appeared a style of religion that accented the capabilities of human reason and the central importance of morality. The other end of the spectrum was anchored by advocates of highly emotional, effervescent religion focused on conversion, and significantly less concerned with systems of doctrine. And in the middle were various shades of the legacy of both Chauncy and Edwards, persons who sought to combine the emotional element in religion with an emphasis on discipline, clerical authority, and formal worship.

In the meantime a further split began to develop within the revivalist camp. Some of those who had been persuaded of the necessity of a work of grace as the indispensable door to the Christian life became disturbed by the continued reception and retention of unconverted members by the churches. For all its emphasis upon conversion, the revival had not led to the abrogation of the lax membership practices that had been introduced by the adoption of the Half-way Covenant. Even when ministers wished to tighten disciplinary procedures, few congregations were willing to accept the rigorous standards implicit in the preaching of their pastors. The most shocking evidence of this fact was the callous ejection of Jonathan Edwards from his Northampton church in 1750 when he insisted upon some evidence of a personal religious experience as a prerequisite to church membership. The unhappiness of the more "experienced" Christians with this lax state of affairs led a considerable number of them to withdraw and to form separate churches of their own.

Although the movement was fairly general throughout New England, the real stronghold of the "Separate" or "Strict" Congregationalists was in eastern Connecticut. It has been suggested that this was a lower-class revolt, but a careful examination of the Separate churches has revealed that they were composed of a representative cross section of the population and included prominent and even wealthy members of their respective communities.[21] The constant factor was the earnestness of their religious concern. In all, no fewer than 98 Separate churches were formed, and there were at least 32 temporary separations. But this scarcely indicates their full strength, for the strong and ultimately overwhelming tendency was for the Separates to become Baptists. The doctrine of believers' baptism, of course, was a fitting expression of the Separates' conception of the church as a community of "experienced" Christians. At least 19 of the Separate Congregational churches became Baptist, but a better indication of the Separates' strength is the additional 130 Baptist churches that were formed by disaffected Congregationalists. Although not participating directly in the earliest New England revivals, the Baptists

---

[21] This is the conclusion reached by Goen as a result of his thorough and careful research. *Revivalism and Separatism*, 188–91.

reaped the largest harvest, siphoning off the strength of the remaining Separate churches to such an extent that they tended to dwindle and die.

The Southern Phase of the Awakening

In the South the Awakening developed more slowly. Although Whitefield preached to large numbers in the South, the way had not been prepared for him by earlier revivals and there was little leadership to conserve the results he obtained. The old, established areas of Virginia were Anglican territory and the Anglican clergy were unsympathetic and even hostile.[22] Other areas were more recently settled and, without existing centers of church life, there had been scant opportunity for revivals to develop. Thus, throughout the South Whitefield blazed the way for the spread of the Awakening instead of consolidating existing interest into a single movement as he had done elsewhere. Later, when the revival took root in Virginia, class differences between Anglicans in the eastern parts of the colony and Baptists and Methodists in the west complicated matters, as they became associated with anti-revivalist and pro-revivalist sentiments, respectively.

The earliest spiritual quickening in Virginia occurred east of the mountains in Hanover County. As a result of Whitefield's influence as he made his way overland to Georgia in December 1739, a few lay people began to meet in private homes to read some of Whitefield's sermons and other devotional literature. A spontaneous revival broke out. As religious concern spread, the homes of the leaders became too small to hold the gatherings and "reading houses" were erected. This was the situation when William Robinson, a graduate of William Tennent's "log college," was sent by the New Brunswick Presbytery on a missionary tour of Virginia during the winter of 1742–43. Those who had erected the "reading houses" invited him to preach and became Presbyterians. Robinson was followed by a succession of revivalist itinerants sent out by the Synod of New York, the most important of whom was to be Samuel Davies, who succeeded Robinson at Hanover in 1747. Under his leadership the revival spread rapidly; numerous churches were organized and brought together in 1755 to form a new presbytery. After Davies' departure in 1759 to become president of Princeton, the Presbyterian activity became less pronounced.

In the meantime the revival broke out in another quarter. In 1754 two brothers-in-law, Shubal Stearns and Daniel Marshall, came to Virginia from Connecticut. They had been converted by Whitefield, became Separate Congregational itinerants, and were then ordained as Baptist preachers. Within a year of their arrival in Virginia they were told of people across the border in North Carolina, where there was no preaching, who would travel 40 miles to hear a sermon. From among these

[22] Rhys Isaac, *The Transformation of Virginia: Community, Religion, and Authority, 1740– 1790* (Chapel Hill, N.C., 1982).

people a church was gathered at Sandy Creek, and from this center no fewer than 125 ministers were raised up in little more than a decade, fanning out in all directions to preach the gospel. Marshall went on to Georgia where, assisted by the "exhortations" of his wife, he labored with almost equal success. From Virginia to Georgia, Separate Baptist churches multiplied at an astonishing rate. At first tension existed between the hyperenthusiastic Separate and the old "regular" Baptist churches formed or reorganized by evangelists from the Philadelphia Baptist Association. By 1787, however, this breach was being healed, first in Virginia and then later in North Carolina, Kentucky, and elsewhere.

As Hanover was the center of Presbyterian expansion and Sandy Creek the center from which radiated Baptist evangelistic activity, so Dinwiddie County was the center of the revival impulse among the Anglicans. It was a delayed response, for no leader appeared until Devereux Jarratt was installed in 1763 as rector at Bath. He had been influenced in his early years by Whitefield, and when he went to England for ordination he had come into contact with both Whitefield and John Wesley. Under Jarratt's zealous preaching his three churches became so crowded that he was compelled to hold services in adjacent groves, and he followed the precedent of Whitefield and Wesley in meeting with the more earnest Christians in small groups.

As early as 1765 two of Wesley's lay preachers had come to America as immigrants — Robert Strawbridge to Maryland and Philip Embury to New York. They were followed by two others in 1769, and in the same year Wesley commissioned the first two of eight officially appointed lay missionaries to serve in America. In 1772 Robert Williams, one of Wesley's lay preachers, appeared in Dinwiddie County and enlisted Jarratt's participation in a more widespread endeavor. Jarratt began to itinerate beyond the bounds of his own parish, and the great assemblies gathered in the open air to hear him preach were impressive. Jesse Lee, one of his young converts, reported:

> I have been at meetings where the whole congregation would be bathed in tears, and sometimes their cries would be so loud that the preacher's voice could not be heard. Some would be seized with trembling and in a few moments drop on the floor as if they were dead, while others were embracing each other with streaming eyes and all were lost in wonder, love, and praise.[23]

With the assistance of several lay preachers, Jarratt was busily forming converts into "methodist" societies. By 1777 as a result of their activity there were 4,379 members of the societies in Virginia and adjoining counties of North Carolina, yet the total for all the colonies was only 6,968. After the Revolution when the societies broke with Anglicanism and formed the Methodist Episcopal Church in 1784, Jarratt expressed

---

[23] W. W. Sweet, *Methodism in American History* (N.Y., 1954), 76.

resentment at the separation. He felt that he had been deceived by the assurances of loyalty that he had received from the lay preachers. Within a few years his bitterness was gone, but he remained within the Anglican fold where his influence contributed greatly to the strength of the evangelical movement within the newly formed Protestant Episcopal Church.

The Impact of the Awakening

The Awakening was much more than the activity of a few conspicuous leaders. It was "Great" because it was general. People everywhere were caught up in the movement, and its influence was spread by innumerable local pastors, passing itinerants, and lay exhorters. No one could escape the excitement or avoid the necessity to declare oneself as friend or foe.

And because the Awakening was general, it played an important role in forming a national consciousness among people of different colonies whose primary ties were with Europe rather than with one another. As a spontaneous movement that swept across all colonial boundaries, generated a common interest and a common loyalty, bound people together in a common cause, and reinforced the conviction that God had a special destiny in store for America, the Awakening contributed greatly to the development of a sense of cohesiveness among the American people. It was more influential in this respect than all the colonial wars the colonists were called upon to fight, more influential in fact than many of the political squabbles they had had with the mother country since the latter as often served to separate as to unite them. Whitefield, Tennent, and Edwards were rallying names for Americans a full three decades before Washington, Jefferson, Franklin, and Samuel Adams became familiar household names. Perhaps it is significant that the Awakening did not reach Nova Scotia until 1776, too late to create the intangible ties that bound the other colonies together.

Institutional Consequences

No exact estimate can be made of members added to the churches by the Awakening, but the number in all denominations was large. Interest in Indian missions was revived. A wide variety of charitable projects, including schools for Indians and the children of indentured servants, were initiated. The role of the laity in the churches was enhanced. The setting of minister against minister undermined ministerial authority at a time when a stress upon a self-authenticating religious experience was freeing the individual from dependence upon clerical opinion. On the other hand, quite paradoxically, the ministerial office was also given added luster by the fame of the revivalists, and the number of young men drawn into the ranks of the ministry rapidly mounted.[24]

A consequence of marked future significance was the remarkable success of Baptist and Methodist itinerants in the conversion of blacks to Christianity. This was the result of their energetic efforts to evangelize the slaves, a task hitherto neglected and not seriously attempted by other Protestant denominations (not even by the Quakers) until plantation missions were organized after 1830. Blacks responded to the exciting preaching of the itinerants and were welcomed into Baptist and Methodist churches on the basis of a surprising degree of equality. They were given formal responsibilities, and the talents of the gifted were utilized as exhorters and preachers in evangelistic endeavors. There often were more black than white members of local churches. Some all-black congregations were formed, and a few blacks served as pastors of mixed congregations.[25]

Apart from the multiplication of churches and the incorporation of blacks within the Christian community, the major institutional survivals of the Awakening came from the impulse that was given to higher education by the necessity to provide educational opportunities for the swelling number of ministerial recruits. Presbyterians were especially active in this endeavor, and many of their ministers established classical academies, similar in character to William Tennent's "log college" and patterned after the small private Presbyterian academies of Ireland and the Dissenting academies of England which at this time enjoyed an educational reputation that was greater than that of the ancient universities. Several colleges — Washington and Lee, Washington and Jefferson, and Dickinson — trace their ancestry back to these early academies. In 1746 the Synod of New York secured a charter for the College of New Jersey (Princeton) which was designed as the capstone of the Presbyterian educational structure, and in 1776 the Hanover Presbytery in Virginia established Hampden–Sydney College. Baptists also organized several academies and in 1764 founded the College of Rhode Island (Brown University) as their major center for training of ministers. In 1766 pro-revivalists among the Dutch Reformed obtained a charter for Queen's College

---

[24] Patricia U. Bonomi emphasizes the health of religious institutions in the eighteenth century in *Under the Cope of Heaven: Religion, Society and Politics in Colonial America* (N.Y., 1986).

[25] For an account of this phase of the Awakening, see W. S. Hudson, "The American Context as an Area for Research in Black Church Studies," *Church History* 3 (1983), 159–70. Baptists and Methodists encountered much opposition and hostility because of their tampering with other people's property, an activity that among other facets of their behavior has caused them to be labeled as a major countercultural force in the South. See R. R. Beeman and Rhys Isaac, "Cultural Conflict and Social Change in the Revolutionary South," *Journal of Southern History,* 46 (1980), 533–34; Isaac, *The Transformation of Virginia,* 161–77.

(Rutgers University). Dartmouth, an outgrowth of an Indian charity school, was incorporated in 1769.

Although the clergy of the English settlements along the seaboard did not have the opportunity to duplicate the work of the priests who accompanied the French traders and trappers on their far-ranging travels through the interior of the continent, the evangelization of those tribes with whom the English came into contact did not suffer neglect.[26] The effect of the Awakening was to pour new enthusiasm into this task. Eleazar Wheelock, Samuel Kirkland, David Brainerd, and for a time Jonathan Edwards were among those who devoted themselves to Indian missions. Brainerd's diary, edited by Edwards, is a moving testament of devotion that tells the story of his experiences among the Indians, and it inspired many others to give themselves to mission work.

The Theological Temper Generated by the Awakening

Evangelicalism, to use the term by which the new surge of spiritual life is usually described, has often been interpreted as a revolt against Calvinism. Although this may have been its ultimate consequence, it was far from that in the beginning. The understanding of the Christian faith as set forth in the great Reformed Confessions was taken for granted. John Wesley was an important exception but, in many respects, even Wesley stood within the Genevan tradition. Evangelicalism, however, was much more a mood and an emphasis than a theological system. Its stress was upon the importance of personal religious experience. If it was a revolt against anything, it was a revolt against the notion that the Christian life involved little more than observing the outward formalities of the religion.

Only in New England was significant theological discussion provoked by the Awakening, and only in New England did clearly defined theological alignments appear. From a theological standpoint the "Consistent Calvinists" or Edwardseans made the most impressive contribution to the debate. This "New England Theology" was fashioned by Jonathan Edwards and his two most influential disciples, Joseph Bellamy and Samuel Hopkins, in an effort to buttress the revival by a bold and intellectually rigorous restatement of those doctrines that they were convinced had been verified by the revival.[27] The truth that redemption was effected by God's sovereign grace alone was to be defended at whatever cost to human pride, and all attempts to substitute moral attainments for the

[26] Anglicans lost heart for Indian missions for many years after the 1622 massacre of 300 colonists, but others did not. For Indian missions, see R. P. Beaver, *Pioneers in Mission* (Grand Rapids, 1966); F. P. Purcha, *Americanizing the American Indians* (Cambridge, Mass., 1973); and Henry W. Bowden, *American Indians and Christian Missions: Studies in Cultural Conflict* (Chicago, 1981).

[27] See Joseph Haroutunian, *Piety Versus Moralism, the Passing of the New England Theology* (N.Y., 1932); and Conrad Wright, *The Liberal Christians* (Boston, 1970).

righteousness that comes only as a gift were to be resolutely opposed. Arrayed against them, especially in the vicinity of Boston, were those charged with being "Arminians"—ministers who regarded Edwardsean doctrines as unduly harsh and as an affront to common sense in that they tended to undermine all morality. The doctrine of original sin, pictured in terms of innocent infants burning in hell, was denounced as inhuman, unreasonable, and indefensible; and the doctrine of predestination was condemned as destructive of all moral effort. Between the embattled extremes was a varied group of middle-of-the-roaders known as "Old Calvinists." Whether more traditionally oriented or more liberally inclined, members of this group were distressed by theological wrangling, viewing it as the consequence of an overly fussy concern for "theological niceties" and advocating instead a "large measure of charity." Ezra Stiles was typical of their point of view when he announced that the reigning theological debate was only a verbal dispute.

> Interrogating so-called Arminians, he found they believed in the redemptive grace of Christ; inquiring of so-called Calvinists, he learned that they did not deny the importance of good works. On the whole, "I cannot perceive any very essential real difference in their opinions respecting the fundamental principles of religion."[28]

In this lack of concern for careful theological distinctions and in the emphasis upon "the fundamental principles of religion," the moderates were more closely akin to the general spirit of Evangelicalism than were the Edwardseans. Evangelicalism as a whole tended to prize a "warm heart" and to be impatient with theological controversy. What distinguished the Edwardseans from other Evangelicals was their firm conviction that a warm heart was not enough. In keeping with the earlier Puritan heritage, they insisted that both heart and head—faith and reason, grace and law—must be brought together in the service of God. Thus the Edwardseans were to provide the major portion of whatever intellectual content Evangelicalism was to have. Without the influence of this theological structure that Evangelicalism took largely for granted, Evangelicalism would have had small staying power. Reduced to little more than sentiment, its thrust would quickly have evaporated. It is of particular importance for American history that Evangelicalism was formed as a compound of an emotional experience of "rebirth" and a commitment of obedience to God's law. This framework for evangelical religion, which took shape in the eighteenth century, also incorporated a view of preaching as a means to promote religion in both of these areas. Various styles of preaching

---

[28] Gaustad, *The Great Awakening*, 130. Stiles was a representative figure through whom many of the tendencies of the age are to be seen. A graduate of Yale, he was pastor at Newport, Rhode Island, and Portsmouth, New Hampshire, before returning to Yale in 1778 as president of the college. See Edmund S. Morgan, *The Gentle Puritan: A Life of Ezra Stiles, 1727–1795* (New Haven, 1962).

came about in the later history of the denominations, but evangelical preaching of the sort that emerged from the religious ferment of the eighteenth century proved the most durable and appealing over time.

Although the Awakening was productive of controversy and strife, it was, paradoxically, at the same time a great unifying force that gave to "four-fifths" of the Christians in America "a common understanding of the Christian life and the Christian faith."[29] Since the revival had penetrated many denominations quite indiscriminately, this common understanding tended to minimize the importance of denominational distinctions and to provide a basis for mutual respect, appreciation, and cooperation. Typical of the new spirit was John Wesley's emphatic declaration that he renounced and detested all distinctions among Christians and refused to be distinguished from other men by anything but "the common principles of Christianity." From "real Christians" he had no desire to be distinguished at all. "Dost thou love and fear God? It is enough! I give thee the right hand of fellowship."[30] This catholicity of spirit was even more conspicuously exhibited in George Whitefield. Whitefield spoke with equal readiness from Anglican, Presbyterian, Congregational, Baptist, and Dutch Reformed pulpits, and he counted men of all denominations among his converts. Preaching from the courthouse balcony in Philadelphia, he raised his eyes to the heavens and cried out:

> Father Abraham, whom have you in heaven? Any Episcopalians? No! Any Presbyterians? No! Any Independents or Methodists? No, no, no! Whom have you there? We don't know those names here. All who are here are Christians. . . . Oh, is this the case? Then God help us to forget party names and to become Christians in deed and truth.

His attitude was echoed by Samuel Davies in Virginia.

> My brethren, I would now warn you against this wretched, mischievous spirit of party. . . . A Christian! a Christian! Let that be your highest distinction; let that be the name which you labor to deserve. God forbid that my ministry should be the occasion of diverting your attention to anything else. . . . It has . . . been the great object of my zeal to inculcate upon you the great essentials of our holy religion, and make you sincere practical Christians. Alas! . . . unless I succeed in this, I labor to very little purpose though I should presbyterianize the whole colony.[31]

In addition to a common theological outlook, a specific understanding of the nature of the Church underlay this broad-minded spirit.

---

[29] Trinterud, *Forming of an American Tradition*, 197.
[30] From *The Character of a Methodist*, reprinted in *The Works of John Wesley*, 4th ed. (London, 1841), VIII, 332–33.
[31] A. L. Drummond, *The Story of American Protestantism* (Boston, 1950), 115, Samuel Davies, *Sermons on Important Subjects* (N.Y., 1842), I, 217–18.

The Denominational Concept

What has been called the "denominational" concept of the church had been elaborated a century earlier by the Dissenting Brethren of the Westminster Assembly of Divines.[32] This concept was to be of decisive future importance in the shaping of American religious life. Denominationalism, as these men used the term, was the opposite of sectarianism. A "sect" regards itself alone as the true Church. By definition a "sect" is exclusive. "Denomination," on the other hand, was adopted as a neutral and inclusive term. It implied that the group referred to is but one member, called or denominated by a particular name, of a larger group — the church — to which other denominations belong. Gilbert Tennent stated the concept with clarity and incisiveness when he declared: "All societies who profess Christianity and retain the foundational principles thereof, notwithstanding their different denominations and diversity of sentiments in smaller things, are in reality but one Church of Christ, but several branches (more or less pure in minuter points) of one visible kingdom of the Messiah."[33]

On the basis of this understanding of the church which acknowledged the unity that existed within the diversity of outward ecclesiastical forms, the Protestant churches were able to develop a functional catholicity that was to find expression in the creation of a whole system of voluntary societies for the promotion of a host of worthy causes. There were societies devoted to missions, Bible and tract distribution, education, charitable enterprises, and a wide-ranging spectrum of moral and social reforms. These societies were to be the instruments into which much of the evangelical fervor released by the Awakening was subsequently to be channeled when the Protestant churches jointly addressed themselves to the task of spreading churches and schools across a continent while devoting themselves, at the same time, to reforming the nation. From a modern perspective, two of the more important causes forwarded by these societies were the abolition of slavery and the emancipation of women. In many ways the full promise for slaves and for women was to remain unfulfilled, but, if much remained to be accomplished, significant progress was made. From the perspective of the early nineteenth century, however, in contrast to that of a later time, the missionary task in its various ramifications was regarded as fundamental to the achievement of all other objectives.

All this, however, was in the future. The immediate problem at hand was the relationship of the colonies to England.

---

[32] The Assembly was summoned in 1643 by the Long Parliament to advise the Parliament in its task of effecting a religious settlement for the nation. Presbyterian sentiment was predominant among the assembled clergy. The Congregational minority became known as the Dissenting Brethren. The case for "denominationalism," as developed by these dissenters, is discussed in Russell E. Richey, ed., *Denominationalism* (Nashville, 1977), 19–42. Jacob Neusner provides an unusually incisive discussion of the same concept in *Understanding American Judaism* (N.Y., 1971), II, 259–77.

[33] Trinterud, *Forming of an American Tradition*, 132.

CHAPTER 4

The Birth
of the Republic

When Edmund Burke in 1775 sought to help his fellow members of Parliament understand the "love of freedom" and "fierce spirit of liberty" that had occasioned the uproar in the colonies over sugar and stamps and tea and taxes, he reminded them that "the people of the colonies are descendants of Englishmen." And then he added:

> England, Sir, is a nation which still I hope respects, and formerly adored, her freedom. The colonists emigrated from you when this part of your character was most predominant; and they took this bias and direction the moment they parted from your hands. They are therefore not only devoted to liberty, but to liberty according to English ideals, and on English principles.

Representative institutions in harmony with English practice had indeed developed very early in all the colonies. Some of the colonial charters were explicit in guaranteeing that the settlers would have "the rights of Englishmen," and the colonists had become accustomed through long practice to the idea that they could not be taxed except by their own consent as expressed in the colonial assemblies.

Religion and Politics

Although the "love of freedom" had deep and ancient roots in English society, it had been nurtured and transformed into a "fierce spirit of liberty" during the first half of the seventeenth century when the religious issue had come to the fore and had become inextricably intermingled with

the liberties of Englishmen. During the course of the constitutional struggle in England, it became evident to the participants that certain theological convictions had definite political implications, and these implications
were rather fully explored and explicated by both royalists and parliamen-
tarians before the nation finally regained its equilibrium. It was the emotion and spirit generated in the struggle between king and Parliament that
Burke had in mind when he noted that the colonists were not only Englishmen but "Protestants, and of that kind which is the most adverse to all
implicit subjection of mind and opinion."

The Puritan Political Heritage

Those Protestants whom Burke described as "the most adverse to all
subjection of mind and opinion" had their rootage in Reformed or Calvinist Christianity. It has been said of the early Calvinists that they feared
God so much that they could not fear any man, be he king or emperor.
And they had much to fear from men, for almost everywhere the Reformed churches were "churches under the cross" — suffering persecution and struggling to survive. But they remained undaunted, sustained in
part by a firm confidence in God's overruling providence and impelled by
a strong conviction that the chief end of man is to glorify God and insisting
that God is glorified by full and complete obedience. When John Knox
informed Queen Mary that "right religion takes neither origin nor authority from worldly princes but from the eternal God alone" and then
told her that subjects therefore must not "frame their religion according
to the appetite of their princes," he was speaking in an accent that was
familiar to all sons of Geneva.[1]

The Reformed churches were prodded into political theorizing. Although they remembered the apostle Paul's admonition that Christians
must be subject to "the powers that be," they were not of a temper to
patiently endure bloody repression if a plausible excuse for active resistance could be found. Goaded by the burnings in England under Mary
Tudor, the persecution in Scotland under Mary Stuart, the wars of religion in France, and the massacre of the Dutch by the Spanish troops of the
Duke of Alva, the Reformed leaders explored every possible concept that
could be utilized to justify resistance and rebellion. Rights derived from
natural law and from the origin of government in a compact between the
ruler and the ruled were explicated, and the role of lesser magistrates as

[1] See John T. McNeill, "The Democratic Element in Calvin's Thought," *Church History*
(1949), 153–71; and W. S. Hudson, "Theological Convictions and Democratic
Government," *Theology Today* (1953), 230–39.

guardians of the liberties of people was carefully defined. Even tyrannicide, in exceptional circumstances, was defended.[2]

Doctrines of resistance and rebellion were purely negative features of Reformed political thought. From a positive point of view, a distinct preference was exhibited for the checks and balances of a "mixed state." Noting with characteristic irony that "it very rarely happens that kings regulate themselves so that their will is never at variance with justice and rectitude," Calvin himself had suggested the importance of broadening the franchise so that the self-interest of the one may be checked by the self-interest of the many. "It is safer and more tolerable for the government to be in the hands of the many that they may afford each other mutual assistance and admonition, and that if any one arrogate to himself more than is right, the many may act as censors and masters to restrain his ambition." "No kind of government is more happy than this, . . . and I consider those most happy people who are permitted to enjoy such a condition" in which they have the right and the duty to "exert their strenuous and constant efforts" to preserve their liberties.[3]

This was the seedbed of the Puritan political thought that reshaped the English constitution through the ordeal of civil war and became so deeply rooted in the consciousness of Englishmen that the ejection of James II from the throne in 1688 was effected by a "bloodless" revolution. Defenders of the royal prerogative had few doubts as to the source of the rebellious and seditious notion of the time. Richard Bancroft, chaplain to Elizabeth's Archbishop of Canterbury and soon to be archbishop himself, pointed an accusing finger at Geneva in his book *Dangerous Positions and Proceedings* (1593). James I echoed the accusation at the Hampton Court Conference in 1604. And in 1663 Robert South repeated it, saying: "In our account of the sons of Geneva, we will begin with the father of the faithful (faithful, I mean, to their old antimonarchical doctrines and assertions), this is, the great mufti of Geneva" — John Calvin.

The fact that this "fierce spirit of liberty" was part of the intellectual baggage carried to the New World by the Puritans has been obscured by two much-quoted statements of John Winthrop and John Cotton. "A democracy," said Winthrop, "is among most civil nations accounted the meanest and worst of all forms of government." "Democracy?" Cotton

---

[2] See, e.g., *A Defense of Liberty Against Tyrants: A Translation of the Vindiciae contra Tyrannos*, ed. H. J. Laski (London, 1924), and John Ponet, *A Shorte Treatise of Politike Power*, facsimile reproduction in W. S. Hudson, *John Ponet: Advocate of Limited Monarchy* (Chicago, 1942).

[3] John Calvin, *Institutes of the Christian Religion*, IV, xx, 8; and *Commentary on Micah*, 5:5. For a later explication of the necessity for checks and balances, see the preface to John Cotton's *The Keys of the Kingdom of Heaven* (1644), reprinted in A.S.P. Woodhouse, *Puritanism and Liberty* (London, 1938), 293–98.

asked rhetorically. "I do not conceive that ever God did ordain it as a fit government either for church or commonwealth."[4] Winthrop and Cotton, of course, used the word in its classical meaning which had no connotation of indirect representation. The democracy they repudiated was not the "mixed" government that the nineteenth century became accustomed to calling democracy. Cotton's inclusion of "church" in his rejection of democracy should make it clear that a definition of terms is required, for Cotton was a major architect of the "congregational" form of church government.[5] Even Thomas Jefferson did not believe that democracy "would be practicable beyond the extent of a New England township."[6] What Winthrop and Cotton were advocating, and what the Founding Fathers sought to establish, was a "mixed government" with a separation of powers that would provide "guards for their future security."

No one was more aware than John Cotton that all men and especially men in power are prone to corruption. "Let all the world," he declared, "learn to give mortal man no greater power than they are content they shall use, for use it they will. . . . It is necessary that all power that is on earth be limited. . . . It is counted a matter of danger to the state to limit prerogatives, but it is a further danger not to have them limited." Winthrop told the men of Hingham that in signing the covenant they had agreed to submit to the rulers that were thus set over them for their own good, but this admonition had an important qualification—unless they could prove that their rulers were violating the good they had been appointed to serve.[7] This was the common conviction. Thus, although minority rights were not cherished with equal ardor by all Protestant churches in America, most of them through tradition, conviction, and experience had developed an ingrained antipathy to arbitrary rule and had been taught that upon just occasion people had the right and even the duty to rebel.

[4] R. C. Winthrop, *Life and Letters of John Winthrop* (Boston, 1869), II, 430; and Cotton's "Letter to Lord Say and Seal" in *The Puritans,* ed. Miller and Johnson, I, 209.

[5] It has often been noted that experience gained in self-governing New England Congregational churches contributed to the political views of the colonists. Less seldom recognized was the "fierce spirit of liberty" generated by the Anglican "vestry system" in the southern colonies and also the familiarity with representative government in Presbyterian and other churches.

[6] *The Constitution Reconsidered,* ed. Conyers Read (N Y., 1938), 106.

[7] John Cotton, *An Exposition of the Thirteenth Chapter of Revelation* (London, 1656), 72, as reprinted in *The Puritans,* ed. Miller and Johnson, I, 213. For Winthrop, see Perry Miller, "From the Covenant to the Revival," in *The Shaping of American Religion,* ed. J. W. Smith and A. L. Jamison (Princeton, 1961), 334–35. It is made clear by Edmund Morgan, *The Puritan Dilemma: The Story of John Winthrop* (Boston, 1958), that Winthrop's (and also Cotton's) emphasis was usually upon the duty of obedience.

Fears Generated by Anglican Aggressiveness

In the colonies the Puritan political heritage had not been allowed to fade into the past as mere ancient history, nor had the memory of distant events that surrounded that heritage with deep emotion been permitted to grow dim. Provoked by an Anglican aggressiveness that aroused old fears of ecclesiastical tyranny, both pulpit and press rehearsed past history to counter what was considered a present threat. And because the royal power and the episcopal pretensions were so closely linked, the controversy generated a widespread spirit of disaffection that in the course of time was transformed into a deeply rooted rebellious temper. Since the most prominent of the immediate grievances that led to the American Declaration of Independence were economic and political, the importance of the ecclesiastical issue as a major factor in precipitating the American Revolution frequently has been neglected.[8]

The Glorious Revolution of 1688 which brought William and Mary to the English and Scottish thrones had a marked effect upon Anglican fortunes in the New World. Under James II the Church of England had been given scant support in the colonies, and numbered few adherents, and had been officially established only in Virginia. This situation was altered by the Revolution. Dissenting "dissidence" at home was temporarily quieted by the Act of Toleration, and the Anglican bishops were freed from their almost complete preoccupation with the domestic problems created by a Roman Catholic king. Thus the way was cleared for a more aggressive Anglican policy in the colonies. With the support of a sympathetic Court, it now became possible to marshal sufficient pressure to secure Anglican establishments in Maryland, South Carolina, and the city of New York, with North Carolina and Georgia later being brought into line.

The Society for the Propagation of the Gospel (S.P.G.) was designed to spearhead and implement the new Anglican thrust. It had been organized in 1701, with royal and archiepiscopal blessing to send "orthodox clergymen" to the colonies to instruct such as lacked "the administration of God's Word and Sacraments" in the "principles of true religion." If the clause in the charter that defined the purpose of the Society had been interpreted to mean providing a ministry for the numerous communities in the middle and southern colonies that lacked any ministry whatsoever, the Society would have aroused little opposition. The Society, however, was determined that Anglicanism should shed its regional character, and

---

[8] Carl Bridenbaugh, *Mitre and Sceptre: Transatlantic Faiths, Ideas, and Politics, 1689–1775* (N.Y., 1962), explored in detail this aspect of the Revolutionary background. For another aspect, see Norman C. Hatch, *The Sacred Cause of Liberty: Republican Thought and the Millennium in the American Revolution* (New Haven, 1977). For a discussion of fears about the possible loss of ecclesiastical independence, see Bernard Bailyn, *Ideological Origins of the American Revolution* (Cambridge, Mass., 1967).

this meant expansion into the older, settled areas north of Maryland. Consequently the charter was interpreted as a directive to proselyte members of other communions. In 1750, for example, one third of the S.P.G. missionaries were stationed in New England where there already was at least one "orthodox minister" in every town and where the converts to Anglicanism were drawn almost exclusively from the ranks of professing Christians. Elsewhere in the colonies S.P.G. activity was similarly restricted to a great degree to older communities that already had a settled ministry, and the zeal of its missionaries was primarily engaged in making Anglicans out of Quakers, Presbyterians, Baptists, Lutherans, and Reformed.

Under such circumstances it is scarcely surprising that friction developed—a friction that was augmented, as Jonathan Edwards and the "Associated Ministers of Hampshire" explained, by the "uncharitable and unchristian spirit" of the missionaries in "intimating that our ministry is no ministry, not having had episcopal ordination," and thereby inferring with self-evident satisfaction that all other "churches are no churches of Christ, and that our people are to be looked upon as strangers to the commonwealth of Israel—a tenet or principle which came from Rome and which in years past has been disclaimed in England and is still by all the other reformed churches in Europe." The "grand business" of the missionaries, a correspondent of the *Boston Evening Post* declared, "seemed to be not to convert men from paganism to Christianity but to proselyte Protestant Dissenters to the Church of England, as if they imagine there can be no salvation out of that church."[9]

Other irritations and grievances, some of them profoundly disturbing, stemmed from what William Smith, Jr., of New York called the Anglican "lust for dominion." Anglican clergy in the middle and northern colonies sought to impress the local populace by holding their conventions in the presence of the governor and by having them preceded by a public procession of the clergy in gowns and cassocks. This ostentation was a minor annoyance but it was not calculated to reduce friction. More serious were deliberate harassments, such as the arrest of Francis Makemie for preaching in New York City; the ejection of a Presbyterian minister at Jamaica, New York, with an S.P.G. missionary installed in his place; repeated interventions of the S.P.G. to prevent non-Anglican churches in New York from being incorporated so that title to their property might be secure; the order of the Board of Trade that no schoolmasters from England were to be permitted to teach in New Hampshire without a license from the Bishop of London; the attempt of the missionaries to thwart the founding of the College of New Jersey by the Presbyterians, their efforts to subvert the interdenominational character of King's College and the College of Philadelphia, their scheming to gain control of

[9] Bridenbaugh, *Mitre and Sceptre,* 79–80, 90.

Harvard and Yale, their role in frustrating the establishment of a Presbyterian college in North Carolina; and the successful intimidation of printers so that for a time there was no freedom of the press for non-Anglicans in New York. Even the granting of a charter to enable Congregationalists to carry on mission work among the Indians was denied. Ill feeling was intensified when news was received that the plight of the Dissenters in England had worsened after Queen Anne came to the throne, with the disabilities imposed by the Occasional Conformity Act and the Schism Act being added to those of the Test and Corporation Acts.[10] Nor were reports of the burning of Dissenting meetinghouses by English mobs reassuring.

It was, however, the persistent efforts of S.P.G. missionaries to persuade the British government to establish an Anglican episcopate in America that did more than anything else to awaken old fears and to spread a spirit of dissaffection. The proposal to send bishops to regularize the status of colonial Anglicanism seems innocuous enough if one fails to take into account the close link that existed between Anglican ecclesiastical authority and British political authority. To many of the colonists, bishops were a symbol of incipient tyranny; and Anglican activity in America had done little to disabuse them of the notion that powers, once granted to bishops, would be extended and abused. Jonathan Mayhew put the point succinctly when he stated: "People have no security against being unmercifully priest-ridden but by keeping all imperious bishops and other clergymen who love to lord it over God's heritage from getting their feet into the stirrup at all."[11] Even so, the traditional fear of bishops might not have evoked such a concerted and long-sustained campaign of opposition had the proposal not been promoted as part and parcel of a plan to secure a tax-supported Anglican establishment in all the colonies and had it not, in order to facilitate this goal, involved a scheme for regrouping the colonies in more efficient administrative units which would necessitate the withdrawal of the existing colonial charters. The struggle against bishops thus came to be regarded by many as a struggle to defend both the civil and the religious liberties of the colonists.

A further alienation occurred when the S.P.G. missionaries sought to advance their cause by suggesting that an American episcopate would bind the colonists more closely to England. No argument could have been better calculated to antagonize the other churches, for its plain implication was that their members were disloyal people. Nor did the missionaries hesitate to spell out this implication. In seeking to counter the antibishop

---

[10] The Test and Corporation Acts excluded non-Anglicans from governmental positions. The Occasional Conformity Act tightened this restriction and the Schism Act required all teachers to be licensed by a bishop and to teach nothing but the Anglican catechism. Had the latter act been enforced, it would have suppressed all schools run by Dissenters and would have taken from Dissenters the education of their children.

[11] A. L. Cross, *Anglican Episcopate*, (N.Y., 1902), 145.

attack, they accused "dissenting" leaders of being "avowed republicans," "enemies to monarchy," and a "restless and turbulent faction" whereas if the Church of England were properly established, the populace would quickly be reduced to "passive obedience" since the Anglican clergy "inculcate the great principles of loyalty and submission to government." An article in the *Boston News-Letter* in 1750 reached back to the Hampton Court Conference of 1604 to find the proper slogan to state the case for episcopacy as the indispensable support of monarchy: "The good old saying, 'No Bishop, no King,' however grating it may be to some people, ought to be the standing maxim of the English government."[12]

Although the tactical skill and political connections of the Dissenting Deputies[13] in London thwarted successive schemes to secure an American episcopate, the fears aroused created a smouldering fire of discontent and provided repeated occasion for preachers to utilize their sermons for purposes of political instruction. The campaign for bishops had been launched by the first S.P.G. missionaries and had been pushed with intermittent vigor in succeeding decades, but in the 1760s the agitation was stepped up, and a mounting militancy reached its peak in 1770. This coincided with the new economic and political policies of the government which were to result in a general conflagration. Within this context, according to the *St. James's Chronicle*, "stamping and episcopizing" were commonly regarded as "only different branches of the same plan of power"; and Ezra Stiles indicated that much of the opposition to the Stamp Act was based on a recognition that if "a Parliamentary revenue had been established independent of the [colonial] Assemblies," the door would have been opened to the appropriation of funds "for half a dozen bishops on this continent." John Adams put it more bluntly: "If Parliament could tax us, they could establish the Church of England with all its creeds, articles, tests, ceremonies, and tithes; and prohibit all churches as conventicles and schism shops."[14]

In the seventeenth century the Church of England had reaped a whirlwind of disaster when Archbishop Laud identified it so completely with the ill-considered economic and political policies of Charles I that the church became an equal victim with the crown in the Revolution that followed. In the eighteenth century the role was reversed. The colonial structure came tumbling down at least partly because the Church of England identified the crown so intimately with its own "lust for dominion" that it became an albatross about the neck of the government. The

---

[12] Bridenbaugh, *Mitre and Sceptre*, 102, 181, 262.

[13] A committee of lay representatives of "the Three Denominations" (Congregationalists, Presbyterians, and Baptists) which was formed in 1732 to direct the political agitation of English Dissenters in their struggle to secure the repeal of restrictive legislation. See B. L. Manning, *The Protestant Dissenting Deputies* (N.Y., 1952).

[14] Bridenbaugh, *Mitre and Sceptre*, 239, 259; Anson Phelps Stokes, *Church and State in the United States* (N.Y., 1950), I, 234.

precise weight to be given ecclesiastical grievances as a contributing cause of the American Revolution is impossible to determine, but John Adams, the most reflective and perceptive participant in the events that led to war, always insisted that "the apprehensions of episcopacy contributed . . . as much as any other cause to arouse the attention not only of the inquiring mind but the common people and urge them to close thinking on the constitutional authority of parliament over the colonies." Such apprehensions took on a particularly urgent tone as Americans increasingly perceived the English church and crown both as hopelessly corrupt and as an imminent threat to subvert by their influence the religious superstructure of America.[15]

Deism

Although a pervasive Puritanism as recast by Evangelicalism was the dominant religious emphasis in colonial America, a minimal faith known as Deism had become fashionable in some upper-class circles during the decades immediately preceding the American Revolution. Sophia Hume, a Quaker writer in South Carolina, had vigorously warned her countrymen of "infidelity and deism" as early as 1748.[16] Several of the most conspicuous leaders of the struggle for independence (George Washington, Thomas Jefferson, Benjamin Franklin, and Thomas Paine were notable examples) were Deists.

Deism had a double rootage. It may be traced back to seventeenth-century men of "latitude" in England who sought to overcome division among Christians by suggesting that only those affirmations on which all Christians agree are essential articles of faith. Rejecting dependence upon bibilical revelation and appealing only to unaided natural reason, Deists reduced the "essentials" of religion to a simple fivefold affirmation that God exists, that he is to be worshipped, that the practice of virtue is the true worship of God, that people must repent of wrongdoing, and that there are future rewards and punishments. To these five points American Deists added a belief in God as a governing and overruling Providence who guides and determines the destinies of nations.

If Deism was partly the product of latitudinarian sentiment, it was also related to the rationalism associated with the "Age of Reason" or the "Enlightenment." The period from the Peace of Westphalia (1648) to the French Revolution (1789) was a time of rapid scientific advance best epitomized in the work of Sir Isaac Newton. To many contemporaries Newton seemed to have solved all the chief problems of astronomy, optics, physics, and mathematics. Alexander Pope voiced this estimate when he wrote:

[15] *The Works of John Adams,* ed. C. F. Adams (Boston, 1850–1856), X, 185.
[16] Sophia Hume, *An Exhortation to the Inhabitants of South Carolina* (Philadelphia, 1748), 137.

> Nature and Nature's Law lay hid in night.
> God said 'Let Newton be!' and all was light.

As a result of his studies, Newton was thought to have discovered "a universal law of nature" that banished mystery from the world.[17] The universe was simply a vast mechanism—intelligible, harmonious, and thoroughly rational—the product of God the Great Mathematician. It was within this context that two chief publicists of Deism, John Toland in *Christianity Not Mysterious* (1696) and Matthew Tindal in *Christianity as Old as Creation* (1730), affirmed that the "essentials" of religion are those truths that can be known by human reason alone without the aid of any special revelation.

The alliance of Christians with Deists in carrying forward the Revolution was not as strange as it may seem to be, for Deists did little more than appropriate Puritan political ideas. English Puritans as early as the 1640s had made a distinction between the realm of nature and the realm of grace, between natural revelation and special revelation. By the end of the seventeenth century this distinction had become integral to the thinking of representative figures ranging from Increase Mather through Jonathan Edwards and his heirs to Jonathan Dickinson, Samuel Davies, and John Witherspoon.[18] As long as Deists made no direct attack upon "revealed" religion (see Chapter 6), Christians had no difficulty uniting with Deists for common political ends on the basis of the shared assumptions of "natural" religion.

William Penn, Algernon Sidney, and John Locke served as transmitters of Puritan political ideas to the Revolutionary generation. Locke was perhaps the most important. His influence was exerted by his *Treatises on Government* (1690) and his *Letter Concerning Toleration* (1689), both of which were written in connection with the Revolution of 1688. In the former he asserted that all peaceful governments were established by the consent of the governed in order to protect their natural rights to life, liberty, and property, and that whenever this trust is betrayed the people have the right to resist. The statement of the "antient" rights of Englishmen in the Magna Carta (1215) formed the historical point of reference for this line of thinking.

Locke's political views were largely a distillation of concepts that had long been current coin in Calvinist political theory—a fact that John Adams acknowledged[19]—and had become fundamental postulates of a

---

[17] Newton had no such idea, for he spent much of his time doing "biblical arithmetic" in an attempt to date the millennium.

[18] See Conrad Wright, *The Liberal Christians* (Boston, 1970), 17–20.

[19] *Works*, VI, 4. For an explication of this point, see W. S. Hudson, "John Locke: Heir of Puritan Political Theorists," in G. L. Hunt, *Calvinism and the Political Order* (Philadelphia, 1965). For Penn, see W. S. Hudson, "William Penn's *English Liberties*: Tract for Several Times," *William and Mary Quarterly*, (1969), 578–85.

large portion of the English people in earlier conflicts between king and Parliament. Although Thomas Jefferson wrote the Declaration of Independence, the key paragraph that justified the resort to arms could quite easily have been written by a Puritan divine. When it came to writing a constitution for the new nation, the happier view of human nature implicit in John Adams' assertion that unaided reason is "a revelation from its maker which can never be disputed or doubted" gave way to a more pessimistic estimate.[20] Even those who thought people were good enough to win heaven by their own efforts were skeptical about statesmen making the grade and insisted that the exercise of power must be checked by adequate safeguards. The stories illustrating the adage "power corrupts" that came to Americans in the form of the popular English publication *Cato's Letters* drove this point home in dramatic fashion.

The Winning of Independence

During the years prior to the Revolution "rational religion" exerted little influence in America except among "intellectuals" of the coastal ports and some plantation owners of the South. Few of those who regarded themselves as emancipated from traditional Christian doctrine had any desire to promote their views among the populace at large. Believing that orthodox religion served to inculcate principles of private and public morality among the common people, the rationalists tended to maintain at least a nominal connection with the existing churches and to contribute to their support. Thus to the extent that religious concerns played a decisive part in enlisting mass support for the colonial cause, this support of necessity was marshaled by the orthodox churches.

The Attitude of the Various Denominations

Not all the churches, of course, supported the war with Great Britain, nor did any single denomination present an unbroken front. There were both Tories and Patriots in every religious group, as well as many who were apathetic. Nevertheless the general attitude that was to characterize each of them would not have been difficult to predict.

The Church of England had a long tradition of intimate identification with the English government, and in the colonies this governmental relationship constituted its major source of strength. It is not surprising therefore that the Anglican clergy, with a few notable exceptions, were zealous Tories who condemned the conflict as an unjustified rebellion against constituted authority. The Anglican laity in the South, on the

---

[20] For an analysis of the basic Puritan-Calvinist assumptions reflected in the U.S. Constitution, see H. Richard Niebuhr, *The Kingdom of God in America*, 48–87. See also Henry F. May, *The Enlightenment in America* (N.Y., 1976), 48–65, 88–99, 155–64.

other hand, gave strong support to the struggle for independence. The pacifist groups—Quakers, Mennonites, Moravians, and Dunkers—held themselves aloof as a matter of principle. The Dutch and German Reformed and the Lutheran churches had no real stake in the perpetuation of British rule. Whereas many sought to avoid taking sides in the conflict, the majority ranged themselves on the side of the colonists. This was also true of Roman Catholics and Jews, with Charles Carroll among the former contributing notable service to the colonial cause. These latter groups, however, were relatively small. The more significant support came from the Congregational, Presbyterian, and Baptist churches.

The Congregationalists had early nurtured a tradition of independence in the colonies they had founded, and later British rule came to be associated in their minds both with Anglican proselyting activity and with pressure to give increased recognition to the status of the Church of England as the official church of the governing authority. But above all, Congregationalists had been fed a steady diet of "election sermons" that emphasized concepts of fundamental law, constitutional rights, limited government, and the duty to resist abuses of power—all of which were notions calculated to create a climate of opinion opposed to any infringement of the people's liberties.[21]

These latter concepts which were so important in generating a revolutionary temper were not, of course, the exclusive possession of the Congregationalists. Having been formulated by early Calvinist political theorists and further refined by English Puritan and Scottish Presbyterian divines, they were shared in America by Presbyterians, Baptists, and others who stood within the Reformed tradition. Indeed, as we have seen, they had been popularized in the "political Calvinism" of John Locke, and in this form they had been appropriated by many who regarded themselves as otherwise quite emancipated from key doctrines of the Reformed understanding of the Christian faith.

The Presbyterians and the Baptists embraced these ideas the more zealously because of the disabilities to which they had been subjected in several of the colonies. Even in New England where Congregationalists often made life difficult for Baptists, the Baptists responded by accusing the Congregationalists of being disloyal to their own tradition and by asserting that the Baptists were the true heirs of the founders of New England.[22] In Virginia both Presbyterians and Baptists were thrown into a

21 Election sermons belonged in the class of "occasional sermons" that were preached not only on election days but on other public occasions as well, such as ordinations, funerals, and so forth. "Regular" sermons, which usually differed in tone from occasional sermons by virtue of their emphasis on piety, made up the vast majority of the sermons audited by colonists, especially in New England. See Harry S. Stout, *The New England Soul: Preaching and Religious Culture in Colonial New England* (N.Y., 1986), 27–31, 54–56.
22 This was the whole thrust of the argument of Isaac Backus in his *History of New England, with Particular Reference to . . . the Baptists* (Boston, 1777–96).

perpetual state of disaffection by irritations arising from Anglican tactics of oppression. The attitude of the Scotch Irish among the Presbyterians was further colored by bitter memories of the ill treatment their fathers had received at the hands of the English in northern Ireland.

The Role of the Clergy

In 1781 when arch-Tory Peter Oliver reviewed the course of the Revolution in his *Origin and Progress of the American Rebellion,* he suggested that if one wished to understand the inflamed public opinion that swept the colonies into war one must look to "Mr. Otis's black regiment, the dissenting clergy."[23] They certainly were key figures, for their influence penetrated remote communities that were seldom reached by newspapers and books. And if it is true, as a British official reported of the people of rural Connecticut, that "they are all politicians and Scripture learnt," this was the result of the work of the preachers. Practical politics may have been learned at the town meeting, but the undergirding political theory was picked up from the Sunday sermon and the weekly lecture as well as from the annual election sermon. So well rehearsed were these common folk in political thought that they knew all the arguments, delighted in the subtleties of debate, and were familiar with the facts of past crises that pointed up the present moral. Ezra Stiles could refer to "half a dozen bishops on this continent and a long string of &c. &c. &c.," in perfect confidence that the reader would recognize the allusion to be to the "Et cetera Oath" which had troubled the consciences of Englishmen more than a century before. Thus a few cliché-studded sentences were often sufficient to evoke a broad context of meaning. Perhaps the general run of the populace was best informed in New England, but elsewhere less widespread literacy and less ample access to the press made people even more dependent upon the preachers for information concerning issues of the day.[24]

The role of the clergy was not restricted to fostering and perpetuating notions of fundamental and "inalienable" rights. What Peter Oliver had in mind when he spoke of the importance of "Mr. Otis's black regiment" was the indispensable aid they provided in enlisting active support by "preaching up" the Revolution in innumerable "fast day" and recruiting sermons. This they did in a curiously roundabout fashion. Although American rights were defended, there was little stress upon American righteousness and few direct and forthright attempts to enlist divine aid against the British. Their understanding of God's relationship to his people in terms of a covenant that involved more responsibilities than privileges left scant room for such unabashed presumption, and they knew that

---

[23] James Otis, a Boston lawyer, was one of the most conspicuous and effective leaders in arousing anti-British sentiment.
[24] Bridenbaugh, *Mitre and Sceptre,* 189, 259.

a simple invocation of the powers of heaven was no way to secure the
assistance of a Supreme Governor whose favor was far from capricious.[25]

The preachers and those taught by them knew that under the providential government of God the occasion for troubles and disasters must be
sought within rather than without. Thus they viewed the present affliction
visited upon the colonies as less the result of the iniquity of the British than
the consequence of the infidelity of the Americans. The remedy therefore
was to confess their sins and to mend their ways. Only then could they

[25] For an analysis of this type of approach, see Perry Miller, "From the Covenant to
Revival," in *The Shaping of American Religion*, ed. J. W. Smith and A. L. Jamison, 322–68.

Cradles of Liberty.   When Peter Oliver complained of "Mr. Otis's black
regiment," he was thinking of preachers in churches throughout the
colonies, two of which are reproduced here. The Midway church (*left*) is
known as "Georgia's Cradle of Liberty." Two members were signers of the
Declaration of Independence. The present structure was built in 1792, the
previous one having been destroyed by the British. Plans for a new meeting
house for the First Baptist church of Providence, Rhode Island (*right*), were
adopted in 1784 and carried out with dispatch. Erected "for the public
worship of God, and also for holding Commencement in," the meeting house
has, as a cherished possession in its steeple, a 1775 bell inscribed "For
freedom of conscience this town was first planted. . . . This church is the
eldest and has not recanted." (Left: *Courtesy of Midway Museum.* Right:
*Courtesy of the Rhode Island Historical Society, RHI (X3) 812. Photo by Norman
S. Watson.*)

expect that God would impart the necessary wisdom, energy, and will to push the war to a successful completion.

The successive "recommendations" of the Continential Congress that days of "public humiliation, fasting, and prayer" be observed played upon this theme as a repetitive refrain, expressing the hope that "we may with united hearts and voices unfeignedly confess and deplore our many sins, and offer up our joint supplications to the all-wise, omnipotent, and merciful Disposer of all events; humbly beseeching him to forgive our iniquities, to remove our present calamities, to avert those desolating judgments with which we are threatened" (1775); summoning the colonists to "implore the mercy and forgiveness of God, and beseech him that vice, prophaneness, and exortion and every evil may be done away and that we may be a reformed and happy people" (1777); lamenting the fact that "too few have been sufficiently awakened to a sense of their guilt, or warmed with gratitude, or taught to amend their lives and turn from their sins, so he might turn from his wrath" (1779); and asking God's gracious intervention "to make us sincerely penitent for our transgressions; to prepare us for deliverance, and to remove the evil with which he hath been pleased to visit us; to banish vice and irreligion among us, and to establish virtue and piety by his divine grace" (1780).

This call to repentance, revival, and reform was a familiar theme to all who had been nurtured in the piety of the early Puritans and their revivalist successors. And it had always elicited not a failure of nerve but a vigorous response, for a program of action in terms of obedience to the ordinances of God was always implicit in their summons to repentance. It may seem strange to a later generation that this theme of abnegation would have been coupled with another theme from their past that demanded immediate and concerted action against any magistrate who violated the fundamental rights of the people. But to the great mass of the religiously oriented in the Revolutionary generation there was no contradiction. These rights, if variously derived, were divinely ordained, and to defend them — even when their abrogation was viewed as punishment for their sins — was part of their Christian obedience. The outcome was always in the hands of God, but since he uses men as instruments to serve the purposes of his providential government, the call to repentance and humiliation was at the same time a summons to battle.

Religious Freedom

The securing of religious freedom in America is sometimes viewed as a sequel to the winning of independence, but this is a mistake. Philip Schaff was right when he asserted that the whole question of religious freedom had been settled prior to the formation of the national government by the previous history of the American colonies.[26] Of the original 13 colonies, 4—Rhode Island, New Jersey, Pennsylvania, and Delaware—had long been fully committed to a policy of religious liberty, and the Anglican establishments in 5 of the remaining colonies—in New York, Maryland, North Carolina, South Carolina, and Georgia—quickly toppled after the outbreak of hostilities when the supporting prop of English authority was withdrawn. The speedy action of New York in repealing all laws or acts that "may be construed to establish or maintain any particular denomination of Christians" was typical. Indeed, the North Carolina Assembly anticipated the repudiation of British authority when it refused in 1773 to renew the Vestry Act, an action that had the practical effect of bringing the establishment there to an end. Only in Virginia, and in Massachusetts, Connecticut, and New Hampshire, was there any delay; and even in these four areas the struggle for religious liberty was carried on during the war years as part of the revolutionary struggle itself. In Virginia as early as June 12, 1776, an effort was made to forestall the popular tide and to preserve some remnant of the establishment by adopting a "Declaration of Rights" that asserted that "all men are equally entitled to the free exercise of religion."[27]

Obviously the urgent necessity that the war imposed to find a basis of unity among people who were religiously diverse was a compelling consideration in this rapid shift of many of the former colonies to a policy of full religious freedom. But the story is much more complex than simple necessity would suggest. For one thing, the shift was facilitated by a growing spirit of harmony and good will among many of the denominations. The Great Awakening had done much to promote this irenic ecclesiastical temper, bridging religious barriers in much the same way as it had tended to dissolve colonial boundaries by the sweeping tide of new religious life and activity. At the same time the major non-Anglican religious groups also were being drawn together to resist Anglican encroachments, and both a catholic spirit and a developing national consciousness were fostered by the interdenominational and intercolonial committees of correspondence that were set up to coordinate this resistance. But an even more important factor in the movement toward full and complete religious freedom was a developing awareness among the colonists of the meaning of the American experience.

Although all non-Anglican churchmen cherished the security and safety they had found in the vast expanse of the New World, the classic interpre-

---

[26] Schaff, *Church and State in the United States* (N.Y., 1888), 23. The literature dealing with the church–state issue in America is voluminous. Much of the relevant source material has been assembled in Stokes, *Church and State in the United States.*

[27] The motion for its adoption was made by a conservative, Edmund Pendleton, who viewed the declaration as a means of relieving the pressure for the more radical action of disestablishment. Stokes *Church and State in the United States,* I, 380.

tation of their common experience which gave meaning to the American adventure was fashioned by the New Englanders.[28] As clear a statement as any of this meaning was supplied by Cotton Mather in an election sermon before the General Court of Massachusetts early in the 1690s. "What went ye into the wilderness to see?" the forefathers were asked rhetorically.

> And the answer to it is not only too excellent but also too notorious to be dissembled. Let all mankind know that we came into the wilderness because we would worship God without that Episcopacy, that Common Prayer, and those unwarranted ceremonies with which the "land of our forefathers' sepulchures" had been defiled. We came hither because we would have our posterity settled under pure and full dispensation of the gospel, defended by rulers that should be ourselves.

It is true that these early settlers were seeking freedom for themselves and not for others, but they were constantly being needled by their fellow Congregationalists in England to adopt a more liberal policy than that of reminding those who differed from them that they had equal freedom to establish settlements of their own in the American wilderness. By the early decades of the eighteenth century this more liberal policy had been forced upon them by the concessions they had been compelled to grant Anglicans, Baptists, and Quakers. Thus the tables were turned when the Anglicans launched their drive for ecclesiastical power in New England. Formerly the Congregationalists had squirmed under charges of intolerance, but now they could pin the label of bigotry upon the Anglicans and could remind them that the New England Congregationalists conceded more freedom to Anglicans than the Anglicans in England were willing to concede to Congregationalists.

Under this Anglican pressure, New Englanders increasingly turned to recasting the story of their past to bring it into accord with the necessities of the present. The Founding Fathers were pictured as apostles of liberty, and the need to maintain intact the liberties that had been bequeathed to them was constantly reiterated. Typical was the pointed application given by Thomas Prince in the dedication of his *Chronological History of New England* (1736) in which he spoke of

> the worthy Fathers of these plantations, whom yourselves and posterity cannot but have in everlasting honor, not only for their eminent selfdenial and piety wherein they set examples for future ages to admire and imitate, but also for their great concern that the same vital and pure Christianity and

---

[28] This was in spite of the fact that the economic model of development that eventually triumphed in America originated in the Chesapeake and the South. See Jack P. Greene, *Pursuits of Happiness: The Social Development of Early Modern British Colonies and the Formation of American Culture* (Chapel Hill, 1988).

LIBERTY, both *civil and ecclesiastical*, might be continued to their successors, for which they left their own and their fathers' houses in the most pleasant places then on earth with many of their dearest relatives, and came over the ocean into this then hideous wilderness.

By 1760 Ezra Stiles was declaring:

> The right of conscience and private judgment is unalienable; and it is truly the interest of all mankind to unite themselves into one body for the liberty, free exercise, and unmolested enjoyment of this right. . . . And being possessed of the precious jewel of religious liberty, a jewel of inestimable worth, let us prize it highly and esteem it too dear to be parted with on any terms lest we be again entangled with that yoke of bondage which our fathers could not, would not, and God grant that we may never, submit to bear. . . . Let the grand errand into America never be forgotten.[29]

And five years later, in an essay on canon law, John Adams rehearsed once again the history of New England and issued a peremptory summons: "Let the pulpit resound with the doctrines and sentiments of religious liberty," for there is "a direct and formal design on foot to enslave America."

So effective a propaganda device was not neglected in other colonies. In New York, William Livingston shrewdly included the Dutch forefathers with the English when he reminded the governor in 1755 that

> the greatest number of our inhabitants are descended from those who with a brave and invincible spirit repelled the Spanish tyranny in the *Netherlands,* or from those who for their ever-memorable opposition to arbitrary measures of King Charles I were constrained to seek a refuge from the relentless sword of persecution in the then inhospitable wilds of AMERICA. From such ancestors we inherit the highest relish for civil and religious LIBERTY.

The following year the Anglican William Smith of Philadelphia sent word to London that "the impartial Presbyterian historian," William Smith, Jr., of New York, had explained the prevailing discontent of the people as the product of their desire "for an equal universal toleration of Protestants" and their aversion to "any kind of an ecclesiastical establishment." Twelve years later Livingston asserted that all good and loyal Protestants affirm "the natural right of every man to choose his own religion." Everywhere the religious issue was inextricably entangled with the revolutionary struggle. From South Carolina the Anglican Commissary, Charles Martyn, reported to the Bishop of London that the principles of most of the colonists "are independent in matters of religion as well as republican in those of government" and that "it would be as unsafe for an American bishop . . . to come hither as it is at present for a distributor of stamps."

---

[29] Bridenbaugh, *Mitre and Sceptre*, 3.

The watchword that united them all was "liberty, both civil and religious." Little wonder that, with the cry of religious liberty having been constantly upon their lips, the Assemblies in those areas where Anglicanism had been established took immediate steps at the outbreak of war to give substance to one of the major slogans under which the colonists were being called upon to do battle.[30]

All the details of what was involved in a policy of religious freedom, to be sure, had not been worked out. In most of the newly independent colonies, for example, voting was restricted to Christians, Trinitarian Christians, or Protestants. In Massachusetts, Connecticut, and New Hampshire, those in control were confident that a policy of religious liberty had long since been put into practice. To be sure, their policy had differed from colonies where no faith enjoyed any privileges. As Ezra Stiles explained it, "the happy policy of establishing one sect without infringing on the essential rights of others is peculiar to the three New England provinces where Congregationalism is the establishment." Basic to this "happy" situation was the dominant Congregational polity. This polity, he contended, provided a guarantee against ecclesiastical despotism, since each congregation enjoys sole power in the regulation of its own affairs. Moreover, other religious groups are permitted to exist, and although all inhabitants are taxed for the support of religion, they are allowed to assign their taxes to a church of their choice. This latitude, Stiles concluded, made possible "the friendly cohabitation of all."[31] Obviously this was an idealized portrait. Isaac Backus thought it a fraud. In a shrewd propaganda move, he turned the tables and insisted that Baptists, with their uncompromising defense of full religious liberty, were the true heirs of the Founding Fathers of New England. Although Backus was unrelenting in his attack upon the remaining ecclesiastical privileges of the New England establishment, the crucial struggle for religious liberty was to be fought in Virginia.

Although the penalties imposed on religious dissent in Virginia were progressively eliminated during the war years as a result of Baptist and Presbyterian pressure, the Anglicans who dominated the "unreapportioned" Assembly had continued to fight a rear-guard action in defense of the establishment. Their last endeavor was the attempt in 1784, after the coercion imposed by the necessity to maintain united support for the war effort had been removed, to regain some measure of tax support for the Anglican church by levying a "general assessment," to be distributed impartially among all Christian churches. It was this "general assessment," again as a result of Baptist and Presbyterian pressure, that was defeated as inconsistent with the principles of liberty. Since the proposed benefits would be restricted to Christian churches, the point was made that the

[30] *Ibid.,* 167, 176, 249, 304.
[31] *A Discourse on the Christian Union* (Boston, 1761), 37, 43, 97–99.

state would be required to determine what constitutes Christianity and thus would be compelled to set up its own standard of orthodoxy. Furthermore, "the same authority which can establish Christianity in exclusion of all other religions may establish with the same ease any particular sect of Christians in exclusion of all other sects" and "the same authority which can force a citizen to contribute threepence only of his property for the support of any one establishment may force him to conform to any other establishment." In January 1786, the issue was settled with the adoption of the "Bill for Establishing Religious Freedom," which rejected the whole idea of any multiple establishment as well as any religious test for public office.[32]

When the delegates assembled to draft the U.S. Constitution, the controversy in Virginia had been brought to an end and for most Americans the issue of religious liberty was no longer a subject for debate. If the Constitution in its primary form failed to deal with the issue beyond providing that "no religious test shall ever be required as a qualification to any office or public trust under the United States," it was not because there was any question at this point but because the instrument of 1787 gave the federal government no powers to deal with religious matters and it was assumed that no other guarantee was needed. As soon as it became apparent that an affirmative statement was necessary to win ratification by reluctant states, the necessary affirmation was promptly made by amendment—an amendment carefully devised to establish religious freedom, defined in terms worked out in Virginia, as binding national policy. The restrictions of the federal Bill of Rights did not apply to acts of the individual states, but only Massachusetts, Connecticut, and New Hampshire, with their emasculated Congregational establishments, remained out of step with the rest of the country. Long before the courts by invoking the Fourteenth Amendment (1868) imposed federal policy upon the states, Connecticut (1818), New Hampshire (1819), and Massachusetts (1833) had fallen into line with guarantees in their own constitutions that gave all religious groups a purely voluntary status.

Partisans of differing camps have quarreled as to who should receive primary credit or blame for the government's surrendering all control over the religious life of its citizens. In many respects this is a fruitless debate. Beyond the decisive necessity imposed by the simple fact of religious diversity, claims and counterclaims can easily be made. The Virginia "Bill for Establishing Religious Freedom" was drafted by Thomas Jefferson, and Jefferson was both a "rationalist" and an ardent advocate of full and complete religious liberty. But other "rationalists" were not as clear as Jefferson was at this point. Washington favored the "general assessment" in Virginia; Franklin had favored an American episcopate and was not

---

[32] The arguments were presented in the "Memorial and Remonstrance" of 1784 drafted by James Madison. Both documents are in Gaustad, *A Documentary History of Religion*, I, 259–67.

unduly disturbed by the Congregational establishment in New England; and John Adams was vigorous in his defense of the New England pattern. The low-pressure religion of the pre-Revoluntary "rationalists," on the whole, did not lend itself to a crusading spirit, and an establishment that did not interfere with private reflection was frequently viewed as a good thing for the masses.

Few of the more orthodox religious groups, on the other hand, presented an entirely unbroken front in support of full and complete religious freedom. The Congregationalists developed an intricate defense of their own distinctive solution to the problem. At least a majority of the Presbyterian clergy in Virginia were ready to settle for a "general assessment" in contrast to the lay elders, who were adamant in rejecting it. Even some Baptist churches in New Hampshire accepted the status and legal privileges of establishment in their respective towns. What seems clear is this. The latter created the problem, popularized the orthodox Protestant conviction expressed by Jefferson that all "legislators and rulers, civil as well as ecclesiastical," are "but fallible and uninspired men" (a conviction that struck at the heart of any rationalization of enforced conformity), and committed the war effort to the slogan of "liberty, both civil and ecclesiastical."

For good or ill — whether as a result of mere necessity, the influence of "rational" religion, or principles that had been resounding from orthodox pulpits for more than a generation — the revolutionary struggle committed the new nation at its birth to a policy of complete voluntarism in religion. Freed from threats of governmental interference, the churches were also denied the possibility of governmental support.

Separation of Church and State

A curious misunderstanding was to develop concerning the First Amendment: "Congress shall make no law respecting an establishment of religion nor prohibiting the free exercise thereof." A *New York Times* editorial of April 23, 1960, began with the words: "We start with the premise, shared by every American who believes in the constitutional principles on which our country is founded, that religion has no proper place in American politics." This was a curious statement because when the First Amendment was adopted no one thought that "separation of church and state," to use the terminology of the Supreme Court, implied any separation of religion and politics. The colonial clergy, according to their differing convictions, both "preached up" and "preached down" the American Revolution. They debated, for example, the issue of God-given rights. Since then, political issues have never been absent from American pulpits. In similar fashion, political leaders cast their thought within religious categories and used religious rhetoric to express political convictions.

The separation of church and state is a separation of institutions — a separation of "church" and "state." Ecclesiastical institutions have no connection with the state. They shall not be "established"; that is, they shall receive no state support, patronage, or privilege. Nor shall religious institutions be subject to any state control. Any interference with the "free exercise of religion" is strictly forbidden. No individual shall be penalized for belief or unbelief. Churches shall be wholly voluntary, dependent upon purely persuasive powers to marshal support to maintain themselves and to make their influence felt.

This seems very clear, plain, and simple, but the terms should be plural rather than singular. Americans have neither a monolithic church nor a monolithic state. What we do have are churches and a multiplicity of governmental units that come into contact at many different points and in many different ways. The principle of separation is clear but the line of separation follows a meandering course that must be repeatedly defined, adjudicated, and applied under a variety of circumstances in specific cases. What must be kept in mind is that the principle of institutional separation and its strict application has been of great utility both to the nation and to the churches. It has contributed to public peace and tranquility by avoiding the religious antagonisms that have lacerated public life in Europe. At the same time, under conditions imposed by the American constitution, religious institutions of all traditions have flourished and exerted influence in the shaping of American society.

PART II

The New Nation

1789–1865

1774	Shaker "Mother Ann" Lee comes to America with eight followers
1784	Methodist Episcopal Church constituted in America
1784	John Carroll appointed "Superior of the Missions" for Roman Catholic Church in America
1790	Revivals among Congregationalists in New England
1790	U.S. population 3.9 million
1790	Philadelphia becomes federal capital of United States. Washington, D.C. founded and becomes capital in 1800
1791	English Parliament carries motion for abolition of slave trade
1793	U.S. law compels escaped slaves to return to owners
1794	"Whisky Rebellion" in Pennsylvania
1796	Tennessee admitted as a state
1796	New York Missionary Society founded by Presbyterians, Baptists, and Dutch Reformed
1796	James McGready settles in Kentucky
1801	Thomas Jefferson inaugurated as president
1800	Philliip William Otterbein forms United Brethren in Christ Church
1800	Peter Cartwright preaches in frontier
1800–03	Camp meetings in Kentucky and Tennessee
1801	"Plan of Union" between Presbyterians and Congregationalists goes into effect
1801	Presbyterian Barton W. Stone organizes revival at Cane Ridge, Kentucky
1802	Presbyterians appoint Standing Committee on Missions
1802	Yale President Timothy Dwight leads revival
1805	Hosea Ballou publishes universalist *Treatise on Atonement*
1807	Thomas Campbell arrives from Ireland
1808	United States prohibits importation of slaves from Africa
1808	John Carroll made archbishop of diocese of Baltimore
1808	Andover Theological Seminary founded
1810	U.S. population 7,239,881
1811	John H. Hobart consecrated Episcopal Bishop of New York. Promotes "High Church" liturgy
1812	James Madison defeats DeWitt Clinton for the presidency
1814	British force burns Washington, D.C.
1815	Americans defeat British at battle of New Orleans
1816	Interdenominational American Bible Society and the American Education Society formed
1817–25	Construction of Erie Canal between Buffalo and Albany
1818	United States and Canada agree on border (49th parallel)
1819	William Ellery Channing preaches sermon on "Unitarian Christianity" in Baltimore
1819	United States purchases Florida from Spain
1820s	Charles Grandison Finney introduces "new measures" revival techniques in New York
1820–69	Princeton Seminary conservative Presbyterianism under Charles Hodge
1820	Washington Colonization Society founds Liberia from repatriation of African slaves
1821	Presbyterian Auburn Seminary founded in western New York
1821	Presbyterians form Domestic and Foreign Missionary Society
1821	Emma Willard founds Troy Female Seminary
1825	Interdenominational American Tract Society formed
1825	American Unitarian Association formed

1828	Nathaniel Taylor publishes "Advice to the Clergy" outlining New Haven theology
1828	Jackson elected as president
1829	Presbyterian Lane Seminary founded in Cincinnati
1830	U.S. population 12.8 million
1830	Joseph Smith's translation of *The Book of Mormon* published at Palmyra, New York
1831	William Lloyd Garrison begins publishing Abolitionist periodical "The Liberator"
1832	Oberlin College founded. Charles Finney later becomes President
1832	Alexander Campbell publishes *Delusions; An Analysis of the Book of Mormon*
1833	Beginning of Whig party in America
1834	Hartford Seminary established in Connecticut
1835	Revivalist Charles G. Finney publishes "Lectures on Revivals of Religion"
1836	Ralph Waldo Emerson publishes "Nature"
1836	Presbyterian Union Theological Seminary founded in New York
1836	William Miller publishes computations predicting Second Coming, "about" 1843
1837	Mary Mason Lyon founds Mount Holyoke Female Seminary
1837	American Presbyterians split into "Old" and "New" School
1839	Reformer Frances E. Willard born
1841	Unitarian Minister George Ripley helps found Brook Farm
1841	Universalist Minister Adin Ballou founds Hopedale Community near Milford, Massachusetts
1843	John W. Nevin of Mercersburg publishes *The Anxious Bench*, an attack on "new measures" revivalism
1843	Phoebe Palmer publishes *The Way of Holiness*
1843	Perfectionist Wesleyan Methodist Church formed
1844	Orestes A. Brownson converts from Unitarianism to Roman Catholicism
1844	Methodist General Conference adopts anti-slavery rule
1844	Mormon leader Joseph Smith killed in Illinois
1844	Brook Farm becomes Fourierist phalanx
1844	Young Mens Christian Association founded in England
1845	Southern Baptist Convention formed
1845–48	War with Mexico
1847	Evangelical Lutheran Synod in Missouri founded
1847	Horace Bushnell publishes *Christian Nurture* promoting Christian education and pointing out limits of revivalism
1848	Spiritualism becomes popular following revelations of Fox sisters in Rochester
1848	John Humphrey Noyes establishes community at Oneida, New York
1850	U. S. population 23 million
1852	Roman Catholic Church becomes largest ecclesiastical body in nation
1852	First Plenary Council of American Roman Catholics held in Baltimore
1852	Harriet Beecher Stowe publishes *Uncle Tom's Cabin*
1857	New School group splits from Presbyterianism
1857–59	"Businessmen's" lay revival
1858	Isaac Hecker founds Catholic Paulist Fathers
1861	Abraham Lincoln inaugurated as President. Outbreak of Civil War
1864	"In God We Trust" first appears on U.S. coins

CHAPTER 5

The Republic and the Churches

The winning of independence presented to the American people a prospect that was at first exhilarating and then sobering. The initial exuberant optimism was voiced by Ezra Stiles in the Connecticut election sermon of 1783, entitled *The United States Elevated to Glory and Honor.*

> This will be a great, a very great nation, nearly equal to half Europe. . . . Before the millennium the English settlements in America may become more numerous millions than that greatest domain on earth, the Chinese Empire. Should this prove to be a future fact, how applicable would be . . . [our] text [Deut. 26:19] when the Lord shall have made his American Israel high above all nations which he has made—in numbers, and in praise, and in name, and in honor.
>
> I am sensible some will consider these as visionary utopian ideas; and so they would have judged had they been told . . . at the battle of Lexington that in less than eight years the independence and sovereignty of the United States should be acknowledged by four European sovereignties, one of which should be Britain herself. How wonderful the revolutions, the events, of Providence! We live in an age of wonders; we have lived an age in a few years; we have seen more wonders accomplished in eight years than are usually unfolded in a century.

Nor was Stiles dismayed that the churches were to be dependent solely upon their powers of persuasion, for he was confident that in a free market truth would prevail. "Here Deism will have its full chance; nor need libertines [any] more to complain of being overcome by any weapons but the gentle, the powerful ones of argument and truth. Revelation will be found to stand the test to the ten thousandth examination."[1]

---

[1] The sermon is reprinted in John W. Thornton, *The Pulpit of the American Revolution* (Boston, 1860). See pp. 440–441, 471.

But when the exhilaration of the moment was past, there were second thoughts. The war left the former colonies exhausted, impoverished, and disorganized. Soon the government of the Confederation was mired in confusion, and the very grounds of promise—expanse of territory, multiplying population, and diversity of interest—came to be seen as dangers that threatened the nation. Hopefulness gave way to anxiety. Several decades were to elapse before it seemed clear that the multiple experiment in independence, republicanism, federal union, and religious liberty would be crowned with success. In the interim, Americans were sustained by the conviction that had nerved them in the struggle for independence —the belief that God had a special vocation in store for America.

The Mission of America

It is somewhat misleading to speak of the religious pluralism of the United States. From the beginning there was a pluralism of religious bodies, denominations, churches. But most of these had a common understanding of the Christian faith, an understanding that under the impact of the Awakening came to be known as "evangelical" religion. In addition to the common faith of the churches, there was also a "general" religion that was not pluralistic; a "civic" religion that was the religion of most people; a "religion of the republic" with its own beliefs, myths, and symbols, its own ceremonies and rituals, its own days of remembrance and thanksgiving. The religion of the churches and the religion of the republic existed side-by-side. Since they were regarded as mutually supportive, the distinction between them often was blurred. Still, the operating assumption was that the nation had its own independent religious vocation.[2]

The Religion of the Republic

The theoretical basis for distinguishing between the vocation of the nation and the vocation of churches had been developed in the 1640s by English Puritans, who were dismayed that religious differences should result in civil war. They posited a distinction between the realm of nature and the realm of grace. The realm of nature was God's "great kingdom, the world." The realm of grace was "his special or peculiar kingdom, the kingdom of grace." In the first, God rules "every natural man" by "the light of nature to a civil outward good and end." In the second, God rules the Christian by his special revelation in Christ to an inward and

---

[2] See R. N. Bellah, "Civil Religion in America," *Daedalus*, 96 (1967), 1–19. See also Elwyn A. Smith, *The Religion of the Republic* (Philadelphia, 1971); Conrad Cherry, *God's New Israel* (Englewood Cliffs, N.J., 1971); and S. E. Mead, "The Nation with the Soul of a Church," *Church History*, 36 (1967), 262–83.

spritual end. Whereas the religion of the churches is available only to the "saints" through the gift of faith, natural religion is available to all men through "natural reason," that is, through the lessons of history, including the history of the Hebrew people, that make plain the manner of God's providential dealings with civil communities. "General religion," William Penn called it; beliefs and principles, including the Ten Commandments (the epitome of natural law) common to Christian and Jew alike. By the end of the seventeenth century, this distinction had received its most influential expression in John Locke's famous *Letter Concerning Toleration* (1689).[3]

Throughout the colonial period many Americans had viewed themselves as sharing in some decisive way the role in history that they believed God had reserved for England. The Revolution brought about a shift in thinking at this point, making it clear to the citizens of the new republic that a headstrong and heedless England had forfeited her place in God's plan for the nations. Even prior to the war some Americans were audacious enough to believe that the colonists alone were God's new Israel. After the war this became the general conviction. Through his providential control of events, God had fashioned the United States as a new instrument to effect his purposes for mankind. Thomas Jefferson, Benjamin Franklin, John Adams, and other members of the Constitutional Convention were as vigorous as any clergyman in asserting that the United States had come into being as a grand design of Providence for "the illumination of the ignorant and the emancipation of the slavish part of mankind over all the earth."[4]

The faith of the new republic was neither sectarian nor parochial. Its roots were Hebraic. Its explication was cast in Hebraic metaphors — chosen people, covenanted nation, Egyptian bondage, promised land. Its eager millennial expectation was expressed in the vivid imagery of the Hebrew prophets. Its potentially unbridled exuberance was kept in partial check by an Hebraic awareness that divine displeasure could quickly bring divine judgment upon the nation.[5] Nor was the faith of the republic parochial. Members of the Revolutionary and post-Revolutionary generation frequently referred to themselves as "citizens of the world." The blessings they had won were blessings that of right belonged to all people. And the cautionary reminder that "the eyes of the world are upon you" remained a standard item in the rhetoric of the nation.

---

[3] For this distinction, see A. S. P. Woodhouse, *Puritanism and Liberty* (London, 1938), Introduction, 38–43. For Locke, see George L. Hunt, *Calvinism and the Public Order* (Philadelphia, 1965), 115–16, 118–24.

[4] *Works of John Adams*, ed. C. F. Adams (Boston, 1850–56), I, 66.

[5] See W. S. Hudson, "Fast Days and Civil Religion," *Theology in Sixteenth and Seventeenth Century England: Papers Read at a Clark Library Seminar, February 6, 1971* (Los Angeles, 1971).

There were two versions of the mission of America. The initial version stressed the role of the United States as "a light to the nations," forwarding the emancipation of mankind by the contagion of its example and the power of its attraction. The second and later version emphasized the American role as "the liberator of the oppressed."

The firm belief in the contagious influence of American example was never more eloquently expressed than by Lyman Beecher in an address at Plymouth in 1827.

> To accomplish . . . changes in the civil and religious condition of the world, revolutions and convulsions are doubtless indispensable. . . . To the perfection of this work a great example is required of which the world may take knowledge, and which shall inspire hope and rouse and concentrate the energies of man. But where could such a nation be found? It must be created for it had no existence upon the earth. Look now at the history of our fathers and behold what God hath wrought . . . , a powerful nation in full enjoyment of civil and religious liberty, where all the energies of men . . . find scope and excitement on purpose to show the world by experiment of what man is capable. . . .
>
> When the light of such a hemisphere shall go up to the heavens it will throw its beams beyond the waves; . . . it will awaken desire and hope and effort and produce revolutions and overturnings until the world is free.
>
> From our revolutionary struggle proceeded the revolution in France and all of which followed in Naples, Portugal, Spain, and Greece. And though the bolt of every chain has been again driven, they can no more hold the heaving mass than the chains of Xerxes could hold the Hellespont vexed with storms. Floods have been poured on the rising flame, but they can no more extinguish it than they can extinguish the fires of Etna. Still it burns, and still the mountain heaves and murmurs. And soon it will explode with voices and thunderings and great earthquakes. Then will the trumpet of Jubilee sound, and earth's debased millions will leap from the dust, and shake off their chains, and cry, "Hosanna to the Son of David."[6]

In the interim preceding that glorious day, the United States would continue as an "asylum for the oppressed," drawing to herself the tired, the poor, the huddled masses yearning to be free. Likewise, by the simple power of attraction, the new nation would bring the blessings of liberty to all North America as settlers in more distant parts of the continent petitioned to be received into the Union.

The second version of the mission of America was no less idealistic. Unlike the "example to the nations" theme, the second version stressed a more active role. This was the servant image of a nation called to help liberate the captive and the oppressed. It was foreshadowed in Thomas Jefferson's purchase of Louisiana, and it found expression in Andrew

[6] For Beecher's address, see W. S. Hudson, *Nationalism and Religion in America* (N.Y., 1970), 99–105.

Jackson's determination to "extend the area of freedom," in subsequent military adventures, and in the sacrificial foreign mission activity of the churches. The latter enterprise, among other objectives, sought to banish ignorance, superstition, poverty, and disease in far corners of the earth as a prelude to Beecher's day of Jubilee when the oppressed everywhere would shake off their chains and the whole world would be free.

Unfortunately a servant image is easily transmuted into a master image, with the master image being justified (through benefits conferred) as no more than an extension of the servant role. Still a tension remained between those who wished simply to liberate and those often equally idealistic, who viewed themselves as tutors to mankind. Senator Albert J. Beveridge, who insisted that God had made Americans stewards of civilization and their brothers' keepers, was a conspicuous exemplar of the muscular Americanism that sought to impose American ways, institutions, and enterprise on peoples who were less than willing to receive them. This robust self-righteous vision of America's mission always encountered resistance. The resistance was not always successful, but it had sufficient rootage in tradition to maintain a degree of ambivalence in the public mind as to America's role in world affairs, whether it was to be that of an example, a servant, or a benevolent master.

The major counter to an uninhibited imperialist thrust was an acknowledgment, deeply grounded in American consciousness, that America's election was conditional. "Covenant mercies" presuppose "covenant duties" was the way John Higginson phrased it in his preface to Cotton Mather's *Magnalia*. The sense of divine vocation was paralleled by a sense of divine judgment, by an awareness that the judgment of God is harshest on those who are most favored. Again and again Americans were cautioned that desolation and destruction is the fate of a wayward people, that the United States has no unqualified promise from God that it will endure, and that God is prepared to raise up another people unto himself if those entrusted with his mission should fail him.

Church Religion

A distinction of "civil religion" from "church religion" is helpful in understanding both within the context of the American sense of mission. "Civic religion," the "religion of the republic," was *public* religion, a religion available to all through natural reason. "Church religion," although technically not a privatized religion, nevertheless was more intensely personal and focused above all on individuals and their salvation rather than the nation and its mission. The one provided a bond that united the nation and gave it a reassuring sense of a God-given vocation; the other rescued individuals from sin, reconciled them to God, and established them in the paths of virtue.

Although civic religion and church religion could be viewed as somewhat autonomous, they were not unrelated. Both fell within the scope of God's ultimate purpose for mankind, and their respective millennial visions often became intermingled. Moreover, both were generally regarded as mutually supportive. Church religion, free and unconstrained, depended upon the devotion to liberty that stood at the heart of the national faith. On the other hand, it was clear to most proponents of "reasonable" religion (including Benjamin Franklin, for example) that, for the rank and file of the populace, a more personal "experienced" religion was indispensable in a society based largely on voluntary obedience.

A Society of Voluntary Obedience

In his later years Jefferson expressed confidence that everyone would one day be able to act rationally in serving the common good on the basis of natural reason alone. But even Jefferson in the early days of the republic exhibited a pragmatic concern for church religion, being convinced of its utility in inculcating morality and virtuous behavior among the people. Others less pragmatic and more devout were equally convinced that the heart must be touched to secure the voluntary obedience required in a society designed to maximize liberty and minimize coercion. In a self-governing society that presupposed the common consent and voluntary obedience of most citizens, few could regard the future with equanimity in the absence of a prevailing sense of moral obligation. Hence the dual emphasis—an emphasis on "the religion of the republic" common to all, and an emphasis on "church religion," a more personal faith that was not of the republic but was regarded by many as indispensable to the well-being of the republic. It was for this reason that, when Lyman Beecher voiced his concern for the republic, he stressed the need for "revivals."

Colonial experience had taught leaders of the churches that "spiritual" or "evangelical" religion was most readily fostered in and through revivals. Many of the churches, however, were ill prepared to undertake aggressive action to promote a resurgence of church religion. Church life had been disrupted by the war. Pastors had marched off with the troops, congregations had been scattered, meetinghouses had been requisitioned as barracks, colleges established for training ministerial recruits had been forced to close, synods and associations had been unable to meet. When President Witherspoon of Princeton and President Stiles of Yale acknowledged that God had blessed the American people beyond all expectation in the winning of independence, they both knew that before the churches could give themselves wholeheartedly to renewing the "spiritual" life of the nation, the churches had many institutional problems of their own to put in order.

Participating in the Mission

American understanding of national mission revolved around the belief that the benefits of life in America as "the Promised Land" were sustained by virtue of the ongoing covenant. The covenant, however, was a delicate instrument, and the relationship that it structured between God and the nation was liable to deterioration in the event that Americans failed to live up to their obligations. Most Americans assumed that by vigilance and diligent effort they could fulfill the conditions of the covenant. Accordingly, they were relatively optimistic about the nation's future. Others, however, worried that the nation was straying from the intentions of the founders, and consequently took a decidedly pessimistic view of the possibilities for continued security and prosperity under the covenant.

Covenant tied together the nation's past, present, and future. Optimists envisioned a process in which the nation would become progressively more decorated with the ornaments of prosperity, democratic government, social justice and compassion, goodness and peace — all for the glory of God, who eventually would return as Christ to crown the nation's faith. Revivalism, which was in most cases closely linked with reform, was generally postmillennial in its view of history. Those associated with it understood their role in the unfolding of the mission of America essentially as combat against deviations from the pristine faith and morals of the founders, as well as pursuing the enlargement of American Christianity through preaching and missionary activities. Other nonrevivalistic forms of religion, mostly within the mainline churches, also manifested at various times this kind of reformist activity and optimism about the nation's future.

Pessimists, on the other hand, took a premillennial view. Surveying the intellectual and social changes that were taking place in the culture, they concluded that America had drifted too far from its obligations to God. They expected an imminent end to such apostasy in the form of destruction of the wicked in a great cosmic cataclysm, followed by the return of Christ to reward the "faithful remnant." Premillennialism was most often associated with new or sectarian religions, which appeared and occasionally flourished on the margins of the culture. Reflection on the mission of America, then, could lead persons to embrace widely different scenarios of national destiny, and to adopt a style of behavior that ranged from an active involvement in reform to a relatively passive awaiting of God's terrible judgment.

The Reordering of Denominational Life

Although no denomination escaped the disruption and dislocation of the war years, they survived the conflict with varying fortunes. Anglicans, Quakers, Mennonites, and Moravians suffered most. Congregationalists and Presbyterians were less affected. Baptists and the as-yet-unorganized Methodists actually prospered, multiplying in number. The Revolution was a time of troubles for the peace churches. Often their members were subjected to fines, abuse, and public opprobrium. Conflicting loyalties led to defections that reduced their membership. Moravians, Mennonites, and Dunkers withdrew into greater isolation as small enclaves within the larger society. This was less true of Quakers, who lacked the defensive rampart of another language. Quakers on occasion were to move into the world to exercise an influence far greater than their numbers warranted, but the war helped introduce the internal divisions that ushered in what Howard Brinton called their period of "conflict and decline." Never again were Quakers to be one of the major religious denominations in America.

Anglicans

The Church of England was the greatest casualty of the American Revolution, stripped almost overnight of its privileges, prestige, and support. As the church of the royal officials it was disliked and distrusted, and its unpopularity was augmented by the ardent Toryism of many of its clergy, most of whom "to the utmost of their power opposed the spirit of disaffection and rebellion." Its ranks were also depleted by the Methodist defection in the South and by the emigration to Canada of "United Empire Loyalists" in the North. In the end only a remnant survived the war, and this remnant continued to diminish.

The surviving Anglicans faced a triple coercion. First, to be indigenous to America, an explicit break with the church that acknowledged the King of England as its "supreme governor" was required. Second, since supervision by the Bishop of London's Commissaries had ended, a new governing structure had to be devised. Most urgent was the problem posed by a shortage of clergymen, most of whom had fled. At this point Anglicans were plagued by dependence upon England. Not only was it impossible to secure ordination in America, English ordination required an oath of allegiance to the British crown.

An American bishop was the basic requirement. Samuel Seabury, urged by ten Connecticut clergymen, secured episcopal consecration from the nonjuring bishops of Scotland, but this independent action was resented. The major roles in organizing an American church were played by William White and William Smith. White was rector of Christ Church in Philadelphia and chaplain to the Continental Congress. Smith's long association was with the College of Philadelphia but at the time he was in Maryland as rector at Chestertown. White was the one who rallied support, and Smith did the committee work. As a result of their efforts a General Convention met in 1785 to frame a constitution for the Protestant Episcopal Church, to revise the liturgy, and to arrange for consecration of bishops. White and Samuel Provoost of New York were sent abroad to be consecrated, reconciliation with Seabury was effected, and a fully equipped church met for the first time in the General Convention of 1789.[7]

Still the new church looked forward to no very hopeful future. Bishop Provoost relinquished his episcopal duties in 1801, convinced that the church would "die out with the old families." Others also believed that no more than a languishing life of brief duration could be expected.[8] It was not until a new generation of men — most notably Bishops Griswold, Moore, Chase, and Hobart — infused new vigor into its leadership that the Protestant Episcopal Church began to make a significant recovery.

Congregationalists, Presbyterians, and Baptists

At the time of the formation of the new nation, the "three old denominations" of English Dissent, linked to one another by common adherence to the doctrines of the Westminster Confession, were the largest American denominations. In contrast to the Anglicans, they had survived the war with increased prestige, each having been strongly identified with the colonial cause. At the beginning of the conflict Congregationalists had the largest number of churches and members, with Presbyterians ranking second. Baptists lagged considerably behind in a virtual standoff with the Anglicans. But whereas Anglican strength disintegrated during the war, Baptist strength multiplied with astonishing rapidity. So marked was Baptist growth that by 1800 Baptists, as the popular wing of the Puritan–Reformed phalanx, had become the largest American denomination.

Outwardly the Congregationalists of New England were well prepared for independence. They had the largest number of churches as well as wealth, prestige, education, and able leaders. In 1760 Ezra Stiles had calculated that a century hence Congregationalists would have a "population" of 7 million, and in 1783 he still was confident that Congregationalists and Presbyterians would far outdistance all other denominations in number of adherents. The promise was there but, in the event, his calculations proved hopelessly wrong. Despite outward signs of strength, Congregationalists were troubled by internal weaknesses, and energy was diverted to waging a rear-guard defense of the special privileges they possessed in New England.

Presbyterians were equally well equipped for independence. They too had numbers, wealth, learning, and able leaders. They also enjoyed the prestige of being strongly identified with the winning side of a war some had labeled a Presbyterian rebellion. "When the war is over," an agent of Lord Dartmouth had declared, it will become apparent that "Presbyterianism is really at the bottom of the whole conspiracy."[9] Furthermore,

---

[7] F. V. Mills, *Bishops by Ballot: An Eighteenth-Century Ecclesiastical Revolution* (London, 1978).

[8] See L. W. Bacon, *A History of American Christianity* (N.Y., 1907), 213, 232.

[9] Trinterud, *Forming of an American Tradition*, 250. "Presbyterianism," of course, was used in the broad sense, which included Congregationalists.

Presbyterians had the advantage of numerical strength on what was to be the growing edge of the country — a fact that led Theodore Roosevelt to call the Scotch-Irish Presbyterians America's first frontiersmen. Moreover, with the breach between the Old and New Side factions healed in 1758, Presbyterians were able to move quickly to fashion an effective structure to meet the needs of an expanding nation — local presbyteries being drawn into four regional synods and these in turn linked to a national General Assembly which met for the first time in 1789. Finally, as population moved westward, Presbyterians were to inherit considerable Congregational strength.

Of real significance was the fact that by the end of the colonial period most Presbyterians and Congregationalists had come to think of themselves as a single denomination. Ministers moved freely between the pulpits of the two groups, and the first three presidents of the Presbyterian college at Princeton were New England Congregationalists. In the years immediately preceding the Revolution, these intimate fraternal relationships produced a variety of joint committees, and this bond was formalized by an exchange of official delegates between their respective church judicatories. The common identification was further reinforced by the tendency of Congregationalists, especially in Connecticut and Rhode Island, to refer to themselves as Presbyterians.

Following the Revolution, Presbyterians and Congregationalists renewed and strengthened the ties that united them. The practice of exchanging delegates — with full right "to vote in all questions" — was revived. This "union" was further implemented when westward migration brought about an intermingling of Presbyterians and Congregationalists in the new settlements. Instead of dividing "the sparse population holding the same faith," as John Blair Smith put it, into "two distinct ecclesiastical organizations" and thus preventing "each from achieving those means of grace that both might sooner enjoy but for such division," it was proposed that Presbyterians and Congregationalists be encouraged to form union churches in frontier areas.[10] In 1801 this "Plan of Union" was put into effect, and seven years later it was strengthened by an "Accommodation Plan" that provided for more complete unity between the two denominations in a "uniform system of church government." For the next three decades Presbyterians and Congregationalists were to all intents and purposes a single denomination in New York, Ohio, Indiana, Illinois, Michigan, and Wisconsin.

In New England two factors forced Congregationalists to be content with the church structure they had been able to forge prior to the war. For one thing, their status as state churches in Massachusetts, Connecticut, and New Hampshire inhibited them from fashioning any official structure

---

[10] The Plan of Union is printed in Smith, Handy, and Loetscher, *American Christianity*, I, 545–47.

that would have provided a link across state lines. Moreover, a strong emphasis upon local autonomy had developed which fostered vigorous resistance to the surrender of local prerogatives. The jealous defense of local rights was most pronounced among those who were not church members but who, as inhabitants of the towns, controlled many of the outward affairs of the state-established churches.

Lack of central organization was not necessarily a liability, as Baptists and later Disciples were to demonstrate. Nor was it an insuperable obstacle to cooperative endeavors, for Congregationalists appropriated the English technique of using voluntary societies of individuals to forward their corporate concerns — a technique permitting quick response to immediate needs and flexibility in marshaling support. It also facilitated joint efforts of Congregationalists and Presbyterians without raising too many ecclesiastical complications.

The major weakness of Congregationalism was division within its own ranks. The Great Awakening created a split between revivalists and anti-revivalists. This led to schisms with large numbers of the revival faction being siphoned off into "Separate Congregational" and Baptist churches. As early as 1760 Ezra Stiles reported that there were already 22,000 Baptists in New England compared with 60,000 to 70,000 Congregational church members. During the next 50 years the gap steadily narrowed. There also had been an upper-class defection to Anglicanism, and by 1800 Methodists were making significant inroads.

Congregationalism was also torn by doctrinal dissension. The differences initially were matters of temperament and cultural outlook. The "liberal" faction, centered in and about Harvard, represented a softening of the characteristic tenets of Calvinism. Thoroughly alarmed by these "Arminian" tendencies, Jonathan Edwards and his heirs occupied themselves with fashioning a tightly argued defense of a consistent Calvinism. The ensuing warfare was intense. Revivalism as a line of demarcation was inexact. Between the two extremes was a large body of moderate traditionalists who at the outset had made common cause with the anti-revivalism of the "liberals," although later they came to acknowledge the utility of revivals. Party lines became increasingly polarized even in eastern Massachusetts. In 1808 Andover Theological Seminary was founded as a bulwark of orthodoxy, and after the explosion of 1815 (see Chapter 7), Congregational ranks were further depleted as the liberal wing found its spiritual home in Unitarianism.

The growing diversity in New England was accompanied by unrelenting attack upon the remnants of the Congregational establishments, and Congregationalists became preoccupied with defending what remained of the "Standing Order." At best this was a delaying action, for acts of disestablishment were passed in Connecticut in 1818, in New Hampshire in 1819, and in Massachusetts in 1833. It was only then that Congregationalists found "in their new insecurity and nakedness a kind of self-respect and self-reliance that made for good health."[11] A degree of doctrinal unity was restored by the conversion of the moderate conservatives to a revivalist point of view and by the defection of the Unitarians. By this time, however, the opportunity that had been theirs had been lost. Although New England exported vast segments of its population to the West, much Congregational blood in the newer regions was flowing through Presbyterian veins as a result of the agreement between the two denominations which did not fall apart until after 1837.

By 1800 Baptists had become the largest of the "three old denominations" of English Dissent, with twice as many adherents as any other religious group. In spite of striking gains they were to make in the West, Baptists were far from a frontier phenomenon. The greatest gains were made in the East. Throughout the nineteenth century most centers of Baptist strength were along the seaboard—in Maine, New Hampshire, Massachusetts, New York, Pennsylvania, the Carolinas, and Georgia.

Noah Worcester, a Congregational minister, was puzzled by the surge of Baptist growth, and in 1794 he sought to account for it in his *Impartial Inquiries Concerning the Progress of the Baptist Denomination*. As reasons for their success, he mentioned the "coldness" of ministers and members of other denominations, the sympathy and respect gained from persecution, the advantage they had been able to take of revivals, the confident use they made of "irrelevant" Scripture, and finally "the want of qualifications in some Baptist teachers." Baptists did profit from revivals, for a stress upon the necessity for a "conversion" experience gave added weight to the doctrine of believers' baptism, and the appeal to Scripture was persuasive to those who had been taught to accept Scripture as their final authority. But Worcester's explanation of the influence exerted by "some Baptist teachers" who lacked "qualifications" (i.e., education) probably missed the point. "Many people," he said, "are so ignorant as to be [more] charmed with sound than sense."

> To them the want of knowledge in a teacher . . . may easily be made up and overbalanced by great zeal, and affecting tone of voice, and a perpetual motion of the tongue. If a speaker can keep his tongue running . . . and can quote memoriter a large number of texts from . . . the Bible, it matters not to many of his hearers whether he speaks sense or nonsense.

Except in the back country of the South, not many of the Baptist preachers were unusually emotional in their preaching, nor did they prize an unlearned ministry. As Baptists multiplied in the closing decades of the eighteenth century, they were busy with projects for establishing academies and a college, and after the turn of the century they became increasingly active in promoting ministerial education. But, overwhelmed by the

[11] E. S. Gaustad, *Historical Atlas of Religion in America* (N.Y., 1962), 42.

rapidity of their growth, Baptists had little opportunity to enforce educational standards. Mature men who exhibited gifts of leadership were called into service, and this readiness to utilize what leadership was available was one of the secrets of their growth. As was to be true of the Methodists, the Baptists helped fill the vacuum left by the shortage of ministers among those denominations that adhered more rigidly to formal educational requirements.

Methodists and "Christians"

Prior to 1784 Methodists were not a church but only a "religious society" nominally related to the Church of England.[12] Local Methodist societies had been formed in America during the decade prior to independence, mostly in the Chesapeake Bay region and southward through Virginia to North Carolina. One would suppose that the Revolution would have had the same disastrous effect upon Methodists as it had upon other Anglicans,

[12] John Wesley's tracts, *A Plain Account of the People Called Methodists* and *The Character of a Methodist,* are reprinted in Harry Emerson Fosdick, ed., *Great Voices of the Reformation* (N.Y., 1952), 499–513.

Barrett's Chapel.   One mile north of Frederica, Delaware, this chapel is known as the "Cradle of Methodism." Here Francis Asbury and Thomas Coke met in 1784 and laid plans to organize the Methodist Episcopal Church in America.   *(Reprinted by permission of the publisher, from Elmer T. Clark,* An Album of Methodist History, *copyright Abingdon-Cokesbury Press, Nashville, 1952, p. 179.)*

for John Wesley was equally vocal in his opposition to American independence. Furthermore, all but one of the lay preachers Wesley had sent out to the colonies returned to England after the outbreak of hostilities. Francis Asbury was the significant exception. When Barrett's chapel was being built in Delaware during the war years, an observer voiced the common estimate of Methodist prospects: "It's no use putting up so large a dwelling for Methodists, for after the war a corncrib will hold them all."[13] This may have been the popular opinion, but it was wrong. The eager and contagious enthusiasm of the Methodist societies thrust forward native lay preachers to replace the departed English itinerants, and Asbury spent much of his time in the saddle supervising them. As a result, membership of the societies roughly doubled during the Revolution. Perhaps Methodists benefited from the suspicion with which they were viewed by the Tory Anglican clergy, but their great growth was basically little more than additional documentation of the truism that for the next three quarters of a century the future in America—numerically speaking—belonged to those groups that could provide an ample supply of ministerial leadership, even if much of that leadership was restricted to lay preachers. The rapid growth of Methodism also owed much to Asbury's particular attention to the poor. "We must suffer with the poor," he said, "if we labor for the poor." Though he was personally authoritarian in his overseeing the development of early American Methodism, Asbury rejected any notion of the office of minister as a representation of gentlemanly refinement and elevated class or social status. Rather, lay preachers under Asbury's direction engaged the lower classes on their own terms, preaching in the vernacular, accepting popular idioms into worship, and offering persons not only a sense of belonging and involvement in the movement, but the opportunity to join its leadership. Asbury's mission accordingly was in step with the mood of emergent democracy, and Methodism, like other populist movements that were to appear in the first part of the nineteenth century, made large numbers of converts utilizing what Nathan Hatch has called "the democratic art of persuasion."[14]

American Methodists seized upon the winning of independence as an opportunity to form themselves into a separate church. With so many of the Anglican clergy gone, John Wesley was prevailed upon in 1784 to ordain ministers for his American brethren so that they would not be denied the consolation of the sacraments. Although he was violating the laws of the Church of England, Wesley was convinced that ordination by presbyters was valid when dictated by necessity, and he found justification for it in the practice of the ancient church at Alexandria where presbyters had even ordained bishops. Thomas Vasey and Richard Whatcoat were

---

[13] J. M. Buckley, *A History of Methodists in the United States* (N.Y., 1986), 186.
[14] Nathan O. Hatch, *The Democratization of American Christianity* New Haven, 1989), 13; and Asbury quoted on page 85.

the two men ordained, and they sailed for America accompanied by the Rev. Thomas Coke, whom Wesley appointed to be "joint superintendent" with Asbury "over our brethren in North America." After their arrival, the "Christmas Conference" of 1784 was convened at Baltimore, Asbury was ordained, and the new Methodist Episcopal Church was constituted.

"The Revolutionary War now being closed and a general peace established," wrote Jesse Lee, the first official historian of Methodism, "we could go into all parts of the country without fear; and we soon began to enlarge our borders and to preach in many places where we had not been before."[15] The borders were enlarged and numbers also. In 1784 at the time of the Christmas Conference, Methodists had numbered almost 15,000. Six years later, in 1790, there were 57,631 members. By 1820 they had overtaken the Baptists and had become the largest American denomination. A major reason for the astonishingly rapid spread and growth of Methodism was the adoption of the "circuit system" Wesley had devised for his English societies. Thus the new church was equipped with a highly mobile ministry of traveling preachers who covered a vast territory instead of being tied to a single locality. The more intimate nurture of the flocks they gathered was provided by local lay preachers and class leaders. No system was more admirably designed for moving quickly into new territory, whether that territory was in older settled regions of the seaboard or over the mountains into the new communities of the frontier. In both areas Methodists met with equal success. Had they not put down deep roots in the East, they would not have been able to move so boldly into the West with the initial tide of migration.

Wesley was partly responsible for a second denomination that took shape in the early years of the new republic. It sprang from an effort to achieve unity among Christians by avoiding party names and "human" creeds and by adhering strictly to New Testament precedents in worship and government. Although his societies were nominally related to the Church of England, Wesley taught his followers to be impatient with theological points that served to divide "experienced" Christians from one another. To those seeking admission to his societies, Wesley wrote:

> Methodists do not impose in order to their admission any opinions whatever. Let them hold particular or general redemption, absolute or conditional decrees; let them be churchmen or dissenters, Presbyterians or Independents, it is no obstacle. . . . [Methodists] think and let think. One condition, and only one, is required—a real desire to save the soul. Where this is, it is enough; they desire no more; they lay stress upon nothing else; they only ask: "Is thy heart herein as my heart? If it be, give me thy hand."[16]

---

[15] *Short History of the Methodists* (Baltimore, 1810), 84.
[16] Quoted by W. W. Sweet, *The American Churches* (N.Y., 1948), 46–47.

Leaders of the Great Awakening in America had exhibited a similar spirit and urged their converts to "forget party names," laboring instead to deserve the name "Christian" as their "highest distinction." These men were thinking primarily of the unity of spirit that bound together members of different denominations, permitted them to acknowledge one another as Christians, and impelled them to work together in common tasks without seeking partisan advantage. But there were to be others who thought that this type of thinking, which affirmed the unity of all "experienced" Christians, should lead to the abandonment of all denominational divisions. Believing that a return to the practices of the early church would provide a basis upon which all Christians could unite, their program of action was expressed in Thomas Campbell's slogan: "Where the Scriptures speak, we speak; where the Scriptures are silent, we are silent."

This sentiment first appeared in 1784 among a group of Virginia Methodists led by James O'Kelly. Impressed by the revivalist emphasis upon the name "Christian" as the bond that unites, they resolved to be known by no other name. In 1801 a similar movement was initiated in New England when Abner Jones, a Vermont Baptist, became convinced that "sectarian names and human creeds should be abandoned and that true piety alone . . . should be made the test of Christian fellowship and communion." Three years later in Kentucky the happy relationship with Methodists in the great camp meeting revivals persuaded several Presbyterian ministers, including Barton W. Stone, that Christians could and should live together in love, and they resolved to be known by no other name. A fourth point of origin was in western Pennsylvania where Thomas Campbell settled after his arrival from Ireland in 1807. As a student at Glasgow he had been deeply influenced by Scottish Evangelicalism, and he was dismayed that in America he was not permitted to invite all Christians to participate in the communion service. In 1809 he organized the "Christian Association of Washington County, Pa.," and issued a *Declaration and Address* to summon Christians of every denomination to abandon unscriptural doctrines and usages and to restore the original unity and purity of New Testament Christianity. A month later he was joined by his son Alexander, who became the best-known leader of the western "Christians," or "Disciples of Christ."

There was little communication between the eastern and western "Christians." In the East the "Christians" were gradually brought together in the General Convention of the Christian Church, a body that united with Congregationalists in 1931. In the West the Campbellites and the Stoneites coalesced to form the larger "Christian" group. (The Campbellites tended to prefer the name "Disciples of Christ.") Although the Christian movement failed in its objective to unite all Christians, it did succeed in becoming one of the larger Protestant denominations.

"Christian" churches were partly the product of a Wesleyan concern to bridge divisions among denominations, but there was more explicit evidence of the spreading influence of Wesleyan theology. From a small beginning in New Hampshire, Free-Will Baptists penetrated much of the New England hinterland and upstate New York. Nor was the German-speaking population of the mid-Atlantic states immune to Wesleyan influence. Jacob Albright became a Methodist in 1790, began to preach among the Germans of the mid-Atlantic area in 1796, and, after forming his converts into what came to be called the Evangelical Association, was elected its bishop in 1807. Philip William Otterbein, a German Reformed minister in Baltimore, also appropriated Methodist theology and techniques, forming the United Brethren in Christ Church in 1800.[17]

Roman Catholics

Unlike Judaism, whose adherents were not greatly augmented numerically until after the Civil War, Roman Catholicism experienced steady growth after the Revolution. Prior to independence Roman Catholics were a small minority, many of them landed gentry, concentrated almost exclusively in Maryland and Pennsylvania. The Quebec Act of 1774 had placed the territory between the Ohio and Mississippi rivers within the province of Quebec; this aroused ill feeling among some ardent patriots who regarded it as evidence that the British government was ready to surrender this vast inland empire to Roman Catholicism, and it was used as a religious issue to whip up anti-British feeling. By the end of the war, however, apprehensions thus generated had been largely forgotten. Charles Carroll had rallied his co-religionists in Maryland to the colonial cause, and Irish Catholics in Pennsylvania had demonstrated their unwillingness to dishonor the memory of their fathers by any hesitancy to fight the English. This display of loyalty plus French military support allayed former suspicions, and the birth of the republic ushered in an era of general good feeling.

The Roman Catholic Church in the colonies had been under the jurisdiction of the Vicar Apostolic in London; but independence made this arrangement inappropriate. In 1784 John Carroll, a cousin of Charles Carroll, was appointed "superior of the missions" with full responsibility to direct the affairs of the church in the United States, and six years later he was elevated to episcopal rank. In 1808 the diocese of Baltimore was given metropolitan status with Carroll as archbishop.

In the new republic the Catholic Church experienced many growing pains. The number of adherents mounted rapidly, partly as the result of the acquisition of older settlements along the Mississippi but more largely a consequence of new immigration from Ireland and southern Germany.

---

[17] In 1946 the Evangelical Association and the United Brethren combined to form the Evangelical United Brethren Church.

Tension between older members and more recent arrivals was often acute, and this complicated the task of maintaining an orderly development of church life. The installation of refugee priests from France as pastors of Irish congregations also aroused resentment.

"Lay trustees" posed one of the more serious problems. All churches in America had been vexed by the self-assertiveness of the laity, and the Roman Catholic Church was no exception. In the immediate postwar years, Americans in general were especially conscious of their "rights" and "liberties" and were determined not to be pushed around. The effect of this pervasive spirit upon Roman Catholics was explained by Archbishop Ambrose Maréchal of Baltimore in 1818.

> The American people pursue with a most ardent love the civil liberty which they enjoy. For the principle of civil liberty is paramount with them, so that absolutely all the magistrates from the highest to the lowest are elected by popular vote. . . . Likewise all the Protestant sects . . . are governed by these same principles, and as a result they elect and dismiss their pastors at will. Catholics in turn, living in their midst, are . . . exposed to the danger of admitting the same principles of ecclesiastical government.[18]

They were not only exposed to the danger; many succumbed to it. As early as 1786 the trustees of St. Peter's Church in New York City asserted their right to choose and dismiss their pastor, and three years later the congregation of Holy Trinity Church in Philadelphia followed the example of St. Peter's in choosing their own pastor. Similar acts of disobedience occurred elsewhere. A congregation at Norfolk went so far as to assert that the bishop, according to the "civil rights and religious liberties" guaranteed by the laws of Virginia, had no authority to interfere in the affairs of any congregation or in "any of their religious matters whatever." Even where overt defiance was absent, chronic friction was frequent. It was not until the custody of property was transferred to the bishops that the situation was finally regularized.

The flood of Roman Catholic immigrants constituted the greatest problem of the church during these years. No fewer than 1 million immigrants of Roman Catholic background arrived in the United States between 1790 and 1850. Had it not been for extensive assistance from abroad in the form of both funds and personnel, the task of ministering to these new Americans would have been completely impossible. As early as 1791 the French Sulpicians founded St. Mary's Seminary in Baltimore to provide training for a native priesthood, but throughout the nineteenth century major reliance had to be placed upon men sent from Europe. The religious orders rendered notable service, especially in the field of education.

---

[18] *Documents of American Catholic History,* ed. J. T. Ellis (Milwaukee, 1955), 219. For a discerning account of the tensions, see James Hennesey, "Square Peg in a Round Hole," *Records of the American Catholic Historical Society of Philadelphia,* (1973), 167–95.

Colleges, academies, and parochial schools were established. By 1840 there were at least 200 parochial schools, staffed in part by American sisterhoods which had been growing in number since 1800. The controversy over tax support for parochial schools which was to agitate the life of the nation for more than a century was initiated in 1840 when Bishop John Hughes of New York petitioned for Roman Catholics to be given a proportionate share of New York City public education funds for their parochial schools.

By 1852, when the First Plenary Council of American bishops was held, the Roman Catholic Church had become the largest ecclesiastical body in the nation, and a number of noteworthy converts testified to its growing indigenous character. Among these converts were Elizabeth Bayley Seton, who founded the Sisters of Charity; Orestes A. Brownson, whose pilgrimage led him from Presbyterianism into the Universalist and then the Unitarian ministry before he became a Roman Catholic in 1844; and Isaac Hecker, a colleague of Brownson at Brook Farm (see Chapter 8), who became the founder of the Paulist Fathers. Compared with total membership, however, converts did not bulk large. Throughout the rest of the century Roman Catholicism continued to gain its great strength from immigration.

Estimating the Influence of the Churches

Although Roman Catholicism made notable numerical gains during the first half of the nineteenth century, Protestantism in its varied ecclesiastical forms remained overwhelmingly predominant. Religious pluralism as a significant feature of American life was a post–Civil War development that reached its culmination in the twentieth century. By then non-Protestant groups had burgeoned as a result of new patterns of immigration, and Protestantism itself had become fragmented into separate camps by geographical, racial, and theological lines of demarcation that had little to do with the earlier denominational divisions. Unlike the earlier denominationalism, the new lines of Protestant division progressively eroded the earlier Protestant consensus.

During its early years, as we have seen, the United States was a two-religion country, with neither faith being pluralistic in any fundamental sense. The one religion was of the republic, and the other was generally regarded as indispensable to the well-being of the republic. "This country," declared Samuel Worcester, "which . . . we may call *our own*, is still *not our own*. God owns it all."[19] God had his design for the nation as well as for the churches. Thus the American Revolution as well as the Great Awaken-

[19] *Our Country and Our Work* (Salem, 1843), 7.

ing could be viewed as a prelude to God's perfecting of earthly existence. And although the two faiths were not necessarily related, still they were complementary and not antithetical, each having its own role to perform.

Subsequent chapters will detail the response of the churches to the larger problems bequeathed to them and the nation by independence. The goal of the churches was a godly nation. Although there is room for debate as to the adequacy of their understanding of what this implied and the propriety of the means they employed in forwarding the goal, one should not be misled in estimating the influence of the churches by interpreting early nineteenth-century church-membership statistics as if they are comparable to twentieth-century statistics. Church statistics are always uncertain and ambiguous, but it is probable that the estimated increase in church membership from 1 out of every 15 persons in the total population in 1800 to 1 out of every 8 in 1835 is reasonably accurate. The doubling of membership is significant at a time when requirements for membership had not been notably relaxed. The point at which misunderstanding occurs is when early nineteenth-century church membership is compared with post–Civil War and twentieth-century church membership, for they are not comparable. The American people were not as "unchurched" in 1800 as the statistics imply, nor was there as much expansion of the church-related portion of the population after 1835 as swelling membership statistics seem to indicate. In fact it remained relatively stable throughout the remainder of the century. The confusion was introduced by a progressive relaxation of membership requirements. The number of people attending Sunday morning worship in the 1830s was usually three times the membership of a church. Furthermore, churches customarily computed their "constituency" (those nominally related but not members) as approximately twice the number of attendants.[20] In terms of twentieth-century definitions of church membership (when what was once "constituency" had become "membership"), the increase in

---

[20] Seymour Lipset noted the unanimity with which foreign observers commented on the "exceptional religiosity" of American society from 1830 to World War I and observed that there had been no drastic change in religious adherence during this extended period. *The First New Nation* (N.Y., 1963), 141–50. Allen Wiley, a pioneer presiding elder, provides specific evidence of the early definition of membership when he reported the membership of the Crawfordsville (Indiana) Methodist District for the 1837–38 conference year as roughly 3,000 whereas those present at services numbered 12,000. Wiley, "Methodism in Southeastern Indiana," *Indiana Magazine of History* (1927). An English Congregationalist visiting Lexington, Kentucky, in 1835, reported that two Presbyterian churches had 300 members and 1,200 at services; two Baptist churches had 200 members and about 1,000 attendants; two Methodist societies had 400 members and 1,100 attendants. Andrew Reed and James Matheson, *A Narrative of the Visit to the American Churches* (N.Y., 1835), I, 132. See also E. S. Gaustad, *Historical Atlas of Religion in America*, 158; and Robert Baird, *Religion in America* (N.Y., 1856), 378.

church members from 1800 to 1835 would have been from approximately 40 percent to about 75 percent of the population. The estimate of church "constituency" may have been overoptimistic, but the translation of the statistics into twentieth-century terms is sufficiently arresting to confirm reports of contemporaries that by 1835 the churches had won a conspicuous place in the life of the new nation.

But this is to anticipate the story. The initial outlook for the churches was far from auspicious. Most had little reason to expect that by the 1830s Alexis de Tocqueville would report that "there is no country in the world in which the Christian religion retains a greater influence over the souls of men than in America."[21]

[21] *Democracy in America*, ed. Phillips Bradley (N.Y., 1945), I, 303.

CHAPTER 6

Protestant Expansion and Consolidation

It took most Protestant churches until about 1800 to regroup and reorder their forces. The initial gloom, shared by Congregationalists and Episcopalians, was voiced by the Presbyterian General Assembly in 1798 when it bewailed the "general dereliction of religious principle and practice among our fellow citizens." Hidden behind the lamentation of prevailing impiety was a demoralizing recognition that these denominations were rapidly being outpaced in number of adherents by Baptists and Methodists. Still, there was sufficient conventional irreligion to disturb those who believed that the health of society depended upon moral principles and virtuous habits inculcated by true religion. More alarming was the aggressive Deism of Thomas Paine, Ethan Allen, and Elihu Palmer, for they launched a frontal attack upon the whole concept of revealed religion.[1]

Deist sentiment was not new in America, but hitherto it had been confined to an aristocratic elite who frowned upon widespread dissemination of their views because they believed that the "superstitions" of revealed religion did little harm and actually had the beneficial effect of promoting morality among the common people, thereby helping preserve good order in society. In the first flush of enthusiasm evoked by the French Revolution, however, Deism was transformed into a popular movement. Pamphleteers began to attack the churches as enemies of progress. Although Robert Baird later spoke of the French Revolution as that "volcano" that for a time "threatened to sweep the United States into its fiery stream," the danger was more apparent than real.[2] It is true that "deistical societies" were formed and college students took delight in shocking their elders by calling each other Voltaire and Rousseau, but in

---

[1] See C. A. Koch, *Republican Religion* (N.Y., 1933).
[2] *Religion in America* (N.Y., 1844), 102.

retrospect it is clear that this "radicalism" had no deep rootage. Unlike in Europe, there was no deep-seated anticlerical sentiment to nourish such activity. At the time, however, the danger posed by French "infidelity" seemed real and threatening. The depraved "state of nature" that engulfed France following 1793 dismayed Americans generally and was utilized to discredit the Deist movement. It also provided churchmen with an effective hortatory device to rouse the churches and summon them to action.

By 1800 the churches had become aware of another problem that was of continuing concern — the problem presented by the flow of population into the fertile valleys beyond the mountains. Even prior to Independence, small pockets of settlement were to be found south of the Ohio River. After 1790 this westward migration became a stampede. Population spread quickly to the Mississippi River. Kentucky was admitted as a state in 1792, Tennessee in 1796, Ohio in 1803, Louisiana in 1812, Indiana in 1816, Alabama in 1817, Illinois in 1818, Mississippi in 1819. By 1821 the Mississippi River was sufficiently breached for Missouri to become a state. Then, without waiting for the intervening territory to be occupied, the rush to the Pacific began.

As early as 1760 Ezra Stiles had called attention to the importance of the West, and a sense of alarm was created when it became apparent that soon the balance of political power would be in the hands of those who were migrating in such numbers to the newer settlements. The great fear was that the people of the West, being far removed from the civilizing and Christianizing influence of the settled communities of the East, would revert to "barbarism" and subvert the moral order of society. Throughout the first half of the nineteenth century, an insistence upon the urgent necessity to find means of countering the lapse of the West into barbarism was a repetitive refrain on the lips of earnest churchmen.[3] John England, Roman Catholic bishop of Charleston, South Carolina, recognized the crucial importance of what was to become the heartland of the nation when he declared, "Give us the West, and we shall take care of the East."[4]

Establishing churches and providing a ministry in the newer settlements was to be a task of overwhelming magnitude, but it would be a mistake to draw too sharp a distinction between the East and the West, between conditions of life in the older settlements and on the frontier. The frontier rapidly receded and the new settlements quickly assumed the characteristics of the areas from which the settlers had come. Life in the Kentucky and Tennessee hills did not differ greatly from life in the back country regions of Virginia and the Carolinas. Plantations of the southern seaboard were duplicated in Alabama and Mississippi. Replicas of the mansions of Charleston dotted the banks of the Ohio. Farther north, along the

---

[3] The most eloquent statement of the threat was Horace Bushnell's *Barbarism, the First Danger,* (N.Y., 1847). See also Lyman Beecher's *A Plea for the West* (Cincinnati, 1835).
[4] Schaff, *America,* 187.

trail of westward-migrating Yankees through western New York, Ohio, Michigan, Illinois, and Iowa, farmhouses and villages were almost indistinguishable from those of New England.

Nor did the manner of life differ greatly after the first years. It was a rural society both East and West, and in both there was relative isolation for those who desired it. A European traveler in the East was apt to be as impressed with stretches of woodland as with expanses of open fields. In 1790 there were only six communities with as many as 8,000 inhabitants —New York, Philadelphia, Boston, Charleston, Baltimore, and Salem— and these as seaports were far from typical. And the West almost immediately began to produce port cities of its own. By 1820 Cincinnati and New Orleans were cities of consequence. By 1830 Pittsburgh, Rochester, Buffalo, Louisville, and St. Louis were thriving centers with a population that ranked them among the top cities of the country. A decade later Cleveland, Detroit, Chicago, and Milwaukee had become boomtowns of importance.

There were differences, to be sure. The population in the West was younger and more uninhibited. Migration was a selective process. As a rule only the more adventurous and sturdy spirited were willing to undertake the long trek to unsettled areas. But basically the population mirrored its own background. Where there were many who tended to be crude, turbulent, and illiterate, as was true along the tributaries of the lower Ohio, they did not differ greatly in these respects from the inhabitants of the regions whence they had come. In religion, the strands linking the West to the East were equally evident. Methodists tended to be exuberant wherever they were. Kentucky revivalists were mostly products of Virginia and North Carolina. The revivalists who preceded and followed Charles G. Finney in western New York made repeated tours of New England. Lyman Beecher on one occasion, it is true, said that if Finney ever came to New England, he would meet him at the border and fight him all the way to Boston. But later it was Beecher himself who invited Finney to come to Boston. Edwin S. Gaustad has called attention to the fact that during the first half of the nineteenth century the churches were engaged not only in a "conquest of the West" but also in a "reconquest of the East," and both of these conquests were closely interrelated and can be understood only as part of a single surge of new religious life and activity.[5]

The Second Awakening

As was to be expected in the light of past experience, an initial reaction of Protestant churches to the need for action was a renewed emphasis upon the tried and proved expedient of revivalistic preaching. This preaching,

[5] *Historical Atlas of Religion in America,* 37, 42.

in turn, helped provoke the great wave of revivals, known as "the Second Great Awakening," which swept back and forth across the country for almost two generations.

The onset of the Second Awakening is difficult to chart,[6] for it appeared in many localities almost simultaneously. The earlier colonial Awakening had continued to some degree among both Baptists and Methodists. And during the 1790s scattered revivals had appeared among Congregationalists in more remote sections of New England. In Virginia the most significant event was a revival among students at Hampden–Sydney and Washington colleges in 1787, which sent 30 to 40 men into the Presbyterian ministry. Joined by James McGready, a graduate of the "log college" at Washington, Pennsylvania, these young men fanned out into the Carolinas, Kentucky, and Tennessee and were responsible for the quickening religious interest which culminated in 1800 in a widely attended revival in Logan County, Kentucky. Excitement generated in Logan County spread rapidly throughout Kentucky and Tennessee; back into the Carolinas, Virginia, and western Pennsylvania; then northward into new settlements beyond the Ohio River. In central and western New York there were revivals of sufficient scope in 1800 for local annalists to refer to that year as the year of "the great revival." And in 1802 there was a revival at Yale where, as the result of a notable series of chapel sermons by Timothy Dwight, a third of the students professed conversion. President Dwight stumbled into the revival inadvertently. Distressed by "freethinking" views among the students, he boldly launched an attack to demonstrate that the only alternative to godliness was first anarchy and then despotism. The intensity of the response was surprising. It convinced Dwight that revivals could be exploited as an effective antidote to "infidelity," and this he proceeded to do.

The revival at Yale was significant for several reasons. Dwight commanded wide respect among conservatives, and under his leadership the heirs of the moderate antirevivalist party in New England were brought into the revivalist camp. It was also significant in terms of the students it sent out to become leaders of the revival campaign, most notably Lyman Beecher and Nathaniel W. Taylor. Beecher was to be the great organizer and promoter of the New England Awakening, and Taylor was the theologian who worked out the appeal and provided the intellectual defense.[7] Finally, through the contagion of Yale's example, the revival spread to other colleges and became an established institution on most American campuses with the number of "hopeful converts" being regularly reported. In this way additional leadership was recruited.

The new revivalism was markedly different from the revivalism of the first Awakening under Jonathan Edwards when the outpouring of God's

---

[6] See B. A. Weisberger, *They Gathered at the River* (Boston, 1958); and J. B. Boles, *The Great Revival, 1787–1805: Origins of the Evangelical Mind* (Lexington, 1972).
[7] See S. E. Mead, *Nathaniel W. Taylor* (Chicago, 1942).

spirit was regarded as a by-product of the faithful preaching of God's Word. Christians "waited" for these earlier revivals, Calvin Colton remarked, "as men are wont to wait for showers of rain, without even imagining that any duty was incumbent upon them as instruments."[8] In the Second Awakening a change began to be introduced. More and more preachers sought to provoke a revival by utilizing "means" that were calculated to cause hearers to make a decision and to make it right. Thus the revival became a technique — a technique that had been taking shape earlier, but never had it been quite so instrumental in character. Heretofore the revival had always in a sense been an end in itself. Now it became an adjunct to other ends, and a discourse could be written on "The Necessity of Revivals of Religion to the Perpetuity of Our Civil and Religious Institutions."[9]

The early revivals in the West were not dissimilar in character to those in the East, but there was a more effervescent emotionalism. The western revivalists were dealing with a moving, floating, migrating population, and they were operating in areas where opportunities for Christian nurture were few and often nonexistent. Consequently they had to push for much quicker decisions than their eastern contemporaries. Subject to this coercion, revivalists in the West tended to turn on all the heat they could and make a concentrated appeal to the emotions. This was especially true in Kentucky and Tennessee where much of the early population was unusually rough, turbulent, and unlettered. In the upland regions of the South, whence they had come, opportunities for schooling had been scant, and uninhibited displays of religious emotion frequent. Many of them were like Augustus Longstreet's "honest Georgian" who "preferred his whiskey straight and his politics and religion red hot."

Camp Meetings

A distinctive feature of frontier religious life was the camp meeting,[10] a technique developed by the fiery Presbyterian minister James McGready. McGready stormed into Kentucky in 1796 to become pastor of three small congregations in Logan County on the Tennessee border — a section Peter Cartwright labeled "Rogue's Harbor." Of the area, Cartwright said: "There was not a newspaper printed south of the Green River, no mill short of forty miles, and no schools worth the name. We killed our meat out of the woods, wild; and beat our meal. . . . As for coffee, I am not sure that I ever smelled it for ten years."[11] Among these backwoodsmen, McGready's impassioned preaching elicited a growing response. Many, he

---

[8] *History and Character of American Revivals of Religion* (London, 1832), 2–6.

[9] It was published as an article in *The Spirit of the Pilgrims* of 1831.

[10] C. A. Johnson, *The Frontier Camp Meeting* (Dallas, 1955); and D. D. Bruce, *And They All Sang Hallelujah: Plain-folk Camp-meeting Religion* (Knoxville, 1974).

[11] Cartwright was a Methodist circuit rider, and his *Autobiography* is a vivid and fascinating account of frontier life.

reported, were struck with "an awful sense of their lost estate." But it was not until 1800 that their pent-up emotions burst loose.

A four-day sacramental meeting was held at Red River in June. Two Presbyterian ministers, William Hodges and John Rankin, were there to assist McGready, and the two McGee brothers—William, a Presbyterian minister, and John, a Methodist minister—were also present. During the first three days McGready, Hodges, and Rankin spoke, and several times the audience was reduced to tears. On the final day, John McGee—the Methodist brother—could restrain himself no longer. He rose and began to exhort the people "to let the Lord Omnipotent reign in their hearts." When a woman "shouted" for mercy, he moved to her side.

> Several spoke to me: "You know these people. Presbyterians are much for order. They will not bear this confusion. Go back and be quiet." I turned to go back and was near falling, [but] the power of God was strong upon me. I turned again, and losing sight of fear of man, I went through the house shouting and exhorting with all possible ecstacy and energy.

Soon the floor was "covered by the slain" and "their screams for mercy pierced the heavens." According to McGready, the most notorious "profane swearers and Sabbath-breakers" were "pricked to the heart" and many were "crying out 'what shall we do to be saved?'"[12]

News of the excitement at Red River spread rapidly, and it was duplicated at Gasper River in July where makeshift tents were erected to accommodate people coming from distances as great as 50 and 100 miles. Underbrush was cleared away so services could be held out-of-doors. Success at Gasper River led to the staging of other camp meetings, which drew larger and larger crowds. The most famous of them all was at Cane Ridge in Bourbon County the following summer, when the number attending was variously estimated from 10,000 to 25,000. Even 10,000 was a striking total at a time when Lexington, the largest settlement in the state, had only 1,795 inhabitants.

Whatever the actual numbers may have been at the camp meetings, there was abundant confusion. Preachers of every denomination attended and were encouraged to exhort the throng simultaneously from preaching stands erected at suitable distances. People would drift from one stand to another. They would gather in smaller groups to hear recent converts relate their experiences, then burst into hymns of praise. With "the traditionally slow cycle of guilt, despair, hope, and assurance" being compressed into a few days or even hours, the emotional stress was agonizingly intensified and it cut deep into normal restraint. Not only were there outbursts of weeping and shouts of joy; in the frenzied excitement of the moment individuals were suddenly swept into physical "exercises"—

---

[12] Johnson, *The Frontier Camp Meeting*, 34–35.

falling, running, jumping, jerking, barking—which were attributed to the smiting power of the Holy Spirit. Accounts of these physical manifestations were undoubtedly exaggerated by both friendly and hostile witnesses but were sufficiently numerous to arouse misgivings in the minds of many.

The camp meetings caused the faithful to rejoice. There is no way to prove that they elevated the moral tone of communities along the tributaries of the Ohio, but in 1801 George Baxter, president of Washington College in Virginia, had no doubts on this score.

> I found Kentucky . . . the most moral place I had ever been. A profane expression was hardly ever heard. A religious awe seemed to pervade the country. Upon the whole, I think the revival in Kentucky the most extraordinary that has ever visited the church of Christ; and all things considered, it was peculiarly adapted to the circumstances of that country. . . . Something of an extraordinary nature seemed necessary to arrest the attention of a giddy people who were ready to conclude that Christianity was a fable and futurity a dream. This revival has done it. It has confounded infidelity, awed vice into silence, and brought numbers beyond calculation under serious impressions.[13]

More tangible evidence of the beneficent effect of camp meetings was the swelling membership of the churches. In Kentucky alone between 1800 and 1803 Baptists gained more than 10,000 members, and Methodists had an equal number of accessions. Presbyterian growth may have been as large, but it was obscured and then reduced by a triple secession.

Many Presbyterians were disturbed by the camp meeting extravagances they had helped foster. In 1805 the General Assembly expressed stern disapproval when it announced that "God is a God of order and not of confusion, and whatever tends to destroy the comely order of his worship is not from him." The disenchantment of the General Assembly had been hastened by the tendency of Presbyterian camp meeting revivalists to accept "the doctrine of grace as held by the Methodists" and by their laxity in enforcing educational standards for ordination. Both issues led or were leading to schism. The first, centering on doctrine, was the "New Light" schism of 1803 which, under the leadership of Barton W. Stone, was quickly transmuted into the Kentucky wing of the "Christian movement." The second had its beginnings in 1805 when the Cumberland presbytery was dissolved by the Synod of Kentucky for ordaining "illiterate" exhorters. The problem of the presbytery had been to find ministers for mushrooming churches. When repeated appeals to the General Assembly proved unavailing, revivalist members of the presbytery formed what was to become the Cumberland Presbyterian Church. A third secession took place in 1805 when Shaker emissaries from New York won a

[13] Quoted from the *Methodist Magazine* (London), (1803), 93, by L. W. Bacon, *A History of American Christianity* (N.Y., 1907), 237.

considerable number of Presbyterians in Kentucky and southern Ohio, including three ministers, to the peculiar tenets of Ann Lee (see Chapter 8).

If Presbyterians had trouble handling the energies generated by camp meetings, Methodists did not. They were accustomed to noise and excitement and to "on-the-job" training for their preachers. Furthermore, the theology of camp meeting exhorters with its implicit rejection of predestination and its explicit emphasis upon salvation as potentially available to all, which proved so divisive among Presbyterians, posed no problem for Methodists. This was the gospel they had preached from the beginning. At Gasper River it was Methodist preacher John McGee who set the theological tone for camp meetings by demonstrating that the hardest sinners would respond if it was made clear by a blunt approach that in winning one's way to heaven the help of the Holy Spirit would not be denied the truly penitent.

Within a few years camp meetings had become almost a Methodist preserve. By 1811 Methodists were holding their own camp meetings — at least 400 of them scattered throughout the country. As camp meetings were domesticated by Methodists and adapted to conditions of life in other sections of the nation, much of the frenzied excitement of the first years disappeared. Grounds were policed, admittance was restricted, crowds were carefully controlled, and the meetings became much more sober, dignified, and orderly. By the 1830s, even among Methodists, camp meetings had become occasions when the faithful gathered to combine an annual outing with an opportunity to listen to inspirational addresses. Ultimately the camp grounds — at Chautauqua, New York; Ocean Grove, New Jersey; Junaluska, North Carolina; Oak Bluffs, Massachusetts; Bayview, Michigan; and elsewhere — became conference centers or summer resorts.

The camp meeting as such did not play a great part in the development of American religious life because it was the product of the scattered population and isolated life of frontier society. When this isolation was replaced by settled communities with a social life of their own, the death knell of the camp meeting as an effective evangelistic technique had been sounded. A new technique — the protracted meeting — was developed to marshal the group pressure that camp meetings had demonstrated to be so successful in inducing conversions.

New Measures

A distinctive thrust of the Second Awakening took shape in central and western New York under the aegis of Charles G. Finney.[14] Until Finney

[14] Whitney R. Cross, *The Burned-over District: The Social and Intellectual History of Enthusiastic Religion in Western New York* (Ithaca, N.Y., 1965), a case study of the westward transit of New England culture, details Finney's activities.

appeared, the northern phase of the Awakening, for the most part, had been kept firmly in the hands of settled ministers and only ordinary "means of grace" had been used. Even when the "gifts" of a traveling evangelist such as Ashahel Nettleton were utilized, the evangelist stayed with the local pastor, preached the Sunday sermons, delivered an extra lecture or two, participated in the prayer meeting, and visited the homes. Disorder and confusion were discouraged. If an audience began to show signs of undue emotion, the people were apt to be dismissed and the distraught counseled in private. Finney was too impatient to put up with such restraint. Before his conversion in 1821, Finney did not think Christians were really sincere. How could they believe that people "were on the verge of hell and yet be so indifferent in regard to this terrific fact"? If he were ever converted, he said, he would be a Christian in earnest and "pull men out of the fire."

At 29 Finney, a lawyer in Adams, New York, was by his own confession a sinful, worldly man. He attended the Presbyterian church, led the choir, and debated theological points with the pastor. But the dazzling insight that led to his conversion was the product of his own reflection. While walking to his office one morning, it dawned upon him that salvation was much simpler than he had supposed. All that was needed to receive it was "my own consent to give up my sins and accept Christ." As he remembered it, he stopped in the middle of the street and said to himself, "I will accept it today or I will die in the attempt." He recalled the Scripture: "Then shall ye go and pray unto me, and I will hearken unto you" (Jer. 29:12). To Finney this was a contract and that night his prayers were answered with a "mighty baptism" that overwhelmed him. "The Holy Spirit descended upon me in a manner that seemed to go through my body and soul. . . . I wept aloud with joy and love; and I do not know but I should say, I literally bellowed out the unutterable gushings of my heart." The next morning when a deacon of the church reminded him of a case in court that was set for ten o'clock, Finney's response was immediate and decisive: "Deacon B——, I have a retainer from the Lord Jesus Christ to plead his cause, and I cannot plead yours."[15]

Finney pursued his theological studies under George W. Gale, the Presbyterian pastor at Adams, and began to make preaching expeditions to nearby communities. In 1824 a Female Missionary Society sent him on a missionary tour of Jefferson County. He began at Evans Mills and Antwerp, where he converted "the great mass of the population." He had equal success in other communities. Six feet two inches in height, with great piercing eyes that had an uncanny hypnotic effect, he was a commanding figure in the pulpit. He had few mannerisms. He spoke the simple language of everyday life. He said that he merely talked about

---

[15] Finney's account of his conversion is printed in Smith, Handy, and Loetscher, *American Christianity*, II, 19–24.

things the preachers preached about, but he did it with a bluntness few could evade. In 1825 he moved into the Mohawk valley. The village of Western caught fire. Then Rome exploded, and Utica, Boonville, and Vernon were swept by the conflagration. By this time Finney was attracting national attention. He was wanted everywhere at once. In 1817 he went to Wilmington, Delaware, spent the winter in Philadelphia, and in 1828 made a foray into New York City.

Finney is said to have arrived in New York City with "his backwoods invasion of civilization" at about the time Andrew Jackson entered the White House. The comment is misleading, for neither Finney nor Jackson was a back country rustic. Finney was trained as a lawyer, had mastered the points of theology with sufficient thoroughness to write a highly regarded book on systematic theology, and ended his career as a professor and then president of Oberlin. His great talent was to make complicated doctrines as clear and sensible as the multiplication table. He noted that his success was greatest with business and professional classes. Rochester, scene of his greatest triumph, was typical in this respect. "The exceptional feature," Whitney Cross observed, "was the phenomenal dignity of this awakening. No agonizing souls fell in the aisles, no raptured ones shouted hallelujahs. . . . The great evangelist, in an unclerical suit of gray,' acted like a lawyer arguing . . . before a court and jury,' talking precisely, logically, with wit, verve, and informality. Lawyers, real-estate magnates, millers, manufacturers, and commercial tycoons led the parade of the regenerated."[16]

The controversial feature of Finney's revivals were his "new measures." As a lawyer, he refused to be inhibited from winning his case by being restricted to conventional means. His were the tactics of a trial lawyer. He said "you" instead of "they" when speaking of the wicked, and on occasion did not hesitate to mention a notorious sinner by name. The "convicted" were brought forward to the "anxious bench"—a front pew roughly analogous to the witness stand—where attention was centered upon them and where they dramatized the struggle for heaven in the soul of everyone. Women, to the scandal of many, were encouraged to testify and pray in public. The greatest "innovation" was Finney's adaptation of the revival to an urban environment. The entire community was mobilized by bands of workers visiting the homes. Prayer meetings were held at "unseasonable hours"—unseasonable, that is, for farmers. And the conventional routine of stated services—Sunday sermons and a weekday lecture—was displaced by special services held each night and prolonged for hours in inquiry sessions. This was the "protracted meeting"—a community-wide revival campaign of several weeks' duration—which was designed to marshal the group pressure in settled areas that the camp

[16] *The Burned-over District*, 155. For a detailed analysis, see P. E. Johnson, *A Shopkeeper's Millennium* (N.Y., 1978).

meeting had been so effective in fostering on the frontier. In a real sense, the protracted meeting was the camp meeting brought to town.

The protracted meeting also was representative of revivalism as a "results-oriented" activity. Evangelical preaching was aimed at awakening the heart of the listener as well as presenting a coherent view of the nature of the relationship of the individual to God. It also made no secret of the fact that preaching itself was the most effective means by which to bring about the intended results (e.g., a new birth and moral enlightenment). It was this view that guided Finney when he wrote of religious revival in 1834: "It is not a miracle, or dependent on a miracle, in any sense. It is a purely philosophical result of the right use of the constituted means — as much so as any other effect produced by the application of means."[17]

Although the urban phase of the Second Awakening can be seen most clearly in the person and activity of Finney, it must not be supposed that it was the work of a single man.[18] There were others who were already proceeding along the path he was to take, and Finney gathered about him many zestful young graduates of the revival-infected colleges, and he established training institutes for other young converts. In more remote areas his methods were widely copied — among Lutherans and Dutch Reformed as well as among Presbyterians, Congregationalists, Baptists, and Methodists. Even Quakers under the leadership of a visiting Englishman, Joseph John Gurney, conformed to the general pattern.[19] In 1832 Albert Barnes of Philadelphia reported that there was scarcely "a city or town or peaceful hamlet" in the country that had not been "hallowed" by a revival. A decade later Robert Baird noted that revivals had become "a constituent part of the religious system" to such an extent that "he who should oppose himself to revivals, as such, would be regarded by most of our evangelical Christians as, *ipso facto*, an enemy to spiritual religion itself."[20]

Role of Women

A striking feature of the revivals was the predominance of women among the converts. Women may or may not have been more religious than men, but for women a conversion experience could provide some release from the constraints of male domination. It could be something of a declaration

---

[17] *Lectures on Revivals of Religion* (N.Y., 1835), 12. A description of the "new measures" is also included in the book. For a broader discussion of the sort of "scientific" view of religion that Finney represented in an early form, see Theodore Dwight Bozeman, *Protestants in an Age of Science: The Baconian Ideal and Antebellum Religious Thought* (Chapel Hill, N.C., 1977).

[18] Daniel Nash, Jedediah Burchard, James Boyle, Luther Myrick, Jabez Swan, and Jacob Knapp were a few of the better-known men who actively promoted the revival.

[19] See D. E. Swift, *Joseph John Gurney* (Middletown, Conn., 1962).

[20] Quoted by S. E. Mead in *The Ministry in Historical Perspectives*, ed. H. R. Niebuhr and D. D. Williams, 226, 227.

of independence, for it was a renunciation of the past and involved a resolute determination to pursue a new independent pattern of life. "The new birth," Donald G. Mathews has said, "was just what it was represented to be, a new entry into a new kind of life," often to the consternation of those upon whom a woman had been psychologically dependent.[21]

The ritual following conversion and preceding church membership also contributed to a woman's sense of self-confidence. She was expected to stand before the congregation and publicly profess her faith by relating her conversion experience. In many circles women, like children, were expected to be seen and not heard. For a woman to become the center of attention by engaging in an act of public speaking to an attentive audience conferred upon her a claim to respect and honor. "She had stood up in meeting on her own," says Mathews, and expressed "some of her most private thoughts which were accepted by the community as significant and praiseworthy." She also had learned to cite biblical texts and the preacher's opinions to counter pronouncements of other males, thus finding room for additional maneuver.

More important than these primary aspects of evangelical religion in creating psychological and social space for women was the way in which evangelists such as Finney used females in the organizational work of the revivals. In similar fashion female auxiliaries to the voluntary societies provided opportunities for women to participate in affairs outside the home, assume responsibility, and perfect leadership skills. Initially the auxiliaries were local groups, primarily responsible for accumulating funds for charitable and missionary projects, but in the end they served as channels to participation in affairs on the national scene. Moreover, on occasion women in a more direct fashion would burst the bonds of male authority to function in a mixed society. This occurred when a woman's account of her conversion was so profoundly moving that she would be asked to repeat her testimony and thus become in effect a traveling evangelist. This phenomenon was most common among Wesleyan groups (i.e., groups with a Wesleyan theology such as Methodists and Free Will Baptists), although it had long been commonplace among Quakers. Mrs. Chloe Willey's conversion by a Baptist itinerant in New Hampshire—a story replete with faintings, visions, and extraordinary discernments of good and evil in the world—had set something of a standard for the genre when it was published in 1807. Such stories effectively established women's reputations and led to some women to become "prophetesses" with groups of their own.[22]

Finally, imbued with the sense of mission generated by evangelicalism, the enthusiasm of women readily spilled over into their own specific

[21] See *Religion in the Old South* (Chicago, 1977), 103–9.
[22] Mrs.Chloe Willey, *A Short Account of the Life of . . . Mrs. Chloe Willey* (Amherst, N.H., 1807).

Methodist Circuit-Rider.   The ubiquitous Methodist circuit-rider was never daunted by the weather.   *(Courtesy of the Library of Congress.)*

concerns, the most prominent of which were female education and woman's suffrage (see Chapter 8).

Missionary and Educational Activity

Although revivals swelled membership rolls and generated enthusiasm and energy, Protestant expansion was primarily the product of missionary activity. This was the principal means employed as the frontier marched westward to the Pacific. This was true even in the camp meeting territory bounded by the watershed of the Ohio. Here the groundwork had been laid by men sent out to gather congregations and establish churches. Even among Methodists who utilized camp meetings most widely, the meetings did no more than supplement the regular work of churches carried on from day to day by circuit riders and class leaders.

Prior to the Second Awakening, the typical form of missionary activity was for presbyteries, associations, and synods to secure the release of settled pastors for brief periods so that they could go on missionary tours of newer settlements. On these tours the pastors would seek out professing Christians, attempt to win new converts, and where possible establish churches. The major burden was carried by those bodies located nearest the frontier, since other synods and associations were less advantageously located to participate in this informal type of missionary endeavor.

By 1800 it was apparent that a more systematic approach to missionary activity was needed. With the stampede to the West that began in 1790, distances became too great and new settlements too numerous to be left to the haphazard and intermittent efforts of pastors on leave as short-term missionaries. For a task so large the full resources of the churches had to be marshaled. Recognition of this need coincided with the onset of the Second Awakening, which quickened missionary interest and concern. The consequence was that the energies released by the revivals were channeled into a new missionary thrust.

Early Missionary Societies

It has often been noted that whenever the English are confronted by an urgent need, the instinctive reaction is to form a committee or "voluntary society" of like-minded friends to do what needs to be done. In England this had been the technique of securing quick and concerted action throughout the seventeenth century, and in the eighteenth-century societies had been formed for a variety of ends, including the reformation of manners, the promotion of Christian knowledge, and the propagation of the gospel. With the rise of new evangelical zeal at the end of the century, this folk pattern of response found expression in the formation of foreign mission, Bible, and tract societies. Nor had the colonists been oblivious to the advantages of the voluntary society technique. They used it to promote Indian missions, to forestall an American episcopate, to mobilize resistance to the Stamp Act, and—through committees of public safety —to initiate the Revolutionary struggle.

With this heritage, it was inevitable that voluntary societies would be formed to enable the churches to match the increasing pace of settlement with a more systematic and widely supported missionary endeavor.[23] The beginning of the new era in mission activity is usually dated from the founding of the New York Missionary Society in 1796 by Presbyterians, Baptists, and Dutch Reformed. The primary object of this society, however, was to promote Indian missions. The Missionary Society of Connect-

[23] C. I. Foster, *An Errand of Mercy: The Evangelical United Front* (Chapel Hill, N.C., 1958).

icut, organized by Congregationalists in 1798, was the first society to undertake the establishment of churches in frontier areas. Baptists followed suit with the Massachusetts Baptist Domestic Missionary Society in 1802. Presbyterians were more ambivalent. For more than a generation they were unable to make up their minds whether to channel their efforts through voluntary societies or the General Assembly. Actually they did both. They formed the Western Missionary Society in 1800, they participated in several New York societies, and at the same time the General Assembly in 1802 appointed a Standing Committee on Missions. Episcopalians were preoccupied with internal problems. Not until 1821 was their Domestic and Foreign Missionary Society organized. Methodists were also tardy in forming their first missionary society (1819), but they had little need of this type of organization since every conference was in effect a missionary society and every itinerant a missionary. As soon as a traveling elder was recruited, a circuit would be laid out that would take him to the newest settlements no matter how remote. A Presbyterian missionary in Kentucky paid tribute to the effectiveness of the Methodist system when he reported that wherever he went a circuit rider had preceded him.

> I at length became ambitious to find a family whose cabin had not been entered by a Methodist preacher. . . . I traveled from settlement to settlement . . . , but into every hovel I entered I learned that the Methodist missionary had been there before me.[24]

Nothing daunted the circuit riders. This was made clear by the common remark, when people wished to describe the severity of a blizzard or cloudburst, that "nobody was out but crows and Methodist preachers."

The touring missionaries, whether Presbyterian, Congregational, or Baptist, functioned in much the same way as the circuit riders.[25] They preached wherever they could gain a hearing, and had an ample supply of books and pamphlets to distribute. Instead of forming "classes," they formed any small cluster of hopeful Christians into a "conference." The goal of the missionaries was to transform one of the conferences as soon as possible into a church and to win sufficient support to become settled pastors. This allowed the sending society to utilize its funds to send out additional missionaries. For his part, the former traveling missionary provided supervision to neighboring conferences, seeking to nurture them into full-fledged churches.

The transition from conference to church was not always easy to effect, for this implied assuming responsibility for paying the preacher, and money was scarce. But if money was scarce, land was not. Life was simple and one could readily become self-supporting. Ministers often supple-

[24] A. H. Redford, *History of Methodism in Kentucky* (Nashville, 1868–1876), 530.
[25] See M. W. Armstrong et al., *The Presbyterian Enterprise*, 106–8, for an extract from the journal of a Presbyterian "circuit-rider."

mented their meager stipend by tilling a few acres. Sometimes they supported themselves until a church was strong enough to maintain them. The latter practice was most common among Baptists, particularly on the southern frontier. Typical in this respect was Joab Powell of Tennessee, who experienced a call to preach as a Baptist minister. Not waiting for a missionary society to send him, he went to Missouri where he spent 20 years farming and preaching, before moving on to Oregon where he gained fame as an itinerant revivalist. As early as 1757 the Synod of Philadelphia noted that Presbyterians in the newer settlements "were highly pleased with the prevailing principle that gospel ministers should work for their living and preach for charity" with the result that many have "struggled and earned their bread in a great measure with the sweat of their brows."[26] Three quarters of a century later in Illinois, a Baptist missionary encountered the same spirit. He had preached 69 sermons and baptized 22 persons, and the people had said to him, "We love to hear you preach. Come as often as you can." But when he reminded them that "the laborer is worthy of his hire," they began to grumble about "missionary-beggars" and "money-hunters."[27]

A clash of cultures along the Ohio River aggravated the problem. Farther north, eastern-educated missionaries were readily accepted. In western New York, Aaron Kinne reported in 1793 that "the principal part of the inhabitants are directly or indirectly from New England and retain the spirit and manners of their native states," being "exemplary in their reverence for the Sabbath, zeal for religious worship, and the decent manner in which they attend." There were exceptions, as at Tioga on the Pennsylvania border where people were "intemperate," "contentious," and pleased to be "without law, without order, without Sabbaths, and without God in the world."[28] On the southern frontier, preachers had learned to address themselves to analogues of those at Tioga, and ill feeling flared when the two streams of migration met. People from south of the Ohio were accustomed to a stronger brew than missionaries were prepared to provide. Missionaries reminded Peter Cartwright, a rough-hewn Methodist circuit rider, of "pale lettuce growing under the shade of a peach tree." He told one of them that he should "quit reading his old manuscript sermons and learn to speak extemporaneously" or "the Methodists would set the whole western world on fire before he could light his match."[29] Glasgow-educated Alexander Campbell was equally contemptuous of the products of the "priest factories" who had not learned to speak the idiom of the people. Missionaries who came into the area with the northern stream of migration, on the other hand, often sent back disparaging reports of preachers schooled by the necessities of the southern

[26] *Ibid.*, 69.
[27] C. B. Goodykoontz, *Home Missions on the American Frontier*, 205.
[28] *Ibid.*, 113.
[29] W. W. Sweet, *Religion on the American Frontier*, III, 257–58.

frontier. John Mason Peck, pioneer Baptist missionary in southern Illinois and Missouri, reflected this bias when he declared that one third of the preachers in this region were "doing positive injury to religion" and another third were able to render no more than "minor service."[30] Given these conflicting views, it is understandable that antimission sentiment should have arisen. Still it was localized and, apart from enclaves among Baptists, did not long endure.

Voluntary Societies and a National Strategy

The initial decades of the nineteenth century witnessed, first, the proliferation of voluntary societies and, then, their coordination in the interest of a unified strategy for the nation as a whole.[31]

The earliest societies were local and regional missionary societies devoted to establishing churches. Other societies serviced the mission enterprise — Bible and tract societies furnished necessary literature, Sunday school societies provided religious instruction for children, and education societies established colleges and seminaries to supply trained missionary personnel and pastors. A third group of societies promoted humanitarian causes and projects for moral and social reform. Societies became so numerous and varied that Orestes Brownson complained that "matters have come to such a pass that a peaceable man can hardly venture to eat or drink, to go to bed or get up, to correct his children or kiss his wife" without the guidance and sanction of some society.[32]

The picture of confusion that one might gain from the multiplicity of societies would be misleading. There was purpose in the apparent disorder. To understand this, one must appreciate what was regarded as the peculiar genius of the voluntary society. The voluntary society, first of all, was an instrument for quick and concerted action by concerned individuals with no need to wait until some official body could be persuaded to act. A few friends could take the initiative and then, through the society they created, proceed to enlist the broadest possible support for the attainment of a single objective. Members of a society might be divided on other issues, but on this single issue they could unite. Furthermore, by limiting a society to a single objective, the possibility of its energies' being diverted and diluted by other concerns would be avoided. "Concentrated action is powerful action" was the way the manifesto of the American Bible Society put it. Finally, the voluntary societies which united "the best hearts, the most willing hands, and the most vigorous and untiring enterprise" in common tasks were regarded as the heaven-sent means by which

---

[30] Goodykoontz, *Home Missions on the American Frontier*, 33.

[31] For the unified strategy, see Foster, *Errand of Mercy*, 160. It is placed in context by R. T. Handy, *A Christian America* (N.Y., 1971); Nathan Hatch, *The Democratization of American Christianity* (New Haven, 1989).

[32] Stow Persons, *American Minds* (N.Y., 1958), 160.

the divided denominations could pool their efforts to meet particular needs.[33]

Four factors converged to give the voluntary societies their distinctive character. First, Protestants had become increasingly conscious of the ties binding them together. S. S. Schmucker of the Lutheran seminary at Gettysburg declared that whereas each evangelical "denomination must naturally prefer its own peculiarities," it is a "dangerous error" to regard "these peculiarities as equal in importance with the great fundamentals of our holy religion held in common by all." In similar vein Samuel Miller at Princeton said "it would never occur to us to place the peculiarities of our creed among the fundamentals of our common Christianity." Albert Barnes was even more explicit, asserting that "the church of Christ is not under the Episcopal form, or the Baptist, the Methodist, the Presbyterian or the Congregational form exclusively; all are, to all intents and purposes, to be recognized as parts of the one holy catholic church."[34]

Second, the revival campaigns stressed a doctrine of "disinterested benevolence" that had been elaborated by Samuel Hopkins and Nathaniel W. Taylor.[35] Sin was defined as including "selfishness," and the effect of conversion was to shift "the controlling preference of the mind" from a "preference for self-interest" to a "preference for disinterested benevolence." If one's conversion was genuine, it was insisted, this shift in the preference of the mind would express itself in action. The conversion experience, therefore, was not the end of the Christian life but only its beginning. Working was as necessary as believing, and working meant participating fully in every good cause.

Third, in clarifying their understanding of conversion as a transformed life, the revivalists sought to place Christian perfection in line with older Puritan ways of thinking. Nathaniel W. Taylor and Lyman Beecher led the way in making the adjustment, but Asa Mahan and Charles G. Finney gave widespread currency to perfectionist ideas among non-Wesleyan Protestants and elaborated them in ways that were congenial to Methodist piety.[36] The result was a blending of a rational outline of doctrine and duties with emotional religion.

Fourth, the concern of churches was not simply to evangelize individuals but also to remake society. They were heirs of the millennial tradition voiced by Mark Hopkins, president of Williams College, when he declared that the time was coming when "wars, and intemperance, and licentious-

---

[33] Smith, Handy, and Loetscher, *American Christianity,* I, 555; and Lyman Beecher writing of national needs in *The National Preacher,* 3 (1829), 154.

[34] Schmucker, Miller, and Barnes are quoted by S. E. Mead in *The Ministry in Historical Perspectives,* ed. H. Richard Niebuhr and D. D. Williams, 222–24.

[35] See selection from Hopkins illustrating his view in Smith, Handy, and Loetscher, *American Christianity,* I, 539–45. For Taylor, see *ibid.,* II, 28–36.

[36] See Timothy L. Smith, "The Doctrine of the Sanctifying Spirit," *Wesleyan Theological Journal,* 13 (1978), 93–94.

ness, and fraud, and slavery, and all oppression" shall be brought to an end "through the transforming influence of Christianity."[37] Although this was to be "the Lord's doing," Christians could help speed the coming of the perfect society by promoting revivals, establishing churches, and participating in the host of societies designed to counter the evils Hopkins had listed as well as others he had neglected to mention.

The societies had local beginnings but were pulled together into national organizations to coordinate their work throughout the country. This was particularly true after 1818 when the fight to save the establishment in Connecticut was lost, thus permitting Lyman Beecher — the real architect of the voluntary system in America — to devote full attention to transforming the societies into "a gigantic religious power," thoroughly "systematized" and "compact" in organization.[38]

There was little difficulty in combining most local reform and service societies into national organizations on an interdenominational basis. The American Bible Society and the American Education Society were the earliest, formed in 1816; the American Colonization Society was next in 1817; then the American Sunday School Union was formed in 1824, the American Tract Society in 1825, the American Temperance Society in 1826, the American Peace Society in 1828, and the American Antislavery Society in 1833. Unlike the reform societies, the Sunday school and tract societies had to take extra precautions to preserve their interdenominational character. The publishing committee of the American Tract Society, for example, was composed of an equal number of Baptists, Congregationalists, Dutch Reformed, Episcopalians, and Presbyterians who were charged with protecting their denominational "peculiarities," it being believed that there was sufficient common ground to load each tract with an ample measure of "divine truth." The missionary and education societies were of a different character. Their task was to establish churches and train ministers. This necessitated organization on a denominational basis. The Presbyterian United Domestic Missionary Society was reorganized in 1826 as the American Home Missionary Society and it became the arm of the Presbyterian–Congregational coalition. Similar national societies were formed for the other denominations.

The whole cluster of national societies has sometimes been referred to as the "benevolent empire." Their activities were closely coordinated through a series of "interlocking directorates." Most of the leadership at the national level was concentrated in a relatively small group; and the annual meetings, held in New York in May, were so scheduled that one could participate in most of them. They did not act alone, an auxiliary society assured its members in 1826. They moved together "harmoniously" and thus formed "so many parts of the grand whole" in seeking to

---

[37] Ralph Gabriel, *The Course of American Democratic Thought* (N.Y., 1940), 36.
[38] Gilberg H. Barnes, *The Anti-Slavery Impulse, 1830–1844* (N.Y., 1933), 17.

fulfill "that last command of our ascended Lord, Go and spread the influence of the gospel over every creature.'"[39]

Attention is given the reform impulse in a subsequent chapter. Here the focus is on the concern with the importance of the growing cities and with the West. Impelled by the conviction that the cities were citadels that must be captured at all costs, Lyman Beecher had gone to Boston in 1826, Albert Barnes accepted a call to Philadelphia in 1830, and Charles G. Finney was persuaded to become a pastor in New York City in 1832. The cities were strategic for two reasons. They were centers of an influence that radiated to the remotest hamlet, and they were repositories of concentrated wealth. Although Bible, tract, Sunday school, and missionary societies devoted great attention to the religious life of the cities, the leaders were equally concerned with mastering the wealth of the urban centers. "The purposes of Christianity," declared Barnes, "require that that wealth should be consecrated to the Redeemer," and consecrating it to the Redeemer meant, among other things, devoting it to the work of the benevolent societies.[40] So successful was this enlistment of wealth that by 1834 total annual receipts of the societies exceeded $9 million.

The West became of even more urgent concern than it had previously been when Andrew Jackson's election as president in 1828 dramatized the shift of political power to the West. "The strength of the nation," a report of the American Home Missionary Society in 1829 declared, "lies beyond the Alleghany. The center of dominion is fast moving in that direction. The ruler of this country is growing up in the Great Valley. Leave him without the gospel and he will be a ruffian giant."[41] With this in mind the whole voluntary society apparatus launched a great "saturation" campaign to save the Mississippi valley and thus save the nation. The goal was a Bible for every family, a Sunday school in every neighborhood, a pastor in every locality, and tracts in abundance. Each of the societies—Bible, tract, Sunday school, missionary—was assigned its allotted task, and a single agent frequently worked for several societies. The statistics tell an incredible story of Bibles shipped, tracts distributed, Sunday schools organized, and churches established. So successful was the operation that, by 1833, the societies were beginning to turn their attention to the South, where population was scattered and ignorance seemed widespread.

Contributions to Education

For those who feared that "barbarism" would overtake the nation, the provision of adequate educational opportunities was a primary concern. Both the political order of America and the ecclesiastical order of Protes-

---

[39] Foster, *Errand of Mercy*, 143, 154.

[40] Albert Barnes, *Sermons on Revivals* (N.Y., 1841), 96. See also 109–10.

[41] W. B. Posey, *The Presbyterian Church in the Old Southwest, 1778–1838* (Richmond, 1952), 111. For the valley campaign of 1829–31, see Foster, *Errand of Mercy*, 190–205, and Hudson, *American Protestantism*, 84–90.

tantism presupposed a literate laity and, with only minor dissent, an educated leadership. In the West the Ordinance of 1785 had set aside land in every township for the maintenance of publicly supported elementary schools. Even so, some time usually elapsed in newly opened territory before these schools could be brought into operation, and during this period ministers often filled the breach by serving as schoolmasters.

It was in the area of secondary and higher education, however, that the churches made their greatest contribution. Presbyterians and Congregationalists were the most active in founding academies and colleges. Baptists followed their example, as did Methodists after a delayed beginning. Other denominations made contributions in proportion to their numbers. For the greater part of the nineteenth century, most secondary and collegiate education was carried on under denominational auspices. Of the 516 colleges and universities founded before the Civil War, only a few had no religious affiliation. Academies were often the product of an individual minister's zeal for learning, whereas the dominant motive in founding colleges was to provide an educated ministry. The classical education offered served also as preparation for other professions. This permitted enlistment of community as well as denominational support. It is interesting that denominational rivalry played small part in the founding of colleges and academies. There was little competition and little territorial duplication. A location preempted by one denomination was usually respected by the others. Still, the mortality rate was high. Some infant enterprises were left stranded by changing patterns of settlement, some were victims of mismanagement, and many were inadequately staffed.

Founding of theological seminaries was another Protestant activity. Prior to 1800 specifically theological education, as distinguished from the classical education given aspiring ministers in the colleges, was commonly acquired under the direction of older clergymen. Such supervised training combined advanced study with practical experience, but there was a growing conviction that more adequate preparation could be given in a graduate professional school. New Brunswick Theological Seminary, which traces its beginnings to 1784 when instruction was initiated in New York City, antedated the general movement which is usually considered to have begun with the founding of Andover Theological Seminary in 1808. In the next few years the movement spread rapidly in most denominations.

Part of the energy generated by revivals was directed toward efforts to provide educational opportunities for females and blacks. Emma Willard's Troy Female Seminary (1821) and Mary Lyon's similar endeavor at Mt. Holyoke (1837) are the most frequently cited examples of the former concern, but many female seminaries flourished in the South and elsewhere.[42] Lincoln University in Pennsylvania, founded in 1854, and Wil-

[42] Leonard I. Sweet, "The Female Seminary Movement and Woman's Mission in Antebellum America," *Church History*, 54 (1985), 41–55.

berforce in Ohio, founded in 1856, are specific examples of the latter concern—provision of educational opportunities for those of African antecedents who had gained their freedom. Earlier, New York Central College, established in 1843 in McGrawville, New York, by abolitionist Baptists, regarded the education of blacks, who constituted a significant portion of its student body, as central to its mission. But it was Oberlin College (1832) that put the whole thrust of evangelical religion together.

Oberlin was dedicated to "universal reform," being rescued financially in 1835 by the Tappan brothers, New York City merchants who stipulated that Finney serve as professor of theology and that the student rebels expelled from Lane Theological Seminary because of antislavery activity be accepted as students. Both women and blacks were admitted to the course of instruction. Its name[43] and the words *learning and labor* on its seal indicated that, like many evangelical colleges of the time, Oberlin was founded as a manual labor school to put into practice the latest educational theory, which stressed the blending of head, hand, and heart in the instructional process. Although the central purpose of Oberlin, in keeping with its revivalist concerns, was to send out well-equipped ministers and missionaries, there was scarcely a reform proposal that did not find ready reception and nurture in the congenial "perfectionist" atmosphere of the college.

The Mood of the South

Although academies and colleges multiplied in the South as they did in other parts of the country, there was less self-generated activity by the voluntary societies. Perhaps the climate, before the advent of air conditioning, slowed the pace of life. More likely the absence of the highly organized and systematic procedures of the bustling cities of the North was responsible. It could not have been because the mood in areas of the South where evangelical religion was strong was any less exuberant and optimistic than in the North. Baptists, Methodists, and Presbyterians may have had fewer resources in the South than elsewhere, but they had done their work well.

Andrew Johnson, the future president but at the time a youthful adherent of Andrew Jackson, reflected the eager optimistic spirit of the time. He was addressing his constituents in the First Congressional District of Tennessee. He told them that democracy and Christianity

> are going along, not in divergents, not in parallels, but in converging lines —the one purifying and elevating man religiously, the other politically. . . .

---

[43] A life of the Swiss Protestant Johann Frederick Oberlin (1740–1826), which gave impetus to the manual labor movement, was published by the American Sunday School Union in 1830. A year later Lewis Tappan and others founded the Society for Promoting Manual Labor in Literary Institutions.

At what period of time they will have finished the work of progress and elevation is not now for me to determine, but when finished these two lines will have approximated each other—man being perfected both in a religious and a political point of view.

As he continued, Johnson became lyrical in his vision of the future, noting that as the lines converge, then can

proclamation be made that the millennial morning has dawned and that the time has come when the lion and the lamb shall lie down together, when the "voice of the turtle" shall be "heard in our land," when ". . . the glad tidings shall be proclaimed . . . of man's political and religious redemption, and that there is "on earth, peace, good will toward men."[44]

Overseas Missions

Thus far, attention has been centered on the new nation, but the religious enthusiasm of the Second Awakening could not be contained within national boundaries. Not only the nation but the world was to be redeemed. News of the Orient had been seeping back into New England during the early years of the Awakening. This was the era of the clipper ships and the Pacific trade, and every ship that returned to Salem or Boston brought tales of distant lands and strange people. Also, exciting reports of William Carey's pioneering missionary venture in India were being published in the religious press, and funds were being collected in Philadelphia and elsewhere for his support. In 1810 the "banding" of a number of students at Andover Theological Seminary—not far from Salem—to offer themselves for foreign-mission service led to the founding of the American Board of Commissioners for Foreign Missions.[45] Two years later, five of the students—Samuel Newell, Adoniram Judson, Luther Rice, Samuel Nott, Jr., and Gordon Hall—set sail for India. Judson became persuaded of the validity of Baptist contentions while on shipboard, and when he arrived in India he discovered that Rice had come to share his views while sailing on board another ship. When Judson went on to Burma, Rice returned to America to enlist Baptist support for Judson's mission. By 1850 the foreign mission work of all denominations called for an annual expenditure of about $650,000.

---

[44] Dixon Wector, *The Saga of American Society* (N.Y., 1937), 100. *The Papers of Andrew Johnson*, ed. L. P. Graf and R. W. Haskins (Knoxville, 1970), II, 176–77. For discussion of the home as a center of piety and as a safe context for the expression of emotion, see Jan Lewis, *The Pursuit of Happiness: Family and Values in Jefferson's Virginia* (NY, 1983), and D. G. Mathews, *Religion in the Old South* (Chicago, 1977).

[45] See W. E. Strong, *The Story of the American Board* (Boston, 1910). An overseas mission had been anticipated by David George when he sailed for Sierra Leone in 1792 after having established a black church in Nova Scotia. Jamaica, Haiti, and Liberia also became scenes of missionary activity by blacks from America.

Protestant expansion in America during the decades that followed the formation of the new nation was part of a much larger movement of Protestant resurgence whose achievements led Kenneth Scott Latourette to describe the nineteenth century as "the great century" in the history of Christianity.[46] In Britain and on the continent of Europe, as well as in America, a sweeping tide of evangelical religion brought new life to Protestant churches at a time when the Roman Catholic Church was waging a defensive struggle against the forces of nationalism and "liberalism" in Roman Catholic lands. It was not until the end of the century that the Roman Catholic Church, either in America or elsewhere, was to be able to abandon its defensive posture. In the meantime, the Protestant churches in America were not without pressing problems of their own.

[46] Latourette's primary focus was upon the achievements of the far-flung missionary enterprise. Only by a repetitive refrain of superlatives could he describe what had taken place. "Never before in a period of equal length had Christianity or any other religion penetrated for the first time as large an area as it had in the nineteenth century." "Never before had any religion been planted over so large a portion of the earth's surface." "Never before had Christianity, or any other religion, been introduced to so many different peoples and cultures." "Never before had so many hundreds of thousands contributed voluntarily of their means to assist the spread of Christianity or any other religion." "Never before . . . had Christians come so near the goal of reaching all men with their message." "Never had it exerted so wide an influence upon the human race." "Measured by geographic extent and the effect upon mankind as a whole, the nineteenth century was the greatest thus far in the history of Christianity." *A History of the Expansion of Christianity* (N.Y., 1937–45), IV, 1, 4; V, 469; VI, 442, 443, 450; VII, 450.

CHAPTER 7

Countervailing Trends and the Triumph of Methodism

The evangelical religion of the first third of the nineteenth century bred a spirit of unity that was expressed both in the revivals of the period and in the activities of the voluntary societies. The societies were explicitly designed to secure the broadest possible cooperation in common tasks. And indispensable to the success of a revival in any community was the participation of a major portion of the churches, for without this broad participation the necessary psychological climate and group pressure could not be created. "The spirit of sectarianism," therefore, was the great "hindrance" and "quencher" of revivals; and Finney constantly warned his helpers not "to dwell upon sectarian distinctions or to be sticklish about sectarian points."[1] With Christians working side-by-side in the revivals and in the societies, further impetus was given to the development of cordial relations among the major denominations.

There were discordant notes, however, in the midst of the harmony. The Great Awakening of the colonial period, with its "New Lights" and "Old Lights," and "New Sides" and "Old Sides," had demonstrated that revivals could divide as well as unify. And the Second Awakening was equally productive of controversy and division. The reactions surprisingly were quite diverse. The doctrinal harshness of revivalist preaching, on the one hand, contributed to the Unitarian and Universalist defections; its doctrinal laxity of revivalism helped produce a reaction that led to a revived confessionalism. Still others found the lax churchmanship of the evangelicals disturbing, and this led to J. W. Nevin's stress upon the

[1] Calvin Colton, *History and Character of American Revivals*, 116 17. Finney, *Lectures on Revivals of Religion*, 2nd ed. (N.Y., 1835), 369.

importance of the priestly office and the sacramental life and to John Henry Hobart's zealous defense of what he considered to be the primitive church order. All the dissenters, whatever form their protest might take, reacted strongly against what Horace Bushnell called the "artificial fireworks" and the "jump and stir" of the revivals.

Unitarians and Universalists

Although Unitarianism (i.e., antitrinitarianism) in Boston was the product of many influences, its roots went back to the "liberal" tendencies that developed during the time of the first Great Awakening, and during the succeeding years there had been a steady but barely perceptible drift toward greater emphasis upon the human role in redemption.[2] By the time Ashbel Green, a young Presbyterian minister from Philadelphia who was later to be president of Princeton University, made a tour of New England in 1791, he found many of the Boston ministers to be unsound in the faith. Among them, he reported, were Arminians, Universalists, Arians, and one professed Socinian. Ten years later Archibald Alexander, then president of Hampden–Sydney College in Virginia, found the situation in Boston even more dismaying. Heretical notions of all types abounded, and the only agreement he could discover was a rejection of the doctrine of the Trinity.[3]

The reports of Green and Alexander are somewhat misleading, for heretical doctrines were not being openly proclaimed. The only overt break occasioned by the theological ferment had occurred not among the Congregationalists but at King's Chapel, the former church of the royal governor. In 1782 the Episcopalian proprietors of the Chapel, being unable to obtain a minister, had invited James Freeman, a recent graduate of Harvard, to serve as reader. In deference to his scruples, the liturgy was revised to eliminate trinitarian references and the Athanasian and Nicene Creeds were omitted, and in 1787 the congregation proceeded to ordain him as its pastor. The Congregational clergy were much more cautious. Without the problem posed by a set liturgy, most of them were content to let "sleeping dogmas lie." Orthodox doctrines were not openly opposed and rejected; they were quietly ignored. A clearcut party alignment appeared only when Henry Ware, a known liberal, was elected to the professorship of divinity at Harvard in 1805, which led to the founding of Andover Seminary in 1808.

A definite separation did not take place until after 1815. The event that brought the uneasy truce to an end was the publication in Boston of a

[2] See Conrad Wright, *The Beginnings of Unitarianism in America* (Boston, 1955); and E. M. Wilbur, *A History of Unitarianism . . . in America* (Cambridge, Mass., 1952). Fresh perspectives are provided by Wright in *The Liberal Christians* (Boston, 1970).
[3] Wilbur, *History of Unitarianism*, 399.

chapter from the *Memoirs* of Theophilus Lindsey, which reproduced letters that had been written to the English Unitarian leader by several of the New England "liberals." One letter noted that, although most of the Boston clergy were Unitarian in sentiment, "the controversy is seldom or never introduced into the pulpit." But now names had been named and sentiments had been exposed, and there was little hope of preventing an open breach. A pamphlet war ensued with Jedidiah Morse writing a tract entitled *Are You of the Christian or the Boston Religion?* and John Lowell replying in kind with one entitled *Are You a Christian or a Calvinist?*

The classic exposition of Unitarian doctrine was William Ellery Channing's Baltimore sermon on "Unitarian Christianity" which he delivered in 1819 at the ordination of Jared Sparks.[4] The foundation was the inspired Word of God made manifest in the Scriptures; but, being "written for mankind" and "in the language of men," the meaning of Scripture must be sought "in the same manner as that of other books." The special divine office of Christ as Savior was not questioned. Though Jesus was not God, he was sent by the Father to effect the "moral and spiritual deliverance" of humankind; that is, to rescue people "from sin and its consequences, and to bring them to a state of everlasting purity and happiness." The basic issue that set them apart was their optimistic view of human nature. There is an "essential sameness" between God and man, declared Channing, and "all virtue has its foundation in the moral nature of man." The great significance of Jesus is that he leads and entices men to divine perfection. Having been made for "union" with the Creator, the "infinite perfection" of the Creator is "the only sufficient object and true resting place for the insatiable desires and unlimited capacities of the human mind." Later the Unitarian position was to be summarized in James Freeman Clarke's Affirmation of Faith: "The fatherhood of God, the brotherhood of man, the leadership of Jesus, salvation by character, and the progress of mankind onward and upward forever."

Publication of the extract from Lindsey's *Memoirs* precipitated a struggle for the possession of church property. Often the Trinitarians constituted a majority of church members, but the courts ruled in 1820 that church property was vested in the "parish," which embraced both church members and nonmembers. In many instances, with all eligible voters of the parish or town participating in the decision, even a minority Unitarian faction among church members was able to gain title to the property. Oliver Wendell Holmes' "One-Hoss Shay" was supposed to be a symbol of the sudden crumbling of "Calvinism," but it collapsed only in eastern Massachusetts; and even there only momentarily, for within a brief time orthodox Congregational churches were reestablished in almost every parish. When the American Unitarian Association was formed in 1825, it

---

[4] The sermon has been reprinted many times. A portion of it is in Smith, Handy, and Loetscher, *American Christianity*, I, 493–502.

numbered 125 churches, 100 of them in Massachusetts, most within 40 miles of Boston, a fact that led the irreverent to quip that the Unitarians believed in the fatherhood of God, the brotherhood of man, and the neighborhood of Boston.

Unitarianism, on the whole, was the faith of well-to-do, urban New Englanders who rejected the notion of human depravity. Universalism was its counterpart among less urbane, rural folk who were repelled by the idea of eternal damnation and thus led to affirm the doctrine of universal countervailing salvation. Their mood in part was reflected in the reaction of a 17-year-old New Hampshire girl to uninhibited revivalist preaching: "We went this evening to hear Lorenzo Dow, a famous Methodist preacher, his appearance was enough to frighten one and his preaching disgusted all—the meeting house was crowded full. Think we should have been as wise if we had staid home."[5]

Although Universalism had been brought to America by John Murray in 1770, it did not gain much headway until after Elhanan Winchester, a Baptist minister, was converted in 1781. The next year Charles Chauncy's universalist-flavored *Salvation for All Men* appeared in print. Later under the leadership of Hosea Ballou, whose *Treatise on Atonement* was published in 1805, Universalists adopted an antitrinitarian position and, except for social status, became indistinguishable from Unitarians. As a lower-class denomination, the Universalists competed with Methodists and Wesleyan-oriented Free-Will Baptists for the allegiance of the common people. Although the Universalists were concentrated initially in rural New England, they moved into the newer settlements of the West with such success that by 1850 they had more than twice as many churches as the Unitarians.

The Resurgence of Old School "Confessionalism"

The protest against revivalism was not limited to the "liberal" wing of the churches. Orthodox Calvinists also were alarmed by what they considered to be the dangerous narrowing of the distinction between Calvinism and Arminianism that was being effected by Nathaniel W. Taylor and Lyman Beecher in the interest of getting results, and the "new measures" employed by Finney in New York State seemed to them clear confirmation of the unhappy practical consequences that the narrowing entailed. Nathaniel Emmons, one of the most distinguished heirs of Jonathan Edwards, grumbled in his old age about the "undue excitements" of "modern" awakenings; and Asahel Nettleton, who had been one of the earliest

---

[5] Alice Felt Tyler, *Freedom's Ferment* (Minneapolis, 1944), 29.

leaders of the Second Awakening, was worried about the harm that was being done by "the imprudence of a few zealous individuals." Others complained that the revivals were becoming the work of "revival-makers" rather than a work of God. Even at Andover, which, after a period of staid orthodoxy had become a seedbed of revival preachers, anxiety began to re-emerge.

Although strict Calvinists among the New England Congregationalists fretted and chafed over the concessions that were being made, their dissent was muted by the necessity to maintain a united front to fight disestablishment and then to counter the Unitarian threat. Open conflict did not break out until 1828 when one of Taylor's more disturbing sermons, *Concio ad Clerum* ("Advice to the Clergy"), was published. The sermon dealt with the crucial issue of man's natural depravity and insisted that sin "is man's own act, consisting in a free choice of some object rather than God as his chief good." The "circumstances" of man's nature make it certain that he will sin, but he has "power to the contrary."[6] The sermon made it clear to the conservatives that the New Haven Theology (or the "New Divinity" of Yale) had departed from orthodox Calvinism at one of its most essential points. The Yale group, on the other hand, argued that they were only offering a more acceptable and convincing explanation of the doctrine. The conservatives, finding the explanation unacceptable, raised the cry: "Shall we sustain our Calvinism or see it run down to the standard of Methodists and laxer men?"[7]

The pattern of response had been set at Andover, where Jedidiah Morse persuaded the founders of the seminary to "guard against the insidious encroachments of innovation" by shackling the institution to the *Westminster Shorter Catechism* and the so-called Andover Creed based upon Samuel Hopkins' restatement of the views of Jonathan Edwards. The center of the controversy was in Connecticut, where a Pastoral Union was formed in 1833 and steps were taken to found a new seminary to combat the influence of Yale. The following year the (Hartford) Seminary was established at East Windsor and Bennet Tyler was summoned from Portland, Maine, to assume the presidency. The integrity of both the Pastoral Union and the seminary was carefully guarded by Articles of Agreement which defined Calvinism in terms that would exclude any New Haven sentiments. The rift which was to continue for many years amounted to an open schism among the loosely organized Congregational churches.

A similar alarm among Presbyterian conservatives precipitated the formation of what came to be known as the Old School party in opposition to the New School or New Divinity men. The Presbyterian conservatives worked in close alliance with the strict Calvinists of New England, and as

---

[6] The sermon is reprinted in Sydney E. Ahlstrom, ed., *Theology in America* (Indianapolis, 1967), 213–49.

[7] S. E. Mead, *Nathaniel W. Taylor*, 221.

early as 1827 the Presbyterian *Christian Advocate*, published in Philadelphia and edited by Ashbel Green, was accusing the professors at Yale of promulgating doctrines that subverted the principles of orthodoxy. The ensuing controversy was marked by a whole series of heresy trials, beginning in 1831 when charges were brought against Albert Barnes in Philadelphia and ending in 1835 with the arraignment of Lyman Beecher before the Presbytery of Cincinnati. In each instance, after appeal to higher judicatories, the charges were dismissed, but the trials contributed greatly to the inflamed climate of opinion which led in 1837 to the exclusion of four New School synods in New York and Ohio from the Presbyterian church.[8]

Although the theological issue was the most obvious factor in the division of 1837, the division was partly the product of a geographically based power struggle within the Presbyterian denomination, and lurking in the background was the disruptive issue of slavery. From the beginning Pennsylvania had been the center of power and prestige within the Presbyterian fold, but by 1828 its position of dominance had been badly eroded. In that year Green noted that, whereas there were 196 licentiates and ministers in Pennsylvania, New York had 426. The damaging aspect of this imbalance was the fact that the New York ministers were within the New England rather than the Pennsylvania orbit of influence. Beecher, who had gone west to become president of the newly established Lane Theological Seminary, was certain that his trial for heresy was triggered by men of the Philadelphia – Pittsburgh axis who were alarmed at the prospect of a New England man rising to leadership in Cincinnati.

Within the Old School party, theological and political concerns reinforced each other. The growing strength of the New School party heightened the apprehensions that had been aroused by the shifting emphasis of the New England Theology. To strengthen its position, the Old School group raised the issue of church government. The "union" with the Congregationalists had been welcomed initially by all parties within the church. Ashbel Green, for example, had been one of the leading proponents of the Plan of Union. But now the arrangement was brought under attack. Since the rival political power of the New School party was chiefly concentrated in the churches, presbyteries, and synods which had been formed under the provisions of the articles of "accommodation," these bodies were now denounced as being faulty in their constitutional foundation. Furthermore, since the great instrument of the New York – New School advance had been the independently controlled American Home Missionary Society and American Education Society, the Old School men

---

[8] The Old School – New School controversy is illuminated by documents reproduced in Maurice W. Armstrong et. al., *The Presbyterian Enterprise,* 146 – 71. See also G. M. Marsden, *The Evangelical Mind and the New School Presbyterian Experience* (New Haven, 1970).

demanded that these societies be repudiated and that all denominational funds be channeled through denominational boards that would be fully committed to the church's confessional position.

With the exception of a single year, the Old School party had not been able to gain control of the General Assembly prior to 1837. The balance of power was represented by Princeton Theological Seminary, and the faculty there hesitated to commit its influence to any program that would divide the church. Princeton regarded itself as the theological center of Presbyterian life, and it had looked with misgiving upon the establishment of Auburn Seminary in 1818 and Lane in 1829. But it was the founding of Union Theological Seminary in New York by New School men in 1836 that threw Princeton, though not without some reservations, behind the political program of the Old School party. The new seminary in New York City could only be regarded as a direct challenge to Princeton's central role in the life of the church.

During the months preceding the General Assembly of 1837, the Old School faction organized carefully to obtain a maximum representation, and when the Assembly met it proceeded with dispatch to carry out the Old School program. The "union" with the Congregationalists was abrogated, the relationship with the American Home Missionary Society and the American Education Society was severed, and three synods in New York and one in Ohio were expelled from the church. The following year, after attempting unsuccessfully to gain readmittance, the New School Presbyterians organized as a separate body that, with the adherence of scattered presbyteries and churches in other parts of the country, was roughly equal in size to the Old School body.

Although he took no great part in the division of 1837, Charles Hodge became the great theologian of Old School Presbyterianism. He had been appointed to a professorship at Princeton Seminary in 1822 and remained there for 50 years, sharing in the training of over 3,000 ministers and contributing more than any other single person to the shaping of American Presbyterianism. He was deeply influenced by Swiss orthodoxy, and a strong confessionalism became the hallmark of his theology. Hodge was convinced that "no such thing exists on the face of the earth as Christianity in the abstract. . . . Every man you see is either an Episcopalian or a Methodist, a Presbyterian or an Independent, an Arminian or a Calvinist. No one is a Christian in general."[9] His theological system was based solidly on the Westminster Standards and other Reformed confessions which he sought faithfully to expound and defend. It was with this in mind that he boasted that "a new idea never originated" at Princeton Seminary while he was there. His great monument and the source of much of his later influence was his three-volume *Systematic Theology*, explicitly designed as a

[9] *Biblical Repertory and Theological Review*, 8 (1836), 430.

defensive rampart against all doctrinal aberrations.[10] Although Hodge attempted to keep Presbyterianism in a theological straitjacket, it has been pointed out that his learning, doctrinal rigor, respect for confessional tradition, and insistence upon intelligible discussion did much in succeeding years to prevent anti-intellectual tendencies, sentimentality, and emotional partisanship from overwhelming theological concern.

During the 1830s the Baptists also were torn by an Old School–New School division that was in part a reaction to the growing influence in their ranks of the New England Theology.[11] The Baptist Old School party, however, failed to capture the denominational machinery that, above the associational level, existed solely in the form of voluntary societies. A defection thereupon occurred both in the East and in the West, but the defensive posture that these "Primitive Baptists" adopted became so permeated by an antimission spirit that the defecting churches and associations were left to eke out no more than a dwindling existence.

A revived confessionalism among the Reformed and the Lutherans came from another quarter. Both groups had been heavily infiltrated, first by Wesleyan doctrines, then by the more moderate evangelicalism of early Princeton, and finally by Taylorism and its associated Finneyite "new measures." In 1822 five ministers withdrew on doctrinal grounds from the Dutch Reformed Church, but their adherents were able to maintain only a meager church life until 1857 when the Christian Reformed Church was established on a strong confessional base by Dutch immigrants in Michigan. Not only did the new church prosper, its influence had the effect of drawing the older Dutch church back to a more conservative position.

A theological shift among the German Lutherans followed much the same pattern. S. S. Schmucker, graduate of Princeton and president of the Lutheran seminary at Gettysburg, was the great symbol of the Lutheran adjustment to the American theological climate.[12] It was Schmucker who

---

[10] It is necessary to speak of "later" influence, for Hodge's *Systematic Theology* (N.Y., 1872–75) was not published until the last years of his life. Prior to this time his influence was mediated primarily through the classroom and his articles in the *Biblical Repertory and Theological Review* (later known as the *Princeton Review*).

[11] The theological issue was clearly delineated by Thomas Smiley (1759–1832), who was to become an Old School leader, in a letter to John Davis, April 27, 1811, and in his manuscript "History of the Chemung Association," 88–102, both of which are in the Samuel Colgate Baptist Historical Collection. Smiley, a pastor on the New York–Pennsylvania border, was shocked and dismayed by "the high Hopkinsian or all but fully Arminian sentiments" of the "Eastern missionaries" sent out by the Baptist board in Boston. For the missionaries' account of their tours through the Chemung River area, see the *Massachusetts Baptist Missionary Magazine*, 2 (1808–10), 302–7; and the *American Baptist Magazine*, 1, (1817–18), 269–71.

[12] See J. A. Brown, *The New Theology* (Philadelphia, 1857); Vergilius Ferm, *The Crisis in American Lutheran Theology*; and E. Clifford Nelson, ed., *The Lutherans in North America* (Philadelphia, 1975).

issued in 1838 a *Fraternal Appeal* summoning all branches of evangelical Protestantism in America to unite in a single Apostolic Protestant Church, and who with other "liberal" leaders exerted strong influence on behalf of "new-measures" revivalism. The defeat of the Americanizing Lutherans, however, was foreshadowed by the arrival in Missouri of a group of immigrant Germans from Saxony the following year. They had left Germany because they could "see no possibility of retaining in their present home" the "pure and undefiled" faith of the historic Lutheran confessions and thus had felt "duty bound to emigrate and to look for a country where this Lutheran faith is not endangered."[13]

With their numbers augmented by continuing immigration, the Missouri group at a meeting in Chicago formed the Evangelical Lutheran Synod of Missouri in 1847. Other equally conservative synods were formed by immigrants from other parts of Germany — the Buffalo Synod in 1845, the Wisconsin Synod in 1850, and the Iowa Synod in 1854. Although these synods engaged in doctrinal controversy among themselves, the conspicuous leader who influenced them all and who played a large part in the reshaping of American Lutheranism as a whole was Carl F. W. Walther. As his biographer reports, he was "easily the most commanding figure in the Lutheran church in America during the nineteenth century." Another scholar has noted that Walther "stood almost alone in the nineteenth century American theological scene as one fully aware of the crucial importance of the problems of Law and Gospel to the Christian faith." In this respect he anticipated "the emphasis of Karl Barth and the 'Luther renaissance' of the next century, but by the same fact he doomed himself to attack and misunderstanding in his own time."[14]

The great wave of German immigration did not leave Lutheranism in the eastern part of the United States unscathed. Not only was pressure exerted by the newer synods in the West, but immigration also altered the theological complexion of the older synods in the East. By the 1850s, even at Gettysburg, Schmucker was displaced in influence by Charles Philip Krauth, who was urging the churches to maintain their fidelity to the traditional Lutheran standards. Later his son, Charles Porterfield Krauth, devoted his attention to inaugurating a liturgical and sacramental renaissance among American Lutherans, and at this point his interests closely paralleled those of John W. Nevin. As a third-generation American, Krauth was an especially effective advocate of a revived confessionalism in the English-speaking Lutheran churches.[15]

[13] A. R. Wentz, *A Basic History of Lutheranism* (Philadelphia, 1955), 116.
[14] D. H. Steffens, *Carl F. W. Walther* (Philadelphia, 1917), 10; Sydney E. Ahlstrom, "Theology in America," in *The Shaping of American Religion*, ed. J. W. Smith and A. Leland Jamison, 275.
[15] See Charles Porterfield Krauth, *The Conservative Reformation and Its Theology* (Philadelphia, 1871); and Adolph Spaeth, *Charles Porterfield Krauth*, (N.Y., 1898).

"High Church" Sentiment: John W. Nevin and John Henry Hobart

While others were fighting defensive battles against New School doctrines and assuming a rigid stance behind their confessional ramparts, John W. Nevin—the chief spokesman for what came to be known as "the Mercersburg theology" or "evangelical catholicism"—was undertaking the more positive task of restoring the sacramental life of the churches that, in his view, had been wrecked by rampant revivalism.[16] Born of Scotch-Irish parents in 1803, Nevin attended Union College and Princeton Seminary, where he was the prize student of Charles Hodge. In 1829 he became a professor at Western Theological Seminary, a Princeton outpost at Allegheny, Pennsylvania. There his antislavery views involved him in constant controversy and, although theologically fully in accord with Old School views, he was violently attacked because he regarded the expulsion of the New School synods in 1837 as an unconstitutional act. Convinced that his future usefulness at Western had been impaired, he accepted a call in 1840 to the struggling German Reformed theological seminary at Mercersburg, a move that was interpreted to him as merely a shift from the "Scotch Reformed" branch of the church to the "German Presbyterian" branch. In the isolation of Mercersburg, Nevin underwent the radical theological reorientation that caused him to break with Princeton orthodoxy at three crucial points: its lack of any sense of historical development, its individualistic view of the church, and its Zwinglian view of the sacraments.

Many influences, some of long standing, combined to produce Nevin's change of front. Not the least of these was the influence of Coleridge, but Nevin reported that it was the writings of J.A.W. Neander, the German church historian, that had actually awakened him from his "dogmatic slumber." Neander taught him that Christianity was a life, an experience, a communion with invisible realities, rather than a dogmatic system. This enabled him to appreciate diverse doctrinal conceptions and to find in all the diversities a movement toward a divinely ordained purpose. Finally, at Mercersburg, Nevin was introduced to a psychology, based upon Hegel, which he discovered had direct bearing on doctrines of the Incarnation, the mystical union of Christ and the believer, and the presence of Christ in the Eucharist.

Nevin's shift to a new theological position was signalized in 1843 by the publication of *The Anxious Bench*, a forthright attack upon the "new-measures" revivalism that had invaded the German Reformed churches and which Nevin regarded as "unfavorable to deep, thorough, and intelligent

---

[16] See James H. Nichols, *Romanticism in American Theology: Nevin and Schaff at Mercersburg* (Chicago, 1961).

piety," "fatal to the true idea of devotion," and "injurious to the worship of God."[17] His major work, *The Mystical Presence: A Vindication of the Reformed or Calvinistic Doctrine of the Holy Eucharist,*[18] was published three years later, and it brought him into a head-on clash with Hodge—a clash that ended with Nevin demolishing Hodge's attempt to marshal support from the Reformed confessions.

In contrast to those who understood Christianity as a relationship of individuals to Christ who are only subsequently brought together to form the church, Nevin held that individuals do not constitute the church. The church is not something added to the gospel; it is an essential part of the gospel. It is the context within which men have access to Christ's saving presence, the means by which the living Christ gives himself to his people. It was constituted and continues to be constituted as a "whole" through communion with Christ rather than being simply the sum total of predestined individuals—past, present, and future. Central to Nevin's understanding of communion with Christ was his conception of the Eucharist. "The question of the Eucharist," he declared, "is one of the most important belonging to the history of religion. It may be regarded indeed as in some sense central to the whole Christian system. For Christianity is grounded in the living union of the believer with the person of Christ; and this great fact is emphatically concentrated in the mystery of the Lord's Supper."[19] Thus it is in the mystical participation of the faithful in the life of Christ through the sacrament of the Lord's Supper that the church is most truly the Church.

Liturgical reform, ecumenical concern, and questions of ministerial order were other subjects to which Nevin devoted his attention. His thought was enriched and in some instances explicated by his colleague Philip Schaff, who arrived in Mercersburg from Germany in 1844. Nevin's views aroused much opposition from defenders of New School doctrines and practices, and after the Civil War the German Reformed Church was bitterly divided between the Nevinists and the anti-Nevinists. Competing educational institutions were established and the denomination barely escaped actual schism.

Of Nevin it was said, "He is always instructive, even when he is in error."[20] Unfortunately, few were instructed, for he moved in a restricted circle. He belonged to a small denomination and taught in a remote seminary. But the main reason for his failure to be heard was the fact that he addressed himself to issues that were not to be keenly felt until the twentieth century.

---

[17] *The Anxious Bench* (Chambersburg, Pa., 1843), 56.

[18] Extensive selections from *The Mystical Presence* are reprinted in Ahlstrom, *Theology in America*, 374–426.

[19] *The Mystical Presence* (Philadelphia, 1846), 51.

[20] J. H. Nichols, "John Williamson Nevin," in *Sons of the Prophets*, ed. H. T. Kerr (Princeton, 1963), 81.

In some respects John J. Hobart, Episcopal bishop of New York, was a kindred spirit to Nevin. His emphases were much the same as those of the Mercersburg theologian, but he really lived in another world. Hobart's interest was practical rather than theological. Unlike Nevin he was stirred by no ecumenical vision and he had little appreciation of historical development. Hobart was a strict "denominationalist," a "sectarian" in the eyes of Evangelicals.

Consecrated bishop in 1811, Hobart spent the remaining 19 years of his life in a burst of activity directed to reviving the flagging fortunes of the Protestant Episcopal Church in the state of New York. He was constantly on the move visiting the churches of his diocese and establishing missions. He wrote and compiled handbooks as practical aids to the laity: *Companion for the Altar, Companion for the Festivals and Fasts, The Pocket Almanac, The Church Catechism, The Christian's Manual on Faith and Devotion.* He rebuked those who participated in the interdenominational voluntary societies, and to counter the influence of those societies he organized the Protestant Episcopal Tract Society, the Protestant Episcopal Sunday School Society, and the New York Bible and Common Prayer Book Society. In a church that was predominantly "Low Church" or "Evangelical" in sentiment, Hobart was proud to acknowledge the name "High Churchman," and the explication of what it meant to be a High Churchman was the constant theme of his annual "charges."

A "Low Churchman" to Hobart was one "who deprecates the distinguishing characteristics of the Church or who is lukewarm or indifferent in advancing them," whereas the "High Churchman" exhibits "an eminent degree of attachment to the essential characteristics of the Church and zeal for their advancement." The essential characteristics were "those of the first and purest ages of Christianity, of the age of the apostles, of martyrs and confessors," and Hobart dedicated himself to arresting "the progress of an indifference and laxity of opinion" that threatened the destruction of the Church as "it was constituted by its divine head."[21]

Hobart rejected what he called the "invidious distinction" that so many made "between the doctrine and the institutions of the gospel." Both, he insisted, "have a divine origin" and "are inseparably connected." Indispensable to the being of the Church are the "essential elements of doctrine, ministry, sacraments, and worship." In developing this fourfold form of the Church, Hobart displayed little creative thought. His liturgical interest was limited to defending the existing Episcopal liturgy as embodying evangelical truth in the "purest" language of devotion. Although he regarded the sacraments as central and indispensable and thought that "he hazarded his salvation if he refused or neglected to receive these means and pledges of divine favor," he considered the bread and wine to

---

[21] E. C. Chorley, *Men and Movements in the American Episcopal Church* (N.Y., 1946), 143, 146.

be no more than "symbols and memorials of the body and blood of Christ." His interest in doctrine was equally commonplace. The point of his central concern was the ministry, as he made clear when he declared that the true High Churchman adheres "in all essential points to the faith, ministry, and worship which distinguished the apostolic and primitive Church, and particularly to the constitution of the Christian ministry under its three orders of bishops, priests, and deacons."[22]

Lawful ministers, Hobart maintained, are "those who derive their authority from Christ himself by regular succession from the apostles." Consequently, there cannot be "a lawful bishop, priest, or deacon who hath not had episcopal consecration or ordination." Episcopacy is essential and "unchangeable because it is the originally constituted mode of conveying that commission without which there can be no visible ministry, no visible sacraments, no visible Church." Thus "we continue in the fellowship of the apostles when we adhere to the ministry of bishops, priests, and deacons who have been from the apostles' times." Nor did Hobart hesitate to draw the harsh conclusion that offended so many of his fellow Episcopalians: "I could not maintain the divine authority of the Episcopal ministry without denying the validity of a nonepiscopal ministry."[23]

Scholars have speculated as to the source of Hobart's uncompromising churchmanship, which ran so counter to the spirit of his age. One clue is to be found in his family tradition, for his grandfather was a New Englander who had become an Episcopalian. Another influence may have been a feeling of defensiveness which developed during his college days in the Presbyterian atmosphere of Princeton. More decisive was the influence of his father-in-law, Thomas Bradbury Chandler, who had led the fight for a colonial episcopate and who had taken care to make sure that his daughter was "well instructed in the doctrines of primitive episcopacy." Whatever their source, Hobart's views — which represented only a minority opinion in his own time — were destined to become, after having been enriched and deepened by insights derived from the Oxford Movement in England, one of the dominant currents in the life of the Protestant Episcopal Church in the twentieth century.[24]

By the mid-nineteenth century, views analogous to those of Hobart developed within Baptist ranks. This "High Church" sentiment, which emphasized apostolic succession through an unbroken line of New Testa-

---

22 *Ibid.,* 143–44, 147.
23 *Ibid.,* 142, 184, 186–87.
24 The Oxford Movement was initiated in 1833 by John Keble (1792–1866) with a sermon on "National Apostasy" and was carried forward through a series of *Tracts for the Times,* the first of which was published by J. H. Newman (1801–90) in the same year. The aim of the movement was to win support within the Church of England for the "High Church" views that had been explicated by seventeenth-century divines. A dominant motif of the movement was its renewed interest in primitive and medieval Christianity.

ment churches, was the distinctive characteristic of a group of Baptists who called themselves "Landmarkists." The name was derived from the tract *An Old Landmark Reset* (1854) by James M. Pendleton,[25] but the basic tenets, which included a refusal to recognize other "societies" as true churches and a rejection of "alien immersion" and "pulpit affiliation" with non-Baptists, had been set forth by James R. Graves three years earlier at a meeting in Cotton Grove, Tennessee. Although the major Baptist bodies repeatedly repudiated the Landmarkists, their "High Church" views gained wide currency in the South by the end of the century.

Transcendentalism

Little more than a decade after the founding of the American Unitarian Association, the Boston churches were torn again by a new reformation led by rebellious young preachers, members of the "Transcendental Club," which first met in the home of George Ripley.[26] In addition to Ripley, the more prominent of the rebel clergymen were Ralph Waldo Emerson, Theodore Parker, James Freeman Clarke, Frederic Henry Hedge, William Henry Channing, and Orestes Brownson. They were ably abetted by several influential lay recruits, such as Bronson Alcott, Henry David Thoreau, Margaret Fuller, and Elizabeth Peabody. Repelled by what they regarded as the cold logic of their Unitarian elders and deeply influenced by Coleridge's *Aids to Reflection,* the Transcendentalists sought to reconcile the rationalism of their fathers with the romanticism of their age by introducing a strong note of mysticism into Unitarian formulations.

Since they were eclectic in their approach to truth, it is difficult to characterize the Transcendentalists. No two of them agreed at every point; and although some exhibited intense individualism, others displayed a passionate zeal for communal life. James Freeman Clarke on one occasion suggested that their group might be called "the Club of the Like-Minded" because "no two of us thought alike." They were, nonetheless, bound together by what they called "the spiritual principle" — a principle that was articulated in three major agreements: an insistence upon divine immanence, a dependence upon intuitive perception of truth, and a rejection of all external authority. Every created thing had deep religious meaning, and they found "sermons not just in stones but in bean rows at Walden Pond and mud puddles on Boston Common." They were called Transcendentalists, said Ripley, because they believed "in an order

[25] See selection reprinted in Smith, Handy, and Loetscher, *American Christianity,* II, 108–12.
[26] See William R. Hutchison, *The Transcendentalist Ministers* (New Haven, 1959). For basic documents, see *The Transcendentalists: An Anthology,* ed. Perry Miller (Cambridge, Mass., 1950).

of truths which transcends the sphere of the external senses." Since "the truth of religion does not depend on tradition, nor historical facts, but has an unerring witness in the soul," they refused to acknowledge any authority beyond themselves. The Transcendentalist, Emerson declared, "believes in miracles, in the perpetual openness of the human mind to the new influx of light and power; he believes in inspiration and ecstasy." The individual soul is linked to God, and through the gift of intuition — instinct, imagination, insight — the soul can penetrate beyond the outer shell of life and consummate union with God by participating in the life of the "oversoul."[27]

Andrews Norton and other old-line Unitarians were horrified by this "latest form of infidelity" and were restrained from ejecting the Transcendentalists from the Unitarian fellowship only by an awareness of the scandal that a heresy trial among the Unitarians would create. Consequently the members of the Club were permitted to proceed in their churches with their program of reformation. Unlike Nevin, who had been spurred by Coleridge to move in a more churchly direction, the Transcendentalists were led by their romantic vision to a quite contrary emphasis. They sought to turn their churches into free religious associations in which the distinction between clergy and laity would disappear and worship would be so ordered that leadership might be rotated.[28] Furthermore, their goal was a comprehension that would embrace the best elements of all former religious systems and within which radical movements would not be looked upon as heresies but as "providential" clues to some need that God wished the churches to fulfill.

The Mediating Theology of Horace Bushnell

After several false vocational starts, which included teaching, journalism, and law, a quiet conversion experience in the solitude of his own room sent Horace Bushnell to Yale Divinity School and to the pastorate of the North Congregational Church in Hartford, Connecticut, where he was to spend the rest of his active pastoral life.[29] Bushnell was both "conservative" and "liberal" in his emphases, finding much of Christian truth in the older tradition of New England and yet appropriating and incorporating into his thinking insights derived from the Unitarian critique. He could speak of "free," "self-governed" individuals, and yet emphasize the way in which individuals are bound, either for good or for evil, by the organic

---

[27] Hutchison, *Transcendentalist Ministers*, vii, 29; Tyler, *Freedom's Ferment*, 48; O. B. Frothingham, *George Ripley* (Boston, 1882), 84–85.

[28] Transcendentalism was not so enamored of the notion of "free association" as to overlook the importance of structure in social life. See Anne Rose, *Transcendentalism as a Social Movement, 1830–1850* (New Haven, 1981).

[29] See Barbara M. Cross, *Horace Bushnell* (Chicago, 1958).

character of the communities—family, church, neighborhood, and nation—in which they exist. His endeavor was to be a mediator, reconciling the intimations of Christian truth to be found in diverse theological camps. Bushnell's views won little acceptance prior to the Civil War, but later became of major importance in preparing the way for the New Theology of the 1870s and 1880s.

Bushnell, Nevin, and the Transcendentalists all acknowledged the decisive influence of the "mysticism" of Coleridge and Schleiermacher, but each domesticated this dual influence in different ways. The Transcendentalists were led to reject the past and to reduce the church to a pragmatically justified religious association. Nevin, on the other hand, experienced no such compulsion, for he had been freed to appropriate the past by a sense of historical development derived from reading Neander. Thus his appreciation both of the past and of the Church as an embodiment of Christ had been enhanced by the stress on mystic communion. Bushnell's approach to the past was similar to that of Nevin, but for Bushnell it was made possible by a theory of language. To him language was an imprecise instrument. Words are but "faded metaphors" that cannot be transferred from mind to mind with their meaning clear and transparent. Each word is organically related to its own history, to the history of the one who uses it and of the one who hears it, and to the situation in which it is used. With these variables, all creedal statements and even the words of Scripture must be understood in a "spirit of accommodation," for they are but linguistic and hence poetic attempts to speak the unspeakable. Christian truth was something that lay behind doctrinal propositions, but Bushnell did not sympathize with the Unitarian rejection of creeds. They were testimonies to that which lay beyond them and he was ready to accept them all, for "when they are subjected to the deepest chemistry of thought . . . they become so elastic and run so freely into each other that one seldom need have any difficulty in accepting as many as are offered him."[30]

Bushnell is best remembered as the author of *Christian Nurture* (1847) which, while not his most important work, was one of the most influential books ever to be published in America. It was a criticism of revivalism and a plea for what in its broadest sense could be called Christian education. With his understanding of language as a social phenomenon, Bushnell was driven to recognize the formative influence of the community of faith. No person exists in isolation. All live within a social context that shapes and determines character. There is no reason to suppose that a child of believing parents cannot "grow up in the Lord." Take any scheme of human nature you please, Bushnell declared, and you will find nothing in it "to forbid the possibility that a child should be led, in his first moral act, to

---

[30] "Preliminary Dissertation on Language," in *God in Christ* (Hartford, 1849), 81–83.
   See also H. Shelton Smith, ed., *Horace Bushnell* (N.Y., 1965), 69–105.

cleave unto what is good and right." Instead of assuming that "the child is to grow up in sin, to be converted after he comes to mature age," the "aim, effort, and expectation" should be that he may "grow up a Christian and never know himself as being otherwise." The great trouble with revivalism, as Bushnell saw it, is that as a result of its "jump and stir" the ordinary operations of God's grace tend to be "swallowed up and lost in the extraordinary," and people are led to believe that the only entrance into the Christian life is through a convulsive conversion experience in a revival meeting.[31]

Bushnell was not opposed to revivals. He believed that they rendered a necessary service to those who have been caught in the web of the kingdom of evil. Sin no less than virtue can be transmitted by the social context.

> Evil, once beginning to exist, inevitably becomes organic and constructs a kind of principate or kingdom opposite to God. . . . Pride organizes caste and dominates in the sphere of fashion. Corrupt opinions, false judgments, bad manners, and a general body of conventionalisms that represent the motherhood of sin, come into vogue and reign. And so, doubtless, everywhere and in all worlds, sin has in its nature to organize, mount into the ascendant above God and truth, and reign in a kingdom opposite God.[32]

With God's help and the Christian nurture provided by family and church, no one need sink into the slough of sin; but if that has occurred, then a drastic rebirth to change the "reigning love" is necessary. As early as 1838 Bushnell had published an article in the *Quarterly Christian Spectator* "to establish a higher and more solid confidence in revivals," an article in which he insisted that "nothing was ever achieved in the way of great and radical change without some degree of excitement; and if any one expects to carry on the cause of salvation by a steady rolling on the same dead level, and fears continually lest the axles wax hot and kindle into a flame," that person "is too timorous to hold the reins of the Lord's chariot." Although not everyone needed "a fireball shot from the moon," some did.[33]

As Bushnell reconciled revivalism to the ordered life of home and congregation, so he reconciled the major contentions of the Unitarians with an evangelical understanding of the Christian faith. He refashioned his conception of God, man, Christ, and the Atonement to take the force from the Unitarian critique, and in the process reached back to Jonathan Edwards for themes that helped him make his case. He reaffirmed the Trinity by acknowledging that it applied only to God as revealed and not

---

[31] *Christian Nurture* (N.Y., 1923), 4, 10; "Spiritual Economy of Revivals of Religion," *Quarterly Christian Spectator*, (1838), 143–45.

[32] *Nature and the Supernatural* (N.Y., 1858), 135.

[33] *An Argument for "Discourses on Christian Nurture"* (Hartford, 1847), 16.

as ultimate being, as descriptive not of his person but of the modes of self-disclosure by which he makes himself known as Father, Son, and Spirit. In similar fashion, Bushnell bridged the gap between the natural and the supernatural without allowing them to become indistinguishable.

The fate that befalls most mediators was not withheld from Bushnell. He was appreciated at one point and criticized at another. No one seemed completely happy with his solutions. He was saved from being subjected to a heresy trial only by the withdrawal of his church from the local Congregational association which was dominated by Bennet Tyler, president of Hartford Seminary and leader of the Old School forces in Connecticut. But Leonard Bacon (1802–81), pastor of the Center Church in New Haven who had stood astride the Taylor–Tyler controversy, pronounced what was to be the growing conviction when he said that "brother Bushnell is essentially sound."[34] During the second half of the century, Bushnell's "progressive orthodoxy" was to sweep through many of the seminaries, and men who had been deeply influenced by him were to be among the most distinguished preachers in the land.

The Triumph of Methodism

Whatever the future verdict was to be, the men discussed in this chapter represented lost causes in their own generation. They were minority voices in a time of evangelistic urgency. The tide was running in another direction, and the decades immediately preceding the Civil War witnessed the triumph of the distinctive emphases of Methodism in practically all the denominations.

Earlier defections to Methodist views and techniques had produced a cluster of new ecclesiastical bodies such as the United Brethren, the Evangelical Association, the Free-Will Baptists, the Cumberland Presbyterians, and the greater part of the Christian movement. But more significant than these defections was the fact that the Calvinism of the other denominations was becoming so diluted as to be unrecognizable. Taking their lead from Nathaniel W. Taylor, the revivalists had placed such stress upon the ability of the sinner to acquire conversion as in effect to transform Calvinism into an operational Arminianism. Finney illustrated the progression. He was first a Presbyterian, then a Congregationalist, but his theology became more and more that of the Methodists until he finally embraced the Wesleyan doctrine of Christian perfection. By mid-century Robert Baird was testifying that it was necessary in all progressive churches "to preach to sinners as if they believed them to be possessed of all the powers of moral agency, capable of turning to God, and on this account, and no other, inexcusable for not doing so."[35]

---

[34] Roland H. Bainton, *Yale and the Ministry* (N.Y., 1957), 124.
[35] *Princeton Review*, 22 (1850), 204.

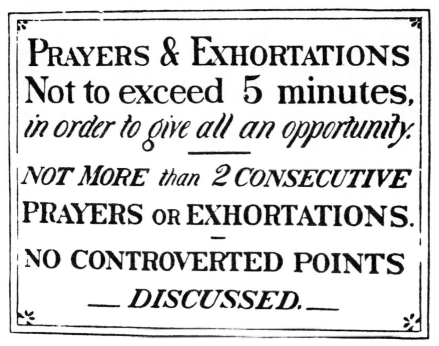

PRAYERS & EXHORTATIONS
Not to exceed 5 minutes,
in order to give all an opportunity.

NOT MORE than *2 CONSECUTIVE*
PRAYERS OR EXHORTATIONS.
NO CONTROVERTED POINTS
— *DISCUSSED.* —

Token Used at Noonday Prayer Meetings in 1858.   They were led by laymen, and a strict time-limit on participation was imposed. Such union meetings spread throughout the country, north and south, east and west. *(Reproduced from T.W. Chambers,* The Noon Prayer Meeting, *New York, 1857, courtesy of Edwin S. Gaustad.)*

Curiously enough, Baird's comment appeared in — of all places — the *Princeton Review*. Old School Presbyterians had been greatly distressed by the infiltration of Arminian views and Finneyite techniques — the "results-oriented" religion — into their denominational life, but after the break of 1837 they exhibited astonishing alacrity in climbing on the bandwagon and turning again to revivalism as "the only effective weapon in the church's arsenal for turning back the tide of uncouthness, materialism, and moral disintegration."[36] Ultimately Barnes, Beecher, and even Finney were defended in the pages of the *Princeton Review*; and James W. Alexander could refer with equal approval to the Calvinist and Arminian revivals of the past, saying: "Accidents may vary but the essence is the same."[37] Charles Hodge was the architect of the theory that permitted Old School Presbyterians to reverse their basic commitment. He did this by adopting Jonathan Edwards' distinction between natural ability and moral inability and then glossing over the distinction to such an extent

[36] Elwyn A. Smith, *The Presbyterian Ministry in American Culture* (Philadelphia, 1962), 214.
[37] *Ibid.*, 215.

that his position was not dissimilar to that of New School revivalists.[38] With even Old School Presbyterians no longer untainted, it is apparent that "the Methodist age" of American Protestantism had reached maturity.

The "prayer meeting" or "businessmen's" revival of 1857–59 serves as a symbol of how thoroughly the piety of the revivalists had become domesticated in the American scene. This was a laymen's revival, growing out of noonday prayer meetings sponsored by the New York Y.M.C.A. and being carried forward by Y.M.C.A.s in other cities throughout the country. The emphasis upon "holiness" and "the higher Christian life" that characterized the revival was a reflection of the influence of Finney's doctrine of Christian perfection, but the revival itself was in the hands of the laity and revealed little theological sophistication. Its major feature was its thorough respectability. Unlike earlier revivals, it seems to have evoked no opposition. A contemporary report noted that "there was remarkable unanimity of approval among religious and secular observers alike, with scarcely a critical voice heard anywhere."[39]

There was some superficiality in this "Methodist" or "evangelical" piety, but its achievements were not inconsiderable. Philip Schaff, when reporting the American scene in 1854 to his former colleagues in Berlin, felt compelled to confess that, despite his reservations, "the United States are by far the most religious and Christian country in the world." "Table prayer," he noted, is "almost universal," "daily family worship" is the rule "in religious circles," and church attendance is "inseparable from moral and social respectibility." In contrast to Berlin, where there were only 40 churches for a population of 450,000 with an attendance at public worship of no more than 30,000, New York with a population of 600,000 had "over 250 well-attended churches, some of them quite costly and splendid." In Brooklyn the proportion of churches to the population was even larger, and a similar state of affairs prevailed elsewhere.[40]

The Continuing Importance of Preaching

Preaching, which was the centerpiece of the lay revival of the 1850s, was central to the development of religion in America over the course of the nation's history. Preaching had always been the most effective way to engender in persons a deep regard for Scripture and to impress upon them a sense of moral obligation. After the Revolution, when a political vision rooted in respect for the voice of the people became culturally dominant, preaching acquired particular importance as "the democratic

[38] For a discussion of the Old School "capitulation," see Smith, *The Presbyterian Ministry*, 220–24.
[39] J. E. Orr, *The Second Evangelical Awakening* (London, 1949), 21.
[40] Schaff, *America*, 11, 35, 56, 78.

art of persuasion."[41] Preaching became an instrument for the proliferation of popular religious movements, but at the same time it remained the cornerstone of religious life in those churches where authority traditionally was vested in ordained clergy.

From the earliest settlement of Massachusetts, the sermon served not only as a means for the promotion of religious doctrine, but as a vehicle for the expression of ideas about the political meaning of America. John Winthrop's exhortation to his fellow travelers on board the *Arbella* in 1629 outlined a social order grounded in faith and guided by divine providence. Winthrop's blending of religious and civil themes was a strategy common among dissenting bodies in England, and it foretold the emergence of the sermon in America as the principal means whereby the relation between religion and national identity was delineated. Not all of the thousands of sermons heard by a New Englander over a lifetime were aimed at clarifying the meanings of Winthrop's "city on a hill." Many sermons were preached simply to encourage piety or to explain points of doctrine. What mattered was the capability of the sermon to function *both* as an instrument of religious exhortation and teaching *and* as a means of expression of religio-political conceptualizations. The sermon was a versatile and fluid form of communication. That fluidity was essential to the adaptation of the sermon to a wide variety of contexts, as America grew and changed as a nation.

From seventeenth-century Puritan sermons that featured lengthy explications of doctrine, to the emotional sermons of the Great Awakening, to the unabashedly political sermons of the Revolutionary War years, the form evolved over the years. In the nineteenth century the sermon was adapted to a much wider range of functions. For John Nevin the sermon was a means to encourage ecumenism, whereas Ralph Waldo Emerson used the sermon to provoke his audiences to reflection on the beauty of God and nature. Charles Finney designed a program of "new-measures" conversionist techniques around the sermon, and William Channing sought to enlighten his audiences to the path of rational progress. In the course of working out their religious beliefs, these ministers came to understand the role of the sermon in different ways. Those diverse understandings were reflected in their various utilizations of the sermon as a dramatic device for communication.

As ministers adapted the sermon to suit their messages, certain styles of preaching became associated with certain ministers. During the Great Awakening, the personality of George Whitefield was unmistakably associated with the rousing sermons he preached throughout the colonies. The same was true with Charles Finney and his "new-measures" preaching in New York beginning in the 1820s. With the emergence in the nineteenth century of a remarkably wide range of perspectives on religion

[41] Nathan O. Hatch, *The Democratization of Christianity* (New Haven, 1989), 211.

came many different styles of preaching. Many new movements sprang from the rich religious ferment of the time, as older denominations underwent change and sometimes division from within. As an increasingly large number of religious groups competed for members, preachers sought ever more diligently to devise styles of communication and dramatization that affected their audiences. The result was that the personality of the preacher to an increasing extent became the most significant component of American homiletics. By 1877 Phillips Brooks, the Episcopal bishop of Boston's Trinity Church, was informing Yale Divinity School students that preaching was the transmission of religious truth through the contagion of a strong personality.[42] In the twentieth century, and especially in the age of electronic media, this view influenced a great many religious leaders—Protestant, Catholic, and Jewish.

Preaching was an important component of the religion of Jews in America. Jews who migrated to America from Europe brought with them little in the way of a preaching tradition that corresponded to the emphases in Protestantism. The rabbi was essentially a teacher whose responsibilities revolved around the application of the Torah to the circumstances of the congregation. Jewish culture was rich with folktales, however, that transmitted moral lessons and offered spiritual insight, and thus to some extent accomplished the sorts of things that Protestants might expect from a sermon. Under the influence of Protestantism in America, this form of Jewish sermonizing was developed to form a significant part of the religious life of a congregation. Some Jewish congregations enlarged the role of the rabbi to include regular preaching, and other congregations went so far as to create a new office in the synagogue, that of "preaching minister." Accordingly, preaching ability became an important consideration in evaluating a rabbi's talents, and the sermon eventually became a regular feature of the Jewish liturgy.

An early instance of the emergence of preaching in a Jewish congregation in America took place in a Sephardic congregation in Philadelphia. In 1829 Isaac Leeser, the newly elected cantor, began to preach regular sermons. Leeser later observed that "at that period, the duties of the minister were confined to the conducting of the public worship in the synagogue and elsewhere, and it was not accepted that he should be at the same time a preacher and exhorter."[43] Over time the congregation became accustomed to Leeser's exhortations, giving official approval to the practice in 1843. Other congregations soon afterward came to expect regular preaching, and as rabbis began to come to America after 1840, they learned to adapt to the expectations of their congregations. None was

---

[42] See *Lectures on Preaching* (New York, 1877); Raymond W. Albright, *Focus on Infinity: A Life of Phillips Brooks* (N.Y., 1961), 187–89.

[43] Leeser is quoted in Leon A. Jick, *The Americanization of the Synagogue, 1820–1870* (Hanover, N.H., 1976), 61.

more successful in this regard than Isaac Meyer Wise, who arrived in Albany in 1846 and whose preaching, according to Leeser who visited him there, was eloquent and gratifying.

Preaching had long been an important part of Roman Catholic religious life. In the course of the Catholic liturgy, the priest traditionally had delivered a homily, which was shorter and generally less elaborate than the Protestant sermon. The form of the Catholic sermon, however, was as fluid as the Protestant. Preaching from the pulpit, a priest could explain doctrine, exhort his audience to greater devotion, transmit the evolving social viewpoint of the church, promote morality, or address pressing local issues. Sometimes the priest took a verse of Scripture as a point of departure for the homily, whereas at other times he began with a message from the bishop or the Pope.

Among some Protestants, the sermon came to be understood as the primary means by which divine grace was communicated to persons. This was never the case in the Catholic Church, where the homily remained but one part of Catholic services. The American context gave rise to an increased Catholic concern with preaching, however. In fact, among some of the so-called Roman Catholic Americanists of the nineteenth century, the sermon came to occupy an elevated place in church services. In the mid-nineteenth century Isaac Hecker of New York, a convert from Methodism and a Catholic priest, incorporated into his missionary campaign the revivalistic style of Protestant preaching, with very favorable results. Hecker later was admonished by the Vatican for seeking to "Americanize" Catholicism, but his belief in the importance of the sermon illustrates the trend toward progressively greater attention to the homily in Catholic worship. By the mid-twentieth century, Catholic seminary curriculum included a very substantial commitment to homiletics, and Catholic congregations had come to expect carefully crafted sermons as a part of their weekly services.

Preaching was particularly important in African-American congregations, and the figure of the black preacher loomed large in the slave world as well as in the segregated world of free blacks. African-American hopes and aspirations, as well as recollections of bondage, were focused on the figure of the preacher, who served not only as a spiritual guide and exhorter, but as the only person tolerated by whites as a voice for the African-American community. "The Preacher," wrote W.E.B. DuBois, "is the most unique personality developed by the Negro on American soil. A leader, a politician, an orator, a 'boss,' an intriguer, and idealist, —all these he is. . . ."[44]

Methodist and Baptist churches had welcomed blacks as members, and unlike many other churches they were prepared to offer them a share of the authority exercised by church leaders. Blacks with the "gift of preach-

---

[44] W.E.B. DuBois, *The Souls of Black Folk* (Chicago, 1903), 190.

ing" were enlisted to serve as exhorters and in numerous instances as preachers and pastors. These black preachers were taught to read and some were eventually ordained, but most commonly they continued as exhorters. Black preaching, encouraged by revivalistic Methodist and Baptist churches in the nineteenth century, featured an emotional style of preaching, oftentimes a kind of shouting, or as DuBois wrote, a "Frenzy."[45]

In addition to the evangelical themes of sin, rebirth, and salvation, black preaching was characterized by references to Old Testament stories about the enslavement of the Jews and their eventual liberation. In the hands of black preachers, these stories served not only as spiritual sustenance, but as commentary on the predicament of blacks throughout American history, and as inspiration for continuing their struggle against racist inequality. During the nineteenth century the sermon came to be the chief means by which African-American communities expressed their disappointments, hopes, and political and social visions. It was through the sermon that Dr. Martin Luther King inspired popular support for the civil rights movement in the 1960s.

Women who believed themselves called to the ministry but who were denied ordination in the churches also became itinerant preachers. This was by no means an easy undertaking for women, who had little in the way of models for their calling. Nancy Towle, who traveled extensively as a preacher in the 1820s and 1830s, recollected her call to preach as a confusing experience: "I sometimes felt a longing desire to go 'into all the world and preach the Gospel to every creature.' In imagination I was there; and in dreams of the night I was there. . . . But, nevertheless, I was not able to understand, how this could be, consistently required of me."[46]

Some women preached through a connection with a denomination, as was the case with Susan Humes, who acquired a reputation as a preacher at Methodist camp meetings in New England in the early 1820s.[47] Other women preachers charted new territory. Phoebe Palmer of New York, a member of the Methodist Episcopal church, undertook highly successful evangelistic tours in the United States and Canada and was instrumental in organizing the Holiness movement. In her lengthy defense of female preaching, *Promise of the Father* (1859), she argued that inspired preaching warranted a woman's "overstepping the precincts of her own church fold."[48] Like African-Americans, women in the nineteenth century discovered that a reputation as an effective preacher could give them public standing on a level with an ordained minister. And in the religiously

[45] *Ibid.*, 191.
[46] Nancy Towle, *Vicissitudes Illustrated, in the Experience of Nancy Towle* (Portsmouth, N.H., 1833), 22.
[47] *Ibid.*, 37–38.
[48] Palmer, *Promise of the Father* (Boston, 1859), 357.

charged culture of nineteenth-century America, that was no mean accomplishment.

By the mid-nineteenth century, persons from all corners of society were preaching sermons of many different sorts. In practice, preaching came to represent freedom and democracy in America. In fact, one historian has concluded that by the time of the Civil War "the sermon had become a metaphor for the culture of America."[49] It was no accident that Herman Melville presented the central theme of *Moby Dick* (1851) in a sermon preached by Father Mapple in Whaleman's Chapel. And what was Mapple's conclusion about the nature of duty to God? "To preach Truth in the face of Falsehood."[50]

[49] William B. Lawrence, "The History of Preaching in America," *Encyclopedia of the American Religious Experience*, ed. Charles H. Lippy and Peter W. Williams, 3 (N.Y., 1988), 1317.
[50] Melville, *Moby-Dick, or The Whale* (N.Y., 1947), 46.

CHAPTER 8

Utopianism, Millennialism, and Humanitarianism

The first half of the nineteenth century in the United States was a time of eager expectancy, unbridled enthusiasm, and restless ferment. A new nation and a new world were being born, and to many anything and everything seemed possible. It was a period when the comet's tail was said to have swept America and everyone went a little mad. "We are all a little wild here with numberless projects of social reform," Emerson wrote to Carlyle in the autumn of 1840. "Not a reading man but has a draft of a new community in his waistcoat pocket." The hyperbole is obvious.

Not everyone went mad. Many were sufficiently prosaic to think that nothing more than a watch belonged in a waistcoat pocket. Still there were many who were not of the mind or spirit to keep their expectations under control. Although European visitors were impressed by the popularity and vigor of conventional religion, they were also struck by the many new ways to heaven being fashioned in America and by the strenuous efforts of others to give the heavenly existence earthly embodiment.

Two factors combined to produce the unusual religious ferment of these years. One was the social context. The other was the religious climate. In the American environment there was an absence of tradition and a sense of pregnant possibility that encouraged a spirit of experimentation. Nor was this experimentation inhibited by law. Unlimited freedom had been granted religious expression, no matter how eccentric it might be. And an abundance of cheap land and open space provided an unequaled opportunity to implement and institutionalize religious ideas. If the context was hospitable to innovation, the actual impetus that gave rise to most of the novel cults, sects, and movements was the climate of opinion generated by successive waves of revivalism.

Noah Worcester had pointed out in 1794 that the "sects" had profited from revivals, and this continued to be true (although it was also true that revivals often functioned as catalysts for unity among the large denominations). Successive harvests were to be reaped by the Shakers, the Mormons, the Oneida community, the Millerites, the Spiritualists, and a host of smaller and more transient groups. The revivals left many individuals distraught and torn by anxiety; and, having tried without success to gain a sense of assurance in their own churches, they were in a receptive mood to listen to new prophets who offered definite guarantees of spiritual security. Although the emotional disturbance that revivalism left in its wake explains why even the most bizarre groups, once established, could garner adherents, it does not account for their origin. Here it was the spirit — ideas, attitudes, hopes — fostered by the revivals that played the creative role.

Three emphases stimulated by revivalistic preaching were of decisive importance in creating the climate of enthusiasm out of which the new cults, sects, and communities emerged. For one thing, the revivalists demanded an immediate confrontation with God. This often took the form of an ecstatic vision or mystical illumination that could easily be interpreted as a new revelation. Second, the revivalists placed increasing stress upon the possibility of perfect sanctification, thus arousing a hunger for holiness and a life free from sin. Finally, they tended to dwell upon the ancient millennial expectation of a golden age to come, whether inaugurated by the personal return of Christ or established through the preaching of the gospel. All the groups that deviated from the norm of conventional religion during these years stemmed from at least one of these emphases, and most represented a blending of all three.[1]

The Utopian Vision

A prominent feature of the first half of the nineteenth century in America was the rise and decline of a variety of communal societies. All of them were impelled by a vision of an ideal or perfect life which they sought to actualize. These societies were never numerous, nor was the total number of adherents great. Most of them quickly appeared and as quickly disappeared. Only a few maintained themselves for any considerable period of time. Some were nonreligious in origin and orientation, and these exhibited the least staying power. Some were imported from abroad — the Rappites at "Harmony" in western Pennsylvania and later at "Harmony" in Indiana; the Separatists of "Zoar" in Ohio; the followers of William Keil at "Bethel" in Missouri and "Aurora" in Oregon; the Amana Society

---

[1] See A. L. Jamison, "Religions on the Christian Perimeter," in *The Shaping of American Religion,* ed. J. W. Smith and A. L. Jamison, 197–202.

(The Community of True Inspiration) at "Ebenezer" near Buffalo and then in Iowa; the community of Swedish immigrants established by Eric Janson at Bishop Hill in Illinois. With the partial exception of William Keil's Rappite seceders, all of these immigrant groups remained isolated from American life. But there also were indigenous communal societies. Of the indigenous communities where men and women sought sanctification in a perfect society, the Shaker settlements of Ann Lee and the Oneida community of John Humphrey Noyes were the most important. The Transcendentalist ventures at Fruitlands, Brook Farm, and Hopedale, on the other hand, were more typical in that they illustrated the pathos of shattered hopes that was the lot of most of the communal enterprises.

The Shakers

The followers of Ann Lee (1736–84) provide an outstanding example of the blending of new revelation with perfectionist and millenarian ideas in the formation of a communal society.[2] Although "Mother Ann" had come to America with eight followers in 1774, the United Society of Believers in Christ's Second Appearing was not organized until 1787, three years after her death, when a former Free-Will Baptist preacher took charge and gave the Society its definitive shape.

Ann was the wife of a blacksmith in Manchester, England, and the mother of four children, all of whom died in infancy. She had become a member of a small group of Shaking Quakers who were crying out warnings of Christ's approaching second advent and predicting that famine and pestilence were about to descend upon the wicked. The distinguishing feature of their worship, which gave them their name, was the frequency with which they would be "seized with a mighty trembling, with a violent agitation of the body, running and walking on the floor, with singing, shouting, and leaping for joy."[3] In 1770 Ann became the vehicle of a revelation that the root of human depravity and the source of all evils afflicting mankind was the sex act. This was the forbidden fruit, the original sin of Adam and Eve. In the words of a Shaker hymn:

> As lust conceived by the Fall
> Hath more or less infected all;
> So we believe 'tis only this
> That keepeth souls from perfect bliss.

---

[2] See Edward D. Andrews, *The People Called Shakers: A Search for the Perfect Society* (N.Y., 1953); and Henri Desroache, *The American Shakers: From Neo-Christianity to Presocialism* (Amherst, Mass., 1971).

[3] See contemporary account in Smith, Handy, and Loetscher, *American Christianity*, I, 586–96. Also D. W. Patterson, *The Shaker Spiritual* (Princeton, 1980).

The basic summons was to a celibate life, and it was about this emphasis that Ann gathered her first little company of disciples.

After leaving England and settling in Watervliet, New York, Ann gained no new adherents until 1779, when a revival at New Lebanon proved so disturbing that it brought Joseph Meacham and several members of his congregation into the fold. Other recruits were won as scattered revivals began to appear in western Massachusetts and Connecticut. During the final four years of her life, Ann was reported to have performed miracles that convinced her followers that she was Christ in his "second appearing," making manifest the female element in the Godhead and inaugurating the beginning of the millennium by gathering a faithful remnant out of the churches of Antichrist.

In 1787, three years after the death of Mother Ann, Joseph Meacham assumed leadership of the group, gathered the members into several "families" for communal living, drafted the constitution of the United Society, and elaborated and systematized Shaker doctrine. Everything was carefully regulated, and the violence of the earlier physical manifestations was subdued and reduced to a ritualistic dance (e.g., "square order shuffle"; "circle dance") in which worship was expressed by the body as well as by speech and song. In the new order that was at hand, all that had been "earthly, sensual, devilish" would become "spiritual, divine, and heavenly," and the whole endeavor of the Shakers was to live a life of perfection as preparation for the perfect state promised to them. Since there would be no further need for the propagation of the human race in the new age, the inclusion of celibacy among the 12 virtues that must be pursued and practiced did not seem unreasonable.

Under Meacham's leadership the Society experienced a surge of growth with the onset of the Second Awakening. Within five years ten communities with more than 2,000 members had been formed in Maine, New Hampshire, Massachusetts, Connecticut, and New York. A second period of growth began in 1805 when emissaries were sent west to reap a harvest in the wake of the great Kentucky revival, including two of the prominent leaders of the revival — Richard McNemar and John Dunlavy. By 1825 there were at least 20 communities scattered throughout Ohio, Indiana, and Kentucky, as well as in New England and New York, and within a few years the Society had about 6,000 members.

Economically the Shakers prospered from the start. Farming was the basis of their economy, but they quickly developed successful commercial and handicraft enterprises. After 1837 the various communities were troubled by a wild burst of spirit-inspired communications that created a deep fear of any further enthusiasm. After this loss of fervor and with the waning of rural revivalism, the Shakers attracted fewer and fewer new members. Although the communities remained prosperous, a steady decline in numbers had set in by 1850. A century later only a handful of elderly men and women remained.

The Oneida Community

Whereas the Shakers were seeking perfection in celibacy, others were going to the opposite extreme with their claims to holiness and even venturing into unorthodox or curiously ordered sexual relationships. Opposed to the "spiritual wifery" that swept through certain perfectionist circles, John Humphrey Noyes was at the same time the most conspicuous perfectionist leader who placed a stamp of approval upon a departure from the accepted code of sexual relationships.[4]

Noyes was a product of the Finney revivals. A graduate of Dartmouth and the son of a successful Vermont businessman who was prominent in state politics, Noyes had begun the study of law when Finney captured him for the ministry and sent him off for a year at Andover Seminary and two years at Yale Divinity School. When he asserted that conversion brought complete release from sin, he was refused ordination. This, however, did not keep him from preaching wherever he could find groups of like-minded perfectionists and from giving further study to what he called "the Sin system, the Marriage system, the Work system, and the Death system." After much pondering, he concluded that it was necessary to create a society in which conditions would be favorable to the practice of perfection. He was later to declare that, as "the revivalists had for their great idea the regeneration of the soul," he had as his great idea "the regeneration of society, which is the soul's environment."[5]

Noyes' communitarianism was based on three fundamental doctrines. The first was total security from sin, but this security was so defined that it did not eliminate the need of discipline and improvement. The second was the conviction that the millennium had been introduced in A.D. 70, but had been obscured by spurious postmillennial growths of the second and third centuries. The third was the insistence that, since the saints were equally yoked in dedication to their faith, the practice of primitive Christian communism — a communism that included the marriage relationship — was the only logical arrangement.

Noyes gathered a small group in Putney, Vermont, and in the early 1840s instituted a communism of property. When this communism was extended in 1846 by putting into operation his theory of "complex marriage," the local citizens were aroused; to avoid the possibility of being mobbed, the community was reestablished at Oneida, New York, two years later. A major stroke of luck was the conversion of Samuel Newhouse, the inventor of a highly effective small-animal trap. Trap manufacturing placed the community on a sound financial basis, until it was

---

[4] See Lawrence Foster, *Religion and Sexuality: Three American Communal Experiments* (N.Y., 1980); M. L. Carden, *Oneida: Utopian Community to Modern Corporation* (N.Y., 1977); and Louis J. Kern, *An Ordered Love: Sex Roles and Sexuality in Victorian America: The Shakers, the Mormons and the Oneida Community* (Chapel Hill, N.C., 1981).

[5] J. H. Noyes, *History of American Socialism* (Philadelphia, 1870), 24. See also Tyler, *Freedom's Ferment*, 186.

replaced as the chief industry by silverplate ("Community Plate") production. But economic considerations were incidental. The philosophy of the community was stated by Noyes in these words:

> Our warfare is an assertion of human rights; first the right of man to be governed by God and to live in the social state of heaven; second the right of woman to dispose of her sexual nature by attraction instead of by law and routine and to bear children only when she chooses; third the right of all to diminish the labors and increase the advantages of life by association.

These principles, he insisted, must find expression in "one living organization before the Kingdom of Heaven can come." Thus, personal sanctification and social regeneration went hand-in-hand.[6]

Although Noyes fashioned a detailed and closely supervised pattern of life for the community, including procedures for "mutual criticism" and innovations in the education of children, it was the theory and practice of "complex marriage" that gained its notoriety for the community. This theory, which regarded each woman in the group as the wife of every man and every man as the husband of every woman, was instituted on religious grounds. Noyes' followers thought of themselves as saints purified by religious experience and disciplined to the practice of absolute fellowship among themselves by a total love of God. As a consequence, they believed there was a basic incompatibility between absolute good will among the regenerate and the exclusive legal and physical bonds of conventional marriage. "Sexual communion," Noyes insisted, "differs only in its superior intensity and beauty from other acts of love" and it contributes to true mutuality. But when sexual communion is restricted to acts of "special love" it becomes unsocial and dangerous to communal interests. The Oneida perfectionists resented the charge that they were practicing "free love," for sexual intercourse among them was "organized" rather than promiscuous, and they believed it was inspired by true spirituality.

For 30 years the community remained true to its original ideals, but pressure from the outside world persuaded Noyes in 1879 to abandon the practice of "complex marriage." This in turn led to the abandonment of communal ownership of property the following year. A joint-stock company was formed, the shares were distributed among the former communitarians, and silverplated tableware became the chief reminder of their former effort to institutionalize a sinless life and thus provide a foretaste of the kingdom of God.

Transcendentalism's "Wild Oats"

When Emerson spoke of the draft of utopia to be found in almost every reading man's waistcoat pocket, he was thinking preeminently of some of his fellow Transcendentalists, for in a curiously romantic way they also

---

[6] Cross, *The Burned-over District*, 335, 337.

had appropriated the perfectionist and millenarian tendencies of the time. Emerson himself remained skeptical, but others were driven by an overpowering desire to anticipate the millennium by perfecting human institutions. Three small communal societies—Fruitlands, Brook Farm, and Hopedale—were the product of what in retrospect can be seen as their moment of aberration.[7]

Louisa May Alcott's *The Transcendental Wild Oats* is a fictionalized account of Bronson Alcott's venture in communal living at Fruitlands, which began with high hopes in the spring of 1843 and collapsed before winter set in. Believing that "our freer, but yet far from freed, land is the asylum . . . for the hope of man," Bronson Alcott was convinced that only in America could "the second Eden . . . be planted in which the divine seed is to bruise the head of Evil and restore Man to his rightful communion with God in the Paradise of Good." This was his vision of Fruitlands. Unfortunately, what might have been at least a summer's idyl was spoiled by the domineering spirit of Charles Lane, a dour ascetic Englishman, who was determined that every natural human desire should be denied. One by one the members slipped away, the crops were left unharvested, and Lane finally departed to join the Shakers.

Brook Farm was a happier experiment. George Ripley, Unitarian minister and leading member of the "Transcendental Club," was its founder and director. In 1840, before resigning from the pulpit of his Purchase Street congregation in Boston, Ripley had told his parishioners that it was the business of Christianity to overthrow every social evil, and Brook Farm was designed to be, "if not the sunrise," at least "the morning star" of the new day in which the thinker and the manual laborer would be united in a noncompetitive society.

Most of the literary lights of the time participated at Brook Farm either as members, visitors, or supporters. The intellectual life at the Farm was exciting, and the social life, which included plays, dances, picnics, and boating parties, was gay. Since the members were better dreamers than farmers, the community was dependent upon outside support except for the income derived from its school, which was recommended by the Harvard faculty as an excellent place to send young boys who aspired to become college students. In 1844, however, the members became entranced by the ideas of the French socialist Charles Fourier (1772–1837) and decided to turn Brook Farm into a Fourierist phalanx. This necessitated conforming to a rigid theory of social organization and involved establishing industries, forming specialized labor groups, and ritualizing sexual relations. Money was borrowed, the school was neglected, and in

---

[7] See Clara E. Sears, *Bronson Alcott's Fruitlands, with Transcendental Wild Oats by Louisa Alcott* (Boston, 1915); Zoltan Haraszti, *The Idyll of Brook Farm* (Boston, 1937); Adin Ballou, *History of the Hopedale Community* (Lowell, Mass., 1897); Mark Holloway, *Heavens on Earth: Utopian Communities in America* (N.Y., 1966).

1846 a fire left the community insolvent. By this time many of the sponsors had lost interest, having been diverted by newer fads, and in 1847 the community wound up its affairs. Later Nathaniel Hawthorne looked back with nostalgia to "our beautiful scheme of a noble and unselfish life" at the Farm. "How fair in that first summer appeared the prospect that it might endure for generations, and be perfected as the ages rolled by into the system of a people and a world. Were my former associates now there — were there only three or four of those true-hearted men still laboring in the sun — I sometimes fancy that I should direct my world-weary footsteps thitherward and entreat them to receive me for old friendship's sake."

The community at Hopedale was a less dilettantish effort. Established near Milford, Massachusetts, in 1841, it managed to maintain itself for 15 years. Adin Ballou, a Universalist minister, was the founder and guiding spirit. He was not a member of the "Club," but was a Transcendentalist nonetheless and a friend of Channing and Parker. Since "it was one of the declared objects of Christ's labors to inaugurate the kingdom of heaven on earth," Ballou was convinced that "the imperative duty" of Christ's disciples is "to pray and to work for that sublime end." Working meant "actualizing" New Testament teachings in order to initiate a world movement toward the perfect life. Some 30 persons responded to Ballou's summons to subject themselves to "all the moral obligations" of the religion of Jesus and to take the lead in banishing from the world "all things known to be sinful against God or human nature." Ten years later the community had grown to nearly 200 members and was a moderate financial success. But when Ballou retired from active leadership, it was decided that the common fund would be more productive if diverted to private enterprise, and in 1856 the whole project was liquidated. The failure, Ballou remarked with sadness, was not financial but "moral and spiritual" — "a deficiency among its members of those graces and powers of character which are requisite to the realization of the Christian ideal of human society."

Other Variant Religious Groups

Utopian communities that sought to reproduce the heavenly existence in earthly institutions were but one manifestation of the religious ferment of the first half of the nineteenth century. Other variant groups came to the fore in which the perfectionist motif was more subdued. Such groups as the Mormons, the Millerites, and the Spiritualists were no less symptomatic of the energies released by the prevailing religious climate, but they found their primary orientation in some other point of emphasis — in a new and supplementary revelation, in the reduction of the millennial expectation to a definite timetable of events, in the sudden bursting of the barriers to the spirit world.

THE

BOOK OF MORMON:

AN ACCOUNT WRITTEN BY THE HAND OF MOR-MON, UPON PLATES TAKEN FROM THE PLATES OF NEPHI.

Wherefore it is an abridgment of the Record of the People of Nephi; and also of the Lamanites; written to the Lamanites, which are a remnant of the House of Israel; and also to Jew and Gentile; written by way of commandment, and also by the spirit of Prophesy and of Revelation. Written, and sealed up, and hid up unto the Lord, that they might not be destroyed; to come forth by the gift and power of God unto the interpretation thereof; sealed by the hand of Moroni, and hid up unto the Lord, to come forth in due time by the way of Gentile; the interpretation thereof by the gift of God; an abridgment taken from the Book of Ether.

Also, which is a Record of the People of Jared, which were scattered at the time the Lord confounded the language of the people when they were building a tower to get to Heaven: which is to shew unto the remnant of the House of Israel how great things the Lord hath done for their fathers; and that they may know the covenants of the Lord, that they are not cast off forever; and also to the convincing of the Jew and Gentile that Jesus is the Christ, the Eternal God, manifesting Himself unto all nations. And now if there be fault, it be the mistake of men; wherefore condemn not the things of God, that ye may be found spotless at the judgment seat of Christ.

BY JOSEPH SMITH, JUNIOR,

AUTHOR AND PROPRIETOR.

PALMYRA:

PRINTED BY E. B. GRANDIN, FOR THE AUTHOR.

1830.

Title Page of the First Edition of the Book of Mormon, *printed by the author. (Courtesy of Lowell H. Fewster and the Ambrose Swasey Library, Colgate Rochester Divinity School.)*

The Mormons

The Church of Jesus Christ of Latter-day Saints which was to create for itself a great intramountain empire in the West had its origin in the remarkable story of Joseph Smith, who in 1816 at the age of ten had come with his parents from Vermont to the vicinity of Palmyra, New York.[8] Here he absorbed much from the religious excitement of what came to be called "the burned-over district." Smith later reported that he was greatly disturbed by the religious controversies that swirled about him. "In the midst of this war of words and tumult of opinions, I often said to myself, what is to be done? Who of all these parties be right? Or are they all wrong together?" Troubled by these anxieties, he "retired to the woods" to seek wisdom of God. His prayer was answered by the appearance of two heavenly personages — the Father and the Son — who told him to hold himself apart from the contending denominations, for a special task was to be given him. After a period of testing in which he received a series of further revelations, he was guided by the angel Moroni to discover long-buried golden plates that told the story of the Nephites and Lamanites, descendants of a lost tribe of Israel, who had inhabited the American continent centuries before. Among them Christ had appeared after his resurrection and had established the proper church order. The Lamanites, progenitors of the Indians, had apostatized and had defeated the faithful Nephites in a battle in which all the Nephites except Mormon and his son Moroni were slain. The records of this ancient people were buried by Moroni in the hill Cumorah, and it was there that Smith discovered them together with the translating spectacles that enabled him to decipher what he later described as the Reformed Egyptian hieroglyphics of the text. In 1830 Smith's translation of the *Book of Mormon* was published at Palmyra.

This new scripture provided a basis for resolving the sectarian jangling that Smith had found so disturbing, for it gave an authoritative judgment upon almost every issue that was in dispute. This fact was quickly recognized by Alexander Campbell, who pointed out in his *Delusions: An Analysis of the Book of Mormon* (1832) that the golden plates had anticipated and given a definitive answer to "every error and almost every truth discussed in New York for the last ten years," including "infant baptism, ordination, the trinity, regeneration, repentance, justification, the fall of man, the atonement, transubstantiation, fasting, penance, church government, religious experience, the call to the ministry, the general resurrection, eternal punishment, who may baptize, and even the question of freemasonry, republican government, and the rights of man." And the *Book of Mormon* even provided for the future adjudication of controversy by insisting that

---

[8] A recent account of Mormonism is L. J. Arrington, *The Mormon Experience* (N.Y., 1979). See also Jan Shipps, *Mormonism: The Story of a Religious Tradition* (Urbana, Ill., 1985).

anyone who denies "the revelations of God" and says "that they are done away, that there are no revelations, nor prophecies, nor gifts, nor speaking with tongues and interpretation of tongues" denies "the gospel of Christ."

It is scarcely surprising that one of the first converts to embrace the new revelation was Sidney Rigdon, an ex-Disciple minister who had once contested Campbell's leadership, for the *Book of Mormon* stressed many of the basic themes of Campbellite preaching—free grace, free will, repentance, restoration, plainness of doctrine, opposition to "priestcraft," rejection of infant baptism, and even the distinctive Campbellite doctrine of baptism "unto the remission of sins." Nor in view of this heritage is it surprising that when young Joseph Smith on October 30, 1830, met with five friends in Fayette, New York, to restore "the Church of Christ in these last days," he should have chosen the typically Campbellite designation of "Church of Christ" for his reincarnation of the ancient order of church life. Four years later, at the instigation of Rigdon, the name was changed to the Church of the Latter-day Saints, and in 1838 it was given its present expanded form.

Another theme of the *Book of Mormon*, which had wide appeal to people who were stirred by the romantic nationalism of the time, was the portrayal of America as the promised land—"a land which is choice above all other lands," a land to which none shall come "save they shall be brought by the hand of the Lord." Indeed, the whole biblical setting of the drama of salvation was transferred to American soil. To the successive declarations of political, economic, diplomatic, and intellectual independence penned by Jefferson, Clay, Monroe, and Emerson was now added a declaration of religious independence. The Old World heritage was rendered both obsolete and irrelevant, for the restoration of the true church depended upon the recovery of an independent American tradition that extended back to the time of the Babylonian Exile and was validated by the postresurrection appearance of Christ in America.

Prior to forming the new church, Smith had a revelation in which John the Baptist appeared and ordained him and Oliver Cowdery[9] to the "Priesthood of Aaron, which holds the keys of the ministering of angels, and of the gospel of repentance, and of baptism by immersion for the remission of sins." Thus equipped, he was directed to form the church by a revelation that designated "Joseph Smith, Jun., who was called of God and ordained an apostle of Jesus Christ, to be the first elder of this church," and "Oliver Cowdery, who was also called of God, an apostle of Jesus Christ, to be the second elder of this church." At the first meeting of the church, Smith's full office was made clear by a further revelation that

---

[9] Cowdery was Smith's clerical assistant. While in Vermont prior to moving to Palmyra, Cowdery had embraced some "extraordinary doctrines, apparently involving millennial expectations and direct revelation as well as some mysterious treasure hunting." Cross, *Burned-over District*, 38–39.

stated that he should "be called a seer, a translator, a prophet, an apostle of Jesus Christ, an elder of the church through the will of God the Father and the grace of your Lord Jesus Christ," with the added admonition that the church should "give heed unto all his words and command-ments . . . for his word shall ye receive as if from mine own mouth."

By 1830 the new scripture had been published, the new church formed, and the new prophet designated with powers of immediate revelation to deal with troublesome problems as they arose. In the course of time more distinctive doctrines were elaborated—a plurality of gods, for example, as well as of wives—which set the Mormons further and further apart from the generality of Christians. Adaptations of Masonic ritual were intro-duced, marriage for time and eternity was adopted, baptism for the dead was instituted, and the priesthood of Melchizedek was restored by the miraculous intervention of Peter, James, and John. Mormon millennial-ism, on the other hand, remained moderate and never became the focal point of enthusiasm. Its perfectionism was restrained, and the communi-tarianism introduced by Rigdon at Kirtland, Ohio, owed more to the Campbellite stress on the authoritative example of the New Testament church (see Acts 2:44–45; 4:34–35) than to any perfectionist drive. The communal tendencies were not central, being sustained by the exigencies of their hegira, and the United Order of Enoch—a form of cooperative economic activity—was never transformed into a full communism. Still it was clear that the Mormons were not a part of conventional society, and their separateness created antagonism. This hostility, in turn, increased their sense of separateness, and the sense of separateness encouraged further innovation.

The impact of Joseph Smith's new church in the area of its origin was scant, for it was removed almost immediately to Kirtland, Ohio, where Sidney Rigdon's congregation provided a larger nucleus of adherents. The growth of the church was astonishing, and new recruits were won in Missouri to where missionaries had been dispatched in a fruitless endeavor to convert the Indians. Trouble at Kirtland, stemming in part from the failure of Smith's "Anti-Banking Company" (so named to circumvent the legislature's refusal to grant a bank charter) in the Panic of 1837, led to shifting the base of operations to Independence and then Far West, Mis-souri. Pitched battles there brought about another removal, this time to Nauvoo, Illinois, where Smith attempted to establish a semi-independent domain. The tragic murder of Smith by an angry mob in 1844 while he was confined in the jail at Carthage precipitated one of the epic stories of American history—the heroic trek of the majority of the Mormons under the leadership of Brigham Young to a new "Zion in the Wilderness." Sheltered by the mountains surrounding the basin of the Great Salt Lake, they at last found a measure of peace and security. By 1870 the number of Mormons in the intramountain region exceeded 140,000, many of them converts who had been won abroad.

The Millerites

The movement that created the greatest flurry of excitement during the years of religious ferment had as its focus a specific date for the literal fulfillment of the ancient expectation that Christ would return in glory to rule upon the earth. In various forms the millennial hope had been a consistent theme of revivalistic preaching, and the increasing number of magnitude of revivals heightened the interest of many in the Second Coming. By 1825 references to the belief that the return of Christ was approaching became more numerous, and the phenomenal awakening of 1831 convinced many that it must be near. This millennial expectation was in part a reflection of the overpowering optimism and perfectionist temper of the American people, but the Panic of 1837 gave it another turn. With their buoyant optimism dissipated by the distress attendant upon an economic depression, many found in millennialism a compensatory substitute for their shattered hopes. An immediate judgment day became the simplest solution to all earthly problems, the shortest possible cut to millennial perfection, a panacea that would set all things right at a single stroke.

William Miller, a farmer at Low Hampton, New York, was the key figure in the Adventist excitement of the late 1830s and early 1840s.[10] After his conversion in 1816 he had become a member of the Baptist church and began to study the Bible with particular attention to the last times. Interested in calculating the date of Christ's return, he probably found the clue that pointed to 1843 in the Boston edition of the British *Christian Observer* or a similar publication. By nimble arithmetic (years of 360 days — twelve 30-day months — instead of 365), he was able to prove to his satisfaction that "God in his wisdom has so interwoven the several prophecies that . . . they tell us the same things." In 1828 he felt a "call" to tell the world of his discovery that Christ would come "about 1843." "I tried to excuse myself," he later explained. "I told the Lord that I was not used to speaking . . . that I was slow of speech and slow of tongue. But I could get no relief." By 1831 he developed sufficient courage to begin to issue local warnings by sharing his discovery with neighbors and friends. He was asked to discuss his views in a nearby church, and he suddenly found that on this one subject at least he was eloquent. Invitations multiplied and he began to gain a measure of local fame. Although he was never ordained, Miller's ministerial status was somewhat regularized in 1833 with a license to preach.

Although revivalism had bred a mentality that predisposed many to become ready converts to Miller's dating of the end of time, three events combined to give him a more than local reputation. The first was the

[10] See Ernest Sandeen's chapter, "The Millenarian Tradition in the United States, 1800–1845," in his *The Roots of Fundamentalism* (Chicago, 1970); also F. D. Nichol, *The Midnight Cry* (Washington, D.C., 1944).

publication in 1836 of his computations in book form under the title *Evidence from Scripture and History of the Second Coming of Christ, About the Year 1843*. The second was the Panic of 1837, which created for the book an unusually receptive audience. The third was the chance discovery of Miller by Joshua V. Himes at Exeter, New Hampshire, in 1839 while Miller was on a speaking tour of New England. Minister of a Christian Connection church in Boston and an indefatigable promoter, Himes had all the gifts that a century later would be associated with Madison Avenue. He immediately sensed the potency of the message of the plain-spoken farmer, and attached himself to Miller as his manager and publicity agent. He equipped Miller with a great chart displaying Miller's calculations in graphic form, purchased the biggest tent in the country for Miller's meetings, edited two journals—the *Midnight Cry* in New York and *Signs of the Times* in Boston—and helped found others in Philadelphia, Cincinnati, Cleveland, Rochester, and Montreal. Other evangelists were recruited and sent on speaking tours; camp meetings were organized; children's books, catechisms, tracts, pamphlets, and even a hymnbook, *The Millenial Harp*, were published.

Despite vigorous condemnation of the movement by the majority of ministers and ridicule by neighbors and friends, thousands were convinced by Miller's detailed calculations. Members of all denominations were enlisted, for the Adventist cause was nonsectarian and noncreedal, but Baptists, Free-Will Baptists, and "Christians" seem to have been the most susceptible. At the height of the Millerite fever there were probably more than 50,000 convinced believers and there may have been as many as a million others who were skeptically expectant.

Miller had been hesitant to be more specific than to say that Christ would return "about 1843," but in January 1843 he announced that *this* year (from March 21, 1843, to March 21, 1844, taking into account the change in the calendar year) must see the end of time. The tension mounted as the year progressed, and was heightened by the appearance of a comet in the heavens. Meetings grew larger and converts more numerous, but March 21, 1844, came—and time still continued. On May 2, Miller confessed his error and acknowledged his disappointment, but one of his followers called attention to Habakkuk 2:3 and Leviticus 25:9 and announced that there obviously was to be a "tarrying time" of seven months and ten days. October 22, 1844, was to be the day of Christ's triumphant return and people were rallied once again with the slogan: "The Tenth Day of the Seventh Month." Miller was finally converted to the new date: "I see a glory in the seventh month which I never saw before. Thank the Lord, O my soul! . . . I am almost home. Glory! Glory! Glory! I see that the time is correct." The excitement revived, and the number living each moment as if it were their last exceeded that of the preceding summer.

With the second disappointment, most of those who had been caught up in the movement were completely disillusioned. The reaction of others was often bitter. Miller, for example, was excommunicated by the Baptist church at Low Hampton, and in 1849 he died, discredited and almost forgotten. A few became Shakers, giving that group its last important influx of new members. Some remained steadfast in their hope, believing that only a minor error in calculation had been made. They met in Albany in 1845 to form a conference that later splintered into three groups, the largest of which was the Advent Christian Church. Others, persuaded by Ellen Gould White that Christ's failure to appear was due to a neglect of proper Sabbath observance, formed the nucleus of what was to be the Seventh-day Adventist Church.

The Spiritualists

Before the Millerites had fully recovered from their disenchantment, "the Rochester rappings" of the Fox sisters in 1848 created a new sensation that led to the development of modern Spiritualism.[11] The way had been prepared by the teachings of Emmanuel Swedenborg (1688–1772), whose views had become something of a vogue among religious liberals and whose works had just been republished in a new English edition. Swedenborg claimed to have received communications from the spirit world by which knowledge of all things in the heavens and below the heavens had been given him. Interest in his teachings was reinforced by the spread of Mesmerism, which utilized the strange power of "animal magnetism" to produce a hypnotic trance that was thought to point to the basic laws of the spirit world and to give promise of unlocking the mysteries of the life beyond. All that was needed to transform these embryonic ideas into Spiritualism was a mechanism for communicating with the dead, and it was such a device that was supplied unwittingly by two young girls, Maggie and Katie Fox.

The "rappings" began at Hydesville, New York, as a childish prank which some adults took seriously and which was exploited by an older sister who lived in nearby Rochester. Soon the Fox sisters were holding public seances and notable converts were being won, including Horace Greeley, editor of the *New York Tribune*. By 1851 seven Spiritualist periodicals were being published, and six years later the number had increased to 67. The Universalists provided the most recruits, and although interest began to subside prior to the Civil War, the movement found institutional expression in a number of enduring Spiritualist "associations." Drawing upon a wide range of religious and psychological writings, and fueled as well by the emergent movement for women's rights, Spiritualism and female mediumship enjoyed several flurries of renewed enthusiasm. In

[11] See R. L. Moore, *In Search of White Crows: Spiritualism, Parapsychology, and American Culture* (N.Y., 1976); Ann Braude, *Radical Spirits: Spiritualism and Women's Rights in Nineteenth-Century America* (Boston, 1989).

1888 the Fox sisters acknowledged their hoax and demonstrated how they had produced the "rappings" by cracking their toe joints; but this exposure had little effect upon convinced believers.

The Humanitarian Impulse

Utopian communities and novel sectarian emphases were not the only expressions of religious ferment. Most of the enthusiasm generated by the Second Awakening was devoted to more conventional enterprises in which the concerns of the evangelically awakened often paralleled those of the heirs of Channing. The revivalists were generally postmillennialists who assumed that an era of peace, justice, and goodness would precede the return of Christ. Consequently where there were revivals, there must be reform. Every aspect of society began to be subjected to eager scrutiny in order to scour and purify the earth in preparation for God's final act of redemption. Scarcely any phase of American life was left untouched. Temperance, Sabbath observance, world peace, profanity, vice, women's rights, slavery, the condition of penal institutions, educational innovations—all became objects of concern. The whole impulse was carefully articulated in a series of related societies and closely integrated with revivalistic efforts, as was made clear in 1835 by Theodore Dwight Weld in a letter to Lewis Tappan.

> God has called some prophets, some apostles, and some teachers. All the members of the body of Christ have not the same office. Let Delevan drive temperance, McDowell moral reform, Finney revivals, Tappan antislavery, etc. Each of these is bound to make his own peculiar department his main business, and to promote collaterally as much as he can the other objects. I have no doubt but Finney has erred in not giving as much collateral attention to antislavery as the present emergent crisis demands. And I am equally certain that I have not done as much collaterally to promote temperance and revivals while I have been lecturing on slavery as I ought.[12]

The revivals provided the impetus, summoning men and women to battle against sin; and the reform movements were the implementation of the thrust toward the coming kingdom of righteousness. The task of those who enlisted in the struggle was put succinctly by Finney: "Every member must work or quit. No honorary members."

The Expanding Concern

Whereas initially the reforms were mainly limited to rectifying individual vices—such as infidelity, drunkenness, Sabbath breaking, dueling, gambling, and profanity—by methods of persuasion, the concern quickly

---

[12] *Letters of Theodore Dwight Weld*, ed. G. H. Barnes and D. L. Dumond (N.Y., 1934), I, 243.

expanded to include larger social issues. The masthead of the *New York Evangelist* illustrated the broadening of the reform impulse. In 1831, when it was insisting that "the emancipation of the world must engross the desires . . . and the enterprise of the world," the masthead announced that the paper was "Devoted to Revivals, Doctrinal Discussion and Religious Intelligence." In 1835 it added "Practical Godliness," and in 1837 "Human Rights." World peace was an early preoccupation, and colonization in Africa was promoted to solve the problem of slavery. Later antislavery sentiment was channeled into a demand for "immediate emancipation." Prison reform captured the interest of some, and a noted group of women spearheaded interest in female education and women's rights. The latter concerns culminated in the 1848 Seneca Falls Convention, held in the heart of Finneyite territory and convened by Elizabeth Cady Stanton, who had been introduced to evangelical reform activity first by her cousin and then by her husband.

Although Lyman Beecher in 1827 listed "monopoly of the soil" and the factory system as twin evils to be combatted, economic problems did not bulk large in the thinking of evangelical reformers. This was partly because they tended to think that individual conversions would remedy the ills of poverty, but primarily it was because an abundance of unsettled land in a largely agrarian society served as an escape valve for economic discontent. Antislavery agitation had deep economic implications, of course, and some dabbled with peripheral urban and labor problems when they established havens for out-of-work sailors and formed societies to reclaim prostitutes from their shame. The Panic of 1837 brought further hesitant steps in the direction of a social gospel. In 1842 revivalist Edward N. Kirk stressed the need to ferret out the causes of poverty and to apply remedies. In 1851 an influential Presbyterian layman, Stephen Colwell, published *New Themes for the Protestant Clergy* in which he advocated legislative enactments to better the condition of workingmen. Two or three years later the *Independent* began to urge programs of urban renewal which would have as their aim low rents, clean buildings, and healthy surroundings.

Although the reform activity in the beginning was a balanced thrust, with each reform being seen as part of a larger strategy, there was a tendency among many to move in the direction of what was called "ultraism" or "one-ideaism." This was a passionate concentration upon one particular reforming cause as the panacea for all human ills. Temperance, for example, tended to be thought of by many as the remedy for poverty, vice, corruption, brawling, ill health, premature death, and marital discord. The benefits to be derived from securing the rights of women were sometimes viewed from a similar universal perspective. Reforms of diet, dress, and education also became the objectives of specific crusades. Ultimately, the growth of antislavery sentiment terminated the "ultraist" dispersal of the reform movement by the simple expedient of focusing attention on the sin of slavery and absorbing the reformist energies and personnel into this one great cause.

The Slavery Controversy

Of all the reform crusades, the one that disrupted the churches and shook the nation to its foundations was the antislavery movement.[13] Other reform movements had taken an individualistic turn that enabled the existing denominations for the most part to contain them. They had developed within the context of revivalism, and most of them were no more than urgent summons to individuals to free themselves from the entanglement of sin. The antislavery crusade, as conducted by the evangelicals, had begun with the same emphasis. Although the adoption of the British motto — "immediate emancipation" — seemed to imply a drastic abolitionism, it was interpreted to mean "immediate emancipation gradually accomplished" or "gradual emancipation immediately begun." The emphasis was upon persuasion and a personal renunciation of slavery as sin. The campaign of Theodore Dwight Weld and his band of rebels recruited at Lane Theological Seminary and later expanded to a biblical "Seventy" exhibited all the characteristics and methods of revival meetings. The immediatism they preached was an immediate repentance of the sin of any personal involvement in and support of the slave system. However gradual the emancipation was to be, there was a point at which persuasion would end and abolition would be required, and as antislavery sentiment was intensified it became increasingly difficult to keep the movement from demanding that its moral standard be imposed and enforced by legislative action. As a convention of Christian abolitionists in Hamilton, New York, resolved in 1845: "Those who admit the sinfulness of slavery . . . and yet vote for oppression, or for those who are connected with pro-slavery parties, are guilty of the most inconsistency; and are underserving the name Christian patriots, and unworthy to be recognized as the true friends of downtrodden Christianity."[14]

The disruptive effect of antislavery agitation was accentuated because it appeared at a time when an equally aggressive proslavery movement was developing. During the first third of the century, many in the South were quite as critical of slavery as anyone in the North, but by the 1830's this sentiment had declined and highly vocal champions of the South's "peculiar institution" were beginning to dominate southern opinion. An influential factor in this shift was the increasing importance of cotton in the

[13] See G. H. Barnes, *The Antislavery Impulse, 1830–1844* (N.Y., 1933); D. L. Dumond, *Antislavery: The Crusade for Freedom* (Ann Arbor, Mich., 1961); and Bertram Wyatt-Brown, *Lewis Tappan and the Evangelical War Against Slavery* (N.Y., 1971).

[14] Quoted in John R. McKivigan, *The War Against Proslavery Religion: Abolitionism and the Northern Churches* (Ithaca, 1984), 147.

South's economy and the accompanying conviction that profitable cotton production depended upon slave labor. The bitter attacks of northern abolitionists also contributed to the consolidation of pro-slavery sentiment in the South, as did the anxiety aroused by the growing minority status of the slaveholding states in a rapidly expanding nation.

Thomas R. Dew, professor of political economy at the College of William and Mary, laid down the basic lines of the slavery defense in 1832 when he argued that slavery not only had been from earliest times the chief means of advancing civilization but it had been established by divine authority.[15] Southern clergymen picked up this final point and began to respond to the antislavery arguments by appealing to the sanction of Scripture and by depicting the abolitionists as anti-Christian atheists who reject the Word of God. "We defend the cause of God," Benjamin Morgan Palmer, minister of the First Presbyterian Church of New Orleans, was to declare.

The Disruption of the Churches

The disruptive effect of the slavery issue upon the churches was foreshadowed by its role in the hidden agenda of the Presbyterian Old School – New School division in 1837, and it was more clearly evident in the formation of perfectionist "union" churches and in perfectionist defections among Methodists, Baptists, and Lutherans. Perfectionist tendencies, of course, always threatened to get out of hand. The revivals had multiplied conversions so rapidly that it became increasingly easy to overlook the great obstacle that man's sinful nature placed in the path to perfection and to believe that it was only an individual's willful perversity that caused him to temporize with sin. Thus many were moving into a perfectionist phase, which emphasized the abolition of sin almost to the exclusion of any preoccupation with creed, just at the moment that slavery was coming to be regarded by many as the one great sin. Since the established denominations tended to play down slavery in the interest of maintaining denominational unity, they appeared increasingly to be condoning sin.

Although this perfectionist antislavery sentiment was to become widespread, its early focal point was in upper New York State. As early as 1835, the reorganized Central (formerly Oneida) Evangelical Association, with 15 ministers, 8 licentiates, and 7 churches, was proposing that it be considered as the nucleus of a network of true churches free from all sin to which all right-minded congregations could repair as they found their old denominations entangled in unrighteousness. "Union of feeling and senti-

[15] See *The Pro-Slavery Argument as Maintained by the Most Distinguished Writers of the Southern States* (Charleston, S.C., 1852); and W. S. Jenkins, *Pro-Slavery Thought in the Old South* (Chapel Hill, N.C., 1935).

Three Stalwarts. Elizabeth Cady Stanton, Harriet Beecher Stowe, and Julia Ward Howe. Stanton adopted Amelia Bloomer's dress reform as well as short hair. (Elizabeth Cady Stanton, photograph from Brown Brothers; Harriet Beecher Stowe, courtesy of the National Portriat Gallery, Smithsonian Institution, Washington, D.C.; Julia Ward Howe, reproduced from an 1861 photograph in Julia Ward Howe, Reminiscences, 1819–1899, *Boston, Houghton Mifflin Co., 1899.)*

ment," ran the resolution, can never be obtained until the churches "abandon their exclusive creeds and incorporate nothing in their articles that will shut off their fellowship with any child of God." The one thing demanded by these "union" churches was an unequivocal stand against slavery, since "proslavery or apparently neutral churches are anti-Christian." By 1855 there were no fewer than 83 of these "union" churches in New York State alone, and others were scattered through New England and the Middle West. In addition the entire Genesee Association was read out of the Congregational fold in 1844 for its perfectionist tendencies.[16]

New York State was also the center of antislavery agitation among Methodists. In spite of the attempt of the national General Conference in 1836 to stifle discussion of the issue, hundreds of petitions demanding disciplinary rules against slavery continued to flood in from New York, especially from the Genesee conference. The bishops resorted to expulsions and discriminatory appointments in an endeavor to silence the antislavery forces, and at the 1840 General Conference they maintained their ironclad control in the face of petitions signed by 10,000 laymen and 500 preachers. Between 1839 and 1842 isolated groups in New England, New York, and Ohio began to withdraw from the church, and finally in 1843 at a meeting in Utica the Wesleyan Methodist Church was formed on a typically perfectionist platform which included abolitionism as one of its tests for membership.

Baptists suffered a similar defection that extended from Maine through New York to Michigan. It took shape in the formation of a competing Baptist Free Mission Society in 1843 and in the establishment of New York Central College at McGraw, New York. Among Lutherans an antislavery faction of 21 perfectionist congregations in central New York in 1837 formed the Franckean Synod, which denied membership to anyone who sanctioned the principle of slavery.

These were minor schisms, and their growth was nipped by a shift in the policy of the major bodies. Responding to the increasing pressure of antislavery sentiment, the Methodist General Conference of 1844 adopted a strengthened antislavery rule that preserved the unity of the northern section of the church at the expense of the southern portion which departed the following year to form the Methodist Episcopal Church, South. The Baptist foreign and home mission societies also were forced to take a firmer stand, which resulted in the formation of the Southern Baptist Convention in 1845. The Congregationalists, as a regional denomination, were able to move into the abolitionist camp without suffering disruption, although the Disciple or "Christian" churches were too loosely affiliated to suffer schism. The Old School and the New School Presbyterian churches, having divided in 1837, sought to muffle the controversy in order to avoid further division. The New School group

---

[16] Cross, *Burned-over District*, 261, 278–81.

succeeded in doing so for a time but it finally split in 1857, whereas the Old School churches forestalled any break until after the Civil War began. Lutherans were torn by controversy, but the General Synod was able to steer a neutral course. The Episcopalians and the Roman Catholics tended to remain aloof from the controversy. Remaining aloof, of course, often meant that the proponents of a slave-based social order were free to speak, whereas their opponents were urged to avoid creating dissension by remaining silent.

The division of the churches was prophetic of the political division that was to follow. By 1860 the crisis was at hand. As soon as the outcome of the presidential election was certain, the South Carolina legislature summoned a state convention that met on December 20, 1860, and unanimously declared "that the Union now subsisting between South Carolina and other states under the name of 'The United States of America' is hereby dissolved." Four months later Fort Sumter was shelled and the Civil War had begun.

During the agitation preceding the conflict, women had emerged for the first time to play a significant political role. Some were important in enlisting financial support; some devoted themselves to organizational tasks; others took to the platform as eloquent advocates of abolition. The Grimké sisters from South Carolina, Sarah and Angeline, toured New England as agents of the Anti-Slavery Society. And there were others.

When Theodore Parker said that Lyman Beecher was "the father of more brains than any man in America," he was thinking not only of Beecher's sons, Henry Ward, Edward, Charles, and Thomas K., but of his equally gifted daughters. Harriet gained fame by her writing. Catherine's great contribution was in education, desiring to secure "professional advantages of education for my sex equal to those bestowed on men." She wrote, she agitated, she established female seminaries and colleges, and she organized societies to support her educational ventures. Isabella joined forces with Elizabeth Cady Stanton and fought with equal zeal for the "great and holy work" of woman suffrage. All were opposed to slavery, but it was Harriet Beecher Stowe who probed the conscience of the nation with her emotion-laden indictment of slavery in *Uncle Tom's Cabin* (1852).[17] And after the war began, it was another young woman, Julia Ward Howe, who provided the stirring words of "The Battle Hymn of the Republic" — with its closing line "as he died to make men holy, let us die to make men free" — as the marching song of the Northern armies.

Both North and South, preachers marched with the troops — some to bear arms, others to serve as chaplains. Prayer meetings were a familiar feature of life in the camp. In the field, the sound of hymn singing echoed across the lines. In the Confederate armies especially, a continuing revivalistic fervor was often maintained. The concern of people at home for the

---

[17] See Marie Caskey, *Chariot of Fire: Religion and the Beecher Family* (New Haven, 1978).

troops was expressed through such agencies of churchmen as the United States Christian Commission (the Civil War equivalent of the World War II USO) whose agents distributed incidental necessities—including mittens, scarves, taffy, writing paper—and wrote letters to loved ones for the seriously wounded or illiterate. The Red Cross, under the inspiration of Clara Barton, won its spurs in assisting the personnel of the Sanitary Commission. But the most fateful feature of the war was its fratricidal character and its magnitude. It was a war that bruised almost every family in the land, changed the face of the nation, and created new problems both for the country and for the churches.

PART **III**

Years of Midpassage

1865–1918

1848	Elizabeth Cady Stanton organizes women's rights conference in Methodist church in Seneca Falls, New York
1857	Herbert Spencer publishes *Progress, Its Law and Cause*
1857	William A. Muhlenberg establishes Episcopal deaconness order in New York
1859	Charles Darwin publishes *The Origin of Species*
1861–65	Civil War
1863	Emancipation Proclamation freeing slaves effective January 1
1864	Vatican issues *Syllabus of Errors*, condemning separation of religion from civil affairs
1864	New School and Old School Presbyterians in South unite
1865–77	Reconstruction
1865	Ku Klux Klan founded in Pulaski, Tennessee
1865	American Christian Commission organized for urban missionary work
1866	Black Members of the Methodist Protestant Church form the African Union Colored Methodist Protestant Church
1867	Free Religious Association formed to promote freedom and progress
1869	Completion of transcontinental railroad
1870	U.S. population 38.5 million
1870	First Vatican Council
1870	Black members of the Methodist Episcopal Church, South, form independent Colored (Christian) Methodist Episcopal Church
1870–80	Emergence of liberal Protestantism
1872	Madame Helena P. Blavatsky establishes the Theosophical Society
1872	Jerry MacAuley founds Water Street Mission in New York, later organizes Convention of Christian Workers (1886)
1872	Warren Felt Evans publishes Swedenborgian *Mental Medicine*
1872	Uniform Lesson Plan adopted by Methodist Sunday schools
1873–75	Dwight L. Moody's triumphal tour of the British Isles with chorister Ira D. Sankey
1874	Women's Christian Temperence Union formed
1874	John H. Vincent founds summer training institute at Chautauqua, New York
1875	Mary Baker Eddy publishes *Science and Health with Key to the Scriptures*
1876	Felix Adler founds Society for Ethical Culture
1876	Cardinal James Gibbons publishes *The Faith of Our Fathers*
1878	Ex-Methodist preacher William Booth founds Salvation Army in London; introduced in America two years later
1880–1910	Heresy trials in Protestant seminaries. "Dispensationalism" and premillennialism among conservatives
1881	Church of God founded in Indiana
1883	Brooklyn Bridge opens to traffic; population of New York 1.3 million
1883	Theodore T. Munger publishes liberal *The Freedom of Faith*
1884	Knights of Labor condemned in Quebec by papal decree
1885	Josiah Strong publishes *Our Country*, promoting global dissemination of Anglo-Saxon "civil liberty" and "spiritual Christianity"
1886	Black Baptists form National Baptist Convention
1887	Nativist American Protective Association founded
1888	Student Volunteer Movement organized
1889	Moody Bible Institute in Chicago accepts its first students

1889	William Henry Holcombe coins the term "New Thought"
1889	Charles and Myrtle Filmore launch periodical *Modern Thought* to publicize Unity School of Practical Christianity
1889	Andrew Carnegie articulates notion of stewardship in *Gospel of Wealth*
1889	Catholic University established in Washington, D.C.
1890	U.S. population 63 million
1890	Mormon church revises views on polygamy to accord with Supreme Court decision to prohibit it in 1879
1891	Pope Leo XIII issues encyclical *Rerum Novarum* supporting labor
1892	William Rainey Harper and John D. Rockefeller found University of Chicago, which pioneers "scientific" approach to religious education
1893	Foreign Missions Conference of North America founded
1893	World Exhibition in Chicago; World's Parliament of Religions meets in Chicago
1894	Pullman strike in Chicago ended by federal troops
1894	Open and Institutional Church League formed to promote urban reform in education
1894	Manufacturing in United States surpasses combined output of Great Britain and Germany
1895	Church of the Nazarene founded in Los Angeles
1896	Theodor Herzel writes Zionist *The Jewish State*
1895–99	Papal warnings against "Americanist" Catholicism of Gibbons, Ireland, O'Connell, and Keane, ending with explicit condemnation by Leo XIII
1896	Robert G. Ingersoll publishes *Why I Am An Agnostic*
1897	Congregational minister Charles M. Sheldon publishes best-selling *In His Steps or What Would Jesus Do?*
1898	Spanish-American War
1898	Baptist theologian William Newton Clark publishes liberal *Outline of Christian Theology*
1898	Young Men's Buddhist Association founded
1900	Baptist Temple in Philadelphia the nation's largest congregation
1900	Publication of dispensationalist *Scofield Reference Bible*
1900	U.S. population 76.2 million
1900–10	Nine million immigrants enter United States
1902	William James publishes *The Varieties of Religious Experience*
1903	W.E.B. DuBois writes *The Souls of Black Folk*
1906	Upton Sinclair's novel *The Jungle* reveals conditions in Chicago Stockyard
1906	Father John A. Ryan publishes *A Living Wage*, which fuels minimum-wage-law movement
1907	Social Gospel leader Walter Rauschenbusch publishes *Christianity and the Social Crisis*
1908	Federal Council of Churches organized
1914–18	World War I
1920	U.S. population 106 million
1920	League of Nations organized in Paris; U.S. Senate votes against joining
1920	Eighteenth Amendment launches Prohibition
1920	Nineteenth Amendment establishes the right of women to vote
1924	Johnson–Reed Act drastically restricts annual immigration and assigns quotas based on nationality

CHAPTER 9

Post–Civil War America

The Civil War was a watershed between an old and a new America. The American people became much more heterogeneous in background. The advent of modern science drastically altered the intellectual climate. And the quickening pace of industrialization created new centers of power in national life.

The changing composition of the population was one of the conspicuous contrasts between the old and the new America. After 1840 a sharply increasing percentage of the population was of foreign birth. From 1850 to 1860 the number of foreign born had increased 84.4 percent. From 1860 to 1870, in spite of the dislocation of war, there was a further increase of 34.5 percent. The first great influx had come from Ireland and Germany, but before the end of the century many nations were contributing to the growing number of new Americans. In contrast to the overwhelming predominance of British elements in the population at the beginning of the century, only a small percentage of the new arrivals were from England, Scotland, and Wales. By 1900, out of a population of 75 million, one third were either of foreign birth or children of foreign-born parents. Of these 25 million new Americans, 8 million were German in background; 5 million were Irish; 2½ million had come from Austria, Hungary, Poland, and Italy; another 2½ million had come from the Scandinavian countries; 850,000 were French Canadians; and 774,000 had come from Russia. In addition to these totals, there were several million grandchildren of the immigrants who had arrived in the 1840s, 1850s, and 1860s.

A second contrast between the old and the new America was the radical shift in the intellectual climate. Geology, in the person of Charles Lyell, had been busy rewriting the Genesis account of the origin and early history of the earth. But it was the new biology, as set forth by Charles Darwin in his *Origin of Species* (1859), that was to become the chief symbol of the intellectual revolution. The idea of evolution was not new. It had been championed by Hegel and Comte, and the writings of Herbert

Spencer were to be more important than those of Darwin in pointing up the full implications of evolutionary thinking. Spencer adopted the doctrine of evolution as a unifying philosophical principle and sought to apply it to all phenomena. *Progress, Its Law and Cause* (1857) set forth the basic thesis that was elaborated in his subsequent writings: *First Principles* (1862), *Principles of Biology* (1864–67), *Principles of Psychology* (rev. ed., 1870–72), *Principles of Sociology* (1876–96), and *Principles of Ethics* (1892–93). With this evolutionism penetrating every realm of thought, a new history began to be written which was based on the application of evolutionary theories to the understanding of the past. And this new historical understanding bolstered the developing "higher criticism" of the Bible — first in Germany and then in Britain and America — which many were to find so disturbing.

A third feature of post–Civil War America was a marked shift in the center of power. Before the war the agrarian democracy envisaged by Jefferson still reigned supreme, although the lure of the city had begun to replace the lure of the West among young men of spirit and ambition. The census statistics for the decade 1840 to 1850, which revealed that the population of the cities had increased 90 percent whereas the population of the country as a whole had increased only 36 percent, gave a foretaste of what was to come. Ten years later, in 1860, the capital invested in industry, railroads, commerce, and urban property was greater than the value of all the farms. The Civil War had "the effect of a hothouse" on this industrial growth. Military needs and currency inflation caused the mills to roar louder and the blast furnaces to flame higher. By the time Ulysses S. Grant took the oath of office as president of the United States, there was no longer any doubt that the dominant influence in American life had shifted from the rural countryside to the burgeoning urban communities. The successive efforts of Grangers, Greenbackers, and Populists to dislodge the commercial and industrial interests from the centers of power simply confirmed the fact that they were fighting a lost cause, for they never were able to win more than regional victories.

Each of these facets of post–Civil War society was to pose critical problems for the churches, but their full significance did not become clear for a decade or two. In the meantime, there were pressing problems that demanded immediate attention.

Reconstituting the Nation

When Abraham Lincoln stood on the windswept fields of Gettysburg and spoke of those who "four score and seven years" before had "brought forth on this continent a new nation, conceived in liberty, and dedicated to the proposition that all men are created equal," he was recalling the theme that had given meaning and significance to the sense of American nationhood. But now this venture had been brought into question. Although Lincoln looked forward to the time when "this nation, under God, shall have a new birth of freedom," there was no blinking the stark, stubborn, present fact that the American people were engaged "in a great civil war, testing whether that nation, or any nation so conceived and so dedicated, can long endure."

The Bond of Religion

From the beginning of national life, religion had served as a bond of unity that helped overcome the divisive effects of competing local interests and regional concerns. The Great Awakening had done much to make the several colonies emotionally one by binding them together in a common cause, generating a common loyalty, fostering common sentiments, and thrusting forward a common leadership. But it was a theological interpretation of the American past, present, and future that had contributed most to making them one nation. What had welded together the diverse peoples of the colonies — Englishmen, Scots, and Germans; Georgians, Virginians, and New Yorkers — was the consciousness of being summoned to a God-given mission. God had "designed this continent . . . to be the asylum of liberty" and had selected America to be an example to the nations. There was scarcely anyone who had not believed with Lyman Beecher that the establishment of the United States "in the full enjoyment of civil and religious liberty" had been a "design of Heaven" to demonstrate to the world "by one great successful experiment of what man is capable" and thereby to awaken among peoples everywhere the "desire and hope and effort" that would produce "revolutions and overturnings" until the whole world was free. It was this conviction that had given Americans whatever sense of common nationality they had, and it was this conviction that gave such moving power to the few brief words spoken by Lincoln at Gettysburg.

As tension had mounted between the North and the South, there had been agonized efforts to preserve the unity of the nation by reminding people of their God-given vocation. But the slavery question proved so disruptive that not even the churches could be kept from separating, and their divisions were prophetic of the tragedy that was to follow. Few had believed that the war could come. The notion that the nation could descend to fratricidal strife was unthinkable to most Americans. "There must be no war" had been a repetitive refrain. But the war had come, and its effect was shattering. The great "experiment" had gone wrong. The protective hand of divine Providence seemingly had been removed. No longer could Americans picture themselves as an example to the nations. Nor could they ease their tortured spirits by placing the blame for the disaster upon extraneous circumstance. The responsibility could not be sought beyond the American people themselves. No outside nation was involved. No foreign influence played any part in precipitating the tragedy. The machinery of peace was at hand in the orderly procedures of national life, but it had not been utilized.

The traumatic effect of the war was doubly compounded when what had been the bond of union was twisted to serve the cause of division. It was both natural and appropriate for the churches, North and South, to provide chaplains for the combatants and to organize agencies to minister to the temporal as well as the spiritual needs of the soldiers. It was no less natural for them to seek God's blessing and to claim divine sanction for their opposing armies, but it was profoundly disconcerting and disturbing. Those on both sides of the Mason–Dixon line in theology and piety were brothers, yet they offered contradictory prayers. In both North and South, the God who had made them a nation was being reduced to the partisan of a section.[1] When the bond that had united them was being utilized by apologists in both camps to justify the resort to arms, it was clear that the war itself must somehow be brought within the scope of a larger design of God if the nation were to be reunited.

Although not many gave themselves to this latter task, Lincoln was struggling throughout the war years to find a larger meaning to the conflict than that suggested by any simple alliance of Providence with either the North or the South.[2] Displaying a deeper theological perception than many preachers, he wrote to John Hay in 1862 that "it is quite possible that God's purpose is something different from the purpose of either party; and yet the human instrumentalities, working just as they do, are of the best adaptation to effect his purpose. I am almost ready to say that this is probably true; that God wills this contest, and wills that it shall not end yet." Later in the same year he told a congressional delegation that he believed that God "will compel us to do right in order that he may do these things, not so much because we desire them as that they accord with his plans for dealing with this nation." And then he continued: "Sometimes it seems necessary that we should be confronted with perils which threaten us with disaster in order that we may not get puffed up and

---

[1] Two Presbyterian theologians, J. H. Thornwell and R. L. Dabney, were the most effective apologists in linking the position of the South with the cause of God and religion. Thornwell declared that "the Scriptures not only fail to condemn slavery, they as distinctly sanction it as any other social condition of man." To call slavery sinful, therefore, is to reject the Bible. "Our policy," wrote Dabney, must be "to push the Bible argument continually" and force the enemies of slavery to reveal their true infidel colors. Presbyterians, of course, were not alone in this enterprise. Episcopalians, Baptists, and Methodists played their part. Even John England, Roman Catholic bishop of Charleston, wrote a sturdy defense of slavery on biblical grounds. For representative statements, see Smith, Handy, and Loetscher, *American Christianity*, II, 177–78, 182–86, 201–10.

[2] See W. J. Wolf, *Lincoln's Religion* (Chicago, 1974); J. H. Moorhead, *American Apocalypse: Yankee Protestants and the Civil War* (New Haven, 1978); and C. C. Goen, *Broken Churches, Broken Nation* (Macon, Ga., 1985).

forget him who has much work for us yet to do." In his Second Inaugural
Address, he reverted once again to this theme.

> On the occasion corresponding to this four years ago, all thoughts were
> anxiously directed to an impending civil war. . . . Neither party expected
> for the war the magnitude or the duration which it has already at-
> tained. . . . Each looked for an easier triumph, and a result less fundamen-
> tal and astounding. Both read the same Bible, and pray to the same God; and
> each invokes his aid against the other. It may seem strange that any men
> should dare to ask a just God's assistance in wringing their bread from the
> sweat of other men's faces; but let us judge not, that we be not judged. The
> prayers of both could not be answered — that of neither has been answered
> fully.
>   The Almighty has his own purposes. . . . If we shall suppose that Ameri-
> can slavery is one of those offenses which, in the providence of God, must
> needs come, but which, having continued through his appointed time, he
> now wills to remove, and that he gives to both North and South this terrible
> war, as the woe due to those by whom the offense came, shall we discern
> therein any departure from divine attributes which the believers in a living
> God always ascribe to him?
>   Fondly do we hope — fervently do we pray — that this mighty scourge of
> war may speedily pass away. Yet, if God wills that it continue until all the
> wealth piled by the bondman's two hundred and fifty years of unrequited
> toil shall be sunk, and until every drop of blood drawn with the lash shall be
> paid by another drawn with the sword, as was said three thousand years ago,
> so still it must be said, "The judgments of the Lord are true and righteous
> altogether."

Lincoln was not alone in exploring the theme of God's hand in the
conflict. Of the theologians who picked it up and elaborated it, Horace
Bushnell and Philip Schaff were most prominent.[3] Like Lincoln, they both
saw the war as the product of the guilt of the whole nation, the humiliation
of an arrogant and boastful people, a supreme hour of trial designed to aid
the nation to fulfill rather than to forfeit its destiny. Slavery had been the
Achilles' heel of a nation called to exemplify what it meant for all people
to be created free and equal, but slavery was not the sin of the South
alone. The evil was inherited by the whole nation. Nor was slavery the real
cause of the war. The real issue was whether or not the American people
were to be a true people capable of fulfilling their destiny. Hitherto —
"half-loyally and half-lawlessly" — Americans had claimed a self-made and
thus a false nationality. Too many had thought of the nation as their own
creation and had never given themselves fully to it. The several states had
"simply kenneled under the Constitution" and had not been merged and
compacted into a true nation.

---

[3] See W. A. Clebsch, *Christian Interpretations of the Civil War* (Philadelphia, 1969). Also
T. J. Pressly, *Americans Interpret Their Civil War* (N.Y., 1962).

As the product of the collective guilt of the American people, the war was an act of divine judgment. But to Bushnell and Schaff it was more than that, for it presented the possibility of redemption and renewal. Believing that without the shedding of blood there is no atonement, they viewed the war as a sacrificial and cleansing tragedy that contained within it the possibility not only of preserving but also of regenerating the nation. The "baptism of blood" was thus to be seen as an act of divine mercy through which the nation could be reborn, purged of its sin, and recalled to its proper vocation. Upon the anvil of suffering and under the hammer of a providential God, it was hoped that what had been only a federation made up by a temporary surrender of power would be forged into a true nationhood. It seemed clear to them that nothing less than a common tragedy was sufficient to effect the reconciliation that would unify a heterogeneous population into the free and responsible society that from the beginning had been God's intention for the American people.

What Lincoln, Bushnell, and Schaff were seeking to do was to restore to the American people their former bond of union by helping them understand that even in the war itself God's will was being worked out in the life of the nation. The verdict of the war could then be accepted with grace both by those who gained the triumph and by those who suffered defeat, for by this reappropriation and reinterpretation of the American experience the conflict could be transmuted into something more than an occasion for future bitter memories. It was with this thought in mind that Lincoln looked forward to the future task as he brought his Second Inaugural Address to a close with words that have never been forgotten:

> With malice toward none; with charity for all; with firmness in the right, as God gives us to see the right, let us strive on to finish the work we are in; to bind up the nation's wounds; to care for him who shall have borne the battle and for his widow and orphan — to do all which may achieve and cherish a just and lasting peace among ourselves, and with all nations.

The Failure of Reconstruction

Having compressed into four years a bloody slaughter that was comparable in magnitude only to the losses inflicted over a decade and a half by the Napoleonic wars, it was to be expected that festering sores would be left that would complicate and long delay the task of binding up the nation's wounds. Still there were many factors that could be counted upon to facilitate the healing process, not the least of which was the general weariness of the people with the war. The generous spirit exhibited by Grant in victory and the dignified acceptance of defeat by Lee had the immediate effect of tending to minimize recrimination. Reconciliation was further eased by "mystic chords of memory" that stretched back beyond the strife to the common history that had been shared. Having been schooled in the providential view of history, many were prepared to accept the outcome of the war as a clear manifestation of God's will for the nation. Reduced to its simplest form, the plain implication of the providential understanding of defeat was stated by a young South Carolinian: "I think it was in the decrees of Almighty God that slavery was to be abolished in this way, and I don't murmur."[4] Other Southerners found it possible to take the more positive view articulated by Bushnell and Schaff. Stephen Elliott of Georgia and Richard H. Wilmer of Alabama were conspicuous examples of theologians who were able to find in the war grounds for gratitude to God for settling "the meaning of the Constitution," restoring to the American people "one undivided country," and making clear the true mission of the nation.[5] Within this perspective, both Lee and Lincoln had served as instruments in the hands of God to effect his purposes; and it was this understanding that made it possible for both men to be lifted from the status of partisan leaders to that of national heroes.

Unfortunately the universal esteem in which Lincoln and Lee came to be held was deceptive, for the reconciliation was destined to be incomplete and a unified national life was never fully reestablished. However decisive the war had been, the peace proved to be inconclusive. In the absence of strong leadership, the national government could not agree on what to make of its victory. Efforts at reconstruction were delayed, confused, indecisive, and of short duration.[6] There was little evidence of that "firmness" to "strive on to finish the work we are in" of which Lincoln had spoken. Some, to be sure, sought to gain political advantage by "waving the bloody shirt," but this did not conceal the increasing disposition in the North to leave the South to its own devices and to get on with the business of tapping the national till and reaping the profits of a booming economy. Seldom in history has a nation been so heedless of the fruits of victory. The issues that had stood at the center of the conflict were subordinated to partisan politics and the task of restoring the Union by protecting the fundamental rights of all its people was neglected.

As soon as it was apparent that little support was to be given the law-abiding elements in the South, unrepentant extremists became convinced that their cause was not wholly lost. Bands of hoodlums — Jayhawkers, Red Shirts, Knights of the White Camellia, and Klansmen — were recruited to intimidate law-abiding citizens by night-riding forays of pillage and torture. With amazing rapidity, unreconstructed malcontents gained control of the former secessionist states, silenced the dissent of other white Southerners, and put blacks "in their place" — a place that

[4] Quoted by S. E. Mead, *Lively Experiment*, 143.

[5] Clebsch, *Christian Interpretations of the Civil War*.

[6] See J. H. Franklin, *Reconstruction After the Civil War* (Chicago, 1961); C. Vann Woodward, *Reunion and Reaction: The Compromise of 1877 and the End of Reconstruction* (Boston, 1951); and Lawanda and J. H. Cox, *Politics, Principle, and Prejudice, 1865–1866* (N.Y., 1963).

sometimes afforded them less protection than their previous status as slaves. While Lee continued to be revered, General Nathan Bedford Forrest, Grand Wizard of the Ku Klux Klan, became the romantic hero that young white Southerners of spirit were encouraged to admire and emulate.

Although the outward ties of national life had been restored by the war, the resulting unity was far removed from that true nationhood that some had dared hope would be the consequence of the baptism of blood through which the American people had passed. In 1880, to be sure, Atticus G. Haygood, Methodist president of Emory University, preached a Thanksgiving sermon on "The New South"[7] in which he repeated the theme that had been articulated by Elliott and Wilmer. But many of his fellow Southerners did not heed his appeal to recognize that the abolition of slavery had been a blessing and that their duty now was to rejoin the Union in spirit as well as in fact. As early as 1865 another Methodist preacher in Mississippi had exhorted the South: "If we cannot gain our *political*, then let us establish our *mental* independence."[8] Actually, in the vacuum created by the withdrawal of national leadership, a very large degree of political independence was achieved, and this fostered a growing mental independence. The successful defiance of the brief effort at Reconstruction along the lines of a national policy made it possible for many Southerners to ignore the verdict of the war and to cling to an understanding of the American Constitution that had few points of contact with either the realities of the past or the necessities of the future. This essentially romantic interpretation of the American experience left the South intellectually and emotionally isolated from the rest of the nation. There was no conversion to an understanding that the nation was anything more than a mere aggregation of sovereign states. What unity there was had been achieved by leaving the major issues—as far as the South was concerned—unresolved, and from these unresolved issues a later generation was destined to reap a bitter harvest.

The Southern Churches

The independent regional course of development that the South was permitted to pursue following the Civil War fostered a growing sectional self-consciousness that was to manifest itself in the religious as well as in the political and intellectual life of the southern states. There were some ecclesiastical links with the rest of the nation. Denominations that had not divided over the issue of slavery prior to the Civil War experienced no great difficulty in resuming their former unified denominational life. For

---

[7] Reprinted in Smith, Handy, and Loetscher, *American Christianity*, II, 372–77.
[8] K. K. Bailey, "Southern White Protestantism at the Turn of the Century," *American Historical Review*, 68 (1963), 618.

them there was no prewar heritage of bitterness to overcome, and they had had scant time to develop the vested interests of an independent institutional life.

The ease with which the latter denominations effected the reunion of their severed branches is illustrated by the Protestant Episcopal Church. Although a separate Episcopal church had been formed in the South following Secession, the fact that a schism had occurred was never recognized or accepted by northern Episcopalians. At the General Convention of 1862, the roll call included the southern dioceses — an action that implied that the missing bishops and deputies were only temporarily absent. The next convention was held in October 1865, six months after Lee had surrendered. Prior to the convention, the presiding Bishop wrote to all the southern bishops inviting them to attend and assuring them of a cordial welcome. The response to the invitation was varied. Those who attended, however, were received with such friendly warmth that a month later the General Council of the southern Episcopal church voted that, since the circumstances that had brought it into existence had ceased, the southern dioceses were free to renew their former affiliation.

The denominations that were able to reunite, however, represented only a minority of southern church members. The three major denominations were the Methodists, Baptists, and Presbyterians. The Methodists and Baptists had gone their separate ways since 1845. Although there was much initial sentiment for reunion in both communions, the Methodist Episcopal Church, South, and the Southern Baptist Convention had become too firmly established to be quickly dismantled. Time was needed to untangle the existing institutional structures, but each year of delay made the prospect of success less promising as a result of the steadily increasing southern regional self-consciousness. By 1869 the Methodist *Richmond Christian Advocate* was declaring, "We consider reunion neither possible nor desirable."[9]

The Presbyterian division was more recent but it was complicated by an earlier schism. Since 1837 the Presbyterians had been divided into Old School and New School bodies. In 1857 the New School Presbyterians divided over the issue of slavery, and in 1861 the southern Old School Presbyterians formed a separate church. In 1864 the New School and Old School Presbyterians in the South united. Thus at the close of hostilities the major body of Presbyterians was confronted by a three-way split. The first task seemed to be the healing of the breach in the North as a preparatory step to ending the schism between North and South. This occasioned delay, for negotiations initiated in 1866 were not brought to a successful conclusion until 1870. By this time an intense sectional spirit had reasserted itself in the South, and Presbyterians were to be no more

[9] Sweet, *Virginia Methodism* (Richmond, 1955), 285.

successful than Methodists or Baptists in bridging the institutional barriers that had been erected.

The three large southern denominations justified their separate existence by constantly reminding themselves that Southerners were "a different people,"[10] and over the years their ecclesiastical isolation helped to give substance to their assertion. Several factors combined to produce this result. The most obvious, of course, was the mere fact of institutional separation, which left most of the southern churches out of touch with the developing religious life of the rest of the nation. Equally important in giving the religious and ecclesiastical ethos of the South its own distinctive cast was the nostalgia that caused Southerners to idealize the past and to look askance at any innovation in either thought or practice. And further heightening the insularity of the southern churches was their role as the only available vehicle for the institutional expression of sectional feeling. Politically the South was divided into several states. Economically the South was not homogeneous and its new commercial and industrial ventures were tied to northern financial centers. Thus the southern Methodist church, the southern Presbyterian church, and the Southern Baptist Convention were the only institutional links that bound the South together. Although the regional character of these denominations contributed to the popular esteem in which they were held throughout the South, this culturally grounded popularity tended to insulate them further from the larger Christian community.

The folk-religion of the southern churches was further heightened by

[10] The *New Orleans Christian Advocate* was to declare in 1880 that the "civilization of the two sections, and the customs and character of the people are in many things diverse. . . . One broad distinction is that the Southerner, as a matter of honor and principle, minds his own business, while the inborn nature of the North is to meddle. The South is tolerant, courteous, and refined in its contact with people in the ordinary associations of life. The North has a prying, inquisitive disposition, and is bent on bringing every one to its way of thinking and doing."

There are also differences in religion. "There is a south side to churches and religion, not so much in regard to their creeds, articles of religion, and church polity, as in the type of piety that prevails. Methodists and Presbyterians in the South profess the same faith as Methodists and Presbyterians in the North, and yet they are not the same people. The political meddling of the Northern churches is, of course, one difference. . . . There is a secularity about them, and a style that brings them into near fellowship with worldly enterprises and organizations. They *run* things up there—churches as well as factories and railroads. The style of their preaching is in contrast with ours, and is largely of the politico-sensational order. The North has been over-run with professional evangelists, whose methods and teachings have in many instances done harm. People raised in these churches, and imbued with their spirit, if converted, are apt to be essentially defective in the higher traits of Christian character. With many excellent people and exemplary Christians among them, and with much that is good and worthy of imitation in their church work, there is a spirit and practice, and a type of religion, that we should regret to see in our southern churches." Quoted by H. D. Farish, *The Circuit Rider Dismounts* (Richmond, 1938), 148–49.

an adherence to the doctrine of "the spirituality of the church." This concept had first been formulated by a Presbyterian, John Holt Rice. When it became apparent in 1827 that the slavery issue was apt to disrupt church life, Rice suggested that the church should "confine itself to making good Christians" and not concern itself with matters beyond its competence, such as the civil arrangements of society. By this means a bifurcation was introduced that permitted the churches to condone slavery while condemning card playing and dancing, and that was reflected in the subsequent attitude of southern Methodist bishops who rejoiced that their church held aloof from political questions and was "satisfied to perform her own legitimate duties."[11]

Basically, however, the southern churches preserved and perpetuated the popular evangelicalism of the immediate prewar period, stressing sentimental preaching, periodic revivals, and heartfelt religion. Although outsiders could point to many defects, including a rigid biblicism that sometimes tended to become obscurantist, there were also manifestations of an impressive vitality that on occasion broke the bonds of established custom. This southern evangelicalism was not distinctive in itself. Parallel expressions were to be found in other sections of the country. What made it distinctive was its almost complete predominance throughout the South and its success in withstanding any fundamental change in either thought or practice over a long period of time.

The Churches and the Freedmen

When he assumed the presidency in 1861, Abraham Lincoln had noted the obligation imposed upon him by the Constitution to see that "the laws of the Union be faithfully executed in all the States." A month later he issued a call for 75,000 volunteers in order to fulfill this constitutional duty. Combinations "too powerful to be suppressed by the ordinary course of judicial proceedings" had arisen, and this left him with no alternative but to utilize the armed forces of the United States "to cause the laws to be duly executed." The integrity of the nation was at stake, and the fundamental issue of the conflict that followed was the preservation of the nation. The precipitating cause of the war, however, had been the issue of human bondage, and before the strife was over the system of human slavery had been brought to an end by executive proclamation. As a consequence of the presidential action and the later constitutional amendment, American blacks—for the first time in any significant numbers—were given an opportunity to determine their own destiny. Legal and extralegal restrictions were to limit this freedom, and its exer-

[11] E. T. Thompson, *The Spirituality of the Church* (Richmond, 1961), 21; Sweet, *Virginia Methodism*, 298; S. S. Hill, *Southern Churches in Crisis* (Boston, 1968).

cise was to prove hazardous in many localities. Nonetheless, the Emancipation Proclamation marked the beginning of a new era.

Educational Work Among the Freedmen

Almost immediately after the outbreak of the war, the need of fugitive slaves who were soon to become freedmen was self-evident — a need for food, clothing, shelter, work, and protection. But perhaps the greatest need was education, for throughout much of the South it had been illegal to teach a slave to read. Although some slaveowners found it to their advantage to evade the law, the great mass of blacks were illiterate. It was at this point that northern churches felt that they could best help, and a whole cluster of agencies — Julius H. Parmalee listed 79 — were organized for this purpose.[12] The early interdenominational Freedmen's Aid Commissions quickly gave way to more firmly established denominational societies and boards, and their work was strongly supplemented for a five-year period after 1865 by the Freedmen's Bureau of the federal government.

As early as September 1861, a representative of the American Missionary Association reported that among the "contrabands" at Fortress Monroe in Virginia there were many, both parents and children, who were delighted by the prospect of learning to read, and before the end of the month classes had been organized to provide them with the necessary instruction.[13] Shortly thereafter a representative of the American Baptist Home Mission Society was at Fortress Monroe to investigate conditions among the black refugees, and later another representative gave a dismaying account of the plight of the 15,000 "contrabands" in Washington, D.C., and Alexandria, Virginia. "What are we to do for the freedmen which are being thrown in increasing numbers upon our hands?" he asked. "One thing is certain, they must not be neglected." The response of the Society was an appeal for funds to send missionaries "to engage in such instruction of the colored people as will enable them to read the Bible and to become self-supporting."[14]

At the end of the war there were three and a half million freedmen, and most of the denominations participated in the attempt to rectify the consequences of two centuries of neglect. The most extensive work was that of the American Missionary Association, a society primarily Congregational in support and personnel. By the end of 1863 it had 83 teachers in the field, and by 1867 the number had increased to 528. Among the surviving institutions that the Association fathered are Fisk, Atlanta, and

[12] "Freedmen's Aid Societies," U.S. Department of Interior, Office of Education, *Bulletin No. 38* (1916), 268–95.

[13] A. F. Beard, *A Crusade of Brotherhood* (Boston, 1909), 121.

[14] *Baptist Home Missions in North America* (N.Y., 1883), 398–99.

Tougaloo universities; Talladega College; and Hampton Institute. Northern Methodists and Baptists also carried on broad-scale programs among the freedmen, whereas more modest contributions were made by northern Presbyterians, Disciples, Episcopalians, Quakers, and Roman Catholics. The southern white churches exhibited a brief flurry of interest in black education at the end of the war, but hostile sentiment in the South soon put an end to almost all official activity. Isolated individuals continued to provide help, and by 1880 there were signs of a renewed interest in black education among southern Methodists, Baptists, and Presbyterians. The editor of the *Alabama Christian Advocate*, however, still spoke for many southern Christians in 1883 when he sought to squelch the emerging concern for black education in his denomination by calling it a "form of negrophilism" that smacks of "Yankee fanaticism."[15]

The men who went South to aid the blacks frequently were distinguished persons. The Baptist missionary-teachers were typical in this respect. J. G. Binney had been president of Columbian College (now George Washington University) and a missionary to Burma; Nathaniel Colver was professor of biblical theology at Morgan Park Theological Seminary (later the Divinity School of the University of Chicago); Marsena Stone was a professor at Denison University; Joseph T. Robert had taught modern languages at Iowa State University and was president of Burlington University when he accepted a call to go to Augusta, Georgia; J. W. Parker had gained distinction during a 20-year pastorate in Cambridge, Massachusetts; and Henry M. Tupper and Charles H. Corey were recent graduates of Newton Theological Seminary, one having served as an army chaplain and the other as an agent of the United States Christian Commission during the war. The young women who volunteered for service in the South were equally able and devoted.

The beginnings were crude and meager. Most of the pupils could neither read nor write, and those who could had little further training. Housing was a major problem. Few whites dared sell or lease a building to the missionaries. In Richmond they had to make do with an old slave pen known as "Lumpkin's Jail." In Raleigh two old log cabins and a dilapidated cotton shed served to house the fledgling institution that was established. In Nashville an abandoned government building was purchased. And the missionaries were subjected to all manner of harassment by rougher elements among the whites. They were ostracized and threatened, and on occasion the school buildings were burned. Even the church press of the South invited the "white cravatted gentlemen from Andover" and the "pretty Yankee girls" to go home.[16]

The opposition to the missionary-teachers was based on a determination to keep the black "in his place." "He is and must continue to be," declared

---

[15] Farish, *The Circuit Rider Dismounts,* 196–97.
[16] Franklin, *Reconstruction,* 52.

the *New Orleans Christian Advocate* in 1867, "the laboring man of the South, because he is not fitted . . . for anything higher."[17] Particular scorn was directed at the idea of providing blacks with a classical education. The Rev. Samuel A. Steele of Mississippi declared: "*Hic, haec, hoc* will be the ruin of the African." Actually, of course, little classical education was provided. In addition to instruction in the most rudimentary subjects, most of the curriculum was preempted by industrial arts, agriculture, and homemaking, with due attention being given to Bible study. Prior to the twentieth century only a handful of institutions attained anything that even resembled a collegiate status. But the contribution that was made by those who gave themselves in sacrificial service to the education of ex-slaves was great. Two thirds of them were women, and an eloquent tribute was paid them by one who had been lifted from ignorance to enlightenment by their endeavors.

> These noble women left homes, their friends, their social ties, and all that they held dear . . . to labor among the recently emancipated slaves. Their courage, their self-sacrificing devotion, sincerity of purpose, purity of motive, and their unshaken faith in God were their pass keys to the hearts of those for whom they came to labor. . . . Their monument is builded in the hopes of a race struggling upward from ignorance. . . . As long as the human heart beats in grateful response to benefits received, these women shall not want a monument of living ebony and bronze.[18]

The Black Denominations

Black Baptist churches were to be found in the South prior to 1790 but these were few and isolated.[19] Most blacks belonged to existing churches. This also was true in the North, where a few served as pastors, but separate congregations began to be organized whenever a sizable black community developed. Among Methodists two independent denominations appeared at an early date. The African Methodist Episcopal Church, organized in 1816, grew out of a separation from other Methodists that occurred in Philadelphia in 1784; and the African Methodist Episcopal Zion Church, organized in 1820, stemmed from a similar separation in New York in 1796. Among Baptists, local African congregations were formed in Boston in 1805, in New York in 1807, and in Philadelphia in 1809. There was a parallel movement in the West. In 1836 the Providence Baptist Association was formed of churches in Ohio, and in Pittsburgh, Detroit, and Buffalo. In 1838 the Wood River Association brought together churches in Illinois. Fifteen years later, in 1853, the Western Colored Baptist Convention was established. Although there was a Negro

---

[17] R. M. Cameron, *Methodism and Society in Historical Perspective* (N.Y., 1961), 209.
[18] Beard, *Crusade of Brotherhood*, 234.
[19] See A. J. Raboteau, *Slave Religion: The 'Invisible Institution' in the Antebellum South* (N.Y., 1978).

Congregational church in New Haven, Connecticut, in 1829, this was exceptional. Most independent African churches were either Baptist or Methodist.

In the South, black membership also was concentrated in Baptist and Methodist churches, and the black members of these churches sometimes far outnumbered the white members. In Richmond, Virginia, for example, there were 387 white members of the First Baptist Church in 1841 and 1,708 black members. In 1846 the First Baptist Church of Charleston, South Carolina, had 261 white members and 1,382 black members; at Georgetown, South Carolina, there were 33 whites and 798 blacks; at Natchez, Mississippi, there were 62 whites and 380 blacks. These figures were not exceptional; a similar situation prevailed among the Methodists. In isolated instances separate black churches were organized, but few, if any, of them were permitted to be fully independent. The property was held by white trustees and the congregations were subject to the supervision of neighboring white-controlled churches. The single attempt of the African Methodist Episcopal Church to penetrate the South prior to the Civil War was quickly stamped out.

The religious lives of black slaves had taken shape in secret prayer meetings and rituals in the swamps and woods at night as much as in the chapel or yard. Moreover, even when slaves assembled to hear a white minister preach, it was their singing of spirituals that emphasized struggle and freedom that set the tone for the meeting.[20] It is scarcely surprising that the defeat of the South should have been accompanied by the withdrawal of most blacks from white-controlled churches. For one thing, the mere act of leaving was a symbolic expression of their new freedom. Furthermore, few congregations were prepared to give blacks any different status than they had had as slaves. They were still expected to sit in the back seats or the gallery and were given no voice in church affairs. Even had the churches pressed for some tangible integration, it is unlikely that the mass of blacks would have gone along. As slaves they had had enough of white churches. Some of the preaching addressed specifically to them had not been particularly inspiring, if Molly Finlay's report was at all typical. "He just say, 'Serve your masters; don't steal your master's turkey; don't steal your master's chicken; don't steal your master's hog; don't steal your master's meat; do whatsoever your master tell you to do.'"[21] Nor, even with the best of intentions, could white ministers have spoken pointedly and effectively to their needs, for the white ministers had not experienced what it meant to be a slave.

Black Episcopalians and Presbyterians defected in large numbers. The Episcopalians made no effort to form them into a separate church, and the Presbyterians waited until 1898 to transfer its black remnant into a new

[20] *Ibid.*
[21] Hodding Carter, *The Angry Scar: The Story of Reconstruction* (N.Y., 1959).

Afro-American Presbyterian Church. The smaller Cumberland Presbyterians acted more expeditiously, organizing the Colored Cumberland
Presbyterian Church as a separate body in 1874. Two other small withdrawals occurred when black members of Primitive (Old School) Baptist
churches in the South established a separate organization in 1865 called
the Colored Primitive Baptists in America, and when black members of
the Methodist Protestant Church in 1866 formed the African Union
Colored Methodist Protestant Church. The Roman Catholic Church also
suffered defections, with the greatest number being lost in Louisiana, the
center of Roman Catholic strength in the South.

The Methodist Episcopal Church, South, which had had a black membership of 207,766 in 1860, had become an all-white body by 1870. A
considerable number of the blacks who had belonged to the southern
Methodist church were formed into new congregations by missionaries of
the northern Methodist church. But the greatest harvest of black Methodists in the South was reaped by the African Methodist Episcopal Church
and the African Methodist Episcopal Zion Church. The former body grew
from 20,000 members in 1864 to almost 400,000 20 years later, whereas
the latter group increased from 6,000 to approximately 300,000 during
the same period. In 1866 the remaining 49,000 black members of the
Methodist Episcopal Church, South, were placed in a separate conference,
and four years later they were set adrift to pursue an independent existence as the Colored (Christian) Methodist Episcopal Church.

The largest number of blacks were Baptists, and they rapidly outdistanced their only rival—the Methodists. This surge of growth was due
perhaps to the ease with which Baptist congregations could be formed.
Black Baptist state conventions were organized in North Carolina in 1866,
and in Virginia and Alabama in 1867. Within a few years every southern
state had its own black Baptist convention. After several abortive attempts
to establish a national organization, the majority of black Baptists were
brought together in 1886 to form the National Baptist Convention.

The black churches made striking gains in membership that far surpassed the growth of other churches. Prior to the Civil War the percentage of blacks who were church members was less than half that of the
white population. By 1916 it was slightly larger, having increased from
about 11 per cent to approximately 43 percent. The popularity of the
church among blacks stemmed at least in part from the fact that it was one
of the few institutions that was exclusively their own. Cut off from most
areas of social and political life, blacks found in the church an opportunity for self-expression, recognition, and leadership. It was hardly a coinci-
dence that until well into the twentieth century most of the outstanding
black leaders had been ministers, for the ministry provided one of the few
opportunities for leadership open to blacks. Furthermore, the church was
the primary agency of self-help in the black community, where the family
historically had been undermined by slavery—families routinely were

broken up for sale—and by the large-scale migration of family members to the North that began in the late nineteenth century. The church played an important role in maintaining group cohesion under difficult circumstances and in fostering the self-respect that is gained only through the exercise of independent responsibilities.

Renewal of Home Missionary Concern

Apart from the South, where the white churches shared the impoverishment of their region, the post–Civil War years witnessed a marked resurgence of missionary activity. For more than two decades after 1840, the mission thrust of the churches had been blunted by a variety of circumstances. The theological disputes spawned by Finneyite "new-measures" revivalism had proved to be divisive and distracting, and the available energy had been further sapped by the task of countering the disaffection created by the Mormons, Millerites, and Spiritualists. The attention of the churches was also diverted by the increasing demands of the slavery controversy, and finally the war itself had thrust to one side all other preoccupations. By the time the smoke had cleared from the battlefields, however, the earlier theological controversies had been forgotten and the churches in the North were ready to redirect to other pressing tasks the energy that had been devoted to ministering to the soldiers. Part of this energy was preempted by needs in the South, but the needs of the West and of the multiplying cities were not forgotten.

Church Extension in the West

The endeavor of the churches to match the pace of the westward migration was a continuation of their missionary activity on the earlier frontier, but "church extension" now became a more popular term than "home missions" to describe this activity. Although a fairly substantial society had been established along the Pacific coast prior to the Civil War, the population was augmented in the postwar years as people began to settle the intervening territory.

Three enticements that drew people to the newer West were mining, cattle, and wheat. The initial discovery of gold in California had been followed by similar discoveries—including silver and copper—in Colorado, Arizona, Idaho, and Montana. Then the discovery that cattle could live on the prairie grass that stretched from the Missouri to the mountains and could survive the winter without shelter led to the creation of a great cattle empire. And when it became clear that it was feasible to raise winter wheat on the plains, there was a swelling influx of homesteaders. The whole development was spurred by the extension of railroads throughout the area, with the first transcontinental track being completed in 1869.

Establishing churches in the new West was an unusually difficult enterprise, for the early population was scattered and transient. In the mining camps, the inhabitants—mostly men—had been stirred by a lust for gold. They had come not to establish homes but to make a "killing." Few men could have cared less than the miners about the desirability of establishing churches. When G. A. Reeder, a Methodist missionary at Yuma, attempted to hold meetings in the schoolhouse, he found himself preaching to empty seats. It was not until he took up a "position on the chief corner of the town, having the wholesale liquor establishment for my 'backing,' all the leading saloons near by, and a score of liquor dealers and drinkers within hearing," that he was able to make any impression on the community.[22] Effective missionary endeavor was equally difficult in the cow country, for it also had a floating population of men who were not greatly addicted to the practice of religion. Unlike the miners, the cowhands were not even gathered into temporary communities. The homesteaders provided a more stable population, but even among them a drought or a disastrous grasshopper infestation might provoke a further migration that would suddenly deplete the membership of a newly established church. With few exceptions, it was not until trading centers began to develop along the railroads that the churches were able to establish themselves on a permanent basis.

Methodists led the westward march of the churches, with Presbyterian, Congregationalists, and Baptists only a step behind.[23] The Methodist Church Extension Society was founded in 1864, and the Presbyterian and Baptist boards also allocated funds for the evangelization of the West. After the long period in which it had merged its interests with the Presbyterian, Congregationalism developed a resurgent denominational consciousness and it was determined not to allow itself to be eclipsed on the new frontier. The Congregational General Council, which met in Boston in 1865, authorized the raising of a rather astonishingly large sum to be used in the West, and thereafter Congregationalists engaged in a surge of church-building activity. By 1882 there was not a western state or territory in which Congregationalism was unrepresented. Baptists pioneered in the use of "chapel cars" that were shunted onto railroad sidings and used as places of worship until church buildings could be constructed. Baptists also persuaded the Union Pacific and Central Pacific railroads to give them a site for a church in every village along their rights-of-way. C. C. McCabe of the Methodist Church Extension Society rode up and down the western lines establishing churches, and he boasted that the Methodists

---

[22] W. C. Barclay, *History of Methodist Mission,* Vol. III, *Widening Horizons* (N.Y., 1957), 242.

[23] In addition to Barclay, see R. T. Handy, *A Christian America: Protestant Hopes and Historical Realities* (Oxford, 1971); C. M. Drury, *Presbyterian Panorama* (Philadelphia, 1952); C. B. Goodykoontz, *Home Missions on the American Frontier* (Caldwell, Idaho, 1939); C. L. White, *Century of Faith* (Philadelphia, 1932).

were building more than one Methodist church for every day in the year and proposed to make it two a day.

Other religious bodies were also represented in the West. The Disciples expanded into the new territory mostly through individual initiative until the church extension board was formed in 1884. The Episcopalians organized the whole area into missionary dioceses, but they were hampered by the problem of recruiting a sufficient number of ministers to implement their ambitious plans. Unitarians established a few churches, and the Lutherans exhibited real strength among German and Scandinavian immigrants who took up land in the West. Roman Catholics were to be found in increasing numbers in the mining centers, and their ranks were swelled by the acquisition of those territories in the Southwest that had a Spanish-speaking population (a development that would have major consequences for Catholicism in the next century). Furthermore, largely through the instrumentality of Bishop John Ireland of St. Paul, Minnesota, colonies of Roman Catholics from Ireland were established in the northern tier of states.

Urban Revivalism

While the churches were busy evangelizing the West, they continued to be concerned with the population flowing into the cities. The rural area of the nation was being enormously expanded as the frontier receded before the plows of the homesteaders, but even this expansion did not counterbalance the denuding of the older rural areas as young people left marginal farms to man the mills and the stores in the new communities that were springing up at every important railroad junction. And an even greater attraction was being exerted by the major metropolitan centers that were developing at key points throughout the country. In the 1830s Finney, Beecher, and Barnes had experimented with conducting revivals among urban people; and the "prayer meeting" revival of 1857–59 was an urban phenomenon. A fully systematized urban revivalism was to be a major contribution of Dwight L. Moody to American church life. Whereas Finney's great successes were won in communities where the population rarely exceeded 10,000,[24] Moody achieved fame by galvanizing into action the religious forces of cities with a million or more inhabitants. Finney's triumphs in Western, Utica, Rome, and Rochester were duplicated by Moody in London, New York, Philadelphia, Boston, and Chicago.

If the new revivalism was shaped and systematized by Moody, it was fathered and promoted by the Y.M.C.A.[25] The move to the cities tended

---

[24] Rochester, with a population of 14,404 in 1835, was the major exception.

[25] Out of a similar concern, women in 1858 began organizing Y.W.C.A.'s to surround young women in the cities with Christian influence. See C. H. Hopkins, *History of the Y.M.C.A. in North America* (N.Y., 1951).

Moody in England. He first gained fame in 1875 when he preached for four months at the Hippodrome in London. His great success as a revivalist in America came after his return from England. *(Courtesy of the Library of Congress.)*

to relax the ties of habit, social pressure, and emotional association that had bound the new arrivals to the church in their former places of residence. The Young Men's Christian Association was a British import designed to counter this tendency among teenage boys who were striking out on their own for the first time. The Boston Y.M.C.A., organized on the British model in 1851, was quickly duplicated in other cities. Its prospectus expressed its hope of becoming "a social organization of those in whom the love of Christ has produced love to men; who shall meet the young stranger as he enters our city, take him to the church and Sabbath school, bring him to the Rooms of the Association, and in every way throw around him good influences, so that he may feel that he is not a stranger, but that noble and Christian spirits care for his soul."

Initially established as "a mission of the evangelical churches to young men," the eager members of the "Y" soon turned the tables and transformed the Y.M.C.A. into a mission to the whole community. They collected funds to aid the destitute and cared for the sick in lodging houses, but their principal activity was evangelistic — working in rescue missions, organizing Bible-study groups, distributing tracts, and going out to preach on street corners. Soon they were to become the chief agency of the churches in promoting communitywide revival campaigns. It was through participation in activities of the Chicago Y.M.C.A. that Moody was introduced to organized evangelistic work and induced to forsake his commercial pursuits to devote himself wholly to the business of conducting revivals.[26]

The "business" of conducting revivals is an appropriate term for Moody. Not only was he a businessman, he looked like a businessman, talked like a businessman, took things in hand like a businessman. By utilizing every technique of efficient business promotion — "planning, organization, publicity, vast sums of money, a host of workers, skillful executive direction" — Moody was able to demonstrate that citywide revivals could be produced almost at will, and in the process he became the first and foremost representative of a new breed of professional evangelists. Whitefield, Wesley, Nettleton, and Finney had made revivalism a full-time profession, but the "new breed" was distinguished by their strong emphasis not just on "results," but on the efficient business methods to be employed in obtaining them. Had Moody not been deflected from his business career, it is likely that with his ebullient energy and talent for organization he would have carved out a financial empire for himself analogous to those of such friends and supporters as Cyrus McCormick, Marshall Field, and John Wanamaker. As it was, he made a fortune in religious work, but gave it all away so that at his death his only estate was $500, which he did not know he had.

Moody was born in Northfield, Massachusetts. He went to Boston at the age of 17 to enter his uncle's shoe business, and two years later, in 1856, he shifted to Chicago to take advantage of the greater opportunities offered by that lustily growing city. "I can make more money here in a week than I could in Boston in a month," he wrote to his brother. Within five years he had an upper-bracket income and a comfortable nest egg in the bank. Having professed conversion in Boston, he displayed equal vigor in church work. In Chicago he participated in the activities of three different churches, organized a mission Sunday school, dragooned

[26] See J. F. Findlay, *Dwight L. Moody: American Evangelist* (Chicago, 1969).

passers-by into the noonday prayer services of the Y.M.C.A., and was chairman of its visitation committee. In 1861, finding Y.M.C.A. work— where every person was a potential customer—much more challenging than the shoe trade, he abandoned his business career to give full time to the "Y." The war years were spent commuting to army camps as an agent of the United States Christian Commission (the Civil War equivalent of the USO of World War II), while at the same time continuing to look after his mission Sunday school. In the final year of the war, he organized the Illinois Street Church for graduates of his mission who felt ill at ease in the other churches of the city.

After the war, Moody became something of a civic institution in Chicago. "Every man has his own gifts," he said. "Some start things; others can organize and carry them on. My gift is to get things in motion." Operating on the basis that "it is better to get ten men to work than to do ten men's work," he soon had a host of projects under way, most of them connected with the Y.M.C.A., of which he had now become "librarian and agent." By a clever scheme of financing he was instrumental in erecting a spacious building—including an auditorium that would seat 3,000 persons—for the work of the association. At the dedication in 1867 he gave unabashed expression to his aggressive spirit: "When we stop trying to enlarge our work for the Lord and raise money for it, we shall become stale and stupid. . . . We must ask for money, *money*, MORE MONEY at every meeting; not for the support of the Association—as it now is—but to enlarge its operations." Shortly after its completion the building burned down, and before the embers were cool Moody solicited sufficient new subscriptions to replace it.

In the meantime, through informal talks at meetings and by shrewdly observing the successes and failures of the preachers who conducted services at his Illinois Street Church, Moody was gaining skill as an evangelist—a skill he perfected in addresses at Y.M.C.A. and Sunday school conventions. It was a triumphal two-year tour of the British Isles from 1873 to 1875, however, that made him a public figure with a national reputation. A chance encounter with two philanthropic laymen on a visit to England in 1872 in connection with his Y.M.C.A. work had led to an invitation to come back the following year to conduct a series of evangelistic meetings. Taking Ira D. Sankey with him as his song leader, the tour began inauspiciously at York. Minor triumphs in the north of England were followed by major victories at Edinburgh and Glasgow. When London was invaded for a four-month period, the total attendance at the meetings was more than 2½ million.

With the unbroken series of successes of the British campaign having been reported in sensational terms by the press, Moody was greeted on his return to the United States by the query as to what he would do in America. If there was a question in the minds of others, there was no question in his. He had found his vocation. As a New England country boy, he knew that "water runs down hill," and he was convinced that in the life of the nation "the highest hills are the great cities." If we can stir the cities, he contended, "we shall stir the whole nation." In the next five years he duplicated his British triumphs in America. Beginning in Brooklyn, where a skating rink was remodeled to hold the crowds, he moved on to Philadelphia for the winter, with John Wanamaker purchasing a freight warehouse to serve as an auditorium. In New York, P. T. Barnum's Hippodrome was rented; and in Chicago and Boston, where no buildings of sufficient size could be found, tabernacles were constructed. From Boston, after a period spent in the smaller New England cities, he went on to Baltimore, St. Louis, Cleveland, and San Francisco.

An editorial in the *Nation* (March 9, 1876) commented that "the Moody and Sankey services are an old-fashioned revival with modern improvements." The improvements were mostly highly efficient methods of organization. Everything was carefully planned in advance. Nothing was left to chance. There were committees for finance, prayer, publicity, home visitation, Bible study, music, tickets, and ushering. An executive committee was appointed to make sure that all the other committees functioned properly. No advertising device was neglected, and considerable sums were spent on posters and newspaper notices. When someone complained that it was undignified to advertise religious services, Moody replied that he thought it more undignified to preach to empty pews. Cities were divided into districts, and squads of workers were trained and sent out to visit each home. Notables were recruited to grace the platform. Sankey's music was a great attraction, as was that of the massed choirs. And the singing of gospel songs by the congregation was a stirring experience.

Moody indeed was accomplished at the "business" of revival, but his sermons were anything but businesslike. He employed a warmhearted, slap-dash, no-nonsense, colloquial style of preaching that established complete rapport with those who attended and persuaded vast numbers to proceed to the inquiry rooms, where they were given "decision cards" to sign for the use of local pastors in following up the conversions that were professed. Like Finney before him and Billy Sunday who followed him, Moody was a "folksy" preacher who fashioned anecdotes into vehicles to transmit his message from the pulpit to the congregation. Indeed, so adept was Moody at relating instructive stories, that a large number of his anecdotes were collected and published. And if he did not manage to reach his audience with his stories and illustrations, he would employ other rhetorical devices, following his own advice: "If one method don't wake them up, let us try another."[27]

Moody never pretended to be anything more than a layman. Such theology as he had was rudimentary at best. Finney had written a book of

---

[27] Dwight L. Moody, *Anecdotes and Illustrations of D. L. Moody Related by Him in His Revival Work* (Chicago, 1877); *How to Conduct Evangelistic Services and Prayer Meetings* (Springfield, Mass., 1876), 4.

almost 1,000 pages to explain the points at which he differed from orthodox Calvinist doctrine. Even had he had the necessary training, Moody
would never have thought of embarking upon such an enterprise. Once
when Moody was confronted by a woman who said that she did not believe
in his theology, he answered: "My theology! I didn't know I had any."[28]
He insisted that instead of troubling his hearers with the disconcerting
intricacies of theology, he simply stuck to the "three R's" of the gospel:
"Ruin by sin, Redemption by Christ, and Regeneration by the Holy
Ghost." God loves everyone, and all that you need to do to be saved is to
believe that Christ died for you. To the man who said, "I am so constituted I can't believe," Moody said, "Men can believe if they will. It is not
because men cannot believe; it is because they will not believe." The
central fact, as far as Moody was concerned, was that any man can obtain
salvation. He called attention to Acts 17:30 — God "commandeth all men
to repent" — and insisted that this left no room for questions of innate
depravity, predestined election, and human inability. "When God commands anything, he gives you the power to obey," said Moody. "We are
free agents. God allows us to choose." And it was a very simple choice, a
"fair, square, practical" choice, that permitted no neutrality: "We are
either for God or against him."

To those who criticized either his methods or his message, Moody had a
stock reply: "It doesn't matter how you get a man to God provided you get
him there." And to most of the churchmen of the time this was a persuasive answer. Endorsements of his campaigns cut across almost all denominational lines and embraced almost all shades of theological opinion,
for he had developed what seemed to be a quick and easy system to reach
the unchurched masses of the cities. After a few years, however, it became
clear that Moody was not reaching "the masses." His audiences, as was
repeatedly pointed out, were made up of "the better class of people." Nor
was there much evidence, in spite of claims to the contrary, that the
campaigns boosted the rate of growth of the churches. Moody's greatest
contribution was to lift the morale of the churchgoing segment of the
population, to infuse it with new enthusiasm, and to stimulate giving to a
wide variety of Christian enterprises. All of this amounted to a project of
enlarged self-understanding for churchgoers, and a clearer sense of identity, especially over other groups. Sankey advanced that project by com-
posing hymns that helped persons effectively organize and conceptualize
their social experience.[29]

[28] This disclaimer was a quip and not true; see S. N. Gundry, *Love Them In: The
Proclamation Theology of D. L. Moody* (Chicago, 1976).

[29] W. G. McLoughlin made a careful statistical analysis that indicates that the Moody
campaigns had little effect, either in Britain or America, in increasing church
membership. *Modern Revivalism*, 202–6, 262–67. For an analysis of the appeal of
Moody's message in America, see Sandra Sizer, *Gospel Hymns and Social Religion: The
Rhetoric of Nineteenth-Century Revivalism* (Philadelphia, 1978).

Moody exerted his more lasting influence on the college campuses, where the students were greatly impressed by his openhearted spirit of devotion. A surprising feature of his student conferences at Northfield was their distinctly liberalizing effect. Moody found it helpful to invite as featured speakers some of the ablest theological scholars, who were competent, as Moody was not, to deal with the acute threats to their faith that the students were experiencing as a result of the new scientific inquiries and the new biblical studies. In spite of feeling himself singularly ill equipped to speak to students, Moody was successful in deeply influencing many of the "first minds" of the college campuses, including Henry Drummond, George Adam Smith, John R. Mott, Robert E. Speer, Sherwood Eddy, and Charles Foster Kent.

The Sunday School Movement

The other great evangelistic enterprise of the Protestant churches following the Civil War was the Sunday school movement. Since early in the century, missionaries of the American Sunday School Union had been busy establishing Sunday schools for the children of the nation, and they had been given powerful support when Horace Bushnell, in *Christian Nurture* (1847), argued the need to supplement revivals with "more natural" and "more constant means of grace." Though the Sunday School Union continued to exist, the dynamic new agency was to be the International Sunday School Association. This was a popular lay enterprise that carried forward the whole endeavor in a burst of new enthusiasm and devotion.

As was true of so many religious movements in the latter part of the nineteenth century, Dwight L. Moody was the chief instigator, having conceived the idea of breathing new life into Sunday school work and having recruited B. F. Jacobs, a Chicago wholesale grocer and real-estate man, to forward the project. Described by his friends as "a steam engine of a man," Jacobs quickly became the key figure. He captured control of the informal conventions assembled at the time of the Sunday School Union meetings, and turned them into an independent organization that promoted city, county, state, and national conventions of Sunday school workers. The movement was frankly interdenominational, and its goal was to multiply through united effort the number of communities throughout the land where the influence of the Christian religion reigned supreme. This was to be done by enlisting, training, and inspiring a corps of dedicated teachers in every community to revitalize the Sunday school and to supplement its traditional instructional purpose with a definite evangelistic objective. The heart of the project was a highly efficient county-convention system that utilized mass rallies to kindle ardor and zeal while at the same time introducing the workers to new methods and providing them with a modicum of training. So great was the enthusiasm awakened at the rallies that a convention often became the occasion for a revival in the city in which it was held.

One of the major innovations, adopted at the insistence of Jacobs by the national convention of 1872, was the Uniform Lesson Plan. This was a plan proposed by John H. Vincent, who had become editor of Methodist Sunday school publications in 1868. The idea was to have each class within a Sunday school, and Sunday schools of all denominations, studying the same lesson each week. The plan had at least two distinct advantages. For one thing, "next Sunday's lesson" became a bond of union between members of different denominations and thus contributed to a growing sense of Protestant solidarity. An equally great advantage was that it facilitated lesson preparation. Teachers of all age groups and of all Protestant denominations could be gathered on Saturday afternoon to study the lesson they were to teach the following day.

Vincent also was responsible for spearheading the development of teacher-training institutes. These institutes were designed primarily for prospective teachers and sought to equip them with tested methods of Bible teaching before they assumed any instructional responsibilities. The institute idea caught on quickly and swept across the country. In Chicago it found more elaborate institutional expression in the establishment of the Moody Bible Institute in 1886. At Chautauqua Lake in western New York, the summer training institute founded by Vincent in 1874 developed into the elaborate summer program of the Chautauqua Institution.

Within a very brief time, the Sunday school — benefiting from its surge of popularity — had begun to replace revivalism as the primary recruiting device of the churches. No longer was it merely a children's school. Adult classes were formed that frequently rivaled the stated services of the church in attendance. Slogans such as "Each one win one" were adopted, and the whole program of instruction marched forward inexorably each year to "Decision Day." So great was the enthusiasm that by the end of the century annual Bible school parades had become a fixture in many communities, with the mayor and other civic notables ensconced in the reviewing stand. In 1910, when the Adult Bible Class Federation held its national convention in Washington, Congress adjourned to witness the parade. The following year at San Francisco the parade was headed by a platoon of mounted police, and there were 10,000 men in the line of march, each with a Bible, carrying banners and singing hymns and official delegation songs. A more sober but scarcely less ecstatic expression of this enthusiasm was reflected in the 1888 Beecher lectures at Yale in which H. Clay Trumbull rehearsed the beneficent influence that was being exerted by the Sunday school. As a result of "God's blessing on the revival and expansion of the Bible school as his chosen agency for Christian evangelization and Christian training," Trumbull declared, "Bible study and Bible teaching have a prominence never before known in the world's history," and "vital godliness is shown and felt in unprecedented potency in the life and progress of mankind."[30]

The eager optimism of the Sunday school workers was not shared by everyone. The more thoughtful were aware of the serious problems being posed for the churches by the new intellectual climate and the new industrial growth. Furthermore, it was now becoming evident how drastically the shape of American religious life was being altered by immigration. Previously the population of the United States had been relatively homogeneous. After the Civil War, as immigration steadily mounted, it became much more heterogeneous. And this shift in the make-up of the population was immediately reflected in the proportionate strength of the various religious groups. By the end of the century the Lutherans had outdistanced the Presbyterians and were exceeded in number of adherents among Protestants only by the Methodists and the Baptists. Judaism had become a sizable community, Eastern Orthodoxy had been launched on its American career, and even Buddhism had made its appearance on the Pacific coast. But the most spectacular feature of the post – Civil War years was the growth of the Roman Catholic Church.

[30] *The Sunday School: The Lyman Beecher Lectures* (Philadelphia, 1888), 142. An unusually discerning overall account of the Sunday school movement has been provided by Robert W. Lynn and Elliott Wright, *The Big Little School: Sunday Child of American Protestantism* (N.Y., 1971). See also Theodore Morrison, *Chautauqua* (Chicago, 1974).

CHAPTER 10

The New Americans

The influx of millions of Europeans into the United States during the 50 years from Appomattox to the assassination of Archduke Franz Ferdinand at Sarajevo was a phenomenon comparable only to the migrations that overwhelmed the Roman Empire in the fifth and sixth centuries. The invasion was spurred by the spreading ganglia of the iron horse which had begun to bind the nation into a single economic unit on the eve of the Civil War. Even in the midst of the fighting, Congress had sped with lavish grants the advance of the railroads to the Pacific coast, thereby opening the whole continent to settlement and creating a market, national in scope, that served as a powerful stimulus to commercial and industrial growth. With free farms awaiting the enterprising, employers bidding for cheap labor, and steamship companies drumming up passengers, the surge of immigrants broke all precedents. From 1865 to 1900 no fewer than 13½ million foreigners entered the United States. The pace at which they arrived was even greater after the turn of the century, when almost 9 million immigrants passed through the ports of entry from 1900 through 1910. What this influx meant to the life of the nation can be fully understood only when it is remembered that the population of the United States at the close of the Civil War was little more than 30 million.

The Irish and German invasions had begun prior to the war, with the incoming tide of Irish attaining major proportions during the "hungry forties" and the influx of Germans gaining momentum after the abortive Revolution of 1848. By the 1870s, when German immigration had reached floodtide and outstripped the Irish, the wave from Scandinavia had begun. Finally, from southern and eastern Europe came waves of Italians, Poles, Croats, Czechs, Slovaks, Hungarians, Greeks, Russians, and Romanians to work the mines, man the factories, and ply the needle in the garment trades.

Many of the Germans and most of the Scandinavians pushed on to the farmlands northwest of Chicago, but the other nationality groups tended to cluster in the cities. The ethnic composition of the cities changed in startling ways. Boston ceased to be the citadel of the Cabots and the Lodges and became the stronghold of the Kellys and the O'Briens. Other cities received a strong German, Polish, or Italian coloration. New York, as the chief port of entry, became a polyglot center of many nationalities. So rapid was the change that the number of foreign born in Chicago, for example, in 1890 nearly equaled the entire population of the city in 1880. The concentration of new Americans was even greater in some of the small industrial cities, where almost all the inhabitants had been recruited abroad to staff the mills. Charles A. Beard, in describing the impact upon American society of the incoming tide of cheap labor, commented that "not since the patricians and capitalists of Rome scoured the known world for slaves—Celts, Iberians, Angles, Gauls, Saxons, Greeks, Jews, Egyptians, and Assyrians—to serve them" had the world witnessed such a drastic alteration in the composition of a social order as occurred in America during these years.[1]

The Response of the Older Americans

It is not surprising that so great a flood of immigrants should have created alarm among many of the older Americans. Peaceful coexistence seldom comes naturally. Tension usually develops whenever differing social groups first come into contact.

Nativist Concerns

The reasons for the sense of alarm that fostered a resurgence of nativist sentiment during the 1880s and 1890s were mixed. Apprehension built up at almost every level. There was a *cultural* concern at the introduction of differing folkways, customs, mores, and patterns of behavior. *Social* apprehensions were aroused by the poverty, illiteracy, and unsanitary habits of many of the immigrants. Whether the immigrants were herded into slums or created slums, there was widespread agreement that they constituted a social hazard. Even at best they had had a bad start. They were fleeing a life of poverty; and long, unsanitary voyages across the Atlantic meant that many of them went from the ship to the hospital to be cared for at public expense. Francis J. Lally has reported that a New York almshouse commissioner sadly exclaimed: "Many of them had far better been cast into the deep sea, than linger in the pangs of hunger, sickness, and pain, to draw their last agonizing breath in the streets of New York."[2] Not only did these new Americans tax the public dole, they committed crimes far out of proportion to their number. The *political* impact of the

---

[1] *The Rise of American Civilization* (N.Y., 1927), II, 247.
[2] *The Catholic Church in a Changing America* (Boston, 1962), 29–30.

new arrivals was expressed in the saying that the immigrants "landed on Monday and voted on Tuesday," being met at the dock by the "bosses," quickly registered, and then were shepherded to the polls. Although this overstated the situation, the shifting of control in the cities from the native born to the foreign born was bound to produce unhappy reactions even without the suspicion that the immigrant vote was being manipulated. From an *economic* point of view, the new Americans also were not an unmixed blessing. They did provide cheap labor for an expanding America, but not too many of the native born appreciated this fact. Much more evident to them was the way in which the immigrants tended to depress wages and lower the standard of living by competing with the existing labor force.

All of these factors were heightened by the sense of an alien intrusion into American life. The various nationality groups tended to cling together in "ghettos" of their own, separating themselves from the rest of the community. Many spoke no English. They were suspected of exalting foreign ties and cherishing foreign ideals. To many native Americans it seemed that the America they had known was doomed unless the immigrant invasion could somehow be checked.

In the post–Civil War period labor leaders were the first to voice alarm at the threat posed by the incoming tide from Europe. At a later date even so uncompromising a "social liberal" as John A. Ryan (1869–1945) of Catholic University was to advocate restricting the flow of immigration. Only small victories, however, were won. The first general immigration law, adopted in 1882, excluded only convicts, lunatics, idiots, and those likely to become public charges. Nine years later polygamists and those suffering from dangerous diseases were banned. It was not until 1917 that a literacy test was imposed, and the highly restrictive "quota" system was not adopted until 1924.[3]

Protestant–Catholic Tensions

Nativist sentiment frequently had religious overtones, with Roman Catholicism being depicted as part of an international conspiracy to subvert the free institutions of America. This had been the theme of Samuel F. B. Morse, inventor of the telegraph, in a series of letters entitled "A Foreign Conspiracy Against the Liberties of the United States" which he wrote to

---

[3] The renewed immigration after World War I coincided with a period of economic recession and brought renewed agitation for restrictive legislation. A temporary measure was adopted in 1921 limiting the number of immigrants annually to 3 percent of the foreign born of each nationality resident in the United States in 1910. Three years later the Johnson–Reed Act restricted total annual immigration to 150,000 and assigned quotas to each nationality on the basis of its present representation in the population. A complete prohibition of Japanese immigration made the exclusion of Orientals almost complete.

the *New York Observer* in 1834. During this early period, such prominent Protestant leaders as Lyman Beecher, Horace Bushnell, and Albert Barnes believed that there was a deliberate design by Roman Catholics to capture middle America, which was to be the great battlefield where the destiny of the world would be decided. The Order of United Americans (the "Know-Nothing" party of the 1850s) both fed upon and generated this fear, but it subsided with the onset of the conflict between North and South. The conspiracy theme was revived in 1887 with the formation of the American Protective Association (A.P.A.) at Clinton, Iowa, whose members were pledged to endeavor "to strike the shackles and chains of blind obedience to the Roman Catholic church from the hampered and bound consciences of a priest-ridden and church-oppressed people." The A.P.A. was a fringe group that flourished most in areas where Roman Catholics were least numerous, as in Iowa, Nebraska, and Kansas. Although the A.P.A was an active political force that won local victories, it was bluntly rebuffed in its attempt to influence national politics, and it withered away within a few years. Anti-Catholic feeling, nevertheless, continued to persist among some segments of the American population.[4]

Although Joseph H. Fichter has suggested that anti-Catholicism in the United States was more largely rooted in ethnic than religious antagonisms,[5] the religious element should not be unduly minimized. It is true that much of the hostility to Roman Catholicism was generated by its "foreignness." And it is likely that native-born Catholics would have continued to be accepted, like other Americans, had Catholic immigrants not arrived in such overwhelming numbers. Moreover, nativist sentiment was not absent among Roman Catholics. Native-born Roman Catholics often were dismayed by the Irish immigrants, criticizing their lack of cleanliness, their boisterous conduct, their raucous laughter, their disgraceful fights. The Irish in turn frequently denounced the Germans with as much vigor as other nativists. In 1854 the Boston diocesan paper, the *Pilot*, welcomed a decline in immigration, urged the tightening of the naturalization laws, and was of the opinion that if the Know-Nothings succeeded in obstructing the Germans, posterity would overlook their crimes of bigotry. A few decades later, Archbishop John Ireland alerted the Associated Press to the "general un-American character" of the American German Catholic Assembly. German Catholics exhibited similar hostility to still-newer immigrant groups. And when Roman Catholics in the southern states were urged to welcome co-religionists from Ireland

---

[4] The excesses of the earlier anti-Catholic movement have been described in detail by R. A. Billington, *The Protestant Crusade, 1800–1860* (N.Y., 1938). For the later movement, see D. L. Kinzer, *An Episode in Anti-Catholicism: The American Protective Association* (Seattle, 1964). John Higham associates anti-Catholicism with other kinds of nativism, including anti-Semitism and racism. See *Strangers in the Land* (N.Y., 1960).

[5] "The Americanization of Catholicism," in McAvoy, *Roman Catholicism and the American Way of Life*, 116–17.

and Germany, they insisted that only those who would be friendly to southern interests be sent. "We must not," they declared, "warm vipers into life that may sting us when they grow warm."[6] Although all this is true, religious concerns were present in the tension between Protestants and Roman Catholics.

Protestants, of course, did not constitute a single homogeneous anti-Catholic bloc, a fact that Archbishop Ireland acknowledged and Robert D. Cross has documented.[7] Expressions of friendship and good will were not uncommon, and such organizations as the A.P.A. seldom reflected responsible Protestant opinion. There were nonetheless serious fears and apprehensions, stimulated in part by the harsh anti-Protestantism of some Roman Catholics. Michael Muller, a Redemptorist Father, did little to foster good feeling when he published *The Catholic Dogma: Out of the Church There Is No Salvation* (1886). His purpose in writing the book, he said, was to refute "those soft, weak, timid, liberalizing Catholics, who labor to explain away all the points of Catholic faith offensive to non-Catholics, and to make it appear there is no question of life and death, of heaven and hell, involved in the difference between us and Protestants." There were other Catholics who denounced Protestants as infidels, and even the suggestion by a bishop in 1870 that non-Catholics could be persons of good faith and good character was sufficient to cause him to be called "a Luther or a Lucifer." Ten years later, Augustine Thébaud, a Jesuit who had been in America since 1838, insisted that Protestants who "profess to be friendly to Catholics" are not sincere. And Archbishop John Hughes of New York denounced as "Protestant priests" Catholic clergymen who enjoyed good relations with Protestants.[8]

Further antagonism was aroused by the generally negative attitude of some Catholics toward American life as a whole. The influential *Church Progress* of St. Louis was not particularly tactful when it made unfavorable comparisons between the United States and the Catholic nations of Europe, and the statement of Condé Pallen that American culture "exhales an atmosphere filled with germs fatal to Catholic life" was hardly calculated to win friends. This negativism was most conspicuous among German-speaking Catholics. Anton Walburg, a leading priest in Cincinnati, was emphatic in his criticism of the United States. In 1889 he depicted American culture as a "hotbed of fanaticism, intolerance, and radical ultra views on matters of politics and religion." Even the language, he insisted, was so permeated with Protestant ideas that an English-speaking Catholicism could never prosper. In contrast to the United States, Walburg

---

[6] W. E. Wright, "The Native American Catholic, the Immigrant, and Immigration," in McAvoy, *Roman Catholicism and the American Way of Life*, 213–14, 216. See also C. J. Barry, "The German Catholic Immigrant," *ibid.*, 199; and Robert D. Cross, *The Emergence of Liberal Catholicism in America* (Cambridge, Mass., 1958), 92.

[7] Cross, *The Emergence of Liberal Catholicism in America*, 30, 32–37, 44, 48, 52, 65.

[8] *Ibid.*, 51–52, 56.

pointed to Germany as standing "foremost in the ranks of civilized nations," and he advised Americans to stop worrying about getting involved
in European quarrels since the United States was too weak to defeat
Ecuador, let alone a European power.[9]

Although mutual animosities fostered mutual estrangement, Protestant
uneasiness had its basic rootage in apprehensions concerning the changes
that a continuing massive Roman Catholic immigration might introduce
into American society. The existing social order, which embodied in so
many ways the ideals and moralities of evangelical Protestantism, seemed
to many thoughtful people to be in danger of being completely subverted.
The most obvious, if perhaps the most superficial, threat was the challenge
to two of the most conspicuous folk moralities of American Protestantism
—Sabbath observance and temperance. The "Continental Sunday" of the
immigrant groups both scandalized and spread consternation in the Protestant camp. And Protestants, long schooled in the evils of strong drink,
noted with dismay that these new Americans were bringing "their grog
shops like the frogs of Egypt upon us."[10]

Of more serious concern were the attacks leveled by Catholics against
the public schools. Universal public education had been fostered as a
counter to the project of that "old deluder Satan" to keep people from a
knowledge of the Scriptures, and the "little red schoolhouse" was regarded, along with motherhood and the home, as one of the most cherished institutions of American life. Although it was understandable that
Catholics might wish schools of their own, nothing could have been better
calculated to raise Protestant hackles than the attempt to drum up support
for parochial education by attacking public education. The public schools
were described as "godless," and those who defended them were charged
with being "fanatics." Bishop Bernard McQuaid called the public school
system "a huge conspiracy against religion, individual liberty, and enterprise," and Michael Muller regarded it as a disease that would "break up
and destroy the Christian family" and described the public schools as
"hotbeds of immorality" where "courtesans have disguised themselves as
school-girls in order the more surely to ply their foul vocation." Zachariah
Montgomery was convinced that free love would be the ultimate consequence of free public education. "Free teaching draws after it free books,
free clothes, free food, free time," he contended. "All this is going very
far with the communists. . . . If we admit a right . . . to take the child
out of the family, they will ask next for the wife." Other Catholics were
convinced that not everyone should be taught to read, for this would serve
to make them unfit for the station in life into which they had been born.
Still others argued that godly innocence was more often associated with
childlike ignorance than with worldly knowledge. A few, appalled by the

[9] *Ibid.*, 26, 28, 72, 90.
[10] Lally, *The Catholic Church in a Changing America*, 29.

thought of a system that mixed innocents with the "crime-steeped progeny of the low and vile," went so far as to urge that all free (i.e., public)
education be abandoned.[11]

Perhaps the greatest apprehension was aroused by the fear that Roman
Catholicism might serve to undermine American democracy. Although no
more than a small minority of the American people may have shared the
conviction of the radical nativist fringe that massive Catholic immigration
was a deliberate plot to overthrow the free institutions of America, there
were many who feared that the tenets and spirit of Roman Catholicism
were antithetical to religious and political liberty. The memory of events
in Europe after the defeat of Napoleon in 1814 and after the abortive
revolutions of 1848–49 did little to reassure them, and they were equally
disturbed by the condemnations contained in the *Syllabus of Errors* of
1864 and by the decrees of the Vatican Council in 1870. Moreover, in the
encyclical letter *Immortale Dei* (The Christian Constitution of States) of
1885, Leo XIII had explicitly affirmed the right of the papacy to judge
when the affairs of the civil order must yield to the superior authority of
the Roman Church.[12] And somewhat later the Vatican newspaper *Osser-
vatore Romano* pointed out that "as the Pope is the sovereign of the
Church . . . , he is also the sovereign of every other society and of every
other kingdom."[13] Some comments by American Catholics were no more
reassuring. An article in the *American Catholic Quarterly Review* in 1877
dismissed the Declaration of Independence as a flock of vague clichés, and
five years later a pastoral letter of the bishops of the province of Cincinnati
took a dim view of the notion that a people should rule themselves.[14]

Other Catholics, most notably Cardinal James Gibbons, Archbishop
John Ireland, and Bishop John J. Keane, were as disturbed as most Protestants by the reactionary stance of the conservative wing of the Roman
Catholic Church in America. They resented both the aspersions cast upon
the public schools and the innuendoes that suggested that the American
form of government was less desirable than the nondemocratic regimes of
Europe. They repeatedly voiced their own approbation of American democratic principles, and were forthright in condemning the antidemocratic
views of some of their fellow Catholics. In contrast to the conservative
Catholics, the liberals were widely acclaimed and publicly honored by
Protestants. Gibbons was invited to preach in Protestant pulpits, Keane
gave the Dudleian lecture at Harvard, and a Baptist minister affectionately
addressed Ireland as "my archbishop." The result of the Catholic ambiva-

---

[11] Cross, *The Emergence of Liberal Catholicism in America*, 95, 96, 98, 131–32, 135–36.
[12] For the *Syllabus of Errors*, see Smith, Handy, and Loetscher, *American Christianity*, II,
112–15. The constitution promulgated at the Vatican Council in 1870 and the
encyclical *Immortale Dei* are reprinted in W. S. Hudson, *Understanding Roman
Catholicism* (Philadelphia, 1959), 37–45, 66–90.
[13] Cited in Cross, *Emergence of Liberal Catholicism*, 60.
[14] *Ibid.*, 99.

lence was a degree of ambivalence in the Protestant mind, with varying opinions being held as to the future course that the Roman Church would pursue in America.

Protestant Ministries to the Immigrants

The Protestant approach to the newcomers to the American scene was motivated by a varying mixture of religious concern, humanitarian sentiment, patriotic fervor, and anti-Catholic feeling that interpreted the incoming tide as part of a carefully laid plot to capture the United States for the Pope. Many believed, however, that the "safety and welfare and Christian civilization of our country depends in no small degree upon transforming" the immigrant "into a true American," and that "nothing but Christianity, as incarnated in American Protestantism," can accomplish this end. The new arrivals, declared mission executive Charles A. Brooks, must be "born again of the American spirit."[15] In spite of attempts to enlist support for mission work among immigrants by equating Protestantism with patriotism, the literature of the time makes it clear that much of the motivation was rooted in a truly humanitarian and religious solicitude for the friendless and poverty stricken. Methodists, for example, were as assiduous in their work among Lutherans from Sweden and Calvinists from Hungary as they were among Roman Catholics from any land.

Apart from informal "welfare" or "relief" programs, the major response of Protestant churches to the presence of the new Americans was a strenuous effort to provide them with a religious ministry in their own language. Later, as a phase of their expanding humanitarian activity, the churches developed a systematized program of "Christian Americanization" or "Christian Friendliness" to assist the immigrant families in making a successful adjustment to American life. Women were enlisted to go into the homes to show mothers how to cook the food available in American stores, to teach them English, to help them prepare for naturalization examinations, and generally to befriend them.

Almost every Protestant denomination developed foreign-language ministries. Mission work was established among the Germans, Scandinavians, French Canadians, Italians, Poles, Hungarians, Czechs, Romanians, and Portuguese. Baptists, for example, maintained a ministry to 21 different nationality groups in as many different languages. The recruiting of a "native ministry" to labor among their fellow immigrants was haphazard at first, but as soon as any specific group began to arrive in significant numbers, training institutes were organized to train converts for mission work. Foreign-language "departments" were established in theological seminaries to provide more adequate ministerial training. Baptists were

---

[15] H. B. Grose, *Aliens or Americans?* (N.Y., 1906), 237, 255; C. A. Brooks, *Immigration: Its Extent, Its Effect on America, Its Call to the Churches* (N.Y., 1915), 8.

typical in this respect, establishing a German department at Rochester Theological Seminary in 1858; a department for Swedish, Danish, and Norwegian students at the seminary in Chicago in 1871; a French-Canadian department at Newton in 1889; and an Italian department at Colgate Theological Seminary in 1907. "So ample were these facilities," Aaron I. Abell reported in his study of urban Protestantism, "that by 1900 a body of clergymen ready to meet all calls for independent or assistant pastorates had come into existence." As early as 1895 the problem of the Congregationalists had become one of sufficient financial support rather than of available personnel, for their home missionary society reported that the once "greatest desideratum — trained Congregational pastors — to supply these churches of foreign tongues, is now supplied in a degree almost beyond our power to use, through Oberlin and Chicago theological seminaries, whose well-equipped graduates stand ready to enlarge the field of our missionary service wherever the means are at the command of this society to employ them."[16]

Although by no means negligible, the number of non-English-speaking immigrants added to the membership of churches of British background accounted for only a small fraction of the new Americans. As was to be expected, it was the churches of their homelands that experienced the great surge of growth.

Adjustments and Tensions Within Roman Catholicism

The most spectacular development in American religious life during the latter half of the nineteenth century was the growth of the Roman Catholic Church. In spite of repeated alarm that vast losses were being suffered among those who came to America, the Roman Catholic Church was remarkably successful in retaining the allegiance of Catholic immigrants.[17] Although the number of Roman Catholics had rapidly mounted during the pre–Civil War years, giant strides in membership took place in the decades that followed. The 4 million Catholics of 1870 increased to 6 million in 1880. Ten years later the total was 9 million, and in 1900 it was 12 million. By 1920 every sixth person and every third church member was a Roman Catholic.[18]

---

[16] A. I. Abell, *The Urban Impact upon American Protestantism* (Cambridge, Mass., 1943), 182, 183.

[17] The myth of vast losses was exploded by Gerald Shaughnessy, *Has the Immigrant Kept the Faith?* (N.Y., 1925). See also J. P. Dolan, *Catholic Revivalism* (Notre Dame, Ind., 1978).

[18] For a scholarly account, see J. J. Hennesy, *American Catholicism: A History of the Roman Catholic Community in the United States* (N.Y., 1981). Key documents of American Catholicism are printed in J. T. Ellis, *Documents of American Catholic History*, rev. ed. (Milwaukee, 1962).

Institutional Development

The challenge presented to the Roman Catholic Church by the immigrant flood was prodigious. The immigrants were poor. They came from different countries, spoke different languages, and—within the limits of their common faith—had different traditions and customs and loyalties. Even had they not been poverty stricken, they came in such numbers that the task of recruiting priests, erecting parishes, and building churches seemed almost insurmountable. Financial help did come from Europe. From France the Society for the Propagation of Faith had sent more than $6 million by 1914. Additional help came from similar societies in Germany, Austria, and Switzerland. But the major financial burden was carried in America. In terms of personnel, assistance from abroad was much more important and substantial. Religious orders and congregations sent over priests, lay brothers, and nuns, with Ireland, Germany, France, and Belgium contributing the greatest number. Secular priests also were dispatched. Although bishops constantly stressed the importance of encouraging vocations to the priesthood and founded seminaries to provide the necessary training, it was the recruits from abroad who made it possible for the ranks of the clergy to swell from slightly more than 2,000 in 1860 to 6,000 in 1880, to 12,000 in 1900, and to 17,000 in 1910. Nor was it an easy task to maintain effective oversight of the multiplying parishes. New dioceses were constantly being formed, and by 1914 exceeded 100, grouped in 14 provinces.

Prior to the period from 1846 to 1850 when five new provinces were constituted, there had been but a single province—that of Baltimore—in the United States. Beginning in 1829, the bishops met approximately every three years in a provincial council to deal with their common problems. When other provinces were established, this procedure had to be altered. In place of the provincial gatherings, plenary councils of the whole American episcopate were summoned to coordinate the work of the church on a national basis. The first plenary council met in 1852, the second in 1866, and the third in 1884.[19] Thereafter such national councils were either suppressed or suspended, presumably to avoid the dangers implicit in the idea of a national church. A similar concern had dictated the refusal of Rome to accede to the petition of the bishops that the archbishop of Baltimore be granted the place of primacy among the bishops in the United States. In place of these alternatives, both containing the potential hazard of undue independence, an Apostolic Delegate (papal representative) was appointed in 1893 to provide the necessary coordination and direction for the American church. With the structure of government having been thus completed and with the arrangement functioning effectively, Pius X on June 29, 1908, removed the church in

[19] For these councils, see Peter Guilday, *A History of the Councils of Baltimore, 1791–1884* (N.Y., 1932).

the United States from the jurisdiction of the Congregatio de Propaganda Fide. The effect was to place the Roman Catholic Church in America on a basis of equality with older branches of the church in Europe and to bring to an end its missionary status.

The resources of manpower, money, and ingenuity were further taxed by the policy of developing a whole system of Catholic education. The first provincial council of Baltimore in 1829 declared it to be "absolutely necessary that schools should be established in which the young may be taught the principles of faith and morality while being instructed in letters." In 1852 the first plenary council re-emphasized the need for parochial schools, and in 1884 the third plenary council decreed that schools, if possible, should be established in every parish within the next two years. Support for the program of parochial education, however, was not as uniform as these decrees suggest. German Catholics were among the most ardent proponents of parochial schools, viewing them as a means of preserving their German language and culture. Liberal prelates, such as Gibbons, Ireland, and Keane, preferred to work out an accommodation with public education as a means of integrating Catholics more fully into the mainstream of American life. A hard-fought struggle ensued, with Irish conservatives such as Archbishop Michael A. Corrigan of New York City and Bishop McQuaid of Rochester giving the Germans staunch support. Ultimately the issue was settled by papal intervention in favor of a complete system of parochial education, with deviations being tolerated if judged necessary by a bishop in the light of local conditions.

Progress in fulfilling the ideal of a school in every parish was slow. Had the Roman Catholic population not been concentrated in the major cities and in a few largely self-contained rural enclaves, the whole project would have been doomed from the start. Even with this concentration, parochial education was made possible only by the sacrificial devotion of the members of sisterhoods who were recruited to staff the schools. In spite of the fact that the council of 1884 had decreed that within two years every parish must have its own school, parishes so equipped had increased only from 40 percent to 44 percent by 1892. Thereafter, with dissidence having been quelled, progress was more rapid. In 1914 the parochial schools enrolled over 1 million pupils, had over 20,000 teachers, and were maintained at a cost of over $15 million per year. But even an achievement of this magnitude was not enough, for a large proportion of Catholic children were still being educated in public schools.

Interest in secondary education lagged, with the total enrollment in 1915 being less than 75,000. Colleges and universities, on the other hand, were beginning to receive vigorous support after a long period of precarious existence.[20] Georgetown, St. Louis, Fordham, Notre Dame, and Holy

---

[20] Of 38 colleges established between 1791 and 1850, only 7 survived. Maynard, *The Story of American Catholicism* (N.Y., 1941), 474.

Cross, among others, had become strong institutions, and in 1884 the third plenary council took action to establish the Catholic University of America as a full-fledged graduate institution to serve as the capstone of the Catholic educational structure.

"Americanism"

In addition to other problems, Roman Catholics had the difficult task of adjusting people of diverse nationality both to one another and to the American environment. Moreover, America was a mission territory under the propaganda until 1908. To weld Irishmen, Germans, Italians, Czechs, French Canadians, and many others into a single church was a taxing effort. Tension often was acute. The earlier trustee controversy was in part a rebellion of the Irish against the imported French priests who had been displaced from their homeland by the Revolution of 1789. After the Civil War the German–Irish tension came to the fore, and in the 1890s Polish dissatisfaction produced a schismatic movement that resulted in the formation of the Polish National Catholic Church.[21] In 1914 a parallel Lithuanian National Catholic Church was organized.

The German–Irish issue, which had long smoldered and had been reflected in the school controversy, was brought to a head in 1891 when the St. Raphael Society of Switzerland, with Peter Paul Cahensly as its secretary, in a petition to Rome declared that in the United States the Roman Catholic Church had lost 10 million souls through failure to make proper provision for them in their own language. As was true of other nationality groups, provision had been made for the establishment of German congregations under the leadership of German-speaking priests. And of the 69 bishops in 1886, 15 were of Germanic extraction. But this was not enough for the St. Raphael Society, which had been founded to aid German-speaking immigrants. In its petition to the papacy the Society proposed that each of the nationality groups in America be organized into separate dioceses. This attempt to fragment the church in America by institutionalizing Old World divisions was rejected by the papacy, but it serves to illustrate a difference in point of view as to the proper strategy to be pursued in the United States.

Most of the German leadership was convinced that the way to hold the immigrants was to keep them isolated from American life. German culture, customs, and language were defended with the slogan "Language Saves the Faith," and it was insisted that only priests proud of being German, and schools in which German was the language of instruction,

---

[21] In 1916 the Polish group reported a membership of 28,245. Consecration of its bishops had been obtained from the Old Catholic Church in Europe, a small Dutch group that had refused to accept the decrees of the Council of Trent. Old Catholics in Germany and Switzerland had been alienated by the dogmatic pronouncements of the first Vatican Council in 1870.

could save German Catholics and their children from being de-Catholicized. To those who contended that "we are apostles to bring the people to Christ . . . , not to maintain or implant a nationality or to spread a language," the *Herald des Glaubens* responded that priests who voiced such sentiments "would rather see several million Germans go to hell than forego the opportunity to convert a few hundred Yankees."[22]

The Germans, of course, were not alone in believing that the only way to prevent defections was to insulate the faithful and to resist all accommodation to the American environment. Some of the most influential Irish bishops, although not concerned with the language problem, were equally determined that no concessions should be made to American culture. There were others, however, who believed that resistance to Americanization not only created unnecessary antagonism and impeded the winning of converts, but actually was a policy calculated to speed the defection of those who had been Catholics in their homelands. If being an American meant ceasing to be a Catholic, they had little doubt of the choice that many, especially their children, would make. Isaac Hecker and the Paulist Fathers, the order of missionary priests Hecker had founded in 1859, were the most conspicuous advocates of this point of view, but it also found strong support among members of the hierarchy, notably from the triumvirate of Gibbons, Ireland, and Keane.

Gibbons' *The Faith of Our Fathers* (1876) was one of the most successful Catholic apologetics ever written in English, and the response it elicited seemed a clear demonstration of the effectiveness of the Americanizing tactic. At the centenary in 1889 of Baltimore's establishment as a diocese, Gibbons re-emphasized the Americanist theme, saying that Carroll's aim had been "that the clergy and people — no matter from what country they sprung — should be thoroughly identified with the land in which their lot was cast; that they should study its laws and political constitution and be in harmony with its spirit; in a word, that they should become, as soon as possible, assimilated to the social body in all things pertaining to the common domain of civil life." And then, turning to the present, Gibbons called upon his contemporaries to emulate Carroll. Ireland was even more emphatic, believing that people unwilling to be assimilated did not deserve to be admitted to the country and that anyone who did not rejoice in the blessings of America "should in simple consistency betake his foreign soul to foreign shores, and crouch in misery and subjection beneath tyranny's sceptre."

> We should live in our age, know it, be in touch with it. . . . We should be in
> it and of it, if we would have its ear. . . . For the same reason, there is
> needed a thorough sympathy with the country. The Church of America
> must be, of course, as Catholic as even in Jerusalem or Rome; but as far as

---

[22] *Roman Catholicism and the American Way of Life,* ed. McAvoy, 192–94; Cross,
Emergence of Liberal Catholicism, 25–26, 91–92.

her garments assume color from the local atmosphere, she must be American. Let no one dare to paint her brow with a foreign taint or pin to her mantle foreign linings.[23]

But it was not simply a tactic that the liberal coterie had adopted. They were fully committed to American democracy, glorying in it, believing in it, and willing to defend it. "If I had the privilege of modifying the Constitution of the United States," declared Gibbons, "I would not expunge or alter a single paragraph, a single line, or a single word of that important instrument."

> The Constitution is admirably adapted to the growth and expansion of the Catholic religion, and the Catholic religion is admirably adapted to the genius of the Constitution. They fit together like two links of the same chain.

Furthermore, these Americanizers believed that America had a mission to the world. God intended America to be more than a "motherland," asserted Keane. "She was meant to be a teacher through whose lips and in whose life he was to solve the social problems of the Old World."[24]

The leaders of the liberal contingent also were certain that America could teach lessons in religion as well as in politics. The role of the laity was emphasized and lay congresses were organized. Close clerical supervision and direction were minimized by a stress upon the necessity for individual initiative in the apostolate of the church. The contemplative life exalted by most of the religious orders tended to be disparaged. "An honest ballot and social decorum," Ireland contended, "will do more for God's glory and the salvation of souls than midnight flagellations or Compestellan pilgrimages." Protestants were not to be regarded as implacable enemies but as "brothers to be brought back to the fold." Love and persuasion should replace harsh polemic. The technique of seeking to exert religious influence through the formation of a Catholic political party, a practice widely adopted in Europe, was likewise decried. Even the almost automatic identification of American Catholics with the Democratic party ("Have you heard the news? John Danaher has become a Republican!" "It can't be true. I saw him at mass just last Sunday.") was deplored on the ground that it deprived Catholics of influence because the Democrats took them for granted, whereas the Republicans felt no obligation to them.[25]

The 1880s and 1890s were heady years for the liberals, but they were

[23] Roemer, *Catholic Church in the United States*, 303–4; Maynard, *Story of American Catholicism*, 511; Cross, *Emergence of Liberal Catholicism*, 89.

[24] J. T. Ellis, *Perspectives in American Catholicism* (Baltimore, 1963), 124; Cross, *Emergence of Liberal Catholicism*, 184.

[25] Maynard, *Story of American Catholicism*, 514; Cross, *Emergence of Liberal Catholicism*, 187.

also years when the issue of "Americanism" was being sharply drawn.[26] The peak of the liberal ascendancy was reached in 1893 at the 17-day Parliament of Religions held in conjunction with the Chicago Columbian Exposition. The American archbishops, presumably influenced by Ireland, had decided that the Parliament presented a signal opportunity to present Catholic truth to those outside the fold. At the opening session, Archbishop Patrick A. Feehan gave an address of welcome, and Cardinal Gibbons (he had received the red hat in 1886) led the assembly in the Protestant version of the Lord's Prayer. Bishop Keane presented two papers, read an address prepared by Gibbons, and presided on the day assigned for a specifically Catholic program. Although those who participated felt that a real service had been rendered the Catholic Church, others were scandalized by the appearance given by Catholic participation of waiving the Roman claim to unique and final truth. By sharing the platform with every religious sect "from Mohammedanism and Buddhism down to the lowest form of evangelicalism and infidelity," the participating bishops were accused of having taken a dangerous first step toward "indifferentism." Even prior to this, in an article in the *American Catholic Quarterly Review,* the vicar general of Archbishop Corrigan had charged Ireland, Gibbons, and Keane of being guilty of the "liberalism" condemned by the *Syllabus of Errors.*[27]

Many issues, in addition to those strictly related to "Americanism," contributed to the coalescing of two parties in the church, each striving for ascendancy. There were differences of opinion over parochial schools and the language question, tensions between nationality groups, differing attitudes toward "temperance," and debates as to the position the church should take with regard to the Knights of Labor and the "single-tax" proposal of Henry George. The establishment of Catholic University in 1889 had been displeasing to many. Some feared it as a rival to their own institutions. Some were opposed to its location in Washington, where students would be exposed to the corrupting influences of the nation's capital. Others were dismayed that an undergraduate college for women would be adjacent to a campus where priests and members of religious orders would be pursuing graduate studies. Still others were alienated by the "progressive" auspices under which the university had been established and by the pretension of its board of trustees to serve as a standing council of the church. The latter pretension was related to a centralizing tendency which also aroused antagonism. Gibbons was being encouraged

---

[26] The two indispensable books dealing with the "Americanism" controversy are Cross, *Emergence of Liberal Catholicism,* and T. T. McAvoy, *The Great Crisis in American Catholic History, 1895–1900.* (Chicago, 1957). The latter volume makes full use of archival material. It was reprinted under a new title, *The Americanist Heresy in Roman Catholicism* (Notre Dame, Ind., 1963).

[27] McAvoy, *The Great Crisis in American Catholic History,* 76–77.

James Cardinal Gibbons (1834–1921), Archbishop of Baltimore for Forty-Three Years. (Courtesy of the Library of Congress.)

to assume the role of spokesman and unofficial primate of the church by exploiting the precedence he derived from being the archbishop of Baltimore and the only American cardinal, and the archbishops had begun to function as a committee in a way that seemed to abridge episcopal liberties. Perhaps as important as any of these issues in the process of polarization was the personal rivalry of Archbishops Ireland and Corrigan, each of whom aspired to be the next American to possess a cardinal's hat. Thus ties of friendship, common convictions and ideals, and mutual antipathies were involved in the struggle that was to take place.

When Archbishop Francesco Satolli was sent to represent the papacy at the Chicago World's Fair in 1892, he was privately instructed to adjudicate the controversies among American Catholics and to make known at an appropriate time that Leo XIII wanted him to remain in America as a resident apostolic delegate to ensure that unity would be maintained. For a variety of reasons, nearly all the bishops were opposed to the appointment of any such permanent papal representative in the United States. Ireland was the major exception to this opposition. He sensed the hopelessness of resistance and decided to seek advantage by being the first to welcome the establishment of an apostolic delegation in Washington. He was confident that Satolli could be won to the liberal cause. Ireland's confidence was buttressed by the favor he had enjoyed at Rome during a visit of the preceding year, and by Leo XIII's apparent sympathy with progressive views. Furthermore, Denis J. O'Connell, rector of the American College in Rome and a close collaborator of the liberal triumvirate, had been assured that Satolli would restore unity by driving Corrigan "to the wall."[28] Ireland therefore was far from dismayed when Satolli announced that he had received a papal commission appointing him as apostolic delegate in the United States.

For a time Ireland's hopes seemed to be confirmed. Satolli's early decisions were generally in harmony with the views of the liberals. The first indication that their fortunes were to suffer reverse came in 1895 when Leo XIII issued the encyclical letter *Longinqua Oceani* to the American church. After praising the notable accomplishments of American Catholics and noting the absence of any hostile legislation in the United States, Leo added the disturbing comment that it "would be very erroneous to draw the conclusion that in America is to be sought the type of the most desirable status of the Church." Indeed, the church in America "would bring forth more abundant fruits if, in addition to liberty, she enjoyed the favor of the laws and the patronage of the public authority." Ireland was so upset by this reprimand that he canceled a previous agreement to write an explanatory article on the anticipated encyclical for the *North American Review*. The encyclical was followed by a series of further blows. A papal warning later in 1895 against taking part in "promiscuous assemblies" was obviously directed against the liberals' enthusiasm for parliaments of religion. The most shocking rebukes were the forced resignation in 1895 of Denis O'Connell as rector of the American College in Rome and the equally involuntary resignation in 1896 of Keane as rector of Catholic University. When news of Keane's dismissal reached Bishop McQuaid, he wrote jubilantly to Corrigan:

---

[28] Cross, *Emergence of Liberal Catholicism*, 180. McAvoy cites evidence that Leo did not really favor either faction. *The Great Crisis in American Catholic History*, 89–90.

> The failure of the University is known at last. . . . What collapses on every
> side! Gibbons, Ireland, and Keane!!! They were the cock of the walk for a
> while, and dictated to the country, and thought to run our dioceses for us.[29]

Several things had combined to change the attitude of Rome toward the
liberal triumvirate. First, the appointment of Satolli had given the papal
court its own independent source of information concerning American
affairs, and his recommendations increasingly favored the conservatives.
After initially relying on the advice of the liberal prelates, Satolli had been
won to the views of their opponents through the influence of Joseph
Schroeder, one of the few staunchly conservative professors at Catholic
University. Second, Leo XIII himself had taken a conservative turn,
having become disappointed by the failure of his liberal tactic to win
support for the restoration of the temporal power of the papacy. Third,
the central issues of the dispute in America had been carried to Europe,
where they accentuated existing unrest and dissension. Ireland had toured
France in 1892, calling upon the French to emulate the Americans; Keane
had spoken in a similar vein at Brussels in 1894; Gibbons had been equally
eloquent at Rome some years earlier, and many of the speeches and
writings of the Americanizers had been translated and circulated in Europe. The conservatives were no less active, with William Tappert reporting in Cologne that the American liberals had surrendered to rationalism,
and Joseph Schroeder telling another German audience that they were
attacking the universality of the church and undermining the authority of
the papacy. The net result of this dual incursion was to win some support
for the liberals but also to arouse an even more powerful opposition.
Fourth, a papal rebuke of McQuaid for an intemperate attack upon
Ireland had given McQuaid an opportunity to make a detailed reply and
to state fully the conservative concern. He warned the Pope of a "false
liberalism" in America "that, if not checked in time, will bring disaster on
the Church." It may have been this communication that tipped the scales
against the progressive prelates, because Rome had already witnessed the
appearance of "modernism" in Europe, and was wary that America might
embrace it as well.[30]

The liberal triumvirate refused to be daunted by its several defeats and
immediately launched a counteroffensive, including the Fribourg Conference. This in turn provoked a detailed indictment of their views in an
article in the February 1897 issue of the *American Ecclesiastical Review.*
The liberals were accused of "an excessive 'flaunting' of American patriotism at the expense of Catholic loyalties; an undue reliance upon scholarship as a source of truth, coupled with a disregard for doctrinal uniformity; extreme libertarianism within the Church to the detriment of sound

[29] Maynard, *Story of American Catholicism,* 518–19.
[30] McAvoy, *The Great Crisis in American Catholic History,* 124–25.

hierarchical principles; and a muting of Catholic truths in order to attract converts from Protestantism."[31] The article went on to declare that the church could be saved from this dangerous "American religious liberalism" only by the direct and forthright intervention of Rome. The sole liberal victory was Schroeder's forced departure from Catholic University at the beginning of 1898, but the price of this small triumph was to strengthen the demand for a formal condemnation of "Americanism." Meanwhile, the "jingoism" of the American press in the months preceding the declaration of war against Spain heightened and consolidated European opposition. It gave substance to the insistence of the Catholic conservatives that all forms of expansionism by the barbarous Americans were aimed at the destruction of the civilization of Christian Europe.

On January 22, 1899, Leo XIII issued a condemnation of what had become known as "Americanism" in the letter *"Testem Benevolentiae,"* which he addressed to Cardinal Gibbons.[32] Although the purpose of the condemnation was "to put an end to certain contentions" that had "arisen lately" among American Catholics, the pretext for the letter was the controversy aroused by the publication in 1897 of an abridged French translation of Walter Elliott's *Life of Father Hecker* (1891).[33] Ireland was informed by Cardinal Rampolla, the papal secretary of state, that centering attention on the Hecker biography was designed to ease the embarrassment and humiliation of submitting to the papal directive. "The words of the letter," Ireland was told, would "allow us to say that the things condemned were never said or written in America" but "were set afloat in France" as a result of the translation and interpretation of the Hecker biography in a foreign language. He was further told that he should do his best "to spread this view." This was "small comfort," wrote Ireland, "but we must make the most of it." And then he added: "In my letter to the Pope, I accepted the letter, swore against all the opinions condemned in it, which I said had never been heard in America, and declared it an insult to America to have linked such extravagances with the name of Americanism."[34]

Ireland was joined by Gibbons and Keane in coupling submission with a

---

[31] Cross, *Emergence of Liberal Catholicism*, 198.

[32] The encyclical is reprinted in Smith, Handy, and Loetscher, *American Christianity*, II, 336–40.

[33] Ireland had written a glowing introduction for the French translation, Keane had presented a copy to Leo XIII, O'Connell had rushed to the defense of Hecker in a speech during the summer of 1897, and Gibbons defended Hecker in a letter published in France, as "a providential agent for the spread of the Catholic faith" and rejoiced that through the biography Europeans had an opportunity to learn more about him. McAvoy, *The Great Crisis in American Catholic History*, 173–76, 180, 182–83, 200.

[34] For Ireland's letter from Rome, dated February 24, 1899, see *ibid.*, 281.

declaration that "Americanism" was a "phantom heresy"[35] that could only have flourished abroad. The conservatives, however, knew better. The bishops of the province of Milwaukee, incensed at the suggestion that the Pope had been "deceived by false reports" and "had beaten the air and chased after a shadow," affirmed that the condemned opinions had "most assuredly and evidently been proclaimed among us orally and in writing." McQuaid publicly denounced those who said the heresy did not exist, and Corrigan rejoiced that "the monster" had been "struck down dead" by the timely intervention of the Holy See.[36] It was obvious, of course, that Leo XIII had the United States in mind as the seat of the infection. He addressed the letter of condemnation to Gibbons and not to the primate of France, and directed that it be sent to other members of the American hierarchy. Furthermore, Keane was privately but specifically instructed, when appointed archbishop of Dubuque, to heed the warnings contained in the letter to Gibbons. And Ireland was placed under leash and died without his coveted cardinal's hat.

Roman Catholics in America, of necessity, had little time for creative theological reflection. Most of the priests and bishops were forced to be "brick and mortar" men rather than theologians. Their major preoccupation was building new churches and institutions to minister to the tremendous influx of Catholics from abroad. Thus the effect of the condemnation of "Americanism" was only to accentuate the generally conservative temper of American Catholicism. Whatever bold experimentation there had been now gave way to timidity. Discussion and debate within the church largely ceased, and any innovation tended to be viewed with suspicion. The papal condemnation of "Modernism"[37] in 1907 caused scarcely a ripple among American Catholics, although it did contribute further to the theological silence that was to characterize the Catholic Church in the United States for the next few decades.

Other Immigrant Faiths and Accessions

Although Roman Catholicism accounted for the largest number of the religiously affiliated among the new Americans, there were significant accessions to other churches, and several additional faiths were introduced for the first time. Buddhism, for example, made its appearance among Chinese and Japanese immigrants on the West Coast, and a Young Men's

---

[35] The term was coined by Felix Klein, the leader of the Americanizing party in France. The fourth volume of his autobiography, *Americanism: A Phantom Heresy,* was published in an English translation in 1951.

[36] McAvoy, *The Great Crisis in American Catholic History,* 293, 296, 329.

[37] Reprinted in Smith, Handy, and Loetscher, *American Christianity,* II, 340–45.

Buddhist Association was founded in 1898. The annexation of Hawaii, also in 1898, gave added strength to the Buddhist community.

Lutheran Accessions

Of the Protestant groups, the Lutherans benefited most from the growing immigrant tide. By 1910 the Lutherans had become the third largest Protestant denominational grouping, being exceeded in number only by the Methodists and the Baptists. From fewer than 500,000 confirmed members in 1870, they had increased to more than 2,225,000 communicants in 1910. During this period 3 million Germans had entered the country, with perhaps nearly two thirds of them being of Protestant background; and during these same years one and three-quarter million Scandinavians had arrived, almost all of whom were Lutheran by heritage and tradition. Although many of these new Americans were intensely anticlerical and served to swell the ranks of the unchurched, others among them were deeply pious and zealously orthodox.

As far as influence in the general life of the nation was concerned, the Lutheran segment of American church life remained a sleeping giant until after World War I. There were several reasons for this. First, apart from some cities in the Midwest, the overwhelming proportion of Lutherans were located in largely self-contained and self-sufficient rural communities. Second, many of them were further isolated by language barriers. Third, their energies were absorbed by the taxing demands of the attempt to keep abreast of the multiplying population from their homelands. Fourth, they had no organizational unity, being badly divided by national origin, place and time of settlement, and doctrinal differences. Throughout the period prior to World War I, they kept splintering apart, regrouping, and then splintering again. Among German Lutherans, the major bodies were the General Synod, the General Council, the United Synod in the South, the Missouri Synod, and the Joint Synod of Ohio. Scandinavians were represented by the Swedish Augustana Synod, the United Norwegian Lutheran Church, the Norwegian and Hague synods, the Danish Lutheran Church, the United Danish Lutheran Church, and Finnish and Icelandic churches. By 1900 there were 24 different Lutheran groups, with the family tree so complicated by constant reshuffling that it was difficult to chart even their individual histories.

Other Protestant Accessions

Both the older German Reformed (Reformed Church in the United States) and Dutch Reformed (Reformed Church in America) churches profited by the arrival of recruits from abroad. The Christian Reformed Church, though small, gained strength from renewed Dutch immigration, and in 1904 Hungarian Reformed immigrants formed a church of their own. More significant statistically was the growth of the Evangelical

Synod,[38] the American counterpart of the Prussian Union of 1817 (the Evangelical United Church of Prussia) which had brought both Lutherans and Reformed together in a single church. Although the Evangelical Synod had roots that antedated the Civil War, scattered groups of "unionizing" Germans, whose major centers of strength were in the Midwest, were not fully organized as a united body until 1877. Mennonites also multiplied as a result of successive infusions from Switzerland, Prussia, and Russia. But they remained small and divided, with a membership of 54,000 in 1910 distributed among 11 different Mennonite groups.

Judaism and Eastern Orthodox Christianity

Immigration from eastern Europe, which peaked during the two decades that bridged the turn of the century, introduced the ancient churches of the East to the American scene and brought to Judaism the large-scale accessions that made it a major religious community in the United States.

Between 1880 and 1900, more than a half-million Jews entered the country, fleeing the anti-Semitic pressures directed against them in Russia, Poland, Austria-Hungary, and Romania. During the next 14 years more than a million arrived. These were added to an estimated Jewish community of 250,000 in 1880. The figures, however, are somewhat deceptive, for only a small proportion became affiliated initially with a synagogue.

Eastern Orthodox Christians had a long history, antedating the gradual separation within the Roman Empire of the East from the West, the Greek from the Latin, the Byzantine from the Roman. The estrangement of eastern from western Christianity began in the sixth century, and the final breach occurred in 1054 when Rome and the ancient patriarchates of the East found it no longer possible to gloss over the divisive issue of Roman primacy. Of the eastern Christians, the Russian Orthodox have chronological priority in America by virtue of the purchase of Alaska in 1867. Apart from this former Russian territory, the Eastern Orthodox churches became statistically significant in America only in the twentieth century. By 1916 the Russian Orthodox and the Greek Orthodox churches each had a constituency of about 100,000 people. Although Bulgarian, Romanian, Serbian, Syrian, and Ukrainian Orthodox churches had their beginnings in the United States prior to World War I, they were subordinated initially to the jurisdiction of the Russian church.

Since Judaism and Eastern Orthodoxy both reached their full maturity in America after 1920 and since the course of their later development is

[38] The Evangelical Synod should not be confused with the Methodist-oriented Evangelical Association which joined with the United Brethren in 1946 to become the Evangelical United Brethren Church and in 1968 became part of the United Methodist Church. The Evangelical Synod united with the Reformed Church in the United States in 1934 to form the Evangelical and Reformed Church, which united with the Congregational Christian Churches in 1957 to form the United Church of Christ.

intimately related to the problems raised and the issues faced in earlier years, a subsequent chapter provides a more meaningful context for a discussion of their initial growth (Chapter 13).

Difficult as were the growing pains experienced by the churches of the new Americans, the churches of the older Americans had problems of their own during these years. The homogeneity of an evangelical Protestantism that transcended and minimized traditional denominational affiliations had been weakened by newer ecclesiastical separations into northern and southern, black and white churches. Now, in the last quarter of the century, as Arthur M. Schlesinger, Sr., noted, these churches were to be beset with new "pitfalls and perils," being confronted simultaneously with "two great challenges" — the one to their "system of thought," the other to their "social program."[39] The first focuses attention on the new intellectual climate of the post–Civil War period, and the second on the new urban and industrial environment. The response to this dual challenge is the concern of the next two chapters.

[39] Schlesinger's essay, "A Critical Period in American Protestantism, 1875–1900," *Massachusetts Historical Society Proceedings*, 64 (1930–32), 523–48, is reprinted in John M. Mulder and John F. Wilson, eds., *Religion in American History* (Englewood Cliffs, N.J., 1978), 302–17. For Protestantism's response to the twofold challenge, see Robert T. Handy, *A Christian America* (N.Y., 1984), 134–58.

CHAPTER 11

The New
Intellectual Climate

During the post-Appomattox years when many of the Protestant churches were preoccupied with problems related to Reconstruction in the South and missionary expansion in the West and were devoting their energies to revival campaigns and Sunday school work, crucial theological issues were being raised by radical changes in the intellectual climate—issues that could not long be ignored.

Within a decade after the Civil War, practically every important American scientist had been converted to Darwin's theory of biological evolution, and Herbert Spencer's "social Darwinism" was equally influential.[1] Indeed, as early as 1872, the *Atlantic Monthly* was able to report that within the scientific community "natural selection" had "quite won the day in Germany and England, and very nearly won it in America." This new intellectual current penetrated the public consciousness with astonishing rapidity. "Ten or fifteen years ago," Whitelaw Reid declared in an address at Dartmouth in 1873, "the staple subject here for reading and talk, outside study hours, was English poetry and fiction. Now it is English science. Herbert Spencer, John Stuart Mill, Huxley, Darwin, Tyndall, have usurped the places of Tennyson and Browning, and Matthew Arnold and Dickens." And the discussion was not limited to college students. Equally avid interest in the new scientific theories was displayed by the general public, if the amount of space devoted by the popular periodicals and newspapers to academic lectures and debates is an accurate index of what was being read and discussed.

The new biblical studies were another feature of the postwar intellectual climate. These studies, stemming mainly from the German universities but partly the work of British textual critics, utilized the techniques of

---

[1] See Richard Hofstadter, *Social Darwinism in American Thought* (N.Y., 1959).

"scientific history" to exhibit the Bible as a varied compilation of poetry, prophecy, history, and folklore that had been assembled over a period of 1,000 years. The extent of the popular interest awakened by these studies is indicated by the reception that was given in 1881 to the English Revised Version of the New Testament which incorporated the results of scholarly analysis of the text. The *Chicago Times* and the *Chicago Tribune* both printed the entire text, and 200,000 copies of the revised New Testament were sold in New York within less than a week.

Furthermore, the study of comparative religion was coming to the fore as an academic discipline, and it soon became apparent that the non-Christian religions also were of fascinating interest to the reading public. James Freeman Clarke's sympathetic appraisal of *Ten Great Religions* went through 21 editions after it was published in 1871.[2] Toward the end of the century when a World's Parliament of Religions was held in connection with the Columbian Exposition of 1892–93, more than 150,000 people attended its sessions.

Finally, before the century was out the burgeoning "sciences" of psychology and sociology made their appearance as forces to be reckoned with in the intellectual life of the nation. Almost immediately religious phenomena were subjected to psychological and sociological analysis. E. D. Starbuck was one of the pioneers, and his *Psychology of Religion* (1899) was something of an overnight sensation. When William James published his Gifford Lectures, *The Varieties of Religious Experience* (1902), the interest was so great that within a dozen years it had been reprinted 21 times. Ten years later J. H. Leuba pointed up in provocative fashion the disturbing implications of the psychological approach in his *Psychological Study of Religion* (1912). In the meantime, William Graham Sumner had published *Folkways* (1906), a sociological study of human behavior that stressed the socially conditioned character of religion and rejected any notion of absolute or eternal truth.

Each of these several currents of thought constituted a threat to accepted understandings of the Christian faith. The psychological and sociological studies tended to reduce religion to a social phenomenon. The accounts of other religions raised questions with regard to the uniqueness of the Christian faith. Both Darwinian biology and the new biblical studies seemed to undermine the authority of the Bible. How could one reconcile Darwinism with the Genesis accounts of creation? How could one adjust the doctrine of biblical inspiration to take account of errors and contradictions in the biblical text that were noted by the scholars? What was one to make of a composite authorship of the books of Moses, with fragments of the text being assigned to widely separated times? What happened to the prophetic character of the book of Isaiah if parts of it were written by a

---

[2] Clarke's views initially were expressed in an article published in 1857, a portion of which is reprinted in Smith, Handy, and Loetscher, *American Christianity*, II, 160–64.

later, "second Isaiah" who was reporting events rather than predicting them? These were unsettling questions and their disturbing implications were made plain to the thousands who listened to Robert G. Ingersoll — "the notorious infidel" — as he ranged back and forth across the land questioning basic tenets of Christian belief.[3] Other thousands read his lectures — *The Gods* (1872), *Some Mistakes of Moses* (1879), *Why I Am an Agnostic* (1896) — in printed form. On a less popular level, J. W. Draper sought to demonstrate the incompability of science and religion in his *History of the Conflict Between Religion and Science* (1874), a task also undertaken by Andrew D. White in his *History of the Warfare of Science with Theology* (1896).

The pattern of response among Protestants, Roman Catholics, and Jews to the challenge of scientific modes of thought was remarkably similar. There were some who resisted the new intellectual currents and rejected any modification of inherited theological formulations. There were others who came to believe that the traditional forms of faith were no longer relevant and must be discarded and replaced with idioms and practices that were forthright expressions of a scientific world view. A third group occupied an intermediate position between the two extremes, seeking to effect adjustments that would do justice both to the essential elements of the inherited faith and to the newer scientific patterns of thought. The radical tendency never loomed large on the American scene, and the moderate "liberal" tendencies in Roman Catholicism were arrested by papal intervention. But both in Reformed Judaism (see Chapter 13) and liberal Protestant evangelicalism were new modes of thought destined to flourish.

Protestant Liberalism

The mood of most Protestant churchmen at the close of the Civil War was reflected in the proceedings of the Congregational National Council, which met in Boston on July 14, 1865. The assembly listened "with profound attention for two full hours" to an opening sermon on the text "Ask for old paths" (Jer. 6:16), and then proceeded to adopt a Declaration of Faith to serve as a bulwark "for the defense of the Word of God now assailed by multiform and dangerous errors." This was not an entirely ritualistic performance, for the Council was aware of new and urgent problems. But many of the errors it had in mind were those of an earlier generation that the "old paths" had been designed to skirt, and it soon became obvious that signposts pointing to "old paths" were to have only

---

[3] Ingersoll, the son of a Congregational minister, was a great orator who had electrified the Republican convention of 1876 with his famous "plumed knight" speech nominating James G. Blaine for the presidency.

limited utility in helping Christians avoid the perils and pitfalls of the
theologically unmapped terrain of the postwar years.

Henry Ward Beecher, pastor of Plymouth Congregational Church in
Brooklyn from 1847 to 1887 and easily the most prominent preacher of
his time, was one of the earliest to recognize that the mere repetition of
ancient doctrines would no longer do. In 1872, as the first Lyman Beecher
lecturer at Yale, he warned the students of the Divinity School of the
danger they faced of being left behind by "the intelligent part of society."

> There is being now applied among scientists a greater amount of real,
> searching discriminating thought . . . than ever has been expended
> . . . in the whole history of the world put together. . . .
>   If ministers do not make their theological systems conform to the facts as
> they are; if they do not recognize what men are studying, the time will not be
> far distant when the pulpit will be like a voice crying in the wilderness. And
> it will not be "Prepare the way of the Lord," either. . . . The providence of
> God is rolling forward in a spirit of investigation that Christian ministers
> must meet and join.

The one thing ministers cannot afford, insisted Beecher, is to become
"apostles of the dead past" by letting "the development of truth run
ahead of them." Consequently, many seminaries took steps to familiarize
their students with the scientific world view, a program that in the end
produced mixed results for religion.[4]

The Fundamental Issue of Biblical Authority

The most heated initial debate centered on the notion of biological evolution, for it was a dramatic issue and, by its apparent contradiction of the
Bible, Darwin's theory seemed to strike at the very root of a biblically
grounded faith. Charles Hodge, the towering theological oracle of Princeton Theological Seminary, declared in 1874 that "a more absolutely
incredible theory was never propounded for acceptance among men," and
Mark Hopkins, the equally distinguished president of Williams College,
denounced the whole concept as "essentially atheistic." A different verdict, however, had been pronounced three years earlier by Hodge's
neighbor James McCosh, president of Princeton University. "I am inclined to think," he said, "that the theory contains a large body of important truths." If one distinguished the "major assumptions" of the biblical
accounts of creation from their literary form, McCosh saw no reason why
creation as described in Genesis should be regarded as inconsistent with

---

[4] *Yale Lectures on Preaching* (N.Y., 1872–74), I, 87–89. See C. E. Clark, *Henry Ward
Beecher: Spokesman for Middle Class America* (Champaign, Ill., 1978). A perceptive
analysis of the forces behind Beecher's fears and the manner in which they influenced
religion is James W. Turner, *Without God, Without Creed: The Origins of Unbelief in
America* (Baltimore, 1985).

developmental theories. Holding fast to the traditional doctrine of design in nature, he interpreted "natural selection" as the product of "supernatural design."[5]

A similar resolution of the problem was proposed by John Fiske. In his *Outline of Cosmic Philosophy* (1874) and subsequent volumes, he transmuted the struggle for survival into a struggle for the lives of others. Infusing the whole process with divine purpose, Fiske coined the sentence —"Evolution is God's way of doing things"— which was later popularized as a slogan by Lyman Abbot. In the meantime, Henry Ward Beecher had given further impetus to this type of adjustment, announcing in the *Christian Union* (August 2, 1883) that he was "a cordial Christian evolutionist."[6] But perhaps the most reassuring evidence to many faithful Christians that evolutionary views could be assimilated without harm to the Christian faith was provided by Henry Drummond, the author of *Natural Law in the Spiritual World* (1883). This gifted young Scottish theologian was an intimate friend of Dwight L. Moody, and when Drummond visited the United States in 1887, Moody enlisted his aid both at Northfield and in his revival meetings.

The theory of biological evolution was actually the least serious of the intellectual problems the churches were being compelled to face. Whereas it could be handled by construing the first chapter of Genesis allegorically or by contending that the Bible was never intended to be a scientific encyclopedia, other problems could not be sidestepped so easily. This was notably true of the issues that were being raised by the "scientific" study of the Bible, for the new biblical studies were making it increasingly evident that any attempt to justify even the "major assumptions" of the Christian faith by an appeal to the authority of Scripture was fraught with difficulty. Biblical scholars were demonstrating that at many points of Christian doctrine conflicting evidence could be adduced from within the biblical text itself.

In 1867 these difficulties were pointed out by Thomas F. Curtis of Bucknell University in *The Human Element in the Inspiration of the Sacred Scriptures*, and the measure of the confusion he evoked is indicated by the reaction to his book of a fellow Baptist, Henry G. Weston, who was soon to become president of Grozer Theological Seminary. "I am all at sea," wrote Weston, "except so far as a dogged belief in inspiration goes, without being able to define what inspiration' is or what its metes and bounds are." Small wonder Weston was determined to hold fast to a belief

---

[5] See Charles Hodge, *What Is Darwinism?* (N.Y., 1874); and James McCosh, *Christianity and Positivism* (N.Y., 1871).

[6] For Beecher and Abbott, see Beecher's *Evolution and Religion* (N.Y., 1885), and Abbott's *The Theology of an Evolutionist* (N.Y., 1897).

in inspiration, for this had been the major line of defense of the whole dogmatic structure.[7]

The central issue was the authority of the Bible. Few great religions have been so dependent as Christianity upon a sacred book. Preaching elucidated its texts. Prayer claimed its promises. And theology and conduct alike were grounded on its teachings. Although both Protestants and Roman Catholics had long regarded the Bible as the inspired and inerrant Word of God, the Roman Catholic Church found it necessary at the Council of Trent (1545–63) to supplement biblical teaching with that of "tradition," and at the first Vatican Council (1870) to affirm papal infallibility in the interpretation of Scripture and tradition. Protestants, on the other hand, had clung to the sole authority of Scripture, which in the first half of the nineteenth century was almost universally understood in terms of an inspired and infallible text. Since they had no recourse to any supplementary authority, the questioning of biblical inspiration was peculiarly threatening to Protestants. Once this point was surrendered, a thorough reconsideration of the basis of the Christian faith was required. Ultimately Protestants worked out different ways of understanding biblical authority, but first many of them sought in "evangelical liberalism" and "scientific modernism" other sources of authority.

Evangelical Liberalism

The striking feature of the liberal movement in Protestantism that began to take shape during the 1870s was its conservative intent. Leaders of the movement were evangelicals, standing firmly within the church, cherishing their Christian experience, and uncompromising in their loyalty to Christ. They had little in common with the earlier rationalistic liberalism that became dominant in Unitarianism. The central concern was quite explicitly apologetic. They wished to preserve the truth of the gospel as it spoke to the hearts of men. In the face of what many feared might be fatal assaults on the Christian faith, they sought to restate the essential doctrines of evangelical Christianity in terms that would be both intelligible and convincing and thus establish them on a more secure foundation.

Henry Ward Beecher was the most conspicuous of the early liberal leaders and it would be easy to overestimate his importance.[8] The influ-

---

[7] See J. W. Brown, *The Rise of Biblical Criticism in America, 1800–1870* (Middletown, Conn., 1969); and N. H. Maring, "Baptists and Changing Views of the Bible, 1865–1918," *Foundations* (July 1958), 52–78, (October 1958), 30–61.

[8] F. H. Foster made this mistake in *The Modern Movement in American Theology* (N.Y., 1939), devoting a whole chapter to "The School of Henry Ward Beecher." J. W. Buckham also asserted that, next to Horace Bushnell, Beecher was "the greatest liberator of American theological thought." *Progressive Religious Thought in America* (N.Y., 1919), 32.

ence he exerted was great, but he was no theologian. At most he was a popularizer—a "weather cock" some called him. The real theological task of adjusting the inherited formulations of the faith to the new "scientific" climate of opinion was the work of other men.

Although isolated individuals in various parts of the country helped fashion what came to be called the "New Theology" and "Progressive Orthodoxy," the most important contribution was made by a notable group of pastors in prominent New England pulpits, all of whom had been deeply influenced by Horace Bushnell. In neighboring churches on the New Haven green, Theodore T. Munger and Newman Smyth gave new luster to a tradition of distinguished theological preaching that had been exemplified in these same pulpits by Jonathan Edwards, Jr., and Nathaniel W. Taylor. Munger, at the United (Congregational) Church, was the author of *The Freedom of Faith* (1883), which the *New York Times* called the "most forcible and positive expression" of the new theology to appear in this country;[9] and Smyth, at the Center (Congregational) Church, had argued the same case in three pioneering volumes: *The Religious Feeling* (1877), *Old Faiths in New Light* (1878), and *The Orthodox Theology of Today* (1881). In Boston, Phillips Brooks at Trinity (Episcopal) Church and George A. Gordon at Old South (Congregational) Church were making Copley Square a center of the new theological outlook. Washington Gladden was less philosophically inclined, but he was equally creative in his own way and was the most effective propagandist of the new point of view. As early as 1873 he had written for the *Independent* an editorial entitled "Immoral Theology," which exhibited the journalistic flair that won widespread circulation for his subsequent books dealing with current theological issues: *Burning Questions* (1886), *Who Wrote the Bible?* (1891), *Ruling Ideas of the Present Age* (1895), *Seven Puzzling Bible Books* (1897), and *How Much Is Left of the Old Doctrines?* (1899). By the time these books were published, Gladden had left New England in 1882 to accept a call to the First Congregational Church of Columbus, Ohio. All these young men were responding in the immediate post–Civil War years to the practical necessity of relating the Christian faith from week to week to questions that were uppermost in the minds of alert and inquiring congregations.

Meanwhile in theological seminaries a less conspicuous intellectual ferment was taking place, the consequence in part of the stimulus provided by younger members of the faculties who had spent a period of study abroad where they had imbibed the advanced theological thinking of the German universities. The most dramatic shift occurred at Andover Theological Seminary, which had been established in 1808 as a counter to Unitarian tendencies at Harvard and had been shackled with a creed designed to prevent any deviation from orthodoxy. A new type of think-

---

[9] C. H. Hopkins, *The Rise of the Social Gospel in American Protestantism* (New Haven, 1940), 61.

ing began to be introduced at Andover in the 1860s, but no open break occurred until 1880 when William J. Tucker qualified his subscription to the creed.

> The creed which I am about to read and to which I subscribe I fully accept as setting forth the truth against the errors which it was designed to meet. No confession so elaborate and with such intent may assume to be the final expression of the truth or an expression equally fitted in language or tone to all times.[10]

When Edwards A. Park, the last great champion of New England orthodoxy, retired the following year, the liberals were left in complete control. Three years later the faculty began publication of the *Andover Review* to elucidate their "progressive orthodoxy."

Although this developing liberal sentiment was indebted to insights supplied from abroad by Friedrich Schleiermacher (1768–1834) and Albrecht Ritschl (1822–89), it was mediated in part through British scholars and scholarship. It also had indigenous rootage in categories and understandings provided by Horace Bushnell, who earlier had been influenced by Schleiermacher and Coleridge. Bushnell was perhaps the key figure, for in many ways it was Bushnell who eased the difficult transition for evangelical Christians from the old to the new theology. As early as 1844 Bushnell had provided the basis for an adjustment to evolutionary views when he asserted that "growth and not conquest" was "the true method of Christian progress."[11] Through his analysis of the use and limitations of language, he also offered a way of escape from bondage to the verbal forms in which doctrinal statements had been cast. But the real key to the influence Bushnell exerted upon his younger contemporaries was his success in fashioning a definitely Christocentric theology that was based upon Christian experience rather than upon any external dogmatic authority. Thus the believer was no longer under compulsion to find his security in biblical proof texts. He could accept the conclusions of the biblical scholars with relative equanimity and appropriate the results of other scientific investigations without great difficulty because his faith was validated by the inward testimony of the heart. Bushnell had discovered this path of escape from his "arrant doubts" at the very beginning of his

---

[10] See D. D. Williams, *The Andover Liberals* (N.Y., 1941), 28. A thorough analysis of the transformation of Andover, and of changes in religious thought in this period, is in Bruce Kuklick, *Churchmen and Philosophers: From Jonathan Edwards to John Dewey* (New Haven, 1985).

[11] See Buckham, *Progressive Religious Thought*, 11. Bushnell, of course, also had found much that was suggestive in the English theologian Frederick Denison Maurice (1805–72). For some of the points at which he diverged from the German theologians, see Fred Kirshenmann, "Horace Bushnell: Orthodox or Sabellian?" *Church History*, 33 (1964), 49–59.

ministry. What shall I do with the doctrine of the Trinity, he asked, when "logic shatters it all to pieces and I am all at the four winds"?

> I am glad that I have a heart as well as a head. My heart wants the Father; my heart wants the Son; my heart wants the Holy Ghost—the one just as much as the other. My heart says the Bible has a Trinity for me, and I mean to hold by my heart.[12]

Secure in the conviction that "the heart has its reasons, which reason does not know," Bushnell, echoing Pascal, found a freedom denied to those who felt compelled to meet a rationalistic assault with a purely rationalistic defense.

In keeping with their apologetic concern, the starting point of all theology for the heirs of Bushnell in pulpit and classroom was to be found in Christ. Christ stood at the heart of the religious experience they were seeking to defend. Christ alone, declared Egbert C. Smyth of Andover Theological Seminary, "fulfills the aspirations and harmonizes the discords in man's religious history."

> The history of religion leads on and up to him, and he possesses all the resources requisite for its greatest possible future growth. He is the Alpha and Omega; the Absolute, revealed; the Infinite, personally disclosed; the eternal Power that makes for righteousness, realized in the Righteous One. . . . A theology which is not Christocentric is like a Ptolomaic astronomy; it is out of true relation to the earth and heavens, to God and the universe.[13]

Thus, although there was much that earlier generations had affirmed that could be surrendered as nonessential and much that had to be adjusted and accommodated to new knowledge, the person and work of Christ as the clue to the nature of God, the worth of human personality, and the meaning of life were indispensable. His life and teachings constituted "the final principle" of "interpretation," the standard by which all else must be judged. The goal of the New Theology, as William Adams Brown was to point out in 1898 in his inaugural address as professor of systematic theology in Union Theological Seminary, was no more than "the old cry, 'Back to Christ.' Let no theology call itself Christian which has not its center and source in him."

Although these evangelical liberals clung tenaciously to the Bible and repaired to it for consolation and inspiration, they viewed it as a document that recorded the historical experience out of which the Christian faith had emerged, a vivid personal record of suffering and travail that culmi-

---

[12] *Life and Letters of Horace Bushnell,* ed. M. B. Cheney (N.Y., 1880), 56; quoted by Mead, *Lively Experiment,* 136.
[13] *Progressive Orthodoxy,* by the editors of *Andover Review* (Boston, 1886), 35–36.

nated in the disclosure in Christ of true and perfect communion with God. It was a record not of a theology but of an experience that was to be reproduced "in our own times and in our own souls." Although it told them what they knew of Christ, there was no need to seek "scientific arguments for Christian truth," for their own experience of Christ was self-authenticating. "The foundation of spiritual faith is neither in the church nor in the Bible, but in the spiritual consciousness of man."[14] The doctrines that "form the subject matter of theology," declared Brown in his inaugural address, are not "dogmas to be received on authority"; they are "living convictions, born of experience, and maintaining themselves in spite of all opposition because of the response which they wake in the hearts and consciences" of advocates of new ways of thinking.

Few of these men exhibited any great metaphysical interest, but those who did found in idealistic philosophy a way of theologizing that did not depend upon complicated processes of biblical criticism. Some, like George A. Gordon, appropriated the "monistic" form of idealism of which Josiah Royce was the most conspicuous American representative. Others, mostly fellow Methodists, adopted the "personalism" of Borden P. Bowne of Boston University. The greater number, however, were content to give only passing attention to philosophical issues and to structure their theological thinking within more familiar biblical categories. Typical in this respect was William Newton Clarke, the Baptist theologian at Colgate Theological Seminary, whose *Outline of Christian Theology* (1898) was so widely used that it has been called "virtually the Dogmatik" of evangelical liberalism.[15]

The same impulse to reinvigorate the Christian witness by a less stultifying understanding of the Christian faith that stood at the heart of the New Theology found parallel expression in a related movement known by many names but most commonly called "the higher Christian life" theology.[16] Like the New Theology of evangelical liberalism, it stressed the centrality of religious experience and the work of the Holy Spirit, but was less interested in intellectual questions. Wesleyan holiness leaders had long been committed to the idea that conversion should be followed by a baptism of the Spirit, the primary effect of which was purity of life. The

---

[14] See Lyman Abbott, *Reminiscences* (Boston, 1915), 451, 461–62.

[15] The phrase is that of Sydney E. Ahlstrom, "Theology in America," *The Shaping of American Religion,* ed. Smith and Jamison, 292. C. B. Smith described it as "perhaps the most influential book of its kind in American religious thinking." *Current Christian Thinking* (Chicago, 1928), 83. W. A. Brown's *Christian Theology in Outline* (1906) was largely based upon Clarke's text. Kenneth Cauthen, *The Impact of American Religious Liberalism* (N.Y., 1962), 42–43. Insight into the changing attitude toward the Bible can best be gained from William Newton Clarke's *Sixty Years with the Bible* (N.Y., 1909), a moving autobiographical account of the development of his own views through six decades.

[16] See Grant Wacker, "The Holy Spirit and the Spirit of the Age in American Protestantism, 1880–1910," *Journal of American History* (1985), 45–62.

higher Christian life leaders, in contrast, thought of this second transforming religious experience as energizing and empowering believers to
witness for Christ and thus serve the church and society. So closely akin
was the higher Christian life emphasis to some expressions of the New
Theology that it is often difficult to tell within which camp different
leaders should be classified. Both were rooted in churches of a Reformed
rather than a Wesleyan background, both were similar in social and cultural status, and evangelical liberals were no less emphatic in appealing to
the testimony of the heart and religious experience. Some of the latter did
not hesitate to speak of a new apostolate of the Spirit.[17]

The great advantage of both forms of a revived evangelicalism was that
proponents were enabled to maintain what to them was the heart of the
inherited faith without coming into conflict with the intellectual climate of
the modern world. The stress upon self-authenticating religious experience allowed the higher Christian life advocates to bypass for a time many
potentially troublesome issues, whereas the same stress permitted evangelical liberals to bridge the gap between the natural and the supernatural
and to give due recognition to the claims of science and the scientific
method. The acceptance of the idea of development made it possible to
view the Bible in a way that was congenial to both their religious and their
cultural orientation, allowed them to share to varying degrees the growing
confidence in man and his future, and fostered an open-minded attitude
toward differing opinions and new modes of thought.

Scientific Modernism

Although evangelical liberalism continued to be the dominant liberal
current in American Protestantism, a more radical approach to the issue
of the relation of science to religion began to emerge in the first years of
the twentieth century. Those who in retrospect have been called "scientific modernists"[18] stood in marked contrast to the conservative intent of
evangelical liberals, for they viewed as a lost cause the endeavor of the
evangelical liberals to maintain continuity with the inherited faith by
abstracting religion from the realm of scientific verification. These men
recognized that the sanctuary of the heart which the evangelical liberals
sought to preserve inviolate had been invaded by the scientists. "Science,"

---

[17] See *Walter Rauschenbusch's: Selected Writings*, ed. W. S. Hudson (N.Y., 1984), 22, 25,
32–33.

[18] The term was coined by Sidney E. Mead. Although exact lines of demarcation between
the evangelical liberals and the scientific modernists are difficult to draw, there was a
clear difference of intention and emphasis. The liberals were committed first and
foremost to the Christian tradition and from that vantage point attempted to effect
any necessary adjustments. The scientific modernists took their stand with the
presuppositions of science, and then sought to reclaim what they could of the
traditional faith. Complicating the picture is the fact that evangelical liberals frequently
called themselves "modernists."

E. D. Starbuck had proclaimed in 1899, "has conquered one field after another, until now it is entering the most complex, the most inaccessible, and of all the most sacred domain—that of religion." The scientific modernists were impressed by the way in which psychological and sociological analysis was able to explain religious experience, doctrinal concepts, and ecclesiastical practice in terms of inner personal drives and conditioning social forces. Thus they were ready to grant "to the data of religious experience the same scientific status as the data of the physical sciences," and then to fashion a religious faith "out of the materials furnished by the several sciences."[19] They did not seek a complete break with the Christian past, as is made clear in Shailer Mathews' classic definition of modernism—"the use of the methods of modern science to find, state, and use the permanent and central values of inherited orthodoxy in meeting the needs of a modern world."[20] The values of orthodoxy were not to be ignored, but "science" was the arbiter in determining what they were and how they were to be stated and used.[21] It is safe to assume, Mathews asserted, that "scientists know more about nature and man than did the theologians who drew up the Creeds and Confessions." The tendency was to become less concerned with a distinctively Christian witness and more interested in general religious affirmations based on a "scientific world view."

Unlike liberal evangelicalism, which initially was the product of the reflections of men who were pastors of churches, scientific modernism was indigenous to the theological seminaries. The great center was at Chicago, where William Rainey Harper and John D. Rockefeller had established their Baptist super-university in 1892, assembling for that purpose many of the most noted scholars in America. Many pastors found comfort and reassurance and themes for sermons in the reports that filtered down to them from the psychologists and sociologists that religious beliefs integrated personality, fostered mental health, and served socially useful ends; yet the theological professors at Chicago, with John Dewey, Albion W. Small, and George Herbert Mead numbered among their university colleagues, were compelled to face the fundamental theological issue that was raised by the empiricism upon which these new disciplines were based.

The Chicago approach to theology (they hesitated to call it more than a theological method) was not fully elaborated until after World War I, but its basic character was evident much earlier. The key figures of the Divinity School faculty, in addition to a distinguished corps of biblical scholars

---

[19] E. E. Aubrey, "Religious Bearings of the Modern Scientific Movement," in *Environmental Factors in Christian History*, ed. J. T. McNeill *et al.* (Chicago, 1939), 368.

[20] See the portion of Mathews' *The Faith of Modernism* which is reprinted in Smith, Handy, and Loetscher, *American Christianity*, II, 238–45.

[21] A typical monograph was that of George A. Coe, "What Does Modern Psychology Permit Us to Believe in Respect to Regeneration?" *American Journal of Theology*, 12 (1908), 353–68.

headed by Harper himself, were Shailer Mathews, George Burman Foster, Shirley Jackson Case and Gerald Birney Smith; and Edward Scribner Ames—simultaneously professor of philosophy in the university, pastor of the University Church of the Disciples of Christ, and dean of the Disciples Divinity House—also provided strong leadership in the task of theological reconstruction. The dominant emphasis, exemplified pre-eminently by Mathews, was upon a sociohistorical approach to theology that viewed all doctrinal statements as reflections of historic cultural patterns, and consequently were functional and not normative, changeable and not permanent. They were to be tested and applied "in the same way that chemists and historians reach and apply their conclusions," and they must be stated in terms that would make sense to intelligent men and women within the contemporary cultural context. "The God of the scientifically minded will assume the patterns of science."[22]

In spite of the fact that some members of the Chicago group moved to a nontheist position and others found it difficult to find anything either unique or normative in the Christian faith, the influence they exerted in the life of the churches was far from insignificant. This was partly due to the fact that for a period of 30 or 40 years a very large proportion of professors in other theological seminaries received their graduate training at Chicago. Scarcely less important was the fact that most of the key figures remained staunch churchmen and played a leading role in ecclesiastical affairs. Mathews, for example, was president of the Federal Council of Churches from 1912 to 1916 and of the American (Northern) Baptist Convention in 1915. Finally, the men at Chicago exhibited an intensely practical propagandist zeal. Harper set the pattern when he became superintendent of the Hyde Park Baptist Sunday School in order to put his theories into practice, and with the stimulus of Harper's interest the University of Chicago pioneered in the new "scientific" approach to religious education. One of the most effective means of penetration was a scheme of adult education known as the American Institute of Sacred Literature, through which books, pamphlets, and study courses in a steady stream were made available and were widely used in Protestant churches throughout the Midwest.

Protestant Conservatism

Mounting accommodation within Protestantism to the new intellectual climate did not go unchallenged. From the beginning resistance was both vocal and widespread, but the response was mainly limited to dogmatic denials grounded in a pietistic indifference to the new "scientific" studies.

---

[22] *The Faith of Modernism*, in Smith, Handy, and Loetscher, *American Christianity*, II, 240–41; and Mathews, *The Growth of the Idea of God* (N.Y., 1931), 184.

Charles Hodge, in an earlier debate, set the tone of the unyielding defensive posture of the conservative elements when he declared: "We can even afford to acknowledge our incompetence to meet them in argument, or to answer their objections; and yet our faith remains unshaken and rational."[23] There was no prominent theologian to play a constructive role comparable to that of a P. T. Forsyth (1848–1921) in Britain or a Martin Kähler (1835–1912) in Germany, unless the attempt of Augustus H. Strong to find a mediating position qualifies him to be ranked with his European contemporaries.[24] Nevertheless, when defenders of the inherited formulations of the faith chose to fight the battle on the basis of biblical inerrancy, they were astute enough to recognize that the central issue was the authority of Scripture even if they failed to recognize that there may have been a more tenable position than a doctrine of "inspiration" upon which to base their defense.

The Heresy Trials

Congregationalists and Baptists, with their loose form of organization, offered the freest field for the growth of liberal sentiment.[25] Neither denomination had any ready means of taking action to enforce doctrinal conformity. Once installed in a church, a pastor was secure as long as he retained the support of his own congregation, and most of their theological seminaries were independently organized and not subject to denominational control. Although Ezra P. Gould was dismissed from Newton Theological Seminary in 1882 and Nathaniel Schmidt from Colgate in 1896, all northern Baptist seminaries were in the liberal camp by the end of the century. This was also true of Congregational seminaries, with Andover's status having been clarified in 1892 when the Supreme Court of Massachusetts sustained the trustees and voided the action of the Board of Visitors in dismissing Egbert C. Smyth from the faculty.

Methodists had the means of closing ranks to prevent doctrinal innovation, but in the North they exhibited little inclination to do so. In spite of the fact that such men as Nathan Bangs, Daniel D. Whedon, and Miner Raymond had whetted their theological scalpels and used them with great effectiveness in running debates with Calvinists, the Methodists as a result

---

23 *Princeton Review* (1857), 662.
24 See Grant Wacker, *Augustus Hopkins Strong* (Macon, Ga., 1985).
25 The Disciples offered an equally free field, but among them the issue assumed a different form. The division was between those who placed primary emphasis upon the Disciples' traditional theme of the "restoration" of the primitive church and those who gave major stress to the equally traditional theme of Christian unity. Such men as Peter Ainslee and Charles Clayton Morrison gained their chief distinction as advocates of Christian unity. Edward Scribner Ames was one of the most prominent of the "scientific modernists." By 1906 the rigidly biblistic wing of the Disciples—the "Churches of Christ" of the middle South—had gone its separate way.

of their continuing emphasis upon the centrality of heart religion had developed no sharply defined theological position. To the extent that they held to external tests of fellowship, their stress was upon morality rather than dogma. When charges of denying the inerrancy of Scripture were leveled in 1904 against Hinkley G. Mitchell of the Boston University School of Theology and then against Borden P. Bowne, the General Conference of 1908 put a stop to any further proceedings of this type by relieving the bishops of responsibility for investigating charges of erroneous teaching in Methodist schools. Although there were subsequent flurries of controversy among northern Methodists, the official policy of the denomination hewed closely to the line represented by John Wesley's oft-repeated dictum: "Is thy heart as my heart? Then give me thy hand." The Protestant Episcopal Church followed a similar policy of comprehension, with the trial of Algernon S. Crapsey in 1906 being the only conspicuous exception. Even Crapsey probably would not have been summoned to defend his theological views had he not embarrassed his bishop by combining his doctrinal errors with radical attacks upon the existing economic order.

The Lutherans, in contrast to these other denominations, maintained an almost solidly unbroken orthodox front. The most liberal of the major Lutheran bodies—the General Synod of the Lutheran Church in the United States—tightened its discipline in 1895 and affirmed that its doctrinal basis was "the Word of God as the infallible rule of faith and practice, and the unaltered Augsburg Confession as throughout in perfect consistence with it—nothing more, nothing less." Thus the heresy trials that gained so much attention in the public press were largely confined to the reunited Presbyterian church in the North.

Among northern Presbyterians the issue was raised in 1874 when Francis L. Patton of McCormick Theological Seminary lodged charges of heresy against David Swing, pastor of the Fourth Presbyterian Church in Chicago. The local presbytery acquitted him, but when Patton filed notice of his intention to appeal the verdict, Swing resigned and established an independent congregation. During the next decade several other men, including W. C. McCune of Cincinnati, W. W. McLane of Steubenville, Ohio, and J. W. White of Huntington, Pennsylvania, were dismissed from the ministry on doctrinal grounds. The most celebrated trials, however, were those of Charles A. Briggs and Henry Preserved Smith.[26]

The Briggs case was precipitated in 1891 by his inaugural address as the first occupant of the newly created chair of biblical theology in Union Theological Seminary (New York), an address in which he vigorously condemned "the dogma of verbal inspiration."[27] There were two immedi-

---

[26] For the trials, see L. A. Loetscher, *The Broadening Church: A Study of Theological Issues in the Presbyterian Church Since 1869* (Philadelphia, 1954).

[27] A portion of the address is in Smith, Handy, and Loetscher, *American Christianity*, II, 275–79.

ate consequences. First, the Presbyterian General Assembly withheld its approval of his appointment. Second, charges of heresy were filed with the presbytery of New York. Briggs was acquitted by the presbytery, but the General Assembly set aside the verdict and suspended Briggs from the ministry. The veto of his appointment by the General Assembly was brushed aside by the Seminary as irrelevant. Two decades earlier the Seminary had granted the General Assembly the right to confirm appointments to its faculty. In this instance, however, Briggs had been a member of the faculty since 1874 and the Seminary contended that the authority of the General Assembly did not extend to a transfer within the faculty from one chair to another. In the end, the Seminary revoked its earlier grant of authority, severed this somewhat tenuous official connection with the Presbyterian church, and retained Briggs — who solved the problem of his ministerial standing by becoming an Episcopalian.

At the same time the Briggs affair was before the General Assembly, the case of Smith, a professor in Lane Theological Seminary, was also being adjudicated. Smith had come to the defense of Briggs and was convicted of heresy on similar grounds in 1892 by the presbytery of Cincinnati. This meant the end of his relationship to Lane Seminary, but Union Seminary provided him with a haven as librarian. A few years later another Presbyterian member of the Union faculty, Arthur Cushman McGiffert, had charges preferred against him, and to avoid another heresy trial he became a Congregationalist.

The heresy trials failed to halt the growing theological cleavage even among the Presbyterians. Not only did the trials bring the issues to the fore and publicize them, they awakened popular sympathy for the "persecuted." And this sympathy in turn was exploited and heightened by widely read novels such as Margaret Deland's *John Ward, Preacher* and Mrs. Humphrey Ward's *Robert Elsmere*. Henry Van Dyke, minister of Brick Presbyterian Church in New York City, spoke for many laymen when he declared: "This great city wants the bread of life. Don't give it the stone of controversy instead." A church that had cast out a warmly devout Professor Briggs was reminded by Van Dyke that it had

> Something to learn and something to forget:
> Hold fast to the good, and seek the better yet:
> Press on, and prove the pilgrim-hope of youth —
> That creeds are milestones on the path to truth.

If orthodoxy was to flourish, Van Dyke insisted, it must breathe the air of freedom. "The best way to defend the Bible is in the open air and in the light of the facts."[28] His admonitions were not without effect, and after the turn of the century at least two of the Presbyterian seminaries —

---

[28] Tertius Van Dyke, *Henry Van Dyke A Biography* (N.Y., 1935), 129.

Auburn in upstate New York and McCormick in Chicago—were exhibiting definite liberal tendencies.

Centers of Conservative Strength

The theological climate of the country varied from section to section. By the time of World War I, New England had long been the great stronghold of Protestant liberalism. New York State, with its Yankee heritage and "New School" tradition, was scarcely less liberal in its dominant theological mood. The Midwest was generally moderate with leaders of both "right" and "left" exerting influence within the churches. This was the area in which the influence of the University of Chicago, through its "extension" activities, was widely felt. On the Pacific coast the old-line denominations were not deeply rooted but, with a few exceptions, their general tone was conservative. Perhaps more significant, especially in California, was a cultural rootlessness that was beginning to manifest itself in a number of new sects and cults. The South had witnessed a few attempts to break with orthodoxy. Alexander Winchell at Vanderbilt had contradicted the Genesis account of creation in 1878, thereby provoking a pointed censure by the General Conference of the southern Methodist church of those who bend "all the energies of their most exalted genius to the inculcation of theories which are calculated, if not designed, to destroy the credibility of the Holy Scriptures."[29] When Winchell refused to resign, the university abolished his position. The following year Crawford H. Toy was forced to resign from the faculty of the Southern Baptist Theological Seminary at Louisville, Kentucky, for teachings that allegedly undercut the absolute authority of Scripture. And in 1886 James Woodrow, uncle of Woodrow Wilson and professor at Columbia Theological Seminary, was condemned and dismissed from his post by the General Assembly of the southern Presbyterian church for suggesting that the theory of evolution could be reconciled with a "not unreasonable interpretation of the Bible."[30] Such incidents were significant only as an occasion for the closing of ranks by the southern churches against any departure from the inherited theological formulations. A placid and undisturbed orthodoxy continued to prevail throughout the South as a whole.

Pennsylvania and New Jersey stood in marked contrast to their neighboring states to the north, for they were dominated by a vigorous, articulate, and strongly entrenched conservatism. This was the Presbyterian citadel, and it was a Presbyterianism that was shaped by the unyielding orthodoxy of Princeton, Western, and Pittsburgh (United Presbyterian) theological seminaries. Also contributing to the conservative cast of the

---

[29] K. K. Bailey, *Southern White Protestantism in the Twentieth Century* (N.Y., 1964), 10.
[30] *Ibid.*

Middle Atlantic states was the strength of the denominations of German origin. The rallying center of the conservative forces was Princeton Theological Seminary, where the mantle of Charles Hodge had been bequeathed to his son Archibald Alexander Hodge and then to Benjamin Warfield, both of whom were as convinced as the elder Hodge that the truth of the gospel had been definitively set forth in the Westminster Confession of 1646. In response to the issues raised by biblical criticism, the younger Hodge and Warfield fashioned the "Princeton doctrine of Inspiration," which became a major defense of biblical inerrancy.

Meanwhile, throughout the northern half of the United States, a new movement was arising that was to give added strength to the conservative forces. This was a movement that found expression in "prophetic" Bible conferences held annually after 1875 at which premillennial views were discussed and advocated. Although differing interpretations of Scripture were represented, those adhering to the "dispensationalist" speculations of J. N. Darby (1800–82) in England were ultimately to prevail and provide the standard by which all else was to be judged. Premillennialist sentiment in America was spearheaded by a few prominent pastors, a number of itinerant evangelists, and additional leadership supplied by newly established "Bible Schools." Displaying little concern for denominational peculiarities, proponents of the "prophetic" understanding of Scripture were making inroads by 1890 in most Protestant denominations. By 1900 varying views were being crowded out, and the victory of the Darbyites (the "any moment now" group) was sealed by the popularity of the *Scofield Reference Bible*, an annotated edition of the Bible prepared by C. I. Scofield and published in 1909. The Scofield Bible imposed a rigid schematization on the complex biblical materials by dividing Scripture into seven or eight distinct historical eras called "dispensations." According to this scheme, the present dispensation was to culminate "any moment now" in the return of Christ to reign in glory.[31]

Pushed by the rising tide of "dispensationalism," many advocates of "the higher Christian life" theology felt it necessary to choose between the harder-line premillennialism and the more benign evangelical liberalism. The result for those who adopted the premillennialist option was a curious blending of the "holiness" motif of the Keswick conferences in England[32] with the hardline dispensationalism of the Darbyite faction of the prophetic conferences.

Among the conspicuous leaders of the dispensationalist movement, after the publication of Scofield's Bible, were Reuben A. Torrey, J. W.

---

[31] See C. N. Kraus, *Dispensationalism in America* (Richmond, 1958); C. B. Bass, *Backgrounds of Dispensationalism* (Grand Rapids, 1960); and F. E. Gaebelein, *The Story of the Scofield Bible* (N.Y., 1959). For the larger context of "dispensationalism," see E. R. Sandeen, *The Roots of Fundamentalism: British and American Millenarianism* (Chicago, 1970).

Chapman, A. C. Dixon, and James M. Gray, all of whom were related in one way or another to the Moody Bible Institute in Chicago. These men tended to interpret every manifestation of theological liberalism as the work of Satan, and constantly voiced their alarm. This preoccupation with heresy led them to identify specific items of Scripture — such as the verbal inerrancy of Scripture, the virgin birth of Christ, and his personal and imminent return — that could be utilized to spot a heretic by a few pointed questions.

Most Protestant conservatives hesitated to identify themselves with the "Bible School" men, for they were not willing to accept the "dispensationalist" doctrine that colored their premillennialist interpretation of the Bible. On occasion, to be sure, the old-line conservatives welcomed "dispensationalist" support when other issues were at stake. And in 1910 the northern Presbyterian General Assembly appropriated the "dispensationalist" technique when it named five "essential and necessary" doctrines that were to be used as tests of orthodoxy. Though not mentioning premillennialism, these "five points" were adopted by many of the Bible School group as a convenient means of detecting heresy.

Although party alignments did take place in every denomination during the years that bridged the turn of the century, the centering of attention on the theological debates between conservatives and liberals can be misleading. Few of the rank-and-file members of the churches were caught up in the controversy. To the extent that they were theologically self-conscious, the great body of American Protestants were conservative and traditional in their basic beliefs, but not rigidly so. They had no thought of abandoning the faith of their fathers, but, having been subjected to several solvents, their definition of that faith was somewhat imprecise. What was most admired was not the rigid stance of embattled theologians, but the great-heartedness of a Dwight L. Moody, who did not stickle at working with those whom he could not regard as doctrinally sound at all points. In the theologically relaxed atmosphere of late nineteenth-century evangelicalism, the eminent Methodist historian, Daniel Dorchester, spoke for the majority when he rejoiced that theology had become "less scholastic and repulsive," had been "lubricated and broadened," and was "the better for its siftings."[33]

Variant Radical Responses

During these same years much more radical attempts to come to terms with the new intellectual climate were taking place outside the established churches. Most of them were not numerically significant, but they are

---

[32] The Keswick conferences were held each summer for the purpose of "promoting practical holiness," and had been initiated in 1875 by men who had been influenced by Dwight L. Moody during his British tour of 1873–75.

[33] The Problem of Religious Progress (N.Y., 1881), 41.

important in illustrating the ferment that had been precipitated. Some were sober attempts at a thoroughgoing reconstruction of religion without a "supernatural" dimension, and others were impressed by "discoveries" in the field of comparative religion, but the most successful were those that constructed a new "science" out of evidence supplied by mesmerism and utilized it as the basic datum for a whole new system of religious belief. What bound these diverse groups together was a common revolt against any accepted understanding of the Christian faith.

The Religion of Humanity

In 1867 the Free Religious Association was formed by a militant group of young Unitarians who had become convinced that organized Christianity, even in its Unitarian form, had become the chief enemy of freedom and progress. They were devotees of science influenced by the positivist philosophy of Auguste Comte and were persuaded that with the tools of science people could become masters of their own destiny.[34] But to release latent energies and to awaken the necessary idealism for the fashioning of a new society in which the peoples of the world would be united in universal brotherhood, they believed that the inspiration of religion was required. The religion they had in mind betrayed many overtones of the transcendentalism of Ralph Waldo Emerson and Theodore Parker, but its major thrust was toward an empirical and scientific naturalism. Conventional theism was abandoned. This was made clear by Octavius Brooks Frothingham, president of the Association, when he declared in *The Religion of Humanity:*

> Whether there shall be peace or war, rule or misrule, purity or corruption, justice or injustice, . . . are questions which men must answer for themselves. There is no higher tribunal before which they can be carried; there is no super-human or extra-human will by which they can be dealt with. If things go well or ill rests with those who are commissioned to make them go.[35]

The fundamental convictions of the "religion of humanity" — as it was disseminated from the pulpit as well as the lyceum podium — were summarized in "Fifty Affirmations" which Francis Ellingwood Abbot published in each issue of the *Index*, the official organ of the Association. The Affirmations begin with the assertion that "religion is the effort of man to perfect himself." This is the oft-times hidden but universal element in all historical religions, and the objective of free religion is the perfecting of people by emancipating them from outward laws and winning them to a

---

[34] There were other, more explicitly Comtean societies, including the Positivist Society which was formed in New York City in 1871 and two Societies of Humanity, one of which Leon Trotsky attended.

[35] *The Religion of Humanity*, 3rd ed. (N.Y., 1875), 171.

voluntary obedience to the inward fundamental law of true humanity. Perhaps the spirit of this free religion was best expressed in the lines of Walt Whitman:

> If I build God a church it shall be a church to men and women.
> If I write hymns they shall be all to men and women.
> If I become a devotee, it shall be to men and women.[36]

Although the Free Religious Association had its origin in Boston, it had representatives elsewhere. Abbot moved to Toledo in 1870, and the Association's most prominent pulpit was in New York City, where Frothingham preached each Sunday in the Lyric Hall to a congregation that included notable figures in the arts and letters. The watchwords of the movement were freedom and unity, and because its strong-minded members believed so wholeheartedly in freedom, there often was little unity and frequently considerable dissension.[37] By 1890 most of the Free Religionists had been reabsorbed into Unitarianism.

The "religion of humanity" found more permanent institutional expression in the Society for Ethical Culture, founded by Felix Adler in 1876. Adler had been trained for the rabbinate but had revolted against his religious heritage. For a time he was president of both his own society and the Free Religious Association. The Ethical Culture movement was never large. It enjoyed, however, a slow but steady growth as long as Adler lived. In 1926 there were six societies in the United States, with a membership of more than 2,000 and perhaps an equal number of peripheral adherents.

Esoteric Wisdom from the East

Theosophy capitalized, on a more popular level, upon much the same interest that had led to the formation of the Free Religious Association. It also emphasized fundamental truths that lay behind all the great religions, assimilated in a curious way the discoveries of modern science, and stressed the godlike potentialities of men and the universal brotherhood of the human race. The founder of the movement was Madame Helena P. Blavatsky, who came to New York in 1872 and three years later established the Theosophical Society.[38] As the wife of a Russian general, she had led a peripatetic existence in the Orient where she had busied herself accumulating occult lore. She claimed that in Tibet she had been instructed in the esoteric wisdom of the ages by a group of "adepts" or

---

[36] *Walt Whitman's Workshop*, ed. C. J. Furness (Cambridge, Mass., 1928), 43.
[37] For the inability of the Free Religionists to act on the basis of complete freedom, see Stow Persons, *Free Religion: An American Faith* (New Haven, 1947), 93–94.
[38] See C.E.B. Roberts, *Mysterious Madame, Helena Blavatsky* (N.Y., 1931); and A. B. Kuhn, *Theosophy* (N.Y., 1930).

"masters" — gifted seers who stood in direct succession to Moses, Krishna, Lao-tze, Confucius, Buddha, Christ, and other great religious prophets. Her teaching combined many features of Spiritualism with a bowdlerized understanding of Buddhism, and interpreted reincarnation as an extension of the evolutionary process. Indicative of her central emphasis are titles of two of her many books: *Isis Unveiled: A Master Key to the Mysteries of Ancient and Modern Science and Theology* (1877) and *The Secret Doctrine: The Synthesis of Science, Religion, and Philosophy* (1893).

After Madame Blavatsky's death the movement divided into two camps when Mrs. Annie Besant[39] began to replace some of the characteristic Buddhist doctrines with concepts derived from Hinduism. Mrs. Besant, with a suave and cultured Hindu brahmin sleeping outside her door to guard her against intrusion, was the leading sensation at the World's Parliament of Religions in 1893. But the conference with the words of Malachi as its motto — "Have we not all one Father? Hath not one God created us?" — provided an opportunity for other representatives of Eastern religions to gain a hearing. The Vedanta Society, a Hindu cult, had its American origin here in the teaching of Swami Vivekananda. A similar movement was the Yogoda Sat-Sanga, or Self-Realization Fellowship, which taught the Hindu practice of yoga. The Bahá'í faith, of Muslim origin, received some notice in 1893 at Chicago, but its American adherents were more fully enlightened when Abdu'lu-Bahá arrived in 1912. The new religion had been founded in Persia in 1853 when Mirza Husayn Ali announced that he was Bahá'u'lláh — "the Glory of God." Operating from the premise that God is unknowable except through a "manifestation," he claimed to be the manifestation for this age commissioned by divine command to unify humanity within one faith and one order. When he died in 1892 he left a testament appointing his son Abdu'l-Bahá — "the Servant of Glory" — as his authoritative interpreter. With its stress on human brotherhood and the unity of all religion, the Bahá'í faith also insists on full and unquestioning acceptance of Baha'u'llah as the authoritative manifestation of God.[40]

Science, Religion, Health

Interest in "mental healing" had been developing in America prior to the Civil War. It was based on experiments with hypnosis by a German physician, Franz Anton Mesmer (1733?–1815), who concluded that a mysterious magnetic fluid was the explanation for the mental power that one person could exercise over another. Phineas Parkhurst Quimby of Portland, Maine, was one of many who became intrigued by the therapeutic power of mesmerism. Ultimately he became convinced that disease could

---

[39] See the two-volume biography by A. H. Nethercot, *The First Five Lives of Annie Besant* (Chicago, 1960), and *The Last Four Lives of Annie Besant* (Chicago, 1963).

[40] R. H. Stockman, *The Baha'i Faith in America* (Wilmette, Ill., 1985).

be cured by cultivating healthy attitudes—positive thoughts instead of negative ones—through suggestion and without the use of hypnotism. Sickness, he insisted, was the consequence of wrong beliefs. The remedy, therefore, was to displace the erroneous ideas of the ill with healing truth.

One of Quimby's patients was Mary Baker Eddy, the founder of Christian Science.[41] As a child she suffered from nervous disorders. Her ill health continued to plague her through three marriages. Although she was helped by Quimby in 1862 and 1864, she and her followers have insisted that she was guided through her own experience to an original discovery of the divine law of life which surpassed in importance Newton's discovery of the law of gravitation when he saw the apple fall. Whether she built upon the foundation provided by Quimby or gained her insight from a unique revelation, Mrs. Eddy was soon embarked upon an independent healing career based upon the conviction that the Eternal Mind is the source of all being, that matter is nonexistent, that disease is caused by erroneous thought (compounded, to be sure, by the Malicious Animal Magnetism projected by one's enemies), and that power is released through Christian Science to overcome all the illusions that have troubled humanity. "The control mind holds over matter," she declared, "becomes no longer a question when with mathematical certainty we gain its proof and can demonstrate the facts assumed." In Christian Science this proof has been reduced to a scientific statement that "furnishes a key to the harmony of man and reveals what destroys sickness, sin, and death."[42]

In 1875 Mrs. Eddy formed a small group of adherents into a society at Lynn, Massachusetts, and published the first edition of the authoritative textbook of her doctrine, *Science and Health with Key to the Scriptures.* The movement did not prosper, however, until she moved to Boston and established the Massachusetts Metaphysical College to train "practitioners." In 1892 control of the movement was vested in the self-perpetuating board of trustees of "the Mother Church" in Boston. Membership multiplied rapidly thereafter, and the Church, especially through its official organ, the *Christian Science Journal* (later the *Monitor*), addressed a host of practical matters of social reform and family life. By the time of Mrs. Eddy's death in 1910, the Church of Christ, Scientist, with its various local units, had grown to almost 100,000 members.

There were other heirs of Quimby. The most important were his former patients Julius A. Dresser and Warren Felt Evans.[43] The latter was a former Methodist minister who had become a Swedenborgian. Evans

---

[41] Robert Peel, *Mary Baker Eddy: The Years of Discovery* (N.Y., 1966). See also E. F. Dakin, *Mrs. Eddy: The Biography of a Virginal Mind* (N.Y., 1929).

[42] *Science and Health* (Boston, 1875), 9.

[43] See J. A. Dresser, *The True History of Mental Science* (N.Y., 1899); H. W. Dresser, *A History of the New Thought Movement* (N.Y., 1919); and C. S. Braden, *Spirits in Rebellion: The Rise and Development of New Thought* (Dallas, 1963).

began to practice "mental medicine" at Claremont, New Hampshire, and set forth the principles of the new science in a series of books: *The Mental Cure* (1869), *Mental Medicine* (1872), *Soul and Body* (1876), and *The Divine Law* (1881). In Boston other disciples of Quimby who had formed the Church of the Divine Unity were joined by Dresser in 1882. The movement spread rapidly under many names—Mental Science, Higher Thought, Higher Life, and Divine Science. The term "New Thought" was coined in 1889 by William Henry Holcombe, a homopathic physician; and in 1894 this was chosen as the title of a little magazine published in Melrose, Massachusetts. The first national convention was held in San Francisco in 1894 under the auspices of the Divine Science Association and five years later the name of the sponsoring body was changed to the New Thought Alliance. The annual conventions failed to develop any centralized organization and the movement continued to be highly individualistic, with considerable variation in doctrine, and with personal preference dictating the choice of name by local groups. One current, represented by M. J. Barnett's *Practical Metaphysics* (1889), interpreted New Thought doctrine within a theosophical context; another current was strongly influenced by Spiritualism. The most prolific of the New Thought writers were Ralph Waldo Trine (1866–1958) and Emmet Fox (1886–1951), whose books were widely read by people who had no connection at all with the movement. All these currents lived on in various forms of popular religious belief, and acquired renewed importance in the late twentieth century.[44]

A less amorphous expression of the "mind cure" idea was the Unity School of Practical Christianity founded at Kansas City, Missouri, by Charles and Myrtle Fillmore.[45] They were attending New Thought lectures in 1886 when "Truth" came to Myrtle Fillmore, as expressed in the affirmation, "I am a child of God, and therefore I do not inherit sickness." As Myrtle's tuberculosis improved, people were attracted to the Fillmores, and to Myrtle's notion that "spiritual truth is that you are God's own beloved child and that God is ever giving you his wisdom, love, power, life and substance."[46] The Fillmores began to advertise themselves as "Healers and Teachers" and gradually gathered a small group into the Society of Silent Help, a prayer ministry. In 1889 a periodical, *Modern Thought*, was launched to publicize their views, and two years later the name "Unity" was seized upon as more adequately expressing their basic principle.

---

[44] See Robert Fuller, *Mesmerism and the American Cure of Souls* (Philadelphia, 1982), and *Alternative Medicine and American Religious Life* (New York, 1989).

[45] See J. D. Freeman, *The Household of Faith: The Story of Unity* (Lee Summit, Mo., 1951); and C. S. Braden, *These Also Believe* (N.Y., 1949).

[46] Myrtle Fillmore, *How to Let God Help You* (Unity Village, Mo., 1956), 13.

> Unity! . . . Unity! . . . That's the name for our work! The name I've been
> looking for! . . . It embodies the central principle of what we believe: unity
> of the soul with God, unity of all life, unity of all religions, unity of the spirit,
> soul, and body; unity of all men in the heart of truth.[47]

The name of the group subsequently was changed to the Society of
Silent Unity, which later became simply Silent Unity, a "department of
dedicated prayer" within the Unity School. In 1891 another periodical,
Unity, was launched as the official organ of Silent Unity. The Fillmores
denied that they were starting a new sect; they were only teaching a
practical philosophy to supplement the teachings of the existing churches.
Accordingly, the term "school" was chosen over "church" in 1914, when
the Fillmores combined the various programs (e.g., Silent Unity, the
publishing company, and a correspondence school) into the single corporation known as "The Unity School of Practical Christianity."[48]

Unity, for all its practical, down-to-earth emphasis, was far from simple.
It developed a highly complex metaphysical system (including belief in
reincarnation) that incorporated ideas from New Thought, Christian
Science, Theosophy, the Christian Bible, Spiritualism, and Hinduism. The
Fillmores advocated the repeated use of statements of denial and affirmation to assist in opening the mind to the "true self" and binding God's
"wisdom, strength and holiness" to one's consciousness. For the Fillmores,
only "those who have *meditated seriously* upon the source of existence and
stirred up the inner substance and life make very substantial pictures in
the universal ether or kingdom of the heavens.'" Serious meditation thus
was not simply "the thought images of an intellectual thinker," but rather
the activity "of one who has got access to the spiritual substance and life
within."[49] Like other new faiths of the time, Unity promised not only
physical health but economic prosperity. "God will pay your debts," declared Charles Fillmore.

> Do not say money is scarce; the very statement will drive money away from
> you. Do not say that times are hard with you; the very words will tighten
> your purse strings until Omnipotence itself cannot slip a dime into it. Begin
> now to talk plenty, think plenty, and give thanks for plenty. . . . It actually
> works.
>
> Every home can be prosperous, and there should be no poverty-stricken
> homes, for they are caused only by inharmony, fear, negative thinking and
> speaking.[50]

[47] Freeman, *Household of Faith,* 44, 61–62. Cf. Marcus Bach, *They Have Found a Faith*
(Indianapolis, 1946), 223.
[48] Hugh D'Andrade, *Charles Fillmore: Herald of the New Age* (N.Y., 1974), 35–36, 67;
Freeman, *The Household of Faith,* 56–57, 89, 105.
[49] Fillmore, *How to Let God Help You,* 44; Charles and Cora Fillmore, *Teach Us to Pray*
(Unity Village, Mo., 1941), 70–71.
[50] Charles Fillmore, *Prosperity* (Kansas City, Mo., 1938), 103–4, 117.

Unity grew into a vast publishing enterprise and a prayer ministry (Silent Unity). Both services claimed a large following beyond the official Unity membership, including an astonishingly large number of persons from the conventional churches. During the movement's early growth, it was not uncommon for followers to meet in public places such as hotels to hear Unity teachers, and to engage in study and prayer sessions. By 1925, however, Unity leaders had grown wary of non-Unity practices (e.g., occult seances, palm reading) creeping into the fringes of the movement. Though opposed to formal creeds and dogma, the church subsequently adopted a set of rules governing the teaching of Unity classes and the activities at Unity centers. As the activities at Unity centers acquired more definition and structure by the mid-twentieth century, they were referred to as churches.

Such were the disparate religious responses to the new intellectual climate. It was a difficult time for the churches, for their whole system of thought had been challenged at many points. But this was not the only problem with which the churches had to grapple. They had to come to terms at the same time with revolutionary changes in the economic and social order that were created by the rapid pace at which the country was becoming urbanized and industrialized. This challenge demanded changes in practice as well as in thought.

CHAPTER 12

New Frontiers for the Churches

While the mind of America was being reshaped by the intellectual revolution of the years of midpassage from 1865 to 1918, the outward aspects of American life were undergoing swift and bewildering change as a result of rapid technological advance. "Steam and electricity have tremendously increased the pace of life," reported an observer in 1896.

> Everybody is in a hurry. . . . St. Martha is the patron saint of the women, and St. Vitus of the men. Nervous prostration is our characteristic disease. Leisure is a word for whose meaning we consult the dictionary. In the clatter of the train, in the click of the keys at the telegraph office, the spirit of the age finds speech.[1]

The click and the clatter were symbols of a surging industrial advance sped by a flood of inventions. In contrast to the fewer than 62,000 patents that had been issued prior to 1865, the number granted by the Patent Office in the following 35 years was in excess of 637,000. Large-scale steel production was made possible by the introduction of the Bessemer converter. The efficiency of the railroads was multiplied by automatic couplings and Westinghouse air brakes. Refrigerator cars made feasible the centralized slaughterhouses of the meatpackers. The discovery of oil, coupled with the use of tank cars and pipelines, gave further impetus to industrial development. The McCormick binder, the typewriter, the transatlantic cable, the telephone, the incandescent lamp, the electric motor, and the gasoline engine each fostered growing commercial enterprises. Before the end of the century the linotype, the automobile, and the motion picture had made their appearance. Meanwhile, through an increasing utilization of machinery and the adoption of interchangeable

[1] George Hodges, *Faith and Social Service* (N.Y., 1896), 6.

parts, the factory system had been established in almost all areas of production. By 1894 the United States had become the leading manufacturing nation of the world, with its production of manufactured goods surpassing the combined output of its two closest rivals, Great Britain and Germany.

Many rubrics have been used to characterize the impact upon society of this massive industrial development. Some have viewed these years as "the gilded age"; others have called it "the tragic era." To some these were "50 years of progress"; to others they were "years of unrest and corruption." The most obvious label has been "the age of big business," for this was the era of the empire builders—the steel kings, the coal barons, the railroad magnates, the merchant princes, the Napoleons of finance, and the potentates of the stockyards, the oil wells, and the street railways. Another rubric has been "the rise of the city," for these were the years when cities were "springing up and growing great and splendid as it were in a night." A further facet of this adolescent period in the emergence of modern America has been suggested by Harold U. Faulkner's phrase "the quest for social justice." And those who placed the period against a larger canvas have used the term "imperial America" to convey the expansionist spirit of an awakening industrial giant. All these aspects of this new industrial society—the problems and opportunities posed by the city, the economic order, and the outward thrust of imperialism—were to replace the West as urgent new frontiers for the churches.

The Challenge of the Cities

Urbanization spawned a wide variety of human needs, for in its wake came slums, poverty, vice, and political corruption. Each of these needs was to claim the attention of the churches, but the most pressing problem was the basic task of evangelism. Even before the Civil War, extensive sections of rural America had begun to experience a steady and persistent decline in population as people moved from farms and back-country villages to growing commercial centers and newly established mill towns. After the war the process was vastly accelerated. Previously tilled acres reverted to woodland and whole villages disappeared, leaving only a few foundation stones as monuments to the past. The cities, in contrast, were lusty infants. During the three decades from 1860 to 1890, the population of Detroit and Kansas City grew fourfold, Memphis and San Francisco fivefold, Cleveland sixfold, Chicago tenfold, Los Angeles twentyfold, and Minneapolis and Omaha fiftyfold and more. Even such previously major centers as New York, Philadelphia, and Baltimore more than doubled in population. "There is a city of thirty-five thousand added to Chicago, and one of fifty thousand added to New York, every year," reported Josiah Strong in 1887. With the overwhelming proportion of the churches located in rural areas and with many of them left stranded to dwindle and die as people departed, it became more obvious than ever that the future influence of the churches in the life of the nation was to be decisively conditioned by their success or lack of success in evangelizing the cities.

At the outset, most of the urban inhabitants came from the farms and villages of the hinterland where many of them had been regular in church attendance. They may not have been conspicuous for piety and they may not even have been church members, but they had been accustomed to going to church. When they pulled up their roots and moved to the city, this pattern of habit and custom was broken,' the emotional ties to a particular church were severed, and the pressure exerted by the expectation of friends and neighbors was removed. In their new environment, the tendency was for these former churchgoers to drift into "indifference." Later the problem of re-evangelization was complicated by the sweeping tide of population arriving from abroad.

Conspicuous as were the effects of urban revival campaigns, the greatest successes were won in the smaller commercial and industrial centers where social relationships remained relatively intimate. In these communities, where employer and employee lived in somewhat close proximity, patronized the same stores, sent their children to the same schools, and frequently knew each other by name, the churches were able to bridge the gap between the social classes. In this respect the American experience duplicated that of the English churches. Even the Primitive Methodists of England, who were famed for bringing the gospel to people who were "rude, poor, and even brutish," did not bring the gospel to more than a small portion of the urban poor. What success they had was restricted to the smaller industrial settlements.[2]

In larger industrial communities, whether in America, Britain, or France (and presumably in the developing urban concentrations of Belgium, Germany, and northern Italy), the working classes tended to be impervious to the message and ministry of the churches.[3] It was not that the churches had "lost" these people; they never had most of them. If people generally attended church from habit, most of the laboring group who were born in the city never had the habit. It was to this habit of nonattendance that newer additions to the urban labor force conformed.

Among other portions of the urban population, churchgoing was a normal, mannerly, and even a fashionable activity. Signs of the popularity of the churches abounded. The churches were well attended. Costly and imposing edifices were being built to match the increasing prosperity of

[2] K. S. Inglis, *Churches and the Working Classes in Victorian England* (Toronto, 1963), 10–13, 327.

[3] For France, see H. Desroche, *Archives de Sociologie des Religions*, VI (1958), 197–98; cited by Inglis, *Churches and the Working Classes*, 327. The Roman Catholic Church in America provided the major exception, but the strength it developed among working people was closely related to the insecurities of their immigrant status.

their clientele, and congregations vied with one another to possess the tallest steeple as a symbol of wealth and prestige. Pipe organs were installed, paid soloists were employed, and the preachers were polished orators who ranked in status with the most substantial citizens. It was a time during which ministers enjoyed a status matched only by New England's earliest pastors, and it was a "golden age of preaching." The princes of the pulpit — men such as Henry Ward Beecher and T. DeWitt Talmage in Brooklyn, Phillips Brooks and George A. Gordon in Boston, David M. Swing and Frank W. Gunsaulus in Chicago, Russell Conwell in Philadelphia, and Washington Gladden in Columbus — were figures of national prominence, but every city boasted eloquent preachers who could hold their congregations spellbound and who were regarded with deference and respect. Their sermons often were published and were circulated widely among Protestants comfortable in their urban existence. Furthermore, the most influential leaders of business and society — Jay Gould, J. Pierpoint Morgan, John D. Rockefeller, Samuel Colgate, Jay Cooke, Cyrus McCormick, Marshall Field, James J. Hill, William H. Vanderbilt, P. D. Armour, G. A. Sift, A. J. Drexel, John Wanamaker, and many others — were prominent churchmen, active in religious enterprises, and frequently Sunday-school teachers.

To many of the immigrants from abroad, the Roman Catholic Church was the one familiar landmark in a strange and alien land, and its role in easing the transition to a new life in America helped it to retain the loyalty of many of the urban workers. With this single major exception, the great evangelistic successes of the city churches were won among the white-collar workers who had come from the rural areas — not to work in a mill, but to "clerk" in a store or an office — and who aspired to win, if not a fortune, at least a comfortable competence in the city. These young men, with their wives and their children, constituted the greater portion of those who were recruited for the churches by the revival campaigns, the Sunday school, and the Y.M.C.A. Beyond this potentially middle-class group was the hard core of nonchurchgoers — the urban masses, they were sometimes called, the poor, the destitute, the day laborers — who were to constitute a continuing challenge to the churches.

New Techniques for City Churches

In 1865, almost before Grant had had time to haul the artillery from the Virginia battlefields, James S. Yeatman of St. Louis — banker, philanthropist, and head of the Western Sanitary Commission during the Civil War — had drafted a *Circular of Inquiry* calling attention to urban religious needs and proposing that the energy devoted to wartime service to combatants be redirected to peacetime service in the cities. He noted the comparative ineffectiveness of the Protestant churches in urban communities and suggested that they were handicapped by four major deficiencies:

"want of knowledge" of the true "moral condition" of the cities; "lack of organization of the wealth, piety, and labor which exist there"; need of information concerning the "best agencies" for city work; and "want of trained, tried, permanent laborers in the various spheres of city labor."[4] As a result of his initiative, those who had been active in the United States Christian Commission (the agency of the churches in ministering to soldiers) met in Cleveland in the autumn of 1865 and organized the American Christian Commission to help the churches develop a systematic program of urban missionary endeavor. They viewed the task of the Commission as twofold: (1) to ascertain the actual conditions prevailing in the cities and (2) to assemble information concerning the "experience already gained" as to the best methods to be employed to gain the ends desired.

The investigators discovered that most American churches did little in any systematic fashion for those "who neglect the house of God." The city mission societies and the Y.M.C.A., to be sure, sponsored street preaching and tract distribution, and occasionally there were citywide revival campaigns. Although these activities were to be encouraged, the Commission believed that the great need was to recover "the simplicity and entire consecration of the early Christians," when "every disciple was a missionary and every church a missionary society," so that the church itself would reach out to people where they live. The obvious means of doing this was by regular house-to-house visitation of working-class neighborhoods. Many of the poverty-stricken, it was contended, had been alienated "because in their affliction they were not visited," and the only remedy was "personal, living, love-convincing" contact between the churchgoer and the nonchurchgoer. This, of course, demanded lay effort. Pastors of churches in densely populated communities were urged to "seek out and employ all such talent in their congregations as they shall believe to possess qualifications for this important and pressing work."[5]

The volunteer visitation program never worked very successfully. Even when the Evangelical Alliance picked up the idea of a cooperative, monthly, citywide house-to-house visitation and, as a result of vigorous promotion, had put it into operation by 1889 in 40 cities, the actual implementation was sporadic. As an alternative, the utilization of female assistants or women missionaries was strongly advocated. It was recognized that women could be especially effective in going into the homes, and considerable support developed for the establishment of sisterhoods or deaconess orders patterned after the German model. In an eloquent plea for the churches to adopt the German practice, a speaker at the 1868 convention of the Commission asserted that the "theory that woman has no place in the church deprives America of two-thirds of its Christian

---

[4] A. I. Abell, *The Urban Impact on American Protestantism, 1865–1900* (Cambridge, Mass., 1943), 11.

[5] *Ibid.*, 12–13, 15, 33.

Rows of Tenements in New York City.   Often there was one family to a room.
(Courtesy of the Children's Aid Society, New York City.)

force." The eloquence of the proponents of the use of women workers, however, was not sufficient to quell popular hostility. In 1857 William A. Muhlenberg had aroused a storm of opposition among his fellow Episcopalians when he established a deaconess order in New York. A Lutheran attempt after the Civil War was equally abortive. The Methodists were somewhat more successful, but official recognition was withheld until 1889. By the end of the century, the Lutherans and the German Reformed were making extensive use of deaconesses, the Episcopalians had established a training school, and even the Congregationalists and Baptists had taken a few tentative steps toward the employment of deaconesses. The Methodists, however, were far in the lead, having nearly as many deaconesses as all other denominations combined. In the next few years the number of deaconesses began to decline. Perhaps their quaint hats and distinctive dress militated against any continuing popularity. But the battle over the employment of women had been won and the churches generally began to make use of women as church visitors and missionaries.

A second problem highlighted by the Commission and underscored in the actual process of house-to-house visitation was the fact that often no churches were located in the neediest neighborhoods. The city mission societies were encouraged to establish mission chapels in these areas. Most of these were conventional in character. Much more dramatic were the "rescue missions" designed to reach and reclaim the dregs of society — vagrants, alcoholics, former convicts, jobless men, and fallen women. The Water Street Mission in New York was the most famous and the Pacific Garden Mission in Chicago the most successful of these rescue operations, but by the 1880s every city boasted one or more missions of this type. The real pioneer of the movement was Jerry MacAuley, who founded the Water Street Mission in 1872, and his own early career was typical of those to whom he sought to minister. He arrived in New York from Ireland at the age of 13. Living in the streets, he became a petty thief and then graduated to gambling, organized burglary, and drunkenness. At the age of 19 he was sentenced to a 15-year term in prison, and while confined he was converted by an ex-prizefighter. Back on the streets after being pardoned in 1864, he resumed his criminal career until he was finally redeemed by agents of the Howard Mission. He then established his own mission in his former neighborhood, ministering primarily to the men who congregated there.

Among both conventional and rescue missions, there was a growing conviction that attention must be given to immediate material necessities before spiritual needs could be met. The managers of the North End Mission in Boston put it bluntly: "Till the cravings of hunger are satisfied, we cannot develop the moral nature," adding that they believed this to be "the biblical way of reaching the heart."[6] As a result of this conviction, rescue missions of all types launched a wide variety of enterprises which included model tenements for the poor, homes for working mothers, and hospitals for the care of sick children.

Yeatman's initial *Circular of Inquiry* had emphasized the importance of "trained" leadership for the specialized tasks of city work, and a number of institutions were established to meet this need.[7] A further step in this

---

[6] *Ibid.,* 36.

[7] Among these schools were Stephen H. Tyng's Home of the Evangelists (1870) in New York, T. DeWitt Talmage's Tabernacle Lay College (1872) in Brooklyn, and Dwight L. Moody's Moody Bible Institute (1886) in Chicago. The latter institution was designed "to raise up men and women who will be willing to lay their lives alongside the laboring class and the poor and bring the gospel to bear on their lives." They were to do work that ministers could not do — "get in among the people and identify themselves with the people." W. G. McLoughlin, *Modern Revivalism,* 272–73.

direction was taken when followers of MacAuley organized the Convention of Christian Workers in 1886. John C. Collins, a Yale graduate and manager of the Union Gospel Mission in New Haven, was the guiding spirit. By means of annual gatherings, a type of "in-service" training was provided through the sharing of experience with new methods and techniques. Within little more than a decade it had gained more than 2,500 members, and Graham Taylor, professor of Christian sociology at Chicago Theological Seminary, declared that the annual Convention of Christian Workers was "a great exhibit of the work and working forces of modern Christianity" and "as nearly ecumenical a gathering of the church in America as is held on this continent." The *Christian Union*, Henry Ward Beecher's personal journal, was equally enthusiastic, asserting that the stenographic reports of the conventions furnished "the best literature on practical Christian work that can be secured."[8]

Meanwhile a new instrument of urban evangelization made its appearance. This was the Salvation Army.[9] It had been founded in London in 1878 by William Booth, an ex-Methodist preacher. Booth had come to the conclusion that "we can't get at the masses in the chapels," and consequently he was determined to move out into the streets. Organized on the basis of strict military discipline, the Army was geared for a many-sided attack on the problems of the city. The program was spelled out in Booth's famous volume, *Darkest England and the Way Out* (1890). The familiar brass band and tambourines that were used to gather a crowd for street preaching was only an incidental feature of a broad range of activities. Booth aimed to supply the poverty-stricken people of England with at least the three things any dray horse enjoyed — "shelter for the night, food for its stomach, work allotted to it by which it can earn its own corn." In addition to the usual provision made by rescue missions for meals, lodging, and an employment service, the Army moved out into the community with its Slum Brigades, Sewing Battalions, and visiting nurses. Legal aid bureaus were opened, day nurseries for children set up, and rescue homes for prostitutes established. And to give men and women the benefit of a new and wholesome environment, farm colonies were founded. Although the Salvation Army was ultimately to take on the characteristics of a church, its initial intention was to serve only as a recruiting agent of the churches among the most neglected elements of the population.

The Salvation Army was introduced into America in 1880, but its major expansion took place after 1886 when Booth's son, Ballington Booth, was sent over to take charge. A schism occurred in 1896 when Ballington Booth refused to obey his father's order that he return to England.

---

[8] Abell, *Urban Impact on American Protestantism*, 97–98.

[9] The English background is summarized by Inglis, *Churches and the Working Classes in Victorian England*, 175–214. For its American career, see H. A. Wisbey, *Soldiers Without Swords: A History of the Salvation Army in the United States* (N.Y., 1955).

Instead he and his wife founded the Volunteers of America, which patterned its activities after the parent organization but was organized on a more democratic basis.

The Institutional Church

The problem of city churches was complicated by the mobility of the urban population. As commercial establishments encroached upon residential areas and housing grew old and deteriorated, the more prosperous sought newer and more spacious accommodations on the outskirts, leaving room at the center for newer arrivals. Without endowments to sustain them, most churches seemed to face the choice either of following their congregations or of being marooned in poverty and left to eke out a dwindling existence. Rather than subject themselves to a lingering death, many churches elected to follow their congregations and erect new edifices in the areas to which their members had moved. It was this solution to their problem that necessitated the founding of mission chapels in sections formerly occupied by churches. The whole process became deeply disturbing to sensitive Christians as they became aware of what was taking place. Instead of moving the church and then seeking to discharge its responsibility to the people of its former neighborhood by proxy through missions of various types, some proposed that the churches adapt themselves to the changing population of the inner city by adopting and utilizing techniques that were being developed by the missions.

The "institutional church," a strange name, was proposed as a means of enabling churches to survive in central-city areas instead of moving. The problem was to entice new arrivals in changing neighborhoods into existing churches. The solution put forward was for churches to provide the newcomers with a variety of "services" or "added attractions." Edward Judson was the preeminent theoretician of an institutional ministry. He defined an institutional church as "an organized body of Christian believers, who, finding themselves in a hard and uncongenial social environment, supplement the ordinary methods of the gospel — such as preaching, prayer meetings, Sunday school, and pastoral visitation — by a *system of organized kindness,* a congeries of institutions, which, by touching people on physical, social, and intellectual sides, will conciliate them and draw them within reach of the gospel."[10] With the slogan "open church doors every day and all the day," institutional churches became hives of activity with gymnasiums, athletic programs, reading rooms, day nurseries, sewing classes, lecture series, choral societies, drama clubs, concerts, and entertainments.

---

[10] "The Church in Its Social Aspect," *Annals of the American Academy of Political and Social Science,* 30 (November 1908), 436. For an impressionistic appraisal of the institutional church, see G. G. Atkins, *Religion in Our Times* (N.Y., 1932), 69–85.

The honor of establishing the first institutional church probably belongs to Thomas K. Beecher, one of the numerous Beecher progeny, who was pastor of the Park Congregational Church in Elmira, New York, from 1854 to 1900. In 1872 he induced his congregation to build a block-long structure equipped for a full range of services. Mark Twain, a summer resident, described the building with its gymnasium, lecture rooms, library, and free public baths in his *Curious Dreams and Other Sketches* (1872) and commented that "we have at least one sensible but very curious church in America." Within two decades there were many of these "sensible" churches, including Reuben A. Torrey's Open Door Congregational Church in Minneapolis. By 1900 one observer listed 173 churches with a full-blown institutional program and acknowledged that there were probably others that had escaped his attention. In addition, scores of churches were appropriating parts of the institutional program, including Roman Catholic programs such as the St. Louis Verein.[11]

When the Open and Institutional Church League was formed in 1894 to promote "educational, reformatory, and philanthropic" activities by the churches as an evangelistic device, its leaders self-confidently proclaimed that the question "how to reach the masses" had been "practically solved." It was true that institutional churches were experiencing phenomenal growth. By 1900 the Baptist Temple in Philadelphia, in process of fathering what was to become Temple University, had become the largest congregation in America. St. George's Episcopal Church in New York, which had been ready to close its doors when it had only six families left, now numbered 5,000 members. Congregationalists reported that their institutional churches had six times as many additions as the average church. But there were problems. For one thing, an institutional church was an incredibly costly enterprise. Not many churches could command the necessary financial support. St. George's was fortunate in having J. Pierpont Morgan as a member of its initial remnant. St. Bartholomew's, whose parish house was erected by Cornelius Vanderbilt and his mother, had an annual budget of over $1 million.[12] Edward Judson's begging expeditions were successful in tapping the resources of John D. Rockefeller. Furthermore, as Judson noted, the involvements of an institutional program "are so difficult and fascinating that they easily absorb all a minister's time and energy." The tendency is for him to neglect "his study and the care of his flock," to lose "his priestly character," and to become "a mere social functionary."[13] Becoming absorbed in manifold activities that initially were intended to serve as a bridge into church membership, the ideal of mere humanitarian service tended to replace the earlier

11 Many new "suburban" churches also felt they should have a gymnasium with a stage so that they too could adopt the tactic of the "added attractions" by having made adequate provision for athletics and theatricals.
12 Abell, *The Urban Impact on American Protestantism*, 150–51.
13 "The Church in Its Social Aspect," 437.

evangelistic concern. As a result, the congregations of institutional churches, as their novelty disappeared, dwindled almost as rapidly as they had increased. In the end, far from being a means of building up a congregation to support a ministry in areas of deterioration, many institutional churches became social agencies that other churches had to find money and leadership to support. Meanwhile, store-front churches began to make an appearance in the surrounding neighborhoods to demonstrate that "added attractions" were not needed to "draw" people "within reach of the gospel." Few noted the irony of this development.

The Churches and the Economic Order

The decade preceding the great railroad strike of 1877 has been described as the "summit" of American economic complacency. This complacency was as evident among churchmen as it was among other Americans. Leaders of the churches may have disagreed about many things, but they displayed remarkable unanimity in their approbation of the existing economic order and the "principles" or "laws" of political economy that provided its theoretical foundation. Gone was the radical criticism and ferment of the 1830s and 1840s. Henry F. May observed that "in 1876 Protestantism presented a massive, almost unbroken front in its defense of the social status quo."[14] This was equally true of Roman Catholicism. Within a dozen years, however, this situation began to change when people were shocked from their complacency by outbreaks of violent social conflict. Roman Catholics remained cautious,[15] but by the 1890's vigorous demands for social reform were being voiced in every major Protestant denomination. A few leaders were calling for the complete reorganization of society. By the turn of the century the adherents of two antithetical gospels — "the gospel of wealth" and "the social gospel" — were locked in combat and struggling for predominance.

[14] *Protestant Churches and Industrial America* (N.Y., 1963), 91.
[15] Francis J. Lally has pointed out that Roman Catholics gave little evidence of being "socially progressive" prior to the New Deal years. The papal encyclical *Rerum Novarum* (1891) had little immediate impact in America, and the few occasions when Roman Catholics displayed an interest in social reform were "sporadic and mostly short-lived." This was true of the 1919 "Bishops' Program of Social Reconstruction" which did not receive strong support until the 1930s. Participation in the labor movement was the single notable exception to the generally conservative outlook. *The Catholic Church in a Changing America*, 47–48. For an account of developing social consciousness among Roman Catholics, see A. I. Abell, *American Catholicism and Social Action* (N.Y., 1960).

The Gospel of Wealth

For many Americans the years following the Civil War marked the beginning of a period of unrivaled prosperity. Rapidly as the population increased, the nation's wealth multiplied three times as fast. Those who benefited by this tremendous economic expansion were confident that they were living in the best of all possible worlds. The American economy had been tested and had not been found wanting. This smug self-satisfaction lent an aura of eminent reasonableness and even sanctity to the *laissez-faire* economic doctrines that had been fathered by Adam Smith, popularized in America by Francis Wayland,[16] and given strong reinforcement by the teachings of Herbert Spencer. The most persuasive argument for allowing economic self-interest free play was the seemingly obvious fact that it worked for general economic betterment. Perhaps it worked, as the *Congregationalist* put it, because there were "thousands upon thousands of acres of magnificent soil" beyond the Mississippi that could be secured "at a merely nominal price" so that "no man who is blessed with health and willingness to work, be his family large or small, need come to the poorhouse."[17] But it worked nonetheless, at least for a time.

The classic statement of "the true gospel concerning wealth," obedience to which will "solve the problem of the rich and the poor," was written by Andrew Carnegie, the steelmaster of Pittsburgh, and was published in the June 1889 issue of the *North American Review*.[18] Carnegie insisted that "civilization depends" upon the triple law of the "sacredness" of private property, free competition, and free accumulation of wealth. This triple law, which allows free play to economic forces, is indispensable to all progress, and nothing should be permitted to interfere with its operation. Its indispensability is a fact of life that cannot be changed. One can only make the "best of it." It is true that a price is exacted, since the law of competition forces the employer "into the strictest economies, among which the rates to be paid to labor figure prominently," and this creates friction. But even if the operation of the law "may sometimes be hard for individuals," it is "best for the race, because it insures the survival of the fittest in every department" and produces "a wonderful material development" that benefits all. "The laborer has now more comforts than the farmer had a few generations ago," "the farmer has more luxuries than the landlord had," and the landlord has more than "a king could

---

[16] Wayland was president of Brown University and the author of *The Elements of Political Economy* (1837), the most popular textbook on the subject.

[17] March 17, 1870; quoted by May, *Protestant Churches and Industrial America*, 55.

[18] Carnegie's brief dissertation on "Wealth" is reprinted, with other essays, in *Democracy and the Gospel of Wealth*, ed. Gail Kennedy, *Problems in American Civilization: Readings Selected by the Department of American Studies, Amherst College* (Boston, 1949).

then obtain." This inequality is better than the "universal squalor" that would otherwise prevail.

Carnegie's harsh views were somewhat tempered by his view of the proper use of wealth. In words reminiscent of Wesley's slogan, "Gain all you can, save all you can, give all you can," he declared that "the man who dies . . . rich, dies disgraced."[19] Instead of leaving vast sums to one's children or even making humanitarian bequests, Carnegie insisted that one's wealth should be distributed in ways that served the common good during one's own lifetime. Indiscriminate charity, of course, could only serve "to encourage the slothful, the drunken, the unworthy." The race has never been improved by almsgiving, for it rewards vice rather than aids virtue. "Those worthy of assistance, except in rare cases, seldom require assistance." The objective should be to help those who will help themselves. "The best means of benefitting the community is to place within its reach the ladders upon which the aspiring can rise." Parks, museums, libraries, schools are ways of returning surplus wealth to the masses in a form "best calculated to do them lasting good."

Carnegie's gospel of wealth was closely intertwined with the doctrine of stewardship of time, money, and talent that had been staple fare in Protestant moral teaching. It was but a small step for current principles of economics to be translated into laws of God's providential ordering of society. Phillips Brooks, Henry Ward Beecher, and lesser luminaries of the Protestant pulpit embraced the gospel of wealth with fervent devotion, but Russell Conwell—with his lecture on *Acres of Diamonds* (they are in one's own backyard) and his exhortation that everyone has a "duty to get rich"—was its most eloquent clerical spokesman.[20]

Roman Catholics, for the most part, represented an older conservatism that enjoined passivity and acceptance of one's lot in society; God permits poverty as "the most efficient means" of fostering "some of the most necessary Christian virtues." Charity should be directed to the relief of suffering and not to its elimination, for "a country where there are no beggars" would be "a veritable branch of hell." It was suggested that "to let well enough alone is a very wise old saw." Liberal Catholics, on the other hand, took a more positive view of the benefits derived from the

---

[19] Wesley's concern, of course, was different. "Religion," he said, "must necessarily produce both industry and frugality, and these cannot but produce riches." And "whenever riches have increased," religion "has decreased in the same proportion." "Is there no way to prevent this—this continual declension of pure religion?" What way "can we take that our money may not sink us to the nethermost hell? There is but one way, and . . . no other. . . . If those who 'gain all they can,' and 'save all they can,' will likewise 'give all they can'; then the more they gain, the more they will grow in grace." *The Works of John Wesley*, 4th ed. (London, 1840–42), XIII, 246–47.

[20] For Brooks and Beecher, see H. F. May, *Protestant Churches and Industrial America*, 64–72. For Conwell, see W. S. Hudson, *The Great Tradition of the American Churches*, rev. ed. (N.Y., 1963), 180–86. There is no standard text of Conwell's *Acres of Diamonds*, for it underwent constant revision.

free play of economic forces. Bishop Spalding assured a graduating class at Notre Dame that "the organs of the social body" had never been so healthy, and Cardinal Gibbons applauded Carnegie's essay on "Wealth." Archbishop Ireland insisted that "respect" for capital "must be supreme," and he admonished Roman Catholics to stop considering money as evil and — with "will," "energy," "pluck," "push," and "ambition" — to set about acquiring some. "It is energy and enterprise that wins everywhere," he declared with the briskness of an entrepreneur, "they win in the Church, they win in the state, they win in business." In 1890 the *Catholic World* published a minor classic of the gospel-of-wealth literature that pointed out that the three men Christ restored to life were all men of wealth and recommended that, after praying for faith, hope, and charity, Catholics should add the petition: "O Lord! give me good sense. Give me hard, practical, everyday gumption. If I had a little of that, I shouldn't act as foolishly as I generally do; I shouldn't waste my time nor money." The ability to make "frequent and handsome donations" to the church is a "pretty" sure indication "that a man has the right sort of zeal."[21]

Many wealthy men had this "right sort of zeal," for this was a great age of philanthropy. Even without the incentive of benefit to be derived from income-tax exemption, benefactions were large and numerous. George Peabody, with gifts amounting to $8.5 million, was only one of many who, in the words of William Gladstone, demonstrated "how a man may be master of his fortune, not its slave." There were, of course, incongruities symbolized by the image of Daniel Drew as both "master fleecer of the lambs" and "founder of a theological seminary." Jay Cooke presented a curious picture as a skilled corrupter of legislatures and president of the Education Society of the Protestant Episcopal Church. Considerations of self-interest may have spurred the Armour brothers to lavish more than $1 million on a mission in Chicago. But many took their stewardship seriously. John P. Crozer, whose many benefactions included a theological seminary, was not exceptional when he confessed his perplexity "how I shall use, as I ought, the great and increasing stores of wealth which God has bestowed upon me."

> Excuses are so easily framed, and the heart of man so deceitful, that one can easily reason himself into the belief that, all things considered, he has done pretty well. I find such a process of reasoning in my own mind, but calm reflection tells me that I have not done well. I am a very unprofitable servant to so good a Master.

Troubled lest the good he designed be lost in the mere satisfaction of giving, he asked the Lord to direct him "clearly and decisively" to the "path of duty and usefulness." Commenting on Crozer's careful assess-

[21] R. D. Cross, *Emergence of Liberal Catholicism in America*, 107–9, 111–12, 163–64.

ment of his responsibility, Sidney E. Mead observed that "only the sneering souls of the mean in mind" could belittle such transparently "honest and consecrated devotion" to sacred duty.[22]

The Rise of Social Discontent

The prosperity of a booming economy was not equally shared by all sections of the population, and the result was smoldering discontent among both farmers and workingmen. The woes of the farmers, apart from the natural hazards of the weather and periodic insect infestations, were due to their growing dependence upon the railroads and a system of mass marketing, both of which were susceptible to manipulation by the "moneyed interests."[23] The earlier subsistence farming had been replaced by the production of money crops—bought, shipped, and processed by others. Selling in a distant market in open world competition, the farmer purchased his machinery, supplies, and personal necessities in a market subsidized by protective tariffs. And his shifting fortunes from year to year frequently made him dependent upon credit to finance his next crop. The great enemy was the triple alliance of railroads, banks, and tariff-protected industry.

Caught in a web woven by railroad monopolists, buccaneering market speculators, tight-fisted money lenders, and hardheaded industrialists, the farmers rose in sporadic movements of protest and revolt. The Grangers of 1867, the Greenbackers of the 1870s, the Farmers' Alliance of the 1880s, the Populists of 1891, and Bryan's "free silver" campaign of 1896 all were expressions of this agrarian discontent that sought to impose systematic government control over the economic life of the nation to mitigate the plight of the farmers. The *Congregationalist Record* of Boston represented the attitude of most eastern churchmen when it described the leaders of the agrarian protest as "dangerous characters of the inflammable and covetous West." Lyman Abbot of Plymouth Congregational Church in Brooklyn was probably equally representative when he spoke disparagingly of William Jennings Bryan as a western "medicine man" who set up his tent to hawk "one medicine which will cure all the ills to which humanity is subject."[24] The evangelical religion of the rural and village churches of the Midwest and South, however, was implicated in the farm revolt and contributed to its continuing impetus.[25] Unfortunately

---

[22] *The Lively Experiment,* 149.

[23] See R. B. Nye, *Midwestern Progressive Politics: A Historical Study of Its Origins and Development, 1870–1950* (East Lansing, Mich., 1951).

[24] *Ibid.,* 5.

[25] *Ibid.,* 160. The Grange, for example, was and has continued to be closely related to the churches. A related discussion of the role of women in the South is in John P. McDowell, *The Social Gospel in the South: The Women's Home Mission Movement in the Episcopal Church* (Baton Rouge, La., 1982).

the relationship of evangelical religion to rural radicalism has received little detailed study, partly because the religious press gave little attention to the agrarian problem. The religious press was urban oriented, and its attention was absorbed by the much more spectacular labor uprisings.

The plight of the workers was even more serious than that of the farmers. Wages were low, hours were long, and working conditions were almost uniformly bad. Where women and children were employed, they labored from dawn to dusk for a pittance. And the situation steadily worsened, for the mounting national wealth was being concentrated in fewer and fewer hands. As early as 1867 a magazine reported that ten men owned one-tenth of the taxable property in New York City, and it listed their holdings. By 1890 it was estimated that 1 percent of the families of the country received one-quarter of the national income, and seven years later one-tenth of the American people were said to own nine-tenths of the national wealth. Wages, to be sure, were rising. From 1860 to 1881 they increased 31 percent, but prices rose 41 percent and more than offset the gain.[26] The crises came, however, when workers were laid off in large numbers or had their pay cut as the result of recurring financial crashes. The crash of 1873 set off the first crisis. This was followed by the panic of 1884 and then by the disastrous depression of 1893, when Coxey's "army" marched on Washington.

Numerous workingmen's associations were being formed throughout these years, and their efforts to improve the lot of the workers led to large-scale labor warfare. Strikes were frequent and bloody. Four were particularly frightening to the nation as a whole. The first was the railroad strike of 1877 in which pitched battles were fought in many cities, arousing widespread fear of imminent revolution and anarchy. The second was the McCormick Harvester strike of 1886. On May 3 six pickets were killed in a clash with the police. The following day at a protest meeting of the workers in Haymarket Square a bomb was exploded which killed a policeman and injured many others. In the subsequent riot ten more persons died. The third was the Homestead strike of 1892 at the Carnegie Steel Plant in Pennsylvania where 10 were killed and 60 wounded in a battle between the workers and 300 "Pinkerton" men. The fourth, the Pullman strike of 1894 which affected rail transportation in 27 states, was accompanied by widespread burning, looting, and killing, and was finally brought to an end by President Cleveland's use of federal troops.

The reaction of the churches to the revolt of the workingmen was one first of shock and then of panic. Orthodox economic theory had taught them that labor was a "commodity," subject "like all other commodities" to "the imperishable laws of demand and supply," and that in a free

---

[26] See Charles B. Spahr, *An Essay on the Present Distribution of Wealth in the United States* (N.Y., 1896), 128 ff.; Robert Hunter, *Poverty* (N.Y., 1912), 61 ff.; Washington Gladden, *Applied Christianity* (Boston, 1894) 120; W. E. Garrison, *March of Faith*, 62, 120.

country the sole responsibility of government to both capital and labor was "the simple duty of enforcing contracts" and preserving peace.[27] Thus they were more shocked by the riots of the strikers than by the conditions that caused the strikers to riot. The whole fabric of society seemed in danger of being torn apart, and many of the Protestant periodicals responded with almost incredibly brutal denunciations of the workers. The issue is between "law and anarchy," declared the *Independent* on July 26, 1877. The safety of society demands that no concessions be made to rioters. A week later its mood was near hysteria. "If the club of the policeman, knocking out the brains of the rioter, will answer, then well and good; but if it does not promptly meet the exigency, then bullets and bayonets, canister and grape . . . constitute the one remedy and the one duty of the hour." The *Christian Union* agreed. "There are times when mercy is a mistake," it asserted.[28] But there were others who were deeply troubled. Washington Gladden, for example, in the late 1860s had defended the cause of the strikers in North Adams, Massachusetts; and in 1876 he published his first book on social questions, *Workingmen and Their Employers*. By the 1880s many were to share his concern.

Roman Catholics were often equally intemperate in their denunciation of strikes. James R. Bayley, archbishop of Baltimore, took a dim view of labor unions, insisting that "no Catholic with any idea of the spirit of his religion will encourage them," and a Catholic periodical asserted that the proper solution for economic troubles was for the workers to "Pray, Pray, Pray."[29] The Knights of Labor, the first mass labor union, was condemned in Quebec by papal decree in 1884, and Archbishop Corrigan of New York insisted that membership in the Knights was forbidden in the United States as well. Cardinal Gibbons, on the other hand, believed that many of the workers' grievances were just, and he was alarmed by the prospect of major defections from the church if the censure was maintained. In 1888, with the help of Ireland and Keane, Gibbons obtained a ruling from Rome that stated that the Knights could be "tolerated." Gibbons then proceeded to warn the Knights against the use of strikes and boycotts. Even the great labor encyclical, *Rerum Novarum* (1891), provided no clear guidance in America, for the workingmen's associations sanctioned by Leo XIII were to be Catholic societies and were to include employers as well as employees. Joseph Schroeder, the conservative leader at Catholic University, quickly pointed out that these associations were a far cry from anything to be found in the United States.[30]

---

[27] *Watchman and Reflector*, June 4, 1874, quoted by May, *Protestant Churches and Industrial America*, 55; and the *Independent*, July 26, 1877, quoted by Garrison, *March of Faith*, 64.

[28] May, *Protestant Churches and Industrial America*, 92–93.

[29] *The American Apostolate*, ed. L. R. Ward (Westminster, Md., 1952); Cross, *Emergence of Liberal Catholicism*, 118.

[30] *Ibid.*, 118. For Gibbons' defense of the Knights of Labor and for portions of *Rerum Novarum*, see Smith, Handy, and Loetscher, *American Christianity*, II, 377–91.

The Social Gospel[31]

Developing social concern among American Protestants was stimulated in part by influences from abroad. The writings of Thomas Chalmers, the Scottish theologian and philanthropist, exerted the earliest influence in this direction,[32] and immediately after the Civil War interest in the distinctively English "Christian socialism" of Frederick Denison Maurice and Charles Kingsley was aroused by their books and novels.[33] Later the "Christian socialists" of Germany and Switzerland contributed a strong theological emphasis upon the centrality of the doctrine of "the kingdom of God." The chief American precursors were Henry M. Dexter, a New England clergyman who published *The Moral Influence of Manufacturing Towns* in 1848, and Stephen Colwell, a Philadelphia iron merchant who became preoccupied with social problems in the 1850s.[34]

The indifference and, on occasion, the hostility of the churches to the cause of the worker was due largely to ignorance. Consciences were disturbed and sympathy and support were enlisted when the clergy became personally acquainted with the workingman's plight. Typical in this respect was the sturdy defense of the workers in the great Pullman strike of 1894 by William H. Carwardine. He was no student of the labor question. He had no theory to support his opinions. But he was the minister of a Methodist church in Pullman, Illinois, and he was drawn by his immediate and firsthand experience of conditions there into a firm belief in the justice of the strikers' demands. For Washington Gladden, the conversion was not so sudden and dramatic. He was first exposed to the plight of the workers during his pastorate at North Adams, Massachusetts, and when he was called to Springfield he found the situation there much more acute. But his views did not mature until the Hocking Valley coal strike of 1884 when he was minister of the First Congregational Church of Columbus, Ohio. The officials of the coal company were members of his congregation, and Gladden was aware of the lengths to which they were

---

[31] The term "social gospel" did not come into common use until after 1900. Prior to this the term most widely used was "social Christianity." See R. C. White and C. H. Hopkins, *The Social Gospel: Religion and Reform in Changing America* (Philadelphia, 1976); R. T. Handy, ed., *The Social Gospel* (N.Y., 1966).

[32] Chalmers' *The Application of Christianity to the Commercial and Ordinary Affairs of Life* was reprinted at Hartford and at Boston in 1821, at Lexington, Kentucky, in 1822, and at New York in 1855. His *Christian and Civic Economy of Large Towns* was considered to be of such value that an abridgment was published in 1900 by Charles R. Henderson, professor of Christian sociology at the University of Chicago.

[33] English nonconformists, such as Andrew Mearson, A. M. Fairbairn, C. Silvester Horne, John Clifford, and Hugh Price Hughes, may have exerted even greater influence in America because they were not "handicapped by ties with an aristocratic and partly feudal establishment." H. F. May, *Protestant Churches and Industrial America*, 149, 150.

[34] Colwell's books were *New Themes for the Protestant Clergy* (1851), *Politics for American Christians* (1852), and *The Position of Christianity in the United States* (1854). He also wrote the Preface to William Arnot's *The Race for Riches* (1853).

prepared to go to crush the strike and break the union. This they succeeded in doing at great cost to the men and to themselves, only to have a new strike break out a year later. This time the miners won. A contract was signed, and the manager of the company admitted to Gladden that it was much better to bargain with the union over a table than to attempt to deal with a mob.

The social gospel leaders represented no unified point of view. They shared a common concern and they were agreed that the people in the churches needed to be exposed to the "facts." Most Protestants were isolated from the scenes of industrial conflict and had no personal acquaintance with the lot of the worker. To remedy this situation, socially minded clergymen organized forums and study groups to discuss industrial problems and they invited representatives of labor to speak before men's brotherhoods in the churches. In addition, they busied themselves with producing a voluminous literature dealing with social issues from a Christian point of view.[35] But beyond this common pattern of activity, there were deep divergences.

Gladden represented a mild "progressivism" that recognized the rights of labor, advocated municipal ownership of public utilities, and placed strong emphasis upon the Golden Rule as the royal law of brotherhood. The latter theme was picked up and romanticized by Charles M. Sheldon, minister of the Central Congregational Church of Topeka, Kansas, in a parable-novel that was destined to win a place beside *Uncle Tom's Cabin* and *Ten Nights in a Bar Room* as one of the great American tracts. *In His Steps, or What Would Jesus Do?* (1897)[36] was the story of the revolution that occurred in a small city when members of a single congregation resolved to live for a year in accordance with the teachings of Jesus. At the opposite pole from Sheldon's nonprogramatic sentimentalism was the demand for a radical reconstruction of society voiced by such men as George D. Herron, professor of applied Christianity at Grinnell College, and W.D.P. Bliss, an Episcopal clergyman in Boston and guiding spirit of the Society of Christian Socialists. A "scientific" approach to social problems was represented by a Chicago coterie whose chief luminaries were Shailer Mathews, Graham Taylor, and Charles R. Henderson. Social melioration based upon careful sociological analysis was their forte, and they were strong advocates of the utility of "social settlements" in forwarding the necessary process of social adjustment.

---

[35] Typical in this respect was Gladden's own literary output, which included *Working People and Their Employers* (1876), *The Christian League of Connecticut* (1883), *Applied Christianity* (1886), *Tools and the Man* (1893), *Social Facts and Forces* (1899), *Social Salvation* (1902), *Christianity and Socialism* (1905), *The Church and Modern Life* (1908), and *The Labor Question* (1911).

[36] Its circulation has been estimated to have exceeded 20 million copies. Conwell's *Acres of Diamonds* occupied much the same place in the gospel-of-wealth literature.

The social settlements were patterned after Toynbee Hall, a pioneer settlement house established in London in 1884. Their purpose was to bring together a company of university-trained social workers who would live together in the slums where they could study conditions at first hand and initiate projects of social betterment. Two of the best-known American "settlements" were in Chicago — Hull House, founded by Jane Addams, and Chicago Commons, with Graham Taylor as its guiding light. Others were to be found in most of the major cities, usually being established in connection with either a university or a seminary.

In terms of continuing influence, Walter Rauschenbusch was the outstanding prophet of the social gospel. His social awakening occurred during ten years spent as pastor of a small Baptist church of German immigrants in New York City. Participation in Henry George's campaign for mayor helped shape his views, as did his experience among the tenements and his association with two other young pastors, Nathaniel Schmidt and Leighton Williams.[37] In 1897 Rauschenbusch was appointed to the faculty of the Rochester Theological Seminary and in 1907, when *Christianity and the Social Crisis* was published, he was thrust into national prominence. Of equal note was his *Prayers of the Social Awakening* (1910), one of the few devotional classics America has produced.

Rauschenbusch is difficult to classify in relation to other social gospel leaders. His fellow Baptists at the University of Chicago dismissed him as "rhetorical" rather than "scientific." He called himself on occasion a "Christian socialist," but he was careful to distinguish his reformist position from any doctrinaire socialism. Although he did not wholly escape the sanguine temper of his time, he showed few traces of the sentimental optimism that characterized so much of the social gospel literature. As early as 1892 he had rejected the "comforting" doctrine of "the inherent upward forces of nature," and in 1907 he spoke strong words of caution to those who had imbibed the heady wine of inevitable progress. As the title of his last volume, *A Theology for the Social Gospel*, indicates, his interest was much more theological than most of the others, and his great contribution was to clothe the social gospel with passion and a sense of destiny. He did this by relating the social gospel in dynamic fashion to the concept of the kingdom of God, placing it in juxtaposition to the inherited, massive, and stubbornly resistant structures of the kingdom of evil.[38]

Rauschenbusch's flurry of optimism just prior to World War I was rooted in the growing popular support and official recognition that was being won by advocates of the social gospel. The social concern reshaped the curricula of theological seminaries, induced some of them to move

---

[37] Henry George had an astonishing influence in awakening Christian social concern in England. Schmidt, Williams, and Rauschenbusch linked themselves in a Society of Jesus which was later expanded to become the Brotherhood of the Kingdom.

[38] See the Introduction to W. S. Hudson, ed., *Walter Rauschenbusch: Selected Writings*.

from isolated hamlets to urban centers ("What medical school," asked Graham Taylor, "is thus remote from the centers of suffering men, and deprived of hospital clinics?"), and prompted others to provide students with a summer's exposure to urban problems.[39] Most major denominations established commissions to forward social concerns, and in 1908 the Federal Council of Churches (predecessor of the National Council of Churches) was formed to enable churches to deal jointly with the problems of an industrial society. A "Social Creed of the Churches" was adopted,[40] addressing itself "to the toilers of America and to those who by organized effort are seeking to lift the crushing burden of the poor, and to reduce the hardships and uphold the dignity of labor," and pledging them sympathy and help in "a cause which belongs to all who follow Christ."

Apart from sincere concern to combat injustice, this official "social Christianity" was motivated by a desire to overcome an assumed alienation of the workingman from the churches. Gladden had noted that only one-tenth of his congregation were wage earners, whereas the census reported that almost one-fourth of the population were of the laboring class. It is "all too evident," he declared, "that the proportion of working people who attend church is much smaller than the proportion of churchgoers to the entire population."[41] The assumption was that the gap between the churches and the workingmen would be closed if the churches would only exhibit an interest in their plight and support them in their struggle for justice.

Middle-class Protestantism, however, was mistaken in assuming that there was such an alienation of workingmen. They simply did not belong to middle-class churches. Overlooked had been the existence of "a working-class social Christianity" running parallel to "the more widely known and well-studied social gospel" of middle-class critics of society. A study of labor periodicals has made it clear that Christian rhetoric, imagery, and motivation were characteristic of labor leadership and that the workingmen found religious sanction for their discontent and union activities in the evangelicalism of traditional American Protestantism.[42] The tactic of wooing workers into middle-class churches by a show of concern for their plight, however, met with little success. Immediate gains rather than expressions of sympathy interested them. Indeed, the 1896 election witnessed a massive shift in the labor vote from its traditional democratic affiliation to the Republican party of Mark Hanna and William McKin-

[39] Abell, *The Urban Impact upon American Protestantism*, 224–45.
[40] Reprinted in Smith, Handy, and Loetscher, *American Christianity*, II, 396–97. It had been drafted and adopted by the Methodist Episcopal Church earlier in 1908.
[41] From "The Working People and the Churches," *The Independent*, July 23, 1885.
[42] Herbert Gutman, "Protestantism and the American Labor Movement: The Christian Spirit in the Gilded Age," *American Historical Review*, 72 (1966), 74–101.

ley.[43] Practical issues were decisive, for neither party in its urban strong-holds (Republicans in Philadelphia and Chicago, Democrats in Boston and New York) offered programs of thoroughgoing social and economic reform.

The "Progressive" Movement

Middle-class support of "social Christianity" was related to Theodore Roosevelt's "Square Deal" and "Bull Moose" platforms. Most social gospel leaders were involved in "progressive" politics, and the 1912 Progressive party campaign had a strong religious flavor. The party convention had as its theme song "Onward, Christian Soldiers," a response to his ringing challenge to them before the convention met — "We stand at Armageddon and we battle for the Lord." Ministers campaigned openly from the pulpit for the party, and one justified himself by maintaining that, although "it is not the province of the pulpit to say that any man ought to be elected president," it is "the province of every pulpit to say that the principles of the Progressive party should guide the nation for the next four years."[44]

Progressivism, like the social gospel, was almost exclusively a manifestation of middle-class idealism. Middle-class opinion had been deeply shocked by the muckrakers' exposure of widespread vice and corruption, of the ruthless tactics employed by the trusts, and of the special privileges accorded "vested interests" by city governments, state legislatures, and the national Congress. The progressives had no consistent philosophy and their program was a miscellaneous collection of reforms that included direct primaries, women's suffrage, the initiative, referendum, recall, regulation of interstate commerce, revision of banking and currency laws, effective antitrust legislation, municipal ownership of public utilities, the income tax, the eight-hour day, prohibition of child labor, safeguards against industrial accidents and occupational diseases, and either strict regulation of the liquor traffic or its outright prohibition.

The related issues of conspiracies in restraint of trade and the corrupting of government officials were the great objects of concern. When most of the reforms designed to curb the "vested interests," restore power to the people, and eliminate other abuses had been adopted, attention was concentrated upon women's suffrage and the abolition of the liquor traffic as the final goals to be achieved. Each was regarded as something of a universal panacea for the ills of society. The women's vote, it was believed, would strengthen at every point the cause of virtue, morality, altruism,

---

[43] S. P. Hays, *The Response to Industrialism, 1885–1914* (Chicago, 1957), 46–47.

Democrats did not recover their urban strength until the elections of 1928 and 1932.

[44] *Ibid.,* 93.

and humanitarian endeavor. The crusade for prohibition, also integral to the progressive program, was viewed as a general panacea.

The liquor industry with its increasing monopolistic tendencies was regarded by the progressives as the most dangerous and predatory of all big business. It was lavish in its expenditures both to gain desired legislation and to thwart the enforcement of bothersome regulations adopted as concessions to public opinion. Often arrogant in its control of government, the liquor industry had been exposed again and again by the muckrakers as a principal source of political corruption and a strong ally of political reaction. Its links with vice and crime were more indirect but nonetheless real. As a progressive reform, prohibition drew upon the same moral idealism as the rest of the progressive program. It was popularly believed that the abolition of the liquor traffic would eliminate at a single stroke a primary cause not only of political reaction, corruption, vice, and crime, but also of poverty, disease, economic inefficiency, marital discord, and broken homes. Although some of the progressives disliked the reform, believing it to be too extreme, this loss of support was more than compensated by that received from conservative Protestants. But the leadership that pushed the adoption of the Eighteenth Amendment remained with the socially liberal progressives.[45]

The temperance cause had long been gaining ground in the United States, and it had become much more vigorous with the organization of the Women's Christian Temperance Union in 1874. Through the efforts of Frances Willard, rhetoric about the physical and social consequences of alcohol consumption were framed within the view of temperance as a moral cause.[46] The emphasis shifted from temperance to total abstinence to a full-scale attack upon the saloon. By 1900 5 of the 45 states had adopted statewide prohibition laws that banned the manufacture and sale of intoxicating beverages, and others had made provision for local option. The big thrust, however, was launched with the formation of the Anti-Saloon League in 1895, an agency that was to become an instrument of sophisticated political action. It was manned by socially progressive Protestant churchmen, and also enlisted the support of liberal Catholics.[47] As was true of the progressive movement as a whole, the drive for prohibition found its greatest strength in an alliance between the old-stock middle-class element in the cities and the rural and small-town population, both groups being staunchly Protestant and united in their determination to rid the cities of vice, crime, poverty, and corruption. Unless this was accom-

[45] See J. H. Timberlake, *Prohibition and the Progressive Movement, 1900–1920* (Cambridge, Mass., 1963).

[46] The influence of the W.C.T.U. was great. For Frances Willard, the key figure in the organization, see Ruth Bordin, *Women and Temperance* (Philadelphia, 1981).

[47] Bishop John J. Keane attended the Anti-Saloon League's founding convention, Archbishop Ireland served as one of the vice-presidents, and Catholic clergymen regularly addressed subsequent conventions.

plished, it was feared that the growing influence of the cities would subvert the character of American society and thwart all further attempts at progress and reform. Men and women who favored the movement pledged their support in writing, sometimes signing a capital "T" alongside their name to indicate that they were opposed to consumption of any kind of alcohol, including beer and wine. Consequently, those entirely opposed to alcohol became known as "T-totalers."

The drive to suppress the liquor traffic had the great advantage of enlisting the support of both liberal and conservative Protestants, and in the end it became a great Protestant crusade. By April 1917, 26 states had gone "dry," and before the end of the year a constitutional amendment to ban the liquor traffic had been passed by Congress and was submitted to the states for ratification. With the approval of 45 of the 48 states, the Eighteenth Amendment came into effect on January 16, 1920. Later in the same year the Nineteenth Amendment, which established the right of women to vote, came into operation. Of the major reforms sought by the progressives, the only unfinished business was a federal ban on child labor. The national child labor statute was declared unconstitutional by the Supreme Court in 1918, and subsequent attempts to secure a child labor amendment were to be unsuccessful.

Imperialism and World Missions

A third frontier of the new industrial society of urgent concern to the churches lay beyond the seas. Conscious of its growing industrial power, the United States began to assume a more positive and vigorous role in international affairs. Foreign trade mounted rapidly and American entrepreneurs were eager to exploit the untapped markets of Latin America and eastern Asia. James G. Blaine, as secretary of state under Presidents Garfield and Benjamin Harrison, championed vigorous action to expand American economic and political influence abroad, and negotiated reciprocal trade agreements and arbitration treaties to further American interests. As early as 1878 a U.S. naval base was established on the Samoan Islands and the process of reducing the Hawaiian Islands to an American possession had begun. President Cleveland's bold defiance of Great Britain in the Venezuelan crisis of 1895 was symptomatic of the new temper that led to the Spanish-American War of 1898 and to the prompt support of Panama's revolt against Colombia in 1903. As an aftermath of the war with Spain, Puerto Rico, Guam, and the Philippines were claimed as U.S. possessions, and "protectorates" were established in several Caribbean countries. Meanwhile the United States was intervening in China to preserve an "open door" for American commerce.

Dollar Diplomacy and Religion

American imperial expansion was accompanied by a mounting enthusiasm among the churches for overseas missions. In its more bellicose form this enthusiasm was utilized as an excuse for territorial aggrandizement and what came to be called "dollar diplomacy." This was the note struck by President McKinley when he sought to explain to some Methodist friends how he had come to change his mind with regard to the acquisition of the Philippine Islands.

> I am not ashamed to tell you, gentlemen, that I went down on my knees and prayed Almighty God for light and guidance more than one night. And one night late it came to me this way. . . . There was nothing left for us to do but to take them all and to educate the Filipinos and uplift and civilize and Christianize them, and by God's grace do the very best we could by them, as our fellow men for whom Christ also died.

Senator Albert J. Beveridge was not troubled by such hesitation and uncertainty, and his defense of annexation was positive and to the point.

> We will not renounce our part in the mission of the race, trustee under God of the civilization of the world. . . . He has marked the American people as his chosen nation to finally lead in the regeneration of the world. This is the divine mission of America. . . . The judgment of the Master is upon us: "Ye have been faithful over a few things; I will make you ruler over many things."

The possibility of a different interpretation of scripture was made clear when Senator George F. Hoar rose to his feet in response to Beveridge and quoted another biblical text: "The Devil taketh him up into an extremely high mountain and showeth him all the kingdoms of the world and the glory of them and saith unto him, 'All these things will be thine if thou wilt fall down and worship me.'"[48]

Without the results of public opinion polls, there is no way to determine which senator represented majority opinion in the churches. Many shared the militant spirit of Senator Beveridge, but influential churchmen who had supported the conflict with Spain as a war of liberation in keeping with America's anticolonialist tradition were appalled when it became an occasion for launching the United States on an imperial career of overseas expansion.[49] When their efforts to exclude provisions for annexation from the peace treaty were defeated, they mounted a continuing campaign to

---

[48] Charles S. Olcott, *The Life of William McKinley* (Boston, 1916), II, 110–11; Mark Sullivan, *Our Times, the United States, 1900–1925* (N.Y., 1926–35), I, 47–48; Garrison, *March of Faith,* 174.

[49] W. S. Hudson, "Protestant Clergy Debate the Nation's Vocation, 1898–99," *Church History,* 42 (1973).

promote the cause of peace and international justice. Peace societies multiplied. Dollar diplomacy and the "big stick" (the naval construction program) were attacked. The newly organized Federal Council of Churches trained young people for foreign mission work, inspiring them with the ideal of human brotherhood and a warless world. On February 10, 1914, 29 of America's most distinguished religious leaders—Protestant, Roman Catholic, and Jewish—formed the Church Peace Union to coordinate their separate activities into a single thrust for a peaceful settlement of international disputes. Andrew Carnegie provided an endowment to underwrite the program. So great was his optimism that he included as a proviso of his gift that "after war is abolished" the income may be used "to relieve the deserving poor . . . , especially those who have struggled long and earnestly against misfortune and have not themselves to blame for their misfortune."[50] The first project of the new organization was to aid in the establishment of the World Alliance for International Friendship through the churches. This was accomplished in August 1914, the month that marked the beginning of World War I.

The Evangelization of the World

When William R. Williams, a scholarly Baptist preacher, wrote in 1846 that "our heavenly Father has made us a national epistle to other lands,"[51] he was reiterating a conviction that had long been held by most American Christians. In the nineteenth century, however, Great Britain had taken the lead in the foreign-mission enterprise and the United States was the junior partner. At the close of the century this role was reversed.

The expansion of American commercial and political interests abroad riveted the attention of the churches upon the needy people beyond the seas. In 1885 Josiah Strong, in a little book entitled *Our Country*, summoned the churches of America to assume their full responsibility for the Christianization of the world.[52] American ideals, he insisted, rather than its national power should be the focal point of concern in America's relationship to other lands. The Anglo-Saxon race in general and the American people in particular, he contended, were the bearers of two great interrelated ideas—"civil liberty" and "spiritual Christianity." And but for the "salt" provided by the second, the first would "speedily decay." These in turn are the "two great needs" of all mankind.

[50] Charles S. MacFarland, *Pioneers for Peace Through Religion: Based on the Records of the Church Peace Union* (N.Y., 1946), 22.
[51] John R. Bodo, *The Protestant Clergy and Public Issues, 1812–1848* (Princeton, 1954), 241.
[52] *Our Country: Its Possible Future and Its Present Crisis*, ed. Jurgen Herbst (Cambridge, Mass., 1963). The quotations that follow are taken from Chapters XIV and XV, pp. 201–3, 205, 210, 212, 215–18, 252, 256.

> Without controversy, these are the forces which, in the past, have contrib-
> uted most of the elevation of the human race, and they must continue to be,
> in the future, the most efficient ministers to its progress.

The obvious corollary of this fact was that "the Anglo-Saxon [in the
United States, all immigrants by the alchemy of the 'melting pot' quickly
became Anglo-Saxons[53]], as the great representative of these two ideas,
the depository of these two great blessings, sustains peculiar relations to
the world's future" and "is divinely commissioned to be, in a peculiar
sense, his brother's keeper."

Strong was more eloquent than exact in his terminology. His words
sound "racist," but he states that Anglo-Saxon superiority "is due in large
measure to its highly mixed origin," it being "almost universally admitted
by ethnologists that the mixed races of mankind are superior to the pure
ones." Thus the Anglo-Saxon is not to be defined in terms of a racial
strain but as the heir of a dual tradition — "civil liberty" and "spiritual
Christianity" — of which the Anglo-Saxon is the custodian. And the influence of these twin concepts served as a corrective to the inevitable temptation to exercise tyrannical domination over other peoples. In the United
States, as a result of this cultural tradition, all immigrants by the alchemy
of the "melting pot" were considered Anglo-Saxons. This occurred as
soon as they learned to speak English. Nor did Strong explain the energy
and vigor of the Anglo-Saxon in terms of "blood" or "genes." It was
largely the product of climate and diet.

As Strong reviewed past history, it was evident to him that, with "two
hands," God had been "preparing in our Anglo-Saxon civilization the die
with which to stamp the people of the earth" and at the same time,
through the revolutionary ferment that contact of Christian with heathen
was creating, had been "preparing mankind to receive our impress."

> The door of opportunity is open in all the earth; organizations have been
> completed, languages learned, the Scriptures translated, and now the
> triumph of the Kingdom awaits only the exercise of the power committed to
> the church.

Whether the perils that threaten to delay "the coming of the kingdom
wherein dwelleth righteousness" will be permitted to retard its advance
"is now being swiftly determined" by the men and women of this generation. Living as they do in one of the plastic moments of history, Strong
declared, "it is fully in the hands of the Christians of the United States,
during the next ten or fifteen years, to hasten or retard the coming of
Christ's kingdom in the world by hundreds, and perhaps thousands, of
years."

Strong's stirring summons elicited a remarkable response the following

[53] *Ibid.*, 203.

summer among the students gathered for a conference at Dwight L. Moody's Mt. Hermon School. The enthusiasm was sparked by Robert P. Wilder, who had just graduated from Princeton, and he was aided and abetted by Luther D. Wishard, secretary of the Student Y.M.C.A. at Princeton, and John R. Mott, a student at Cornell. Before the conference was over, an even 100 had volunteered for foreign-mission service. The delegates carried their contagious enthusiasm back to their campuses, Wilder made a whirlwind tour of the colleges, and by the end of the succeeding year the number of volunteers had grown to more than 2,000.[54] In 1888 the growing enthusiasm was channeled into a permanent organization, the Student Volunteer Movement, which adopted as its slogan "the evangelization of the world in this generation." For the next three decades this organization was to enlist the very ablest men and women on the college campuses of the nation and to send them to the far corners of the earth.

The motivation that lay behind this surge of foreign-mission interest was varied. A. T. Pierson and A. J. Gordon, both of whom played a part in arousing Wilder's concern, were premillennialists who believed that the gospel had to be preached throughout the world as a prerequisite to the second coming of Christ. Others were distressed at the thought of millions of souls being lost forever. J. Hudson Taylor at the Student Volunteer convention at Detroit in 1894 declared:

> There is a great Niagara of souls passing into the dark. . . . Every day, every week, every month, they are passing away! A million a month in China . . . are dying without God.[55]

Democratic and humanitarian sentiment, however, seems to have played the strongest role in winning support for missions. Robert E. Speer, who with Wilder and Mott constituted the great triumvirate of the Student Volunteer Movement, emphasized this when he asserted that the great need for the world was "to be saved from want and disease and injustice and inequality and impurity and lust and hopelessness and fear."[56]

The whole foreign-mission enterprise was marked by widespread interdenominational cooperation. Not only did the mission boards recruit their personnel through the joint endeavors of the Student Volunteer Movement, they allocated territory on a comity basis in the mission fields and formed interdenominational councils in mission lands for purposes of consultation and sharing of experience. At home the work of the denominational boards was coordinated through the formation of the Foreign Missions Conference of North America in 1893, and later it was also

---

[54] R. W. Braisted, *In This Generation: The Story of Robert P. Wilder* (N.Y., 1941).

[55] *The Student Volunteer Enterprise: Addresses and Discussions of the Second International Convention of the Student Volunteer Movement for Foreign Missions* (N.Y., 1910), 48.

[56] *Christianity and the Nations: The Duff Lectures for 1910* (N.Y., 1910), 29.

coordinated through the International Missionary Council which grew out of the Edinburgh conference of 1910. In 1902 the Missionary Education Movement was launched to quicken missionary interest in all the major denominations. A continuing problem, of course, was to provide sufficient financial support for the youth who were offering themselves in increasing numbers for missionary service. A Presbyterian layman, John B. Sleman, Jr., sought to meet this need. He had been deeply moved when thousands of college students had gathered in Nashville in 1906 for a Student Volunteer convention. As a result of his prodding, the Laymen's Missionary Movement was organized in the autumn of that year to challenge laymen throughout the nation to match the devotion of youth with the dedication of their dollars. Until the outbreak of World War I, the Laymen's Missionary Movement was carried forward with the same surge of enthusiasm that characterized the Student Volunteer Movement.

The years of midpassage following the Civil War had introduced many changes into American life and had presented the churches with multiple problems of adjustment. These problems had been met with varying degrees of success, but never were they tackled with more exuberance than during the first decade and a half of the new century, which Gaius Glenn Atkins described as "the age of crusades." The unusual moral idealism and superabundance of zeal that found expression in the allied enterprises of the missionary movement were channeled into a whole galaxy of causes, only a few of which have been noted in this chapter. World War I brought to an end all these peaceful crusades by diverting the idealism and zeal of the American people into the one great crusade to end war and make the world safe for democracy through military power.

World War I also marked the end of the years of transition. The great tide of immigration from Europe was cut off in 1914 when the German armies smashed through Belgium and into France. The economic effect of the war was to hasten the process of industrial development and to bring to maturity the urban world of modern America. In most parts of the country the agrarian democracy of earlier years was to be little more than a memory as back-country villages and smaller cities were brought within the orbit of great metropolitan centers.

The changes introduced by World War I were not immediately apparent. By the time the United States entered the war in 1917, the attention of the American people had long been absorbed by the dramatic news of the conflict in Europe. When the United States joined the struggle, President Wilson's "Fourteen Points" made the issues at stake seem clear cut, and the churches responded to the national summons with zeal and unanimity. Few voices of dissent were heard as "preachers presented arms," utilizing their sermons to depict the iniquity of the Central powers and the righteousness of the Allied cause. Prominent clergymen exhibited their enthusiasm for the president's crusade by volunteering to go abroad with the troops as Y.M.C.A. workers. Others served at home as "Minute Men," promoting the sale of Liberty Bonds. Then, with American troops having scarcely arrived on the field, the war ended. So quickly had it rushed to its conclusion that only the most perceptive had had time to contemplate the possibility that the old days were gone and that the world would never be the same again.

PART IV

Modern America

1918–

1873	Reform Rabbi Isaac M. Wise helps found Union of American Hebrew Congregations
1875	Jewish Reform seminary, Hebrew Union College (Cincinnati) founded
1879	Charles Taze Russell publishes *Food for Thinking Christians*, outlining beliefs of Jehovah's Witnesses
1882	Russian government enacts harsh anti-Jewish laws
1886	Conservative Jewish Theological Seminary founded in New York City
1890–15	Ex-baseball player Billy Sunday popular revivalist
1897	The Church of God in Christ founded
1910–15	Amzi C. Dixon and Ruben A. Torey publish *The Fundamentals*
1911	Pentacostal Holiness Church organized
1914	Assemblies of God founded in Arkansas
1917	National Catholic War Council formed
1917	National Baptist Convention splits into the National Baptist Convention, Inc. and the National Baptist Convention of America
1918	Maryknoll Fathers begin sending missionaries abroad
1919	John A. Ryan writes Roman Carholic pamphlet on reform *Social Reconstruction*
1919–20	Interchurch World Movement undertakes ambitious campaign to Christianize the world
1923	Aimee Semple McPherson (Foursquare Gospel Church) builds Angelus Temple in Los Angeles
1925	Bruce Barton pictures Jesus as business executive in *The Man Nobody Knows*
1925	United Church of Canada founded
1925	A copy of the Bible costs three dollars
1925	Scopes "monkey trial" at Dayton, Tennessee
1928	George N. Shuster complains of American Catholic anti-intellectualism in *The Catholic Spirit in America*. John Tracy Ellis and Thomas F. O'Dea follow in 1950s
1929	Stock market crash; beginning of Depression
1930s	Popular Roman Catholic radio priest Charles E. Coughlin
1930	Frank Buchman launches "First Century Christian Fellowship" at Calvary Episcopal Church in New York City
1930	Greek Archdiocese of North and South America established
1931	Joseph "Judge" Rutherford introduces the name "Jehovah's Witnesses" for members of Zion's Watch Tower Society
1932	Reinhold Neibuhr voices discontent with Protestant theology in *Moral Man and Immoral Society*
1932	Catholic League for Social Justice established
1932	Franklin D. Roosevelt elected president
1933	Dorothy Day helps found Catholic Worker movement
1934	Reconstructionist leader Mordecai M. Kaplan publishes *Judaism as a Civilization*
1937	Association of Catholic Trade Unionists formed
1938	Frank Buchman forms a "Moral Re-Armament" group
1939–45	World War II
1940	U.S. population 132 million
1940	Virgil Michel begins to institute liturgical innovations at Benedictine abbey in Minnesota
1942	Fundamentalist National Association of Evangelicals formed
1946	Elijah Muhammad founds Nation of Islam
1946–53	Communist witch hunts promoted by Senator Joseph McCarthy
1947	Catholic Archbishop of St. Louis ends segregation in diocesan schools; Washington D.C., diocese follows
1948	State of Israel established

1948	Trappist monk Thomas Merton writes best-selling *The Seven Story Mountain*
1948	World Council of Churches is formed in Amsterdam
1949	Radio celebrity Monsignor Fulton J. Sheen publishes *Peace of Soul*; later becomes television priest
1950	National Council of Churches formed to coordinate mission and education activities
1950	U.S. population 150 million
1952	Norman Vincent Peale writes *The Power of Positive Thinking*
1952	"Revised Standard Version" of the Bible published
1954	Council of Eastern Orthodox Youth Leaders of America formed
1954	Supreme Court ends "separate but equal" doctrine in public education
1956	Martin Luther King, Jr., leads bus boycott in Montgomery, Alabama
1957	Billy Graham preaches highly successful revival in New York City
1957	United Church of Christ formed
1959	Castro leads overthrow of Battista in Cuba
1960	John F. Kennedy elected first Catholic president; 42.1 million (of population of 179 million) are Roman Catholics
1962–65	Second Vatican Council
1962	Consultation on Church Unity (COCU) organized
1962	Protestant Episcopal Church consecrates J. M. Burgess, a black clergyman, as Suffragan Bishop of Massachusetts
1963	Martin Luther King, Jr., addresses civil rights advocates during march on Washington
1963	President Kennedy assassinated
1965	Black Muslim leader Malcolm X assassinated
1965	Catholic Traditionalist Movement objects to Vatican II changes
1967	Israel wins Six-Day War
1968	United Methodist Church organized
1968	Pope Paul VI issues Encyclical "Humanae Vitae" against all artificial contraception
1969	70 percent of those questioned in Gallup poll feel that influence of religion is declining in United States
1968	Martin Luther King, Jr., and Robert Kennedy assassinated
1972	National Coalition of American Nuns issues "Declaration of Independence" demanding equality
1976	Episcopal church approves the ordination of women to be bishops and priests
1977	The Orthodox Church in America selects its first American-born prelate
1978	John Paul II becomes Pope
1979	The Moral Majority, organized by Reverend Jerry Falwell, spearheads rise of "new religious right."
1982	Reverend Sun Myung Moon, leader of Unification Church, sentenced to prison term for tax fraud
1982	Federal court overturns Arkansas law requiring teaching of creationism
1984	President Ronald Reagan, championing the causes of conservative religious supporters, proclaims anti-abortion National Sanctity of Human Life Day
1985	Amy Eilberg ordained first female Conservative rabbi (following Sally Preisand's ordination in Reform tradition in 1972)
1987	Television evangelist Jim Bakker confesses sexual improprieties, loses control of PTL organization, and is later given stiff sentence for misuse of church money
1988	Merger of Lutheran churches creates Evangelical Lutheran Church in America
1989	Barabara C. Harris ordained first female bishop in Episcopal church
1990	Population of United States 247 million
1990	Supreme Court rules against traditional sacramental use of peyote by Oregon Indians
1990	In City University of New York study 9 out of 10 Americans identify themselves as religious

CHAPTER 13

The Shifting Religious Configuration

By 1914, when the onset of World War I brought to an end the massive influx of new Americans, the religious configuration of the nation had been sharply modified. Mounting Roman Catholic immigration had continued to reduce the numerical predominance of Protestantism, and in the two decades preceding the outbreak of war, both Judaism and Eastern Orthodox Christianity made the striking gains that transformed them into numerically significant communities. At the same time, marked Lutheran growth, the emergence of new "disaffected" Protestant groups, and the growing strength of black churches had altered the Protestant spectrum.

Judaism

Of all the religious traditions and groups that emerged into relative numerical prominence for the first time at the turn of the century, Judaism had the longest history. As children of Abraham, the ancient Hebrews had known troubled times and prosperous times, times of strife and times of peace. Their epic included escape from bondage in Egypt, only to spend 40 years in the wilderness before reaching the Promised Land. Recurring wars ended with exile in Babylon, whence many returned to rebuild the temple in Jerusalem. Greeks and Romans came as conquerors, followed by an heroic insurrection. Again the temple was destroyed and the Jewish people were further dispersed into almost all parts of the known world. Here and there, scattered in small communities, from Spain to India and from northern Africa to the Danube and the rivers of Gaul, the Jews survived. Sometimes they prospered; frequently they were harried; and always the dispersion continued. In 1654, fleeing from Portuguese harassment in Brazil, 23 Jews arrived in New Amsterdam as initial representatives of what was to become one of America's major faiths and in time the largest Jewish community in the world.

Jewish life found its focus in the giving of the Law to Moses some 3,000 years ago and in the consciousness of being a people chosen of God to exhibit both his righteousness and his mercy.[1] The Temple in Jerusalem was the center of Jewish worship. The synagogue appeared for the first time during the Babylonian exile and was given definite shape by Ezra after the return to Jerusalem, where it occupied a subordinate position to the renewed Temple worship. Among Jews of the Diaspora (those living outside Palestine), except for a rare pilgrimage to Jerusalem, the synagogue provided the sole opportunity for communal worship. Although its prayer services were modeled after the Temple service, the central emphasis was upon the instruction of the people rather than upon priestly acts performed in a sacred place. The Torah (the Law contained in the Pentateuch, the five books of Moses) was read and explained and applied to the needs of daily life. When the Temple was again destroyed in A.D. 70, synagogue worship took on heightened significance as a corporate reminder of the ancient bond symbolized by the Temple and its Ark of the Covenant.

Closely related to the developing life of the synagogue were the rabbis. The rabbis, or teachers, were businessmen or workers who had devoted their leisure to studying the heritage of Israel and, as learned scholars, had been recognized as competent authorities of Jewish law. Although they had no official relationship to the synagogue, the rabbis had always played a prominent role in synagogue life as spokesmen and interpreters of God's claim upon his people. After the shattering events of A.D. 70, the rabbis gained a more central position. Broken and forlorn, the members of the scattered Jewish communities were groping for guidance and comfort. The rabbis gave them both. In their teaching they reinterpreted the Law to make it applicable to the new situation and combined this instruction with glowing words of encouragement and hope. Official leadership, to be sure, did not belong to the rabbis. Others conducted the services of worship, reciting the prayers and reading from the Torah. But it was the rabbi who won the full respect and esteem of the community. More than a millennium was to pass, however, before it became customary to provide the rabbi with a salary. Even as late as the fifteenth century this was far from a universal practice.

Life in America introduced a significant change in Jewish life. In medieval Europe a pattern of Jewish life developed that was perpetuated in some areas until the twentieth century. These European Jewish communities

---

[1] For Jewish faith and practice, see Milton Steinberg, *Basic Judaism* (N.Y., 1947), and Arthur Hertzberg, *Judaism* (N.Y., 1961). Jacob Neusner, *American Judaism: Adventure in Modernity* (Englewood Cliffs, N.J., 1972), and Joseph Blau, *Judaism in America* (Chicago, 1976), are compact accounts of the American Jewish experience.

were tightly knit enclaves set apart from the larger community. An individual Jew had no independent civic status. But within the ghetto there was considerable self-government, with the Jewish leadership being responsible for maintaining order, levying taxes to satisfy the demands of the civil government, and imposing additional assessments to meet their own communal needs. The synagogue was but one of several communal institutions, and it both embraced and was controlled by the total Jewish community.[2] In America these self-contained Jewish enclaves disappeared. The synagogue became the primary institution of Jewish life, with membership a matter of individual choice. Instead of one synagogue, there could be several within a given area. And the synagogue was controlled by its own congregation rather than by the whole Jewish community.

The first Jews to arrive in America were "Sephardim," Jews of Spanish or Portuguese antecedents who came by way of Brazil beginning in 1654, but they never came in large numbers. Until the last decade of the nineteenth century, most American Jews were "Ashkenazim," German-speaking Jews from central Europe. Both groups were thoroughly orthodox, differing in ritual but not in doctrine. What may be called Jewish denominationalism dates from 1802 when a group of Philadelphia Jews who wished to adhere to the practices of the Ashkenazic rite formed a separate synagogue. This was a time of small beginnings, of course, for in 1825 there were only about a half-dozen active congregations in the United States and in 1848 there were no more than 50. In the latter half of the century, however, the number rapidly multiplied.

Reform Judaism

From the beginning Jews had a love affair with America. Almost everywhere throughout the world, Jews had been forced to regard themselves as a separate entity, living apart from the general community and governing themselves, to the extent that they were permitted to do so, by Talmudic law.[3] In the United States the legal restrictions that fostered this isolated life were absent. Jews could become full citizens. They could be Americans of Jewish faith rather than an alien people. True, the United States was not a perfect society. Numerous ills needed to be remedied. But, with political rights having been followed by economic advance and growing acceptance, Jews felt more completely at home than they had in the lands from which they came. They accommodated themselves to American society.

In this situation a growing number of Jews came to regard many of their ancient laws as anachronistic. Specific sources of embarrassment were some of the ancient folk customs associated with synagogue worship, and

---

[2] See Nathan Glazer, *American Judaism* (Chicago, 1972), 18–19.
[3] The Talmud is a distillation of the biblical interpretation and wise counsel of the ancient rabbis.

the general lack of decorum and dignity of the religious services. An initial attempt to simplify synagogue worship and to make it more comprehensible and appealing was made at Charleston in 1824. Although this was abortive, a similar effort in 1836 was more successful. The first congregations that were founded to foster Reform were Har Sinai of Baltimore in 1842 and Emanu-El of New York in 1845.

American Jews, of course, were few in number. The great impetus for Reform came from Germany, where the Jews had been emancipated by constitutional changes. At Frankfort-on-the-Main in 1843 the Frankfort Society of the Friends of Reform was organized and issued the following declaration:

> First, we recognize the possibility of unlimited development in the Mosaic religion. Second, the collection of controversies, dissertations, and prescriptions commonly designated by the name Talmud possesses for us no authority from either the doctrinal or practical standpoint. Third, a Messiah who is to lead back the Israelites to the land of Palestine is neither expected nor desired by us; we know no fatherland except that to which we belong by birth or citizenship.[4]

These were to be the classic guiding principles of Reform Judaism. As a result of the storm of protest the declaration aroused among the more conservatively inclined, many German Jews sympathetic to Reform emigrated to the United States where they greatly strengthened the Reform cause.

The great leader of Reform Judaism in America was Isaac M. Wise, who arrived in the United States in 1846. He served as rabbi of a small congregation in Albany until 1854, and then spent the rest of his career in Cincinnati. His great concerns were to effect a national organization to give some unity to the independent Jewish congregations, and to establish a college to train rabbis. Primarily through his efforts the Union of American Hebrew Congregations was formed in 1873, and the Hebrew Union College was founded in 1875. His Reform views were promoted through the *American Israelite*, a paper he founded and edited. In the area of doctrine he discarded belief in a personal Messiah and in the resurrection of the dead. He also made a distinction between the Torah of God (the Ten Commandments) and the Torah of Moses (the rest of the Pentateuch), the latter being an application of divine truth to specific circumstances and becoming outdated as conditions changed. In terms of practice he insisted upon equal rights for women (family pews, for example, instead of segregation by sex), and introduced into the service the use of both English and instrumental music. The prayer book he compiled was a simplification of the traditional liturgy modified to conform to his views. Other reformers were much more radical than Wise, making a sharper

---

[4] David Philipson, *The Reform Movement in Judaism* (N.Y., 1931), 122.

break with the past, introducing original prayers into the service, and substituting Sunday for Sabbath worship. Wise's adjustment to the problem posed by a Saturday morning service was to shift it to Friday evening, an innovation that had little support during the nineteenth century but became the general practice by the middle of the twentieth century.

By 1880 Reform had become the dominant version of American Judaism, although a placid orthodoxy continued to find expression in scattered synagogues. The extent to which Reform leaders were willing to effect accommodation to American life, however, was soon to create a further division. The growing restiveness of a minority who were nominally within the Reform camp was brought to a head in 1883 by the serving of shrimp (a violation of the dietary laws) at a banquet honoring the first graduates of Hebrew Union College. This produced a deep emotional shock among some of the more conservatively inclined. Rallied by Sabato Morais, the disaffected groups in 1886 founded the Jewish Theological Seminary in New York City, an institution that was to become the chief center of Conservative Judaism. Occupying a middle position between Reform and Orthodox Judaism, the Conservative synagogues did not prosper greatly until the atrocities of the Nazi era in Germany heightened the sense of Jewish identity and created a desire among Jews to reemphasize the historic continuities of Judaism.

The Great Immigration

The wave of Jewish immigrants who poured into the United States for three and one-half decades after 1880 introduced a new strain into American Judaism and changed the character of the whole community. In 1880 there were 250,000 Jews in the United States,[5] mostly German in background, and widely dispersed throughout the country. Most of them were related to the synagogue, that is, to a Reform Temple. By 1914 the Jewish segment of the population numbered 3 million. This new Jewish population was markedly different in cultural background and represented a quite different type of Judaism. The recent arrivals were refugees from eastern Europe. They were poverty stricken and heterogeneous. They came from different lands, and their common Yiddish tongue was spoken in varied dialects. A few were distinguished scholars, but some were illiterate and most were without skills. Unlike the older Jewish inhabitants, they crowded into the eastern cities.

The Jewish flight from eastern Europe was a response to harsh anti-Semitic pressures and pogroms. In 1882 the Russian government issued a

---

[5] Interpretation of Jewish statistics is complicated by the fact that until well into the twentieth century, numbers were computed in terms of "heads of families." Nor are Jewish statistics comparable to those of most other religious bodies, for they usually refer to total Jewish population rather than to synagogue membership.

series of decrees designed to make Jewish life impossible. The objective was stated with cynical frankness by the Tsar's most trusted advisor: "One-third of the Jews will emigrate, one-third will be baptized, and one-third will starve."[6] A similar policy was pursued elsewhere in eastern Europe, most notably in Romania and Galicia (Austrian Poland). The pressure continued with varying intensity until the outbreak of World War I.

Among Jews of eastern Europe there were three responses to the tragic condition in which they found themselves. The majority, without hope of securing full status as citizens through political and social assimilation in the lands of their birth, retreated into rigid orthodoxy, finding inner security in unquestioning piety and strict observance of the Torah. Their cultural outlook was little affected by cultural movements among the peoples about them. A second group, those who had had some contact with contemporary thought, reacted in a fashion quite different from that of the Jews of Germany and America. Instead of seeking to create a Reform Judaism that would be consonant with modern culture, they tended to renounce Judaism and identify themselves with radical antireligious movements of social reform. The passion and intensity with which the religious Jews of eastern Europe clung to traditional forms of thought and practice made the prospect of altering these forms seem hopeless, whereas the political structures were so repressive and class oriented that only a thoroughgoing social revolution seemed to offer the possibility of emancipation. Emerging from this second group was a third faction, rather insignificant at the outset, which cast its revolutionary fervor into a nationalistic mold. Taking their cue from the liberation movements of Poles, Czechs, Ukrainians, and other oppressed peoples of eastern Europe, these "Lovers of Zion" emphasized the national rather than the religious character of Judaism and began to think in terms of securing emancipation through the establishment of a Jewish state. Each group was represented in the east European immigration.

Nathan Glazer has reported that the Jewish immigrants who came from eastern Europe were "a frightening apparition" to "the established, middle-class, Americanized German Jews of the 1880s."

> Their poverty was more desperate than German Jewish poverty, their piety more intense than German Jewish piety, their irreligion more violent than German Jewish irreligion, their radicalism more extreme than German Jewish radicalism. It is not surprising that the American Jews viewed this immigration with mixed feelings, and some even suggested the possibility of deflecting or preventing it.

The American Jews did not know which was the most objectionable: the strident orthodoxy of the immigrants (as distasteful to the dignified Or-

[6] Bamberger, *The Story of Judaism,* 324.

*New Year's Worshippers in Front of a Tenement Synagogue.   (Courtesy of the
Bain Collection, Library of Congress.)*

thodox who opposed Reform as it was to the adherents of Reform synagogues), the antireligious views of the social radicals, or the political
separatism of the Jewish nationalists. By the end of the century, however,
the antipathy had been pushed sufficiently to one side for the leaders
of the older Jewish communities to engage in strenuous efforts to "uplift"
the immigrants and ease their adjustment to American life. One specific
project of considerable future significance was the injection of new life

into the Jewish Theological Seminary, which had slowly been dying as its original base of tradition-oriented synagogues had dwindled. Under the leadership of Cyrus Adler, the financial support of Reform Jews was enlisted to transform the seminary into an agency for civilizing the east Europeans by providing them with modern English-speaking rabbis. A fund of more than a half-million dollars was collected for this purpose. Solomon Schechter was brought from England to be the new president, and a distinguished faculty was assembled.

Reconstructionism and Zionism

By 1920, 80 percent or more of the Jewish population in the United States was of east European descent, and adherents of Reform Judaism were far outnumbered by members of Orthodox synagogues. Those unaffiliated with any synagogue, however, exceeded the combined total of all religious Jews, and the proportion of the unaffiliated was growing. The flight from Judaism, which had begun in the old country, was accelerated as a concomitant of the process of Americanization. Repelled by the "foreignness" of the religious observances of their parents, children of Orthodox immigrants drifted into indifference to religion. Few exhibited any inclination to transfer their loyalties to more modern synagogues. The results of a 1935 survey in New York City, which revealed that approximately 75 percent of Jewish young people between the ages of 15 and 25 had attended no religious service during the preceding year, were not regarded as atypical.[7] Social centers, growing out of such social agencies as the settlement houses and the Young Men's and Young Women's Hebrew Associations, were more often the focal points of Jewish life than the synagogues.

A creative response to this situation was the Reconstructionist movement led by Mordecai M. Kaplan of Jewish Theological Seminary. Kaplan's views evolved out of the synagogue center movement which he initiated in 1918. Others had experimented with making the synagogue more attractive by developing "institutional" temples patterned after the institutional churches of the Protestants, but Kaplan's aim was a new type of Jewish community, with its focus not religion but "Jewishness." His approach to religion was sociological. He sought to strengthen Judaism by relating it closely to all aspects of Jewish life — political, cultural, intellectual, and philanthropic. His central contention, fully elaborated in *Judaism as a Civilization* (1934), was that Judaism was not a religion but a religious civilization in which nonreligious as well as religious Jews shared. The synagogue should be the rallying center of Jewish people and Jewish culture even for those who did not feel strongly about Jewish religion. Traditional rituals and ceremonies were viewed as important for their

[7] Glazer, *American Judaism*, 85.

instrumental value as cement that helped bind the Jewish people together. There was little place in Kaplan's thinking for the supernatural: "To modern man, religion can no longer be a matter of entering into a relationship with the supernatural. The only kind of religion that can help him live and get the most out of life will be the one which will teach him to identify as divine or holy whatever in human nature or in the world about him enhances life."[8]

Conservative Judaism, with its ambivalent stance between Reform and Orthodox Judaism, was best equipped to assimilate Kaplan's Reconstructionist emphasis upon both tradition and modernity. In general, the Conservative synagogues adopted Kaplan's policy of fostering a broad, inclusive Jewishness while rejecting the more radical features of his philosophy.

Closely allied to Kaplan's view of Judaism as a civilization was the older Zionist view of Judaism as a nation. Zionism had east European roots among the nineteenth-century "Lovers of Zion" but was given its more definitive shape by Theodor Herzl, a Viennese reporter who was present in Paris at the trial of Captain Alfred Dreyfus. In 1894 Dreyfus had been falsely charged with treason and was subsequently convicted, a victim of virulent anti-Semitic feeling in the French army. In a state of high emotional excitement Herzl wrote a pamphlet entitled *The Jewish State* (1896). The only salvation for Jews, he insisted, was national rebirth. This necessitated a homeland, preferably in Palestine. Herzl was hailed by many as a prophet, and in 1897 the first World Zionist Congress was held in Basel, Switzerland.

The Zionist issue became the subject of prolonged debate. Although Zionist leaders tended to be nonreligious, many Orthodox Jews embraced Zionism since it could be reconciled with the ancient expectation of the restoration of Israel. Conservative Jews had even fewer reservations and tended to become ardent Zionists. Reform Jews, on the other hand, were generally hostile, viewing Judaism as a religion and advocating a policy of assimilation at other points. After Hitler's persecution of the Jews began in 1933 and thousands of German Jews emigrated to Palestine, the Zionist question became much less theoretical. By 1935 a majority of the Reform rabbis had moved into the Zionist camp, and in that year the Central Conference of American Rabbis abandoned its official policy of opposition to Zionism and adopted in its stead a position of neutrality. The subsequent holocaust, in which 6 million Jews were murdered by the Nazi state, further strengthened both the Zionist cause and the sense of Jewish solidarity. When the State of Israel was established in 1948, American Jews rallied to ensure its survival by raising astonishingly large sums through the United Jewish Appeal to aid the resettlement of refugees who were streaming into Israel from many parts of the world.[9]

---

[8] Mordecai Kaplan, *The Meaning of God in Modern Jewish Religion* (N.Y., 1985).
[9] The total amount raised in 1948 was $201 million. In subsequent years the amount declined, but in 1955 it still exceeded $100 million.

Jewish Religious Revivals at Midcentury

Although the Hitler years heightened Jewish self-consciousness and drew many into participation in Jewish activities, there was no great return to the synagogue. The surge of growth in synagogue membership was to be a phenomenon of the post–World War II period. In 1937 the *American Jewish Year Book* estimated that the Reform congregations had 50,000 member families. The Conservative congregations, having gained recruits from the children and grandchildren of Orthodox immigrants, numbered some 75,000 member families. The Orthodox congregations had the largest constituency, with about 200,000 families. Thus the combined synagogue membership represented between 1 and 1.5 million Jews, not much more than one-fourth of all the Jews in the country. By 1956 there was a marked change. Synagogue life was flourishing, with most of the gains having been made in the last decade. Member families of Reform temples numbered 255,000, a fivefold increase over 1937. The growth rate of Conservative synagogues was smaller, but their member families had almost tripled in number and stood at 200,000. Although Orthodox Judaism was a declining portion of the Jewish religious community, it too was exhibiting signs of vigorous life, and its intellectual center, Yeshiva College, had become a flourishing university.

Apart from numbers, there was a marked increase in the practice of piety. The proportion of Jewish population attending religious services at least once a month increased from 18 percent in 1947 to 31 percent in 1955. Even among Reform Jews there was a strong tendency to reemphasize traditional values, customs, and ceremonies. The Friday evening family Kiddush with its candle lighting became more common and holidays more widely observed. In the mid-1950s it was said somewhat skeptically that the modern Jew "does more" but "knows less." This verdict was scarcely supported by available evidence. Not only had there been a vast increase in the number of children receiving a Jewish education through weekday classes, the Sunday school, and Jewish day schools, but publishers had discovered that there was a growing market among adults for books dealing with Jewish theology and religious life.

The revival of synagogue life may have been related to a change in the Jewish community. In the 1930s Jews had been predominantly working class in status, but by the 1950s only a small segment could be classified as "blue-collar" workers. As a result of a zeal for education, second- and third-generation east European Jews were successful in imitating earlier Jewish immigrants by moving into business and the professions. Their children and grandchildren also shifted their place of residence from the inner city to better neighborhoods and then to the suburbs. Having become a more homogeneous and prosperous community, mid-twentieth-century Jews tended to conform to the churchgoing pattern of other middle-class Americans. They conformed in other ways as well: in their denominationalism, in the lay control and autonomy of congregational life (there was no "chief rabbi" as in Europe), and in their activism and emphasis on Judaism as a "way of life," not doctrine.

By 1960 there were stirrings of a deeper religious concern. On university campuses some Jewish students, reacting against the affluent lifestyle and the seeming spiritual void represented by suburban temples, began to exhibit interest in discussing Jewish mysticism, spiritual discipline, and personal faith. A few sought to develop a renewed or parallel Judaism of their own in communes or "covenanted" communities. Although older members of the Jewish community did not resort to such drastic solutions, many shared the same longing for meaning that transcended their daily routine.

The establishment of the State of Israel also posed a problem for thoughtful Jews. It pushed to the fore the issue of defining Judaism in more specifically religious terms. Attachment to the land of Israel and hope for eventual return, whether Judaism was religiously or culturally defined, had been one of the bonds of Jews of the Diaspora (dispersion). When it became clear that millions of Jews chose to remain where they were when the way to return was open, the need for a rationale for a continuing Diaspora became urgent. If a cultural Judaism was unable to satisfy the spiritual hunger of individuals, it was equally unrealistic to expect Jews in America to find a meaningful existence merely by living vicariously in another land. They had to live where they were and no emotional tie to Israel, however strong, could provide the meaning derived from a common religious vocation to which Jews everywhere had a contribution to make.

With astonishing rapidity, Jewish scholars began to mine the rich resources of Jewish mystical piety. Some younger Jews were especially drawn to the Hasidic mystical enthusiasm that had its beginnings in eighteenth-century eastern Europe, attracted partly by the countercultural aspects of Hasidic communal life, but more interested in the Hasidic experience of encounter with God than in rituals and customs. Martin Buber had explicated the teachings of the Hasidic masters,[10] but youthful Jews set about exploring the riches of Hasidic texts for themselves. The mystical piety of Abraham Heschel, who had insisted that Jews by attuning their "yearning to the lonely holiness of this world" will "aid humanity more than by any particular service," became more influential than hitherto.[11] The issue of vocation, so important to Jews of the Diaspora, was a central concern for a group of distinguished scholars, including Eugene Borowitz, Norman Lamm, and Seymour Siegel. Known as "Covenant theologians," they defined the Jewish people in terms of a relationship with God, insisting that God established a special covenant with the Jews that imposes on

[10] *Hasidism and Modern Man* (N.Y., 1958).
[11] For a moving account of his views and lively faith, see *The Earth Is the Lord's* (N.Y., 1950), and also *Man Is Not Alone* (N.Y., 1951).

them a special vocation that has relevance and meaning for all humanity. If Vatican II was to open windows and allow fresh air to penetrate the closed confines of Roman Catholicism, it is clear that a freshness of thought and a deepening of spirituality was also penetrating a Judaism that was in danger of ceasing to be a living religion.

Eastern Orthodox Christianity

The Eastern Orthodox churches also have a long history.[12] They look back to the early Christian Fathers, and to Athanasius, the Cappadocians, Pseudo-Dionysius, and "the seven ecumenical councils" as the source of their tradition. Perhaps Orthodox Christianity can best be identified in terms of the two separations that gave the Orthodox churches their geographical locus. The first separation, which took place in the fifth and sixth centuries, was that of the smaller eastern churches — the Nestorians of Syria, Persia, and ultimately China, and the Monophysites (the Jacobite and Coptic churches) of Armenia, Syria, Egypt, and Ethiopia. The second separation was the product of a growing cleavage between the Greek-speaking and the Latin-speaking areas of the old Roman Empire. Although the ecclesiastical division was beginning to be apparent as early as the sixth century, the final separation is commonly dated from 1054. As a result of these two separations, Eastern Orthodoxy was bounded on the east and the west, but it was able to expand to the north among the Slavic peoples. As the Greek power of Byzantium dwindled, the newer Orthodox churches of the north increased in importance. After the fall of Constantinople in 1453, Moscow — "the third Rome" — tended to assume Byzantium's role as protector of the Orthodox world.

The Orthodox Churches

Distributed throughout eastern Europe, in Russia, and along the eastern coast of the Mediterranean, Orthodox Christianity is a family of self-governing churches, united by a common faith and order. Apart from areas of more recent expansion, these churches are the ancient Patriarchates of Constantinople, Alexandria, Antioch, and Jerusalem; the national churches of Russia, Romania, Serbia (Yugoslavia), Greece, Bulgaria, Georgia (U.S.S.R.), Cyprus, Czechoslovakia, Poland, and Albania; and the Holy Monastery of Sinai. Although the Patriarch of Constantinople is known as the Ecumenical or Universal Patriarch and enjoys a position of special honor, he has no power to intervene in the affairs of any church

---

[12] See Nicolas Zernov, *Eastern Christendom* (London, 1961); Ernst Benz, *The Eastern Orthodox Church: Its Thought and Life* (Chicago, 1963); and Timothy Ware, *The Orthodox Church* (Baltimore, 1963).

other than his own. His position is much like that of the Archbishop of
Canterbury in the Anglican communion, which is also composed of self-
governing churches spread throughout the world. Because the overwhelming proportion of Orthodox Christians (perhaps as many as 55
million) were for many years behind the "iron curtain," it is difficult to
estimate their total number. The four ancient Patriarchates have more
than 2.5 million adherents, and the churches of Greece and Cyprus have a
combined total of almost 8 million adherents.

Although the Orthodox have much in common with Roman Catholics,
there are significant differences in emphasis, practice, and even doctrine.
The whole mood is much more mystical and much less legalistic. The
mode of baptism is triple immersion. Communion is in both kinds, the
communicant receiving both the bread and the wine. Infants are confirmed and receive communion immediately after being baptized. Statues
(rounded images) are not permitted, and in their stead icons (paintings
and mosaics) are used. Priests may marry prior to ordination, but bishops
must be unmarried. The date of Easter is different (being reckoned by the
Julian rather than the Gregorian calendar), and church architecture is
distinctive. The doctrines of purgatory and the immaculate conception of
Mary are not generally accepted; and instead of extreme unction for the
dying, the sick are anointed for the recovery of health. The most crucial
difference is the authority Roman Catholicism confers upon the Roman
Pontiff as the vicar of Christ and the infallible teacher and ruler of the
faithful. Where Roman Catholics insist upon obedience to the Bishop of
Rome, Orthodox Christians stress the role of the bishops in the government of the church and the authority of General Councils in the determination of matters of faith.

Orthodoxy in America

Eastern Orthodoxy had its beginnings in North America when missionary
monks came to Alaska in the 1790s and succeeded in converting many of
the natives. A seminary was established at Sitka in 1848 and a diocese was
formed in 1867 when Alaska became a territory of the United States. In
1872 the seat of the diocese was transferred to San Francisco, and in 1905
to New York. In addition to the Russians, a few Greek communities had
churches prior to 1900, but the major Orthodox influx came after the
turn of the century. During the latter years of the great Jewish immigration, Slavic peoples (and Romanians) were also arriving from eastern
Europe. Many of the non-Jewish east Europeans were Roman Catholic,
but a large portion were Orthodox. Unlike the Jews, these other east
Europeans did not crowd into the coastal cities. They had been recruited
to labor in the mines and steel mills, and hence they were dispersed
throughout Pennsylvania and along the periphery of the Great Lakes. The
significant exception to this pattern of Orthodox settlement was repre-

sented by non-Slavic immigrants, principally Greeks and Syrians (including Armenians), who, as independent entrepreneurs, were widely scattered throughout the country.

From a total membership of not more than 100,000 in 1900, the number of Orthodox in the United States had risen to more than 2 million in 1960,[13] subdivided into at least 15 national or jurisdictional groups. Before World War I all Orthodox Christians in America were under the jurisdiction of the Russian church, since it was the Russians who first brought Orthodox Christianity to the United States. The subsequent multiplicity of jurisdictions was a consequence of the Russian Revolution of 1917. With the Russian church becoming involved in a difficult and controversial relationship to the new Soviet regime, each of the Orthodox nationality groups formed separate organizations.

The Orthodox churches in America had a confused history in the post–World War I years as a result of the readjustments that then took place. The Greek church has been the largest (1.5 million members in 1962) and most stable, but it was troubled by such disorders and frictions that it was not until 1930 that its life was fully regularized as the Greek Archdiocese of North and South America. The Russians experienced a fourfold split based mostly on varying interpretations of their relationship to the Patriarch of Moscow. The Ukrainians in America not only separated from the Russians, they suffered a threefold division among themselves. The Albanian, Bulgarian, Romanian, Serbian, and Syrian Orthodox were not fragmented, but their churches did not become fully stabilized in organization until around 1930.

Troubled by cultural and administrative divisions, the Orthodox churches in America gained stability only after World War II. Several theological seminaries were established, and those in New York and Boston became distinguished centers of theological scholarship. There also was evidence of growing sentiment for unity. In 1954 the Council of Eastern Orthodox Youth Leaders of America was formed and drew together most of the Orthodox youth organizations; and in 1960 a committee of Orthodox bishops began periodic meetings under the presidency of the Greek archbishop. The Orthodox churches also exhibited vitality in adjusting to the American environment. The use of English in worship, the introduction of mixed choirs and instrumental music, the installation of pews, the development of parish organizations, and the adoption of church dinners as an important aspect of church life were the kind of adaptation that other immigrant bodies had made prior to becoming integrated into American life. There were several attempts, mostly by

[13] According to the *Year Book of the American Churches*, the total in 1960 was 2,680,633. This figure is no more than an approximation, for Orthodoxy, like Judaism, has tended to estimate its adherents in terms of total ethnic or national groups. Membership is generally reported in round numbers.

former Episcopalians, to form an indigenous Orthodox church that would be at the same time both more American and more "catholic" and thus attract converts from other traditions. These met with little success, received little encouragement from Orthodox leaders, and enlisted only a handful of adherents.

"Disaffected" Protestants

One consequence of religious liberty is the opportunity for disaffection to find free and open expression. Many groups born of disaffection in the nineteenth century lived on into the twentieth century, some growing in strength, others declining. Among those that have been discussed in preceding chapters are Mormonism, Millerism, and Spiritualism; New Thought, Christian Science, and Unity; Theosophy, Baha'i, and the Vedanta Society. But other groups were to have a surge of growth in the post–World War I years. Of these, with the exception of the Fundamentalist movement (see Chapter 17), the Holiness and Pentecostal churches and Jehovah's Witnesses were perhaps the most conspicuous. These latter groups were more traditional in orientation than those previously considered. One might refer to them as "sects" rather than "cults."[14] They are best described as disaffected Protestants, for they claimed no new revelation and their intention was to recover past tradition.

The Holiness Movement

The quest for perfect sanctification or holiness is as old as Christianity. In nineteenth-century America it had received powerful reinforcement from the generally optimistic temper of the time ("Jacksonian perfectionism"), from the hunger for holiness generated by the revivals, and from the pervasive influence of the strong Wesleyan emphasis upon the doctrine of Christian perfection.[15] Among the non-Methodists who responded to this

[14] As is true of many words, "cult" and "sect" have a variety of meanings. In this context, "cult" is used to denote those groups that are based on a claim to new revelation and/or the authoritative teaching of a new prophet. A cult tends to be forward looking and frequently is eager to come to terms with what is considered to be "modern" thought. On the other hand, "sect" (from the Latin "secare," which means "to cut" or "cut off") is used to denote groups that make no claim to new revelation but instead seek to recover what they regard as an important but neglected aspect of past tradition. In the process, they emerge as new and separate incarnations of tradition.

[15] Wesleyan perfectionism was defined by nineteenth-century Methodists in terms of a "second blessing"—a work of grace (sanctification) subsequent to conversion (justification) which imparted perfect love of God and liberation from sin. Wesley never claimed sanctification for himself, and sometimes he seemed to imply that it was the culmination of a growth in grace rather than an instantaneous experience. For Wesley's views, see Harold Lindström, *Wesley and Sanctification*, trans. H. S. Harvey (London, 1946).

"perfectionist" climate of opinion, Charles G. Finney and his colleagues at Oberlin were the most prominent. Beginning in 1839 the Oberlin group exhibited a growing interest in "the higher Christian life," and through their influence the concern for sanctification penetrated most Protestant denominations during the decades immediately preceding and following the Civil War.[16] The holiness revival, however, found its preeminent expression among Methodists, where it was sparked in the North by the enthusiasm of a remarkable woman, Phoebe Palmer, and where it gained momentum through her evangelistic tours and through the organizational efforts of the National Association for the Promotion of Holiness. In the South, Mary Cagle contributed similar energy to the movement.

Methodism as a whole continued to be concerned with the quest for holiness in the latter half of the nineteenth century.[17] In spite of this unanimity, it was nonetheless a potentially disruptive emphasis, for it tended to cultivate an absolutist state of mind that brooked no compromise. This was illustrated by the Wesleyan Methodist defection of 1843, which demanded moral perfection on the slavery issue. After the Civil War the disruptive issue was the growing "worldliness" of Methodists.

Methodists had been a plain people — plain in dress, behavior, and worship. But as Methodism gained in numbers, wealth, and social status, signs of laxity began to appear. As early as 1856 the stringent rules prohibiting the use of specific items of dress were reduced in the *Discipline* to a general admonition — an admonition that was not sufficiently rigorous to deter Bishop Matthew Simpson's wife from appearing in ruffled silk, expensive lace, and fine jewelry. A similar loss of simplicity in worship occurred as costly edifices were built, and choirs, organs, and instrumental music were introduced. A correspondent of the *Christian Advocate* reported in 1868 that in the cities of the western states — in Ohio, Indiana, Michigan, Wisconsin, Illinois, and Iowa — the tendency was to erect "one hundred thousand dollar churches" where "wealth and style and fashion gather, and the poor have not the gospel preached to them." Two years earlier a writer in the same journal had noted with satisfaction that "by virtue of the habits which religion inculcates and cherishes, our church members have as a body risen in the social scale, and thus become socially removed from the great body out of which most of them were originally

---

[16] For Asa Mahan's statement of the Oberlin views, see selection in Smith, Handy, and Loetscher, *American Christianity*, II, 42–48. Wesleyan and Oberlin perfectionism had much in common, but the former tended to stress the instantaneous change wrought by the "second blessing," whereas the latter emphasized the more gradual change resulting from growth in grace. See Timothy L. Smith, *Revivalism and Social Reform* (N.Y., 1957), 108–12, and J. L. Peters, *Christian Perfectionism and American Methodism* (N.Y., 1956).

[17] Southern bishops constantly emphasized this theme, and northern bishops were equally firm, declaring in 1884 that "the mission of Methodism is to promote holiness." *The History of American Methodism*, ed. E. S. Bucke (N.Y., 1964), II, 614–18.

gathered." Although he regarded this development as "natural" and "not undesirable," there were some who regarded it as a betrayal of the summons to holiness.[18] By the end of the century grievances were multiplying, with notice being taken of the "church theatricals" and "fairs" that were being held, and of the increasing number of church members who "dance, play cards, attend theaters, [and] absent themselves from revivals."[19]

A foretaste of what was to be a continuing disaffection was supplied in 1860 with the formation of the Free Methodist Church at Pekin, New York. Taking its stance on the declaration that "those who are sanctified wholly are saved from all inward sin" and "all their thoughts, words, and actions are governed by pure love," the new church proceeded to denounce the proud and aspiring, to voice opposition to all "superficial, false, and fashionable" Christians, and to demand of church members an affirmative response to the question: "Will you forever lay aside all superfluous ornaments and adorn yourself in modest apparel . . . , not with broidered hair or gold or pearls or costly array?" Organs, instrumental music, and pew rentals were also condemned.[20]

The Free Methodist revolt was restricted to three relatively small areas in western New York, Michigan, and Illinois, but in the 1880s evidence of more widespread disaffection found expression in the formation of numerous independent Holiness groups throughout much of rural America, and in some urban contexts as well. Although some of these "come-outer" groups were composed of people from various denominations, the larger portion were formed by dissident Methodists. By the 1890s local fellowships had begun to coalesce into larger groupings. Most were to remain numerically unimportant, but a few were to exhibit a capacity for sustained growth during the first half of the twentieth century. One of these was the Church of God (Anderson, Indiana), founded in 1881 with a dual stress on holiness and Christian unity. From its initial base in the rural Midwest, it spread gradually into the South and to the Pacific coast. Another group, the Christian and Missionary Alliance, was founded by a Presbyterian minister, A. B. Simpson, in New York City in 1887. But the most successful was the Church of the Nazarene, established by a Methodist district superintendent at Los Angeles in 1895, which numbered 874,000 members by 1988. By this date the Holiness groups, including the Salvation Army, had a total membership of more than 2.5 million.[21]

[18] W. C. Barclay, *History of Methodist Missions,* Vol. III (N.Y., 1957), 49; May, *Protestant Churches and Industrial America,* 62.

[19] *History of American Methodism,* II, 624.

[20] *Ibid.,* 346, 352, 356, 357n., 359.

[21] See Timothy L. Smith, *Called unto Holiness: The Story of the Nazarenes* (Kansas City, Mo., 1962).

The Pentecostal Churches

Growing out of the Holiness movement were the "pentecostal" churches, having a combined membership in 1960 of approximately 1.5 million. Their distinguishing feature, in addition to faith healing, was an emphasis on baptism in the Holy Spirit, manifested by speaking in unknown tongues.

Modern Pentecostalism was first known as the Latter Rain Movement, a name derived from the "former rain" and "latter rain" of Joel 2:23, interpreted as a dual prophecy of the speaking in tongues on the first Pentecost (Acts 2:4) and of the descent of the Spirit immediately prior to Christ's premillennial return. The movement originated in 1901 among students of C. F. Parham's Topeka Bible College, but its greatest momentum came from the 1906 Azusa Street revival in Los Angeles initiated by Parham's student, W. J. Seymour, a fledgling black preacher. The Azusa Street Mission became a nursery of Pentecostal leadership, with Florence Crawford establishing headquarters in Portland, Oregon, and C. H. Mason and G. B. Cashwell planting the seed in what proved to be the highly receptive soil of southern Appalachia. The Church of God in Christ, the largest black Pentecostal group, was shaped and nurtured by Mason, and Cashwell's ardent preaching led to A. J. Tomlinson's Spirit baptism. Tomlinson's activity, supplemented by R. G. Spurling's preaching, led to a bewildering array of Church of God organizations. The largest (170,261 members in 1960; 505,755 in 1987) is known as the Church of God (Cleveland, Tennessee). There were three offshoots with the same name—two with headquarters in Alabama, one with headquarters in Cleveland. Confusion was somewhat reduced when the latter group adopted the designation Church of God of Prophecy.[22]

Apart from the Church of God groups of the Southeast, most other Pentecostal bodies were more Reformed than Wesleyan in background. The Pentecostal Holiness Church, organized in 1911, belongs to this wing of the movement, but the largest group is the Assemblies of God founded in 1914 at Hot Springs, Arkansas. The Assemblies of God differs from the Wesleyan wing of the movement in that its proponents regard sanctification as a gradual process rather than an instantaneous work of grace. Consequently, for them, speaking in tongues is an independent experience of the Holy Spirit. Beginning with an initial membership of 6,000, the Assemblies of God numbered over 41,000 adherents in 1926; 318,478 in 1950; 508,602 in 1960; and 1,256,982 in 1989. Furthermore, they had launched a bold foreign-mission program and had won notable successes in many parts of the world.

---

[22] See Vinson Synan, *The Holiness–Pentecostal Movement* (Grand Rapids, 1971), and C. W. Conn, *Like a Mighty Army*, rev. ed. (Cleveland, Tenn., 1977).

A more streamlined Pentecostalism was represented by the Foursquare Gospel of Aimee Semple McPherson. With a magnetic personality, striking beauty, a flair for the dramatic, and an ability to turn the unfavorable publicity generated by her sensational adventures to her own advantage, Mrs. McPherson gathered a large following in Los Angeles where she erected in 1923 the Angelus Temple, which quickly became a major tourist attraction. Emphasizing Christ as Savior, Healer, Baptizer, and Soon-Coming King, Sister Aimee gathered branches of her Foursquare Gospel Church in various parts of the country. After Mrs. McPherson's death, her son Robert continued her work. The rate of growth slowed, but the church remained strong, especially in the Pacific Northwest, with a membership of 181,594 in 1987, up from 82,624 in 1960.

Millennialism

Although premillennial views were held by some Holiness and Pentecostal groups, other disaffected Protestants seized upon the expectation of Christ's return to judge the quick and the dead as their major theme. This emphasis offered both present and future consolation to those who felt alienated by the "fashionable" churches of the privileged classes. Part of the comfort was the assurance that the established denominations were clearly apostate, and further consolation was gained from the belief that the tables would soon be turned, with the mighty being put down and the humble exalted, the hungry being filled with good things and the rich sent away empty.

The "dispensationalism" of the Darbyites and the Scofield Bible (see Chapter 11) had made significant inroads among members of many of the older churches during the latter years of the nineteenth century, and after 1920 it produced a growing number of independent Bible churches and gospel tabernacles. It also contributed to Fundamentalist defections. An older premillennial tradition in America, stemming from the Millerite excitement of the 1840s, was represented by the Seventh-day Adventists and the smaller Advent Christian group. After maintaining a modest witness for more than half a century, the Seventh-day Adventists, who had been known chiefly for their sanitariums and for fathering the breakfast-food empires of the Kelloggs and the Posts, experienced a surge of new life in the twentieth century. From 62,211 members in 1906, they grew to 110,998 in 1926, to 237,168 in 1950, and to 317,852 in 1960. But these statistics tell less than half the story, for twice this number of Seventh-day Adventists were to be found outside the United States as a result of far-flung missionary endeavor. Quite surprising in view of their firm belief in the imminent end of the world was their heavy investment in publishing houses, hospitals, homes for the aged, and especially educational institutions. Not only did they maintain numerous academies, colleges, graduate schools, and both a theological seminary and a medical and dental school, they also established a widespread network of elementary schools. Noting their many good works, one observer has commented that seldom, while expecting a kingdom of God from heaven, has a group worked so diligently for one on earth.[23]

Of all the Adventist or millennial groups, Jehovah's Witnesses have been the most conspicuous and vigorous.[24] After the onset of the depression in 1929, the Witnesses often seemed omnipresent, selling the *Watchtower* on busy street corners, and ringing doorbells endlessly in an effort to gain an opportunity to present their message of salvation. Then with the end of World War II, Kingdom Halls began to multiply. But it was their encounters with the law that gained the Witnesses most notoriety. Much of their trouble stemmed from their refusal to salute the flag, register for the draft, and permit their children to receive blood transfusions. Not only did these several refusals bring them before the courts, but they served to engender a popular hostility that found expression in attempts to harry the Witnesses by charging them with minor infractions of municipal codes — disturbing the peace, trespassing, violating Sunday "blue laws," and peddling without a permit.

The Witnesses have been known under a variety of names — Millennial Dawnists, International Bible Students, the Watchtower Bible and Tract Society, Russellites, and Rutherfordites. The founder was Charles Taze ("Pastor") Russell, a haberdasher and member of a Congregational church in Allegheny, Pennsylvania, who had been troubled by the notion of eternal damnation and by doubts as to the reliability of the Bible. "Stumbling," as he put it, upon an adventist preacher, he found help that was sufficient to reestablish his "wavering faith." By 1872 Russell was meeting with a group of earnest Christians to examine the teaching of Scripture "relative to the coming of Christ and his kingdom."[25] Soon he had elaborated a millennial scheme of his own. In 1879 he began the publication of a magazine. The following year he published his first book, *Food for Thinking Christians.* In 1884 he formed his adherents into the Zion's Watch Tower Society. To disseminate his message, Russell trained "preachers" and issued a constant stream of publications, including a multivolumed *Studies in the Scriptures.* Attention was focused on 1914 as the year when "the kingdoms of this world" will be brought to an end, and "the full establishment of the Kingdom of God will be accomplished."[26] When the year passed without the expected heavenly intervention, a reexamination of Scripture disclosed that it was Christ's return "in spirit" that had taken place in 1914, and that this was a prelude to his visible

[23] Gaustad, *Historical Atlas of Religion in America,* 115.

[24] H. H. Stroup, *The Jehovah's Witnesses* (N.Y., 1945); Marley Cole, *Jehovah's Witnesses* (N.Y., 1955); and J. A. Beckford, *The Trumpet of Prophecy* (N.Y., 1975).

[25] Stroup, *Jehovah's Witnesses,* 4, 6.

[26] *Jehovah's Witnesses in the Divine Purpose* (Brooklyn, 1959), 55.

return to lead the righteous into battle against the hosts of evil. This imminent Armageddon would mark the beginning of the millenium.

When Pastor Russell died in 1916, his following was not large, but positions of leadership in the Society were sufficiently coveted to occasion a severe struggle for power. The victor was Joseph Franklin ("Judge") Rutherford, legal counsel of the Society and Russell's attorney in his imbroglio over the sale of "miracle wheat." Judge Rutherford injected new life into the Society, substituted his writings for those of Pastor Russell, popularized the slogan "Millions now living will never die," introduced the name "Jehovah's Witnesses" (1931), and equipped the Witnesses with phonographs so that they could utilize transcriptions of his talks in their house-to-house calls. As before it was a personality-centered operation, with Rutherford replacing Russell as the authoritative teacher and leader. All this was changed when Rutherford died in 1942. This time there was no "palace intrigue," no struggle for control, for a collective leadership took over and the "personality cult" was eliminated.[27] A board of directors assumed control with Nathan H. Knorr as president. Unsigned pronouncements replaced the writings of Rutherford, and the portable phonographs disappeared. Henceforth the Witnesses were trained to do their own talking instead of relying on the transcribed voice of a leader.[28]

With Rutherford's death, Jehovah's Witnesses entered the period of their greatest growth. Activity was stepped up both at home and abroad. During World War II the worldwide membership almost doubled, increasing from 115,240 to 207,552. The rate of growth was even greater during the next five years, with membership reaching 456,265 in 1952. By 1960 the number of Witnesses throughout the world was nearly 1 million, with the United States accounting for slightly more than one-quarter of the total.

The message, elaborated successively by Russell, Rutherford, and the directorate headed by Knorr, was calculated to appeal to the multiple resentments of those who are euphemistically described as the "culturally deprived." The central contention was that Satan's power is wielded through "the religious, commercial, and political combine" which is united in oppressing the righteous.[29] These three elements in society are so intimately linked that each does the bidding of the others. All churches and religious organizations are "tools of Satan" and are utilized by the clergy as a means of securing cash income. The clergy both support and are supported by the proud and arrogant commercial class which dominates, subjugates, and exploits the poor. The wealthy in turn are protected by the governments of the world, all of which are equally wicked

[27] Cole, *Jehovah's Witnesses*, 107–8.
[28] *Ibid.*, 211–12.
[29] See Stroup, *Jehovah's Witnesses*, 155–61.

since they are ruled by Satan. The righteous, however, are not without hope, for the evils of the world are soon to be rectified at the battle of Armageddon when the forces of Jehovah led by Jesus will defeat the hosts of Satan.

Although few of the Holiness, Pentecostal, and millenarian groups were as direct or as comprehensive in their appeal to the frustrated and the resentful as Jehovah's Witnesses, they all tended to thrive among those who for one reason or another felt either alienated or disinherited. And since this was a common feeling among many upwardly mobile, lower-income Americans, these diverse expressions of disaffection — including the related Fundamentalist groups — represented a combined membership in 1960 of almost 8.5 million persons.

The Black Churches

In many ways black religious life reflected the patterns and trends that prevailed in the general religious life of the nation. Most larger "white" denominations had black members. Some of these black members belonged to predominantly white congregations, but most were in separate black congregations. These "integrated" churches, however, accounted for only a small fraction of black church membership, for the overwhelming proportion of blacks belonged to black denominations. Outwardly these denominations closely resembled the churches of the white majority, but this outward resemblance was somewhat deceptive.

As a result of social forces to which blacks were subjected, a separate black world had been created. The black church was partly the product of this segregated society with a distinctive life of its own.[30] The worship featured liturgical innovations designed to encourage group participation. The theology stressed both the consolations of heaven and the this-worldly promise of a near-approaching Day of Jubilee. Congregational singing was deeply moving. Both the emotional pitch of the services and their eschatological focus found expression in the "spirituals," which have been called the most original and enduring contribution of the black church.[31] With most avenues of social expression cut off and with the ministry one of the few professions open to blacks, the church assumed an

[30] See C. G. Woodson, *The History of the Negro Church* (Washington, D.C., 1945), and E. F. Frazier, *The Negro Church in America* (N.Y., 1971). For the ambivalent relationship to the larger American community, see G. S. Wilmore, *Black Religion and Black Radicalism* (N.Y., 1972), L. I. Sweet, *Black Images of America* (N.Y., 1976), and James M. Washington, *Frustrated Fellowship: The Black Baptist Quest for Social Power* (Macon, Ga. 1986).

[31] See Howard Thurman, *The Negro Spiritual Speaks of Life and Death* (N.Y., 1947), and D. J. Epstein, *Sinful Tunes and Spirituals: Black Folk Music to the Civil War* (Champaign, Ill., 1977).

importance that has seldom been duplicated among other groups.[32] Since there was little opportunity elsewhere for a black to gain recognition and exercise authority, there often was a scramble for leadership. This highly competitive situation led to numerous schisms, withdrawals, and reorganizations. Black Methodists splintered into at least eight denominational bodies, the largest ones being the African Methodist Episcopal Church; the African Methodist Episcopal Church, Zion; and the Christian Methodist Episcopal Church. Perhaps as many as 70 percent of black church members were Baptists, and their strength is explained at least in part by the ease with which an individual pastor could pursue an independent course. But the Baptists suffered a major denominational schism in 1917 when the National Baptist Convention split into two rival organizations— the National Baptist Convention, Inc. and the National Baptist Convention of America. A later breach resulted in the Progressive National Baptist Convention.

The large-scale movement of black population into the major industrial centers of the nation, which began during World War I and continued thereafter at a steadily mounting tempo, introduced marked changes into black church life. Many urban churches became much more formal and restrained. The emotionalism of earlier days declined, "spirituals" were sung less frequently, the itinerant evangelist was less prominent, and preaching, although still the foundation of church life, gave less emphasis to otherworldly aspects of the faith. Attention was increasingly devoted to advancing the interests of blacks through practical action. The Supreme Court decision of 1954, which put an end to the "separate but equal" doctrine in public education, triggered a massive civil rights movement in which the black churches played the predominant role. A spectacular illustration of this was the bus boycott in Montgomery, Alabama, in 1955–56, which was sparked by Rosa Parks' refusal to move to the back of a bus, was led by the local black clergy, and made Martin Luther King, Jr., a national figure. Subsequent "freedom rides" to eliminate discrimination in interstate travel, "sit-ins" and "demonstrations" to obtain equal access to public accommodations, and voter registration drives were usually planned and organized in the black churches and often were led by their pastors.

The growing decorum and "worldliness" of many of the city churches produced much the same reaction among some of the new black urban dwellers as had occurred among segments of the white population. Tiny store-front churches, which reproduced the intimacy and informality of the rural churches, multiplied, and the Holiness and Pentecostal movements found ready recruits among blacks who looked back with nostalgia to the uninhibited emotionalism of their childhood religious experience.

---

[32] By the 1930s a larger proportion of blacks were church members than was true of members of the white population.

Where It All Began. Rosa Parks being fingerprinted in Montgomery, Alabama, for refusing to move to the back of the bus on September 1, 1955. *(Photograph from Wide World Photos.)*

A whole cluster of new black denominations emerged—the Church of God in Christ, Christ's Sanctified Holy Church, Church of the Living God, House of the Lord, Apostolic Over-coming Holy Church of God, Fire-Baptized Holiness Church of God, Triumph the Church and King- dom of God, Church of Our Lord Jesus Christ of the Apostolic Faith, Bible Way Churches of Our Lord Jesus Christ, Kodesh Church of Imman- uel, and Free Christian Zion Church of Christ. Most were small—some almost minuscule in membership—but taken together they had almost 750,000 adherents in 1960. The Church of God in Christ accounted for half of this total. Founded in 1897 with a stress on sanctification and on the gift of tongues, the Church of God in Christ experienced rapid growth after 1936, numbering 392,635 members in 1960.

Like urban whites who toyed with the teachings of Psychiana, the Rosicrucians, the "Mighty I Am," and Zen Buddhism, blacks also devel- oped exotic cults in the urban environment.[33] The House of Prayer for All

[33] See A. H. Fauset, *Black Gods of the Metropolis* (Philadelphia, 1971).

Nations of Bishop "Sweet Daddy" Grace was a product of the Depression
years which gained added income from the sale of Daddy Grace coffee,
Daddy Grace cold cream, and Daddy Grace toothpaste. Although Daddy
had given God a vacation, the faithful were assured they need not despair,
for they could still be saved by grace — Daddy Grace. The Peace Mission
of Father Divine was equally bizarre, for he claimed to be God and his
followers were "angels." In 1932 he established "heavens" in Harlem
where he fed thousands. Later Philadelphia became a major center. After
World War II, the Peace Mission lost much of its momentum. Both Daddy
Grace and Father Divine emphasized nonracial brotherhood, but other
movements took an opposite tack. The "Black Jews" of W. S. Crowdy,
F. S. Cherry, and W. A. Matthew, for example, stressed black separateness
and superiority. A similar view was represented by Marcus Garvey's
"Black Nationalists" who appealed to "the God of Africa," and Drew
Ali's "Moorish Americans" who rejected the white gods and turned for
inspiration to the Koran. In the 1960s the "Black Muslims" of
Elijah Muhammed's Islam, which blended emphases derived from Garvey
and Drew Ali, was reported to be the fastest-growing movement among
blacks in America.[34] This seemed an overenthusiastic verdict until the
brief but charismatic leadership of Malcolm X and the conversion of
Cassius Clay (Muhammad Ali) gave major impetus to the Muslims. Overenthusiastic or not, the comment called attention to unusual ferment
among urban blacks, and Muslim growth pointed to a forthcoming repudiation of "Negro" and adoption of "black" as the proper term of
identification.

Mid-Twentieth Century Religious Profile

An accurate assessment of the balance of religious forces in the United
States is difficult to make. Several shifts took place during the first half of
the twentieth century, but available statistics are not always comparable.
As officially reported, Protestant church membership in 1960 was approximately 64 million, the Roman Catholic total was 42 million, the number
of Jews was 5.5 million, and the Eastern Orthodox total was roughly 2.65
million. But the Roman Catholic figure included baptized infants, whereas

[34] C. E. Lincoln, *The Black Muslims* (Boston, 1961), 44. See also Malcolm Little,
Autobiography of Malcolm X (N.Y., 1965). Wallace Deen Muhammad, assuming
leadership on the death of his father, Elijah Muhammad, in 1975, gave the Nation of
Islam both a new direction and in 1980 a new name, American Muslim Mission.

Protestant statistics generally did not.[35] Jewish and Eastern Orthodox figures, on the other hand, tended to be estimates of total ethnic or national groups rather than of specific religious affiliation.

Within Protestantism significant shifts in numerical strength took place during the post–World War I period. Methodists increased from 7.6 million to 13.15 million between 1916 and 1960, but were displaced as the largest Protestant grouping by the Baptists, who had grown from 7 million to 21 million. Lutherans surged forward from 2.5 million to 8 million to become the third largest Protestant group. Presbyterians and Reformed slipped to fourth place with a gain from 2.8 million to 4.8 million. The growth of the Protestant Episcopal Church from 1.1 million to 3.3 million was somewhat deceptive, for the first figure was communicant membership and the second was the total number of baptized. The merger of the Congregational Christian Churches with the Evangelical and Reformed Church put the United Church of Christ in sixth place with 2.2 million members in 1960. A group that had only a tenuous relationship to Protestantism, the Latter-day Saints, or Mormons, had grown from 450,000 to 1.6 million between 1916 and 1960.[36]

Although interesting and illuminating in some respects, such a traditional classification of the relative strength of various Protestant groupings serves to obscure one of the most significant shifts that was taking place in twentieth-century Protestantism.

The traditional classification was largely based upon differences in polity and church government, which had little relationship to the divisive

[35] Information supplied by the U.S. Census Bureau and the American Institute of Public Opinion indicates that the Protestant–Roman Catholic membership figures give a rather accurate picture of proportionate strength. A Census Bureau study in 1958 reported that of 119,330,000 Americans 14 years of age and older, 66.2 percent (78,952,000) regarded themselves as Protestant, 25.7 percent (30,669,000) regarded themselves as Roman Catholic, 3.2 percent (3,868,000) regarded themselves as Jewish, 1.3 percent (1,545,000) identified themselves with other faiths, and 3.6 percent (4,300,000) claimed no religious preference or were not reported. Protestant predominance is reduced to rough conformity with official membership figures when active identification, as reflected in church attendance, is taken into account. A survey by the America Institute of Public Opinion in 1958 reported that 44 percent (34,740,000) of those who considered themselves Protestant attended church the preceding Sunday, whereas 74 percent (22,700,000) of those who considered themselves Roman Catholic attended.

[36] The long-established smaller religious groups met with varying success in the twentieth century. The Mennonites doubled their membership in the 1916–60 period (from 80,000 to 160,000), as did the Church of the Brethren (100,000 to 200,000). The rapid growth of Christian Science ended about 1940, after having tripled in number of churches during the preceding three decades. Quakers, Unitarians, and Universalists, on the other hand, had steadily declined during the first 40 years of the century, but each of them made small but significant recoveries after World War II.

issues of the twentieth century, for the latter were theologically and sociologically grounded in a way that bypassed the older distinctions. The traditional classification fails to give adequate weight, for example, to the 1.5 million members of Holiness churches, the 1.5 million members of Pentecostal bodies, and the 500,000 members of Adventist or Premillennialist groups. Moreover, some of the smaller Baptist, Methodist, Presbyterian, and Reformed groups should more properly be classified as part of the 4.8 million members of Fundamentalist denominations. And the Fundamentalist total ought to be even larger to take into account many individual churches, such as the Park Street Congregational Church in Boston and the Tenth Street Presbyterian Church in Philadelphia, which held Fundamentalist views and actively supported Fundamentalist agencies.[37] What is needed in place of the traditional grouping of Protestants into denominational families is a classification that takes into account the actual realignment within American Protestantism.

The old-line Protestant group at mid-century was composed of those mildly "liberal" or "progressive" denominations affiliated with the National Council of Churches. Frequently referred to as "cooperative Protestantism," these bodies represented a constituency of some 37 million members. Approximately 24 million conservative Protestants were "noncooperative" in the sense that they were not affiliated with the National Council of Churches.[38] These included such major groups as the Southern Baptists with over 10 million members, and almost 5 million Lutherans belonging to the American Lutheran Church and the Lutheran Church – Missouri. In addition there were 8.5 million "disaffected Protestants," members of Fundamentalist, Adventist, Holiness, and Pentecostal churches. This classification does not produce neat packages, for it does not take into account the fracturing of Protestantism along racial lines. Nor do the formal figures give any hint that "disaffected Protestantism," having given up hope of gaining control of the major denominations of "cooperative Protestantism," continued to exhibit astonishing vitality during the 1930s and 1940s and was succeeding in penetrating old-line denominations at the grass-roots level.[39] Many individuals and congregations grouped with "cooperative Protestantism" actually were providing major support for the institutions of the "disaffected."

---

[37] Their respective pastors, Harold J. Ockenga and Donald Grey Barnhouse, were prominent Fundamentalist leaders.

[38] Some did have their own cooperative organizations, such as the National Association of Evangelicals, the smaller American Council of Churches, and a variety of cooperative missionary, evangelistic, educational, and publishing agencies. See Joel A. Carpenter, "Fundamentalist Institutions and the Rise of Evangelical Protestantism, 1929–1942," *Church History*, 49 (1980), 62–75.

[39] *Ibid.*, 65–68.

The emergence of Judaism and Eastern Orthodox Christianity as prominent components of an American religious scene that was becoming ever more multiform and diverse has been discussed in some detail. Major Protestant and Roman Catholic developments during the period that followed World War I, however, were more complicated and need further attention before the bubbling ferment affecting all religious groups in the 1960s, followed by a turn to conservatism, can be assessed.

CHAPTER 14

Protestantism's Uneasy Journey to the Comfortable Fifties

For American Protestantism, World War I marked the end of an era. Kenneth Scott Latourette observed that "Protestant Christianity had entered the nineteenth century on a rising tide" and noted that it had come to the end of the century "on a rapidly ascending curve."[1] The momentum of almost 200 years of vigorous advance had not yet been spent, and the new century found Protestantism at the peak of its apparent strength and influence. Churches were crowded, financial support was generous, programs were proliferating, and a host of good causes elicited eager and ardent devotion. It was a time of unusual moral idealism generated in part by a widespread determination among church members to "win the world for Christ in this generation." By the time Warren G. Harding was installed in the White House, however, much of the contagious enthusiasm exhibited by the churches had begun to be dissipated. By 1925 the usual indices of institutional health—church attendance, Sunday school enrollment, missionary giving—showed a downward trend that was to continue for at least a decade. Although not many at the time were aware that the forward thrust was seriously blunted, it is clear in retrospect that by the middle 1920s an ebb tide had set in.[2]

---

[1] *A History of the Expansion of Christianity* (N.Y., 1937–45), IV, 458; VI, 5.
[2] See Robert Handy, "The American Religious Depression, 1925–35," *Church History*, 29 (1960), 2–16.

The Transitional Years

The blunting of the long Protestant advance was foreshadowed by the fate of the Interchurch World Movement of 1919 and 1920. This was an ambitious enterprise, launched with a flourish of trumpets, that was designed to push to rapid completion the task of Christianizing the world, a Christianizing that was defined in terms of "the complete evangelization of all of life." The major Protestant denominations cooperated to make a detailed survey of urgent needs both at home and abroad, to chart a common strategy for meeting them, to allocate specific responsibilities to the different mission boards, and then, through a concerted campaign patterned after the great wartime drives for funds, to secure the necessary financial resources to carry out the plans.[3] Each denomination had its own financial goal and its own "movement" or campaign for funds, and these coordinated drives were to be supplemented by a general campaign that would tap the supposedly vast potential support of public-spirited citizens who could not be reached through denominational channels. At first a goal of $300 million was suggested, then $500 million, and the final figure was $1 billion, with $335 million to be raised initially. Although large sums were raised by the participating denominations,[4] the joint campaign was a costly and dismal failure that left the denominational mission boards saddled with debts incurred in the cooperative phases of the endeavor.

The failure of the Interchurch World Movement can be attributed in part to the economic recession of 1920–22. Prospects for success also were blighted by the report of the Movement's commission of inquiry which surveyed the needs of the steelworkers and their families. The inquiry coincided with the 1919 strike of the steelworkers, which sought the elimination of the 12-hour day and the 7-day week. The sympathetic tenor of the commission's report was not calculated to win the support of wealthy public-spirited citizens, which was one of the objectives of the campaign. But there were more deep-seated reasons for the failure. A marked shift in the mood of the American people was perhaps the most important. Moreover, long-smoldering tensions within Protestantism broke out into open conflict at the close of the war, diverting to interne-

---

[3] For objectives of the Movement, see H. W. Schneider, *Religion in the Twentieth Century*, 95ff. The scope is indicated by a survey to ascertain "all the facts about the religious, social, moral, physical, and economic environments through the world." D. B. Meyer, *The Protestant Search for Political Realism*, 9. The full story is told by Eldon Ernst, *Moment of Truth for Protestant America* (Missoula, Mont., 1974).

[4] The New World Movement of the Northern Baptists was the most successful on the basis of per capita giving, but only half the $100 million goal was raised. Methodists, with five times as many members, raised the largest total amount. The much more modest $40 million goal of the Methodist Centenary Movement was far exceeded, with more than $100 million being subscribed. But in the end the Methodists had many unpaid pledges and soured hopes.

cine strife energies that might have been otherwise employed. And finally, Protestantism was beginning to reap the consequences of a long period of acculturation.

The Postwar Generation

For two decades Protestants had been engaged in a series of crusades to refashion the face of America and to reshape the life of the world (see Chapter 12). The war itself was but the greatest of these crusades, enlisting as it did the idealism generated by the churches in "a war to end war" and to "make the world safe for democracy." The United States had entered the conflict with banners flying, but it proved to be a dirty, unheroic war which few participants remembered with anything but distaste. The peace proved equally disappointing. Little idealism was apparent in the treaty negotiations at Versailles, and Woodrow Wilson was pilloried at home as a fool trapped by the wily diplomats of Europe. Harding's call for a "return to normalcy," a summons to put aside idealistic crusades and far-flung responsibilities, mirrored the mood of a tired and disenchanted people. Small wonder, in this climate of opinion, that the new crusade envisioned in the Interchurch World Movement met with so disappointing a response.

The postwar generation, however, was suffering from a more severe malady than mere weariness with crusades. Nor was the disenchantment that stemmed from the machinations of the diplomats at Versailles sufficient to account for the waning of idealism. The latter was more largely the product of a profound revolution in morals. Wars tend to be followed by a breakdown in public and private morality, and World War I was no exception. For many people the war was a liberating experience. Young men were uprooted and introduced for the first time to the amoral standards of army life. Women were drawn from their homes to engage in war work. The movement of population into the cities was accelerated. Each of these represented a break with accustomed patterns of life. But the war also imposed its own restrictive discipline. Those at home were driven to strenuous exertion by the effort to win the war, and those in the army were subjected to the unpleasant regimentation of military life. From this perspective, it was the end of the war that brought a welcome release from the stern requirements of duty and evoked a heartfelt desire to relax and enjoy the satisfactions of a less disciplined existence. This mood, quite apart from the brutalizing effect of war, was normal for a postwar period. Parallels in other postwar epochs can be found for the scandals of the Harding administration and the heedless preoccupation of the business community with making "a fast buck." But these were symptoms only of a widespread moral laxity that was mostly covert and did not represent an open flouting of accepted standards of morality. The more serious malady was a candid and undisguised revolt that bluntly attacked the whole system of traditional manners and morals.

The revolution in morals of the 1920s is most frequently depicted in terms of "flaming youth" and the "jazz age," of "speakeasies" and "gang wars." But it was more than this. It was a revolution that affected all classes of society and tore people loose from their old moorings. Its roots are extraordinarily difficult to assess. As William E. Leuchtenburg has pointed out, historians have given the revolution almost no attention,[5] and others have naïvely attributed it almost solely to the breakdown of law enforcement occasioned by prohibition. It can be seen in part as an aftermath of war, but its fundamental rootage was more remote. Techno-logical advance had multiplied material satisfactions and weakened reli-gious sanctions, and the booming prosperity of the 1920s was a heady experience. The "status revolution" which undercut the authority of those who traditionally set the moral standards—the "professional" classes (ministers, lawyers, teachers), the "rural gentry," and the "urban patricians"—was also involved. Not least in importance was the erosion of family solidarity, which was one of the consequences of increasing urbani-zation. But it was the popular appropriation of insights derived from the teachings of such men as John Dewey and Sigmund Freud that contrib-uted as much to the new hedonism as anything else. "Self-expression" and "self-fulfillment" became magic words, and anything that smacked of "repression" was regarded as a threat to the "psyche." These tags of popular understanding distorted carefully devised philosophies, but they had the effect of giving a supposedly scientific imprimatur to self-indulgence.

The prophets of the moral revolt were literary figures—Theodore Dreiser, Sinclair Lewis, H. L. Mencken, George Jean Nathan, F. Scott Fitzgerald, and other luminaries. Their rebellion took the form of a frontal attack on what they called America's "puritanism"—an epithet for anything that interfered with the new freedom. Religion was dismissed as antiquated, false, and absurd—a blend of prudery, cant, and sanctimo-niousness from which individuals must emancipate themselves if their spirits were not to be suffocated. To Joseph Wood Krutch, "sin" and "love" were empty words, and he insisted that "all the capital letters in the composing-room cannot make the words more than that which they have become—shadows, as essentially unreal as some of the theological dogmas which have been completely forgotten."[6] Concerned with the individual rather than society, with private rather than public experience, these writers had no interest in social reform. "Doing good" was either a dull business or, as Mencken insisted, "in bad taste." "The great problems of the world—social, political, economic, and theological—do not con-cern me in the slightest," wrote Nathan.

> If all the Armenians were to be killed tomorrow and if half of Russia were to starve to death the day after, it would not matter to me in the least. What

---

[5] *The Perils of Prosperity, 1914–32* (Chicago, 1958), 290.
[6] *The Modern Temper: A Study and a Confession* (N.Y., 1929), 191–92.

concerns me alone is myself, and the interests of a few close friends. For all I care the rest of the world may go to hell at today's sunset.[7]

Not all were as blunt and callous as Nathan, but social nihilism was a fundamental theme of the *avant garde* novelists and poets. Even the care with which most of them avoided adjectives and sought to make do with unadorned nouns and verbs was part of a studied and self-conscious rejection of all idealistic sentiment.

Although the cynical hedonism of the novelists and poets and literary critics blazed the way for many, the revolution in morals found more temperate and prosaic expression in the population as a whole. Spurred on by handbooks of popular psychology and carried forward in home and classroom, the revolution produced a less sin-ridden and more self-indulgent people. But, unlike the despair of the "intellectuals," the popular mood of "the booming twenties" was optimistic, and the new freedom was geared to an undisciplined pursuit of more tangible forms of personal fulfillment. Whereas the intellectuals had lost faith in progress, the great mass of Americans were content to believe that the promises of the past had become the realities of the present. Here the waning of idealism had complacency, and even smugness, as its hallmark, and it manifested itself in the demise of the progressive movement. The only alarm was that directed against those who seemed to threaten the existing order.

In 1912 progressivism, with its zeal for reform, had been triumphant. In a three-cornered race, Taft had been far outdistanced by both his progressive rivals—Woodrow Wilson and Teddy Roosevelt. Moreover, Eugene Debs, the Socialist candidate, had amassed almost a million votes. Four years later Wilson and Hughes, who were almost equally progressive in outlook, had vied for the White House. But in 1920 progressivism was buried under the Harding landslide, and only a remnant could be resurrected by the LaFollette–Wheeler banner in the 1924 campaign.

The churches were not unaffected by this shift in mood of the American people. The demise of progressivism was accompanied by the decline of the social gospel which in prewar years had given American Protestantism much of its verve and contagious enthusiasm. As a typical social gospel project, the Interchurch World Movement was one of the first casualties of the fading idealism. It is true that interest in social Christianity survived in some circles, just as there were still progressives to be found, but it was mostly confined to clerical ranks and had ceased to be important as a powerful ferment in church life. Clergymen who continued to issue social pronouncements were generals with few troops. They were tolerated by their congregations, but their summons to action sparked little response.[8]

---

[7] Quoted in Leuchtenburg, *The Perils of Prosperity*, 150.
[8] A failure to make this distinction weakens Robert M. Miller's otherwise cogent demonstration of a continuing interest in social Christianity in his *American Protestantism and Social Issues, 1919–1939* (Chapel Hill, N.C., 1958).

Even among the clergy, much of the social concern was diverted into a pacifist crusade. Shamed and humiliated by the role of churchmen in propagating hatred during World War I[9] and revolted by the horrors of trench warfare, a large percentage of the clergy vowed that the church should not bless war again and that they would neither support nor participate in any future conflict.

The Fundamentalist Controversy

If the Protestant advance was blunted by the shifting mood of the American people, it also was impeded by an intramural conflict that broke out in 1920 within Protestantism. The protagonists were "Liberals," or "Modernists," who sought to adjust the inherited faith to the new intellectual climate, and "Fundamentalists," who insisted that the old ways of stating the faith must be preserved unimpaired.[10]

Theological tension had been developing for a long time, but it subsided after the heresy trials of the latter years of the nineteenth century. A common enthusiasm for reform made it possible to subordinate theological differences and to gloss over divergent theological positions with pious ambiguities.[11] Almost every prominent professional evangelist regarded himself as being engaged in a work of social reformation. A few, like B. Fay Mills, went all the way with the social gospel. Others, like Sam Jones, Milan B. Williams, Burke Culpepper, William E. Biederwolf, and Rodney "Gypsy" Smith, limited themselves to "civic reform" and stressed "social service." Some, like J. Wilbur Chapman, placed primary stress on personal morality. But whatever emphasis, they tended to be welcomed as allies in the progressive movement for human betterment and were drawn unwittingly into its orbit.[12] And they, in turn, tended to mute points of theological dissent. Not everyone, to be sure, was bemused by this happy state of affairs. The more ardent "dispensationalists" within the revivalist camp were primarily responsible for introducing discord into the general harmony.

Unlike other professional evangelists, the "dispensationalists" had their own scheme of reform, which reflected the general expectancy and enthusiasm of the time, a scheme expressed in terms of their premillennial views. Furthermore, they were not of a mind to compromise their convic-

[9] See R. H. Abrams, *Preachers Present Arms* (N.Y., 1933), as qualified by J. F. Piper, "The Social Policy of the Federal Council of the Churches of Christ," Duke University Ph D. thesis (Durham, N.C., 1964).

[10] Stewart G. Cole, *The History of Fundamentalism* (N.Y., 1931), is an early account of the controversy. See also G. M. Marsden, *Fundamentalism and American Culture: The Shaping of Twentieth-Century Evangelicalism, 1870–1925* (N.Y., 1980), E. R. Sandeen, *The Roots of Fundamentalism* (Chicago, 1970), and T. P. Weber, *Living in the Shadow of the Second Coming: America Premillennialism, 1875–1925* (N. Y., 1979).

[11] See McLoughlin, *Modern Revivalism*, 350–54, 361–63, 386–87, 393, 397, 402, 411.

[12] Biederwolf and Gypsy Smith, for example, were active in the Men and Religion Forward Movement of 1911–14, liberal in leadership with a strong social emphasis.

tions by glossing over theological differences. In 1905 Amzi C. Dixon, shortly to become minister of the Moody Church in Chicago, published a book in which he announced that there could be no reconciliation between science and religion any more than socialism and free enterprise could be reconciled. The duty of the church was to convert individuals, to keep out of politics, and to remember that there could be no true revival that was not led by "believers in the inspiration and infallible authority of the Word of God."[13]

With the help of Reuben A. Torrey, superintendent of the Moody Bible Institute, Dixon prepared a counterattack that culminated in 1910–15 with the publication of 12 small volumes entitled *The Fundamentals,* which sought to reduce the Christian faith to clear essentials. These brief treatises were written by various men but were edited by Dixon and Torrey, and their distribution was financed by two wealthy residents of Los Angeles, Milton and Lyman Stewart. They were sent free of charge "to every pastor, evangelist, missionary, theological student, Sunday school superintendent, Y.M.C.A. and Y.W.C.A. secretary" whose address could be obtained, and eventually 3 million copies were distributed.[14] It is likely that serious strife would have been provoked then had not the agitation been interrupted by the outbreak of World War I.

The career of Billy Sunday—the professional baseball player turned evangelist whose antics in the pulpit did more than anything else to discredit revivalism—bridged the prewar and postwar periods.[15] He was a transitional figure, whose early popularity was derived in part from the alacrity with which he jumped on the bandwagon of civic reform and moral uplift, and who then rode to fame on the crest of the wave of reaction against the social gospel. Even during the early phase, his denunciations of liberal theology were frequent and coarse. He had no use for the "bastard theory of evolution" or for the "deodorized and disinfected sermons" of "hireling ministers" who gave up the old faith to please their liberal parishioners. Furthermore, he complained of those who tried to "make religion out of social service with Jesus Christ left out." He exhibited nonetheless a marked ability to blend his "old-time religion" with the progressive emphasis on reform. He advertised his revivals as "civic cleanups" that would make any town a better place in which to live. He appropriated many of the indictments leveled by the "muckrakers," and this led many progressives and social gospelers to believe that he was buttressing their cause. Even his vulgarity and "vaudeville stunts" were defended as necessary means of reaching the masses. One contemporary

[13] McLoughlin, *Modern Revivalism* 348, 352–53.

[14] *Ibid.,* 352, 370; N. F. Furniss, *The Fundamentalist Controversy,* 12. Charges that fright among wealthy laymen aroused by radical social views accounts for Fundamentalist financial support at this time are unfair.

[15] See W. G. McLoughlin, Jr., *Billy Sunday Was His Real Name* (Chicago, 1955), and *Modern Revivalism,* 400–54.

observer was confident that "it is as a reformer that Mr. Sunday has warmed the hearts of all who desire better things." His ideas of reform, however, turned out to be extremely limited, not extending much beyond the suppression of the liquor traffic.[16]

Sunday was quick to respond to changing climates of opinion. From the beginning he had preached a masculine "muscular" Christianity that equated salvation with decency and manliness ("the man who has real, rich, red blood in his veins instead of pink tea and ice water"), but that stressed as well a strongly emotional rather than a mechanical piety ("Some people pray like a jack-rabbit eating cabbage."). Under the excitement of war this masculine Christianity was transformed into a barnstorming, tub-thumping "100 percent Americanism" that insisted that "Christianity and patriotism are synonymous terms" just as "hell and traitors are synonymous." Soon he was attributing German atrocities to the baneful influence of biblical criticism upon the German people. And when labor unrest developed at the close of hostilities, he was in full cry after all foreign-inspired, godless social radicalism.

In spite of Billy Sunday's diatribes, most prominent Protestant leaders at the end of the war believed that the struggle to win acceptance for new ways of understanding the Christian faith had been won, and they were prepared to resume the humanitarian advance of the prewar years.[17] But Sunday was demonstrating how hostile sentiment could be aroused in the postwar climate. The American people were in no mood for any further tampering with the social order, and it was easy to demonstrate to the satisfaction of many that "modernism" and "communism" were but reverse sides of the same coin.

A decisive factor in thrusting the controversy into public attention was the championship of the Fundamentalist cause by William Jennings Bryan, the "peerless leader" of the old populist element in the Democratic party. When Bryan entered the fray in 1920, he was able to claim a national audience and to use his magic voice and moving rhetoric to transform isolated protests into a more-or-less unified crusade. Soon every denomination was embroiled in conflict. Strenuous efforts were made to ferret out evidence of heresy accompanied by demands that remedial action be taken to guarantee doctrinal orthodoxy. Harry Emerson Fosdick, a Baptist preacher filling the pulpit of the First Presbyterian Church of New York City, added fuel to the flames in 1922 when, dismayed by the demoralizing effects of the Fundamentalist attacks he had observed on a visit to the mission fields of Asia, he seemed to fling down the gauntlet in a sermon entitled "Shall the Fundamentalists Win?"

The qualifying phrase describing the Fundamentalist movement as

---

[16] McLoughlin, *Modern Revivalism*, 399, 410–12, 429, 437.
[17] For the eager enthusiasm of church leaders, see Meyer, *Protestant Search for Political Realism*, 12–13.

"more or less" unified is important, for it did embrace diverse elements. The Bible School "dispensationalists" sought to detect heresy by a summary of key points of faith, including the verbal inerrancy of Scripture, the Genesis account of creation, and the premillennial return of Christ, as the standard of orthodoxy. But this was initially a fringe position. The movement derived much of its strength at the outset from men who stood more squarely within the traditional life of the churches.[18]

Curtis Lee Laws, Baptist editor of the *Watchman-Examiner* who coined the label "Fundamentalist" in 1920 to designate those who were prepared to battle for the "fundamentals" of the faith, was associated with a large body of genuine "conservatives," whose concern was to conserve and defend the integrity of the Christian faith. The key issue, as they saw it, was the authority of the Bible, for Protestantism historically claimed the authority of Scripture for the whole structure of its thought. While continuing to revere the Bible as a treasury of religious devotion, there had been a growing tendency in liberal circles to reject it as being normative. It was suitable for historical study and useful for devotional purposes, but the canons of truth were to be found in religious experience. It was this tendency to forget that the Christian faith had any objective standard of truth that alarmed the conservatives. These men were not obscurantist in their attitude toward modern knowledge. Although they centered attention on the question of biblical authority, few wished to make an issue of evolution, biblical inerrancy, or premillennialism. They represented the type of reaction to the more extreme modernist tendencies that had long been present in Protestant seminaries. The views expressed by John A. Faulkner at Drew Theological Seminary in *Modernism and the Christian Faith* (1921) and by Augustus Hopkins Strong, former president of Rochester Theological Seminary whose *Outlines of Systematic Theology* was widely used as a textbook in the more conservative seminaries, were typical of this broad current of concern. Nevertheless, critics such as those at the University of Chicago warned that fundamentalist premillennialism essentially gave up on the world and consequently conveyed a message that threatened world security.

Strong frankly accepted the doctrine of evolution and the methods of biblical criticism. "Neither evolution nor the higher criticism has any terrors to one who regards them as parts of Christ's creating and educating process." The composite authorship of the Pentateuch and the existence of two Isaiahs did not disturb Strong. "Any honest Christian," he affirmed, ". . . has the right to interpret Jonah and Daniel as allegories rather than histories." The Bible, he insisted, is the record of a progressive revelation, "shaped in human molds and adapted to ordinary human intelligence." It is a "human composition," but it is also "God's Word,"

[18] For this distinction, see the chapter by Norman H. Maring, "Conservative But Progressive," in *What God Hath Wrought*, ed. G. L. Guffin (Philadelphia, 1960), 17–28.

presenting "divine truth in human forms." The danger of historical criticism of the Bible, he declared, is not the method but the presuppositions of those who use it. "'The historical method' of Scripture interpretation, as it is often employed, ends without Christ because it begins without him." It makes the mistake of "treating Scripture as it would treat any unreligious or heathen literature" and ignores the fact that to interpret the Bible properly one must adopt a confessional stance. The point is "not how man made the Scripture for himself, but how God made the Scripture through the imperfect agency of man." To abandon the Bible as the authoritative testimony to Christ and thus in a derivative sense the authoritative ground of faith, Strong contended, would cut the "taproot" and imperil the very existence of Protestantism.[19]

The moderate Fundamentalists, however, were quickly upstaged by more radical elements, whose quarrel seemed to be with almost every facet of modern life. Viewed from this perspective, Fundamentalism can best be understood as a phase of the rural–urban conflict, drawing its strength from the tendency of many who were swept into an urban environment to cling to the securities of their childhood. Although this characterization does less than justice to the moderate wing of the movement, it does point up the fact that in many ways Fundamentalism was as much the product of a cultural as a religious concern. It is significant that it arose among rural-oriented people in the cities before it penetrated the small towns and villages of the countryside. Furthermore, the mores that were emphasized as indispensable to the Christian life had, in the words of H. Richard Niebuhr, "at least as little relation to the New Testament and as much connection with social custom" as did those aspects of behavior that were condemned, and the cosmological and biological notions that were stressed as integral to the gospel were equally culturally conditioned.[20] Fundamentalist sentiment also was not unrelated to the sweeping tide of hyperpatriotism that was so conspicuous a feature of the early 1920s. "One hundred percent Americanism" was regarded as the normal corollary of "old-time religion," and "Back to Christ, the Bible, and the Constitution" was a typical slogan. Isolationism and a renewed nativism were two features of the "siege mentality" that emerged in particularly vivid terms during the "Red Scare" of 1919–20.[21]

The great body of Protestants was never fully committed to either side of the controversy, but when the more belligerent Fundamentalists formed themselves into a power bloc intent on seizing control of various Protestant denominations by placing them in a rigid theological strait-

---

[19] *Outlines of Systematic Theology* (Philadelphia, 1903), ix, 55–62. See also Strong's *Tour of Missions* (Philadelphia, 1918), 177, 181, 186–87, 191, 203.

[20] *Christ and Culture* (N.Y., 1951), 102.

[21] Official Roman Catholic opposition to "modernism" and "Americanism," and advocacy of a return to tradition, likewise contributed to the formation of a siege mentality that mixed well with the conservatism of the period.

jacket, the effect was to push middle-of-the-roaders into a defensive alliance with the liberals. This shift in alignment was clearly evident at Princeton Theological Seminary, long the citadel of Presbyterian orthodoxy and where Fundamentalism had its ablest spokesman in the person of J. Gresham Machen. Nowhere was the Fundamentalist case stated with more clarity and cogency than in Machen's writings,[22] but his ill-advised dogmatism in personal relationships and his determination to dominate the life of the seminary drove even staunchly conservative colleagues to make common cause with the Auburn "Affirmationists."[23] Among Baptists the initiative was seized by a radical triumvirate—J. Frank Norris, William B. Riley, and T. T. Shields—who formed the Baptist Bible Union to promote their views and succeeded in placing their stamp on much of the movement within the Baptist ranks. Here too the bitter-spirited intransigence of the extremists caused some of the prominent early leaders of the movement to defect and work out a policy of coexistence with the liberals. By 1925, when a national comedy was acted out in the "monkey trial" at Dayton, Tennessee, with William Jennings Bryan and Clarence Darrow in the starring roles, the violent language and "smear" tactics of the more vociferous Fundamentalists so alienated public opinion generally that there was little prospect that the Fundamentalists would gain control of any major Protestant denomination. In 1929 Princeton Seminary was reorganized, and Machen left to found Westminster Theological Seminary and the Orthodox Presbyterian Church.

Most denominations continued to be troubled by controversy throughout the 1930s, and among American (Northern) Baptists peace was not restored until after World War II. Although Fundamentalism was a declining force throughout these years in the major denominations, it maintained itself in many local congregations and expanded its influence through the formation of independent Bible churches and the capture of some smaller denominational bodies. A continuing source of strength was its ability to supply, through graduates of Bible Schools, ministerial leadership to impoverished churches.

Protestant Acculturation

Despite the distractions of controversy and the shafts of ridicule directed by "intellectuals" against those who made profession of religious faith, the mood of the old-line Protestant churches in the 1920s was remarkably complacent. Curiously enough, during the decades when Protestantism was reaching the peak of its prestige and apparent influence, the nerve that had impelled two centuries of advance was being cut. A long process

---

[22] See his *Christianity and Liberalism* (N.Y., 1923).
[23] The "Auburn Affirmation" is printed in Armstrong, Loetscher, and Anderson, *The Presbyterian Enterprise,* 284–88.

of theological erosion opened the way to a rather complete assimilation of Protestantism to the model of the world.[24] With its basic theological insights largely emasculated, Protestantism was robbed of any independently grounded vision of life and became more and more the creature of American culture rather than its creator. In this respect the culturally conditioned character of Fundamentalism was typical of Protestantism as a whole, the tension within Protestantism arising primarily out of the differing cultural orientation of the older agrarian and the newer urban society. "If the theology of the fundamentalists was archaic and anachronistic," Sidney E. Mead observed, "that of the liberals was secularized and innocuous."[25]

Although there were exceptions to this general characterization, by and large the Protestant churches had become victims of their own success. They had succeeded in creating a culture that in mood and spirit was recognizably Christian, and then during the first two decades of the twentieth century practically all the reforms that had been proposed to remedy the ills of society had been set in operation. Proud of their achievements and pleased that their mission had been so largely accomplished, the churches relaxed and made peace with the world.

From satisfaction with the culture, it was but a small step to the placing of confidence in the culture to nurture and sustain the Christian faith. Even before the end of the nineteenth century, Phillips Brooks had declared: "I do not know how a man can be an American, even if he is not a Christian, and not catch something with regard to God's purpose for this great land." How else could one explain "all the secular, all the studiously irreligious, all the even blasphemous attempts at education and the development of character"? The most impressive feature of American life, to Brooks, was the way in which men "outside the churches" were impelled by the spirit of America to do that which "the churches and Christianity" seek to do, being led to do "Christian work in the spirit of Christ" even when they "studiously" or "vehemently" disown him.[26] By thus investing the culture with intrinsic redemptive power, scant room was left for any special redemptive work of Christ. The distinction between the Church and the world, between the Christian and the non-Christian, was largely obliterated. The churches, as a result, became increasingly composed of adherents whose religious affiliation was determined more by accident of birth and persistence of custom than by conscious conviction.

The missionary thrust of a religion is one of the most sensitive indices of its vitality. Evidence was accumulating throughout the 1920s of a growing

[24] See W. S. Hudson, *The Great Tradition of the American Churches,* 157–225, and H. Richard Niebuhr, *The Kingdom of God in America,* 164–98.

[25] *The Lively Experiment,* 186. For a defense of liberalism, see W. R. Hutchison, *The Modernist Impulse* (Cambridge, Mass., 1976), esp. 274–87.

[26] *National Needs and Remedies: Discussions of the General Conference of the Evangelical Alliance* (N.Y., 1890), 301–11.

missionary apathy. Missionary giving steadily declined during this period of booming prosperity, and the Foreign Missions Conference reported in 1929 that, in contrast to the 2,700 students who had volunteered for foreign service in 1920, only 252 had volunteered in 1928.[27] It was this waning interest in missions that led to the Laymen's Foreign Missions Inquiry in 1930, whose report in 1932 reflected the questioning of the mission enterprise as it had been traditionally conceived.

The Laymen's Inquiry was instigated and financed by John D. Rockefeller, Jr. Its purpose was to study existing mission projects, evaluate their effectiveness, and determine what was worthy of continued support. Research specialists were sent abroad to collect factual information, and then, armed with data, a "Commission of Appraisal" visited the mission fields before issuing their report.[28] The chairman of the commission and editor of the report was William E. Hocking, professor of philosophy at Harvard. While urging that missionary endeavor be continued, the report declared that there is no ground for "a renewed appeal for the support, much less for the enlargement, of these missions as a whole in their present form and on their present basis." A "big business" bias, which equated centralization with efficiency, was evident in the critical attitude toward all operations based upon separate denominational entities. "A single administrative unit" free of all church control, it was maintained, should be given "administrative direction of missionary effort in all fields." But the report went much farther than this. Not only did it question much of the work that was being done on the mission fields, it brought the whole philosophy of Christian mission under attack. Educational and philanthropic work was commended, but the report insisted that the missionaries should be freed of responsibility for "conscious and direct evangelization." Far from making any overt presentation of the claims of Christ, the missionary must adopt a stance of openness toward other religions and "regard himself as a co-worker with the forces within each such religious system which are making for righteousness." As Christians we must "be willing to give largely without any preaching, to cooperate wholeheartedly with non-Christian agencies for social improvement." The basic philosophy, which was fully explicated two years later by Archibald G. Baker in *Christian Missions and a New World Culture*, was to foster an intercultural penetration that would bring about a synthesis or reconception of all religions into one universal faith.

A similar indecision and hesitancy with regard to any forthright presentation of the Christian faith was evident at home. Home missions under-

[27] See Handy, "The American Religious Depression," *Church History*, 29 (1960), 4–5. The United Stewardship Council reported that per capita gifts for benevolence fell from $5.57 in 1921 to $3.43 in 1929.

[28] *Re-Thinking Missions: A Laymen's Inquiry After One Hundred Years* (N.Y., 1932). The factual material that had been assembled was published in the seven-volume *Laymen's Foreign Missions Inquiry . . . Supplementary Series* (N.Y., 1933).

went the same metamorphosis that was recommended in the Laymen's report, with mission centers being transformed into social agencies. "A decreasing emphasis upon a specific church program and intensification of efforts to help the immigrant worker in the struggle for economic security and social recognition," a study sponsored by the Institute of Social and Religious Research concluded, "suggest themselves as the most constructive items on the future program of mission work."[29] As for the professional evangelists who had sought to maintain the tradition of mass evangelism, their day also was over. No longer able to secure the necessary cooperation of the churches for citywide campaigns, most of them settled down in churches of their own.[30]

The churches were under considerable pressure during these years, quite apart from uncertainty as to their own vocation. Less and less reliance could be placed on habit and custom to maintain active participation in church life. In addition to the free and easy atmosphere generated by the revolution in morals that enabled many to ignore the Sabbath and neglect church attendance without compunction, there were other features of American life that made the task of the churches more difficult. The population was increasingly urban and mobile. Once within the urban orbit, there were many who did not stay put long enough to develop strong ties to a church. Nor could the churches count on the family as an ally to the same extent as formerly, as was made evident by the rising divorce rate and the sharp decline in the practice of family devotions. Automobile production soared at almost a geometric rate, vastly extending the range of an individual's freedom, providing easy access to multiplying golf courses and setting up the family weekend outing as a counter-attraction to the church. Motion pictures and the radio joined the press as rivals of the churches in setting the tone of society.[31] Almost everything —the popular mood, the churches' own sense of uncertainty, urbanization, mobility, competing attractions, the decay of family solidarity— militated against vigorous church life.

One response to this situation was a frenzied effort by some churches to "merchandise" religion with the huckstering methods of Madison Avenue.[32] "Early to bed and early to rise, preach the gospel and advertise,"

---

[29] Theodore Abel, *Protestant Home Missions to Catholic Immigrants* (N.Y., 1933), 107.

[30] McLoughlin, *Modern Revivalism*, 469. C. E. Fuller, M. R. DeHaan, and D. G. Barnhouse captured national audiences by taking to the air-waves with their "Old-Fashioned Revival Hour," "Radio Bible Class," and "Bible Study Hour."

[31] The press provided much less support for the churches than heretofore. The circulation of religious periodicals dwindled, and there was a marked change in the attitude of the nonreligious press. One study has indicated that, whereas about 78 percent of published views of religion in 1905 could be classified as favorable, by 1930 the situation was almost reversed with 67 percent unfavorable. Hornell Hart, "Changing Attitudes and Interests," *Recent Social Trends* (N.Y., 1933), I, 403.

[32] See Miller, *American Protestantism and Social Issues*, 22–26.

ministers were admonished. "Selling Religion—that is the only business of the Church," proclaimed Lewis S. Mudge, stated clerk of the Presbyterian General Assembly, in supplying the churches with five sure-fire tips on how they might best vend their goods. "The old idea that a minister is above stooping to commercial devices must disappear if the church is to grow," the Methodist *Zion's Herald* informed its readers, for "ministers are salesmen with a wonderfully fine 'line' to sell their congregations." The use of printer's ink and brightly illuminated signs to advertise their services, churches were told, could change the cry of "S.O.S." to "S.R.O."—standing room only. Bruce Barton, an advertising executive, made his contribution to the cause by writing a biography of Jesus, *The Man Nobody Knows* (1925), which for two years headed the nonfiction list of best-selling books. Jesus was pictured as a master salesman, psychologist, and forceful young executive, who forged 12 men from the lower ranks into the best management team of all time. As the merchandising of religion became more sophisticated, abuses occurred. Guy Ballard's "I AM" movement, which combined ideas from a wide range of religious traditions and popular religious belief, was put on trial in the 1930s in New York for hoodwinking the elderly with promises and taking their money.

Churches responded to the multiple exhortations with snappy slogans and promotional stunts. "A friendly church" became a familiar slogan that compared favorably with more flashy punchlines such as "Be a Sport —Come to Church" or the hard-sell "Worship Increases Your Efficiency" and "Business Success and Religion Go Together." Catchy sermon topics —"The Irishmen of the Old Testament," "Two in a Bed," "The Mae West of My Bible"—were used as teasers to draw a crowd.

Churches with a more sedate and prosperous clientele sought to maintain their prestige and popularity by the more dignified expedient of constructing impressive gothic cathedrals, and even the less prosperous invested heavily in modest gothic structures. In 1921 the total spent on new church buildings was $60 million. Five years later the total had risen to $284 million. John D. Rockefeller, Jr., explained his interest in spending large sums on the construction of a new home for the Park Avenue Baptist Church on Riverside Drive by saying that he did not want the business community to look down on the churches.[33] Some attempted to make Sunday morning worship more attractive by decorating it with liturgical innovations borrowed from other traditions. Unlike earlier forms of church architecture and liturgical practice which expressed the common faith of the congregation, the new eclecticism betrayed little discernible relationship to any fundamental theological convictions.

These same churches also adopted "progressive" programs of religious education, geared to the immediate interests and capacities of the child.

[33] *Ibid.,* 25.

According to George A. Coe's *Social Theory of Religious Education* (1917), the aim of the new educational program was "the growth of the young toward and into mature and efficient devotion to the democracy of God, and happy self-realization therein." The basic conviction was that religious consciousness is a natural and progressive experience that emerges out of "an experimental pupil–teacher quest for growing values."[34] With this emphasis upon "growth" and a "continuous becoming," there was little point to the old Sunday school "Decision Day." Far from involving any crisis of conversion, church membership was regarded as a routine step in the normal unfolding of human life.

Much church life, of course, remained untouched by these newer expedients, for many congregations refused to adopt cheap appeals to attract a crowd and did not have the financial resources to embark upon a building program or to launch a full-blown program of "progressive" education. Moreover, many of them were still old-fashioned enough to believe that a "life-centered" Sunday school curriculum was no adequate substitute for specific instruction in the Bible. But whatever course individual churches pursued, nothing could obscure the fact that most Protestant churches were suffering a loss of prestige and authority. It was upon churches thus weakened that the blow of the economic depression of the 1930s fell, and the churches suffered from the crippling effect of the economic disaster along with the rest of the nation. Budgets were slashed, benevolent and missionary enterprises were curtailed, and some churches were forced to close their doors.

Variant Protestant "Revivals"

Many people expected that the depression into which the nation was cascaded following the crash of the "great bull market" of 1929 would produce a return to religion. A people shorn of their material possessions, it was believed, would turn to God in some spectacular way. By-and-large they did not. Samuel P. Kincheloe of the Chicago Theological Seminary explained that secularism had become so pervasive that a general revival was impossible.[35] Even churchgoing people looked to Washington instead of to God in their extremity. But there were exceptions. A somewhat *sub rosa* revival did occur among less secularized portions of the population as indicated by the rapidly mounting membership of what Kincheloe dismissed as "minor fundamentalist groups,'" the most striking gains being made by Holiness and Pentecostal churches.

At the opposite end of the social spectrum, a quickening religious

---

[34] See H. Shelton Smith, "Christian Education," in *Protestant Thought in the Twentieth Century,* ed., A. S. Nash (N.Y., 1951), 241.

[35] *Research Memo on Religion in the Depression* (N.Y., 1937), 45 ff., 95.

interest found expression in the "First Century Christian Fellowship" of Frank Buchman.[36] Since 1921 Buchman had been engaged in personal evangelism among students. Becoming convinced that Park Avenue needed conversion as much as the Bowery, a mission to America was launched in 1930 with headquarters in the Calvary Episcopal Church in New York City. The focus was upon "four absolutes" of perfect honesty, purity, unselfishness, and love, and upon "the five C's" of confidence, confession, conviction, conversion, and continuance, which were the five stages of a "changed" life. The basic "house party" technique was supplemented by a traveling team, and sophisticated use was made of news media and propagandist literature, with such titles as *For Sinners Only* (1932), *I Was a Pagan* (1934), *Life Began Yesterday* (1935), and *How Do I Begin?* (1937). In 1939, after the movement was renamed Moral Re-Armament, 30,000 people filled Hollywood Bowl for its second World Assembly. Buchman's emphasis was highly individualistic and no great renewal of church life was effected, but many prominent people professed to have had their lives changed in the "quiet times" of the house parties.

Theological Reassessment

As early as 1928 Episcopal Bishop Charles Fiske was convinced that there was "evidence of a sad disintegration of American Protestantism," a view shared by Unitarian writer William L. Sullivan. In an article on "Our Spiritual Destitution," Sullivan noted that religion had become "timorous, unimaginative, quick with comment upon the contemporaneous, but unable in the authentic manner of its great tradition to judge the contemporaneous by categories that are eternal."[37] Further discontent with Protestantism's theological void and accompanying acculturation was voiced by Edwin Lewis, *Christian Manifesto* (1934), H. Richard Niebuhr, *The Kingdom of God in America* (1937), and Joseph Haroutunian, *Wisdom and Folly in Religion* (1940). Even more stirring was Reinhold Niebuhr's devastating polemics, *Moral Man and Immoral Society* (1932) and *Reflections on the End of an Era* (1934).[38] In spite of the prescience of such men, not more than a handful of ministers were ready to engage in a fundamental theological reconsideration. Harry Emerson Fosdick was a significant exception, having announced in a widely publicized sermon that "The Church Must Go Beyond Modernism."

---

[36] See A. W. Eister, *Drawing-Room Conversion* (Durham, N.C., 1950), and W. H. Clark, *The Oxford Group: Its History and Significance* (N.Y., 1951). For the later Moral Re-Armament phase see *Moral Re-Armament: A Study of the Movement Prepared by the Social and Industrial Council of the Church Assembly* (London: Church [of England] Information Board, 1955).

[37] *Confessions of a Puzzled Parson* (N.Y., 1928), 191; *Atlantic Monthly,* 133 (1929), 378.

[38] Other important books were Walter Lowrie, *Our Concern with the Theology of Crisis* (1932), and George Richards, *Beyond Fundamentalism and Modernism.*

There were several reasons for the lack of response. In the midst of a depression, the working clergy were overwhelmed with the mere task of seeing that bills were paid and church doors kept open. Whatever time was left for reflection tended to be absorbed by efforts to mitigate the plight of their parishioners. Additional energy was siphoned off in an effort to qualify themselves to deal more adequately with the personal problems of anxious and distraught people. More important was the lingering impact of the Fundamentalist controversy. Attention had been centered on peripheral issues, with both parties driven to more extreme positions than they otherwise would have adopted. Alarmed by the controversy's threat to institutional concerns, denominational officials took charge and, in the interest of harmony, were largely successful in ruling theological discussion out-of-bounds in church assemblies.

It was otherwise in the seminaries, where indications of a theological revival had begun to surface in the 1930s. This revival, however, is difficult to characterize, for it found expression in no single theological system or school of thought. Its most common feature was represented by Henry Nelson Wieman's announcement in 1932 of his intention henceforth "to promote a theocentric religion as over against the prevalent anthropocentric one." Influenced by Alfred North Whitehead's process philosophy, Wieman, Douglas C. Macintosh, and also Walter M. Horton moved in a new theological direction that rejected the philosophical idealism of the older liberalism. Destined to be much more influential, however, were views derived from Europe,[39] where the shattered optimism of the postwar years had produced an earlier theological reassessment. Although European-oriented theology in America was generally labeled "neo-orthodox," it was multiform and varied, borrowing insights from such diverse sources as the Jewish thinker Martin Buber, the Russian Orthodox theologian Nicholai Berdyaev, the Spanish existentialist Miguel Unamuno, the French neo-Thomist Jacques Maritain, and the Swedish Lutheran theologians Anders Nygren and Gustaf Aulén. While recognizing this diversity, the European influence can best be summarized as an intermingling of neo-Reformation and existentialist emphases, with Karl Barth and Emil Brunner representing primary stress on the Reformation heritage and Paul Tillich, who came to America in 1933, drawing more heavily on the "existentialism" of Søren Kierkegaard.

Karl Barth was the towering figure of the theological revival. Although fully accepting the historical criticism of the liberal era, Barth took his stand firmly on the Scriptures as interpreted by the Protestant reformers and insisted that it is through Jesus Christ alone that God's Word addresses man. Emil Brunner was not quite so uncompromising in the rejection of natural theology and was at first more influential in the United

---

[39] See S. E. Ahlstrom, "Continental Influence on American Christian Thought Since World War I," *Church History*, 37 (1958), 256–73.

States than his Swiss colleague. Americans found Brunner's strong emphasis on one's apprehension of God being derived from a deeply personal "I–thou" encounter less forbidding than Barth's seemingly more harsh statement of much the same position. Although both Barth and Brunner had been influenced by "the melancholy Dane," Americans were directly exposed to Kierkegaard's writings through translations provided by Walter Lowrie and David Swenson. In differing ways, a type of existentialism represented by Kierkegaard was mediated by the writings of Rudolf Butman and Dietrich Bonhoeffer, the German martyr. Preoccupied with the problem of the agonized conscience (the sense of guilt, estrangement, and frustration that once had been so prominently displayed in revival meetings), these men manifested much the same personal concern and introspective analysis that had become fashionable among the *literati*. The self-acceptance they stressed, however, was grounded in the biblical message of justification by faith alone.

Although the tendencies of the theological revival cannot be reduced to a single consistent point of view, major themes can be identified.[40] The first was a reassertion of the sovereignty of God. Even such a neo-naturalist as Wieman thought in terms of a religion of "grace." Second, there was a much less optimistic evaluation of the human situation, and a much more radical stress on the demonic power of sin. Third, there was a renewed appreciation of the centrality of biblical revelation. Fourth, there was a revival of interest in Christology. Fifth, there was a deepening concern to recover a sense of fullness and wholeness in the life of the church. Finally, there was a tendency among many, while moving to the "right" theologically, to move to the "left" politically. The tone was set by Reinhold Niebuhr's remark in *Reflections on the End of an Era:* "In my opinion, adequate spiritual guidance can come only through more radical political orientation and more conservative religious convictions than are comprehended [at present] in the culture of our era."

For at least three reasons the theological revival was abortive, having little impact beyond the seminaries. First, attention to theological issues was diverted by World War II. Second, attempts at theological reconstruction never got out of the classroom and into the pulpit, to say nothing of making the transition from pulpit to pew.[41] Most important of all, serious theological reflection was overwhelmed by the surging popular "religious revival" which peaked in 1957 when Billy Graham had his "finest hour" in New York City.

---

[40] Several of these themes are illustrated by selections reprinted in Smith, Handy, and Loetscher, *American Christianity,* II, 438–71.

[41] Presbyterians attempted to make the transition with their *Christian Faith and Life Series* of church school materials, but an ill-equipped laity found it difficult to teach and it was gradually phased out. For the point of view of the series, see Armstrong, Loetscher, and Anderson, *Presbyterian Enterprise,* 301–3.

The Religious Revival of the Fifties

By the 1950s it was evident that the United States was in the midst of a religious revival. Critical voices became muted, and religion was riding the crest of a wave of popularity. Church attendance soared, contributions mounted, and unprecedented sums were spent on new church buildings.[42] This was equally true of Protestants, Catholics, and Jews. Publishers discovered that religious books were profitable. The more popular volumes dominated the best-seller lists for extended periods of time. Seldom had religion been held in greater public esteem. The pledge of allegiance was amended to include the phrase "under God," prayer breakfasts were attended by the president and members of his cabinet, a prayer room was installed in the national Capitol, and both the American Legion and the National Advertising Council launched "Back to God" and "Go to Church" campaigns. In 1957 the Census Bureau indicated that more than 96 percent of the American people cited a specific religious affiliation in response to the question: "What is your religion?" Many names among the 96 percent did not appear on any church membership roll, but the fact that they so identified themselves is significant.

The "return to religion" of the 1950s was formless and unstructured, manifesting itself in many different ways and reinforcing all religious faiths quite indiscriminately. It was a comfortable time for the churches, but it cannot be understood apart from the trauma of World War II and its aftermath. Unlike the brief involvement of the United States in World War I, four long years elapsed after Pearl Harbor before peace was restored. Husbands and wives were separated and marriages postponed for what seemed to be an unending period of time. Those left at home spent long hours in the workforce on assembly lines and loading platforms, not for a few months as in World War I, but for two, three, or four years. The developing nostalgia was for the recovery of the quieter time and ties of family, home, and church. Back to normalcy meant the reunion of loved ones and the establishment of new family formations or the reestablishment of old ones. These were the years of the baby boom and of the housing explosion in the suburbs. Seldom had the joys of home and family been more cherished and celebrated. These joys were given added importance by an undercurrent of anxiety. The Depression of the 1930s had been a sobering experience, but among the more thoughtful the "immense and indomitable optimism" of the American people was given a heavier blow when the bombing of Hiroshima and Nagasaki in 1945 demonstrated the potential destructiveness of the unleashed powers of the atom. The uneasy peace of the "cold war" that followed, with its recur-

---

[42] From a base of $26 million in 1945, the amount spent on new churches rose steadily: 1946—$76 million; 1948—$251 million; 1950—$409 million; 1954—$593 million; 1956—$775 million; 1958—$863 million; 1959—$935 million; 1960—$1,016 million. After 1960 a decline set in.

ring crises and continuing conflicts, heightened the sense of anxiety and insecurity.

As a result of what Robert Maynard Hutchins, president of the University of Chicago, called "the good news of damnation," even the world of the secular intellectuals was prepared to listen to the theologians, most notably to Reinhold Niebuhr and Paul Tillich, in a way and to a degree that had not been true for almost half a century. The comment of *Time* magazine in 1956 that Tillich was an intellectual whom even the intellectuals regarded with awe may have been overly exuberant, but it nonetheless reflected the shift in attitude that had occurred. For the most part, however, the revival flowed through more popular channels.

Heirs of the Fundamentalists gave the revival its most vigorous leadership. The way for their new surge of activity had been prepared by the National Association of Evangelicals (N.A.E.), Youth for Christ, and a handful of scholars determined to develop an effective Fundamentalist apologetic. The N.A.E. was formed in 1942 to unite the forces of moderate Fundamentalism,[43] and under the leadership of Harold J. Ockenga it adopted a conciliatory policy designed to capitalize upon the demoralization of the "modernists" and to penetrate the life of major denominations by persuasion from within rather than by leveling criticism from without. In pursuing this goal they successfully appropriated for themselves the name "evangelical" to avoid the Fundamentalist label. Youth for Christ, the second organization spearheading the Fundamentalist recovery, was founded in 1943 to sponsor Saturday night rallies for young people. It quickly became both a recruiting instrument and a training ground for the new "evangelical" leadership. The activity of these two agencies was strengthened by a coterie of young theologians who were willing to engage in the give-and-take of reasoned theological discussion.[44]

The thrust of the new "evangelicalism" was brought into focus by Billy Graham, who had been recruited by Youth for Christ in 1945 to serve as an itinerant evangelist at its rallies. Four years later at a tent meeting in Los Angeles, Graham gained widespread attention through the conversion of three minor celebrities — a local television star, a former Olympic athlete, and an alleged associate of the notorious racketeer Mickey Cohen. The Los Angeles success was followed by an 18-day campaign at the Park Street Church in Boston and in 1950 by a citywide revival in Portland, Oregon. Under the tutelage of Ockenga, Graham expressed a distaste for interdenominational feuds, deplored "fumbling Fundamentalists" who destroyed their effectiveness by intolerance and sectarianism, and an-

---

[43] See J. D. Murch, *Cooperation Without Compromise* (Grand Rapids, 1956).
[44] The most prominent were Carl Henry, Edward Carnell, and Cornelius Van Til. See A. W. Hearn, "Fundamentalist Renascence," *Christian Century*, 75 (1958), 528–30.

nounced a decision to refuse any invitation to conduct a revival that was not tendered by a majority of the Protestant clergy of the host city.[45]

Several factors, in addition to his dashing youthful appearance and generally irenic spirit, combined to further Graham's growing prominence and popularity, which culminated in his dramatic "invasion" of England in 1954. One was a skillful use of sophisticated organizational techniques and an adroit exploitation of publicity media, including his weekly "Hour of Decision" radio broadcast. The second was the care he took to marshal support among all denominations. But the real key to his success, perhaps, was the mounting public anxiety that reached a peak during the Korean conflict and the Red-hunt of the McCarthy era.

The political flavor of Graham's gospel had great appeal to ultraconservative segments of the population. Drawing a contrast with the Garden of Eden where there were "no union dues, no labor leaders, no snakes, no disease," Graham depicted the United States as "falling apart at the seams" as a result of deficit spending, "giveaway" foreign-aid programs, "immorality in high places," the influence of "big labor" and "pinks and lavenders" in Washington, and "the infiltration of the left wing" into schools and churches. The "betrayals" at Yalta and Potsdam, the war in Korea, the bungling United Nations ("they set the policies and we shed the blood and pay the bills") were cited as evidence of the "deadly work" of Communism boring from within and were used to demonstrate that "we are living in the latter days." Since Communism was "masterminded by Satan," it was a mistake to think that Satan can be defeated with "flesh and blood and guns and bullets." Only through a great revival, purging America of "the rats and termites" that are weakening "this nation from within," can the United States be saved and the battle won, for "the greatest and most effective weapon against Communism today is a born-again Christian." The altar call was simple and direct: "If you would be a true patriot, then become a Christian. If you would be a loyal American, then become a loyal Christian." In a political atmosphere charged with suspicion and fear — represented above all by the witch hunts of Senator Joseph McCarthy and the House Un-American Activities Committee the combination of religious conservatism and anti-Communism proved to be appealing to many.[46]

The patriotic motif did not represent the full scope of Graham's message. There was much traditional doctrine, and he often spoke to the more personal needs of people. Here the stress was upon the role of

[45] See John Pollock, *Billy Graham: Evangelist to the World* (N.Y., 1979); Marshall Frady, *Billy Graham: A Biography of American Righteousness* (Boston, 1979); W. G. McLoughlin, *Billy Graham: Revivalist in a Secular Age* (N.Y., 1960); L. I. Sweet, "The Epic of Billy Graham," *Theology Today,* 37 (1980), 85–92.

[46] McLoughlin, *Modern Revivalism,* 505–12.

religion as a consolation that brings "peace of mind, peace of soul, peace of conscience." This latter emphasis points to another prominent feature of the surge of piety of the 1950s—the "cult of reassurance" of which Norman Vincent Peale, minister of the Marble Collegiate Church in New York City, has been called the "high priest."

New Thought, Christian Science, and the Unity School of Christianity had long exploited the reassurance theme in religion, but the full-blown cult of reassurance dates from the publication of Joshua L. Liebman's *Peace of Mind* in 1946, which quickly achieved a phenomenal sale. Liebman was a Jewish rabbi, and preachers of all persuasions, including Monsignor Fulton J. Sheen with his *Peace of Soul* (1949), capitalized upon this newly awakened religious interest.

Of the "peace of mind" evangelists, Norman Vincent Peale most fully captured the public imagination. From his base in New York City he issued a stream of books, including the fabulously successful *The Power of Positive Thinking* (1952). His was a simple "do-it-yourself" faith, calling for the replacement of "negative thought" with "positive thinking," that was strongly reminiscent of the teachings of Charles and Myrtle Fillmore. You can "make your life what you want it to be through belief in God and in yourself," he informed his readers. You must "think, believe, visualize success"—"think big," "believe big," "pray big," "act big." How does one "practice faith?" he asked. "First thing every morning before you arise say out loud, 'I believe,' three times."[47]

Peale was referred to by some as "the rich man's Billy Graham," and the two men did hold each other in high esteem. Although they differed theologically, they shared common political and economic views. Peale was a sponsor of Graham's New York Crusade and, if the number of decision cards received from the Graham organization was an accurate index, his church reaped the largest harvest. Graham in turn regarded Peale as "a born-again Christian" in spite of his obvious self-help Pelagianism.[48]

Although the popular "religious revival" of the 1950s can most easily be depicted by vivid personalities, its substratum was much broader than that suggested by personality cults. Religion-in-general, any religion and all religion, was thoroughly popular, reflecting a simple belief that religion was a "good thing." President Dwight D. Eisenhower stressed the importance of having "faith in faith." Belonging to a church was widely regarded as a badge of respectability. This was the real revival of the 1950s, expressing itself in increased church attendance, increased church giving, increased church building, and increased public esteem.

---

[47] *The Power of Positive Thinking* (N.Y., 1952), 154; *Stay Alive All Your Life* (Englewood Cliffs, N.J., 1957), 22, 104, 211, 263.

[48] Pelagius was a British monk of the fourth-fifth century who denied original sin and the need for divine grace for salvation.

Other Manifestations of Religious Vitality

In spite of the pervasive "folk religion" of the time, many of the clergy and coteries of church members continued their attempts to deal realistically, from a Christian perspective, with some of the more urgent problems of national life.

During World War II the churches demonstrated that they had learned a lesson from the uninhibited exuberance with which they had blessed World War I. The new conflict was viewed much more soberly. The halting of totalitarian aggression was accepted as a necessity. It was recognized, however, that if the ensuing peace was to be secure, the requirements for the establishment of international order must be clearly defined before the victory was won. To this end a conference was summoned in 1942 to meet at Delaware, Ohio, to draft a report on the prerequisites for a "just and durable peace."[49] Seldom has a report received more serious consideration by the churches. Study guides were prepared and few congregations failed to make use of them. Key political leaders declared that the report was of decisive importance in creating the favorable climate of American opinion that was indispensable to the establishment of the United Nations.

Later in the McCarthy era, the Protestant churches performed yeoman service in calling a halt to the witch hunt of those years. All major denominations repeatedly expressed alarm at the threat to freedom implicit in the practice of character assassination, imputation of guilt by association, use of loyalty oaths as a means of thought control, and curtailment of individual rights on the basis of credence given accusations by undisclosed informers. The boldest action was taken by the Presbyterian General Council in a statement of October 21, 1953, to be read to each congregation, which declared that "detestation of Communism" was becoming a "new form of idolatry" that could be as dangerous as Communism itself, that dissent and treason are not identical, and that true believers in God will not play fast and loose with truth to preserve freedom.[50] The firm strictures of official church bodies played no small part in heartening the defenders of liberty in this difficult time and in encouraging the U.S. Senate to meet the issue without equivocation.

Still later the racial crisis elicited the strong leadership of many churchmen.[51] Two years prior to the 1954 Supreme Court decision outlawing segregation in the public schools, the National Council of Churches adopted an official statement, *The Churches and Segregation*, which de-

[49] The "Statement of Guiding Principles" is reprinted in Smith, Handy, and Loetscher, *American Christianity*, II, 522–26.

[50] The statement is reprinted in *ibid.*, 549–55.

[51] See Robert Root, *Progress Against Prejudice: The Church Confronts the Race Problem* (N.Y., 1957).

clared racial segregation to be "diametrically opposed" to the Christian faith. When the decision of the Court was announced, the National Council quickly issued "Suggestions for Action" to guide the churches in helping speed compliance with the law. Unfortunately, instead of proceeding with "all deliberate speed" to carry out the directive, many southern states adopted a "massive resistance" policy that served to create smoldering discontent in black communities. A tragic aspect of the situation was the abdication of responsibility and leadership by southern white churches. After passing a mild resolution commending the Court's decision, the Southern Baptist Convention retreated into silence. The record of other denominations was not notably better, although some local congregations exhibited firm and courageous leadership.

A new phase of the struggle began in 1956 when blacks of Montgomery, Alabama, put an end to segregated seating in the city's public transportation by a mass bus boycott. The leader of the boycott was a young black Baptist minister, Martin Luther King, Jr., who became the principal architect of a drive to attack all forms of segregation through nonviolent action.[52] Other clergymen and particularly black college students rallied to his support, as did leaders of northern white churches. Several organizations, including the Southern Christian Leadership Conference of which King became president, were formed to push a program of nonviolent resistance. By 1962 the movement had spread to northern cities, where the focal point of concern was discrimination in housing, employment, and de facto school segregation.

With a succession of "long hot summers" of increasing tension in prospect, the National Council of Churches created a committee on Religion and Race to coordinate the activities of member denominations. Action programs were set into motion. Special funds to aid victims of economic and legal harassment were established. Prominent churchmen joined picket lines, street demonstrations, and "sit-ins," and the top echelon of official leadership was conspicuously present in the massive "March on Washington" on August 28, 1963, when King stirred the conscience of the nation with his emotion-packed and unforgettable refrain, "I have a dream." In the autumn the nation was shocked by the tragic murder of four black Sunday school children in the wanton Sunday morning bombing of a Baptist church in Birmingham. The following spring, during the Senate debate on the Civil Rights Bill of 1964, a Daily Protestant Assembly was maintained at the Lutheran Church of the Reformation on Capitol Hill. The prayer services of the Assembly were followed by briefings for those who came to make their views known to their legislative representatives. But it was the marshaling of support in local congregations that was of decisive importance in bringing the debate to a successful conclusion.

A further feature of old-line Protestantism at mid-century was a grow-

[52] See his *Stride Toward Freedom: The Montgomery Story* (N.Y., 1958).

Martin Luther King. "I have a dream . . . black and white together."
This was the theme at the peak of his career when he spoke to the
multitude assembled at the Lincoln Memorial during the famed March
on Washington in 1963. *(Photo by Roland Mitchell in* A Martin Luther
King Treasury, *copyright Educational Heritage, Inc., Yonkers, N.Y., 1964,
Courtesy of Wyatt Tee Walker.)*

ing trend toward unity. Throughout the nineteenth century Protestants
were accustomed to work together in voluntary societies of individuals.
Most believed "there were sufficient targets to hit without firing at each
other." In the twentieth century these voluntary modes of cooperation
were replaced by "official" interdenominational agencies to coordinate
home-mission, foreign-mission, and Christian education activities. The

final step in the consolidation of Protestant cooperation was taken in 1950 when these several agencies came together to form the National Council of Churches.[53] The national coordinating structure was paralleled by state and local councils of churches. In rural areas a "grass roots" unity movement developed with the formation of federated and community churches to solve the problem created by a declining rural population. Although there were dissident voices, H. Richard Niebuhr was probably correct when he observed that "the increasing unity of American Protestantism" was "more striking than its apparent diversity."[54]

The typical Protestant pattern in America had been to unite in service while preserving diversity in polity and worship, but the vision of organic unity has had recurrent spokesmen. Numerous proposals for broad-scale union were made, but the suggestion that won most serious consideration was made in 1960 by Eugene Carson Blake, stated clerk of the United Presbyterian Church, speaking in the San Francisco Episcopal cathedral at the invitation of Bishop James A. Pike. A Consultation on Church Unity (COCU) was convened in 1962 to forward a plan of union that would be "both catholic and reformed." High hopes were awakened and nine denominations participated in the continuing consultations.

Denominational "reunions" had more success than more broadly based mergers. Three Methodist bodies came together in 1939 to form the Methodist Church, becoming the United Methodist Church in 1968 with the addition of the Evangelical United Brethren (German Methodist) Church. The 24 Lutheran groups of 1900 were gradually reduced in number until by 1960 almost all Lutherans (96 percent) belonged to 3 major bodies — the Lutheran Church in America, the American Lutheran Church, and the Lutheran Church – Missouri Synod. Several mergers followed, so that by late 1988, the newly created Evangelical Lutheran Church in America included most Lutherans. Meanwhile in 1958 the United Presbyterians had merged with the northern Presbyterians, and in the 1970s northern and southern Presbyterians were brought together to form one church. A merger that bridged traditional denominational lines of division was the formation of the United Church of Christ in 1957 by the Congregational Christian Churches and the Evangelical and Reformed Church.

Closely related to movements of Christian unity in America was a growing concern for ecumenical or worldwide unity, which found expression in the formation of the World Council of Churches in 1948. Several currents of interest combined to produce the World Council. The first stemmed directly from foreign-mission fields, where divisions imported from the West seriously impaired the task of evangelism and weakened the

---

[53] *Christian Faith in Action: The Founding of the National Council of Churches* (N.Y., 1951). See also Samuel McCrae Cavert, *Church Cooperation and Unity in America* (N.Y., 1970).
[54] *The Purpose of the Church and Its Ministry* (N.Y., 1956), 16–17.

small Christian communities that were struggling to maintain themselves in non-Christian societies. Periodic missionary conferences to chart common strategies culminated in the formation of the International Missionary Council at the Edinburgh Conference of 1910. This conference inspired two Americans to pursue alternate paths to unity. Bishop Charles H. Brent, believing that churches should engage in theological discussion to learn from one another and to discover their common faith, was instrumental in organizing the Faith and Order Movement. Charles S. MacFarland took an alternate route. Believing that the way to bring churches together was to have them address themselves jointly to common social tasks, he took the lead in helping initiate the Life and Work Movement. Leaders in all three areas had become accustomed to working together in the World's Christian Student Federation, organized in 1905, and it was natural for them to envision the consolidation of their efforts in an inclusive ecumenical body. Though its formal organization was delayed by World War II until 1948, the World Council immediately achieved a status far exceeding the hopes of those who labored to bring it into being.

The Protestant phase of the "religious revival" has often been dismissed as an expression of mere religiosity—a booming, surging, culture religion, without depth and with little commitment, which was utilized to lend divine sanction to "the American way of life." Although there is evidence to support this indictment and although there was much that was superficial in Protestantism at mid-century, there were deeper currents that were never wholly submerged. There was also earnest probing and a great hunger for faith.

CHAPTER 15

The Maturing of Roman Catholicism

When Pius X issued the apostolic constitution *Sapienti Consilio* on June 29, 1908, he recognized that the Roman Catholic Church in the United States had come of age by bringing to an end its missionary status. Hitherto the church in the United States had been under the jurisdiction and control of the Congregatio de Propaganda Fide in Rome. Henceforth it was to be administered on a basis of equality with the older branches of the church in Europe. But it was not until after World War I that the Roman Catholic Church in America began to exhibit the full marks of maturity as an indigenous expression of the Roman Catholic faith.

The External Marks of Maturity

Maturity is an ambiguous word. It may refer to external manifestations of adulthood, or it may connote an inner temper of mind that is no longer plagued by the insecurities and anxieties of adolescence. Generally in the maturing process, outward evidence of maturity precedes the inward maturation. Here the initial concern is with the external aspects of a "full-grown" American Catholicism.

The Effect of World War I

The outbreak of war in 1914 cut off the massive influx of immigrants that had contributed so largely to the numerical growth of Roman Catholicism. After the war restrictive legislation put an end to renewed large-scale immigration. This meant that for the first time the Roman Catholic Church had an opportunity to become stabilized in the American environment. Throughout the nineteenth century it had been a church of immigrants—heir of many different national traditions. Parishes were identified by national constituencies—Irish, Polish, German, Portuguese, Italian, French, Slovak, Croatian, Hungarian, and Spanish-speaking. It often was difficult to think of them as constituting a single, indigenous church. With the curtailment of immigration, the nationality and language distinctions normally would have tended to disappear over a period of two or three generations, but the process was hastened by the strong Americanizing pressures that were so prominent a feature of World War I and its immediate aftermath. Immigrant languages were abandoned as quickly as possible, and there was a scramble by immigrants to demonstrate that they were 100 percent Americans. Almost within a single decade thereafter, Roman Catholicism ceased to be thought of as an immigrant's church, and by 1955 the "melting pot" had to a great extent eliminated the identification of religion with specific national origins.[1]

A second consequence of the war was a greatly increased organizational unity that was achieved through the formation of the National Catholic Welfare Conference. The last plenary council was held in 1884, when the triumvirate of Gibbons, Ireland, and Keane was intent on limiting diocesan autonomy in the interest of a unified national policy. Since that time the papal delegate and an annual meeting of the archbishops were the only channels through which the activities of the church could be coordinated. In practice this meant that each bishop set his own policy. Neither the delegate nor the archbishops had the necessary administrative staff for overall planning. Although the delegate could intervene in a diocese if an emergency situation developed, the authority of the archbishops was limited to the influence they could exert by persuasion and example. The war, however, created a situation in which specific and detailed centralized action was necessary if wartime needs were to be met effectively. For this purpose the National Catholic War Council was formed in 1917. So "sensible, visible, practical, efficacious" was its work that many bishops became convinced that a peacetime coordinating agency should be continued. After some delay occasioned by a few bishops who feared that their independent powers would be jeopardized, the National Catholic Welfare Conference (N.C.W.C.) was established in 1921.

Initially the work of the N.C.W.C. was divided into five departments—Education, Lay Activities, Press, Social Action, and Missions. Later it was reorganized to embrace almost every area of Catholic interest and concern. The Conference had no independent authority, existing solely to advise and assist the bishops. Nonetheless it gained such prestige that it became an effective instrument for establishing national policy, for issuing

---

[1] See Will Herberg, "The Triple Melting Pot," *Commentary* (1955), 101–8, 243. Later the massive influx of Spanish-speaking Catholics from Puerto Rico, Cuba, Mexico, and elsewhere posed the question of whether this surging tide could be assimilated in similar fashion within two or three generations.

pronouncements in the name of the entire hierarchy, and for fostering a sense of unity and solidarity among American Catholics.

Another mark of growing maturity was the changing role of American Roman Catholics in the field of foreign missions. For almost a century they had been the recipients of assistance from abroad. The war shut off this source of help, and by bringing mass immigration to an end it lessened the need for such aid. The Society for the Propagation of the Faith, with headquarters in Europe, had long been a chief channel through which mission funds had been sent to the United States, but after the war Americans began to supply much of its income. By 1957 about 65 percent of its total budget was being met by gifts from the United States. In terms of foreign-mission personnel the story was much the same. The Maryknoll Fathers had been funded in 1911, but it was not until 1918 that the first missionaries were sent out. By mid-century, however, Maryknoll Fathers were at work in Asia, Africa, Central and South America, and the islands of the Pacific. Meanwhile, other American orders joined the enterprise, and by 1960 Americans represented about one-ninth of the total Roman Catholic foreign-mission force.

Increase in Numbers and Wealth

Growing homogeneity, increasing unification, and vanishing dependence upon aid from abroad were not the only signs of maturity. In terms of numbers the Roman Catholic Church was far more than a lusty infant. By 1920 the *Official Catholic Directory* reported a total of 17,885,000 baptized members.

With the flow of recruits through immigration reduced to a trickle, there was hope of strengthening the church through converts. The number of converts did increase, many the result of mixed marriages. This, of course, was a two-way street, with a Gallup Poll indicating that the movement in both directions was roughly in balance.[2]

Other defections stemmed from the natural tendency of many people to shirk religious obligations, but Roman Catholicism was remarkably successful in holding its own during these years. The officially reported membership was 20,203,702 in 1930; 21,284,455 in 1940; 28,634,878 in 1950; and 42,104,900 in 1960.[3] The latter figure reflects the triple effect of a swelling birthrate, the influx of refugees following World War II, and the "religious revival." In terms of any realistic standards of membership, the church in the United States had become the largest national grouping of Roman Catholics in the world.

---

[2] "Conversion Poll Ends in a Dead Heat," *Christian Century,* 72 (1955), 411.

[3] Inadequate collection of data resulted in an underreporting of membership at least through 1940. Statistical procedures were gradually improved thereafter. See G. A. Kelly and Thomas Coogan, "What Is Our Real Catholic Population?" *American Ecclesiastical Review,* 110 (1944), 377.

In addition to numerical size, the Roman Catholic community in the United States was distinguished by its success in developing the largest private educational system in the world. By 1964 there were 10,902 Catholic elementary schools with more than 4.5 million pupils; 2,458 high schools with 1,068,424 students; 295 colleges and universities with more than 350,000 students; and 596 seminaries with 48,750 seminarians preparing for the priesthood. All this was accomplished with little or no direct aid from public taxation.

A third indication that American Roman Catholicism had moved far beyond its period of infancy was the fact that it had become the wealthiest national church in the Roman Catholic world. By 1920 it had achieved its financial independence and rapidly became a chief contributor to foreign-mission funds. Moreover, as early as 1937 it was estimated that half of Rome's current income was supplied by Americans.[4] A decade later communist takeovers in Poland, Czechoslovakia, Hungary, and Yugoslavia increased the reliance of the Vatican on American support.

Representation in the College of Cardinals is often an index of the importance Rome attaches to a particular segment of the church. Until 1921 there was never more than one prince of the church in the United States, but thereafter the number gradually increased. By 1959 there were six American cardinals, a number approximating Spanish representation and exceeded only by that of France and, of course, Italy. The number of American priests appointed to offices in the Curia and in the Holy See's diplomatic service also reflected the enhanced importance of American Catholicism in the eyes of Rome.

Changing Status of Catholics in American Life

In the first half of the century, attention often was called to the contrast between the number of Catholics and their representation in national leadership positions. The failure to attain prominence in proportion to their numbers was commonly alleged to be the result of a conscious discrimination designed to keep Catholics out of posts of leadership. Few would contend that there were no instances of discrimination, but as an explanation of the lag in status of Catholics in American life, it is much too facile.

First, such an explanation fails to take into account the source of a large portion of Roman Catholic strength. It was derived from recent immigrants, drawn from the underprivileged classes of Europe, who arrived without financial resources. Many were illiterate; of those who were not, many were isolated from the general culture by language barriers. It normally takes at least a generation for children of immigrants to secure

---

[4] William Teeling, *Pope Pius XI and World Affairs* (N.Y., 1937), 133, 158f.

education necessary to qualify for professional positions. More often it is not until the third generation that this occurs.

Second, much of the isolation of Roman Catholics was self-imposed. To hold immigrants true to the faith, tightly guarded enclaves were often created. Language barriers were perpetuated, and children were separated in parochial schools from other children in the community. The Knights of Columbus, the Catholic Youth Organization, the Newman Clubs, the Catholic War Veterans, and even Catholic "Junior Leagues" served to retard assimilation into the general community and thus made it more difficult for Catholics to gain positions of community leadership.

Third, the Catholic Church often projected a negative image. It was most successful in conveying an image of what it was against—birth control, divorce, euthanasia, therapeutic abortion. The Legion of Decency, founded to encourage the production of better motion pictures, became much better known for the films it blacklisted than for those it approved. At several points, including issues relating to public education and American policy toward Franco Spain, Catholic opinion was at variance with that of other citizens. Quite apart from any religious prejudice, Catholic aspirants for public office were sometimes defeated simply because they did not represent majority opinion.

Studies based on information gathered in 1939–40 and in 1948 indicated that Roman Catholics moved up the economic ladder much faster than had generally had been assumed.[5] By the latter date differences in class affiliation were rapidly disappearing. No appreciable distinctions in class, occupation, and education were found between Roman Catholics, Baptists, and Lutherans; and the disparity between Roman Catholics and Methodists was not great enough to be statistically significant.

Roman Catholics gained political prominence at an even earlier date. As was to be expected, urban centers where their strength was concentrated provided the arenas where Catholics first gained roles of political leadership. Later they moved in increasing numbers into positions of consequence in state capitals. If Roman Catholics were underrepresented in some state governments, it was presumably not because of their religion but because state legislatures were apportioned to give undue predominance to rural rather than urban interests.

The nomination of Alfred E. Smith in 1928 as the Democratic candidate for president signaled that Roman Catholics had come of age politically on the national scene. This reversed his failure to gain the nomination in 1924. Even so, Smith faced a hopeless prospect. In 1928 Smith as the Democratic candidate was seeking office in a time of booming prosperity and he had as his opponent a man with a towering reputation as a great humanitarian. Also Hoover, the opponent, as secretary of commerce had guided the nation into such affluence that the slogan "two chickens in

[5] See appendix to Schneider, *Religion in Twentieth Century America*, 225–38.

every pot and two cars in every garage" did not seem unrealistic. Hoover also had the benefit of Republican alliances with big-city machines and organized labor. Later it was said that Smith's religion cost him votes.

Anti-Catholic votes were cast in the election. Methodist Bishop J. M. Cannon of Virginia urged Protestants to "vote as you pray," and in the South the traditional Democratic vote was reduced. But prohibition was as decisive as religion in this defection. Elsewhere "the noble experiment" was not yet a sufficiently emotional issue to cause very many to vote against their pocketbooks. Four years later a vote for one's pocketbook coincided with a vote to end prohibition. Smith's Catholicism apparently gained him more votes than he lost. What else would account for his astonishing achievement in lifting the Democratic percentage of the total vote from 34 percent in 1920 and 28 percent in 1924 to 40 percent in 1928?[6] It is likely that a Protestant would have fared much worse. Not only did Smith lift the Democratic total from 8 to 15 million, he did better in proportion to the Democratic vote for congressmen than any other twentieth-century Democratic candidate prior to Franklin D. Roosevelt. After the election of 1932, Catholic political participation at the national level became commonplace, and John F. Kennedy's election in 1960 finally put to rest the myth that a Catholic could not be elected president of the United States.

Expressions of New Vitality

European Roman Catholics often referred to the "activism" of American Catholicism. With rapidly proliferating parishes to staff, churches to build, and schools to be established, money to be raised and ecclesiastical supervision to be maintained, there was ample cause for energetic busyness. The preoccupation with immediate tasks may explain the absence of any native-born citizen in the ranks of the saints. Mother Cabrini, of course, was elevated to sainthood in 1946, but she was of Italian birth. It is also true that Elizabeth Bayley Seton was canonized in 1970. But on the whole American Catholics have been distinguished for virtues other than those calling for veneration by the faithful. It is appropriate, therefore, to begin a consideration of currents of thought and concern that have characterized American Catholicism by centering attention on its "social program."

The Social Program of the Church

For two decades after its founding, the National Catholic Welfare Conference was regarded in public esteem as almost synonymous with its Social Action Department, headed by John A. Ryan, professor of moral theology

---

[6] R. C. Silva, *Rum, Religion, and Votes, 1928 Re-examined* (University Park, Pa., 1962), 4. Also E. A. Moore, *A Catholic Runs for President* (N.Y., 1956).

at Catholic University.[7] In 1919 Ryan wrote a pamphlet, *Social Recon-struction: A General Review of the Problems and Survey of the Remedies,* which became known as the "Bishops' Program of Social Reconstruction."[8] The document pointed to the need for minimum-wage legislation, regulation of child labor, protection of the right of labor to organize, public housing, a national employment service, and unemployment, industrial-accident, and old-age insurance. With one or two exceptions, the recommendations of the Ryan document became part of the New Deal legislation of the early Roosevelt years. In Ryan's writings, in Catholic urban projects such as the St. Louis Verein, and in Father Edward McGlynn's programs of humanitarian reform, there existed a loosely organized Catholic initiative that was similar to the Protestant Social Gospel in its religiously grounded call for social reform.

Meanwhile other Catholics forwarded the cause of economic justice. The Catholic League for Social Justice was established in 1932. A year later Dorothy Day helped found the Catholic Worker movement. In 1937 the Association of Catholic Trade Unionists was formed. Numerous "labor schools" were established to train union members and help them combat both racketeering elements in the unions and communist infiltra-tion. Moreover, Charles E. Coughlin, the radio priest of the Shrine of the Little Flower in Royal Oak, Michigan, won a large following in the 1930s as a spokesman for social justice. When his weekly broadcasts became tinged with anti-Semitic sentiment, however, his ecclesiastical superiors gradually inhibited him from political activity.

Although the "Bishops' Program of Social Reconstruction" was based on the authoritative papal encyclical *Rerum Novarum* (1891), the stance of the church was ambiguous. Some bishops were lukewarm in their support, and many of the laity were recalcitrant. The cooling of social ardor was especially noticeable after World War II when much of the Catholic press became scornful of "do-gooders" and "bleeding hearts." The disposition to give only nominal acceptance to the "social encyclicals," Bishop William Mulloy declared in 1952, "tended to paralyze the force of the teaching Church in modern American society."[9]

Roman Catholic policy was more firm during the 1950s in the area of racial justice. Ever since the Civil War work among blacks had followed a segregated pattern, but in the 1920s a series of conferences focused attention on segregation in Catholic institutions. The movement began to bear fruit when the Archbishop of St. Louis in 1947 ended segregation in the schools of his diocese. The following year the Archbishop of Washing-ton followed his example, and in 1953 the Bishop of Raleigh, North

---

[7] See F. L. Broderick, *Right Reverend New Dealer: John A. Ryan* (N.Y., 1963).
[8] Reprinted in Smith, Handy, and Loetscher, *American Christianity,* II, 407–14.
[9] Cross, *Emergence of Liberal Catholicism,* 218–19.

Carolina, defied the opposition of Catholics in his diocese and opened the churches, schools, and hospitals under his jurisdiction to people of every race. After the Supreme Court in 1954 declared public-school segregation unconstitutional, the unequivocal stands of Archbishops Robert E. Lucey of San Antonio and Joseph F. Rummel of New Orleans were a heartening feature of the situation in the South.

The tenor of Catholic political thought contrasted sharply with the progressive character of other aspects of the church's social program. Tendencies toward accommodation of Catholic tradition to basic assumptions of American democracy had been arrested by Leo XIII's condemnation of "Americanism" in 1899. The alternative, in terms of official teaching, was to look back to the Middle Ages for normative models, and this alternative was commanded by Leo XIII's encyclicals "The Christian Constitution of States" (1885) and "Christian Democracy" (1901), which rejected doctrines of popular sovereignty, government by consent of the governed, and pernicious notions of freedom of religion, freedom of speech, freedom of assembly, and freedom of the press.[10] The encyclicals conceded that, due to circumstances in any given nation, a full Christian political order may not always be possible or practical. Under certain conditions, therefore, the church will not judge it "blameworthy" for "the people to have a share, greater or less, in the government." Indeed, under certain conditions, "such participation . . . may even be of obligation." This concession was the "out" seized upon by American Catholics familiar with papal teaching to effect a practical adjustment to the necessities of American political life. The theory was explicated by John A. Ryan and Moorhouse F. X. Millar in the widely used textbook, *The State and the Church* (1922).[11] In the area of political thought, since he was forced to acknowledge that Catholic teaching involved "hard sayings" that smacked of intolerance, Ryan was cast into the role of a reactionary.

By the late 1940s, however, Catholic theologians began to challenge Ryan's conclusions. Jesuits John Courtney Murray and Gustave Weigel took the lead with a more dynamic view of Catholic political theory, placing it in historical context and demonstrating that political democracy could be firmly grounded on Catholic principles.[12] Their views were widely accepted. Whatever Ryan's intention may have been, the views expounded in his textbook made it possible for many Catholics in the 1950s to defend Senator Joseph McCarthy's activities on the assumption that they were based on "Catholic" teaching.

---

[10] For the encyclicals, see W. S. Hudson, *Understanding Roman Catholicism.*

[11] Later revised and republished by Ryan and Francis J. Boland under a new title, *Catholic Principles of Politics* (N.Y., 1940).

[12] See Murray's essays, *We Hold These Truths* (N.Y., 1960), and Gustave Weigel, "The Church and the Democratic State," *Thought,* 27 (1952), 165–75.

Intellectual Life

As early as 1928, in *The Catholic Spirit in America*, George N. Shuster voiced the complaint that American Catholicism was intellectually asleep and exhibited "a terrible contempt for thought." In 1940 he renewed the charge that the church had "virtually no use for intellectuals." The absence of a strong intellectual tradition may be attributed to several causes. For one thing, American Catholics had been too engrossed in "brick-and-mortar" enterprises—constructing churches, schools, and other institutions—to allow much energy and imagination to be devoted to intellectual pursuits. Moreover, the average immigrant family lacked both the educational background and the financial resources to foster intellectual interests. Symptomatic of this was the fact that in the late 1940s not a single member of the hierarchy was the son of college-educated parents. Furthermore, the Catholic educational system had emphasized "safeness" at the expense of "excellence" and creative inquiry. But the major reason was the inhibiting effect of the condemnation of "Americanism" and "Modernism." The authoritarian (as opposed to critical-intellectual) style of the Catholic Church, coupled with a sacramentalism that required for its efficacy the participation of church authorities (e.g., priests, bishops), intensified the problem, so that an outright antiintellectualism developed among Catholics in America.

The retreat into "separatism" from American culture that followed Leo XIII's letter of 1899 to Cardinal Gibbons was strongly reinforced by Pius X's comprehensive attack in 1907 on the "modernist" heresies flowing from the historical researches of certain European Catholic scholars. Bishops were instructed to exercise minute supervision of both teachers and students. Three years later a decree was issued requiring all Catholics in positions of responsibility to take a detailed antimodernist oath. Although few in America held the condemned opinions, the effect of the condemnation was to heighten timidity and give full reign to an unquestioning orthodoxy. The spirit inculcated was reflected in the counsel given a young Paulist who was perplexed by intellectual problems. He was advised to "preach the moral law and let dogmas alone."[13]

After World War II the situation began to change. The mingling, especially of priests, with non-Catholics in the armed forces ended Catholic isolation. Also, the educational level of the Catholic population was rising, thrusting to the fore questions hitherto regarded as "too hot to handle." And an awareness of new theological trends in Europe began to seep into academic cloisters. But the decisive factor may have been such verdicts as that expressed by an English observer that "the Catholic church in America has counted for astonishingly little in the formation of

---

[13] W. L. Sullivan, *Under Orders* (N.Y., 1944), 111. T. T. McAvoy spoke of the "theological silence" that descended on the church. See *The Great Crisis in American Catholic History*, 344.

the American intellectual climate." In 1955 John Tracy Ellis of Catholic University created a minor sensation with an indictment of American Catholics for their intellectual abdication, and three years later Thomas F. O'Dea contributed an even more detailed analysis of the problem.[14]

In the meantime a vigorous controversy developed between those who were convinced that the general culture was important to Catholics and necessitated their active involvement in it and those who insisted that a strongly guarded defensive posture was indispensable since Catholicism and modern cultural tendencies were diametrically opposed. The first position commanded massive Jesuit support, with John Courtney Murray and Gustave Weigel the outstanding protagonists. Stressing the obligation of the church to the pursuit of truth and drawing heavily upon new biblical and theological studies in Europe, they believed that one who turned aside from apologetic opportunities involved in friendly contact with non-Catholic scholars was "only a half Catholic." The conservative citadel was the faculty of theology at Catholic University, where Joseph C. Fenton and Francis J. Connell took the lead in viewing the "openness" of the Jesuits as verging on indifferentism. "Polemics" rather than "irenics" was emphasized as the proper approach to error, for any minimizing of the hard sayings of dogma to avoid offense to outsiders was to trifle with the salvation of the faithful.[15] By 1960 the ranks of the "liberals" were swelled by recruits from non-Jesuit orders, new scholarly journals were being published, and a number of Catholic colleges and universities were beginning to be distinguished by the quality of their scholarly contributions and the vigor of their intellectual life.

The Religious Revival

Fulton Sheen and Thomas Merton were two major symbols of the post – World War II religious revival among Roman Catholics. In public esteem Sheen ranked with Billy Graham and Norman Vincent Peale as the preeminent spokesmen of religion during these years. A teacher of philosophy at Catholic University with a gift of speaking intelligibly and convincingly to a mass audience, Sheen gained fame as a radio and television preacher and then as the author of several widely read books. His role in a number of prominent conversions, both before and after being appointed auxiliary bishop of New York, also made him a focus of attention. These conver-

---

[14] D. W. Brogan, U.S.A.: An Outline of the Country, Its People and Institutions (London, 1941), 65; Ellis, American Catholics and the Intellectual Life (Chicago, 1956); O'Dea, American Catholic Dilemma: An Inquiry into the Intellectual Life (N.Y., 1958).

[15] See Fenton, "The Direction of Catholic Polemic," American Ecclesiastical Review, 122 (1950), 48–55; "The Church and God's Promises," ibid., 123 (1950), 295–308; "The Lesson of Humani Generis," ibid., 359–78; and "Catholic Polemic and Doctrinal Accuracy," ibid., 132 (1955), 107–17. See also Connell, "If the Trumpet Give an Uncertain Sound," American Ecclesiastical Review, 118 (1948), 23–30; and "Theological Content of Humani Generis," ibid., 123 (1950), 321–30.

sions, however, did not prevent him from gaining a wide hearing among Protestants as well as Catholics, since he seldom stressed distinctively Roman Catholic doctrine. Merton was a disillusioned sophisticate who had sought peace in many places, including Greenwich Village, and finally found it in the silence of a Trappist monastery in Kentucky. His autobiography, *The Seven Story Mountain* (1948), was on the list of best-sellers for months, and his subsequent writings also aroused widespread interest.

Merton's pilgrimage was part of a striking movement to which his autobiography gave added impetus. Although a Trappist monastery had been established in America early in the nineteenth century, contemplative monasticism, with its vows of perpetual silence and rigorous austerity, failed to prosper in the American environment. At the end of World War II, however, a startling change occurred when hundreds of young men began to forsake the world and give themselves fully to a life of prayer.

The surge of interest in a contemplative life, of course, was restricted to a spiritual elite. A more typical expression of the religious revival was mounting lay participation in the life of the church, much of it associated with the burgeoning parishes of the suburbs. The lay movement was the product of the wedding of traditional American activism with postwar religious enthusiasm and the increased stress of Pius XII on the importance of the lay apostolate. So marked was the development that one clerical observer could speak with confidence of "The Coming Era of the Catholic Layman."[16]

Closely related to the lay movement was a developing liturgical interest that sought to revitalize corporate worship. The religious revival had expressed itself initially among Roman Catholics in the growing popularity of many special nonliturgical devotions — the Forty Hours Adoration of the Blessed Sacrament; novenas to Our Lady of Perpetual Help, Our Lady of Sorrows, Our Lady of Fatima, Our Lady of the Miraculous Medal; and devotions to favorite saints such as St. Ann, St. Jude, St. Anthony, and St. Rita. But attendance at Mass was often little more than fulfillment of solemn obligation. Worshipers frequently had little understanding of the service and sat as mere spectators or performed private devotions by reciting the rosary. This was scarcely an adequate expression of their role as a Christian people or of their lay priesthood, nor did such routine attendance readily relate itself to their apostolate in the world. It was out of concern to renew the life of the church through truly corporate worship that the liturgical movement was born.

The main center of the liturgical revival in American was the Benedictine Abbey at Collegeville, Minnesota, where Virgil Michel was the outstanding pioneer. Through his initiative the periodical *Orate Fratres* (later

---

[16] This was the title of an article by W. R. Fleege in the *Homiletical and Pastoral Review*, 54 (1953), 134–39. For the lay movement, see Leo R. Ward, *The American Apostolate* (Westminster, Md., 1952), and *Catholic Life, U.S.A.* (N.Y., 1959).

known as *Worship*) was founded to promote liturgical renewal. In 1940 annual Liturgical Weeks, conferences for those interested in liturgical renewal, began to be held. In addition to seeking to instruct the faithful in the meaning of the liturgy, two chief goals of the movement were use of the vernacular instead of Latin and adoption of the dialogue Mass in which the people recite the prayers with the priest. Other aims included restoration of the Holy Week Liturgy, encouragement of daily attendance at Mass, and the use of "people's altars" placed in the midst of the worshiping congregation.[17] By 1960 liturgical renewal was receiving widespread support, many innovations had been introduced, and the movement was influencing the architecture of new church buildings.

The Emergence of Hispanic Catholicism

Catholicism originally took root in the Americas through the efforts of Spanish Franciscan, Dominican, and Jesuit missionaries in Mexico and the Caribbean, and eventually in Central America, Peru, and the rest of South America. Financed by the gold-rich royal treasury, over 15,000 missionaries came from Spain to the Americas between 1493 and 1820. The missionary endeavor as a whole was greatly expedited by a proclamation of the crown that every exploration include two priests who were to undertake the conversion of the Indians encountered along the way. The Spanish missions that were thus founded were highly organized centers of learning, agriculture, the arts, and religion. Missionaries learned the native tongues, taught the Indians to read and write Spanish, catechized them, and introduced Spanish ways of farming and animal husbandry. Sometimes the missionaries were extraordinarily successful. At other times they failed to persuade the Indians to convert, and not infrequently they were wiped out by uprisings.

In the course of expanding the mission system, the Spanish developed a tolerance for native religious beliefs and customs. Although they sought to curb practices that they considered idolatrous or superstitious, they nevertheless accepted to some degree the Indians' desire to retain certain aspects of their religious traditions. Accordingly, the Catholicism that developed in Mexico and the American Southwest was marked by the interweaving of local religious custom with Catholic devotions. In Mexico, folk healing and a rich vein of animism survived alongside Catholic doctrine. The widespread display in Mexico of images of the Virgin of Guadalupe, who reputedly appeared to the Indian Juan Diego in 1531, represents something of the supernaturalistic tone and the distinctive emphases of Spanish Catholicism as it developed in the New World.

[17] E. B. Koenker, *The Liturgical Renaissance in the Roman Catholic Church* (Chicago, 1954); P. B. Marx, *Virgil Michel and the Liturgical Movement* (Collegeville, Minn., 1957); A. H. Reinhold, *The American Parish and the Roman Liturgy* (N.Y. 1958).

From Mexico, Spanish missionaries made their way northward to Southwest territories ranging from Texas to California. In these territories, which came into the Union following war with Mexico in 1848, and in Florida, the labors of the missionaries bore fruit for a time. With the arrival of Anglos, however, the Protestant churches rapidly proliferated, so that Catholicism remained dominant only in New Mexico.

In the twentieth century a series of major waves of immigration from the Caribbean, Mexico, and Central America have taken place. Following World War II, Puerto Ricans settled in extreme poverty in New York City, where diocesan officials who did not speak Spanish were ill equipped to incorporate them into church life. Middle-class and professional Cubans who came to south Florida after Fidel Castro's revolution in 1959 adapted more easily to their new surroundings and became a strong Catholic presence. Most important were the many millions of Mexican Americans who flowed continuously into the Southwest in search of economic opportunity. The expanding Spanish-speaking American churches found themselves in a difficult relationship with an Irish-American hierarchy that disapproved of the folk religion aspects of Mexican-American Catholicism. However, as Mexican Americans became more visible, not only in the Southwest but in cities such as Chicago, Detroit, and Atlanta, they exercised a stronger influence on church life, as in the appointment of Patrick Fernandez Flores, a Mexican American, as bishop of El Paso in 1978. But Hispanic churches continue to manifest a distinctive form of Catholicism, which includes not only the aforementioned emphases, but to an increasing extent outspoken advocacy for social and economic justice, and a claim of the right to be different over the demand to assimilate.

Interfaith Relationships

The middle decades of the twentieth century were marked by increasingly friendly interfaith relationships. The National Conference of Christians and Jews, founded in 1928, was one of the instruments for promoting understanding between adherents of different faiths, utilizing local committees to combat prejudice, ill feeling, and strained relationships. Broad Protestant and Jewish support was enlisted, but Catholic participation was extremely limited. Francis J. Connell voiced the prevailing sentiment when he declared that "the association of Catholics with non-Catholics in such organizations and meetings is a grave menace to the faith of our people."[18] This aloofness from interfaith relationships was in striking contrast to the generally warm, friendly, and even cordial attitudes of Protestants and Jews. Even the Eastern Orthodox churches, while main-

---

[18] Cross, *Emergence of Liberal Catholicism,* 212.

taining their doctrinal integrity, felt sufficiently secure to accept membership in both the National and World councils of churches. The Catholic
problem was complicated by tension at several points of social policy and
also by an unresolved difference of opinion as to the proper strategy to be
pursued in a religiously pluralistic society.

Although feelings were exacerbated by Roman Catholic intransigence
on issues of public policy, the greatest problem in reducing tension was the
self-imposed Roman Catholic policy of isolation. As the ecumenical movement gained momentum in the 1920s and 1930s, it was hoped that
Catholics would participate. This hope was dashed in 1928 when Pius XI
issued an encyclical on "Fostering True Religious Unity" (*Mortalium
Animos*) in which he declared that it was unlawful for Catholics to "take
part in these assemblies," and that by giving "such enterprises their encouragement or support" they "would be giving countenance to a false
Christianity quite alien to the one Church of Christ." Throughout the
1940s, however, there was growing restiveness at this blanket prohibition.

In retrospect it is clear that a basis for a new attitude was being prepared
by a revival of biblical studies that made it possible to distinguish the
spiritual from the physical body of Christ. This dual understanding of the
church was susceptible of being interpreted to justify regarding Protestants as "separated brethren" and "brethren in Christ." Although European scholars initiated this new type of thinking, a number of American
Catholics recognized the necessity of breaching the wall of ignorance that
separated Catholics and Protestants in the United States. In 1957, when
John A. Hardon published *The Protestant Churches of the United States*, he
noted that Catholics "often have only the vaguest notion of what Protestants believe, how they worship, and what their religion means to them."[19]
Nor was Hardon alone in this concern. In 1955 George H. Tavard published *The Catholic Approach to Protestantism*, and in 1957 Gustave Weigel
contributed *A Catholic Primer on the Ecumenical Movement*.

The elevation of Angelo Giuseppe Roncalli to the chair of Peter as John
XXIII late in 1958 inaugurated a new era in the Catholic Church. On
January 25, 1959, he announced his intention to summon a General
Council of the Roman Catholic Church to bring the church up-to-date
(*aggiornamento*) through purification and renewal. By opening a few windows he hoped to introduce "some fresh air" into the church and make it
more effective in dealing with the problems of the twentieth century and
provide a basis for furthering Christian unity. When the first session of the
Second Vatican Council convened on October 11, 1962, 17 non-Roman
Catholic churches had responded to an invitation to send "official observers," and the impact of their presence was felt throughout the church.

---

[19] Two years later Jaroslav Pelikan, a Protestant, made a similar admission in the
Introduction to *The Riddle of Roman Catholicism*, stating that many Protestants "know
more about the batting averages of the Yankees or the marriages and divorces of
Hollywood than they do about the life and workings" of the Roman Catholic Church.

In the United States John XXIII's initiatives led to a dramatic shift in the atmosphere of interfaith relationships. Even in terms of pressing social problems there had been little interfaith cooperation, but within a month of the close of the first session of the Second Vatican Council, Protestants, Roman Catholics, and Jews met in a national meeting to chart a common strategy for dealing with the racial crisis. "The bishops were holding back from these meetings out of fear—fear of Rome," one theologian explained. "Now Pope John has given the Church a freedom from fear."[20] The most impressive consequence of the new spirit was the flowering of interfaith discussion in city after city throughout the nation. Reticence gave way to openness and friendliness, and for the first time in more than half a century, Catholic clergy with ease of mind could talk freely with representatives of other faiths about points of difference. Equally impressive was the warmth of the response by clergy of other faiths. No surrender of doctrinal positions was intended or expected, but sympathetic understanding was no longer foreclosed by estrangement.

The several tendencies of growing maturity within American Roman Catholicism—a deepened sense of responsibility to society, a heightened emphasis upon intellectual pursuits, a greater stress on the role of the laity, and an intensified concern for liturgical renewal—had been brought into focus and reinforced by John XXIII and the Second Vatican Council. But this remarkable pontiff, who had been expected to serve only a caretaker role, made a further contribution. By the openness to the "world" he displayed, American Catholics were enabled to shed the last vestiges of an immigrant mentality and with Americans of other faiths they were learning, in the presence of diversity, to live together in a way that was mutually enriching rather than impoverishing. Learning this latter lesson was to be especially important for the years ahead, for both churches and nation were about to enter a troubled time that would tax the wisdom, strength, and resources of everyone.

[20] R. B. Kaiser, *Pope, Council, and World* (N.Y., 1963), 254.

CHAPTER 16

Shattered Hopes and Spreading Disarray

The 1960s began in what seemed to many to be the best of times, but the decade ended in the midst of social turmoil that still larger numbers considered the worst of times. To fully appreciate the change in mood that took place late in the 1960s and early in the 1970s, one must first recall the 1950s as the afterglow of an earlier America.

The Eisenhower years (1952–60) were quiet years of relative affluence and stability. The Korean War ended, Joseph McCarthy was "put down," and most Americans were content to relax and enjoy themselves. Some tumult followed the 1954 Supreme Court decision ordering school desegregation "with all deliberate speed." But even on the racial front, in spite of an emphasis on "deliberate" rather than "speed," there was hopefulness—a confidence that through sit-ins, ride-ins, and legal proceedings steady progress was being made in eliminating discrimination in public accommodations. An important source of calm and hope was President Eisenhower himself. To most people he was a father figure. "We like Ike" was the chant that expressed the majority feeling.

The academic community, to be sure, felt displaced after the heady years of the Roosevelt "brain trust." Their subsequent hero, Adlai Stevenson, had twice gone down to defeat, and "Engine Charlie" Wilson of General Motors was a chief symbol of Eisenhower's "businessmen's government" to which they felt it difficult to relate. Disaffection also surfaced among some theological professors who were critical of the popular "religious revival." Analyses of what was disparagingly called "religion-in-general" ("a passionate faith in the Great Whatever" was William Lee Miller's designation) were accompanied by calls for more substantive renewal than that represented by middle-class piety.

Although the Protestant phase of the post–World War II revival peaked in 1957, Roman Catholic momentum was maintained for a few more years, pent-up disaffection not being fully released until Vatican Council II relaxed the fetters that inhibited public expressions of discontent. The momentum of Judaism continued and was reinforced by a surge of pride in "Jewishness" that followed an unexpectedly quick victory in the Six-Day War of 1967.

Protestantism's Quest for Meaning and Vocation

Awareness of Protestant acculturation and accommodation led to a loss of sense of vocation among the clergy. Not being content with a mere housekeeping role of maintaining the institutional life of the churches and tutored by theologians of a Barthian stamp, clerical leadership at the end of the 1950s once again embarked briefly on the task of theological recovery, seeking to rediscover in the Christian gospel a source of identity and meaning that transcended its cultural expressions.[1] This endeavor, however, was quickly aborted, partly because it was difficult and arduous and partly because the 1960s began with a new flare of hope for society.

New Cultural Accommodations

The new hope was awakened among some theologians and ecclesiastical leaders by the election of John F. Kennedy in 1960. The striking feature of the Kennedy administration was a change in style. "Intellectuals" from the academic community were brought into the inner circles of government. Kennedy had élan, flair, style. He had a romantic aura—youth, a young and beautiful wife, little children. He became a symbol of hope, not only in the United States but—in contrast to the old men of Europe, Adenauer, De Gaulle, De Gaspari—throughout the world. This change in mood produced a change in Protestantism's quest for vocation. If theological leadership spoke disparagingly of culture-bound religion during the Eisenhower era, it was partly because of disenchantment with existing social and cultural prospects. With a more hopeful prospect in view and their former reservations dispelled, some of the same leaders turned to the easier task of seeking a vocation for church and clergy within the society and culture that now seemed open to change. The new quest was pursued along several parallel and often converging paths.

In the field of theology the new optimism found most dramatic expression among a small coterie who styled themselves "radical" or "death of

---

[1] An illustration of the attempted theological recovery was the *Christian Faith and Life Series* developed for Presbyterian church school classes.

God" theologians.[2] Although the term *theology* was retained, there was a forthright rejection of the past (theological language, theological categories, and "God-talk") as no longer meaningful, and acceptance of the present (modern man and secular culture) as normative. With existentialism a strong influence, meaning was sought in the present. One spoke of "doing theology" — an emphasis on "style" (standing beside the neighbor) rather than on "substance" (principles, rules, standards). When one engaged in reflection, it was reflection derived from present action and present experience.

If meaning was to be found in the present rather than the past, the vocation of church and clergy had to be present-oriented. This meant for many a shift from theology to sociology. With consciences sensitized to the plight of the disadvantaged, the scandal of discrimination, and the growing stratification and isolation of various segments of society in self-contained residential enclaves, many churchmen became fascinated with the central city as the place where cleavages could be transcended and injustices rectified.

The preoccupation with the city, as explicated by Gibson Winter in 1961,[3] had a double thrust. The first was a romanticizing of the "inner city" as a locus where all kinds of people could be found—a place, therefore, where experimental ministries could foster "congregations" (groups) that would be truly "inclusive." The motivation was anti-elitist as a counter to the exclusivism of existing churches, but in practice this anti-elitism often degenerated into a paternalistic ghetto type of activity. The second thrust spelled out by Winter was specifically elitist, being preoccupied with social management and utilization of technology to transform the metropolis into the New Jerusalem. The vocation of the clergy was to be "change-agents," social engineers, "evangelizing" the structures of society by infiltrating community organizations and planning commissions, as well as penetrating the corporate structures of business and industry and developing cadres among the professions.

The sociological emphasis led quite naturally to a stress on sociological skill as a means of "doing theology" and discovering a meaningful clerical vocation. A popular way of describing this sociological vocation was to speak of clergymen as "enablers" who initiated community change by helping lawyers, doctors, architects, business executives, and others discover their duty and do it.

[2] See the essays by Thomas Altizer and William Hamilton, *Radical Theology and the Death of God* (Indianapolis, 1966); also Paul Van Buren, *The Secular Meaning of the Gospel* (N.Y., 1963), and Joseph Fletcher, *Situation Ethics: The New Morality* (Philadelphia, 1966). For a critique of this type of present-mindedness, see Kenneth Hamilton, *What's New in Religion: A Critical Study of New Theology, New Morality, and Secular Christianity* (Grand Rapids, 1968).

[3] *The Suburban Captivity of the Churches* (Garden City, N.Y., 1961). The emphases were further elaborated by Winter, *Metropolis as the New Creation* (N.Y., 1963), and by Harvey Cox's best-seller, *The Secular City* (N.Y., 1965).

An alternate way of finding a meaningful role for church and clergy in a present-oriented society was to seek it in the field of psychology. This therapeutic Christianity was derived from a variety of cultural ideologies —from Freud, Jung, Fromm, Erikson. But the most immediately influential figure was Carl Rogers, beginning with his *Casebook of Non-Directive Counseling* (1947) and extending to his *Carl Rogers on Encounter Groups* (1970). Multiform and diverse, the development of therapeutic Christianity is difficult to chart, but its general movement is reasonably clear — from the pastor as individual therapist in a one-to-one relationship to a utilization of group dynamics and group process. Beginning with small groups, the progression was to therapy groups, encounter groups, and group marathons. Sometimes contrived chaos was fostered to free individuals from the ordered structures of church life and thus facilitate creativity, innovation, and self-discovery.

Protestant Disarray

Although "faith" had ceased to "abide" (I Corinthians 13:13) for radical theologians and their fellow accommodationists, "love" was still available, and a cultural confidence gave ground for "hope." For William Hamilton two events of January 4, 1965, signaled the final shift from pessimism to optimism: the death of T. S. Eliot, with his wasteland and hollow men, and the inaugural address of Lyndon Johnson, with its depiction of "the Great Society."[4]

Although Hamilton was late in recognizing it, the promise of "the golden sixties" was not to be fulfilled. The 1960s turned out to be a decade when everything began to go wrong. Beginning with the Bay of Pigs fiasco, the Vietnam intervention, the assassination of President Kennedy in 1963 and later of Martin Luther King and Robert Kennedy in 1968, the decade witnessed mounting unrest, discontent, bombings, and burnings. The civil rights movement achieved its initial goals, but instead of diminishing, the racial crisis intensified. Urban programs multiplied, but the problems of the cities became increasingly intractable and desperate.

The new secular emphases and programs of the churches were scarcely calculated to stimulate church renewal and augment religious interest. The reductionism of "secular theology" had scant appeal and little compelling power. Its most provocative slogan — "the death of God" — appeared at face value to be an announcement of the irrelevance of religion. Psychological therapy, moreover, was no monopoly of the church and required no return to church or religion. Therapy groups were everywhere available to those who wished to embark on a process of self-discovery. The "secular city" (Gibson Winter's "metropolis" as the

---

[4] Altizer and Hamilton, *Radical Theology*, 159.

"new creation") thrust was more preoccupied with action than reflection, more interested in power than piety, more concerned with effecting political coalitions than communicating Christian insight. Small wonder that these emphases were more productive of apathy than renewal, of dissidence than growth. After an initial shock, they even failed to titillate the interest of the nonchurch public.

Old-line Protestant churches were thrown into disarray by the misplaced confidence in the culture. With few social achievements to validate them, the secular thrusts of theologians and ecclesiastics had little impact. In 1957, according to a Gallup Poll, only 14 percent of Americans believed that religion was losing influence. A decade later 57 percent held this opinion. In 1970 those who believed religion was losing influence increased to 75 percent. After 1957 church attendance leveled off and then declined. In 1968 ten of the largest Protestant bodies had fewer members than the preceding year. The United Methodist Church, a denomination that once outpaced all others, leaping forward like a brush fire, in 1972 reported a net loss of 518,000 members in the previous four years.

The old-line churches of cooperative Protestantism continued to post declines in membership throughout the 1970s and into the 1980s. Statistics drawn from the 1970 and 1985 *Year Book of American and Canadian Churches* show the losses sustained by the following typical old-line denominations:

Christian Churches (Disciples of Christ) declined 27.8 percent.
Episcopal Church declined 14 percent.
Presbyterian Church in the U.S.A. declined 15.4 percent.
United Church of Christ declined 16.3 percent.
United Methodist Church declined 14.5 percent.

When measured against growth in population, the actual declines were even greater. The American Lutheran Church and the Lutheran Church in America fared somewhat better with a combined loss of 10 percent during the same years, whereas the ultraconservative Lutheran Church–Missouri Synod, its rapid growth checked by controversy, had a 3.7 percent loss.

Roman Catholic Euphoria, Vacillation, and Dissidence

The rate of Roman Catholic growth peaked in 1959. Thereafter a slowly eroding plateau was maintained until 1965, when the erosion accelerated. The decline in accessions was partly obscured and partly arrested by the heady excitement following John XXIII's election to the papal office in 1958, by John F. Kennedy's election, and by the surprising events of Vatican II. Of the three, the Vatican Council (1962–65) had the most important consequences. Not since the Council of Trent in the sixteenth century had the Church been subjected to such transformation. Few aspects of church life were left untouched—shape and language of worship, devotional practices, ecclesiastical administration, relationships to other Christians, attitudes of clergy and laity. Ripples set in motion by the Council ran far and wide.

Euphoria and Vacillation

If Vatican II initiated profound changes in the Church, expectation of change often outran the speed and extent of reform. The response of most American bishops was hesitant and cautious. They were slow to move, partly out of habit and partly because they had other pressing problems. The heady anticipation of reform made the problems seem less pressing to others, but bishops were not permitted the luxury of ignoring urgent day-to-day needs. The Church was in trouble.

A dramatic decline in conversions was paralleled by declines in accessions by birth and immigration. More serious were declines in the number of seminarians and of religious vocations among young women, accompanied by increases in the number of priests and members of teaching orders returning to lay life.[5] Parochial schools also demanded attention. Even with enrollment dropping and schools closing, the loss of low-paid personnel precipitated a crisis, for this meant greater dependence on more highly paid lay teachers. The problem was aggravated by a questioning of the value and quality of parochial education.[6] There also was the problem of parishes left stranded by the shift of Catholic families from slums to suburbs. New churches had to be built in the suburbs, and inner-city churches were left with half-empty houses of worship and inadequate means of support. Thus bishops had to make agonizing reappraisals of priorities and allocation of resources.

The Roman Curia and the National Conference of Catholic Bishops were slow in issuing guidelines for reforms approved by the Council, and individual bishops were often tardy in instituting reforms once guidelines were provided. The "Constitution on the Sacred Liturgy," for example, was promulgated in 1963; but Cardinal Thomas McIntyre of Los Angeles, who believed lay participation distracted attention from "contemplation of the mystery of the Eucharist," kept the liturgical life of Los Angeles unchanged throughout the decade. Most bishops were less laggard, but

---

[5] Seminarians dropped from 48,046 in 1966 to 22,963 in 1972; nuns from 181,421 to 146,914; lay brothers from 12,255 to 9,740.
[6] See Mary P. Ryan, *Are Parochial Schools the Answer?* (N.Y., 1964).

few kept pace with expectations. Eager young priests with enthusiastic support of youthful parishioners took things into their own hands, embarking on liturgical experiments that sometimes took the form of "underground" or "house" churches but more often were unauthorized innovations introduced into regular worship. Official changes were dramatic enough—use of English instead of Latin, freestanding "people's altars" with the priest facing the people, congregational responses, singing of (often Protestant) hymns.

Gradually other reforms were instituted. The laity were given more active roles. Advisory school boards and parish councils were established. Diocesan priests' councils were set up, and in 1968 these were linked in a National Federation of Priests' Councils. In 1966 bishops sought greater coordination among themselves by electing a president of the National Conference of Catholic Bishops.

Dissidence

A curious result of Vatican II is that it created dissidence both right and left. Apprehension was aroused as well as exhilaration and expectation. The "fish on Friday" syndrome is a convenient way to illustrate the disquiet that followed the ending of compulsory Friday abstinence. Of little consequence in itself, "Friday's fish" was of great symbolic importance in distinguishing Catholics from other Americans. When such a symbol is changed, much else is called into question. And alterations were introduced in other areas of symbolic importance. With the changes, gnawing identity anxieties were awakened.

The Latin Mass was symbolically the most important feature of traditional church life, and the introduction of a vernacular liturgy was a point at which conservative opposition first coalesced. The Catholic Traditionalist Movement issued its first manifesto in 1965. Other groups, such as Catholics United for the Faith, were organized. The National Federation of Laymen urged the withholding of funds from parishes that allowed their schools to teach "humanistic" and "Freudian" values. An anomaly of traditionalist dissidence was that it led to open disobedience of Church authority and to blunt criticism of the Pope. Of Paul VI, William Marra of Fordham grumbled: "He looks at all the heresy that is rampant in the chanceries, and all that he can do is weep."[7]

Among "progressives," the vacillation of the bishops also precipitated a crisis of authority. The Church's teaching began to be questioned on subjects as diverse as the Incarnation, birth control, celibacy of priests, and papal infallibility. The issue of obedience was publicly dramatized in 1967 at Catholic University when Charles S. Curran was denied a promotion recommended by the faculty. To the consternation of authorities, this led

---

[7] "Catholic Right," *New York Times*, March 14, 1971.

to a boycott of classes by faculty and students including large numbers of graduate student priests and nuns. The ecclesiastical authorities capitulated and Curran was promoted.[8]

Caught up in a crisis of change, younger priests were unsure of who they were and what they were to do. Responding to this malaise, the bishops in 1967 sponsored sociological and psychological studies to ascertain the scope of the problem. The results were illuminating. Customary devotional practices were being abandoned. Of younger priests, 60 percent did not pray privately each day, 85 percent did not say the breviary each day, and 50 percent did not say it at all. Of those under 35, 87 percent did not support the official teaching on birth control. Sixty percent of all priests did not think divorce was forbidden by divine law.[9]

The identity crisis of priests was accentuated by the relaxing of their psychological isolation. The 1964 decree on "Ecumenism" led to an extraordinary fraternizing with non-Catholics. Some used their new freedom to engage in dialogues and to experiment with "sensitivity" training. Others began to think of their rights, demanding the right to be heard and to elect their own bishops. Others sought relevance by going into the streets. Participating in the civil-rights march on Selma, Alabama, was an exhilarating experience. Even more dramatic were open housing marches in Milwaukee led by Father James Groppi and involving angry crowds, stern-faced police, and multiple arrests. Opposition to the Vietnam war enlisted articulate groups of priests and led to highly publicized acts of civil disobedience. The celebrated folk heroes of the movement were Fathers Daniel and Philip Berrigan.[10]

Members of women's religious orders also were in revolt. At the 1972 Berrigan conspiracy trial, Sister Elizabeth McAlister was a co-defendant. On April 30, 1972, a dozen nuns disrupted a Mass conducted by Terence Cardinal Cooke at St. Patrick's Cathedral in New York City to protest Catholic apathy toward the Vietnam war. The nuns prostrated themselves in the center aisle before the Cardinal until police dragged them from the cathedral and arrested them for disorderly conduct.

Emancipation of nuns began in 1954 with the founding of the Sisters Formation Conference. Small progress was made until the number of sisters dropped alarmingly. Changes were then rapid and startling. There

---

[8] The capitulation was eased by J. E. Walsh's redefinition of a Catholic university's role being "the Church *learning*" instead of being part of the "*teaching* function of the Church." *Academic Freedom and the Catholic University*, ed. Edward Manier and J. S. Houck (Notre Dame, 1967), 109. Twenty years later Curran was again charged with deviation from Catholic doctrine in his ethics courses, and was barred from teaching in that area at Catholic University. He subsequently left that school to teach elsewhere.

[9] Andrew Greeley, *Priests in the United States* (Garden City, N.Y., 1972), 55–56, 65–66; D. P. O'Neill, *The Priest in Crisis* (Dayton, 1968).

[10] See Daniel Berrigan, *No Bars to Manhood* (Garden City, N.Y., 1970), and Philip Berrigan, *Prison Journals of a Priest Revolutionary* (N.Y., 1970).

were changes in garb (street clothes were adopted by some orders) and experiments in living in small groups without a superior. Many wished to be treated as individuals, to be able to relate more freely with outsiders, and to be relevant to their own moment in time. On July 20, 1967, the *Saturday Evening Post* featured an article on "The New Nuns," and in December the cover story of *Newsweek* was "The Nun: Going Modern." In 1972 the National Coalition of American Nuns issued a "Declaration of Independence," demanding full equality in churches, including women priests.

Episcopal authority was in obvious disarray when priests no longer hesitated to criticize their bishops on issues of policy. The Association of Chicago Priests in 1971 publicly rebuked John Cardinal Cody for failing to represent their views at the National Conference of Catholic Bishops. The focus of their anger was his "silence" on the issue of celibacy when he knew from the survey commissioned by the hierarchy that the majority of priests favored optional celibacy.

Most of the laity seemed unaffected by the stress and strain among the clergy. But the cork was out of the bottle, and the froth had begun to fizz. Unlike their grandparents, who docilely accepted the word of their bishops and priests, they were making up their own minds. A 1971 Gallup survey reported these findings. Attendance at Mass was taken less seriously (only 52 percent attended regularly, and 42 percent did not regard absence as a sin); confession was neglected (63 percent had not made confession in eight weeks); 60 percent neither prayed together as a family nor said the rosary as a private devotion; 78 percent believed their children could still be saved if they left the church. Oddly, when confused about what to believe, almost as many relied on Billy Graham as looked to the teachings of the Pope. There was no open revolt. The teachings of the church were simply quietly ignored by many. This was notably true in matters relating to sex. Seventy-five percent of those of childbearing age believed good Catholics could use contraceptives. Nearly half favored liberalized abortion laws, and 60 percent did not believe that a remarried divorced Catholic was living in sin. When reversed, of course, these statistics reveal that large numbers of Catholics still believed and behaved along traditional lines.

Religion on the Periphery

When Nash K. Burger commented in 1971 that, as a result of a "creeping secularism" in religion, "religious book sales and the numbers of titles published have declined," he was reporting past history.[11] If he had

---

11 *New York Times Book Review*, May 23, 1971. He explained that "religious books" had come to offer little more than "secular answers to secular questions."

glanced at publishers' lists for 1971 he would have noted that new religious titles were again flooding the market, and he also could have noted
that magazine articles were reporting the surprising phenomenon of new
religious interest at a time when church attendance was lagging. Outside
the confines of conventional religion, the time of "creeping secularism"
was over. By 1970 this interest had gained sufficient momentum for Sarah
Davidson to speak of it as a "rush for instant salvation."[12]

The 1960s were a time of mounting disenchantment. The Vietnam war
was the major albatross, but equally dispiriting was the crumbling enthusiasm of youthful idealists when they discovered that idealism had its own
potential for explosions of pent-up anger and rage. Earlier "beatnik"
disaffection with an affluent culture was vastly augmented as the disenchanted adopted changing styles of dress and behavior as symbols of
dropping out of established society. But even the counterculture bred its
own disillusionment when the euphoria of the 1969 Woodstock "rock"
festival was followed by the wanton murder of an innocent bystander at
Altamont. Small wonder that many began to look inward for meaning,
seeking it on the periphery in a home-brewed medley of occult lore, in
mystic teachings of itinerant gurus from the East, or in a new Jesus cult
among the street people. Many of the groups on the periphery originated
in California, where unconventional religions had long flourished.

The Pursuit of Private Heavens

Fascination with astrology, spiritualism, psychic prediction, and a mixed
bag of prescriptions for meeting personal needs — including notions of
reincarnation and astral projection (out-of-body travel) — was not new in
America. Psychedelic and drug-induced consciousness-expanding experiments also had been practiced by Timothy Leary and others, including
Aldous Huxley in California. Witchcraft, as a nature religion and fertility
cult, had ancient rootage. Even the Scientology of L. Ron Hubbard ("the
bridge to total freedom and total power") had connections with nineteenth-century healing fads. And Oriental religions had intrigued Americans since the 1893 World's Parliament of Religions.

After World War II the practice of the occult arts became big business,
but it was primarily addressed to senior citizens. What was new in the late
1960s was a surge of interest and a shift in clientele from age to youth, the
occult having developed great attraction for the under-25 generation and
their folk heroes. Although Jeanne Dixon was the most publicized psychic,
Wanda Moore, a self-styled "Aquarian Child," was more typical of a
glamorous new breed of spiritual counselors. Mascot of a California mo-
torcycle gang, Wanda turned up in Greenwich Village in 1967 to found a
"hard rock" psychedelic club. After six months she retreated to New

[12] *Harpers*, 243 (July, 1971), 41.

Jersey to practice Yoga and immerse herself in occult lore, putting together a patchwork quilt of many things and returning a year later as the New Age Wanda, psychic advisor to the throng of under-30 entertainers and musicians. Others of the occult "glamor elite" practiced witchcraft, including Louise Huebner, official witch of Los Angeles county, and Sybil Leek, author of *Diary of a Witch*. Some younger devotees, turned off by the monetary demands of the professionals, practiced a do-it-yourself religion with accoutrements purchased from occult emporiums. Often they formed rural communes, the nature–religion emphasis of witchcraft being congenial to their concerns.

Less home grown than the occult pursuit was the response to gurus from the East who came to the West with new methods to pursue the quest for private heavens of personal religious experience. In 1968 attention was riveted upon Eastern alternatives to Western religions by the happy guru Maharishi Mahesh Yogi, whose picture adorned the covers of popular periodicals as a result of captivating the interest of Mia Farrow, Shirley MacLaine, the Beatles, the Rolling Stones, and 15,000 lesser mortals with his Spiritual Regeneration Movement. His prescription for "cosmic consciousness" was to practice "transcendental meditation" twice daily for 30 minutes. More colorful were saffron-robed adherents of Hare Krishna, shaven-headed boys and sari-clad girls who gyrated on street corners to the tinkling of little cymbals. Zen Buddhism was a less flamboyant method of seeking enlightenment. Those who turned to Indian mysticism often had used psychedelic drugs for mind expansion and experience beyond normal consciousness, but the path of Zen usually was taken by those who experienced emptiness in ordinary life and yearned for an inner mystical experience that would restore meaning to their existence.

The Jesus Cult

No one knows where or when it began, but by 1967 there were traces of reviving interest in Jesus among the "street people," "cop-outs," and "trippers" of California. Perhaps it began with rock music. The turning of rock to protest themes led to secularized religious themes to express and convey messages of alienation. The rock musical *Hair* had religious overtones. These became explicitly Christian themes in *Jesus Christ Superstar* and *Godspell*. Then "Amazing Grace" and "O Happy Day" hit the top of the charts.

New Christians among hippies, flower children, and drug addicts quickly became known as Jesus Freaks or Jesus People. They were a variegated lot, having no common origin. Although there were spontaneous beginnings elsewhere, the Jesus cult first gained public attention in California. An early group in San Francisco was related to Ted Wise, a sail maker from Sausalito who had been deeply involved in drug use. Late in 1967 he established a coffee house known as The Living Room, forerunner of a commune called The House of Acts. Then Lonnie Frisbee founded a similar commune in southern California, The House of Miracles. Members of these groups dispersed to New Knoxville, Ohio; Rye, New York; and Eugene, Oregon, to extend the influence of the Jesus Way.[13]

By 1970 there were Jesus groups everywhere, representing a surprisingly wide range of ideology. The appeal of Jesus to youth who had become apathetic to organized religion was not unlike the appeal of Oriental religions to some of their friends. With a pervading sense of emptiness and futility, they found in simple gospel texts meaning and direction that released them from drug-oriented routes of escape. Their new commitment, although it did not change their counterculture lifestyle, did result in a shift to sober, disciplined living, coupled with new excitement and purpose. Although diverse, Jesus people shared some common emphases: a nonintellectual insistence on the simple gospel, a belief that they were living in the last times, an espousal by some of pentecostal gifts, a tendency toward communal living, a bias against organized Christianity, a utilization of the music and vocabulary of the youth culture.

It is difficult to assess how many were involved with the Jesus people. There was much coming and going. For some it meant no more than the first step in going back to Kansas, back to a more conventional life. But numbers were not as important as influence. As a result of media attention, Jesus definitely was "in." He even became commercial, and organizations of conservative bent capitalized on the new interest.

The Authoritarian Strain

The Children of God, founded by "Moses" Berg, began as "Teens for Christ" in Huntington Beach, California, in 1968 and demonstrated the appeal of intensely rigid authoritarian discipline. When acutely distraught "flower children" discovered that the counterculture of the street provided little support, it is not surprising that some retreated to the security of a group gathered about a dictatorial father figure. Bluntly anti-establishment and legalistic, the Children of God demanded complete separation (including rejecting their parents) from the world that was soon to perish.[14]

In addition to the Children of God, there were two other rigidly authoritarian groups that gained notoriety in the 1970s. One such group gained worldwide attention in 1978 with a macabre murder-suicide ritual in Jonestown, Guyana. Jim Jones had gathered poor blacks and white social activists in to his Indianapolis People's Temple, moving them in 1965 to

---

[13] See R. M. Enroth et al., The Jesus People (Grand Rapids, 1972).
[14] The date for the end most recently predicted by them is 1993.

rural Redwood Valley in California. A Stanford Law School graduate joined the Temple in 1969 and helped facilitate a move to San Francisco. The People's Temple had a different clientele from the Children of God, garnering its followers not from among the "flower children," but from among those who had been active in civil-rights marches, anti-Vietnam demonstrations, and organizing farm workers. They turned to the charismatic leadership of Jones as a last hope for securing a more humane and just society. The discipline of the Temple was intense. Jones patterned his style of leadership after Father Divine, becoming the personification of God. This may have helped cloak his growing paranoia. In 1973 an agricultural commune was established in Guyana as a refuge from a hostile world, a venture that ended on November 18, 1978 with mass suicide and slaughter.

A third and more stable authoritarian group was generally known as the "Moonies," members of the Reverend Sun Myung Moon's Unification Church. Moon, a Korean, founded his Holy Spirit Association for the Unification of World Christianity in 1954, mingling messianism with anti-Communism while amassing a private fortune. In 1973 he shifted his primary base to the United States, being preceded by emissaries who sought converts by warning of the approaching doom of America because of crime, alcoholism, drug abuse, college radicals, and Communists. Later, at a "God Bless America" rally in Yankee Stadium, Moon said that his purpose was to restore confidence in the American dream.

More was involved than the American dream. As the self-proclaimed Messiah commissioned by Jesus on a Korean mountainside to finish his task, Moon's teachings were to be accepted unquestioningly as divinely revealed. Aided by a Stanford graduate as director of training, Moon won recruits not from the "street" but from psychologically troubled middle-class youth who had yet to make a break with home and family. Enticed by fellow students to conferences where they were surrounded by loving concern, potential recruits were persuaded to attend marathon training sessions that left them exhausted and scarcely able to think for themselves. God's plan for salvation was spelled out, and they were offered one last chance for salvation. Moon was called "father" and his command was: "What I wish must be your wish." When parents objected, recruits were taught to regard them as agents of Satan. Ever smiling and neatly dressed, Moonies were conspicuous as they solicited money for vague humanitarian causes.

Beyond the fringe of conventional religion in the United States, there always have been groups based on fresh revelations and authoritarian leadership. Some of them — most notably the Mormons, the Seventh-day Adventists, and Jehovah's Witnesses — survived and prospered in the years following World War II, even winning adherents worldwide, and their momentum increased in the 1970s and 1980s. None of these three, of course, would be happy to be placed in a classification with the others, for they have little in common beyond illustrating the appeal of self-enclosed groups in an uncertain world.

For Jehovah's Witnesses, the 1970 and 1985 issues of the *Year Book of the American and Canadian Churches* indicate a dramatic increase of 91 percent for a total of 428,046 adherents in the United States, but some say that this does not take into account recent losses. The Church of Jesus Christ of the Latter-day Saints (Mormons) with 3,602,000 members maintained its remarkably rapid growth, posting a gain of 65 percent for the same comparable period. Seventh-day Adventists had a 56 percent gain and a membership of 623,563.

Intramural strife was present within both the latter groups. The issue for Seventh-day Adventists was: What happened in 1844? (See Chapter 3.) Did Christ enter the heavenly sanctuary at that time to begin judging people in preparation for his return? Or did he begin raising up a people as a prerequisite to his return? The issue was raised in 1979 by an Australian scholar, Desmond Ford, at the Adventists' Pacific Union College in California. He insisted that the latter doctrine was necessary to sustain the worldwide outreach of the church. The hidden agenda was the exact authority of Ellen Gould White. One scholar phrased the question: "Are we prepared to test Mrs. White by the Scriptures?" A year later the official answer was given when Ford's ministerial credentials were withdrawn.

Mormons achieved the height of respectability following World War II as a thoroughly American church with a claimed rootage far in the American past. Although its growth was worldwide, it projected an image of all-American young men and women—clean shaven, well dressed, and devoted to the virtues of honesty, diligence, thrift, sobriety, and obedience—as they spread out across the nation from their Utah heartland. Both the church and its members prospered, the latter achieving high posts in business, industry, and government. Still, Mormons were troubled by gnawing problems. The disturbing issue of the place of blacks in the scheme of salvation was partially solved in the 1970s. But the ejection from the church in 1982 of some housewives and mothers who spoke out against the church's organized opposition to the Equal Rights Amendment indicated that the church was not ready to yield to public opinion on every issue. A more serious problem was posed in 1985 by some bombings that were related to the surfacing of letters (later proved to be fraudulent) that raised questions about Joseph Smith's early life and his later account of the finding of the golden plates.

Religion, Nature, and Health

Nature Religion and Holistic Living

In the nineteenth century, Americans had shown considerable interest in religions that were focused on health, especially those that featured "mental healing." In the 1960s that interest re-emerged as a manifestation of "nature religion."[15] Nature religion in America was not an institutional religion or an organized denomination; nature religion was not characterized by a set system of rituals or by systematic theology or by the presence of seminary-trained leaders. It was essentially a perspective on nature, a recognition of a religious dimension to nature, that generated a wide range of behaviors and practices.

Nature religion had deep roots in the nation's past and had appeared in many forms, ranging from Puritan awe at the wilderness of the New World to twentieth-century revivals of pagan religions (from the Latin word *paganus*, which refers to a person from the countryside).[16] We might speak of Henry David Thoreau's experiment at Walden Pond as a form of nature religion. The same could be said of the lifelong mission of the naturalist John Muir. The numerous nineteenth-century attempts to articulate a sense of cosmic order based on theories about magnetism, electricity, and mesmerism likewise were species of nature religion. And the health-reform movements of the nineteenth and twentieth centuries—with their emphasis on diet, on clean living, on balance and harmony in everyday life—embodied a strongly religious perspective on nature. Sometimes, as in the case of nineteenth-century reformer Sylvester Graham (who invented a cracker that still bears his name), a religious perspective on nature was expressed against a background of Christian ideas.[17] In other cases, non-Western, folk, or Native-American traditions served as vehicles to express that sensibility.

"Holistic health" emerged in the 1960s as one form of nature religion, particularly in its incarnation as the "health-food movement." As Americans became increasingly conscious of ecological issues, and as "country living" acquired symbolic power over urban life, so did "natural foods." If the slogan of the nineteenth-century migration from rural America to the city was "The country for health, the city for wealth," so too was it an accurate expression of the attitudes of health-food advocates in the 1970s, but with the emphasis reversed to reflect the desirability of communing with nature and the physical and moral corruption of urban life. The religious dimension to the movement was apparent in the fact that many natural foods stores were operated by religious groups, and particularly by those that favored the wisdom of the East. But the movement had a distinctly moral tone to it as well, as evidenced by the best-selling natural

---

[15] Catherine Albanese, *Nature Religion in America: From the Algonkian Indians to the New Age* (Chicago, 1990), proposes the term and I have adopted it here. She writes that "the term nature religion is my own name for a symbolic center, and a cluster of beliefs, behaviors and values that encircle it" (p. 7). She identifies numerous and varied manifestations of nature religion, ranging from early America attitudes toward the wilderness to twentieth-century holistic health movements.

[16] See Margot Adler, *Drawing Down the Moon: Witches, Druids, Goddess-Worshippers, and Other Pagans in America Today* (Boston, 1986).

[17] See Stephen Nissenbaum, *Sex, Diet and Debility in Jacksonian America: Sylvester Graham and Health Reform* (Westport, Conn., 1980).

foods cookbook *Diet for a Small Planet,* wherein a moral argument about the most efficient use of grain to feed the world's hungry was coupled with meatless recipes. Organically grown fruits and vegetables became, in this atmosphere, more than pesticide-free nutrition. They symbolized American rediscovery of a harmonious relationship with nature.[18]

The health-food movement was an example of the "wellness" approach that often was associated with holistic health. That is, it was predicated on the belief that a proper diet and style of living would prevent illness, improve the quality of life, and promote moral behavior. Other movements associated with nature religion were focused not as much on wellness as on healing of disease. One such movement, Reiki, which began in Japan and became popular in America in the 1970s, was founded on the belief that a properly trained healer could serve as a conduit for a lifeforce energy to flow into a diseased person. The cure of a person's illness in this way, through the mediation of a Reiki master, was understood to be the consequence of a process of bringing harmony and balance into the body and the mind. Healing was understood essentially as a process of "attunement" to natural energy.

Other forms of spiritual healing besides Reiki — such as gemstone (crystal) healing, shamanism, Swedenborgian movements, and so forth — were a part of the religion of the "New Age," which began to take shape in the pages of the Boston *East-West Journal* in the early 1970s, and from there took root among the middle class and especially among upwardly mobile adults. New Age discourse, which featured an emphasis on cosmic harmony, quantum physics, and personal openness to spiritual energy, provided a twentieth-century framework for the reconstitution of nineteenth-century spiritualist impulses.[19]

Development of a Health Ministry

The involvement of the mainline denominations in health concerns had been well established since the mid-nineteenth century, when immigrant Irish Catholics and German Lutherans began constructing their own hospitals. Presbyterians, Baptists, Disciples, Methodists, and Seventh-day Adventists likewise founded a wide-ranging network of sanitariums and health-care institutions shortly thereafter. These denominations viewed their roles first of all as providers of medical care, but they conceived that enterprise as one wing of their overall ministry, so that the hospital served as a setting for the exercise of pastoral care of a specifically religious sort as

[18] David J. Hofford, "Contemporary Folk Medicine," in *Other Healers: Unorthodox Healing in America,* ed. Norman Gevitz (Baltimore, 1988), 222.
[19] Gordon Melton, *Encyclopedic Handbook of Cults in America* (N.Y., 1986), 108, 116; Meredith G. McGuire with Debra Kantor, *Ritual Healing in Suburban America* (Brunswick, N.J., 1988); Robert C. Fuller, *Alternative Medicine and American Religious Life* (N.Y., 1989).

well. With the rise of the hospital as a market institution in the twentieth century, however, the denominations gradually surrendered control to business administrators. Consequently, there was a deterioration of the formal connection between religion and the hospital that marked late-nineteenth-century health care.[20]

The denominations by no means lost interest in religion and health, however. Because they continued to view the hospital as an inviting ground for pastoral work, they set about developing pastoral clinical education programs that trained counselors to appreciate the therapeutic aspect of ministry. Drawing on theoretical works about religion, psychology, and healing—such as Rollo May's *Art of Counseling* (1939), Carl Rogers' *Counseling and Psychotherapy* (1942), and Erich Fromm's *Psychoanalysis and Religion* (1950)—some Protestant theologians advocated the exploration of religion itself as therapy.

By the 1960s, the pastoral counselor who blended psychological and sometimes medical training with a religious perspective on health had become a fixture in the health-care (and especially mental health) field. In the 1950s, the National Institute of Mental Health reported that among persons who pursued counseling for their emotional disturbances, 42 percent first turned to their ministers for help. This impulse rapidly was translated into a process of institutionalizing the minister's role in such cases, with 149 pastoral counseling centers established by 1963.[21] The 1970s and 1980s witnessed further enlargement of an educational infrastructure for the training of pastoral counselors. Although such training revealed some sympathy with the mentality of New Age religion, in most cases it nevertheless remained rooted in theological orthodoxy. This was partly a consequence of warnings by theologians that the goal of therapy was compatible with, but not identical to, traditionally religious concerns about faith and morality.[22]

As religion and health increasingly were linked in both theory and practice, Americans also spoke more of death. The popularity of works such as Elizabeth Kubler-Ross' *On Death and Dying* (1969) and the wide circulation of accounts of "near-death experiences" in the popular press signaled a departure from previous habits of "evasion and concealment"[23]

---

[20] E. Brooks Holifield, *Health and Medicine in the Methodist Tradition* (N.Y., 1986); Paul Starr, *The Social Transformation of American Medicine: The Rise of a Sovereign Profession and the Making of a Vast Industry* (N.Y., 1982). See also the essays in *Caring and Curing: Health and Medicine in the Western Religious Traditions*, ed. Ronald L. Numbers and Darrell W. Amundsen (N.Y., 1986).

[21] E. Brooks Holifield, *A History of Pastoral Care in America: From Salvation to Self-Realization* (Nashville, 1983).

[22] Don Browning, *Religious Ethics and Pastoral Care* (Philadelphia, 1983); Charles Gerkin, *The Living Human Document* (Nashville, 1984).

[23] William F. May, "The Sacral Power of Death in Contemporary Experience," *Social Research*, 39 (1972), 469.

that characterized the American approach to death. Although evasion continued, perhaps most visibly in the rise in popularity of cryonic suspension of the body, there were signs that a new perspective was emerging. Not the least of these signs was the widespread initiation of programs for clergy and laity aimed at developing means to help the dying and the bereaved come to terms with death.

American concern about both health and death intensified during a time in which there was little sense of how all of the various strands of religion in America might join together in such a way as to suggest a new religiously grounded consensus. Lacking the kind of cultural guidance that was available to an earlier generation, frustrated Americans circumscribed their lives a bit more narrowly. Intensely personal matters such as health and death acquired a new prominence, and reflection upon such things formed a large part of the framework for new or resurrected understandings of cosmic harmony and balance.

Although religions of the periphery often gained headlines, their chief significance was that of a barometer indicating a changing climate of opinion. Whatever consensus had existed in the United States as late as the years of the Eisenhower presidency, for good or ill, was gone. Moreover, a radical shift in direction for Roman Catholicism and for a growing segment of Protestantism was taking place at the end of the 1970's and the beginning of the 1980s. Both were marching to the beat of new drummers. Among Roman Catholics official leadership took the initiative in an attempt to restore order and authority in the church. Among Protestants, a more vocal type of grass roots sentiment, responding to a new breed of leadership, was fracturing Protestantism in a more decisive way than had been true previously.

CHAPTER 17

The New Pluralism and the Search for Consensus

The 1960s, like the 1860s, constituted a watershed between an old and a new America.

Sydney Ahlstrom viewed the decade of the 1960s as marking the end of the Protestant epoch in American history. He saw it as the end of a long process in which many factors were involved, including immigration from non-Protestant lands.[1] Catherine Albanese, in a similar vein, spoke of the 1960s as the years when the cultural dominance of Protestantism was brought to a decisive closure. Protestantism, she noted, had provided the foundation for a system of myths and rituals as well as a code of belief and behavior that was acceptable to the large portion of the populace, even to adherents of other faiths.[2] For more than a century and a half this lingering cultural consensus helped bind the many into a sense of being one people, surviving even the trauma inflicted by the Civil War. Whatever the consensus was called, it fell apart late in the 1960s and early in the 1970s and, for the first time, the United States became a truly pluralistic society.

There always had been religious diversity in the United States, a diversity that, if not always welcomed, at least was accepted, protected by the Constitution, and often celebrated as the chief glory of the Republic. But it was a diversity within the context of what Crevecoeur called a new creation — the American. The motto on the great seal *E pluribus unum* (out of many, one), with an emphasis on the *unum*, was the ideal, and in

---

[1] *A Religious History of the American People* (New Haven, 1972), 967–68, 1093–94. Robert Handy suggested that the disestablishment of "the voluntary Protestant establishment" occurred during the 1930s and was confirmed and became fully self-evident in the 1960s. *A Christian America*, rev. ed. (N.Y., 1984), 185–210.

[2] Catherine L. Albanese, *America: Religions and Religion* (Belmont, CA, 1981), pp. 247–281.

many ways it reflected a reality. The concept of denominationalism, with the stress on things held in common, was the basis on which most Protestants adjusted their differences and learned to live together in friendly rivalry. With some lapses, this mode of accentuating commonality was extended to include non-Protestant faiths. Will Herberg, as late as the 1950s, spoke of Protestantism, Catholicism, and Judaism as constituting three acceptable ways of being an American.[3] What all held in common was a feeling of being Americans bound together, not only by an acquired cultural consensus, but by what has been analyzed as civil religion or a religion of the Republic with its own cherished myths, traditions, beliefs, and vocation.

What was new about the new pluralism, it was commonly observed, was that it covered a much broader religious spectrum. The new pluralism was usually depicted in terms of additions to the mosaic of religion in America and to the increased visibility of some old components. The stress also was often placed upon the inclusion of faiths from outside the Judeo-Christian tradition.

It is true that this was one aspect of the new pluralism. An imposing mosque on Massachusetts Avenue in Washington, D.C., adjacent to the residence of the papal delegate, was testimony to the growing presence of Islam in the United States. Elsewhere Buddhist temples served as reminders of the influx of population from Asia. Eastern Orthodox Christianity also was more visible. Both a Greek and a Russian Orthodox church, as well as the national Episcopal cathedral, graced the upper end of Washington's fashionable embassy row. Mormons, with multiplying "stakes" (churches) throughout the land, followed the example of other faiths and built an eye-catching temple overlooking the nation's capital from the hills of Kensington, Maryland. And other groups, once peripheral, were more visible. The religious spectrum was much broader. But the important aspects of the new pluralism were the fracturing of the once-dominant Protestant coalition, and the separatist tendencies within other traditions that shared in the general cultural consensus.

Separatist Tendencies

In a world of change and uncertainty when a sense of stability and well-being are in short supply, separatist tendencies appear. People seek security by withdrawing from the uncertainties of the larger society in search of roots among those who can provide them with a sense of belonging, meaning, and mutual support. Times of uncertainty are times for the closing of ranks around small centers of community, times for the gather-

---

[3] *Protestant-Catholic-Jew* (Garden City, N.Y., 1955).

ing of clans. Martin Marty spoke of this as the tribal instinct,[4] the quest for an intimate bonding that existed in a real or imaginary past.

There was much fragmentation and small-scale clustering during the turbulence of the 1960s, but the first major defection was within the black community. Martin Luther King had marshaled a mass following under the banner of a theology of reconciliation. But in the years after 1966 when Stokeley Carmichael raised the cry of "Black Power" during James Meredith's march to Jackson, Mississippi, an independent course began to be pursued that, unlike the emphases of King, had few affinities with traditional theology. Labels were changed. Negro theologians became black theologians. The stress was on black pride, black church, black religion, black theology, black liberation. The look was back to Africa for "roots," and Afro-American studies became a respected academic discipline.

Two major spokesmen for the theology of black liberation were Albert B. Cleage, Jr., and James H. Cone.[5] Cleage, with a black Christology brought into focus in his Church of the Black Madonna in Detroit, sought to bring black religion into the service of political action, economic pressure, and black separation. Cone related a theology derived from black experience to biblical themes — the bondage of the Israelites in Egypt, the oppression of Christians under Roman rule, the manifestation of Jesus as the Black Christ. Black theology was a strategy for freeing the black mind from beliefs and attitudes that frustrated the thrust for liberation. The cause of liberation took priority over any suffering servant claim of the gospel. "Black theology must say: 'If the doctrine is compatible with or enhances the drive for black freedom, then it is the gospel of Jesus Christ. If the doctrine is against or indifferent to the essence of blackness as expressed in Black Power, then it is the work of the Antichrist.'"[6]

Black liberation theology had great influence, especially in theological schools, but it did not go unchallenged. Others, no less concerned with black awareness, self-esteem, and liberation, held fast to Martin Luther King's vision of a redeemed society of mutual reconciliation. Still, even this involved a degree of separation as a prerequisite to full mutuality.

Few people were more wedded to the American tradition of liberty, both civil and religious, than the Jews; and few exhibited more idealism and compassion for the rights of the underprivileged. They constituted an important component of what has been referred to as the cultural consensus. Although widespread euphoria was generated among Jews by Israel's speedy triumph in the Six-Day War of 1967, a few, most conspicuously in Brooklyn, were less than euphoric. They were more concerned with their immediate situation. Crime in the streets had become common

[4] *The Public Church* (N.Y., 1981), 113–22.
[5] See Cleage, *The Black Messiah* (N.Y., 1968), and Cone, *Black Theology and Black Power* (N.Y., 1969).
[6] Cone, *Black Theology and Black Power*, 121.

in America, and the push for integration precipitated many forms of backlash. Both were present in Brooklyn where Jewish neighborhoods were in transition and hazardous places to live, while "affirmative action" policies threatened the security and advancement of Jews long entrenched in the school system. What made Brooklyn distinctive was not that the backlash was more intense than elsewhere. It was the historical dimension given the plight of the Jews by Rabbi Meir Kahane who, not willing to be intimidated, organized the Jewish Defense League in 1968 with the slogan "Never again." Too long, he insisted, Jews had responded passively to threats to their existence.

Kahane's language and tactics embarrassed leaders of the Jewish community and found scant support among the rank-and-file. But there was a growing feeling of the precariousness of life, a feeling that was reinforced by Israel's near defeat in the Yom Kippur War of 1973. The consequence among some Jews was a shift to conservative politics, in both domestic and foreign policy. And among other Jews there was a stronger emphasis upon Jewishness and Jewish roots.

Eastern religious traditions also became more clearly defined in America during this period of time. With the liberalization of immigration laws in 1965, large numbers of Asians came to America. By 1985, there were over a half-million Asian Indians who had settled in America, 800,000 Japanese Americans, and over a million Chinese Americans. In addition, a great many people left Southeast Asia for American cities such as Lowell, Massachusetts, where the Cambodian and Laotian population grew from a few thousand in 1980 to nearly 30,000 by 1990.

Religion was one of the principal means by which Asian Americans have kept alive their heritage. The richly textured belief systems of Hinduism, Shinto, Buddhism, and Confucianism, including the religious calendar of celebrations and rituals, connects Asian immigrants to their roots and fosters community among them in their adopted country. Japanese and Chinese Americans tend toward folk religion more than to the formal organization of churches. Like Indian Hindus in America, they view the extended family as the primary social context for the practice of their religion.

Like black Christians and Jews who were following their own independent paths, Asian immigrant groups established distinct religious identities for themselves as they became more settled in America. As they did so, a radical shift in direction was taking place in the traditionally white segment of Protestantism and in Roman Catholicism.

The Fracturing of Protestantism

The parts of Protestantism that were growing during the 1970s and 1980s had a distinctly conservative cast, and they were located outside the official structures of the long-established denominations. Southern Baptists were one exception. With their own brand of regional and Baptist identification, Southern Baptists had surged forward after 1920 to become the largest Protestant body in the United States. After 1940 they became increasingly noncooperative. Although many were unhappy with this trend, by the 1970s Southern Baptists, victims of a power struggle, had begun to move steadily in an extreme fundamentalist direction that brooked no dissent. From the large base of over 11 million members reported in the 1970 *Year Book of American and Canadian Churches*, Southern Baptists posted a 25 per cent gain in the next 15 years. Apart from Southern Baptists, who kept to themselves, new Protestant vitality was represented by parallel and sometimes overlapping movements that had taken on new life after being on the scene since early in the century. These movements were what once would have been called the holiness-pentecostal-fundamentalist fringe of Protestantism. By the 1970s they were commonly referred to as "the new evangelicalism" and "the new pentecostalism."[7]

If the religious landscape looked different at the end of the 1980s, it was partly the result of the new confidence and thrust of the evangelicals — what the press called "the born-again movement." To some the new evangelicalism seemed little more than a renamed, and perhaps reborn, version of the old fundamentalism. There were continuities, including an insistence upon a conversion experience, a reliance upon the authority and reliability of the Bible, and an acceptance of the birth, miracles, and resurrection of Christ as supernatural events. But there were also differences. The movement was less monolithic[8] and more broadly based and more socially respectable. The leadership was better educated and more prone to identify with middle-class America. And there was a strong tendency to identify with overtly right-wing politics.

A growing awareness of evangelical strength led *Newsweek* to label 1976 "the year of the evangelical." This was perhaps a salute to the election of Jimmy Carter as president. But the editors could have cited other evidence. Evangelical book publishers were flourishing, penetrating the commercial book market with titles that reached the top of the best-seller lists. Also, student organizations such as Intervarsity Christian Fellowship and Campus Crusade were eliciting strong student support at a time when

---

[7] During the same 15-year period for which churches of cooperative Protestantism reported losses, the Christian and Missionary Alliance posted a gain of 80 percent; Church of God (Anderson, Ind.), 25 percent; Church of God (Cleveland, Tenn.), 103 percent; Church of the Nazarene, 40 percent. The Assemblies of God led the numbers parade, tripling their membership from 626,660 to 1,992,754.

[8] Many were moderate, irenic, and cooperative. But others were contentious and ready to fight along narrowly defined lines. Some were still proud to call themselves fundamentalists, and some of these believed in "biblical separation," not separation of church and state or separation from the world, but separation of the races.

conventional campus religious groups were dwindling. But the most telling evidence, to the public mind, was the fact that it was becoming almost fashionable to be "born again." The ranks of the reborn included rock stars (Bob Dylan), folk singers (Johnny Cash), and a long list of movie stars, professional athletes, and U.S. senators.

An equally striking manifestation of the turn to conservatism was the mushrooming of the "new pentecostalism" within conventional Protestant denominations and the Roman Catholic Church. For 50 years charismatic gifts of healing, miracles, prophecy, tongues, and the interpretation of tongues (I Cor. 12:1–11) had been the domain of small Pentecostal denominations. But late in the 1950s "the pentecostal experience" began to penetrate major Protestant churches without producing defections. It was primarily a lay movement, informal groups being drawn together by mutual unhappiness with a lackluster spiritual life and a common longing for an intimate experience of God's presence.[9]

In terms of national publicity, the charismatic movement, as it was now called, surfaced in 1960 when sensational treatment was accorded Dennis J. Bennett's announcement to his 2,000-member Van Nuys, California, Episcopal congregation of his "pentecostal experience." Within the decade Presbyterians, Methodists, Lutherans, and Baptists also were involved.

The most important institutional bridge between the old and new pentecostalism was the Full Gospel Businessmen's Fellowship, founded by a wealthy California dairyman, Demos Shakerian. The intent was to provide an opportunity for laypersons in the older pentecostal denominations to promote pentecostal renewal without supervision of denominational officials. Meetings of the fellowship were often held in luxury hotels, and their nondenominational character was attractive to persons in conventional churches who did not wish to sever their old affiliations. Oral Roberts also played a key role in transmitting the old pentecostalism to the new charismatic movement. Ordained by the Pentecostal Holiness Church, Roberts began a fulltime faith-healing ministry in 1948. By 1954 his healing services were being carried live on network television. Determined to spread the pentecostal message more effectively, Roberts became a United Methodist in 1968 and founded Oral Roberts University as the world's first charismatic university. He also erected a 60-story hospital, "the City of Faith," next to the campus as testimony to his emphasis on the health of the "whole person" — spiritual, intellectual, physical, and even financial. In 1980 the *Christian Century* named Oral Roberts as one of the ten most influential religious leaders of the decade.

The eruption of pentecostalism within Roman Catholicism began in 1967 with a lay faculty prayer group at Duquesne University in Pitts-

---

[9] See D. E. Harrell, Jr., *All Things Are Possible: The Healing and Charismatic Revival in Modern America* (Bloomington, Ind., 1975), and Richard Quebedeaux, *The New Charismatics* (Garden City, N.Y., 1976).

burgh. An Episcopalian woman invited them to attend an informal pentecostal prayer group at the home of a Presbyterian woman. Shortly thereafter, early in 1967, four of them received a Spirit baptism. Later, at a "Duquesne weekend," about 30 students were touched by the Spirit. The excitement spread to Notre Dame, Michigan State, Michigan, and other university centers. In the late 1970s 20,000 to 30,000 persons were attending an annual "National Conference on Charismatic Renewal in the Catholic Church" at Notre Dame. Although there was much going and coming between Protestant and Catholic pentecostals, Protestants tended to stress tongues as evidence of the initial baptism in the Holy Spirit, whereas Catholics regarded tongues as one of many possible manifestations of the Spirit.

Evangelical and pentecostal influence was most evident in their successful use of radio and television to reach a mass audience. Seventy percent of religious radio programing and 90 percent of religious television were produced under their auspices. Estimates of the amount of revenue raised by the programs varied from $500 million to $1 billion annually. Whatever the sum, the lion's share was garnered by fewer than a dozen ministries.

The "big league" television programs were individually produced. They included "Pat" Robertson's "700 Club" from Virginia Beach, Virginia; Jerry Falwell's "Old Time Gospel Hour" from Lynchburg, Virginia; Rex Humbard's "Cathedral of Tomorrow" from Akron, Ohio; and Jim Bakker's "PTL Club" from Charlotte, North Carolina. Others with audiences and revenues in the millions were Jimmy Swaggart in New Orleans, James Robison in Fort Worth, and two stars in California— Gene Scott in Glendale and Robert Schuller in Garden Grove.[10] Schuller with his "possibility thinking," derived from his mentor Norman Vincent Peale, was sharply criticized by both liberals and conservatives. Still it is clear that his nationally syndicated television program, "The Hour of Power," strongly appealed to theologically unsophisticated evangelicals.

There were differences among the leaders of the Electronic Church. Some were pentecostals; others steered clear of charismatic gifts. A few were nonpolitical, but most did not hesitate to use their programs to promote right-wing causes that often had no visible connection with religion. The similarities, however, among these electronic superstars were much more striking. All directed their message to upwardly mobile people. All were intensely ambitious. All, except Schuller, perceived themselves as modern-day prophets, fervently ringing a tocsin to warn of a perilously close day of final judgment.

"Armchair religion" was the label some attached to the Electronic Church. Nothing much was demanded beyond mailing in a weekly or

---

[10] Billy Graham and Oral Roberts could be included, but their broadcasts began in the 1950s and were not the central focus of their ministries.

monthly check. Still the influence in shaping the mind set of the listener was tremendous. Although listeners to evangelical television programs could relax religiously in their armchairs, they were exhorted to be active politically. When Hodding Carter reviewed David Broder's *Changing of the Guard* (1980), which analyzed the shifts in political power in America, he noted one striking omission. Nowhere did Broder mention "the newly politicized religious fundamentalists" as a significant influence in "the coming years."[11] Traditionally these doctrinally rigid people had been much less inclined to register and vote than the population as a whole. But by 1980 this was no longer true.

Since the 1950s there had been vocal right-wing, fundamentalist, anti-communist organizations such as Billy James Hargis' "Christian Anti-Communist Crusade" and Carl T. McIntire's American Council of Churches. But not many paid them much attention. What was new in the last years of the 1970s was the development of heavily financed evangelical organizations designed to elect right-wing conservatives to national office.[12] On the West Coast Richard Zone established Christian Voice, which boasted 200,000 active supporters, a mailing list of 5 million names, and a $3 million treasury. And in Texas, where television evangelist James Robison never hesitated to link the gospel to extremist politics, several thousand ministers were brought together from the mid-South in the summer of 1980 to listen to Ronald Reagan and to encourage voter-registration drives.

The largest of these organizations was the Moral Majority, founded in 1979 by Jerry Falwell. Falwell had organized the Thomas Road Baptist Church in 1956, meeting with a humble congregation of 35 faithful in the abandoned Donald Duck Bottling Company building in Lynchburg, Virginia. In television broadcasts of his "Old-Time Gospel Hour," Falwell addressed from a fundamentalist perspective the leading issues of the day, including abortion, the Equal Rights Amendment, prayer in public schools, and civil rights. A national audience responded to his preaching by joining the Moral Majority. By the fall of 1980 it reportedly had nearly a half-million members, claimed to have registered 3 million voters, and signed up 72,000 clergymen to serve as precinct workers in addition to accumulating a million-dollar war chest. As religion mixed with politics in the activities of the Moral Majority and similar organizations, such goals as increasing defense spending, curtailing the powers of regulatory agencies, repealing the Panama Canal Treaty, and reinstating diplomatic recognition of Taiwan became major tests of religious orthodoxy.

[11] *Washington Post Book World* (August 31, 1980), 2.
[12] Not all evangelicals were wedded to right-wing politics. A number of young evangelicals sought to relate biblical faith to the problems of hunger, racism, and sexism through such magazines as *The Other Side, Sojourners,* and *Daughters of Sarah.* See also Robert Webber, *The Secular Saint* (Grand Rapids, 1979).

Evangelical leaders were cultivating grass roots support in ways that the churches, with the exception of black churches, had not done since early in the century. And they were doing it more efficiently by means of computerized technology. Grass roots opinion had been neglected by the politically active leadership of the conventional churches, a neglect that limited their effectiveness as spokespersons in forwarding causes for which they had marshaled only partial support among people in the pews. It was not clear at the outset whether evangelicals would be more successful in turning their flocks into a solid voting bloc. In the end, in spite of running against a highly visible "born-again" Christian (Jimmy Carter), Ronald Reagan in 1980 gained great support in areas of evangelical strength. Evangelical support was even more evident in 1984. An indication of this was the contrasting figures obtained in two surveys of 1,000 Southern Baptist ministers. A 1980 poll revealed that 29 percent of these ministers were registered Republicans. Four years later 60 percent reported that they were registered Republicans.[13]

The politicizing of conservative Protestantism, however, should not be misconstrued as a process whereby fundamentalists were drawn away from their traditional theological orientation. For all of their investment in reforming society, fundamentalists continued to believe in the literal return of Christ in the Second Advent, and they were inclined to interpret geopolitical events according to a religiously grounded scheme that led them to expect the end of the world. Billy Graham had preached regularly about the end since the 1950s and Hal Lindsey's vision of doom in *The Late Great Planet Earth* (1970) sold to millions throughout the 1970s and 1980s. And Jerry Falwell, in "Nuclear War and the Second Coming of Jesus Christ" (1980), predicted that the world would end in 1985, following a period of accelerated decay of traditional values. Millennialism and political action were not easily reconciled, but in the fracturing of Protestantism after the 1960s, they emerged nevertheless as leading features of the conservative world view.

By 1990, the wave of evangelical revival had begun to flatten out. Conservative Protestants, in spite of some victories at the polling place, failed in their bid to transform American politics—a failure confirmed by the ill-fated 1988 presidential campaign of "Pat" Robertson. Some of the strident tone of evangelicalism was lost as Presbyterian, Baptist, and Methodist churches, and even to some extent the Roman Catholic Church, had made some room within their ranks for the "born-again" style of religion. More importantly, the public face of evangelicalism suffered from scandals involving its most visible figures. Jim and Tammy Bakker left the "PTL Club" in disgrace amid charges of sexual improprieties and financial misdealings (the latter resulting in a 50-year jail sentence for Jim Bakker, later reduced). Jimmy Swaggart, discovered in a sexual relation-

---

[13] *Christian Century* (August 14–21, 1985), 729.

ship with a prostitute, confessed to his audience, "I have sinned," and faded into a minor-league ministry. Oral Roberts, threatening that God would "call him home" if he did not raise a large sum of money by a certain date, lost credibility as well.

The enduring influence of conservative Protestantism at the institutional level was to be found in the Southern Baptist Convention, where evangelical conservatives embarked on a successful program of power politics within the denomination. Conservatives eventually gained nearly complete control of the national and state organizational apparatus, including a majority of the denomination's 51 colleges and 6 seminaries. Striking institutional gains also were registered by the Assemblies of God under a variety of names for the local units, and the Church of God in Christ continued to exhibit remarkable numerical growth.

Changing the Guard in Roman Catholicism

The 1978 election of a Pole, Karol Wojtyla, as the first non-Italian bishop of Rome in more than 400 years inaugurated a dramatic reversal in the Roman Catholic Church. Unlike the grass roots turn to conservatism in Protestantism, the return to old ways in Roman Catholicism was imposed from above by the new pope.

John Paul II stood in marked contrast to the conventional image of occupants of the papal office. Much younger, he was bold, colorful, and charismatic in personality. With a quick wit and a keen sense of humor, laughter came readily. He related easily to ordinary people, did not hesitate to lead them in singing folk songs, and established instant rapport with great crowds as well as small groups. He was a poet, a sophisticated philosopher, and a skilled linguist. Above all, he had learned the techniques and discipline needed for the church to survive in the hostile environment of a land under communist rule.

The new pontiff turned his attention immediately to the task of reinvigorating his worldwide flock. His technique was to make dramatic and triumphant visits to carefully targeted countries. In January 1979 he visited traditionally anticlerical Mexico and was followed by millions of people as he toured the nation. In June he overwhelmed Poland, his native land, in an eight-day visit that astonished the world. It was as if he were implicitly challenging the government to interfere. At the end of September he made a three-day visit to Ireland where he was welcomed and heard by over half the population. This was followed by a seven-day, six-city conquest of popular sentiment in the United States. Six months later, in May 1980, he visited six new nations in central Africa. And two months later he was in Brazil for a whirlwind tour of that vast and diverse country.

It was clear that John Paul II was not marching to any drum except his own. Wherever he went he neither shortened his step nor lengthened his stride to accommodate local opinion, and he used every opportunity to spell out how he intended to restore order to the Church. A sympathetic observer commented that he was a man with an open heart but a closed mind. He faced issues without equivocation. He was sensitive to human need but unwavering on matters of doctrine and discipline. He was mild with the faithful but stern with the clergy.

During his visit to the United States, John Paul II spoke sharply against abandoning priestly celibacy and ordaining women. Priestly celibacy is a sign of total consecration to God and a reminder of the loyalty priests owe their superiors in the hierarchy. Nor is the priesthood a proper calling for women, and John Paul urged nuns who had discarded their habits to resume their traditional garb.

Perhaps as compensation for the subordinate role assigned women in the church,[14] the new pontiff made every effort in his travels to revive, restore, and exalt the cult of the Virgin—which had been the center of much popular piety but had been played down following Vatican II. To strengthen devotion to Mary, he made it a point to visit the most prominent shrines to the Virgin, as at Guadalupe in Mexico, the shrine of the Black Madonna in Poland (where he led a half-million pilgrims in consecrating their country to Mary), and at Knock in Ireland. John Paul's concern to give renewed prominence to Mary was also related to her role as a model for women in their day-to-day life as mothers. Strengthening family life was strongly stressed, and the Pope made plain his unswerving opposition to birth control, abortion, divorce, extramarital sex, and homosexual relationships.

In Washington and in Brazil, John Paul met with leaders of other Christian churches. At Chicago he spoke of his desire to pursue the ecumenical vision of Vatican II, but he insisted that Catholic doctrine must not be compromised. Meanwhile, steps were taken at the Vatican to bring theologians into line with teaching that received papal approval. By the end of 1979 members of theological faculties had been put on notice. Hans Küng, one of the most liberal and by far the best-known scholar, was notified that he was no longer recognized as an official theologian and was therefore no longer qualified to serve as a member of the Roman Catholic faculty at Tübingen. Elsewhere scholar-priests were reassigned to different duties. Then, during the next six years, other theologians were rebuked, censured, even silenced.

At the same time, John Paul was using his appointive powers to secure control of the Vatican bureaucracy and to consolidate his hold on the bishops. Those who shared his views were rewarded. John O'Connor of New York and Bernard Law of Boston, who were the two American

---

[14] At Philadelphia, in a special mass celebrated by the Pope for those with a religious vocation, the nuns were seated in the basement with closed-circuit television while the priests were ushered into the sanctuary above.

archbishops to be made cardinals in 1985, were among the most vocal in stating that, because of her qualified stand on abortion, Roman Catholics could not in good conscience vote for Geraldine Ferraro, the Democratic candidate for vice-president. The same issue came into play in attempting to force a number of nuns publicly to retract their views under threat of being expelled from their orders.

For many Catholics in the United States, the Pope demanded radical readjustments. His stand on birth control and divorce ran counter to the practice or opinion of most Roman Catholics. His stand on priestly celibacy was opposed by a majority of both priesthood and laity. His views on the role of women were out of step with the views of many. His lagging approach to ecumenism was foreign to the easy relationships that had developed in the United States. His theological traditionalism was not in tune with the thinking of many scholars in Catholic universities and seminaries. Yet there was little public dissent. Most remarkable was the absence of any discussion of the issue of collegiality in the government of the Church. Certainly there were undercurrents, but publicly the whole movement was in the direction of order and discipline.

Pluralism and the State

The First Amendment Asserted

Americans in the late twentieth century were obsessed with litigation. This should not be surprising, for the cultural consensus that had fostered social cohesion had collapsed. With the end of Protestant domination of American culture, familiar and customary ways of understanding social life were stretched beyond their limit to make sense of the pluraformity of American life. Accordingly, individuals and organizations petitioned the courts for judgments in matters that the previous generation would have considered obvious and undeserving of formal judicial consideration.[15]

Court cases involving religion were among the most significant of the 1970s and 1980s. They were also extraordinarily numerous, compared with every other period in the nation's history. A broad spectrum of issues, ranging from education to employment to reproduction, in which consideration of the religious element played a key role, came before the courts in the two decades after 1970. Such appeal to the courts to decide cases in which religious claims — either explicit or implicit — were at stake already had begun to increase in the 1940s. The process accelerated over the course of the next 50 years as the government and the churches sought to come to terms with the new pluralism. During that time, numer-

---

[15] Robert T. Handy, "Why It Took 150 Years for the Supreme Court Church–State Cases to Escalate" *Princeton Seminary Bulletin* 9 (1988), 32–43.

ous laws that reinforced Protestant morality were challenged, and some were repealed.

In 1920, in deciding against several related cases challenging national Prohibition, Supreme Court Justice White wrote without further comment that Prohibition was a matter "intimately concerning the welfare of the whole people." Thirteen years later, when Prohibition was repealed, Americans had decided that their welfare (as far as consumption of alcohol was concerned) was more properly connected with personal morality than with legal control of their behavior. And by 1940, when the Court began to pay closer attention to issues involving religion, the justices were less likely to view cases in terms of "the welfare of the whole people," and more willing to recognize and protect the freedoms of persons outside the religious mainstream. Such was the case that year when the Court unanimously upheld the right of Jehovah's Witnesses to perform their religious duty of seeking converts through door-to-door solicitation. In short, by the 1940s, the courts had taken a step toward recognizing that not all Americans arranged their lives according to an unwritten code of distinctively Protestant coloration.[16]

In the wake of the cultural upheaval of the sixties, the legal consequences of pluralism for relations between government agencies, religious groups, and individuals became dramatically clear. Laws restricting certain activities on moral grounds (e.g., divorce, sexual practices) were repealed, and courts issued opinions reinforcing the separation of church and state. One of the most striking examples of the new mood was the Supreme Court decision in *Wade* v. *Roe* (1971) that protected a woman's right to seek an abortion in the early stages of pregnancy. By way of that decision, the Court gave notice that it did not find traditional Christian moral arguments about the fetus to be as compelling as the necessity for the protection of the rights and privileges of individuals under the Constitution. In a time of social and cultural turmoil, many Americans turned with hope to the Constitution, and drew from it anew a sense of justice and purpose.

American re-embrace of the principles of liberty and equality underlying the Constitution was manifest in many other court cases besides those involving abortion. In the 1970s a series of cases involving the "free exercise" clause of the First Amendment made their way through the nation's judicial system. These cases illustrated how old and new religious groups alike acquired standing that they previously had not enjoyed. In one instance the Supreme Court affirmed a decision of the Wisconsin court exempting Amish from compulsory high school education. The Amish community always has vigorously distanced itself from the main-

---

[16] National Prohibition Cases, 253 U.S. 350 (1920). Glenn Miller, "Church and State," *Encyclopedia of the American Religious Experience*, ed. Charles H. Lippy and Peter W. Williams, 1388. *Cantwell* v. *Connecticut*, 310 U.S. 396 (1940).

stream of American culture. Amish traveled by horse and buggy rather than by car, rejected buttons for old-fashioned hook-and-eye fasteners on their clothing, and strived in numerous other ways to resist the technological culture of modernity. In the early 1970s, a group of Amish refused to enroll their children in public secondary education. Citing religious reasons for their decision, they argued that compulsory education was in effect a form of forced assimilation. The Court, after considering the Amish way of life and the nature of their alternative informal educational system, ruled that the free-exercise clause of the First Amendment protected their interest in keeping their children at home. In a subsequent case arising in Minnesota, the Court ruled that even the Oliver Wendell Holmes dictum that the need to protect public safety over-ruled the guarantee of free speech was not sufficient to require the Amish to display triangular red reflectors on their horse-drawn buggies at night on main travelled roads.[17]

The Amish had begun immigrating in the early eighteenth century, and so had been a denomination well rooted in America at the time of their dispute over high school education in Wisconsin. Another religious group that became involved in a dispute involving the free-exercise clause was the Unification Church of the Rev. Moon. The "Moonies," unlike the Amish, were new arrivals to America in 1973. But like the Amish, certain of their practices stemming from religious belief marked them as a group outside the mainstream of denominational life. Those practices included a regimen for recent converts that included crowded communal life, relatively few hours of sleep each night, a spartan diet, and long days of work in the streets selling flowers or otherwise producing income for the church. In 1977, a group of parents of Unification Church converts petitioned the court in California for a temporary conservatorship (or guardianship) order over their adult children, who, they argued, had been brainwashed by the church. The court noted the strength of religious conviction on the part of the church members and observed as well that they suffered no "grave disabilities" as far as their physical health was concerned. The style of life that the Moonies chose as a part of their religious faith indeed included behavior that might have seemed extremely odd, and perhaps even self-destructive, to observers whose perspective was derived from their mainstream religious background. But the court strongly affirmed several previous rulings in deciding that any judgment about the content of the faith of the Moonies was beyond the reach of the law. Accordingly, the state was not allowed to interfere in the

---

[17] *Wisconsin* v. *Yoder*, 406 U.S. 205 (1972). The "free-exercise" clause of the First Amendment reads: "Congress shall make no law respecting an establishment of religion, or prohibiting the free exercise thereof."

religious life of the Moonies, and the request for conservatorship was denied.[18]

Decisions such as these helped frame a legal mentality that more vigorously extended First Amendment guarantees to groups that historically had existed on the "margins" of the culture. Against the background of legal support, a host of previously invisible or barely visible religious groups came forward through the 1980s to claim their place in the emerging pluralistic order.

Resistance to a Pluralistic State

The efforts of the courts to accommodate religious groups from outside the mainstream were not welcomed by religious conservatives. In assessing the new state of affairs, most conservatives initially did not seek to place blame on religious groups that had recently become more visible. Rather, they lamented more generally what they perceived as the loss of Judeo-Christian influence in society, of the traditional and reliable ways of their parents. Eventually, however, in their calculation of the negatives arising from social change, conservatives began to assign culpability for the undermining of the spiritual dimension to American life. Their criticisms ranged from Vice-President Spiro Agnew's complaint about persons who were "nattering nabobs of negativity" to outright accusations of heresy. For revivalist crusader Billy Graham, the post-1960s religious scene was a time of "false religions and counterfeit cults," of "false teachers" who used "high-sounding words" to beguile persons into their camp. Other religious leaders used similar language in decrying what they perceived as the de-Christianizing of America. Eventually, most conservatives came to believe that the culprits in the overturning of the old order were not so much the "new" religions as the "secular humanists."[19]

G. K. Chesterton once wrote that America was a "nation with the soul of a church." Trying to understand the collapse of cultural Protestantism, conservative religious leaders concluded that a loosely organized group of irreverent and amoral persons were conspiring to exile that soul. Claire

[18] *Katz* v. *Superior Court*, 73 Cal App. 3d 952, 141 Cal Rptr. 234 (1977). A note on this case observes that "because the courts may not inquire into the wisdom of theological tenets, a conservatorship order, which requires a determination of mental competence, may not be based on an inquiry into the substance of an adult's religious belief" (Note 53 N.Y.U. L Rev. [1978], 1269). See also William C. Shepherd, "The Prosecutor's Reach: Legal Issues Stemming from the New Religious Movements," *Journal of the American Academy of Religion*, 50 (1982), 187–214; David G. Bromley and Anson D. Shupe, Jr., *Strange Gods: The Great American Cult Scare* (Boston, 1981).

[19] Billy Graham, *Approaching Hoofbeats* (Waco, Tex., 1983), 106, 104. The term *secular humanism* became a regular part of conversations about religious change in America after Justice Hugo Black referred to secular humanism as a "religion" (*Torcase* v. *Watkins*, 367 U.S. 468 [1961]).

Chambers of the John Birch Society framed the extreme scenario for such a plot, claiming to have identified "an international subversive movement whose aim is no less than world domination by way of destruction of Christianity, traditional morality, and the whole fabric of society." Members of the clergy, in numerous books and articles, elaborated on that theory. A leading figure of the antisecular humanist movement was pastor Tim Lahaye, whose conservative manifesto, *The Battle for the Mind*, added the explicit warning: "If the present interpretation of church–state separation is followed, the church will soon be excluded from everything meaningful in our lives."[20]

Conservatives actively sought to oppose what they perceived as the secularizing force of the courts, and their opposition was nowhere clearer than in their attempts to set an agenda for public education. The leading issue in their program of educational reform was the teaching of evolution in public schools. Previous Christian Fundamentalist attacks on the teaching of Darwinian evolution — such as the one that ended in the Scopes "Monkey" Trial of 1925 — had proved unsuccessful. Nevertheless, in the early 1980s the matter was brought to a head again in Arkansas. The Christian Right, as it was called during the administrations of President Ronald Reagan, had engineered the passage of an Arkansas statute specifying that "creation science" be taught in the schools alongside evolution. "Creationism," or "creation science," referred to an interpretation of human origins that relied largely on the Genesis account. The Arkansas legislature was not alone in its support for the inclusion of creation science in the high school curriculum. Eighteen other state legislatures either had passed a similar bill or were considering doing so. The movement was grounded, however, when U.S. District Court Judge William R. Overton ruled in 1982 that the Arkansas law violated constitutional provisions for the separation of church and state: "Since creation-science is not science, the conclusion is inescapable that the only real effect of Act 590 is the advancement of religion, the unconstitutionality of which there can be no doubt."[21]

Five years later, when the Supreme Court refused to allow a similar Louisiana statute to stand, the creationist cause was seriously crippled. Nevertheless, the New Religious Right continued to influence federal and state policy in matters involving church and state. Part of the reason for that continued influence was the election of Ronald Reagan and George Bush — candidates strenuously promoted by the Religious Right — and their successes as presidents in placing conservative judges on federal

---

[20] Clarie Chambers, *The SIECUS Circle: A Humanist Revolution* (Belmont, Mass., 1977), 393–94; Tim Lahaye, *The Battle for the Mind* (Old Tappan, N.J., 1980), 207. Martin E. Marty suggests that the term *secular humanism* early on was used by religious conservatives to refer to "non Judeo-Christian values, teachings, etc." (*Context*, November 1, 1985, 1).

[21] *McLean* v. *Board of Education*, 529 Supp. 1255 (E.D.Ark [1982]).

benches and in the Supreme Court. The raw political power of religious conservatives had diminished significantly by the late 1980's, but their indirect legacy—conservative courts—became increasingly important.

At the end of the decade, the courts began to take a less tolerant view of groups that historically had developed outside the mainstream. Characteristic of this mood was the decision in the case of *Oregon Department of Human Services* v. *Smith* in 1990, in which the Supreme Court ruled against traditional sacramental use of peyote by Oregon Indians. In other cases that year, a Christian Science couple was convicted for a role in the death of their son because they chose religious healing (which failed) over hospitalization. Laotian Hmong in Rhode Island lost protection of their right to refuse autopsies on religious grounds. Indian Sikhs and Old Amish, who had been exempted from wearing hardhats under a 12-year-old decision, lost that exemption. Orthodox Jews also suffered setbacks to their religious freedom.

As the nation entered the last decade of the century, it was clear that the conservative struggle against "secularizing" forces had lost some of its momentum. However, it appeared that the movement to actively extend First Amendment protections to all religious groups—which was a leading feature of the 1970s and 1980s—was also losing its momentum.

Pluralism and Passivity

Religious and religio-ethnic groups that historically had been dominated by a powerful cultural Protestantism did not overnight become full partners in public life. Deep-seated resentments remained on both sides, preventing a clear view of the new pluralism as it emerged and inhibiting progress in understanding how pluralism would lead to new expressions of the morals and values of the nation. The problem was complicated by the fact that the mood of the 1970s and 1980s was for the most part not conducive to reflection on the nation's future.

In the latter decade especially, and coincident with the Reagan presidency, Americans were extremely anxious about the prospect of nuclear war. The announcement by a blue-ribbon panel of scientists that a "nuclear winter"—predicted as the consequence of any exchange of missiles—could destroy virtually all life on the planet intensified the atmosphere of doubt and gloom. Secretary of the Interior James Watt shrugged off complaints about his advocacy of commercial use of National Park lands with his own warning that since the end was imminent, parks would soon matter no more. And President Reagan repeatedly portrayed Russia as the "evil Empire" and the "focus of evil" in the world, leaving Americans with little hope for a peaceful resolution of differences with the Soviet Union.

In this context of gloom, Americans were not encouraged to explore the meanings of the new pluralism. Religious groups that had recently

become visible and empowered maintained their efforts to establish themselves as full partners and participants in public life. But the general mood
was one of passivity. There was not the kind of creative ferment that took
place in the years following the Great Awakening, or during the emergence of Jacksonian democracy in the early nineteenth century. Reflection
about religion and the nation (where it was present) followed the contours
of the dominant economic doctrine of the period: The assumption was
that religious groups, like individuals, would each fend for themselves,
and that from that activity, the good of the whole would emerge. There
was widespread belief in the importance of religion, but little or no
interest in discovering how *differences* between religious groups arose or
were sustained, or might contribute positively to the well-being of the
nation.

From Many, Toward One

Disenchanted with many aspects of American life and having forgotten
how they had adjusted to ecclesiastical diversity and then to a growing
religious pluralism, Americans in the latter quarter of the twentieth century were confronted with a pluralism more widespread, diverse, and
variegated than anything they had encountered before. What are to be the
bonds uniting so diverse a population?

With many questioning what had been cherished values and having
been disabused of any sense of American mission, how is the United States
to recover a sense of nationhood that unites rather than divides the
American people? The old Hebraic themes may no longer be ample
enough to accommodate so heterogeneous a population. New themes may
need to be identified and elaborated with clarity and persuasiveness,
related to the American past, and spelled out in appropriate myths and
rituals. Both the recovery of health by the churches and the restoration of
a sense of nationhood constitute unfinished business on the agenda of the
American people.

A cultural consensus that will bind the many into a sense of being one
people will not easily be achieved. It is not something that can be imposed
by legislation. In a free society so heavily dependent upon voluntary
obedience, only by moral suasion and free assent can any viable consensus
be reached. Churches and congregations of various religious persuasions
will need to participate. Some tribal groups will survive as enclosed societies, but most tendencies toward tribalism must be mitigated by a degree
of openness in the public sphere. Consensus can only be the product of a
long process.

The old-line churches of cooperative Protestantism are beginning to
regroup. Most of them by 1985 had appointed committees or commissions
to help them find or recover a sense of identity and mission so that they
may know not only who they are, but what they have to share with others

in the fashioning of a common mind. Lutherans, perhaps, are best positioned initially for this task. Having been isolated to varying degrees from American life for a long period, Lutherans have been less subject to the theological erosion which so largely stripped other denominations of an awareness of their continuity with historic Christianity. Thus the resources of the Christian past are more readily available to them. Among assets immediately at hand among Lutherans are a confessional tradition, a surviving liturgical structure, and a sense of community that, however much it may be the product of cultural factors, may make it easier for them than other Protestants to participate effectively in the dialogue of a pluralistic society.

American Catholics, who have been recovering from their disarray partly through papal intervention, are unlikely to permit a retreat into the isolationist or siege mentality that prevailed for several decades after 1900. A triumphalist longing to impose its will upon other segments of society may still linger in the halls of the Vatican, but American Catholics have learned to rely more on discussion and persuasion than coercion.

In a society in which all religious groups have become minorities, any triumphalist ventures into the public sphere have a tendency to become self-correcting. This is a lesson that even fundamentalist Protestants have been learning. An incident at a rally sponsored by Jim Robison's religious Roundtable in 1980 illustrates this point. Bailey Smith, president of the Southern Baptist Convention, created an uproar when he said:

> It is interesting at great political rallies how you have a Protestant to pray, a Catholic to pray, and then you have a Jew to pray. With all due respect to those dear people, my friends, God Almighty does not hear the prayer of a Jew.

In the furor that followed, there were many repudiations of Smith's words, and Jerry Falwell sought to set the record straight.

> This is the time for Catholics, Protestants, Jews, Mormons, and all Americans to rise above every effort to polarize us in our efforts to return the nation to a commitment to the moral values on which America was built.

And then, speaking for the Moral Majority, he wrote:

> We are Catholics, Jews, Protestants, Mormons, Fundamentalists—blacks and whites—farmers, housewives, businessmen, and businesswomen.

Although Falwell's openness remained restricted, he was learning that no mere tribalism would do.[22]

---

[22] The quotations are from Handy, *A Christian America*, 207. The smashing defeat in the 1985 Virginia election of every candidate that had Falwell's blessing was an indication that perhaps he was alienating more voters than he was winning. Falwell responded early in 1986 by founding a Liberty Federation to broaden his base and to divert attention from his Moral Majority.

Black leaders went their separatist ways in the 1970s, but many black mayors in the 1980s were learning that an appeal to a single constituency will not gain success at the polls, and black churchmen were recalling Martin Luther King's insistence that the emphasis must be on reconciliation. Black churchmen are fortunate that the deep spiritual resources of the black churches still remain. Out of long suffering, the possibility exists that black churches can speak a word that few others can speak, a word that will lead to authentic freedom for all people.

Perhaps Harriet Beecher Stowe was right. She depicted Uncle Tom as a Christ figure (a black messiah) whose unswerving loyalty and sacrificial death brought redemption to Charles Shelby and to the two blacks who were the instruments of the brutal torture that ended his earthly life. But it was the third-from-the-last chapter that may have been more prophetic when Stowe placed stress upon a people called of God to deliver black America from its bondage and white America from its lethal folly. Who would they be? A people of "African nationality" was the answer in *Uncle Tom's Cabin*. Whence would they come? Where but from Africa. Out of a period of struggle and conflict, a new era may be born. From its vantage point, the present throes that convulse the nations will be seen as "but the birth-pangs of an hour of universal peace and brotherhood."[23]

Judaism may have its own contribution to make. For 2,000 years adherents of Judaism were compelled to live in two worlds—to maintain their faith while meeting demands for coexistence within a non-Jewish culture and society. Such dual allegiance was not easy to maintain. It required strenuous efforts in "schule" and family to preserve the religious tradition. It was doubly difficult when the coercion of the ghetto was relaxed. Still it could be and was done, even in America where the temptation to abandon a dual allegiance was greatest.

Perhaps the greatest contribution of Judaism to the United States will be to help other Americans understand how the United States can be a truly pluralistic society in which the pluralism is maintained in a way that is enriching rather than impoverishing, a society in which the integrity of different faiths is preserved while their respective adherents engage in open dialogue to clarify their own self-understanding. A pluralistic society is a society of dual commitments that need not be in conflict but can be complementary. From the long experience of Judaism, it may be possible for other Americans to learn how this may be done with both grace and integrity.

---

[23] *Uncle Tom's Cabin* (N.Y., 1976), 300, 302.

Epilogue

What will characterize religion in America as the twentieth century moves toward a close? The prospect seems to be more of the same without any startling new breakthroughs.

A survey commissioned by the Graduate School of the City University of New York provides the most ambitious and comprehensive effort to draw a portrait of religion in America at the beginning of the 1990s. This survey confirms what most scholars have reported about the major characteristics of the American religious scene, modified somewhat by previously unknown details of some minor trends. Nine out of ten Americans claimed a specific religious affiliation, with 86.5 percent of them, or 214 million people, labeling themselves as Christians. Roman Catholics, with 26 percent of the nation's population, are followed in number by Baptists, Methodists, and Lutherans, while less than 2 percent of the population identify themselves as Jews and only 0.5 percent as Muslims.[1] What are we to conclude then about religion in the 1990s?

First, religious pluralism will continue to be the name of the game. This is partly the result of immigration from Asia and Latin America. The immigration factor is less important, however, than hitherto suspected. It comes as a surprise to most observers of the American scene that, according to the careful analysis of the CUNY study, most Asian-Americans in the United States are Christians rather than Buddhists, Hindus, or

---

[1] The Muslim total is sharply below previous estimates which put the Muslim population at 3 million to 6 million. The pollsters speculated that the difference might have to do with Christians from Arab countries who have been assumed to be Muslims. Other finds confirm regional differences in religious identification. While for the nation as a whole only 7.5 percent of the population claimed no religion, 17 percent in Oregon, 14 percent in Washington, and 13 percent in California gave a similar response. Also it is interesting that Muslims and Buddhists are most likely to remain single, and that the likelihood of divorce is generally uniform across all religious groups within a spectrum the ends of which are set by the Greek Orthodox who have the lowest level of divorce (4.4 percent) and the Unitarians who have the highest (18 percent).

Taoists, and that most Arab-Americans are Christians rather than Muslims.

While there had been a striking surge of growth in the 1970s in the Nation of Islam among African-Americans in the United States, this increase had leveled off by 1990 so that only 1.4 million people identified themselves as being Muslims. Forty percent of this total were represented by converts from among the African-American population. Even so, Black Muslims constituted less than 2 percent of the black population, in contrast to the overwhelming percentage of those identifying themselves as Christians.

In addition to the impact of immigration resulting in the presence of one million Buddhists and a half million Hindus, the new pluralism is broader in scope because of both the frequent formation of new religious groups in the United States and the continued fragmentation of older groups. The traditional three-fold division within Judaism (Orthodox, Conservative, Reform), for example, has been expanded to include Reconstructionism and a variety of Hasidic communities. Both Roman Catholics and Episcopalians have experienced new "traditionalist" schisms, while Presbyterian churches now include the Presbyterian Church in America and scattered southern Presbyterian churches. Many have expected a new Baptist group to emerge from the controversies within the Southern Baptist Convention, but Southern Baptists for the most part have found it easier to adapt to the new power structure within their denomination than to fashion a new denominational home for themselves.

New religious groups have appeared regularly in the United States, and this continued to be true in the recent past. The CUNY survey lists a number of smaller religious groups with less than 50,000 members, including Baha'i, Taoism, Rastafarianism and Wiccan. It also reports that New Age religions count 28,000 adherents, a membership that is considered statistically insignificant. Much more important is a shifting in rank among long-established churches. The religious scene continues to change constantly, with some groups moving off the periphery to claim a place closer to the center and others becoming less visible as their social prestige and political influence ebbs. Whereas Mormons, Seventh-Day Adventists, the Assembly of God, and the Church of God in Christ continue to grow in number and social status, some long-established churches of cooperative Protestantism have been experiencing a steady decline in membership.[2]

---

[2] William Hutchison of Harvard Divinity School thought that the American Baptist churches in the north constituted an exception to the declining trend among the churches of cooperative Protestantism. He was misled by confusing statistics, for American Baptists are not an exception. They maintained their numerical total by adding a considerable number of African-American Baptist churches to their total membership. These churches are dually alligned with the Progressive National Baptist Convention and thus do not represent any new growth, being counted twice in overall statistics.

Second, a further characteristic of the American religious scene is the ebbing of "ethnicity" as a factor in the institutional life of churches. This has been notably true among Lutherans and Roman Catholics. For many years ethnic divisions — German, Swedish, Norwegian, Danish, Icelandic —were a prominent characteristic of Lutheran churches. Most of these divisions have disappeared, and churches of the two major groups which have not coalesced with the others embrace members of varied national backgrounds. Roman Catholics once were torn by strong ethnic antagonisms. Separate German, French, Irish, Italian, Belgian, Lithuanian, Slovak and Croat congregations formed often within a stone's throw of one another. The "stones" were customarily verbal. Vivid memories of the antagonisms still remain but the divisions themselves are now mostly only memories. The divisions among Protestant ethnic churches — whether Methodist, Presbyterian, Baptist, or Congregational, whether French, German, Italian, Polish, or Hungarian — are also mostly memories, having disappeared almost as soon as the ethnic enclaves and language bonds vanished.

A third feature of American religious life is the presence of strong movements to foster unity among different faiths. Most of them have been abortive and none seem destined to reduce the current religious pluralism. The reason for this is not difficult to understand. In a free society the corollary of religious freedom (the separation of church and state) is religious diversity. No two persons ever think exactly alike. As soon as a coalition of like-minded religionists develops, one or more of its members espouse some new ideas and begin to attract followers to these new beliefs. In the seventeenth century Jeremiah Burroughs, one of the Dissenting Brethren in England, was acutely disturbed by divisions among Christians. After much reflection he concluded that "perfect unity" and "the perfect man" go together. Thus, in the absence of perfected individuals, religious unity can be secured only within a police state that is willing and able to enforce conformity. To Burroughs's dictum, one may add that "pluralism" and a "free society" also go together.

Fourth, functioning in a free society, churches have long sought new applications of religious ideas through programs of social reform. Quakers early sought reforms that included the abolition of slavery, aiding the poor, educating Indians, protesting against inhumane prison conditions, and establishing asylums for orphans and the mentally disturbed. This spirit of social reform was true of other denominations as well. The mixture of Enlightenment rationalism with evangelical religion gave rise to an emphasis on the active role individuals play in their own spiritual development. Reform coalesced as a form of opposition to whatever obstructed opportunities for self-improvement — in religion as well as in economic and social life. In the nineteenth century, as ever more ambitious programs were mounted, reform became a crusade. Dorothea Dix, activist daughter of a Methodist minister, evinced the religious aspect of reform — which persists today — when she petitioned the Massachusetts legislature to provide care for the insane: "Gentlemen, I commit to you this sacred cause. Your action upon this subject will affect the present and future conditions of hundreds of thousands. In this legislation, as in all things, you may exercise that 'wisdom which is the breath of the power of God.'"[3]

Churches of various denominations often share a common cause in programs of social reform. They recognize their mutual adherence to the principles of democratic equality that are manifest in civil religion. Civil religion is less clearly definable and less obvious than institutional religion. There are no weekly services and no separate organized institutions, but civil religion is no less real. It is a kind of pervasive civic piety that combines nationalism with values and ideals drawn initially from Protestantism but available to people of different faiths because it is phrased in Hebraic terms and metaphors. Civil religion is expressed most cogently in the Preamble to the United States Constitution, in the Declaration of Independence, in Lincoln's Gettysburg Address and in his Second Inaugural, as well as in various national holidays such as Memorial Day, the Fourth of July and the birthdays of both Washington and Lincoln. The consolidation of those two birthdays is an indication of a weakening of civil religion's hold on a large segment of the American people, but civil religion itself is far from dead. In recent years it has made strong appearances in the most recent Republican Presidential campaign, in popular support for the Gulf War, and in reform movements ranging from environmentalism to opposition to Latin American policies.

Fifth, in spite of recent indications of the vitality of religion in the United States, a process of secularization has set in that has profoundly affected the public appearance of religion. In the area of public education the courts have ruled against prayer and religious instruction in state-supported schools. A wider pattern of secularization also has affected higher learning. In order to appreciate this, one needs only to remember that, in the period after World War I during the Fundamentalist controversy of the 1920s, there was an effort to marshal community support to replace the dwindling ability of the churches to support higher education. Princeton, Yale, Vassar, New York University, Western Reserve, the University of Chicago, and scores of liberal arts colleges severed (or lost) their denominational affiliations. In 1990, Furman, Baylor, Wake Forest, and other universities affiliated with the Southern Baptist Convention moved to limit the influence of the denomination in their affairs.

Sixth, whether we are concerned with education or with other areas of American culture in which secularization is visible, we must keep in mind that there is no sure measurement of how the secular supplants the sacred in society. Universities may end their denominational affiliations, but campus ministries such as Intervarsity Christian Fellowship, Campus Cru-

---

[3] Dorothea L. Dix, *Memorial to the Legislature of Massachusetts* (Boston, 1843), p. 32.

sade, Fellowship of Christian Athletes, Hillel, and Newman Centers flourish. Prayers are no longer said in public schools, but American television programming is bursting with religious shows. During a decade in which Wall Street displayed an extraordinary penchant for unethical practices, a remarkable number of men and women became missionaries.

Though we live in an increasingly high-tech world, there are ample signs for the continued pervasiveness of religion. Religious music, including gospel, Christian rock, and some religiously inclined folk and country-and-western music crowd the airwaves. Pop stars incorporate religious themes into their lyrics. The highly developed machinery of the religious press keeps the faithful informed, while thousands of religious bookstores offer devotional best-sellers. Religious slogans appear everywhere on bumper stickers, religious statuettes continue to adorn American dashboards, and religion is always on television.

Religion in America remains complex and multifaceted, a mixture of institutionalized and popular forms, reformist and critical (but conservative as well), resilient and constantly changing. In a nation where the free exercise of religion is protected as a fundamental right of all Americans, we should expect no less.

A final word from Benjamin Franklin is in order. In 1749 Franklin wrote that the study of history was an important part of the school curriculum because it "afford(s) frequent opportunities of showing the necessity of a public religion, from its usefulness to the public."[4] In the end, however, the value of religion has depended on its potential to affect the private lives upon which public life rests. And it has done that not through promises of utility, but through imagination and daring.

---

[4] Benjamin Franklin, *Proposals Relating to the Education of Youth in Pennsylvania* (Philadelphia, 1749), p. 22.

Suggestions for Further Reading

For those who wish to pursue further reading on specific topics, many books and articles are cited in notes adjacent to the text where it is believed they will be most useful. For further guidance, two excellent general bibliographies are available: Ernest R. Sandeen, *American Religion and Philosophy: Guide to Information and Sources* (Detroit, 1978), and Nelson R. Burr, *Religion in American Life: Goldentree Bibliography* (New York, 1971). The latter is a condensation and supplement to Burr's two-volume *A Critical Bibliography of Religion in America*, published as part of *Religion in American Life* (Princeton, 1961). On religion in the South see Charles H. Lippy, *Bibliography of Religion in the South* (Macon, GA, 1985), and especially the valuable essays introducing each chapter. The well-organized collection edited by Charles H. Lippy and Peter W. Williams, *Encyclopedia of the American Religious Experience* (New York, 1988), contains three volumes of essays and bibliography on over one hundred topics. Also valuable is the two-volume collection of essays edited by John F. Wilson, *Church and State in America: A Bibliographical Guide* (Greenwood, CT, 1986, 1987). Other useful reference volumes are: H. W. Bowden, *Dictionary of American Religious Biography* (Westport, CT, 1977); E. S. Gaustad, *Historical Atlas of Religion in America*, 2nd ed., (New York, 1976); A. C. Piepkorn, *Profiles in Belief: The Religious Bodies of North America*, 3 vols. (New York, 1977–79); Peter L. Halvorson and William M. Newman, *Atlas of Religious Change in America* (Washington, D.C., 1978), J. Gordon Melton, *Encyclopedia of American Religions*, 2nd ed., (Detroit, 1987). There are many helpful short articles and profiles as well in the *Dictionary of Christianity in America*, (Downers Grove, IL, 1990), edited by Daniel G. Reid, Robert D. Linder, Bruce L. Shelley, and Harry S. Stout.

Ann T. Fraker has detailed a wide range of resources for classroom use in *Religion in American Life*, (Urbana, IL, 1989). Primary sources useful as supplementary reading in the classroom are collected in E. S. Gaustad's two-volume *A Documentary History of Religion in America* (1982–83).

Other surveys that approach religion as part of the whole of American life are Peter W. Williams, *America's Religions: Traditions and Cultures* (New York, 1990); Martin Marty, *Pilgrims in Their Own Land: 500 Years of Religion in America* (Boston, 1984); Catherine L. Albanese, *America, Religions and Religion* (Belmont, CA, 1981); and Robert T. Handy, *A History of the Churches in the United States and Canada* (New York, 1976). Also useful is George M. Marsden, *Religion and American Culture* (San Diego and New York, 1990). R. Laurence Moore describes the historical roles and cultural contributions of religious groups not associated with the Protestant "mainline" in *Religious Outsiders and the Making of Americans* (New York, 1986).

Accounts of America's "three major faiths" by J. T. Ellis, Nathan Glazer, and W. S. Hudson are included in the University of Chicago's History of American Civilization series. For these traditions, see also: J. P. Dolan, *The Immigrant Church* (1975); J. J. Hennessey, *American Catholicism* (1981); J. L. Blau, *Judaism in America* (1970); Jacob Neusner, *American Judaism* (1972); and R. T. Handy, *A Christian America: Protestant Hopes and Historical Realities*, rev. ed. (1984).

Illuminating analysis of the changes that have taken place in recent decades can be found in Wade Clark Roof and William McKinney, *American Mainline Religion* (1987); Martin E. Marty, *Religion and the Republic: The American Circumstances* (1987); Robert Wuthnow, *The Restructuring of American Religion* (1988); and William R. Hutchison, ed., *Between the Times: The Travail of the Protestant Establishment in America, 1900–1960* (1989).

For other religious traditions, both old and new, see Timothy Ware, *The Orthodox Church* (1963); Constance J. Tarasar, ed., *Orthodox America 1794–1976* (1975); Leonard Arrington and Davis Bitton, *The Mormon Experience* (1979); Jan Shipps, *Mormonism: The Story of a New Religious Tradition* (1985); Stephen Gottschalk, *The Emergence of Christian Science* (1973); Edwin F. Gaustad, *The Rise of Adventism* (1974); B. F. Campbell, *Ancient Wisdom Revived: A History of the Theosophical Movement* (1979); J. J. Penton, *Apocalypse Delayed: The Story of Jehovah's Witnesses* (1985); Jacob Needleman and George Baker, eds., *Understanding the New Religions* (1978); and R. S. Ellwood, *Alternative Altars: Unconventional and Eastern Spirituality in the United States* (1979).

Since 1976, the American Revolution and religious liberty have received renewed attention by Nathan Hatch, *The Sacred Cause of Liberty: Republican Thought and the Millennium in Revolutionary New England* (1977); Mark A. Noll, *Christians and the American Revolution* (1977); William Lee Miller, *The First Liberty: Religion and the American Republic* (1986); Robert S. Alley, ed., *James Madison on Religious Liberty* (1985); Leonard W. Levy, *The Establishment Clause: Religion and the First Amend-*

ment (1986); and Thomas J. Curry, *The First Freedoms: Church and State in America to the Passage of the First Amendment* (1986).

Social and intellectual dimensions of American religious experience have been prominent features of recent historiography. Among such studies are: D. G. Bloesch, *The Evangelical Renaissance* (1973); D. D. Bruce, Jr., *And They All Sang Hallelujah, 1800–1845* (1974); Ruth Alden Doan, *The Miller Heresy, Millennialism, and American Culture* (1987); C. C. Goen, *Broken Churches, Broken Nation* (1985); E. Brooks Holifield, *The Gentleman Theologians: American Theology in Southern Culture, 1795–1860* (1978); S. S. Hill, *The South and the North in American Religion* (1980); W. R. Hutchison, *The Modernist Impulse in American Protestantism* (1976); W. G. McLoughlin, *Revivals, Awakenings, and Reforms* (1978); G. F. Marsden, *Fundamentalism and American Culture, 1875–1925* (1980); Martin E. Marty, *The Public Church* (1981); D. G. Mathews, *Religion in the Old South* (1977); Sidney E. Mead, *The Old Religion in the Brave New World* (1977); D. B. Rutman, *American Puritanism* (1970); D. A. Roozen and Jackson W. Carroll, *Varieties of Religion* (1984); Sandra S. Sizer, *Gospel Hymns and Social Religion* (1978); Cushing Strout, *The New Heavens and the New Earth* (1974); Grant Wacker, *Augustus A. Strong, and the Dilemma of Historical Consciousness* (1985); T. P. Weber, *Living in the Shadow of the Second Coming* (1979); John F. Wilson, *Public Religion in America* (1979); and Ellen Weiss, *City in the Woods: The Life and Design of an American Camp Meeting on Martha's Vineyard* (1987).

The rise of popular religious forms and their relation to traditional religion has been the subject of recent works, including Jon Butler, *Awash in a Sea of Faith: Christianizing the American People* (1990); David D. Hall, *Worlds of Wonder, Days of Judgment: Popular Religious Belief in Early New England* (1989); Nathan O. Hatch, *The Democratization of American Christianity* (1989); Charles H. Lippy, *Twentieth-Century Shapers of American Popular Religion* (1989); Colleen McDannell, *The Christian Home in Victorian America* (1986); Robert Anthony Orsi, *The Madonna of 115th Street* (1985); Ann Taves, *The Household of Faith* (1986); and Peter W. Williams, *Popular Religion in America* (1989). See also Catherine L. Albanese, *Nature Religion in America* (1990).

The transatlantic dimension of religion in America is the subject of recent works by Richard Carwardine, *Transatlantic Revivalism* (1978); Leigh Eric Schmidt, *Holy Fairs: Scottish Communions and American Revivals in the Early Modern Period* (1989); and Marilyn Westerkamp, *Triumph of the Laity: Scots-Irish Piety and the Great Awakening, 1625–1760* (1988). A study that emphasizes ongoing British influence on American "folkways" is David Hackett Fischer, *Albion's Seed* (1989).

Two areas need specific notice. Aspects of African-American religion are discussed in Gerald L. Davis, *I Got the Word in Me and I Can Sing It, You Know* (1987); C. Eric Lincoln, ed., *The Black Experience in Religion* (1974); and Benjamin Quarles, *Black Abolitionists* (1979); A. J. Raboteau, *Slave*

Religion (1978); Milton C. Sernett, *Afro-American Religious History: A Documentary Witness* (1985); L. I. Sweet, *Black Images of America, 1784–1870* (1976); James Washington, *Frustrated Fellowship: The Black Baptist Quest for Social Power* (1986); Robert Welsbrot, *Father Divine and the Struggle for Racial Equality* (1983); David Wills, ed., *Black Apostles at Home and Abroad: Afro-Americans and the Christian Mission* (1982); G. S. Wilmore and J. H. Cone, eds., *Black Theology: A Documentary History* (1979); C. Eric Lincoln and Lawrence H. Mamiya, eds., *The Black Church in the African American Experience* (1990). The role of women is brought into focus by Ruth Bordin, *Women and Temperance: The Quest for Power and Liberty, 1873–1900* (1980); Joan Brumberg, *A Mission for Life* (1980); Nancy F. Cott, *The Bonds of Womanhood: "Women's Sphere" in New England, 1780–1815* (1977); Mary Ewens, *The Role of the Nun in Nineteenth-Century America* (1978): June Fochen, *Movers and Shakers: Women Thinkers and Activists, 1900–1970* (1973); Nancy Hardesty, *Women Called to Witness: Evangelical Feminism in the Nineteenth Century* (1984); Janet James, ed., *Women in American Religion* (1980); Sally Priesand, *Judaism and the New Woman* (1975); Rosemary Radford Reuther and Eleanor McLoughlin, eds., *Women of Spirit: Female Leadership in Jewish and Christian Traditions* (1979); Rosemary Radford Reuther and Rosemary S. Keller, *Women and Religion in America: A Documentary History* (1981, 1983, 1985); L. I. Sweet, *The Minister's Wife: Her Role in Nineteenth-Century Evangelicalism* (1983); and Ann Braude, *Radical Spirits: Spiritualism and Women's Rights in Nineteenth-Century America* (1989).

Index